WORLD TRADE ORGANIZATION

Dispute Settlement Reports

2003
Volume IX

Pages 4389-4820

CAMBRIDGE
UNIVERSITY PRESS

CAMBRIDGE UNIVERSITY PRESS

Cambridge, New York, Melbourne, Madrid, Cape Town, Singapore, São Paulo

Cambridge University Press
The Edinburgh Building, Cambridge CB2 2RU, UK

Published in the United States of America by Cambridge University Press, New York

www.cambridge.org
Information on this title: www.cambridge.org/9780521859998

© World Trade Organization 2003, 2005

First published 2005

Printed in the United Kingdom at the University Press, Cambridge

A catalogue record for this book is available from the British Library

ISBN-13 987-0-521-85999-8 hardback
ISBN-10 0-521-85999-9 hardback

THE WTO DISPUTE SETTLEMENT REPORTS

The *Dispute Settlement Reports* of the World Trade Organization (the "WTO") include panel and Appellate Body reports, as well as arbitration awards, in disputes concerning the rights and obligations of WTO Members under the provisions of the *Marrakesh Agreement Establishing the World Trade Organization*. The *Dispute Settlement Reports* are available in English, French and Spanish. Starting with 1999, the first volume of each year contains a cumulative index of published disputes.

This volume may be cited as DSR 2003:IX

TABLE OF CONTENTS

Page

Japan – Measures Affecting the Importation of Apples (WT/DS245)

JAPAN – MEASURES AFFECTING THE IMPORTATION OF APPLES

Report of the Appellate Body
WT/DS245/AB/R

Adopted by the Dispute Settlement Body
on 10 December 2003

Japan, *Appellant/Appellee*
United States, *Appellant/Appellee*
Australia, *Third Participant*
Brazil, *Third Participant*
European Communities, *Third Participant* New Zealand, *Third Participant*
Separate Customs Territory of Taiwan,
Penghu, Kinmen, and Matsu, *Third Participant*

Present:
Lockhart, Presiding Member
Baptista, Member
Sacerdoti, Member

TABLE OF CONTENTS

TABLE OF CASES CITED IN THIS REPORT

Short Title	Full Case Title and Citation
Australia – Salmon	Appellate Body Report, *Australia – Measures Affecting Importation of Salmon*, WT/DS18/AB/R, adopted 6 November 1998, DSR 1998:VIII, 3327
Brazil – Desiccated Coconut	Appellate Body Report, *Brazil – Measures Affecting Desiccated Coconut*, WT/DS22/AB/R, adopted 20 March 1997, DSR 1997:I, 167
Chile – Price Band System	Appellate Body Report, *Chile – Price Band System and Safeguard Measures Relating to Certain Agricultural Products*, WT/DS207/AB/R, adopted 23 October 2002
EC – Asbestos	Appellate Body Report, *European Communities – Measures Affecting Asbestos and Asbestos-Containing Products*, WT/DS135/AB/R, adopted 5 April 2001
EC – Bananas III	Appellate Body Report, *European Communities – Regime for the Importation, Sale and Distribution of Bananas*, WT/DS27/AB/R, adopted 25 September 1997, DSR 1997:II, 591
EC – Bed Linen (Article 21.5 – India)	Appellate Body Report, *European Communities – Anti-Dumping Duties on Imports of Cotton-Type Bed Linen from India, Recourse to Article 21.5 of the DSU by India*, WT/DS141/AB/RW, adopted 24 April 2003
EC – Hormones	Appellate Body Report, *EC Measures Concerning Meat and Meat Products (Hormones)*, WT/DS26/AB/R, WT/DS48/AB/R, adopted 13 February 1998, DSR 1998:I, 135

Short Title	Full Case Title and Citation
EC – Sardines	Appellate Body Report, *European Communities – Trade Description of Sardines*, WT/DS231/AB/R, adopted 23 October 2002
EC – Tube or Pipe Fittings	Appellate Body Report, *European Communities – Anti-Dumping Duties on Malleable Cast Iron Tube or Pipe Fittings from Brazil*, WT/DS219/AB/R, adopted 18 August 2003
India – Quantitative Restrictions	Appellate Body Report, *India – Quantitative Restrictions on Imports of Agricultural, Textile and Industrial Products*, WT/DS90/AB/R, adopted 22 September 1999, DSR 1999:IV, 1763
Japan – Agricultural Products II	Appellate Body Report, *Japan – Measures Affecting Agricultural Products*, WT/DS76/AB/R, adopted 19 March 1999, DSR 1999:I, 277
Japan – Apples	Panel Report, *Japan – Measures Affecting the Importation of Apples*, WT/DS245/R, 15 July 2003
Korea – Alcoholic Beverages	Appellate Body Report, *Korea – Taxes on Alcoholic Beverages*, WT/DS75/AB/R, WT/DS84/AB/R, adopted 17 February 1999, DSR 1999:I, 3
Korea – Dairy	Appellate Body Report, *Korea – Definitive Safeguard Measure on Imports of Certain Dairy Products*, WT/DS98/AB/R, adopted 12 January 2000, DSR 2000:I, 3
US – Carbon Steel	Appellate Body Report, *United States – Countervailing Duties on Certain Corrosion-Resistant Carbon Steel Flat Products from Germany*, WT/DS213/AB/R and Corr.1, adopted 19 December 2002
US – Countervailing Measures on Certain EC Products	Appellate Body Report, *United States – Countervailing Measures Concerning Certain Products from the European Communities*, WT/DS212/AB/R, adopted 8 January 2003
US – Offset Act (Byrd Amendment)	Appellate Body Report, *United States – Continued Dumping and Subsidy Offset Act of 2000*, WT/DS217/AB/R, WT/DS234/AB/R, adopted 27 January 2003

Short Title	Full Case Title and Citation
US – Shrimp	Appellate Body Report, *United States – Import Prohibition of Certain Shrimp and Shrimp Products*, WT/DS58/AB/R, adopted 6 November 1998, DSR 1998:VII, 2755
US – Steel Safeguards	Appellate Body Report, *United States – Definitive Safeguard Measures on Imports of Certain Steel Products*, WT/DS248/AB/R, WT/DS249/AB/R, WT/DS251/AB/R, WT/DS252/AB/R, WT/DS253/AB/R, WT/DS254/AB/R, WT/DS258/AB/R, WT/DS259/AB/R, 10 November 2003
US – Wheat Gluten	Appellate Body Report, *United States – Definitive Safeguard Measures on Imports of Wheat Gluten from the European Communities*, WT/DS166/AB/R, adopted 19 January 2001
US – Wool Shirts and Blouses	Appellate Body Report, *United States – Measure Affecting Imports of Woven Wool Shirts and Blouses from India*, WT/DS33/AB/R and Corr.1, adopted 23 May 1997, DSR 1997:I, 323

I.   INTRODUCTION

1.   Japan and the United States appeal certain issues of law and legal interpretations in the Panel Report, *Japan – Measures Affecting the Importation of Apples* (the "Panel Report").[1] The Panel was established to consider a complaint by the United States concerning certain requirements and prohibitions imposed by Japan with respect to the importation of apple fruit from the United States.

2.   Following consultations that failed to resolve the dispute, the United States requested on 7 May 2002 that a panel be established to examine the matter on the basis of "measures" maintained by Japan that "restrict[] the importation of US apples in connection with fire blight or the fire blight disease-causing organism, *Erwinia amylovora*."[2] On 3 June 2002, the Dispute Settlement Body (the "DSB") established the Panel with the following terms of reference, in accordance with Article 7.1 of the *Understanding on Rules and Procedures Governing the Settlement of Disputes* (the "DSU"):

> … To examine, in the light of the relevant provisions of the covered agreements cited by the United States in document

---

[1]   WT/DS245/R, 15 July 2003.
[2]   Request for the Establishment of a Panel by the United States, WT/DS245/2, 8 May 2002.

WT/DS245/2, the matter referred to the DSB by the United States in that document and to make such findings as will assist the DSB in making the recommendations or in giving the rulings provided for in those agreements.[3]

Australia, Brazil, the European Communities, New Zealand, and the Separate Customs Territory of Taiwan, Penghu, Kinmen, and Matsu reserved their right to participate before the Panel as third parties.

3.   Before the Panel, the United States claimed that Japan was acting inconsistently with Articles 2.2, 5.1, 5.2, 5.6, 5.7, and 7 of the *Agreement on the Application of Sanitary and Phytosanitary Measures* (the "*SPS Agreement*") and Annex B thereto; Article 4.2 of the *Agreement on Agriculture*; and Article XI of the *General Agreement on Tariffs and Trade 1994* (the "GATT 1994").[4] In the Panel Report, circulated to Members of the World Trade Organization (the "WTO") on 15 July 2003, the Panel found that Japan's phytosanitary measure:

(i)   is maintained "without sufficient scientific evidence", inconsistent with Japan's obligation under Article 2.2 of the SPS Agreement;

(ii)   does not qualify as a provisional measure under Article 5.7 of the SPS Agreement because it was not imposed in respect of a situation "where relevant scientific evidence [was] insufficient"; and

(iii)   is not based on a "risk assessment" within the meaning of Article 5.1 of the SPS Agreement.[5]

4.   As to the claims of inconsistency with Article 7 of the *SPS Agreement* and Annex B thereto, the Panel found that the United States had failed to establish a *prima facie* case under those provisions. Furthermore, having found the measure to be inconsistent with Japan's obligations under Articles 2.2, 5.7, and 5.1 of the *SPS Agreement*, the Panel determined that resolution of several of the remaining claims under other provisions was unnecessary, as such findings would not assist the DSB in making its recommendations and rulings so as to allow for prompt compliance by Japan. Therefore, in an exercise of judicial economy, the Panel declined to rule on the United States' claims under Articles 5.2 and 5.6 of the *SPS Agreement*, Article 4.2 of the *Agreement on Agriculture*, and Article XI of the GATT 1994.[6] In the light of its findings, the Panel recommended that "the Dispute Settlement Body request Japan to bring the phytosanitary measure in dispute into conformity with its obligations under the *SPS Agreement*."[7]

---

[3]   Constitution of the Panel Established at the Request of the United States, WT/DS245/3, 17 July 2002, para. 2.

[4]   The United States had also raised claims under Articles 2.3, 5.3, 5.5, and 6.1-6.2 of the *SPS Agreement* in its request for the establishment of a panel. The Panel observed, however, that the United States did not pursue these claims in any of its submissions. Accordingly, the Panel concluded that the United States had not made a *prima facie* case for any of these claims and therefore declined to make corresponding findings. (Panel Report, para. 8.334)

[5]   *Ibid.*, para. 9.1(a)-(c).

[6]   *Ibid.*, paras. 8.292, 8.303, 8.328, and 8.332.

[7]   Panel Report, para. 9.3.

5.   On 28 August 2003, Japan notified the DSB of its intention to appeal certain issues of law developed in the Panel Report and certain legal interpretations developed by the Panel, pursuant to Article 16 of the DSU, and filed a Notice of Appeal pursuant to Rule 20 of the *Working Procedures for Appellate Review* (the *"Working Procedures"*). [8] On 8 September 2003, Japan filed an appellant's submission. [9] The United States filed an appellee's submission on 22 September 2003. [10] In addition to Japan's appeal, the United States cross-appealed the Panel Report by filing an other appellant's submission on 12 September 2003. [11] With respect to this cross-appeal, Japan filed an appellee's submission on 22 September 2003. [12] On that same day, Australia, Brazil, the European Communities, and New Zealand filed third participants' submissions [13], and the Separate Customs Territory of Taiwan, Penghu, Kinmen, and Matsu notified its intention to attend and make statements at the oral hearing. [14]

6.   The oral hearing in this appeal was held on 13 October 2003. The participants and third participants presented oral statements (with the exception of the Separate Customs Territory of Taiwan, Penghu, Kinmen, and Matsu) and responded to questions put to them by the Members of the Division hearing the appeal.

7.   Our analysis in this Report proceeds as follows:

- we begin with a brief factual background and an examination of the scope of the dispute, including the nature and history of the plant disease at issue, the products addressed by the Panel in its analysis, and the measure challenged by the United States [15];

- we then set out the arguments of the participants and third participants on appeal;

- we next identify the issues raised before us on appeal and, in order to do so, consider the United States' claim that one of the issues argued by Japan in its appellant's submission is not properly before us because it was not identified in Japan's Notice of Appeal;

- we begin our assessment of the case by examining the United States' claim on appeal that the Panel did not have the authority to issue findings with respect to apples other than "mature, symptomless" apples. Because this claim raises the question of whether the Panel was even permitted to pronounce on the subject

---

[8]   Notification of an Appeal by Japan, WT/DS245/5, 28 August 2003, attached as Annex 1 to this Report. Japan's Notice of Appeal challenges only certain findings made by the Panel in the course of its analysis under the *SPS Agreement*; there are no issues on appeal related to the *Agreement on Agriculture* or to the GATT 1994.

[9]   Pursuant to Rule 21(1) of the *Working Procedures*.

[10]   Pursuant to Rule 22(1) of the *Working Procedures*.

[11]   Pursuant to Rule 23(1) of the *Working Procedures*.

[12]   Pursuant to Rule 23(3) of the *Working Procedures*.

[13]   Pursuant to Rule 24(1) of the *Working Procedures*.

[14]   Pursuant to Rule 24(2) of the *Working Procedures*.

[15]   Additional factual aspects of this dispute are set out in greater detail in paragraphs 2.1-2.32 of the Panel Report.

of apples other than "mature, symptomless" apples", we address this claim as a logical antecedent to Japan's claims on the merits of the Panel's findings;

- next, we consider Japan's claims challenging the Panel's findings that Japan's phytosanitary measure at issue is inconsistent with Japan's obligations under Articles 2.2, 5.7, and 5.1 of the *SPS Agreement*; and

- finally, we evaluate Japan's claims under Article 11 of the DSU that the Panel failed to make an "objective assessment of the facts of the case" in the course of its analysis of the United States' claims under the *SPS Agreement.*

II.   BACKGROUND

A.   *The Disease at Issue*

8.   The following summarizes "factual aspects" set out by the Panel in paragraphs 2.1–2.6 of the Panel Report. The disease[16] targeted by Japan's phytosanitary measure in this dispute is called "fire blight", often referred to by the scientific name for its bacterium, *Erwinia amylovora* or *E. amylovora*. Fruits infected[17] by fire blight exude bacterial ooze, or inoculum[18], which is transmitted primarily through wind and/or rain and by insects or birds to open flowers on the same or new host plants. *E. amylovora* bacteria multiply externally on the stigmas of these open flowers and enter the plant by various openings.[19] In addition to apple fruit, hosts of fire blight include pears, quince, and loquats, as well as several garden plants.[20] Scientific evidence establishes, as the Panel found, that the risk of introduction and spread of fire blight varies considerably according to the host plant.[21]

9.   The uncontested history of fire blight reveals significant trans-oceanic dissemination in the 200-plus years since its discovery.[22] *E. amylovora*, first reported in New York State in the United States in 1793, is believed to be native

---

[16]   The Panel defined "disease" as "[a] disorder of structure or function in a plant of such a degree as to produce or threaten to produce detectable illness or disorder … usually with specific signs or symptoms." (Panel Report, para. 2.9)

[17]   "Infection" was defined by the Panel as "[w]hen an organism (e.g., *E. amylovora*) has entered into a host plant (or fruit) establishing a permanent or temporary pathogenic relationship with the host." (*Ibid.*, para. 2.12) In contrast, the Panel noted that the term "infestation" would "[r]efer[] to the presence of the bacteria on the surface of a plant *without any implication that infection has occurred*." (*Ibid.*, para. 2.13 (emphasis added))

[18]   The Panel defined "inoculum" as "[m]aterial consisting of or containing bacteria to be introduced into or transferred to a host or medium". The Panel explained that "[i]noculation is the introduction of inoculum into a host or into a culture medium. Inoculum can also refer to potentially infective material available in soil, air or water and which by chance results in the natural inoculation of a host." (*Ibid.*, para. 2.14)

[19]   Panel Report, para. 2.2.

[20]   *Ibid.*, para. 2.5.

[21]   *Ibid.*, para. 8.271.

[22]   *Ibid.*, para. 2.6.

to North America.[23] By the early 1900s, fire blight had been reported in Canada from Ontario to British Columbia, in northern Mexico, and in the United States from the East Coast to California and the Pacific Northwest. Fire blight was reported in New Zealand in 1919, in Great Britain in 1957, and in Egypt in 1964. The disease has spread across much of Europe, to varying degrees depending on the country, and also through the Mediterranean region. In 1997, Australia reported the presence of fire blight, but eradication efforts were successful and no further outbreaks have been reported. With respect to the incidence of fire blight in Japan, the parties disputed before the Panel whether fire blight had ever entered Japan; but the United States assumed, for purposes of this dispute, that Japan was, as it claimed, free of fire blight and fire blight bacteria.[24]

B.   The Product at Issue

10.   The United States argued before the Panel that the subject of the United States' challenge to Japan's phytosanitary measure at issue is the sole apple product that the United States exports, that is, "mature, symptomless" apples. The United States claimed that such apples constitute a separate, identifiable category of apples and that its categorization is "scientifically supported".[25] Japan did not accept the United States' categorization, arguing that "mature" and "symptomless" are subjective terms and that the distinction has no scientific basis.[26] Furthermore, Japan argued, its phytosanitary measure addressed the risk arising, not only from mature, symptomless apples that develop and spread fire blight, but also from the accidental introduction of infected or infested apples within a shipment of what are thought to be mature, symptomless apples destined for Japan.[27]

11.   In the light of this disagreement about the product scope of the dispute, the Panel identified the product that was subject to the measure at issue. The Panel observed that, if it were to consider the "product" to be limited to mature, symptomless apple fruit, as claimed by the United States, "many aspects of the measure at issue might, *ipso facto*, lose their *raison d'être* and may become incompatible with the *SPS Agreement*."[28] If, on the contrary, the Panel were to conclude that the product at issue was "any apple" fruit exported to Japan from the United States, then it would need to address the justification of all the requirements imposed by Japan as a whole.[29] The Panel also noted that it would be "illogical" to accept the United States' characterization because it would

---

[23]   *Ibid.*, paras. 2.1 and 2.6.
[24]   *Ibid.*, paras. 4.25-4.26.
[25]   *Ibid.*, para. 8.26.
[26]   *Ibid.*, paras. 4.99 and 8.26.
[27]   *Ibid.*, para. 8.28(b).
[28]   Panel Report, para. 8.30. As an example of aspects of the measure that might in this manner lose their *raison d'être*, the Panel refers to the requirements covering pre-harvesting actions to be undertaken with respect to apples. (*Ibid.*)
[29]   *Ibid.*

prevent the Panel from examining certain aspects of the measure that could be relevant, even if not expressly addressing mature, symptomless apples.[30]

12.   In addition, the Panel stated that the request for the establishment of a panel submitted by the United States referred only to "US apples", which is less specific than mature, symptomless apples. The Panel said that the fact that the United States intended to address "only" mature, symptomless apples in its submission did not affect the Panel's mandate.[31] Finally, the Panel observed that scientific methods existed for distinguishing mature apples, and that an apple's susceptibility to fire blight was related to its maturity.

13.   Considering the parties' arguments, as well as the experts' views[32], the Panel determined that the scope of the dispute should not, at a preliminary stage, be limited to mature, symptomless apples. The Panel considered it particularly inappropriate to limit the scope of the dispute before further consideration of the merits of the case in the light of the two assumptions it found to underlie the United States' characterization of the product at issue: (i) that mature, symptomless apple fruit is not a "pathway"[33] for fire blight and (ii) that shipments from the United States to Japan contain only mature, symptomless apples.[34]

C.   The Measure at Issue

14.   The United States argued before the Panel that, through the operation of various legal instruments[35], Japan maintains nine prohibitions or requirements imposed with respect to apple fruit imported from the United States.[36] With

---

[30]   *Ibid.*, para. 8.31. Aspects of the measure that the Panel thought might be relevant, notwithstanding the fact that they did not focus on mature, symptomless apple fruit, included requirements related to apples that *cannot* be exported (that is, prohibitions). (*Ibid.*)

[31]   *Ibid.*, para. 8.32.

[32]   The Panel engaged experts in consultation with the parties, as provided for in Article 11.2 of the *SPS Agreement* . (*Ibid.*, paras. 6.1-6.4)

[33]   We understand the Panel to have used the term "pathway" to describe the steps through which a disease must travel for successful transmission from one plant to a new host plant. We employ the term in this Report in the same manner.

[34]   Panel Report, para. 8.33.

[35]   The Panel identified the following means by which Japan imposed the prohibitions or requirements relevant to this dispute: (i) the Plant Protection Law (Law No. 151; enacted 4 May 1950), as amended; (ii) the Plant Protection Regulations (Ministry of Agriculture, Forestry, and Fisheries Ordinance No. 73, enacted 30 June 1950), as amended; (iii) Ministry of Agriculture, Forestry and Fisheries Notification No. 354 (dated 10 March 1997); and (iv) related detailed rules and regulations, including Ministry of Agriculture, Forestry, and Fisheries Circular 8103. (Panel Report, para. 8.7)

[36]   Panel Report, para. 8.5, citing Request for the Establishment of a Panel by the United States, WT/DS245/2, 8 May 2002; United States' first written submission to the Panel, para. 19; United States' answers to the Additional Questions posed by the Panel, 28 January 2003, para. 2. The nine requirements identified by the United States are as follows:

(a)   The prohibition of imported apples from US states other than apples produced in designated areas in the states of Oregon or Washington;

(b)   the prohibition of imported apples from orchards in which any fire blight is detected on plants or in which host plants of fire blight (other than apple trees) are found, whether or not infected;

respect to the United States' description of the requirements for importation of apple fruit from the United States, Japan claimed that two such requirements amounted merely to "procedural steps" common to all phytosanitary measures [37], and that one of them should actually have been identified as two separate requirements. [38]

15.   The Panel decided to regard the multiple requirements imposed on imported apple fruit from the United States as a single measure to be reviewed under the *SPS Agreement*. [39] With regard to the precise requirements to be considered as the elements of the single measure, the Panel found that the two requirements claimed by Japan to be "procedural" nevertheless constituted "phytosanitary measures" within the definition of the *SPS Agreement* and formed part of the collective set of conditions to be fulfilled for the importation of apple fruit from the United States. [40] The Panel also appears to have agreed with Japan's claim that one of the requirements identified by the United States should actually be understood as two separate requirements. Therefore, the Panel identified the focus of this dispute to be *a* measure applied by Japan to the importation of apple fruit from the United States, which measure consists of the following ten cumulatively-applied elements:

(a)   Fruit must be produced in designated fire blight-free orchards. Designation of a fire blight-free area as an export orchard is made by the United States Department of Agriculture (USDA) upon application by the orchard owner. Any detection of a blighted tree in this area by inspection will disqualify the orchard. For the time being, the designation is accepted only for orchards in the states of Washington and Oregon;

(c)   the prohibition of imported apples from any orchard (whether or not it is free of fire blight) should fire blight be detected within a 500-meter buffer zone surrounding such orchard;

(d)   the requirement that export orchards be inspected three times yearly (at blossom, fruitlet, and harvest stages) for the presence of fire blight for purposes of applying the above-mentioned prohibitions;

(e)   a post-harvest surface treatment of apples for export with chlorine;

(f)   production requirements, such as chlorine treatment of containers for harvesting and chlorine treatment of the packing facility;

(g)   post-harvest separation of apples for export to Japan from fruits destined to other markets;

(h)   certification by US plant protection officials that fruits are free of fire blight and have been treated post harvest with chlorine; and

(i)   confirmation by Japanese officials of the US officials' certification and inspection by Japanese officials of disinfection and packaging facilities.

(Panel Report, para. 8.5(a)-(i) (footnote omitted))

[37]   The two requirements claimed to be "procedural" are items (h) and (i), *supra*, footnote 36.

[38]   Panel Report, para. 8.6. Japan claimed that item (f), *supra*, footnote 36, should be regarded as two separate requirements: one for the chlorine treatment of harvesting containers and one for the chlorine treatment of packing facilities.

[39]   Panel Report, para. 8.17.

[40]   *Ibid.*, para. 8.24.

(b)   the export orchard must be free of plants infected with fire blight and free of host plants of fire blight (other than apples), whether or not infected;

(c)   the fire blight-free orchard must be surrounded by a 500-meter buffer zone. Detection of a blighted tree or plant in this zone will disqualify the export orchard;

(d)   the fire blight-free orchard and surrounding buffer zone must be inspected at least three times annually. US officials will visually inspect twice, at the blossom and the fruitlet stages, the export area and the buffer zone for any symptom of fire blight. Japanese and US officials will jointly conduct visual inspection of these sites at harvest time. Additional inspections are required following any strong storm (such as a hail storm);

(e)   harvested apples must be treated with surface disinfection by soaking in sodium hypochlorite solution;

(f)   containers for harvesting must be disinfected by a chlorine treatment;

(g)   the interior of the packing facility must be disinfected by a chlorine treatment;

(h)   fruit destined for Japan must be kept separated post-harvest from other fruit;

(i)   US plant protection officials must certify that fruits are free from fire blight and have been treated post harvest with chlorine; and

(j)   Japanese officials must confirm the US officials' certification and Japanese officials must inspect packaging facilities. [41] (footnote omitted)

16.   At the oral hearing, neither participant disagreed that the measure identified by the Panel as set out in the preceding paragraph, derived from the application of several legal instruments related to quarantine and other restrictions placed by Japan on imported agricultural products, is the measure before us on appeal. [42]

---

[41]   Panel Report, para. 8.25(a)-(j).

[42]   Japan's and the United States' responses to questioning at the oral hearing.

III.   ARGUMENTS OF THE PARTICIPANTS AND THE THIRD PARTICIPANTS

A.   Claims of Error by Japan – Appellant

1.   Article 2.2 of the SPS Agreement

17.   Japan argues that, when evaluating the United States' claim under Article 2.2 of the *SPS Agreement*, the Panel erred in concluding that Japan's measure, as applied to infected apple fruit *and* to mature, symptomless apples, is maintained without sufficient scientific evidence. In Japan's view, the Panel failed to allocate properly the burden of proof under Article 2.2 because it incorrectly arrived at a conclusion on the United States' claim despite the fact that the United States had failed to establish a *prima facie* case as to either infected apple fruit or mature, symptomless apples.

18.   First, as to *infected* apple fruit, Japan claims that, to establish a *prima facie* case under Article 2.2 with respect to the sufficiency of scientific evidence on the risk of completion of the pathway for transmission of fire blight through infected apple fruit, the United States had to prove either (i) that the pathway would not be completed even if infected apple fruit were exported to Japan, *or* (ii) that Japan's scientific evidence on this risk would nonetheless be insufficient for the measure in question. However, Japan argues, the United States limited its evidence on the issue of pathways for fire blight to transmission of the disease through mature, symptomless apple fruit. Therefore, according to Japan, the United States advanced no factual claim or evidence with respect to infected apple fruit. Indeed, Japan claims, the United States "explicitly disavowed attempts or intent" to establish a *prima facie* case of insufficient scientific evidence on the risk posed by infected apple fruit. [43] In the absence of such a *prima facie* case, Japan argues, the Panel was required to find that Japan had not acted inconsistently with its obligations under Article 2.2.

19.   Japan submits that, the Panel's finding that Japan had acted inconsistently with respect to the application of its measure to infected apple fruit was premised on the Panel's view that Japan bore the burden of proof as regards the risk posed by infected apple fruit. Japan contends that, as the United States had declined to assert and prove a *prima facie* case in respect of infected apple fruit, the United States was not entitled to a presumption that the measure is maintained without sufficient scientific evidence. Citing the Appellate Body Report in *EC – Hormones*, Japan further argues that the Panel's shifting of the burden of proof to Japan was "[p]remature" [44] because it occurred *before* the demonstration of a *prima facie* case by the United States. Therefore, according to Japan, the Panel erred in overlooking the absence of a *prima facie* case by the United States and thereby shifting the burden of proof to Japan.

20.   Japan refers to possible explanations that might justify a panel's finding made without the establishment of a *prima facie* case. Japan contends that these

---

[43]   Japan's appellant's submission, para. 23.
[44]   *Ibid.*, p. 7, subtitle *ii*.

possible explanations are inapplicable to the present case or have no merit in law. First, Japan examines the possibility that a panel might be allowed to find a particular fact—not specifically asserted by the complainant—if the complaining party made a general factual assertion under the provision in question. Japan argues, however, that, in the present case, the United States not only failed to address a particular factual claim on infected apple fruit, but consciously declined to make that factual claim and requested that the Panel delete the finding. Therefore, in Japan's view, there is no *general* factual argument of the complaining party that could serve as an "umbrella" argument under which the Panel could have made a specific finding. [45]

21.   Japan also considers the possibility that a panel may be authorized to "distill" a generalized case from the argumentation of the complaining party, regardless of whether that party in fact has made a particular claim. [46] However, according to Japan, the Appellate Body "*implicitly* rejected this sort of arbitrary distillation of arguments" [47] in reversing the panel's finding under Article 5.6 of the *SPS Agreement* in *Japan – Agricultural Products II*. [48]

22.   Finally, Japan claims that the Panel's conclusion as to *infected* apple fruit could be understandable if the risk of the spread of fire blight through infected apple fruit were a "*defensive plea*", for which the defendant normally bears the burden of proof. [49] However, Japan argues, Article 2.2 does not impose any requirement of proof on the importing Member. As a result, in Japan's view, it is the complainant's burden to prove that there is not sufficient scientific evidence for the measure in respect of a particular pathway, and not the respondent's burden to establish that such evidence exists.

23.   For Japan, the Panel's finding of inconsistency with Article 2.2 is based, in part, on the erroneous finding of a *prima facie* case made with respect to *infected* apple fruit. Therefore, Japan requests the Appellate Body to reverse the Panel's finding that the measure at issue is maintained "without sufficient scientific evidence" within the meaning of Article 2.2 of the *SPS Agreement*.

24.   Turning to Japan's claim as it relates to mature, symptomless apple fruit, Japan claims the Panel did not respect the discretion conferred by Article 2.2 on an importing Member in the evaluation of the relevant scientific evidence. Japan submits that misinterpretation of Article 2.2 led the Panel to conclude, erroneously, that the United States had established a *prima facie* case under Article 2.2 with respect to mature, symptomless apple fruit.

25.   Japan asserts that Article 2.2 does not mandate any specific method for a Member to evaluate scientific evidence. Therefore, in Japan's submission, the provision should be interpreted and applied to allow a "certain degree of discretion" on the part of the importing Member to determine how to choose,

---

[45]   *Ibid.*, para. 30.
[46]   *Ibid.*, para. 32.
[47]   *Ibid.* (original italics)
[48]   Appellate Body Report, para. 143(h).
[49]   Japan's appellant's submission, para. 38. (original italics)

weigh, and evaluate such scientific evidence.[50] Japan argues that the Panel failed to accord such discretion when considering the scientific evidence submitted by Japan, because "the Panel evaluated the scientific evidence in accordance with the experts' view, despite the contrary view of an importing Member (Japan)."[51] As an example of the Panel's improper approach, Japan notes that the Panel found that "mature apples are unlikely to be *infected* by fire blight if they do not show any symptoms", despite the fact that Japan had submitted evidence of an experiment suggesting the contrary.[52]

26.   Japan points out that the Panel's risk analysis differed from the risk assessment undertaken by Japan. According to Japan, the Panel: divided the overall risk of apple fruit serving as a pathway for entry, establishment and spread of fire blight into individual components; identified the level of risk for each component; and reviewed whether the corresponding risk for each component was established with sufficient scientific evidence.[53] In contrast, Japan argues, Japan's assessment of the risk reflects the historical facts of trans-oceanic spread of the bacteria, the rapid growth of international trade, and the lack of knowledge on the pathways of transmission of fire blight. Japan contends that the Panel should not have discarded Japan's approach to risk assessment, which was "reasonable as well as scientific" and derived from "prudence and precaution".[54] Therefore, according to Japan, the Panel's improper analysis of the scientific evidence underlying Japan's measure, failed to recognize the discretion conferred on an importing Member by Article 2.2.

27.   Japan asserts that the Panel, as a result of its misinterpretation of Article 2.2, erroneously found that the United States had established a *prima facie* case regarding mature, symptomless apples. Japan submits that the United States failed to "raise a presumption that there [were] no *relevant* scientific studies or reports"[55] supporting the measure at issue because it did not rebut the following points established by Japan: (i) the unknown cause of the trans-oceanic dissemination of fire blight and (ii) the possibility of a physiologically mature apple being infected and shipped to Japan before showing noticeable symptoms. As a result, in Japan's view, the Panel could not have concluded properly that the measure was inconsistent with Japan's obligations under Article 2.2.

28.   Accordingly, Japan requests the Appellate Body to reverse the Panel's finding that the measure at issue is maintained "without sufficient scientific evidence" within the meaning of Article 2.2 of the *SPS Agreement*.

---

[50] *Ibid.*, para. 76.
[51] *Ibid.*, para. 78.
[52] *Ibid.*, quoting Panel Report, para. 8.139. (original italics)
[53] Japan's appellant's submission, para. 72, citing Panel Report, paras. 8.89, 8.122, 8.139, 8.153, 8.157, and 8.161.
[54] Japan's appellant's submission, paras. 81-82.
[55] *Ibid.*, para. 83, quoting Panel Report, para. 8.106. (original italics)

2. Article 5.7 of the SPS Agreement

29.   Japan challenges the Panel's overly "narrow"[56] interpretation of Article 5.7 of the *SPS Agreement* and its consequent finding that the risk of transmission of fire blight from United States apples to plants in Japan does not constitute a "case[] where relevant scientific evidence is insufficient", as required by Article 5.7.

30.   Japan asserts that, according to the Panel, Article 5.7 does not apply to the present situation of fire blight disease, where scientific studies as well as practical experience exist, because Article 5.7 was designed for situations "where little, or no, reliable evidence was available on the *subject matter at issue*."[57] In Japan's view, this reading of the provision is "far too narrow" because Article 5.7 should also be applied to a situation where, although much literature is found concerning a "certain phytosanitary phenomenon"[58], there are particular aspects of that phenomenon as to which evidence is not available, or questions remain unanswered.[59]

31.   Japan contends that the Panel's reliance on *Japan – Agricultural Products II* for its reading of Article 5.7 is misplaced because the Appellate Body's decision in that case does not *a priori* exclude the application of Article 5.7 even where relevant scientific evidence is sufficient "*in general*".[60] Japan asserts that the phrase "[w]here relevant scientific evidence is insufficient", in Article 5.7, should be interpreted to relate to a "*particular situation*" in relation to a "*particular* measure" or a "*particular* risk".[61] Therefore, Japan argues, different situations concerning the same disease should be considered separately, not in general, for purposes of Article 5.7, because they might involve "two separate sets of evidence or information that are materially different from each other."[62]

32.   Japan submits that the conclusion of the Panel in its analysis under Article 5.7 is premised on its assessment that, as regards fire blight, "scientific studies as well as practical experience have accumulated for the past 200 years".[63] Japan contends that the Panel was not authorized to base its conclusion on the "history" of 200 years of studies and practical experience because the United States did not claim that such "history" undermined Japan's adoption of the provisional measure pursuant to Article 5.7.[64] According to Japan, because the United States had itself not raised such an objection based on the "history" of evidence and experience related to fire blight, the Panel could not draw a conclusion regarding Article 5.7 on the basis of this "history".

---

[56] Japan's appellant's submission, para. 94.
[57] *Ibid.*, para. 93, quoting Panel Report, para. 8.219. (emphasis added by Japan)
[58] Japan's appellant's submission, para. 94.
[59] *Ibid.*
[60] *Ibid.*, para. 95, quoting Panel Report, para. 8.218. (original italics)
[61] Japan's appellant's submission, para. 96. (emphasis added)
[62] *Ibid.*, para. 96.
[63] *Ibid.*, para. 93, quoting Panel Report, para. 8.219; and para. 97.
[64] Japan's appellant's submission, para. 97.

33.   Japan further argues that the Panel's interpretation of Article 5.7 implicitly draws an inappropriate distinction between what Japan identifies as "unresolved uncertainty" and "new uncertainty", and that such a distinction is inconsistent with the text of the *SPS Agreement*. Japan employs the term "unresolved uncertainty" to refer to uncertainty that the existing scientific evidence is not able to resolve despite its accumulation over a long period of time.[65] "New uncertainty", according to Japan, refers to cases where a new risk has been identified and little or no reliable scientific evidence is available on it.[66]

34.   Japan claims that the Panel's interpretation of Article 5.7 would deny its applicability as long as there had accumulated, over the years, scientific studies as well as practical experience on the risk in general. According to Japan, this implies that cases of "unresolved uncertainty" would not be covered by Article 5.7; Japan submits that such "inflexibility" is not based on the text or a proper interpretation of the provision.[67] For Japan, Article 5.7 makes no distinction between "new uncertainty" and "unresolved uncertainty", and thereby encompasses both types of uncertainty.

35.   Japan asserts that the standard in Article 2.2 of "sufficient scientific evidence" requires a rational relationship between the evidence and a *particular* measure. Japan also notes the Appellate Body's characterization in *Japan – Agricultural Products II* of Article 5.7 as a "*qualified* exemption"[68] from the requirement of "sufficient scientific evidence" in Article 2.2. Thus, Japan claims, in the context of Article 2.2, the phrase "cases where relevant scientific evidence is insufficient" in Article 5.7 should properly be understood as referring to "a particular situation in respect of a particular *measure* to which Article 2.2 applies (or a particular risk), but not to a particular *subject matter* in general, which Article 2.2 does not address."[69]

36.   Because Article 5.7 is intended to cover situations of "unresolved uncertainty" as well as "new uncertainty", Japan argues that the "unresolved uncertainty" in this case was improperly discounted by the Panel. Japan asserts that, in the present case, the Panel found that "unresolved, scientific uncertainty" still remained as to the risk of shipment of infected apple fruit, notwithstanding 200 years of experience of fire blight.[70] According to Japan, the experts themselves expressed the need for caution with respect to unresolved uncertainty, as they considered reasonable the continuing requirement of a fire blight-free orchard, and as they voiced strong reservations about the possibility of removing all elements of Japan's phytosanitary measure at once. Japan further argues that a novel experiment it introduced during the Panel proceedings to show the possibility of infection of the inside of apple fruit via pedicel was not challenged by any of the experts consulted by the Panel. For Japan, the results of the experiment indicate that the available information on fruit infection is far

---

[65]   *Ibid.*, para. 98.
[66]   *Ibid.*, and footnote 76 thereto.
[67]   *Ibid.*, para. 100.
[68]   *Ibid.*, para. 102, quoting Appellate Body Report, para. 80. (original italics)
[69]   Japan's appellant's submission, para. 102. (original italics)
[70]   *Ibid.*, para. 106.

from conclusive, contrary to the assertions of the United States. Japan adds that the fact that other countries do not impose phytosanitary measures in response to "unresolved uncertainty" regarding fire blight does not necessarily mean that such uncertainty does not exist or is negligible. Instead, according to Japan, it is the prerogative of each importing Member, corresponding to its appropriate level of protection, to determine if it will accept such uncertainty.

37.   Japan further contends that this case involves "new uncertainty" *as well as* "unresolved uncertainty". Referring to the testimony of the experts, Japan argues that if it has to remove or modify its phytosanitary measure to bring it into conformity with Article 2.2, the impact of this action will create "new uncertainty", as the change to the phytosanitary requirements will result in a new situation of risk, for which little, or no, reliable evidence is available. Therefore, in Japan's view, even under the Panel's unduly narrow interpretation of Article 5.7, this provision should be considered applicable to the present case.

38.   Japan states that the Panel erred by concluding that the first of the four prerequisites for a provisional measure under Article 5.7 (that is, the existence of a case where relevant scientific evidence is insufficient), as articulated by the Appellate Body in *Japan – Agricultural Products II*, was not met. Japan further asserts that the Panel should have examined whether Japan's measure satisfied the remaining three requirements for a provisional measure. Accordingly, Japan requests that the Appellate Body complete the legal analysis with respect to the remaining three prerequisites identified in *Japan – Agricultural Products II* for a provisional measure. [71] In this respect, Japan submits that it satisfies these three remaining requirements.

39.   Japan therefore requests the Appellate Body to reverse the Panel's finding under Article 5.7, to complete the legal analysis, and to find that Japan's measure constitutes a provisional measure pursuant to Article 5.7 of the *SPS Agreement*. [72]

3.   Article 5.1 of the SPS Agreement

40.   Japan appeals the Panel's legal interpretation of Article 5.1 of the *SPS Agreement*. Japan claims that the Panel's finding that Japan has acted inconsistently with Article 5.1 is premised on this erroneous interpretation, in particular, on three legal errors perpetrated by the Panel when applying Article 5.1 in its examination of Japan's risk assessment (referred to by the Panel as the "1999 PRA"). [73]

---

[71]   See *infra*, para. 60.

[72]   Japan's appellant's submission, para. 121.

[73]   The "1999 PRA" refers to the "Report on Pest Risk Analysis concerning Fire Blight Pathogen (*Erwinia amylovora*) - Fresh apples produced in the United States of America", *Ministry of Agriculture, Forestry and Fisheries, Plant Protection Division* (August 1999); Exhibit JPN-32, submitted by Japan to the Panel. This pest risk analysis follows an earlier such analysis deemed by the Panel to be relevant to the entry and spread of fire blight (Panel Report, para. 8.246) and identified by Japan as the "Pest Risk Analysis concerning Fire Blight Pathogen (*Erwinia amylovora*)" (1996); Exhibit JPN-31, submitted by Japan to the Panel. The Panel observed that "the parties agree

41.   First, Japan claims that the Panel improperly interpreted Article 5.1 as requiring the risk assessment to be "specific" to apple fruit. In Japan's view, Article 5.1 requires a "risk assessment"; but does not speak to the precise *manner* in which that risk assessment must be conducted. As such, according to Japan, the requirement of "specificity", identified in *EC – Hormones*, should be understood as referring to the "[specificity of] the risk" rather than to "how a risk assessment is done".[74] On the basis of this understanding, Japan does not find legally significant the Panel's observation that Japan's risk assessment was "conducted on the basis of a *general assessment* of possibilities of introduction of fire blight into Japan, through a variety of hosts, including - *but not exclusively - apple fruit*".[75] Japan emphasizes the fact that it conducted the pest risk assessment for fire blight in accordance with its own "methodology", namely, one that considers "all importation of plants and fruits which could be potential vectors of the bacteria".[76] Selection of such a methodology, according to Japan, is well within the discretion accorded each importing Member by Article 5.1 in the conduct of its risk assessment. Therefore, Japan argues, it would be "erroneous to find the 1999 PRA not specific enough".[77]

42.   Secondly, Japan contends that the Panel read Article 5.1 improperly as requiring Japan to "consider[] any alternative measures other than the[] existing measures."[78] Japan submits that the consideration of alternative phytosanitary measures relates to the "*methodology*" of the risk assessment, which is not addressed by Article 5.1.[79] Japan notes that under its risk assessment methodology, when an exporting Member makes "a specific request and a proposal [for the lifting of the default import prohibition], a risk assessment would have to be made in connection with that particular proposal."[80] Japan argues that its reliance on "cumulative measures" reflects not the inadequacy of its risk assessment, as the Panel suggests, but the "high level of protection" sought to be achieved by Japan.[81] Therefore, in Japan's view, Article 5.1 does not require Japan to have considered alternative measures in its risk assessment.

43.   Finally, Japan argues that the Panel improperly evaluated Japan's risk assessment in the light of information that became available only subsequent to the risk assessment. Japan draws a distinction between (i) compliance with Article 5.1 at the time of the "initial" risk assessment and (ii) "continu[ing]" compliance with Article 5.1 in the light of subsequent information.[82] Japan argues that, in the first case, the importing Member should "fully complete[]" a

---

that the 1999 PRA is the main relevant document" to be evaluated as Japan's risk assessment under Article 5.1 of the *SPS Agreement*. (Panel Report, para. 8.247) At the oral hearing, both participants reaffirmed the focus of the Panel's Article 5.1 analysis to be the 1999 PRA.

[74]   Japan's appellant's submission, para. 129.
[75]   Panel Report, para. 8.270. (emphasis added)
[76]   Japan's appellant's submission, para. 128.
[77]   *Ibid.*, para. 129.
[78]   *Ibid.*, para. 133, quoting Panel Report, para. 8.285.
[79]   Japan's appellant's submission, para. 133. (emphasis added)
[80]   Japan's appellant's submission, para. 133.
[81]   *Ibid.*, para. 134.
[82]   *Ibid.*, para. 136.

risk assessment, consistent with the *SPS Agreement*, and on the basis of "information available at [that] time".[83] In the second case, the requirement of a "full, formal risk assessment"[84] immediately after the discovery of new evidence would be "unreasonable"[85] and, therefore, recently discovered evidence should be considered only "in the context of investigating whether ... the party *continues to comply* with Article 5.1".[86]

44.   With regard to subsequent information, Japan advances three grounds for considering as "unreasonable" the requirement of a "full" risk assessment. First, Japan argues that the importing Member should be given an opportunity to consider whether the recent information necessarily warrants a new risk assessment. Secondly, as there is no requirement under the *SPS Agreement* that a risk assessment be a formal process, and as Japan has already taken into account recent evidence filed by the United States and New Zealand during the Panel proceeding, Japan submits that it has already "substantively fulfilled the risk assessment requirements" of Article 5.1.[87] Finally, Japan notes that a formal risk assessment process takes time to complete and that the review of newly available information is an "on-going process".[88] Because such information comes to an importing Member's knowledge in "piecemeal" fashion, Japan argues, that Member cannot be expected to conduct a "full risk assessment" for every new piece of evidence.[89] Therefore, in Japan's view, "the requirement of a formal risk assessment should mean that the assessment be performed in due course."[90]

45.   Japan therefore requests the Appellate Body to reverse the Panel's findings with respect to Article 5.1 of the *SPS Agreement*.

4.   Article 11 of the DSU

(a)   The Panel's Objective Assessment under Article 2.2 of the *SPS Agreement*

46.   Japan challenges on appeal the Panel's analysis of the completion of the last stage of the pathway for transmission of fire blight from "infected" apple fruit. According to Japan, the errors of the Panel in this analysis constitute a failure to make an "objective assessment of the facts of the case" in accordance with Article 11 of the DSU.

47.   First, referring to the Panel's reasoning in paragraph 8.166 of the Panel Report, Japan argues that the evidence and experts' opinions relied upon by the Panel were focused on the pathway of transmission of fire blight from mature, symptomless apples and did not take into consideration the pathway from *infected* apple fruit. Japan contends that the Panel failed to present how the

---

[83]   *Ibid.*, para. 135.
[84]   *Ibid.*, para. 136.
[85]   *Ibid.*, para. 138.
[86]   *Ibid.*, para. 136. (emphasis added)
[87]   *Ibid.*, para. 137.
[88]   *Ibid.*, para. 138.
[89]   *Ibid.*
[90]   Japan's appellant's submission, para. 138.

evidence related to *mature, symptomless* apple fruit should be applied to the issue of *infected* apples, and therefore, the Panel erroneously relied on such evidence in arriving at a conclusion for *all* kinds of apple fruit.

48.   Secondly, Japan asserts that, in the same paragraph of the Panel Report, the Panel, when considering evidence of experiments of inoculated apples, made a "factual error" [91] in declaring that "discarded apples have not led to any visible contamination, *even when ooze was reported to exist*". [92] According to Japan, this declaration is a mischaracterization of the underlying scientific studies, which actually reported that no ooze was observed, and is inconsistent with other evidence in the Panel record. Such a "material error" in this finding, in Japan's view, "implies that this key paragraph on completion of the pathway was not given careful thought", and is therefore inconsistent with the standard of review in Article 11 of the DSU. [93]

49.   Thirdly, Japan notes that the Panel rejected the United States' argument that the caution emphasized by the experts with respect to changes in Japan's measure should be equated to a "theoretical risk", as such risk was described by the Appellate Body in *EC – Hormones*. [94] In rejecting this characterization, Japan argues, the Panel necessarily viewed the risk from infected apples to be "real" and implicitly recognized that the pathway from infected apples could, in fact, be completed. [95] In Japan's view, the Panel's determination that the risk of transmission of fire blight from infected apples was not "theoretical", cannot be reconciled with its finding on the likelihood of completion of the pathway.

50.   Fourthly, Japan contends that the Panel failed in its analysis to take into account properly the "precautionary principle" and the need for caution that was expressed by the experts. Japan claims that, although the expressions of caution by the experts "do not identify a concrete path of the dissemination of the disease" [96], the Panel's failure to accord them "greater weight" [97] in its evaluation of the evidence is inconsistent with the Panel's duty to make an "objective assessment of the facts of the case" under Article 11 of the DSU.

51.   In the light of these errors in the Panel's assessment of the facts of the case, Japan requests the Appellate Body to find that the Panel failed to discharge its functions under Article 11 of the DSU with respect to is evaluation of the United States' claim under Article 2.2 of the *SPS Agreement*.

(b)   The Panel's Objective Assessment under Article 5.1 of the *SPS Agreement*

52.   Japan claims that the Panel failed to fulfill its obligations under Article 11 of the DSU when evaluating the United States' claim under Article 5.1 of the

---

[91]   *Ibid.*, para. 52.
[92]   *Ibid.*, quoting Panel Report, para. 8.166. (emphasis added by Japan)
[93]   Japan's appellant's submission, para. 54.
[94]   Appellate Body Report, para. 186.
[95]   Japan's appellant's submission, para. 61.
[96]   *Ibid.*, para. 68.
[97]   *Ibid.*, para. 69.

SPS Agreement. In particular, Japan contests the Panel's conclusions that Japan's risk assessment (the 1999 PRA) insufficiently analyzed the "probability" and "pathways" when considering the likelihood of entry, establishment or spread of fire blight.

53.   Concerning the "probability" considered in the risk assessment, Japan challenges the Panel's finding that the 1999 PRA does not provide any "quantitative or qualitative" assessment of the "probability" of entry, establishment or spread of fire blight in Japan.[98] According to Japan, the Panel reached this erroneous conclusion by "ignoring the clarifying material supplied by Japan" and relying solely on its own understanding and interpretation of the risk assessment contained in the 1999 PRA.[99] With regard to the risk assessment's examination of "pathways" of transmission, Japan claims that the Panel again focused exclusively on the text of the 1999 PRA and overlooked Japan's submissions and other explanatory material on the subject. Such a "clear aversion" to considering the additional evidence and explanations submitted by Japan, in Japan's view, constitutes a failure to make an "objective assessment of the facts of the case".[100]

54.   Japan therefore requests the Appellate Body to find that the Panel acted inconsistently with its obligations under Article 11 of the DSU when evaluating the United States' claim under Article 5.1 of the *SPS Agreement*.

B.   Arguments of the United States – Appellee

1.   Article 2.2 of the SPS Agreement

55.   Because the United States agrees with Japan that the Panel erred in making findings as to immature apples[101], the United States limits its discussion under Article 2.2 of the *SPS Agreement* to "mature, symptomless" apples. In this respect, the United States argues that Japan's arguments in favour of reversing the Panel's findings are based either on the re-weighing of evidence before the Panel, or on the imposition of legal standards that are "not found in the SPS Agreement".[102]

56.   The United States first claims that Japan's allegations under Article 2.2 constitute a challenge to the Panel's fact-finding. These allegations, according to the United States, cover the Panel's weighing of the significance of the 1990 van der Zwet study[103] and of the history of trans-oceanic dissemination of fire blight, as well as the Panel's factual conclusions with respect to the possibility of infection of mature, symptomless apples. The United States submits that such a challenge to the Panel's fact-finding may be raised on appeal only in the context

---

[98]   *Ibid.*, para. 130, quoting Panel Report, para. 8.275.
[99]   Japan's appellant's submission, para. 131.
[100]   *Ibid.*, para. 132.
[101]   United States' appellee's submission, para 5. See also, *infra*, paras. 82 *ff*.
[102]   United States' appellee's submission, para 15.
[103]   T. van der Zwet *et al.*, "Population of *Erwinia amylovora* on External and Internal Apple Fruit Tissues", *Plant Disease* (1990), Vol. 74, pp. 711-716; Exhibit JPN-7, submitted by Japan to the Panel.

of a claim under Article 11 of the DSU. The United States notes that Japan does not allege a violation of Article 11 with respect to these issues. Therefore, in the view of the United States, Japan's allegations under Article 2.2 should be rejected by the Appellate Body and the Panel's finding that Japan acted inconsistently with Article 2.2 of the *SPS Agreement* should be upheld.

57.　　The United States rejects Japan's arguments that the Panel failed to give appropriate weight to Japan's interpretation of the evidence, and hence failed to accord the appropriate "discretion" to the importing Member in the evaluation of scientific evidence and the consequent establishment of a phytosanitary measure. [104] According to the United States, the "discretion" enjoyed by importing Members should not prevent a panel from finding that a Members' judgement is unsupported by scientific evidence. In the United States' view, Japan's position is inconsistent with the Appellate Body's statement in *Australia – Salmon* that panels "are not required to accord to factual evidence of the parties the same meaning and weight as do the parties." [105] The United States submits that Japan's position also "echoes" the interpretation proffered by Japan and rejected by the Appellate Body in *Japan – Agricultural Products II.* [106]

58.　　The United States contests Japan's argument that the United States failed to prove the absence of scientific evidence concerning "mature, symptomless" apples serving as a pathway. The United States asserts that Japan "distorts the applicable burden [of proof]": it transforms the requirement of "rais[ing] a presumption" that there was no relevant scientific evidence supporting the measure, into an obligation of "prov[ing] the absence of scientific evidence". [107] The United States contends that the *SPS Agreement* cannot be interpreted as imposing upon the complaining Member the burden of either proving a "negative" [108], or disproving "all speculation on hypothetical risks". [109] According to the United States, Japan itself acknowledged that meeting this burden of proof would be an "impossible" task. [110] In contrast to this impossibility, the United States argues, a complaining party must be given the possibility of raising a presumption of the absence of relevant scientific evidence.

59.　　The United States recalls that Article 2.2 requires that a measure not be maintained "without sufficient scientific evidence". According to the United States, this requirement does not mean that "uncertainty" will be completely eradicated because "uncertainty" is an inherent characteristic of science, which cannot provide absolute certainty, as explained by the Appellate Body in *EC – Hormones.* [111] In the light of this uncertainty that can never be eliminated, the United States rejects as speculative Japan's suggestion that "apple fruit *may have been* the means by which trans-oceanic dissemination of fire blight occurred in

---

[104]　United States' appellee's submission, para. 19, quoting Japan's appellant's submission, para. 76.
[105]　Appellate Body Report, para. 267.
[106]　United States' appellee's submission, para 19, citing Appellate Body Report, para. 82.
[107]　United States' appellee's submission, para. 21.
[108]　*Ibid.*, para. 22.
[109]　*Ibid.*, para. 20.
[110]　*Ibid.*, para. 22, quoting Japan's appellant's submission, para. 85.
[111]　United States' appellee's submission, para. 23, quoting Appellate Body Report, para. 186.

the past" or that "*E. amylovora* bacteria *may* be present in physiologically mature apples".[112] These propositions, the United States claims, are based respectively on allegations that the causes of trans-oceanic dissemination are still unknown, and that the moment of maturity is not precise. Such "speculation", in the view of the United States, cannot constitute "sufficient scientific evidence" in the face of research establishing that mature apples do not serve as a pathway for transmission of fire blight.

60.   Therefore, the United States requests the Appellate Body to uphold the Panel's finding that Japan's measure, as applied to mature, symptomless apples, is maintained "without sufficient scientific evidence" and is therefore inconsistent with Japan's obligations under Article 2.2 of the *SPS Agreement*.

2.   Article 5.7 of the SPS Agreement

61.   The United States supports the Panel's interpretation and application of Article 5.7 of the *SPS Agreement*. It requests the Appellate Body to reject Japan's appeal in this regard and uphold the Panel's findings accordingly.

62.   The United States contends that the mere fact that some uncertainty exists in the evidence before a panel, whether "unresolved" or "new", cannot justify the conclusion that relevant scientific evidence is insufficient. According to the United States, such a conclusion must be based on an assessment of the evidence itself. The United States adds, to illustrate its point, that the uncertainty as to the means by which trans-oceanic dissemination of fire blight occurred is not relevant to the issue of transmission of fire blight by mature apples in the face of "specific, direct, and voluminous" evidence that mature apple fruit does not transmit fire blight.[113]

63.   The United States further contends that the context of Article 5.7 clarifies the concept of "sufficiency" under Article 5.7. The United States notes that the second sentence of Article 5.7 requires Members imposing provisional phytosanitary measures to "obtain *additional* information necessary for a more objective assessment of risk."[114] According to the United States, this provision implies that information necessary for an objective risk assessment is lacking at the time the provisional measure is adopted. The United States finds this implication "logical" because, if sufficient information existed for an objective risk assessment, a provisional measure would be unnecessary.[115] As such, in the view of the United States, the "sufficiency" of evidence relevant to Article 5.7 should be defined in relation to the sufficiency of evidence for an objective risk assessment.

64.   With respect to the concept of "unresolved uncertainty", the United States claims that the examples of "unresolved uncertainty" cited by Japan "do not even

---

[112]   United States' appellee's submission, para. 24. (original italics)
[113]   *Ibid.*, para. 29.
[114]   *Ibid.*, para. 30, quoting Article 5.7 of the *SPS Agreement*. (emphasis added by the United States)
[115]   United States' appellee's submission, para. 31.

constitute relevant scientific evidence."[116] The statements of caution by the experts, according to the United States, were based on policy judgements rather than scientific considerations, as the experts themselves acknowledged. In the view of the United States, these statements cannot be considered *scientific* evidence within the meaning given by the Panel to this term.[117] The United States also argues that the unpublished study cited by Japan cannot constitute uncertainty that leads to a conclusion of insufficient relevant scientific evidence, because the experts did not agree with Japan as to the uncertainty identified by the study. Thus, according to the United States, Japan's purported uncertainties cannot overcome the extensive studies on fire blight on which the Panel relied to determine that relevant scientific evidence was not insufficient.

65. The United States contests Japan's attempt to identify "new uncertainty" that would justify the measure under Article 5.7. The United States claims that uncertainties related to the possible removal of Japan's measure do not render the relevant scientific evidence "insufficient" within the meaning of Article 5.7. Such uncertainties, in the view of the United States, constitute "[h]ypothetical speculation" that does not meet the requirements of Article 5.7, just as speculation cannot satisfy the requirements of Article 5.1.[118] If Japan's interpretation were accepted, the United States contends, "the exception in Article 5.7 would swallow the whole of the SPS Agreement."[119]

66. The United States argues that, in any event, Japan does not meet the remaining three requirements of Article 5.7 set out by the Appellate Body in *Japan – Agricultural Products II*.[120] The United States claims that Japan's measure cannot be based on "available pertinent information", as stated in Article 5.7, because Japan has not cited such information, nor does such information exist given the evidence establishing that the pathway cannot be completed for mature apple fruit. In addition, the United States argues, Japan has not sought to obtain additional information for a more objective risk assessment, as Japan has "disregarded" the evidence on the lack of susceptibility of mature apples to fire blight infection and bacterial presence.[121] According to the United States, Japan has also not reviewed the measure within a reasonable period of time, as Japan "has not examined, let alone sought, information" concerning the critical elements of the pathway for transmission of fire blight.[122] Thus, in the view of the United States, Japan meets none of the requirements set forth under Article 5.7.

---

[116]   *Ibid.*, para. 34.
[117]   The Panel stated that scientific evidence is "evidence gathered through scientific methods" and that it "excludes in essence not only insufficiently substantiated information, but also such things as a non-demonstrated hypothesis." (*Ibid.*, para. 38, quoting Panel Report, paras. 8.92-8.93)
[118]   United States' appellee's submission, para. 42, citing Appellate Body Report, *EC – Hormones*, para. 186.
[119]   United States' appellee's submission, para. 42.
[120]   Appellate Body Report, para. 89.
[121]   United States' appellee's submission, para. 46.
[122]   *Ibid.*, para. 47.

67.   Therefore, the United States requests the Appellate Body to uphold the Panel's finding that Japan acted inconsistently with its obligations under Article 5.7 of the *SPS Agreement*.

3.   Article 5.1 of the SPS Agreement

68.   The United States supports the Panel's interpretation of and analysis under Article 5.1 of the *SPS Agreement*, and therefore requests the Appellate Body to reject Japan's appeal on this issue.

69.   The United States argues first that the Panel properly applied the requirement of "specificity" when evaluating Japan's risk assessment (the 1999 PRA). The United States observes that Japan acknowledges that the 1999 PRA "did not specifically focus on a particular commodity" (in particular, on apple fruit). [123] The United States contests Japan's claim, however, that the lack of a product-specific focus in the risk assessment was only a matter of "methodology" in order to assess the risk of multiple vectors, including that from apple fruit. According to the United States, the Panel's interpretation properly required the assessment under Article 5.1 to be sufficiently specific to the risk at issue. The United States submits that, in order for a measure imposed on a particular product to be "rationally" related to, or based on, an assessment of risks, that measure must "specifically" focus on a "product". [124] That Japan characterizes the lack of such focus in the 1999 PRA as a "methodology" does not, according to the United States, exempt the risk assessment from this specificity requirement. The United States asserts that Japan's risk assessment evaluated the risk related to several hosts but did not sufficiently consider the risks "specifically associated with the commodity at issue: US apple fruit exported to Japan." [125] Therefore, the United States contends, the 1999 PRA failed to meet the requirement of specificity under Article 5.1, as correctly found by the Panel.

70.   Secondly, the United States challenges Japan's argument that, because its "methodology" required a risk assessment in connection with a proposal from an exporting Member, Japan was not bound to consider in the 1999 PRA any alternative measures to those already applied. The United States claims that, as the Panel noted, "nothing in the text of Article 5.1 and Annex A, paragraph 4 suggests that alternative options have to be proposed by the exporting Member." [126] Instead, the United States notes, paragraph 4 of Annex A refers to "SPS measures which might be applied". In the view of the United States, this text makes clear that it is the importing Member's obligation to consider alternative measures to those that it actually applies. In this regard, the United States draws attention to the observations by Dr. Chris Hale and Dr. Ian Smith that the 1999 PRA "appeared to prejudge the outcome of its risk assessment" and that the 1999 PRA seemed to be primarily concerned with showing that "each of

---

[123]   *Ibid.*, para. 50, quoting Japan's appellant's submission, para. 128.
[124]   United States' appellee's submission, para. 51.
[125]   *Ibid.*, quoting Panel Report, para. 7.14.
[126]   United States' appellee's submission, para. 54, quoting Panel Report, para. 7.18.

the measures already in place was effective in some respect" in order to conclude that all were necessary. [127]

71.   Finally, the United States takes issue with Japan's claim that it has satisfied the requirements of Article 5.1 by conducting an "informal risk assessment" on mature, symptomless apples in the course of the dispute settlement proceedings and has reached the conclusion that the latest data presented by the United States and New Zealand are "not yet sufficient" to justify a modification of the current measure. [128] Such a claim, the United States argues, reflects Japan's intention to maintain its measure even in the face of an adverse ruling and, therefore, highlights the need for the Appellate Body to make clear legal findings rejecting Japan's "spurious legal theories". [129] In this regard, the United States submits that, although the Panel correctly found that Japan failed to meet the requirements of Article 5.1, this conclusion could have been reached on a "more fundamental basis": in the United States' view, given the "close relationship" between Articles 5.1 and 2.2, and in the absence of "sufficient scientific evidence" under Article 2.2, the relationship between the measure and the risk assessment lacks the "rational" basis required in order for the former to be "based on" the latter. [130]

72.   The United States therefore requests the Appellate Body to uphold the Panel's finding that Japan's measure, with respect to mature, symptomless apples, is inconsistent with Japan's obligations under Article 5.1 of the *SPS Agreement*.

4.   *Article 11 of the DSU*

(a)   The Panel's Objective Assessment under Article 2.2 of the *SPS Agreement*

73.   The United States understands Japan's argument under Article 11 of the DSU, with respect to the Panel's fact-finding in paragraph 8.166 of the Panel Report, to challenge those conclusions only as they apply to "immature apples". [131] The United States agrees with Japan that paragraph 8.166 of the Panel Report should not be read to apply to "infected" apple fruit, but for reasons different from those proffered by Japan. [132] The United States submits that the Panel was without authority to make any finding on "immature apples" because the United States' claims and arguments were expressly limited to "mature, symptomless" apples. [133] Nevertheless, to the extent that Japan contests the Panel's conclusions in paragraphs 8.166 and 8.168 in relation to mature apples, the United States contends that this claim is without merit.

---

[127]   United States' appellee's submission, para. 55, quoting Panel Report, para. 8.289, in turn quoting *ibid.*, paras. 6.177 (Dr. Hale) and 6.180 (Dr. Smith).
[128]   United States' appellee's submission, para. 56, quoting Japan's appellant's submission, paras. 124 and 137.
[129]   United States' appellee's submission, para. 59.
[130]   *Ibid.*, para. 60.
[131]   *Ibid.*, para. 8.
[132]   *Ibid.*, para. 14.
[133]   *Ibid.*, para. 5. See also, *infra*, paras. 82 *ff.*

74.   The United States emphasizes that claims under Article 11 require a showing that the Panel evinced "deliberate disregard" for evidence or "refuse[d] to consider", "willfully distort[ed]", or "misrepresent[ed]" evidence. [134] In the view of the United States, Japan has failed to meet this "high standard". [135]

75.   First, the United States argues that the Panel had sufficient evidentiary basis for its fact-finding in paragraph 8.166 of the Panel Report as to mature, symptomless apples. According to the United States, the Panel cited studies that had found no vector for "calyx-infested discarded apples", in addition to the experts' statements that other means of completing the pathway were unsupported by the available scientific evidence. [136] In this regard, the United States submits that Japan's allegation of a factual error in the Panel's reference to the existence of ooze as found by these studies, is "irrelevant" to the Panel's finding as to mature, symptomless apples, because ooze can occur only in "immature, infected" apples. [137]

76.   Secondly, the United States argues that Japan's arguments regarding the "precautionary principle" have already been rejected by the Appellate Body in *Japan – Agricultural Products II*. According to the United States, neither the text of the *SPS Agreement* nor the "precautionary principle" compels a panel to find that a pathway for transmission of a disease exists where none of the scientific evidence on record supports that conclusion. This view, the United States claims, is supported by the Appellate Body's discussion in *EC – Hormones* of the "precautionary principle". Furthermore, the United States observes, Japan refers to the experts' statements of caution but acknowledges that "these expressions do not identify a concrete path of the dissemination of the disease". [138] Therefore, the United States concludes, the Panel properly refused to assume, on the basis of generalized statements of "caution", that the pathway could be completed where no evidence attests to that fact.

77.   Finally, the United States challenges Japan's claim that the Panel considered the risk of completion of the pathway to be more than theoretical. The United States observes that the Panel employed the term "unlikely" when characterizing the experts' views on the likelihood of completion of the pathway, but claims that, in doing so, the Panel reflected the reality that science can never state with certainty that an event will never occur. In the view of the United States, this proper approach to risk analysis by the Panel should not be understood to suggest more than a theoretical risk of transmission of fire blight from apple fruit.

78.   The United States therefore requests the Appellate Body to find that the Panel properly discharged its obligations under Article 11 of the DSU when

---

[134]   United States' appellee's submission, para. 10, citing Appellate Body Report, *EC – Hormones*, para. 133.
[135]   United States' appellee's submission, para. 10.
[136]   *Ibid.*
[137]   *Ibid.*, footnote 9 to para. 10.
[138]   United States' appellee's submission, para. 12, quoting Japan's appellant's submission, para. 67.

finding that the last stage of the pathway for transmission of fire blight from mature, symptomless apples would not be completed.

> (b) The Panel's Objective Assessment under Article 5.1 of the *SPS Agreement*

79.   The United States claims that Japan's challenges to the Panel's fact-finding in the course of its Article 5.1 analysis are not properly before the Appellate Body. The United States argues that, in *US – Countervailing Measures on Certain EC Products*, the Appellate Body found that an appellant raising an Article 11 claim must indicate such a claim in its Notice of Appeal.[139] In the United States' view, because Japan did not identify, in its Notice of Appeal, its Article 11 claim with respect to the Panel's findings under Article 5.1, Japan has not appealed this issue in accordance with Rule 20(2)(d) of the *Working Procedures*. Therefore, the United States contends, the Appellate Body should decline to address this aspect of Japan's appeal.

80.   Should the Appellate Body proceed to consider Japan's Article 11 claim with respect to the Panel's analysis under Article 5.1, the United States argues, the Appellate Body should find that Japan has not established the sort of "egregious errors" required to find that the Panel has not fulfilled the requirements under Article 11.[140] In addition, according to the United States, Japan has not contested other "deficiencies" identified in Japan's risk assessment by the experts and accepted by the Panel.[141]

81.   The United States thus requests the Appellate Body to dismiss Japan's claim that the Panel failed to satisfy its obligations under Article 11 of the DSU in the course of evaluating the United States' claim under Article 5.1 of the *SPS Agreement*. Alternatively, the United States requests the Appellate Body to find that these obligations were discharged properly by the Panel when it found that Japan's risk assessment did not evaluate adequately the likelihood of entry, establishment or spread of fire blight from apple fruit.

> C.   *Claim of Error by the United States – Appellant*
>
> *Claim on the "Authority" of the Panel*

82.   The United States argues that, because it presented claims relating only to "mature, symptomless" apples, the Panel erred in analyzing the measure with respect to products other than those identified. In particular, according to the United States, the Panel exceeded its authority by making findings related to *immature* apples and to United States export control procedures. The United States requests the Appellate Body to "reverse the Panel's legal findings and

---

[139]   United States' appellee's submission, footnote 88 to para. 53.
[140]   United States' appellee's submission, para. 53, quoting Appellate Body Report, *Japan – Agricultural Products II*, para. 141.
[141]   United States' appellee's submission, para. 53, citing Panel Report, para. 8.279.

declare the Panel's statements derived from those findings to be without legal effect." [142]

83.   The United States asserts that the issue presented to the Panel was "whether Japan's restrictions on mature, symptomless apples are consistent with the SPS Agreement, and not whether Japan could maintain restrictions on any other product." [143] The United States contends that it pursued this approach because it was seeking to export only mature, symptomless apples to Japan, and that it has laws and "extensive measures" to limit apple exports to apples with these characteristics. [144]

84.   The United States notes that, although its claims were limited to mature apples, the Panel concluded that the measure at issue should be evaluated in the light of its applicability to *all* apple fruit, including immature apples. As a result, according to the United States, the Panel also considered it appropriate to examine those issues related to "control procedures" and requirements for the exportation of apples, because such measures affect whether apples exported to Japan could include immature infected apples. [145] The United States considers as flawed the rationale provided by the Panel to justify its consideration of all apple fruit, and of United States export control procedures.

85.   First, the United States contests the Panel's understanding that the reference in the United States' request for the establishment of a panel to "apples" authorizes the Panel to make findings on apples other than "mature, symptomless" apples. In particular, the United States challenges the Panel's reasoning that a request for the establishment of a panel "is not exclusively a limitation to [a panel's] jurisdiction, it defines it positively too." [146] According to this logic, the United States argues, panels may offer analysis and findings on *any* claims identified in the request for the establishment of a panel, including those not pursued by the complaining party. In the view of the United States, however, it is not the function of dispute settlement panels to conduct a *de novo* review and make findings on claims not pursued, nor is it their function to "theorize" about arguments and evidence that a complaining party *might* have advanced. [147] Moreover, the United States contends that the Panel ignored the limits of its investigative authority recognized by the Appellate Body in *Japan – Agricultural Products II*, wherein the Appellate Body explained that "this authority cannot be used by a panel to rule in favour of a complaining party which has not established a *prima facie* case *based on specific legal claims asserted by it.*" [148] The United States asserts that it made no *prima facie* case with respect to immature apples, and that Japan offered no evidence that United States export control procedures would fail to ensure that only "mature, symptomless"

[142]   United States' other appellant's submission, para. 3.
[143]   *Ibid.*, para. 6.
[144]   *Ibid.*, para. 7.
[145]   United States' other appellant's submission, para. 8.
[146]   *Ibid.*, para. 10, quoting Panel Report, para. 8.32.
[147]   United States' other appellant's submission, para. 10.
[148]   *Ibid.*, para. 11, quoting Appellate Body Report, para. 129. (emphasis added by the United States)

apples were exported. In the view of the United States, therefore, the Panel had no basis to make findings *not* related to mature, symptomless apples.

86.   The United States also observes that the Panel's decision to make a finding based solely on the wording of the claim in the United States' request for the establishment of a panel is inconsistent with panel practice under the current dispute settlement mechanism. The United States argues that, because panels have not made findings on abandoned claims, parties have been able to reasonably assume that claims may be abandoned through lack of argumentation. The Panel's reasoning in this case, according to the United States, "risks prejudicing one or both parties" because it "contravene[s] that assumption". [149]

87.   Secondly, the United States challenges the Panel's claim that it had authority to make findings related to immature apples on the basis of (i) the United States' evidence on its export control procedures and (ii) Japan's argument that the measure at issue would also address the entry of immature or infected apples due to possible lapses in those procedures. The United States contends, however, that it had made no *claim* with respect to immature apples and, as a result, the Panel had no basis to review the measure in relation to immature apples. Furthermore, in the view of the United States, Japan's concerns regarding the possible failure of United States export control procedures could not justify the Panel's finding on immature apples because the sole question before the Panel related to the consistency of Japan's measure, as applied to "mature, symptomless" apples, with Article 2.2.

88.   Thirdly, the United States contends that the Panel erroneously asserted that the definition of "sanitary measure" in paragraph 1 of Annex A to the *SPS Agreement* "does not limit the scope of application of phytosanitary measures to the product that the exporting country claims to export. In order to be effective, a phytosanitary measure should cover all forms of a product that may actually be imported." [150] According to the United States, it is impossible to decide in the abstract what the requirements may be for all phytosanitary measures that a Member might maintain on any product. In any event, the United States argues, the fact that a phytosanitary measure may address risks associated with *certain* types of a product does not mean that the measure conforms to a Member's obligations under the *SPS Agreement* with respect to *all* types of a product.

89.   Finally, because Japan's measure does not relate to export control procedure failures, the United States claims that the Panel's findings on immature apples cannot be justified by reference to the Appellate Body's acknowledgement in *EC – Hormones* that a risk assessment underlying a measure may consider all scientific risks, whatever their origin, including risks from export control procedure failures.

90.   Therefore, as the Panel exceeded its authority , in the view of the United States, in ruling on matters beyond the scope of the dispute, the United States requests the Appellate Body to reverse the Panel's findings with respect to

---

[149]   United States' other appellant's submission, para. 13.
[150]   *Ibid.*, para. 16, quoting Panel Report, para. 8.119.

products other than "mature, symptomless" apples and to export control procedures, and to "declare the Panel's statements derived from those findings to be without legal effect." [151]

D.   Arguments of Japan – Appellee

Claim on the "Authority" of the Panel

91.   Japan claims that the Panel was, not only permitted to address the issue of "infected apple fruit" on the basis of the scope of the Panel's terms of reference that cover Article 2.2 of the *SPS Agreement* and United States apples "in general", but was also obligated to do so because the issue of infected apple fruit was part of the *prima facie* case to be established by the United States. [152]

92.   First, Japan disagrees with the United States' assertion that the Panel should not have addressed the issue of "immature apples" based on the fact that a panel has authority to rule only on specific claims made by the complainant. [153] Japan claims that this erroneous assertion involves two legal principles that should not be confused. The first principle, according to Japan, relates to the "scope of the dispute". [154] Japan submits that the scope of the dispute is determined by the terms of reference in the request for the establishment of a panel, such that a panel should not rule on matters not included in its terms of reference. The second principle, in Japan's view, dictates the onus on the complaining party to establish a *prima facie* case within that scope of the dispute.

93.   Regarding the "scope of the dispute" in the current case, Japan observes that Article 2.2 of the *SPS Agreement* is included in the Panel's terms of reference, and the United States' request for the establishment of a panel makes reference to "US apples" generally, rather than specifically to "mature, symptomless" apple fruit. Japan submits that the Panel's discussion of infected apples under Article 2.2 thus falls well within the scope of the dispute as defined by the request for the establishment of a panel and the terms of reference. According to Japan, addressing infected apples was necessary in order for the Panel to achieve a "satisfactory settlement of the matter", as required in Article 3.4 of the DSU; the fact that the United States did not specifically mention "infected apples" does not deprive the Panel of its right to address this issue.

94.   Concerning the second "principle", Japan asserts that the fact-finding authority of a panel should not be confused with the requirement of establishing a *prima facie* case. In Japan's view, establishing a *prima facie* case is a "requirement of proof" imposed on the complaining party that prevents a panel from finding facts in favour of the complaining party when that party has not

---

[151]   United States' other appellant's submission, para. 3.
[152]   Japan's appellee's submission, para. 2.
[153]   *Ibid.*, para. 3.
[154]   *Ibid.*, para. 4.

asserted those facts. [155] Nevertheless, Japan argues, a panel may find facts not "asserted" by the complaining party if those facts are "asserted" by the respondent. [156] Japan alleges that the assertion of a particular factual claim, even if proven, may not be sufficient to establish a *prima facie* case under the relevant provisions. More specifically, Japan claims, "in order to establish a *prima facie* case of insufficient scientific evidence under Article 2.2 of the SPS Agreement, the complaining party must establish that there is not sufficient scientific evidence for *any* of the perceived risks underlying the measure, or that the measure is otherwise not supported by sufficient scientific evidence." [157] Thus, in the present case, Japan argues, because the issue of "infected apples" is related to the risk addressed in Japan's phytosanitary measure, the United States should have established a *prima facie* case covering infected apples *in addition to* mature, symptomless apples.

95. Japan further argues that, although the Panel acted properly in addressing infected apple fruit, the Panel erred in shifting to Japan the burden of proof on the establishment of the risk of completion of the pathway through infected apple fruit. In Japan's view, it was the United States' burden to establish that it would ship only "mature, symptomless" apples. [158] Japan contends that, because the United States failed to discharge this burden, the only way for the United States to establish a *prima facie* case would be to prove the insufficiency of scientific evidence supporting the view that the pathway could be completed for *infected* apple fruit. According to Japan, this had not been demonstrated by the United States, and, therefore, the burden of proof should not have been shifted.

96. Japan contests the United States' claim that Japan failed to submit evidence on the inappropriateness of the "U.S. [export] control procedures". [159] Japan submits that the United States, not Japan, bore the obligation of proving the efficacy of United States export control procedures for apples. Moreover, Japan observes, it did submit evidence on the failure of United States export control procedures in one specific case, where apple fruit harbouring codling moth larvae was shipped to the Separate Customs Territory of Taiwan, Penghu, Kinmen, and Matsu. Japan submits that this case is "[i]ndisputable evidence that the U.S. [export] control procedures are prone to failure and that they did fail." [160] This evidence was not contested by the experts, nor was it rebutted by the United States, even though it had "ample opportunities" to do so. [161] Notwithstanding these points, Japan argues that the United States' claim regarding the adequacy of its export control procedures raises an issue of fact already decided by the Panel, and the claim should therefore be dismissed by the Appellate Body.

---

[155] *Ibid.*, para. 8.
[156] Japan's appellee's submission, para. 8.
[157] *Ibid.*, para. 9. (original italics)
[158] *Ibid.*, para. 12.
[159] *Ibid.*, para. 14, quoting United States' other appellant's submission, para. 4.
[160] Japan's appellee's submission, para. 17.
[161] *Ibid.*, paras. 21-22.

97.   Japan therefore requests the Appellate Body to reject the United States' appeal on the findings of the Panel under Article 2.2 of the *SPS Agreement*.

E.   Arguments of the Third Participants

1.   Australia

98.   Australia agrees with Japan that the Panel misinterpreted and misapplied Article 2.2 of the *SPS Agreement* and, in doing so, erred in law in finding that Japan acted inconsistently with its obligations thereunder. Concerning the interpretation of Article 2.2, Australia considers that the Panel erred by introducing a requirement under this provision for a phytosanitary measure to be "justified" by the relevant scientific evidence, and not to be "disproportionate" to the identified risk. In Australia's view, this requirement is not supported by the text of Article 2.2 and suggests that the Panel incorporated improperly into that provision the substantive obligations set forth separately in Articles 5.1, 5.3, and 5.6. In doing so, according to Australia, the Panel undermined the negotiated balance of rights and obligations in the *SPS Agreement*.

99.   Australia submits that "Article 2.2 operates to ensure that the body of available scientific evidence related to the risk addressed by the measure is adequate for an assessment of risk required under Article 5.1, but does not include a requirement for the actual measure applied by the Member to be justified by the scientifically identified risk." [162] According to Australia, to read Article 2.2 as requiring a phytosanitary measure to be "justified" by sufficient scientific evidence, as the Panel did, converts impermissibly the phrase "not maintained without sufficient scientific evidence" in Article 2.2 to the phrase "not supported by sufficient scientific evidence". [163] Instead, Australia argues, the issue of whether a phytosanitary measure is "justified" by scientific evidence should be evaluated under Articles 3 and 5 of the *SPS Agreement*.

100.   Regarding the application of Article 2.2, assuming the Panel's interpretation were correct, Australia agrees with Japan that the Panel held implicitly that Japan should bear the burden of proof in establishing that the last stage of the pathway through infected fruit would be completed. Citing the Appellate Body Reports in *US – Wool Shirts and Blouses* and *Japan – Agricultural Products II*, Australia submits that the complaining party has the burden of establishing a *prima facie* case of inconsistency with Article 2.2. Although the United States could have satisfied this burden by establishing a presumption that sufficient scientific evidence did not exist, according to Australia, the Panel failed to make any assessment of whether the United States had raised the necessary presumption with respect to the risk from *infected* apple fruit. Australia notes that the United States made no assertion and presented no evidence on *infected* apple fruit. Therefore, Australia argues, the Panel erred in law by making findings on claims concerning apples other than mature, symptomless apples in the absence of any legal arguments or evidence brought

---

[162]   Australia's third participant's submission, para. 28.
[163]   *Ibid.*, para. 30.

by the United States in support of these claims. In Australia's view, "the legal effect of a reversal of the Panel's findings on apples other than mature symptomless apples must lead to the conclusion that the United States failed to make a *prima facie* case in relation to the specific legal claim on the consistency of Japan's measures under Article 2.2." [164]

101.   Australia also agrees with Japan that the Panel made errors of law and interpretation with respect to Article 5.7 of the *SPS Agreement*, but "does not share Japan's views on the interpretation of Article 5.7." [165] Recalling the findings of the Appellate Body in *US – Wool Shirts and Blouses*, *EC – Hormones*, and *EC – Sardines*, Australia argues that a complaining Member bears the burden of proof in establishing a measure's inconsistency with any provision that is a "fundamental part of the rights and obligations of WTO Members". [166] In Australia's view, these cases also make clear that this burden cannot be discharged merely by characterizing the relevant provision as an "exception" because certain exceptions may nevertheless constitute a "fundamental part of the rights and obligations of WTO Members". In Australia's view, Article 5.7 of the *SPS Agreement* is such an exception because the provision establishes an importing Member's right to impose provisional phytosanitary measures, subject to certain conditions found by the Appellate Body in *Japan – Agricultural Products II*. [167] Therefore, according to Australia, Article 5.7 does not stand in a "general rule-exception" relationship with Article 2.2 that would warrant reversing the burden of proof normally placed on the complaining Member. [168]

102.   Australia further submits that the Panel made several errors in its legal interpretation of Article 5.1 of the *SPS Agreement*. First, Australia agrees with Japan that the Panel erred in its interpretation of the definition of a risk assessment under Article 5.1 of the *SPS Agreement*. Australia submits that the Panel misinterpreted the requirement of "specificity" as applying to the "product at issue" in the context of the risk assessment [169], erroneously introducing a "new standard" [170] of "specificity" that is not warranted by the text of the *SPS Agreement*. In Australia's view, the Appellate Body findings in *EC – Hormones*, consequently applied by the panel in *Australia – Salmon*, discussed "specificity" in the context of requiring a risk assessment to be related to the "risk at issue", not to the "product at issue". [171] Therefore, Australia agrees with Japan that the fact that the 1999 PRA assessed the probability of transmission by more than one vector is not a sufficient basis *alone* for determining that Japan

---

[164]   *Ibid.*, para. 47.
[165]   *Ibid.*, para. 48.
[166]   *Ibid.*, para. 55, quoting Appellate Body Report, *US – Wool Shirts and Blouses*, p. 16, DSR 1997:I, 323, at 337.
[167]   Australia's third participant's submission, para. 66, referring to Appellate Body Report, para. 89.
[168]   Australia's third participant's submission, paras. 65 and 68, citing Appellate Body Report, *EC – Hormones*, para. 104 and Appellate Body Report, *EC – Sardines*, para. 275.
[169]   Australia's third participant's submission, para. 78.
[170]   *Ibid.*, para. 76.
[171]   *Ibid.*, para. 77.

did not assess properly the probability of transmission of fire blight through apple fruit.

103.   Secondly, Australia submits that the Panel "mistakenly" [172] relied on the phrase "as appropriate to the circumstances" in Article 5.1 as context when interpreting "measures which might be applied" in paragraph 4 of Annex A to the *SPS Agreement*. According to Australia, whatever flexibility may be afforded an importing Member in the conduct of its risk assessment by the phrase "as appropriate to the circumstances", such flexibility cannot be interpreted to "annul or supersede the substantive requirements for a valid risk assessment." [173]

104.   Thirdly, Australia submits that there is no legal or textual basis to impose a requirement on a Member to update its completed risk assessment every time new scientific evidence becomes available or existing evidence is challenged. In Australia's view, the obligation under Article 5.1 for a Member to ensure that its "measures are based on an assessment ... of risks" is a constant and objective requirement, which may be assessed by the Panel at the time of its inquiry. However, concerning the conditions for a "risk assessment" under the *SPS Agreement*, as identified by the Appellate Body in *Australia – Salmon*, Australia argues that once a risk assessment has met these conditions, its validity is not subject to ongoing review. [174] Thus, in Australia's view, new scientific evidence is relevant under Article 5.1 for the purpose of determining whether a rational relationship exists between the measure and the risk assessment, but not for determining whether a particular risk assessment continues to satisfy the definition of a "risk assessment" in Annex A to the *SPS Agreement*. In the light of the Panel's errors in interpreting Article 5.1, Australia supports Japan's request to reverse the Panel's findings accordingly.

105.   Australia additionally claims that, with respect to the Panel's failure to make an "objective assessment of the matter" before it, as required under Article 11 of the DSU, Japan's allegations "have merit and deserve close attention". [175] In particular, Australia agrees with Japan's allegation that the Panel failed to make an objective assessment in its analysis under Article 5.1 because it failed to consider all relevant evidence before it. In Australia's view, despite the fact that the Panel indicated that it would consider other materials *in addition to* the 1999 PRA, the Panel does not appear to have gone beyond the 1999 PRA in its examination of evidence. Australia submits that the "Panel's decision to rely heavily on one piece of evidence in its Report, and not to refer to all relevant evidence in its analysis, is a violation of Article 11." [176] Moreover, Australia asserts, the Panel failed to meet the criteria for an objective assessment described in previous Appellate Body Reports because of its failure to provide "adequate reasoning" to support its findings. [177]

---

[172]   *Ibid.*, para. 82.
[173]   *Ibid.*, para. 83.
[174]   *Ibid.*, para. 86.
[175]   *Ibid.*, para. 92.
[176]   *Ibid.*, para. 98. (footnotes omitted)
[177]   *Ibid.*, para. 98.

2. Brazil

106.   Brazil agrees with the interpretation given by the Panel to Article 5.7 and its conclusion that the measure at issue did not satisfy the first requirement of Article 5.7, namely that this be a case "where relevant scientific evidence is insufficient".

3. European Communities

107.   The European Communities agrees with the United States that the Panel should have refrained from making findings with respect to "immature, possibly infected apples" [178], on which the United States had not made any claim. The European Communities asserts, however, that the Panel's error should not affect merely the *scope* of the Panel's findings, but rather the Panel's findings on the merits of the case. The European Communities contends that, in the absence of a *prima facie* case made out by the United States, which required the production of evidence related to *all* apples, the Panel should have reached the conclusion that the United States had failed to prove the incompatibility of the measure at issue with the *SPS Agreement*.

108.   The European Communities argues that the Panel should have begun its analysis by focusing on the risk sought to be addressed by the measure at issue. Instead, in the European Communities' view, the Panel erroneously concluded that it was relevant to differentiate between the risks related to mature and apparently healthy apple fruit, and those related to other apples. By drawing this distinction and analyzing separately the case of apples other than mature, symptomless apples, the European Communities submits, the Panel "made a case for the complainant". [179] According to the European Communities, the United States had argued that mature, symptomless apple fruit represents no risk of fire blight transmission and hence presented a *prima facie* case only for this particular type of apple, not for any other. The European Communities emphasizes that if the premise assumed in any analysis of a phytosanitary measure is that only "hazard-free goods" are exported, then no domestic measure will ever be found to be consistent with the *SPS Agreement*. [180] The European Communities argues that if a complainant desires to base its claim on the fact that it exports solely "hazard-free goods", it should bear the burden of presenting "convincing evidence showing that there is no possibility of fraud or negligence or accident", particularly when there are large volumes of exports of that commodity. [181]

109.   Therefore, the European Communities submits that the United States should have established a *prima facie* case showing that Japan's measure was not necessary or was disproportionate, including with respect to the importation of *infected* fruit. Alternatively, the European Communities contends, the United

---

[178]   European Communities' third participant's submission, para. 4.
[179]   *Ibid.*, para. 10.
[180]   *Ibid.*, para. 11.
[181]   *Ibid.*

States should have provided evidence establishing that *only non-infected* fruit would be exported. Because the United States failed to make any claim or submit any evidence in this respect, and as the Panel found on the basis of the experts' advice that there may be errors of handling or illegal actions, the European Communities agrees with Japan that the Panel should have concluded that the United States failed to make a *prima facie* case on the inconsistency of the measure at issue with the *SPS Agreement*.

110.   The European Communities further disagrees with the Panel's allocation of the burden of proof under Article 2.2. In the European Communities' view, once the Panel found that the scientific evidence was not sufficient to justify the measure as applied to "mature, symptomless apples" [182], it allocated improperly to Japan the burden of proof as regards the risk of completion of the pathway in *immature, infected* apple fruit, for which the United States had submitted no evidence at all. Because the United States had not made a *prima facie* case with respect to apples other than mature, symptomless apples, according to the European Communities, the Panel erred in prematurely shifting the burden of proof to Japan.

111.   With respect to the Panel's analysis under Article 5.7 of the *SPS Agreement*, the European Communities argues that the Panel erred in treating Article 5.7 as an "affirmative defence to a violation of Article 2.2" and in its interpretation of the term "insufficient". [183] Citing the Appellate Body Report in *EC – Hormones*, the European Communities argues that Article 5.7 is not, by its nature, an exception, despite the phrase "except as provided in Article 5.7" at the end of Article 2.2. [184] The European Communities submits that Article 5.7 contains its own set of obligations and that it creates an "autonomous right" to take provisional measures. [185] The European Communities claims that the autonomous nature of this right is confirmed in *Japan – Agricultural Products II*, wherein the Appellate Body explained how a measure may be inconsistent with Article 5.7 in and of itself. Accordingly, in the European Communities' view, it is for the *complaining* party to demonstrate an inconsistency with Article 5.7. Therefore, the European Communities contends that the Panel erred with respect to the allocation of the burden of proof under Article 5.7.

112.   As to the Panel's interpretation of Article 5.7, the European Communities argues that the phrase "[i]n cases where relevant scientific evidence is insufficient" refers to precise occurrences rather than general phenomena. As a result, the European Communities submits that the application of provisional measures under Article 5.7 is permissible in situations where there is insufficient scientific evidence on a "specific issue" that is "key" to defining the nature or extent of a risk, despite the existence of "general information on a given subject". [186] Moreover, the European Communities contends, the term

---

[182]   *Ibid.*, para. 16.
[183]   *Ibid.*, paras. 14 and 21.
[184]   See European Communities' third participant's submission, para. 22, citing Appellate Body Report, para. 104.
[185]   European Communities' third participant's submission, para. 24.
[186]   *Ibid.*, para. 32.

"insufficient evidence" can cover evidence that is "incomplete" or "unconvincing", even if there is a large volume of such evidence.[187] In this regard, the European Communities argues, the sufficiency of the evidence may change over time, for example, as new research casts doubt on the correctness of previously sufficient studies. Thus, according to the European Communities, the Panel erred by interpreting "insufficient evidence" narrowly so as to examine the sufficiency of existing evidence solely on a quantitative rather than a qualitative basis.

4.   New Zealand

113.   New Zealand agrees with the United States that the Panel should not have made findings with respect to immature apples. In New Zealand's view, the United States' claims were related to the WTO-consistency of Japan's measure as that measure applied to *mature* apples, not to other products, such as immature apples. New Zealand asserts that the Panel acted contrary to "established WTO jurisprudence regarding the burden of proof" because it made findings as to issues on which a *prima facie* case was not established by the complaining party.[188] Accordingly, New Zealand submits that the Appellate Body should reverse the Panel's legal findings in respect of immature apple fruit and "declare the Panel's statements derived from those findings to be without legal effect."[189]

114.   As to the interpretation of Article 2.2, New Zealand contests Japan's claim that Article 2.2 should be understood to "allow a certain degree of discretion ... on the part of an importing member to determine the value of the evidence to it and to introduce a particular measure thereon."[190] New Zealand argues that Article 2.2 provides no basis for such a "certain degree of discretion". Instead, according to New Zealand, Article 2.2 requires a rational or objective relationship between the phytosanitary measure and the scientific evidence, and an importing Member's method of evaluating scientific evidence must necessarily be consistent with this requirement of rationality. In New Zealand's view, the "logical conclusion" of Japan's argument is that importing Members would be permitted to accord little weight to relevant scientific evidence and thereby impose phytosanitary measures that have no rational relationship with such evidence.[191]

115.   With respect to the United States' *prima facie* case under Article 2.2 for mature apples, New Zealand argues that Japan has failed to establish an error in the Panel's analysis. First, New Zealand rejects as a basis for error Japan's claim that the Panel evaluated improperly the scientific evidence on the basis of the experts' statements rather than of the views of the importing Member in this case. Not only did the Panel discount the value of the evidence cited by Japan, New Zealand claims, but Japan's reasoning would preclude panels from ever

---

[187]   *Ibid.*, para. 33.
[188]   New Zealand's third participant's submission, para. 3.35.
[189]   *Ibid.*, para. 3.36.
[190]   *Ibid.*, para. 3.09, quoting Japan's appellant's submission, para. 76.
[191]   New Zealand's third participant's submission, para. 3.10.

considering scientific evidence that contradicts the views of the importing Member. Such subjectivity accorded an importing Member, in the view of New Zealand, is inconsistent with the objective relationship that must exist between the phytosanitary measure and the scientific evidence under Article 2.2.

116.   Secondly, New Zealand disagrees with Japan's claim that the United States failed to establish the absence of scientific evidence on material aspects of the risk sought to be addressed by Japan. New Zealand claims that Japan "mischaracterises" the criteria set out by the Panel for a *prima facie* case to be made by the United States.[192] New Zealand states that the Panel, after rejecting Japan's claim that the United States was required to prove positively the insufficiency of the scientific evidence, relied on the Appellate Body Report in *Japan – Agricultural Products II* to find that a *prima facie* case would be made where the United States had raised a *presumption* that sufficient scientific evidence did not exist. Once the Panel found that the presumption had been raised, New Zealand argues, the Panel weighed the evidence before it and found that Japan had not rebutted the presumption. Therefore, in New Zealand's view, the Panel properly found that a *prima facie* case had been made by the United States on its claim in respect of mature apples under Article 2.2.

117.   New Zealand agrees with the Panel's analysis relating to Article 5.7 of the *SPS Agreement*, because the Panel found that the "wealth of scientific evidence"—either "in general" *or* in relation to specific aspects of the risk—demonstrates that the issue of the risk of transmission of fire blight through mature apple fruit is not one upon which there is insufficient relevant scientific evidence as required under Article 5.7.[193] In New Zealand's view, therefore, Japan is incorrect to suggest that the Panel failed to consider the sufficiency of scientific evidence as to the particular elements of the risk at issue. Moreover, concerning Japan's argument that the elimination of the measure would create "new uncertainty", New Zealand submits that this dispute is concerned with the measure at issue, not with measures that may be in place in hypothetical circumstances at some point in the future. As such, the possible uncertainty created by the development of a *new* phytosanitary measure cannot be relied upon to cure the WTO-inconsistency of the *existing* measure.

118.   New Zealand further submits that the Panel's findings in relation to Article 5.1 of the *SPS Agreement* are correct and should be upheld. New Zealand agrees with the Panel that Japan's risk assessment was not sufficiently specific to the matter at issue. In New Zealand's view, the evaluation of the likelihood of entry, establishment and spread of the disease specifically from mature apple fruit is more than an issue of procedure or methodology, as Japan alleges, but a "substantive requirement" of Article 5.1.[194] This requirement, according to New Zealand, does not prevent an importing Member's selection of methodology for conducting its risk assessment, nor does it prevent importing Members from

---

[192] *Ibid.*, para. 3.16.
[193] *Ibid.*, para. 3.19.
[194] *Ibid.*, para. 3.30.

considering several possible hosts simultaneously, provided that a conclusion as to the risk is drawn with respect to the *particular commodity* at issue.

119.   New Zealand also contests Japan's claim that it has conducted an appropriate risk assessment "in the course of this proceeding". [195] New Zealand finds it "astonishing" that Japan "essentially" asks the Appellate Body to find that, on the basis of evidence and arguments advanced by Japan in this dispute, Japan has conducted an "informal" risk assessment that satisfies the standard required by the *SPS Agreement*. [196] In New Zealand's view, the requirement under Article 5.1 of basing measures on a risk assessment would be rendered "devoid of any meaning" because, according to Japan's rationale, an importing Member could avoid conducting a risk assessment until challenged in a dispute settlement proceeding, at which point a "*post facto* risk assessment" would be found to satisfy Article 5.1. [197] Accordingly, New Zealand requests the Appellate Body to uphold the Panel's findings under Article 5.1 of the *SPS Agreement*.

IV.   PRELIMINARY ISSUE: SUFFICIENCY OF THE NOTICE OF APPEAL

120.   We begin our analysis of this appeal with a preliminary issue related to the sufficiency of the Notice of Appeal filed by Japan. [198] In its appellee's submission, the United States argues that Japan's claim under Article 11 of the DSU, as it relates to the Panel's findings under Article 5.1 of the *SPS Agreement*, is not properly before us and requests that we dismiss this aspect of the appeal. [199] According to the United States, Japan did not properly raise this Article 11 claim in its Notice of Appeal, as required by Rule 20(2)(d) of the *Working Procedures* and in the light of the Appellate Body's decision in *US – Countervailing Measures on Certain EC Products*. As a result, the United States asserts, it did not receive the requisite notice of this issue on appeal.

121.   Rule 20(2) of the *Working Procedures* sets forth the "information" that must be contained in a Notice of Appeal:

> *Commencement of Appeal*
>
> ...
>
> A Notice of Appeal shall include the following information:
>
> (a)   the title of the panel report under appeal;
>
> (b)   the name of the party to the dispute filing the Notice of Appeal;
>
> (c)   the service address, telephone and facsimile numbers of the party to the dispute; and

---

[195]   *Ibid.*, para. 3.25, quoting Japan's appellant's submission, para. 124.
[196]   New Zealand's third participant's submission, para. 3.27.
[197]   *Ibid.*, para. 3.28.
[198]   WT/DS245/5, *supra*, footnote 8, attached as Annex 1 to this Report.
[199]   United States' appellee's submission, para. 53 and footnote 88 thereto.

(d)   a brief statement of the nature of the appeal, including the allegations of errors in the issues of law covered in the panel report and legal interpretations developed by the panel.

The Appellate Body recognized, in *US – Countervailing Measures on Certain EC Products*:

> ... the important balance that must be maintained between the right of Members to exercise the right of appeal meaningfully and effectively, and the right of appellees to receive notice through the Notice of Appeal of the findings under appeal, so that they may exercise their right of defence effectively. [200]

The Appellate Body observed in that case that the requirements identified in Rule 20(2) for inclusion in a Notice of Appeal "serve to ensure that the appellee also receives notice, albeit brief, of the 'nature of the appeal' and the 'allegations of errors' by the panel." [201] Thus, an evaluation of the sufficiency of a Notice of Appeal must examine whether the appellee received notice therein of the issues to be argued on appeal.

122.   In *US – Countervailing Measures on Certain EC Products*, the Appellate Body considered an appellee's challenge to the sufficiency of a Notice of Appeal on the basis that, *inter alia*, the Notice of Appeal had not provided the appellee with the requisite notice of the appellant's claim under Article 11 of the DSU. The appellant had alleged in its written and oral submissions that the Panel had failed to make an "objective assessment of the matter before it", as required by Article 11. [202] When considering whether the appellee had been given notice of the Article 11 challenge, the Appellate Body reviewed the Notice of Appeal and observed as follows:

> We do not find any explicit reference to Article 11 of the DSU, or to the language of Article 11 in the Notice of Appeal, or in the attachment to the letter of 13 September 2002. Nor can we discern in either of them any suggestion that the United States was alleging that the Panel failed to make an objective assessment of the matter before it, or an objective assessment of the facts of the case. [203]

123.   The Appellate Body rejected in that case the appellant's submission that its Article 11 challenge was merely an *argument* supporting the broader *claim* raised on appeal with respect to other WTO provisions and that, therefore, no further clarification was required in the Notice of Appeal. [204] In doing so, the Appellate Body acknowledged that claims on appeal under Article 11 of the

---

[200]   Appellate Body Report, para. 62.
[201]   Appellate Body Report, *US – Countervailing Measures on Certain EC Products*, para. 62.
[202]   *Ibid.*, paras. 27 and 73.
[203]   *Ibid.*, para. 72.
[204]   *Ibid.*, paras. 73-74.

DSU are unique when compared with other claims of legal error committed by a panel:

> A *claim* of error by a panel under Article 11 of the DSU is possible only in the context of an appeal. By definition, this *claim* will not be found in requests for establishment of a panel, and panels therefore will not have referred to it in panel reports. Accordingly, if appellants intend to argue that issue on appeal, they must refer to it in Notices of Appeal in a way that will enable appellees to discern it and know the case they have to meet. [205] (original italics)

Therefore, the Appellate Body concluded that the appellee could not have had notice that the appellant intended to challenge the consistency of the panel's evaluation with its obligations under Article 11, and that the appellant sought to have the Appellate Body rule on that matter. [206]

124.   We likewise examine in this case the Notice of Appeal filed by Japan to evaluate whether the United States was on notice that Japan would make claims on appeal under Article 11 of the DSU. Japan claims to have raised on appeal two separate challenges under Article 11 of the DSU: one with respect to the Panel's evaluation of the United States' claim under Article 2.2 of the *SPS Agreement*, and one with respect to the Panel's evaluation of the United States' claim under Article 5.1 of that agreement. [207] Japan's Notice of Appeal identifies, in relevant part, the following alleged legal errors as issues on appeal:

> 1.   The Panel erred in law in finding that Japan acted inconsistently with its obligations under Article 2.2 of the SPS Agreement. This finding reflects the Panel's erroneous interpretation of the rule of burden of proof, and the Panel's failure to make an objective assessment of the matter before it under Article 11 of the DSU.
>
> ...
>
> 3.   The Panel erred in law in finding that Japan's phytosanitary measure was not based on a risk assessment within the meaning of Article 5.1 of the SPS Agreement. This finding is based on an erroneous interpretation of the requirements of a risk assessment under Article 5.1.

125.   Japan's intention to contest the Panel's analysis *under Article 2.2* as inconsistent with the requirements of Article 11 of the DSU is set out clearly and unambiguously. As to the Panel's analysis *under Article 5.1*, however, we note the conspicuous absence of any reference to Article 11 of the DSU, or to the standard of "objective assessment" established in that provision. Indeed, we find in the Notice of Appeal no reference to Article 11 or to the "objective assessment" standard set out therein other than in the context of Article 2.2, quoted above.

---

[205] Appellate Body Report, *US – Countervailing Measures on Certain EC Products*, para. 74.
[206] *Ibid.*, para. 75.
[207] Japan's appellant's submission, paras. 47-70 (Article 2.2) and paras. 130-132 (Article 5.1).

126.   By referring to the Panel's alleged failure to comply with Article 11 of the DSU only in the context of Article 2.2, Japan did not enable the United States to "know the case [it had] to meet" [208] as to the Article 11 claim related to Article 5.1 of the *SPS Agreement*. The Appellate Body has consistently emphasized that due process requires that a Notice of Appeal place an appellee on notice of the issues raised on appeal. [209] It is this concern with due process, reflected in Rule 20 of the *Working Procedures*, that underlay the Appellate Body's ruling on the sufficiency of the Notice of Appeal in *US – Countervailing Measures on Certain EC Products*.

127.   Japan acknowledged during the oral hearing that it did not give the United States notice of its Article 11 claim specifically with respect to the Panel's analysis under Article 5.1 of the *SPS Agreement*. [210] Japan claimed, however, that "since we raised the claim under Article 5.1 of the *SPS Agreement*, this naturally involved some factual issues and ... we can assume that the United States was notified" as to the related Article 11 claim. [211] We disagree. As noted above [212], the Appellate Body determined in *US – Countervailing Measures on Certain EC Products* that Article 11 claims are distinct from those raised under substantive provisions of other covered agreements. It follows from this distinction that notice of an Article 11 challenge cannot be "assumed" merely because there is a challenge to a panel's analysis of a substantive provision of a WTO agreement. Rather, an Article 11 claim constitutes a "separate 'allegation of error'" [213] that must be included in a Notice of Appeal. We therefore reject Japan's assertion that an Article 11 challenge is only a "legal argument" underlying the issues raised on appeal. [214]

128.   Under these circumstances, we agree with the United States that it could not have been on notice that Japan intended to raise an Article 11 challenge to the Panel's evaluation of the United States' Article 5.1 claim. Accordingly, we find that the issue of the Panel's compliance with Article 11 of the DSU, with respect to its analysis of the United States' claim under Article 5.1 of the *SPS*

---

[208]   Appellate Body Report, *US – Countervailing Measures on Certain EC Products*, para. 74.

[209]   For example, Appellate Body Report, *US – Offset Act (Byrd Amendment)*, para. 195; Appellate Body Report, *US – Countervailing Measures on Certain EC Products*, para. 62; Appellate Body Report, *EC – Bananas III*, para. 152; and Appellate Body Report, *US – Shrimp*, para. 97.

[210]   Japan's response to questioning at the oral hearing.

[211]   *Ibid.*

[212]   *Supra*, para. 123, quoting Appellate Body Report, *US – Countervailing Measures on Certain EC Products*, para. 74.

[213]   Appellate Body Report, *Chile – Price Band System*, para. 182, quoting Rule 20(2)(d) of the *Working Procedures*. In this respect, we note the distinction between *claims* and *arguments* in the context of determining whether claims have been properly identified in the request for the establishment of a panel (Appellate Body Report, *EC – Bananas III*, paras. 141-143; Appellate Body Report, *EC – Hormones*, para. 156), and we affirm the Appellate Body's observation in *Chile – Price Band System* that "this distinction between claims and legal arguments under Article 6.2 of the DSU is also relevant to the distinction between 'allegations of error' and legal arguments as contemplated by Rule 20 of the *Working Procedures*." (Appellate Body Report, para. 182)

[214]   Japan's response to questioning at the oral hearing. As discussed, *supra*, at paragraph 123, the Appellate Body rejected a similar contention by the appellant in *US – Countervailing Measures on Certain EC Products*. (Appellate Body Report, paras. 73-74) The Appellate Body made a similar observation in *US – Steel Safeguards*. (Appellate Body Report, para. 498)

Agreement, is not properly before us in this appeal. Consequently, we do not rule on this issue. [215]

V.   ISSUES RAISED IN THIS APPEAL

129.   Japan raises the following four claims, namely, that the Panel:

(i)   erred in finding that Japan's phytosanitary measure is "maintained without sufficient scientific evidence" and is therefore inconsistent with Japan's obligations under Article 2.2 of the *SPS Agreement*;

(ii)   erred in finding that Japan's phytosanitary measure is not a provisional measure under Article 5.7 because the measure was not imposed in respect of a situation where "relevant scientific evidence is insufficient";

(iii)   erred in finding that Japan's phytosanitary measure was not based on a risk assessment, as defined in Annex A to the *SPS Agreement*, and as required by Article 5.1 thereof; and

(iv)   failed to comply with its duty under Article 11 of the DSU because it did not conduct an "objective assessment of the facts of the case".

130.   In addition to Japan's claims on appeal, the United States cross-appeals the Panel Report, claiming that the Panel did not have the "authority" to make findings and draw conclusions with respect to *immature* apples because the United States had limited its claims before the Panel to *mature* apples.

VI.   CLAIM ON THE "AUTHORITY" OF THE PANEL

131.   It is convenient to begin our analysis of the issues raised on appeal with the question of the "authority" of the Panel raised by the United States. [216] In the course of its analysis of whether Japan's measure is "maintained without sufficient scientific evidence" within the meaning of Article 2.2 of the *SPS Agreement*, the Panel sought to evaluate the risk that apple fruit exported by the United States would serve as a pathway for the entry, establishment and

---

[215]   Japan's allegations under Article 11 of the DSU, as they relate to the Panel's analysis of Article 2.2 of the *SPS Agreement*, are addressed *infra*, at paragraphs 217-242.

[216]   We note that the United States argues that a panel cannot "offer analysis and findings" on a claim that was not pursued by the complainant, even though the claim was initially raised in a panel request. (United States' other appellant's submission, para. 10) In other words, the United States contends that a panel does not have the "authority" to make findings and draw conclusions on such a claim. (*Ibid.*) In response to questioning at the oral hearing, the United States indicated that it had not specifically made a "terms of reference claim". We understand from the submissions of the United States that it does not challenge on appeal the "jurisdiction" of the Panel, as defined by the terms of reference, to make findings and draw conclusions on apples exported from the United States to Japan; rather, the United States contends that the Panel did not have the "authority" to make findings and draw conclusions with respect to a claim that the United States did not pursue, that is, a claim relating to apples other than mature, symptomless ones.

spread of fire blight in Japan. Although the United States claims that it exports only mature, symptomless apples to Japan, the Panel did not limit its examination to the risk related to mature, symptomless apples; it also considered the risk associated with apples other than mature, symptomless apple fruit. It did so because Japan had argued that apples other than mature, symptomless apples could be imported as a result of human or technical error, or illegal actions, and the Panel thought that such risks could be "legitimately considered" by Japan. [217] Thus, the Panel concluded that it was entitled to address Japan's assertion that a risk of introduction of fire blight in Japan "could result from a malfunction in the sorting of apples or [from] illegal action in the country of exportation", [218] and rejected the proposition that it should limit its findings to mature, symptomless apples simply because "the United States apparently limits its claims, arguments and evidence to [such apples]." [219]

132.   The United States contends on appeal that the Panel had no authority to make findings and draw conclusions with respect to "immature apples" because the United States advanced no claim regarding such apples. [220] In support of its assertion that a panel cannot rule on a claim that has not been put forward by the complainant, the United States relies on the Appellate Body Report in *Japan – Agricultural Products II*, where the Appellate Body stated that a panel cannot use its investigative authority "to rule in favour of a complaining party which has not established a *prima facie* case [of inconsistency] *based on specific legal claims asserted by it.*" [221] The United States explains that it exports only mature, symptomless apples to Japan and that it has both laws and extensive measures in place to limit apple exports to mature, symptomless apple fruit. [222] The United States observes that Japan offered no evidence, nor did the record otherwise contain any evidence, of the failure or likelihood of failure of United States procedures to ensure compliance with United States control requirements prohibiting the exportation of apples other than mature, symptomless apple fruit. The United States further notes that the measure under challenge in this appeal includes no such control requirements. [223]

133.   In evaluating the "authority" of the Panel to make findings and draw conclusions with respect to all apple fruit, including immature apples, we turn first to the Panel's terms of reference. A panel's terms of reference perform a fundamental function as they "establish the jurisdiction of the panel" [224] and "define the scope of the dispute". [225] In the present case, the terms of reference of the Panel include the following :

---

[217]   Panel Report, paras. 8.85, 8.121, and 8.174.
[218]   *Ibid.*, para. 7.31.
[219]   *Ibid.*
[220]   United States' other appellant's submission, paras. 3 and 15.
[221]   *Ibid.*, para. 11, quoting Appellate Body Report, para. 129. (emphasis added by the United States)
[222]   United States' other appellant's submission, para. 7.
[223]   *Ibid.*, para. 12.
[224]   Appellate Body Report, *Brazil – Desiccated Coconut*, p. 22, DSR 1997:I, 167, at 186.
[225]   Appellate Body Report, *US – Carbon Steel*, para. 126.

> In accordance with Article 7.1 of the DSU, the terms of reference of the Panel are the following:
>
> "To examine, in the light of the relevant provisions of the covered agreements cited by the United States in document WT/DS245/2, the matter referred to the DSB by the United States in that document and to make such findings as will assist the DSB in making the recommendations or in giving the rulings provided for in those agreements." [226]

Document WT/DS245/2, referred to therein, is the request of the United States for the establishment of a panel. That request refers to "measures restricting the importation of US apples in connection with fire blight or the fire blight disease-causing organism, *Erwinia amylovora*". The request then lists the restrictions with which the United States is concerned. We note, first, that those restrictions are applicable to apple fruit produced in the United States for exportation to Japan; their scope is not restricted to mature, symptomless apples. Secondly, the United States' request refers to "US apples", an expression that in our opinion is broader than mature, symptomless apples. For these two reasons, we are of the view that the terms of reference did not limit the Panel to making findings and drawing conclusions with respect to mature, symptomless apples.

134.   We examine next the United States' argument that the Panel had no authority to make findings and draw conclusions with respect to immature apples, because the United States had made no claim regarding immature apples. We are not persuaded by this argument. Before the Panel, the United States claimed that Japan maintains "measures restricting the importation of US apples in connection with fire blight or the fire blight disease-causing organism, *Erwinia amylovora*", and that "[t]hese measures appear to be inconsistent with the commitments and obligations of Japan under Article[] 2.2 … of the *Agreement on the Application of Sanitary and Phytosanitary Measures* (SPS Agreement)." [227] In seeking to establish its claim, the United States put forward arguments and allegations of fact only with respect to mature, symptomless apples. For its part, Japan argued, among other things, that despite controls established by exporting countries, apples other than mature, symptomless apples could be exported to Japan as a result of human or technical errors or illegal actions, and that such apples could serve as a pathway for fire blight. [228] In other words, even though a country seeks to export only mature, symptomless apples, there is a risk that apples other than mature, symptomless apples will be exported to Japan, be infected, and transmit fire blight to Japanese host plants.

135.   The Panel determined that it was "legitimate to consider" [229] the arguments and allegations of fact regarding apples other than mature, symptomless apples put forward by Japan in response to the claim pursued by the United States under Article 2.2. We agree with the Panel. A panel has the

---

[226]   WT/DS245/3, *supra*, footnote 3, para. 2.
[227]   WT/DS245/2, *supra*, footnote 2.
[228]   Panel Report, para. 8.28.
[229]   *Ibid.*, para. 8.121.

authority to make findings and draw conclusions on arguments and allegations of fact that are made by the respondent and *relevant* to a claim pursued by the complainant. The Panel's findings and conclusions with respect to apples other than mature, symptomless apples were in response to the arguments and allegations of fact that were "legitimately" raised by Japan. Therefore, when the Panel made findings and drew conclusions on apples other than mature, symptomless apple fruit, it duly acted within the limits of its authority. [230]

136.   In making this finding, we do not suggest that a panel should rule on claims that are not before it; nor do we disagree with the United States that a party may abandon claims in the course of dispute settlement proceedings. In other words, we see nothing wrong with the United States restricting the scope of its claim subsequent to the issuance of the terms of reference or at any other stage of the proceedings. Undoubtedly, a party has the prerogative to pursue whatever legal strategy it wishes in conducting its case. However, that strategy must not curtail the right of other parties to pursue strategies of their own; nor can the strategic choices of the parties impose a straightjacket on a panel. A respondent is entitled to answer the complainant's case and is not confined to addressing the specific facts and arguments put forward by the complainant, provided that the response is *relevant* to the issues in dispute. Also, a panel is entitled to consider such facts and arguments, provided that it does not exceed its terms of reference. The Panel in this case considered relevant Japan's arguments relating to apples other than mature, symptomless apples, and nothing in the terms of reference prevented the Panel from addressing them. In doing so, the Panel did not rule on a claim that was not before it; rather, it ruled on the very claim it was mandated to address.

137.   The United States points to the absence of evidence on the failure or likelihood of failure of United States' procedures to ensure compliance with United States control requirements prohibiting the exportation of apples other than mature, symptomless apple fruit. [231] According to the United States, the Panel "undertook an analysis of U.S. procedures ... based on a record devoid of evidence on those procedures." [232] The United States also appears to suggest that, in the absence of evidence on United States' export control procedures, the Panel was not entitled to conclude that it was legitimate to consider the risks inherent

---

[230]   In support of the argument that the Panel had no authority to make findings and draw conclusions with respect to immature apples, the United States relies on the finding of the Appellate Body in *Japan – Agricultural Products II* that a panel should not use its investigative authority "to rule in favour of a complaining party which has not established a *prima facie* case of inconsistency based on specific legal claims asserted by it." (Appellate Body Report, para. 129) The United States' reliance on *Japan – Agricultural Products II* is misplaced, for the facts and circumstances that led to the Appellate Body's finding are not the same as those present here. In *Japan – Agricultural Products II*, the Appellate Body found fault with the panel's reliance on expert evidence to rule in favour of the complainant in the absence of a case established by the complainant itself. The circumstances in the present case differ from those present in *Japan – Agricultural Products II*. Indeed, in the present case, the Panel made findings and drew conclusions on apples other than mature, symptomless apples in response to Japan's case.

[231]   United States' other appellant's submission, para. 12.

[232]   *Ibid.*

in errors in sorting apples, or of illegal actions, which might lead to the importation into Japan of contaminated apples. [233]

138.   We are not persuaded by this argument. We point out first that, contrary to what the United States contends, the Panel did not "undert[ake] an analysis" of the United States' export control procedures. The subject matter of the Panel's analysis was the risk of transmission of fire blight through apple fruit. The Panel carried out this analysis in order to evaluate whether Japan's measure is "maintained without sufficient scientific evidence" within the meaning of Article 2.2 of the *SPS Agreement*. Japan had argued, in connection with the question of risk of transmission of fire blight through apple fruit, that it must protect itself against failures in control systems of exporting countries that could lead to the introduction of contaminated apples. [234] In making this argument, Japan referred to export control systems in general, not the specific export control system of the United States. To substantiate the argument, Japan referred to opinions of the experts and to a case of export control failure that occurred in November 2002, involving codling moth larvae found in apples shipped from the state of Washington to the Separate Customs Territory of Taiwan, Penghu, Kinmen, and Matsu. [235] After reviewing Japan's argument, the Panel found that errors of handling or illegal actions were risks that could, in principle, legitimately be considered by Japan [236] and, consequently, the Panel included these risks in the scope of the analysis. [237]

139.   Secondly, we note that, in justifying the finding that errors of handling or illegal actions may legitimately be considered, the Panel also referred to opinions of the experts. [238] Therefore, the United States' allegation that the Panel made its finding in the absence of evidence is incorrect.

140.   Furthermore, contrary to what the United States suggests, we consider that, in any event, the Panel did not need specific evidence of failure or likelihood of failure of United States export control procedures to conclude that errors of handling or illegal actions are risks that may legitimately be considered. The Panel's determination does not relate to the *specific* export control procedures of the United States and does not stem from an assessment by the Panel of such specific procedures. Instead, the Panel's conclusion applies *in general* to errors of handling and illegal actions; it is based on views on the nature of these risks and, in particular, on the opinion of one of the experts that, in plant quarantine, inspections are rarely 100 percent efficient. [239]

---

[233]   *Ibid.*, para. 17; Panel Report, paras. 8.121 and 8.161.

[234]   Panel Report, para. 8.85(d).

[235]   *Ibid.*, para. 4.191.

[236]   *Ibid.*, para. 8.161.

[237]   *Ibid.*, para. 8.121.

[238]   *Ibid.*, paras. 8.160-8.161, citing *ibid.*, paras. 6.15 and 6.71, and paras. 263, 266, 303, 327, 398, and 431 of Annex 3 thereto.

[239]   *Ibid.*, para. 8.160. The Panel refers to a comment made by Dr. Ian Smith, one of the experts retained by the Panel. We note that, in response to questioning at the oral hearing, the United States acknowledged that the conclusion in paragraph 8.161 of the Panel Report that errors of handling or illegal actions are risks that may be legitimately considered is a "general statement" which refers to

141.   Finally, we note that the Panel did not examine the risk of errors of handling or illegal actions *in general* for the purpose of assessing the reliability of the United States' export control procedures or of determining whether apples other than mature, symptomless apple fruit were actually exported from the United States to Japan. The examination by the Panel of the risk of errors of handling or illegal actions *in general* had a more limited objective—that of appreciating the relevance of Japan's allegations on apples other than mature, symptomless apple fruit.

142.   In the light of these considerations, we find that, contrary to the United States' claim, the Panel had the "authority" to make findings and draw conclusions with respect to all apple fruit from the United States, including immature apples.

VII.   ARTICLE 2.2 OF THE *SPS AGREEMENT*

143.   We proceed next to Japan's claim that the Panel erred in finding that the measure is maintained "without sufficient scientific evidence" within the meaning of Article 2.2 of the *SPS Agreement*.

144.   As explained in the previous section of this Report, the Panel decided that it would not limit its analysis to the risk of transmission of fire blight inherent in mature, symptomless apple fruit.[240] Thus, the Panel also considered the risk associated with other apples (that is, immature apples, or mature but damaged apples)[241] that might enter Japanese territory as a result of human or technical errors, or of illegal actions.

145.   In the course of its analysis as to whether Japan's measure is maintained without sufficient scientific evidence within the meaning of Article 2.2 of the *SPS Agreement*, the Panel, on the basis of the information before it, made the following findings of fact:

- Infection[242] of mature, symptomless apples has not been established. Mature apples are unlikely to be infected by fire blight if they do not show any symptoms[243];

- The possible presence of endophytic[244] bacteria in mature, symptomless apples is not generally established. Scientific evidence does not support the conclusion that mature,

---

the efficiency of export control procedures in general, not to the specific export control procedures of the United States.
[240]   See *supra*, para. 131.
[241]   Panel Report, paras. 8.122 and 8.174.
[242]   For the Panel's definition of the term "infection", see *supra*, footnote 17.
[243]   Panel Report, paras. 8.139 and 8.171.
[244]   The Panel defined "endophytic" as follows: "With respect to *E. amylovora*, the term **endophytic** is used when the bacterium occurs inside a plant or apple fruit in a non-pathogenic relationship." (*Ibid.*, para. 2.10 (original boldface))

symptomless apples could harbour endophytic populations of bacteria[245];

- The presence of epiphytic[246] bacteria in mature, symptomless apples is considered to be very rare[247];

- It is not contested that immature apple fruit can be infected or infested[248] by *Erwinia amylovora*[249];

- Infected apples are capable of harbouring populations of bacteria that could survive through the various stages of commercial handling, storage, and transportation[250];

- Scientific evidence does not support the conclusion that infested or infected cargo crates could operate as a vector for fire blight transmission; rather, the evidence shows that *Erwinia amylovora* is not likely to survive on crates[251]; and

- Even if infected or infested apples were exported to Japan, and populations of bacteria survived through the various stages of commercial handling, storage, and transportation, the introduction of fire blight would require the transmission of fire blight from imported apples to a host plant through an additional sequence of events that is deemed unlikely, and that has not been experimentally established to date.[252]

146.   On the basis of these findings of fact, the Panel concluded that scientific evidence suggests a negligible risk of possible transmission of fire blight through apple fruit[253], and that scientific evidence does not support the view that apples are likely to serve as a pathway for the entry, establishment or spread of fire blight within Japan.[254]

147.   For the Panel, a measure is maintained "without sufficient scientific evidence" within the meaning of Article 2.2 of the *SPS Agreement* if there is no "rational or objective relationship" between the measure and the relevant scientific evidence.[255] Given the negligible risk identified on the basis of the scientific evidence and the nature of the elements composing the measure, the Panel concluded that Japan's measure is "clearly disproportionate" to that risk.[256]

---

[245]   *Ibid.*, paras. 8.128 and 8.171.
[246]   The Panel defined "epiphytic" as follows: "With respect to *E. amylovora*, the term **epiphytic** is used when the bacterium occurs on the outer surface of a plant or fruit in a non-pathogenic relationship." (Panel Report, para. 2.10 (original boldface))
[247]   *Ibid.*, paras. 8.142 and 8.171.
[248]   For the Panel's definition of the terms "infection" and "infestation", see *supra*, footnote 17.
[249]   Panel Report, para. 8.171.
[250]   *Ibid.*, para. 8.157.
[251]   *Ibid.*, para. 8.143.
[252]   *Ibid.*, paras. 8.168 and 8.171.
[253]   *Ibid.*, para. 8.169.
[254]   *Ibid.*, para. 8.176.
[255]   *Ibid.*, paras. 8.101-8.103 and 8.180, relying on Appellate Body Report, *Japan – Agricultural Products II*, paras. 73-74, 82, and 84.
[256]   Panel Report, para. 8.198.

The Panel reasoned that such disproportion implies that a rational or objective relationship does not exist between the measure and the relevant scientific evidence and, therefore, the Panel concluded that Japan's measure is maintained "without sufficient scientific evidence" within the meaning of Article 2.2 of the *SPS Agreement.*[257]

148.   Japan challenges the Panel's conclusion, arguing that a *prima facie* case that infected apples would not act as a pathway for fire blight was not made by the United States. Japan contends that, in the absence of such a *prima facie* case, it was not open to the Panel to find a violation of Article 2.2. In addition, Japan argues that the Panel erroneously found that the United States had made a *prima facie* case in respect of mature, symptomless apples. According to Japan, this error resulted from the Panel's improper approach to Japan's risk evaluation, based on a misinterpretation of Article 2.2 of the *SPS Agreement.*[258]

149.   With respect to infected apples, Japan submits that it was for the United States to establish a *prima facie* case that there was no risk that infected apples could serve as a vector for the introduction of fire blight within Japan. The United States did not do so, because it presented arguments and evidence relating only to mature, symptomless apples[259], acknowledging explicitly during the Interim Review that "there is no factual claim or evidence submitted by the United States" relating to the risk associated with infected apple fruit.[260] Absent a *prima facie* case by the United States that there was insufficient scientific evidence on the risk posed by infected apples, the Panel, according to Japan, should have ruled in favour of Japan and found that infected apples could act as a pathway for fire blight.[261] In addition, Japan submits that, by finding that "Japan did not submit sufficient scientific evidence in support of its allegation that the last step of the pathway had been completed or was likely to be completed"[262], the Panel shifted the burden of proof to Japan; and that such a shift constituted an error of law as it was made prematurely, before the demonstration of a *prima facie* case by the United States.[263] Finally, Japan argues that the Panel was not entitled to use its investigative authority to make findings of fact on the risk relating to infected apples because the United States declined to establish a *prima facie* case with respect to this issue.[264]

150.   Regarding mature, symptomless apples, Japan advances a distinct argument, namely, that the Panel should have interpreted Article 2.2 in such a way that a "certain degree of discretion"[265] be accorded to the importing Member as to the manner it chooses, weighs, and evaluates scientific

---

[257]   *Ibid.*, para. 8.199.
[258]   Japan's appellant's submission, para. 71.
[259]   *Ibid.*, para. 22.
[260]   *Ibid.*, para. 23.
[261]   *Ibid.*, paras. 26, quoting Panel Report, paras. 7.31 and 8.154; and para. 27.
[262]   Panel Report, para. 8.167.
[263]   Japan's appellant's submission, para. 33.
[264]   Japan's appellant's submission, paras. 18, quoting Appellate Body Report, *Japan – Agricultural Products II*, para. 129; and para. 36.
[265]   Japan's appellant's submission, para. 76.

evidence. [266] Japan argues that the Panel denied such discretion, as it "evaluated the scientific evidence in accordance with the experts' view, despite the contrary view of an importing Member". [267] Japan contends that its own approach to the risk relating to mature, symptomless apples—an approach that reflects "the historical facts of trans-oceanic expansion of the bacteria" and the rapid growth of international trade, and which is premised on "the fact that the pathways of … transmission of the bacteria are still unknown in spite of several efforts to trace them" [268]—is reasonable as well as scientific because it is derived from "perspectives of prudence and precaution". [269] Consequently, the Panel should have accorded deference to Japan's approach and should have assessed whether the United States had established a *prima facie* case in the light of it. Japan argues that the United States did not establish a *prima facie* case in respect of mature, symptomless apples that reflected Japan's approach. In particular, Japan submits that the United States failed to prove that both the history of trans-oceanic dissemination of fire blight and, the fact that the cause of trans-oceanic dissemination is unknown, are irrelevant. [270]

151.   We will examine successively these two arguments of Japan: first, Japan's case relating to apples other than mature, symptomless apples, and secondly, that regarding mature, symptomless apples.

A.   *Apples Other Than Mature, Symptomless Apples*

152.   It is well settled that, in principle, it rests upon the complaining party to "establish a *prima facie* case of *inconsistency with a particular provision* of the *SPS Agreement*". [271] As the Appellate Body said in *EC – Hormones*:

> The initial burden lies on the complaining party, which must establish a *prima facie* case of inconsistency with a particular provision of the *SPS Agreement* on the part of the defending party, or more precisely, of its SPS measure or measures complained about. When that *prima facie* case is made, the burden of proof moves to the defending party, which must in turn counter or refute the claimed inconsistency. [272]

153.   In this case, the United States seeks a finding that Japan's measure is inconsistent with Article 2.2 of the *SPS Agreement*. Therefore, the initial burden lies with the United States to establish a *prima facie* case that the measure is inconsistent with Article 2.2. In particular, the United States must establish a *prima facie* case that the measure is "maintained without sufficient scientific evidence" within the meaning of Article 2.2. Following the Appellate Body's ruling in *EC – Hormones*, if this *prima facie* case is made, it would be for Japan

---

[266]   *Ibid.*, para. 75.
[267]   *Ibid.*, para. 78.
[268]   *Ibid.*, para. 73.
[269]   *Ibid.*, para. 81, quoting Appellate Body Report, *EC – Hormones*, para. 124.
[270]   Japan's appellant's submission, para. 87.
[271]   Appellate Body Report, *EC – Hormones*, para. 98. (emphasis added)
[272]   Appellate Body Report, para. 98.

to counter or refute the claim that the measure is "maintained without sufficient scientific evidence".

154. That said, the Appellate Body's statement in *EC – Hormones* does not imply that the complaining party is responsible for providing proof of all facts raised in relation to the issue of determining whether a measure is consistent with a given provision of a covered agreement. In other words, although the complaining party bears the burden of proving its case, the responding party must prove the case it seeks to make in response. In *US – Wool Shirts and Blouses*, the Appellate Body stated:

> ... we find it difficult, indeed, to see how any system of judicial settlement could work if it incorporated the proposition that the mere assertion of a claim might amount to proof. It is, thus, hardly surprising that various international tribunals, including the International Court of Justice, have generally and consistently accepted and applied the rule that *the party who asserts a fact, whether the claimant or the respondent, is responsible for providing proof thereof.*[273] (footnote omitted, emphasis added)

155. In this case, the United States made a series of allegations of fact relating to mature, symptomless apples as a possible pathway for fire blight, and sought to substantiate these allegations. Japan sought to counter the case made by the United States, arguing that:

- Japan must protect itself against failures in the control systems of exporting countries that might result in the introduction of apples other than mature, symptomless apples[274];

- it is possible that apples other than mature, symptomless apples (namely, immature apples or mature but damaged apples) could be infected by fire blight; and

- infected apple fruit has the capacity to serve as a pathway for fire blight.[275]

156. Japan was thus responsible for providing proof of the allegations of fact it advanced in relation to apples other than mature, symptomless apples being exported to Japan as a result of errors of handling or illegal actions. We therefore disagree with Japan's contention that the Panel erred because it "shifted the burden of proof to Japan in respect of a factual point that the complainant explicitly declined to prove"[276] or that "the shift of the burden of proof to Japan was made prematurely *before* the demonstration of a *prima facie* case by the United States."[277]

157. It is important to distinguish, on the one hand, the principle that the complainant must establish a *prima facie* case of inconsistency with a provision

---

[273] Appellate Body Report, p. 14, DSR 1997:I, 323, at 335.
[274] Panel Report, para. 8.85(d).
[275] *Ibid.*, para. 8.154.
[276] Japan's appellant's submission, para. 31.
[277] *Ibid.*, para. 33. (original italics)

of a covered agreement [278] from, on the other hand, the principle that the party that asserts a fact is responsible for providing proof thereof. [279] In fact, the two principles are distinct. In the present case, the burden of demonstrating a *prima facie* case that Japan's measure is maintained without sufficient scientific evidence, rested on the United States. Japan sought to counter the case put forward by the United States by putting arguments in respect of apples other than mature, symptomless apples being exported to Japan as a result of errors of handling or illegal actions. It was thus for Japan to substantiate those allegations; it was not for the United States to provide proof of the facts asserted by Japan. Thus, we disagree with Japan's assertion that "the shift of the burden of proof to Japan was made prematurely *before* the demonstration of a *prima facie* case by the United States." [280] There was no "shift of the burden of proof " with respect to allegations of fact relating to apples other than mature, symptomless apples, for Japan was solely responsible for providing proof of the facts it had asserted. Moreover, it was only after the United States had established a *prima facie* case that Japan's measure is maintained without sufficient scientific evidence, that the Panel had to turn to Japan's attempts to counter that case.

158.   Japan also contends that the Panel did not have the authority to make certain findings of fact [281] and, in support of this contention, refers to the Appellate Body's statement in *Japan – Agricultural Products II* :

> Article 13 of the DSU and Article 11.2 of the *SPS Agreement* suggest that panels have a significant investigative authority. However, this authority cannot be used by a panel to rule in favour of a complaining party which has not established a *prima facie* case of inconsistency based on specific legal claims asserted by it. [282]

We disagree with Japan. We note first that we are not persuaded that the findings of the Panel, identified by Japan in relation to this argument, relate specifically to, or address apples other than mature, symptomless apples, as Japan seems to assume. Also, the Appellate Body's finding in *Japan – Agricultural Products II* does not support Japan's argument that the Panel was barred from making findings of fact in connection with apples other than mature, symptomless apples. Those findings were relevant to the claim pursued by the United States under Article 2.2 of the *SPS Agreement*, and were responsive to relevant

---

[278]   Appellate Body Report, *EC – Hormones*, para. 98.

[279]   Appellate Body Report, *US – Wool Shirts and Blouses*, p. 14, DSR 1997:I, 323, at 335.

[280]   Japan's appellant's submission, para. 33. (original italics)

[281]   Japan refers to the following findings of the Panel:

> [W]e are of the opinion that the prohibition of imported apples from any orchard (whether or not it is free of fire blight) should fire blight be detected within a 500-meter buffer zone surrounding such orchard is not supported by sufficient scientific evidence; [and]

> [W]e are of the opinion that the requirement that export orchards be inspected at least three times yearly (at blossom, fruitlet, and harvest stages) for the presence of fire blight is not supported by sufficient scientific evidence. (footnotes omitted)

(Japan's appellant's submission, para. 35, quoting Panel Report, paras. 8.185 and 8.195)

[282]   Appellate Body Report, para. 129; Japan's appellant's submission, paras. 18 and 44.

allegations of fact advanced by Japan in the context of its rebuttal of the United States' claim. The Panel acted within the limits of its investigative authority because it did nothing more than assess relevant allegations of fact asserted by Japan, in the light of the evidence submitted by the parties and the opinions of the experts.

159.   Japan also submits that, "in order to establish a *prima facie* case of insufficient scientific evidence under Article 2.2 of the SPS Agreement, the complaining party must establish that there is not sufficient scientific evidence for *any* of the perceived risks underlying the measure".[283] According to Japan, the Panel should not have concluded that this *prima facie* case had been established unless the United States had first addressed *all* the possible hypotheses—including those for which the likelihood of occurrence is low or rests upon theoretical reasonings—and had shown for each of them that the risk of transmission of fire blight is negligible. We find no basis for the approach advocated by Japan. As the Appellate Body stated in *EC – Hormones*, "a *prima facie* case is one which, in the absence of effective refutation by the defending party, requires a panel, as a matter of law, to rule in favour of the complaining party presenting the *prima facie* case."[284] In *US – Wool Shirts and Blouses*, the Appellate Body stated that the nature and scope of evidence required to establish a *prima facie* case "will necessarily vary from measure to measure, provision to provision, and case to case."[285] In the present case, the Panel appears to have concluded that in order to demonstrate a *prima facie* case that Japan's measure is maintained without sufficient scientific evidence, it sufficed for the United States to address only the question of whether mature, symptomless apples could serve as a pathway for fire blight.

160.   The Panel's conclusion seems appropriate to us for the following reasons. First, the claim pursued by the United States was that Japan's measure is maintained without sufficient scientific evidence to the extent that it applies to mature, symptomless apples exported from the United States to Japan. What is required to demonstrate a *prima facie* case is necessarily influenced by the nature and the scope of the claim pursued by the complainant. A complainant should not be required to prove a claim it does not seek to make. Secondly, the Panel found that mature, symptomless apple fruit is the commodity "normally exported" by the United States to Japan.[286] The Panel indicated that the risk that apple fruit other than mature, symptomless apples may actually be imported into Japan would seem to arise primarily as a result of human or technical error, or illegal actions[287], and noted that the experts characterized errors of handling and illegal actions as "small" or "debatable" risks.[288] Given the characterization of these risks, in our opinion it

---

[283]   Japan's appellee's submission, para. 9. (original italics)
[284]   Appellate Body Report, para. 104.
[285]   *Ibid.*, p. 14, DSR 1997:I, 323, at 335.
[286]   Panel Report, para. 8.141. The Panel also found that "the importation of immature, infected apples may only occur as a result of a handling error or an illegal action". (*Ibid.*, footnote 275 to para. 8.121)
[287]   *Ibid.*, para. 8.174.
[288]   *Ibid.*, para. 8.161.

was legitimate for the Panel to consider that the United States could demonstrate a *prima facie* case of inconsistency with Article 2.2 of the *SPS Agreement* through argument based solely on mature, symptomless apples. Thirdly, the record contains no evidence to suggest that apples other than mature, symptomless ones have ever been exported to Japan from the United States as a result of errors of handling or illegal actions. [289] Thus, we find no error in the Panel's approach that the United States could establish a *prima facie* case of inconsistency with Article 2.2 of the *SPS Agreement* in relation to apples exported from the United States to Japan, even though the United States confined its arguments to mature, symptomless apples.

B.   Mature, Symptomless Apples

161.   We turn now to Japan's arguments in respect of mature, symptomless apples. As we indicated above, Japan contends that the Panel erred in interpreting Article 2.2 of the *SPS Agreement* because the Panel failed to accord a "certain degree of discretion" [290] to the importing Member in the manner in which it chooses, weighs, and evaluates scientific evidence. [291] Japan submitted that, had the Panel accorded such discretion to Japan as the importing Member, the Panel would not have focused on the experts' views. Rather, the Panel would have evaluated the scientific evidence in the light of Japan's approach, which reflects "the historical facts of trans-oceanic expansion of the bacteria" and the rapid growth of international trade, and which is premised on "the fact that the pathways of ... transmission of the bacteria are still unknown in spite of several efforts to trace them." [292] Japan thus argues that the Panel erred in the application of Article 2.2 of the *SPS Agreement*, as it should have assessed whether the United States had established a *prima facie* case regarding the sufficiency of scientific evidence, not from the perspective of the experts' views, but, rather, in the light of Japan's approach to scientific evidence. According to Japan, had the Panel made such an assessment, it would have been bound to conclude that the United States had not established a *prima facie* case that Japan's measure is maintained without sufficient scientific evidence.

162.   We disagree with Japan. As the Panel correctly noted, the Appellate Body addressed, in *Japan – Agricultural Products II*, the meaning of the term "sufficient", in the context of the expression "sufficient scientific evidence" as found in Article 2.2. [293] The Panel stated that the term "sufficient" implies a

---

[289]   In response to questioning at the oral hearing, Japan indicated that the only evidence relating to the export control procedures of the United States that it submitted to the Panel related to a case of codling moth larvae found in apples shipped from the United States to the Separate Customs Territory of Taiwan, Penghu, Kinmen, and Matsu. In our view, there was no reason for the Panel to infer from this that apples other than mature, symptomless ones have ever been exported from the United States to Japan.

[290]   Japan's appellant's submission, para. 76.

[291]   *Ibid.*, paras. 75-76.

[292]   *Ibid.*, para. 73.

[293]   Panel Report, paras. 8.101-8.103 and 8.180.

"rational or objective relationship"[294] and referred to the Appellate Body's statement there that:

> Whether there is a rational relationship between an SPS measure and the scientific evidence is to be determined on a case-by-case basis and will depend upon the particular circumstances of the case, including the characteristics of the measure at issue and the quality and quantity of the scientific evidence.[295]

The Panel did not err in relying on this interpretation of Article 2.2 and in conducting its assessment of the scientific evidence on this basis.

163. As we see it, the Panel examined the evidence adduced by the parties and considered the opinions of the experts. It concluded as a matter of fact that it is not likely that apple fruit would serve as a pathway for the entry, establishment or spread of fire blight in Japan.[296] The Panel then contrasted the extent of the risk and the nature of the elements composing the measure, and concluded that the measure was "clearly disproportionate to the risk identified on the basis of the scientific evidence available."[297] For the Panel, such "clear disproportion" implies that a "rational or objective relationship" does not exist between the measure and the relevant scientific evidence, and, therefore, the Panel concluded that the measure is maintained "without sufficient scientific evidence" within the meaning of Article 2.2 of the *SPS Agreement*.[298] We note that the "clear disproportion" to which the Panel refers, relates to the application in this case of the requirement of a "rational or objective relationship between an SPS measure and the scientific evidence".

164. We emphasize, following the Appellate Body's statement in *Japan – Agricultural Products II*, that whether a given approach or methodology is appropriate in order to assess whether a measure is maintained "without sufficient scientific evidence", within the meaning of Article 2.2, depends on the "particular circumstances of the case", and must be "determined on a case-by-case basis".[299] Thus, the approach followed by the Panel in this case— disassembling the sequence of events to identify the risk and comparing it with the measure—does not exhaust the range of methodologies available to determine whether a measure is maintained "without sufficient scientific evidence" within the meaning of Article 2.2. Approaches different from that followed by the Panel in this case could also prove appropriate to evaluate whether a measure is maintained without sufficient scientific evidence within the meaning of Article 2.2. Whether or not a particular approach is appropriate will depend on the "particular circumstances of the case".[300] The methodology adopted by the Panel was appropriate to the particular circumstances of the case before it and, therefore, we see no error in the Panel's reliance on it.

---

[294] *Ibid.*, paras. 8.103 and 8.180.
[295] *Ibid.*, para. 8.103, quoting Appellate Body Report, *Japan – Agricultural Products II*, para. 84.
[296] Panel Report, para. 8.176.
[297] *Ibid.*, para. 8.198.
[298] *Ibid.*, para. 8.199.
[299] Appellate Body Report, para. 84.
[300] *Ibid.*

165.   Regarding Japan's contention that the Panel should have made its assessment under Article 2.2 in the light of Japan's approach to risk and scientific evidence, we recall that, in *EC – Hormones*, the Appellate Body addressed the question of the standard of review that a panel should apply in the assessment of scientific evidence submitted in proceedings under the *SPS Agreement*. It stated that Article 11 of the DSU sets out the applicable standard, requiring panels to make an "objective assessment of the facts". It added that, as regards fact-finding by panels and the appreciation of scientific evidence, total deference to the findings of the national authorities would not ensure an objective assessment as required by Article 11 of the DSU.[301] In our view, Japan's submission that the Panel was obliged to favour Japan's approach to risk and scientific evidence over the views of the experts conflicts with the Appellate Body's articulation of the standard of "objective assessment of the facts".

166.   In order to assess whether the United States had established a *prima facie* case, the Panel was entitled to take into account the views of the experts. Indeed, in *India – Quantitative Restrictions*, the Appellate Body indicated that it may be useful for a panel to consider the views of the experts it consults in order to determine whether a *prima facie* case has been made.[302] Moreover, on several occasions, including disputes involving the evaluation of scientific evidence, the Appellate Body has stated that panels enjoy discretion as the trier of facts[303]; they enjoy "a margin of discretion in assessing the value of the evidence, and the weight to be ascribed to that evidence."[304] Requiring panels, in their assessment of the evidence before them, to give precedence to the importing Member's evaluation of scientific evidence and risk is not compatible with this well-established principle.

167.   For these reasons, we reject the contention that, under Article 2.2, a panel is obliged to give precedence to the importing Member's approach to scientific evidence and risk when analyzing and assessing scientific evidence. Consequently, we disagree with Japan that the Panel erred in assessing whether the United States had established a *prima facie* case when it did so from a perspective different from that inherent in Japan's approach to scientific evidence and risk. Thus, we are not persuaded that we should revisit the Panel's conclusion that the United States established a *prima facie* case that Japan's measure is maintained without sufficient scientific evidence.

168.   In the light of these considerations, we uphold the Panel's findings, in paragraphs 8.199 and 9.1(a) of the Panel Report, that Japan's phytosanitary

---

[301]   Appellate Body Report, *EC – Hormones*, para. 117.
[302]   Appellate Body Report, para. 142.
[303]   Appellate Body Report, *EC – Bed Linen (Article 21.5 – India)*, paras. 170, 177, and 181; Appellate Body Report, *EC – Sardines*, para. 299; Appellate Body Report, *Korea – Alcoholic Beverages*, paras. 161-162; Appellate Body Report, *EC – Hormones*, para. 132; and Appellate Body Report, *US – Wheat Gluten*, para. 151. See also, Appellate Body Report, *Australia – Salmon*, paras. 262-267; Appellate Body Report, *Japan – Agricultural Products II*, paras. 140-142; and Appellate Body Report, *Korea – Dairy*, paras. 137-138.
[304]   Appellate Body Report, *EC – Asbestos*, para. 161.

measure at issue is maintained "without sufficient scientific evidence" within the meaning of Article 2.2 of the *SPS Agreement*.

VIII. ARTICLE 5.7 OF THE *SPS AGREEMENT*

169.   We turn to the issue whether the Panel erred in finding that Japan's phytosanitary measure was not imposed in respect of a situation where "relevant scientific evidence is insufficient" within the meaning of Article 5.7 of the *SPS Agreement*.

170.   Article 2.2 of the *SPS Agreement* stipulates that Members shall not maintain sanitary or phytosanitary measures without sufficient scientific evidence "except as provided for in paragraph 7 of Article 5". Before the Panel, Japan contested that its phytosanitary measure is "maintained without sufficient scientific evidence" within the meaning of Article 2.2. Japan claimed, in the alternative, that its measure is a provisional measure consistent with Article 5.7.

171.   Article 5.7 of the *SPS Agreement* reads as follows:

> *Assessment of Risk and Determination of the*
> *Appropriate Level of Sanitary or*
> *Phytosanitary Protection*
>
> ...
>
> In cases where relevant scientific evidence is insufficient, a Member may provisionally adopt sanitary or phytosanitary measures on the basis of available pertinent information, including that from the relevant international organizations as well as from sanitary or phytosanitary measures applied by other Members. In such circumstances, Members shall seek to obtain the additional information necessary for a more objective assessment of risk and review the sanitary or phytosanitary measure accordingly within a reasonable period of time.

172.   The Panel found that Japan's measure is not a provisional measure justified under Article 5.7 of the *SPS Agreement* because the measure was not imposed in respect of a situation where "relevant scientific evidence is insufficient".[305]

173.   The Panel identified the "phytosanitary question at issue" as the risk of transmission of fire blight through apple fruit.[306] It observed that "scientific studies as well as practical experience have accumulated for the past 200 years"[307] on this question and that, in the course of its analysis under Article 2.2, it had come across an "important amount of relevant evidence".[308] The Panel

---

[305]   Panel Report, paras. 8.221-8.222.
[306]   *Ibid.*, para. 8.218.
[307]   *Ibid.*, para. 8.219.
[308]   *Ibid.*, para. 8.216.

observed that a large quantity of high quality scientific evidence on the risk of transmission of fire blight through apple fruit had been produced over the years, and noted that the experts had expressed strong and increasing confidence in this evidence. Stating that Article 5.7 was "designed to be invoked in situations where little, or no, reliable evidence was available on the subject matter at issue"[309], the Panel concluded that the measure was not imposed in respect of a situation where relevant scientific evidence is insufficient.[310] The Panel added that, even if the term "relevant scientific evidence" in Article 5.7 referred to a *specific aspect* of a phytosanitary problem, as Japan claimed, its conclusion would remain the same. The Panel justified its view on the basis of the experts' indication that, not only is there a large volume of general evidence, but there is also a large volume of relevant scientific evidence on the specific scientific questions raised by Japan.[311]

174.   Japan challenges the Panel's finding that the measure is not imposed in respect of a situation where "relevant scientific evidence is insufficient" within the meaning of Article 5.7 of the *SPS Agreement.*[312] Moreover, Japan submits that its measure meets all the other requirements of Article 5.7.[313] Accordingly, Japan requests us to reverse the Panel's finding and to complete the analysis regarding the consistency of its measure with the other requirements set out in Article 5.7.[314]

A.   The Insufficiency of Relevant Scientific Evidence

175.   As noted above, Japan's claim under Article 5.7 was argued before the Panel in the alternative.[315] Japan relied on Article 5.7 only in the event that the Panel rejected Japan's view that "sufficient scientific evidence" exists to maintain the measure within the meaning of Article 2.2. It is in this particular context that the Panel assigned the burden of proof to Japan to make a *prima facie* case in support of its position under Article 5.7.[316]

176.   In *Japan – Agricultural Products II*, the Appellate Body stated that Article 5.7 sets out four requirements that must be satisfied in order to adopt and maintain a provisional phytosanitary measure.[317] These requirements are:

      (i)   the measure is imposed in respect of a situation where "relevant scientific evidence is insufficient";

---

[309]   Panel Report, para. 8.219.

[310]   *Ibid.*

[311]   *Ibid.*, para. 8.220.

[312]   We note that Japan does not challenge the Panel's conclusion that in order to assess whether the measure was imposed in respect of a situation where "relevant scientific evidence is insufficient", the Panel had to consider "not only evidence supporting Japan's position, but also evidence supporting other views." (*Ibid.*, para.8.216)

[313]   Japan's appellant's submission, paras. 117-120.

[314]   *Ibid.*, paras. 120-121.

[315]   Panel Report, para. 4.202.

[316]   The Panel's assignment of the burden of proof to Japan to make a *prima facie* case of consistency with Article 5.7 is not challenged on appeal.

[317]   Appellate Body Report, para. 89.

(ii)   the measure is adopted "on the basis of available pertinent information";

(iii)   the Member which adopted the measure "seek[s] to obtain the additional information necessary for a more objective assessment of risk"; and

(iv)   the Member which adopted the measure "review[s] the ... measure accordingly within a reasonable period of time". [318]

These four requirements are "clearly cumulative in nature" [319]; as the Appellate Body said in *Japan – Agricultural Products II*, "[w]henever *one* of these four requirements is not met, the measure at issue is inconsistent with Article 5.7." [320]

177.   The Panel's findings address exclusively the first requirement, which the Panel found Japan had not met. [321] The requirements being cumulative, the Panel found it unnecessary to address the other requirements to find an inconsistency with Article 5.7.

178.   Japan's appeal also focuses on the first requirement of Article 5.7. Japan contends that the assessment as to whether relevant scientific evidence is insufficient should not be restricted to evidence "in general" on the phytosanitary question at issue, but should also cover a "particular situation" in relation to a "particular measure" or a "particular risk". [322] Hence, Japan submits that the phrase "[w]here relevant scientific evidence is insufficient", in Article 5.7, "should be interpreted to relate to a particular situation in respect of a particular *measure* to which Article 2.2 applies (or a particular risk), but not to a particular *subject matter* in general, which Article 2.2 does not address." [323] According to Japan, the Panel "erred by interpreting the applicability of [Article 5.7] too narrowly" [324] and too "rigid[ly]". [325]

179.   It seems to us that Japan's reliance on the opposition between evidence "in general" and evidence relating to specific aspects of a particular subject matter is misplaced. The first requirement of Article 5.7 is that there must be insufficient scientific evidence. When a panel reviews a measure claimed by a Member to be provisional, that panel must assess whether "relevant scientific evidence is insufficient". This evaluation must be carried out, not in the abstract, but in the light of a particular inquiry. The notions of "relevance" and "insufficiency" in the introductory phrase of Article 5.7 imply a relationship between the scientific evidence and something else. Reading this introductory phrase in the broader context of Article 5 of the *SPS Agreement*, which is entitled "Assessment of Risk and Determination of the Appropriate Level of Sanitary or Phytosanitary

---

[318]   Appellate Body Report, *Japan – Agricultural Products II*, para. 89. The third and fourth requirements relate to the *maintenance* of a provisional phytosanitary measure and highlight the *provisional* nature of measures adopted pursuant to Article 5.7.

[319]   Appellate Body Report, *Japan – Agricultural Products II*, para. 89.

[320]   *Ibid.* (original italics)

[321]   Panel Report, para. 8.222.

[322]   Japan's appellant's submission, para. 102.

[323]   *Ibid.* (original italics)

[324]   *Ibid.*, para. 96.

[325]   *Ibid.*, paras. 100-101.

Protection", is instructive in ascertaining the nature of the relationship to be established. Article 5.1 sets out a key discipline under Article 5, namely that "Members shall ensure that their sanitary or phytosanitary measures are based on an assessment ... of the risks to human, animal or plant life or health".[326] This discipline informs the other provisions of Article 5, including Article 5.7. We note, as well, that the second sentence of Article 5.7 refers to a "more objective assessment of risks". These contextual elements militate in favour of a link or relationship between the first requirement under Article 5.7 and the obligation to perform a risk assessment under Article 5.1: "relevant scientific evidence" will be "insufficient" within the meaning of Article 5.7 if the body of available scientific evidence does not allow, in quantitative or qualitative terms, the performance of an adequate assessment of risks as required under Article 5.1 and as defined in Annex A to the *SPS Agreement*. Thus, the question is not whether there is sufficient evidence of a general nature or whether there is sufficient evidence related to a specific aspect of a phytosanitary problem, or a specific risk. The question is whether the relevant evidence, be it "general" or "specific", in the Panel's parlance, is sufficient to permit the evaluation of the likelihood of entry, establishment or spread of, in this case, fire blight in Japan.

180. The Panel found that, with regard to the risk of transmission of fire blight through apples exported from the United States—"normally"[327], mature, symptomless apples—"not only a large quantity but a high quality of scientific evidence has been produced over the years that describes the risk of transmission of fire blight through apple fruit as negligible", and that "this is evidence in which the experts have expressed strong and increasing confidence."[328]

181. Japan also raised specific questions related to endophytic bacteria in mature apple fruit and regarding the completion of contamination pathways.[329] In relation to these specific questions, the Panel made the finding of fact, based on indications of the experts retained by the Panel, that there is a large volume of relevant scientific evidence regarding these questions as well.[330] Moreover, Japan did not persuade the Panel that this scientific evidence is not conclusive or has not produced reliable results.[331]

182. These findings of fact by the Panel suggest that the body of available scientific evidence permitted, in quantitative and qualitative terms, the performance of an assessment of risks, as required under Article 5.1 and as defined in Annex A to the *SPS Agreement*, with respect to the risk of transmission of fire blight through apple fruit exported from the United States to Japan. In particular, according to these findings of fact by the Panel, the body of available scientific evidence would allow "[t]he evaluation of the likelihood of

---

[326] The risk assessment referred to in Article 5.1 is defined in Annex A to the *SPS Agreement*.
[327] Panel Report, paras. 8.87 and 8.141.
[328] *Ibid.*, para. 8.219.
[329] Panel Report, para. 8.220.
[330] *Ibid.*,
[331] *Ibid.*, para. 7.9. See also the Panel's findings of fact in paragraphs 8.128, 8.168, and 8.171 of the Panel Report, made in the context of the Panel's analysis under Article 2.2 of the *SPS Agreement*.

entry, establishment or spread" [332] of fire blight in Japan through apples exported from the United States. Accordingly, in the light of the findings of fact made by the Panel, we conclude that, with respect to the risk of transmission of fire blight through apple fruit exported from the United States to Japan ("normally", mature, symptomless apples), the "relevant scientific evidence" is not "insufficient" within the meaning of Article 5.7.

B. Japan's Argument on "Scientific Uncertainty"

183.   Japan challenges the Panel's statement that Article 5.7 is intended to address only "situations where little, or no, reliable evidence was available on the subject matter at issue" [333] because this does not provide for situations of "unresolved uncertainty". Japan draws a distinction between "new uncertainty" and "unresolved uncertainty" [334], arguing that both fall within Article 5.7. According to Japan, "new uncertainty" arises when a new risk is identified; Japan argues that the Panel's characterization that "little, or no, reliable evidence was available on the subject matter at issue" is relevant to a situation of "new uncertainty". [335] We understand that Japan defines "unresolved uncertainty" as uncertainty that the scientific evidence is not able to resolve, despite accumulated scientific evidence. [336] According to Japan, the risk of transmission of fire blight through apple fruit relates essentially to a situation of "unresolved uncertainty". [337] Thus, Japan maintains that, despite considerable scientific evidence regarding fire blight, there is still uncertainty about certain aspects of transmission of fire blight. Japan contends that the reasoning of the Panel is tantamount to restricting the applicability of Article 5.7 to situations of "new uncertainty" and to excluding situations of "unresolved uncertainty"; and that, by doing so, the Panel erred in law. [338]

184.   We disagree with Japan. The application of Article 5.7 is triggered not by the existence of scientific uncertainty, but rather by the insufficiency of scientific evidence. The text of Article 5.7 is clear: it refers to "cases where relevant scientific evidence is insufficient", not to "scientific uncertainty". The two concepts are not interchangeable. Therefore, we are unable to endorse Japan's approach of interpreting Article 5.7 through the prism of "scientific uncertainty".

185.   We also find no basis for Japan's argument that the Panel's interpretation of Article 5.7 is too narrow for the reason that it excludes cases where the quantity of evidence on a phytosanitary question is "more than little" [339], but the available scientific evidence has not resolved the question. The Panel's statement that Article 5.7 is intended to address "situations where little, or no, reliable

---

[332]   Annex A to the *SPS Agreement*, para. 4.
[333]   Panel Report, para. 8.219.
[334]   Japan's appellant's submission, para. 101.
[335]   *Ibid.*, footnote 76 to para. 98.
[336]   *Ibid.*, para. 98.
[337]   *Ibid.*, paras. 105-110.
[338]   *Ibid.*, para. 110.
[339]   Panel Report, para. 7.8.

evidence was available on the subject matter at issue", refers to the availability of *reliable* evidence. We do not read the Panel's interpretation as excluding cases where the available evidence is more than minimal in quantity, but has not led to reliable or conclusive results. Indeed, the Panel explicitly recognized that such cases fall within the scope of Article 5.7 when it observed, in the Interim Review section of its Report, that under its approach, Article 5.7 would be applicable to a situation where a lot of scientific research has been carried out on a particular issue without yielding reliable evidence. [340]

C. The Panel's Reliance on a "History of 200 Years of Studies and Practical Experience"

186. Japan contends that the conclusion of the Panel regarding Article 5.7 is based on its assessment that, as regards fire blight, "scientific studies as well as practical experience have accumulated for the past 200 years". [341] Japan submits that the Panel was not authorized to rule on the basis of a " 'history' of 200 year[s] of studies and practical experience" [342] because "the United States did not raise any objection to application of Article 5.7 on the basis of [a] 'history' of 200 year[s] of studies and practical experience." [343] In other words, according to Japan, the Panel was not entitled to draw a conclusion regarding Article 5.7 on the basis of such "history" unless the United States had raised an objection based on "history", something that the United States had not done. [344]

187. In the course of its reasoning, the Panel mentioned that, as regards the risk of transmission of fire blight through apple fruit, "scientific studies as well as practical experience have accumulated for the past 200 years". [345] This statement was relevant to the debate under Article 5.7 and was based on the evidence before the Panel. [346] Accordingly, it was appropriate for the Panel to make such a statement irrespective of whether the United States had explicitly advanced an argument based on "history".

188. In the light of these considerations, we uphold the findings of the Panel, in paragraphs 8.222 and 9.1(b) of the Panel Report, that Japan's phytosanitary measure at issue was not imposed in respect of a situation "where relevant scientific evidence is insufficient", and, therefore, that it is not a provisional measure justified under Article 5.7 of the *SPS Agreement*. We note that Japan requested us, in the event we were to reverse the Panel's finding on Article 5.7, to complete the analysis in respect of the other requirements set out in Article 5.7 of the *SPS Agreement*. Given our conclusion, there is no need to do so.

---

[340] *Ibid.*, para. 7.9.
[341] *Ibid.*, para. 8.219; Japan's appellant's submission, paras. 93 and 97.
[342] Japan's appellant's submission, para. 97.
[343] *Ibid.*
[344] *Ibid.*
[345] Panel Report, para. 8.219.
[346] We note that Dr. Chris Hale, one of the experts consulted by the Panel, referred to a historical perspective when he stated that "fire blight had taken 220 years to spread from New York State, USA in 1780, to its latest geographic locations". (*Ibid.*, para. 6.28)

IX.   ARTICLE 5.1 OF THE *SPS AGREEMENT*

189.   We turn now to Japan's allegations of error with respect to Article 5.1 of the *SPS Agreement*. The Panel began its evaluation of the United States' claim under Article 5.1 by noting that both parties effectively identified a document referred to as the "1999 PRA" as the risk assessment to be analyzed in this evaluation.[347] Japan, however, objected to the Panel's consideration of evidence arising subsequent to the 1999 PRA when assessing the 1999 PRA's conformity with the requirements of Article 5.1. Despite this objection, the Panel concluded that it would "consider principally the 1999 PRA as the relevant risk assessment in this case, but we do not exclude that other elements, including subsequent information, could also be of relevance."[348]

190.   On the substance of the claim, the Panel noted first that the United States did not contest the fact that the 1999 PRA properly identified fire blight as the disease of concern.[349] The focus of the United States' claim was that (i) the risk assessment did not sufficiently evaluate the likelihood of entry, establishment or spread of fire blight, and (ii) this evaluation was not performed "according to the SPS measures which might be applied".[350]

191.   As to the first element of the claim, the Panel said that a risk assessment must be sufficiently specific to the risk at issue. In this regard, the Panel observed that the 1999 PRA studied several possible hosts of fire blight, including apple fruit. Recognizing that the risk of transmission of fire blight could vary significantly from plant to plant, the Panel found that the risk assessment was not "sufficiently specific" because "the conclusion of the [1999] PRA [did] not purport to relate exclusively to the introduction of the disease through apple fruit, but rather more generally, apparently, through any susceptible host/vector."[351]

192.   The Panel similarly found the discussion of possible pathways to have "intertwined" the risk of entry through apple fruit with that of other possible vectors, including vectors considered more likely to be potential sources of contamination than apple fruit.[352] The Panel also determined that those parts of the 1999 PRA that specifically addressed apple fruit, although noting the *possibility* of entry, establishment or spread of fire blight through this vector, did not properly evaluate the *probability* of the occurrence of such events. Finally, the Panel recalled the testimony of certain experts, identifying several steps in the evaluation of the probability of entry that had been "overlooked" by the 1999 PRA.[353] In the light of these shortcomings, the Panel concluded that

---

[347]   *Ibid.*, para. 8.247. In response to questioning at the oral hearing, both participants reaffirmed the focus of the Panel's Article 5.1 analysis to be the 1999 PRA.
[348]   Panel Report, para. 8.248.
[349]   *Ibid.*, para. 8.252.
[350]   *Ibid.*, para. 8.253.
[351]   *Ibid.*, para. 8.271.
[352]   *Ibid.*, para. 8.278.
[353]   *Ibid.*, para. 8.279.

Japan's risk assessment did not properly evaluate the likelihood of entry, establishment or spread of fire blight through apple fruit.

193. With respect to the second element of the United States' claim, the Panel observed that a risk assessment, according to Annex A to the *SPS Agreement*, requires an evaluation "according to the sanitary or phytosanitary measures which might be applied". From this language, the Panel determined that a risk assessment must not only consider the particular measure already in place, but also other measures that "*might*" be applied.[354] Because the 1999 PRA did not consider other risk-mitigating measures, the Panel found the risk assessment inadequate for purposes of Article 5.1.

194. Reviewing Japan's evaluation of the measure that was already in place, the Panel acknowledged that the 1999 PRA could be considered to have provided "some" evaluation of the likelihood of entry of the disease and possible mitigation through the existing measure. The Panel noted, however, that, in *Australia – Salmon*, the Appellate Body found that "some" evaluation was insufficient for purposes of Article 5.1 and that a comparison between Japan's evaluation and that of the importing Member in that case reveals the 1999 PRA to be "considerably less substantial".[355] The Panel also noted that the 1999 PRA assumes that the individual components of Japan's measure would be applied cumulatively, without consideration as to their individual effectiveness. The Panel found that the required consideration of alternative measures included an obligation to evaluate whether the independent elements needed to be applied cumulatively and to provide an explanation therefor.[356] As a result, the Panel concluded that, in the 1999 PRA, Japan did not sufficiently conduct its evaluation "according to the sanitary or phytosanitary measures which might be applied".

195. Japan challenges three specific aspects of the Panel's analysis of the 1999 PRA under Article 5.1. First, Japan contests the Panel's finding that the 1999 PRA is inconsistent with the requirements of Article 5.1 because it did not focus its analysis on the risk of fire blight entering through *apple fruit*, in particular. Japan contends that the Panel misinterpreted Article 5.1 and misunderstood the Appellate Body's decision in *EC – Hormones* with respect to the requirement of "specificity" of a risk assessment.[357] Secondly, Japan argues that Article 5.1, contrary to the Panel's interpretation, does not require a consideration of "alternative measures other than [the] existing measures."[358] Finally, Japan claims that its risk assessment should be assessed in the light of evidence available at the time of the assessment, not against evidence that has become available subsequently.[359]

---

[354] *Ibid.*, para. 8.283. (original italics)
[355] Panel Report, para. 8.287.
[356] *Ibid.*, para. 8.288.
[357] Japan's appellant's submission, paras. 127-129.
[358] *Ibid.*, para. 133, quoting Panel Report, para. 8.285.
[359] Japan's appellant's submission, paras. 135-138.

196.   We begin our analysis with the text of the relevant provision at issue, Article 5.1 of the *SPS Agreement*:

> Members shall ensure that their sanitary or phytosanitary measures are based on an assessment, as appropriate to the circumstances, of the risks to human, animal or plant life or health, taking into account risk assessment techniques developed by the relevant international organizations.

The first clause of paragraph 4 of Annex A to the *SPS Agreement* defines the "risk assessment" for a measure designed to protect plant life or health from risks arising from the entry, establishment or spread of diseases as follows:

> *Risk assessment* - The evaluation of the likelihood of entry, establishment or spread of a pest or disease within the territory of an importing Member according to the sanitary or phytosanitary measures which might be applied, and of the associated potential biological and economic consequences ... .[360]

Based on this definition, the Appellate Body determined in *Australia – Salmon* that:

> ... a risk assessment within the meaning of Article 5.1 must:
>
> (1)   *identify* the diseases whose entry, establishment or spread a Member wants to prevent within its territory, as well as the potential biological and economic consequences associated with the entry, establishment or spread of these diseases;
>
> (2)   *evaluate the likelihood* of entry, establishment or spread of these diseases, as well as the associated potential biological and economic consequences; and
>
> (3)   evaluate the likelihood of entry, establishment or spread of these diseases *according to the SPS measures which might be applied.*[361] (original italics)

197.   As the Panel noted, the United States does not claim that Japan's risk assessment failed to meet the first of these conditions.[362] The Panel therefore limited its analysis of Japan's risk assessment to the second and third conditions. The Panel found that the 1999 PRA did not constitute a "risk assessment", as that term is defined in the *SPS Agreement*, because it did not satisfy either of those conditions. Japan challenges aspects of the Panel's analysis with respect to both of these conditions. We consider each of these conditions before turning to

---

[360]   The second clause in paragraph 4 of Annex A to the *SPS Agreement* addresses risk assessments evaluating the "potential for adverse effects on human or animal health arising from the presence of additives, contaminants, toxins or disease-causing organisms in food, beverages or feedstuffs." As such, the second clause does not define the type of risk assessment relevant to this dispute involving the possibility of transmission of fire blight to plants in Japan. (See Appellate Body Report, *Australia – Salmon*, footnote 67 to para. 120)

[361]   *Ibid.*, para. 121.

[362]   Panel Report, para. 8.252.

Japan's argument regarding the evidence that may be relied upon by a panel when evaluating a risk assessment.

A.   Evaluating the Likelihood of Entry, Establishment or Spread of Fire Blight

198.   Japan challenges first the Panel's finding that the 1999 PRA was not sufficiently specific to constitute a risk assessment under the *SPS Agreement* because it did not evaluate the risk in relation to *apple fruit*, in particular. In *EC – Hormones*, in the context of evaluating whether a measure was "based on" a risk assessment, the Appellate Body examined the specificity of the risk assessment relied upon by the importing Member. In that case, the importing Member had referred to certain scientific studies and articles as the risk assessment underlying its measures. In its Report, the Appellate Body described the panel's finding that these materials:

> ... relate[d] to the carcinogenic potential of entire *categories* of hormones, or of the hormones at issue *in general*. ... [They did] not evaluate[] the carcinogenic potential of those hormones when used specifically *for growth promotion purposes*. Moreover, they [did] not evaluate the specific potential for carcinogenic effects arising from the presence in *"food"*, more specifically, "meat or meat products" of residues of the hormones in dispute. [363] (original italics)

199.   The panel in *EC – Hormones* concluded, as a result, that the studies cited by the importing Member were insufficient to support the measures at issue. The Appellate Body upheld these findings, stating that, although the studies cited by the importing Member:

> ... [did] indeed show the existence of a general risk of cancer ... they [did] not focus on and [did] not address the particular kind of risk [t]here at stake - the carcinogenic or genotoxic potential of the residues of those hormones found in meat derived from cattle to which the hormones had been administered for growth promotion purposes - as is required by paragraph 4 of Annex A of the *SPS Agreement*. [364]

The Appellate Body therefore concluded that the risk assessment was not "sufficiently specific to the case at hand." [365]

200.   In this case, the Panel, relying on the Appellate Body's finding in *EC – Hormones*, concluded that the 1999 PRA was not sufficiently specific to constitute a "risk assessment" in accordance with the *SPS Agreement*. [366] The Panel based this conclusion on its finding that, although the 1999 PRA makes determinations as to the entry, establishment and spread of fire blight through a

---

[363] Appellate Body Report, *EC – Hormones*, para. 199.
[364] *Ibid.*, para. 200.
[365] *Ibid.*
[366] Panel Report, paras. 8.267 and 8.271.

collection of various hosts (including apple fruit), it failed to evaluate the entry, establishment or spread of fire blight through apple fruit as a separate and distinct vector. [367] As the Panel stated in response to Japan's comments during the Interim Review, "Japan evaluated the risks associated with all possible hosts taken together, not sufficiently considering the risks specifically associated with the commodity at issue: US apple fruit exported to Japan." [368]

201.   Japan does not contest the Panel's characterization of the risk assessment as one that did not analyze the risks of apple fruit separately from risks posed by other hosts. [369] Rather, Japan claims that the Panel's reasoning relates to a "matter of methodology", which lies within the discretion of the importing Member. [370] Japan contends that the requirement of "specificity" explained in *EC – Hormones* refers to the specificity of the risk and not to the methodology of the risk assessment. [371]

202.   We disagree with Japan. Under the *SPS Agreement*, the obligation to conduct an assessment of "risk" is not satisfied merely by a general discussion of the disease sought to be avoided by the imposition of a phytosanitary measure. [372] The Appellate Body found the risk assessment at issue in *EC – Hormones* not to be "sufficiently specific" even though the scientific articles cited by the importing Member had evaluated the "carcinogenic potential of entire *categories* of hormones, or of the hormones at issue *in general*." [373] In order to constitute a "risk assessment" as defined in the *SPS Agreement*, the Appellate Body concluded, the risk assessment should have reviewed the carcinogenic potential, not of the relevant hormones in general, but of "residues of those hormones found in meat derived from cattle to which the hormones had been administered for growth promotion purposes". [374] Therefore, when discussing the risk to be specified in the risk assessment in *EC – Hormones*, the Appellate Body referred in general to the harm concerned (cancer or genetic damage) *as well as* to the precise agent that may possibly cause the harm (that is, the specific hormones when used in a specific manner and for specific purposes).

203.   In this case, the Panel found that the conclusion of the 1999 PRA with respect to fire blight was "based on an overall assessment of possible modes of contamination, where apple fruit is only one of the possible hosts/vectors

---

[367]   *Ibid.*, paras. 8.268-8.271.

[368]   Panel Report, para. 7.14.

[369]   Japan's appellant's submission, para. 128; Japan's response to questioning at the oral hearing.

[370]   Japan's appellant's submission, para. 127.

[371]   *Ibid.*, para. 129.

[372]   Indeed, we are of the view that, as a general matter, "risk" cannot usually be understood only in terms of the disease or adverse effects that may result. Rather, an evaluation of risk must connect the possibility of adverse effects with an antecedent or cause. For example, the abstract reference to the "risk of cancer" has no significance, in and of itself, under the *SPS Agreement*; but when one refers to the "risk of cancer from smoking cigarettes", the particular risk is given content.

[373]   Appellate Body Report, para. 199. (original italics) In other words, the risk assessment proffered by the importing Member in *EC – Hormones* considered the relationship between the broad *grouping* of hormones that were the subject of the measure and cancer.

[374]   *Ibid.*, para. 200.

considered."[375] The Panel further found, on the basis of the scientific evidence, that the risk of entry, establishment or spread of the disease varies significantly depending on the vector, or specific host plant, being evaluated.[376] Given that the measure at issue relates to the risk of transmission of fire blight through apple fruit, in an evaluation of whether the risk assessment is "sufficiently specific to the case at hand"[377], the nature of the risk addressed by the measure at issue is a factor to be taken into account. In the light of these considerations, we are of the view that the Panel properly determined that the 1999 PRA "evaluat[ion of] the risks associated with all possible hosts taken together"[378] was not sufficiently specific to qualify as a "risk assessment" under the *SPS Agreement* for the evaluation of the likelihood of entry, establishment or spread of fire blight in Japan through apple fruit.[379]

204.   Japan contends that the "methodology" of the risk assessment is not directly addressed by the *SPS Agreement*. In particular, Japan suggests that, whether to analyze the risk on the basis of the particular pest or disease, or on the basis of a particular commodity, is a "matter of methodology" not directly addressed by the *SPS Agreement*.[380] We agree. Contrary to Japan's submission, however, the Panel's reading of *EC – Hormones* does not suggest that there is an obligation to follow any particular methodology for conducting a risk assessment. In other words, even though, in a given context, a risk assessment must consider a specific agent or pathway through which contamination might occur, Members are not precluded from organizing their risk assessments along the lines of the disease or pest at issue, or of the commodity to be imported. Thus, Members are free to consider in their risk analysis multiple agents in relation to one disease, provided that the risk assessment attribute a likelihood of entry, establishment or spread of the disease to each agent specifically. Members are also free to follow the other "methodology" identified by Japan and focus on a particular commodity, subject to the same proviso.

205.   Indeed, the relevant international standards, which, Japan claims, "adopt both methodologies"[381], expressly contemplate examining risk in relation to

---

[375]   Panel Report, para. 8.270.
[376]   *Ibid.*, reads, in relevant part:
    The scientific evidence submitted by both parties leaves no doubt that the risk of introduction and spread of the disease varies considerably according to the host plant, with nursery stock and budding material identified as known sources for the spread of fire blight in some cases.
[377]   Appellate Body Report, *EC – Hormones*, para. 200.
[378]   Panel Report, para. 7.14.
[379]   We note our understanding that the Panel did not base its finding on, nor make any reference to, whether the *SPS Agreement* requires a risk assessment to analyze the importation of products on a *country-specific* basis. Neither participant in this appeal has asked us to find that the definition of "risk assessment" in the *SPS Agreement* mandates an analysis of risk specific to *each country* of exportation. As a result, we make no findings with respect to whether such a *country-specific* analysis is required in order to satisfy a Member's obligations under Article 5.1 of the *SPS Agreement*.
[380]   Japan's appellant's submission, paras. 127-128.
[381]   Japan's appellant's submission, para. 128, quoting "Guidelines for Pest Risk Analysis", *International Standard for Phytosanitary Measures*, No.2 (Rome 1996), Food and Agriculture Organization of the United Nations; Exhibit JPN-30, submitted by Japan to the Panel;

particular pathways. [382] Those standards call for that specific examination even when the risk analysis is initiated on the basis of the particular pest or disease at issue [383], as was the 1999 PRA. Therefore, our conclusion that the Panel properly found Japan's risk assessment not to be sufficiently specific, does not limit an importing Member's right to adopt any appropriate "methodology", consistent with the definition of "risk assessment" in paragraph 4 of Annex A to the *SPS Agreement*.

206. We therefore uphold the Panel's finding, in paragraph 8.271 of the Panel Report, that Japan's 1999 Pest Risk Analysis does not satisfy the definition of "risk assessment" in paragraph 4 of Annex A to the *SPS Agreement*, because it fails to evaluate the likelihood of entry, establishment or spread of fire blight specifically through apple fruit.

---

and "Pest Risk Analysis for Quarantine Pests", *International Standard for Phytosanitary Measures*, No.11 (Rome 2001), Food and Agriculture Organization of the United Nations; Exhibit USA-15, submitted by the United States to the Panel.

[382] For example, the *International Standard for Phytosanitary Measures*, No.2, states at page 14:

The final stage of assessment concerns the introduction potential which depends on the pathways from the exporting country to the destination, and the frequency and quantity of pests associated with them. ...

The following is a partial checklist that may be used to estimate the introduction potential divided into those factors which may affect the likelihood of entry and those factors which may affect the likelihood of establishment.

Entry:
- opportunity for contamination of commodities or conveyances by the pest

...

Establishment:
- number and frequency of consignments of the commodity

...

- intended use of the commodity

...

(Exhibit JPN-30, submitted by Japan to the Panel, *supra*, footnote 381)

Similarly, the *International Standard for Phytosanitary Measures*, No.11, provides at pages 13-14:

All relevant pathways should be considered. ... Consignments of plants and plant products moving in international trade are the principal pathways of concern and existing patterns of such trade will, to a substantial extent, determine which pathways are relevant. Other pathways such as other types of commodities ... should be considered where appropriate. ...

...

Factors to consider are:
- dispersal mechanisms, including vectors to allow movement from the pathway to a suitable host
- whether the imported commodity is to be sent to a few or many destination points in the [pest risk analysis] area

...

- intended use of the commodity

...

(Exhibit USA-15, submitted by the United States to the Panel, *supra*, footnote 381)

[383] See *supra*, footnote 382.

B. *Evaluating the Likelihood of Entry, Establishment or Spread of Fire Blight "According to the Sanitary or Phytosanitary Measures Which Might Be Applied"*

207.   Japan also challenges the Panel's finding that Japan "has not ... properly evaluated the likelihood of entry 'according to the SPS measures that might be applied'."[384] According to the Panel, the terms in the definition of "risk assessment" set out in paragraph 4 of Annex A to the *SPS Agreement*—more specifically, the phrase "according to the sanitary or phytosanitary measures which might be applied"—suggest that "consideration should be given not just to those specific measures which are currently in application, but at least to a potential range of relevant measures."[385] Japan acknowledged that it did not consider policies other than the measure already applied.[386] However, according to Japan, this "again relates to the matter of methodology", which is left to the discretion of the importing Member.[387]

208.   The definition of "risk assessment" in the *SPS Agreement* requires that the evaluation of the entry, establishment or spread of a disease be conducted "according to the sanitary or phytosanitary measures which might be applied".[388] We agree with the Panel that this phrase "refers to the measures *which might* be applied, not merely to the measures which *are being* applied."[389] The phrase "which might be applied" is used in the conditional tense. In this sense, "might" means: "were or would be or have been able to, were or would be or have been allowed to, were or would perhaps".[390] We understand this phrase to imply that a risk assessment should not be limited to an examination of the measure already in place or favoured by the importing Member. In other words, the evaluation contemplated in paragraph 4 of Annex A to the *SPS Agreement* should not be distorted by preconceived views on the nature and the content of the measure to be taken; nor should it develop into an exercise tailored to and carried out for the purpose of justifying decisions *ex post facto*.

209.   In this case, the Panel found that the 1999 PRA dealt exclusively with the " 'plant quarantine measures against *E. amylovora* concerning US fresh apple fruit', which have been taken by Japan based on the proposal by the US government since 1994".[391] The Panel also found that, in the 1999 PRA, no attempts were made "to assess the 'relative effectiveness' of the various individual requirements applied, [that] the assessment appears to be based on the assumption from the outset that all these measures would apply

---

[384]   Panel Report, para. 8.285. See Japan's appellant's submission, para. 133.
[385]   Panel Report, para. 8.285.
[386]   Japan's response to questioning at the oral hearing.
[387]   Japan's appellant's submission, para. 133.
[388]   Annex A to the *SPS Agreement*, para. 4.
[389]   Panel Report, para. 8.283. (original italics)
[390]   *Shorter Oxford English Dictionary*, 5th ed., W.R. Trumble, A. Stevenson (eds.) (Oxford University Press, 2002), Vol. I, p. 1725.
[391]   Panel Report, para. 8.284, quoting 1999 PRA, § 3-1. Japan confirmed, in response to questioning at the oral hearing, that the 1999 PRA considered no phytosanitary measure other than the one in place.

cumulatively" [392], and that no analysis was made "of their relative effectiveness and whether and why all of them in combination are required in order to reduce or eliminate the possibility of entry, establishment or spread of the disease." [393] Moreover, the Panel referred to "the opinions of Dr Hale and Dr Smith that the 1999 PRA 'appeared to prejudge the outcome of its risk assessment' and that 'it was principally concerned to show that each of the measures already in place was effective in some respect, and concluded that all should therefore be applied'." [394] In our opinion, these findings of fact of the Panel leave no room for doubt that the 1999 PRA was designed and conducted in such a manner that *no* phytosanitary policy other than the regulatory scheme *already in place* was considered. Accordingly, we uphold the Panel's finding, in paragraph 8.285 of the Panel Report, that "Japan has not ... properly evaluated the likelihood of entry 'according to the SPS measures that might be applied'."

C. Consideration of Scientific Evidence Arising Subsequent to the Risk Assessment at Issue

210. Finally, Japan argues that "Japan's PRA *was* consistent with Article 5.1 of the SPS Agreement at the time of the analysis, because conformity of a risk assessment with Article 5.1 should be assessed against the information available at the time of the risk assessment." [395] According to Japan, a risk assessment should be evaluated solely against the evidence available at the time of the risk assessment, such that a Member that fulfils the requirement of a risk assessment when adopting a measure is not held to have acted inconsistently with Article 5.1 upon the discovery of subsequently-published scientific evidence. [396]

211. During the oral hearing, we invited Japan to identify what evidence, arising subsequent to the 1999 PRA, had been relied upon by the Panel in evaluating Japan's risk assessment under Article 5.1. Japan was unable to point to any such evidence. We also asked the participants what the legal consequence would be for the Panel's finding under Article 5.1 if we found, as Japan requests, that the Panel was not permitted to examine evidence post-dating the 1999 PRA. The United States suggested that there would be no consequence for this dispute because the risk assessment was "inadequate" at the time it was completed. [397] Nor did Japan identify any consequence of such a finding on our part.

212. The Panel concluded that Japan's measure could not be "based on" a risk assessment, as required by Article 5.1, because the 1999 PRA did not satisfy the definition of "risk assessment" set out in paragraph 4 of Annex A to the *SPS Agreement*. [398] The Panel determined that the definition of "risk assessment" was not satisfied because the 1999 PRA failed to meet the two elements discussed

---

[392] Panel Report, para. 8.288.
[393] *Ibid.*
[394] *Ibid.*, para. 8.289. (footnotes omitted)
[395] Japan's appellant's submission, para. 135. (original italics)
[396] *Ibid.*, para. 135.
[397] The United States' response to questioning at the oral hearing.
[398] Panel Report, paras. 8.290-8.291.

above, namely, that a risk assessment (i) "evaluate the likelihood of entry, establishment or spread of " the plant disease at issue, and (ii) conduct such evaluation "according to the SPS measures which might be applied".[399]

213. As we see it, Japan was unable to identify any scientific evidence relied upon by the Panel, but published after the issuance of the 1999 risk assessment, because the Panel did not, in fact, base its finding on such evidence. The Panel's analysis focused almost exclusively on the risk assessment itself to determine whether the 1999 PRA satisfied the legal requirements the Panel found in the *SPS Agreement*. The Panel identified those requirements as the need to assess a risk with a certain degree of "specificity", to evaluate probability rather than possibilities, and to evaluate the likelihood of entry "according to the sanitary or phytosanitary measures which might be applied".[400] Beyond the text of the 1999 PRA, the only scientific information relied upon by the Panel relates to its finding on "specificity": on this point, the Panel determined that "scientific evidence submitted by both parties leaves no doubt that the risk of introduction and spread of the disease varies considerably according to the host plant".[401] From this finding of fact, the Panel concluded that Japan's risk assessment was not "sufficiently specific to the matter at issue" because it did not examine the risk in relation to apple fruit in particular.[402]

214. In stating that its finding of fact was based on "scientific evidence submitted by both parties", the Panel did not cite those studies or provide any indication of whether those studies dated from before or after Japan's risk assessment. Japan does not assert that this scientific evidence, or any other scientific evidence underlying the Panel's conclusion with respect to Article 5.1, was not available to Japan at the time of the risk assessment. We also note that the Panel record includes relevant scientific evidence adduced by both parties that arose *before* Japan's risk assessment.[403] Such evidence could have reasonably formed the basis for the Panel's conclusion that the risk from fire blight varies according to the host plant. Under these circumstances, we are not persuaded that, when analyzing the conformity of the 1999 PRA with Japan's obligations under Article 5.1, the Panel relied on scientific evidence that was not available to Japan at the time it conducted its risk assessment.

215. As Japan failed to establish that the Panel utilized subsequent scientific evidence in evaluating the risk assessment at issue, it is not necessary for us to express views on the question whether the conformity of a risk assessment with

---

[399] *Ibid.*, paras. 8.280, 8.285, and 8.288.
[400] See, for example, *ibid.*, paras. 8.268, 8.270-8.271, 8.274-8.278, 8.284, and 8.287-8.288.
[401] *Ibid.*, para. 8.271.
[402] *Ibid.*
[403] See, for example, R.G. Roberts *et al.*, "The potential for spread of *Erwinia amylovora* and fire blight via commercial apple fruit; a critical review and risk assessment", *Crop Protection* (1998), Vol. 17, No. 1, pp. 19-28, at p. 24; Exhibit JPN-5, submitted by Japan to the Panel and Exhibit USA-4, submitted by the United States to the Panel; T. van der Zwet *et al.*, "Population of *Erwinia amylovora* on External and Internal Apple Fruit Tissues", *Plant Disease* (1990), Vol. 74, No. 9, pp. 711-716, at p. 711; Exhibit JPN-7, submitted by Japan to the Panel; and S.V. Thomson, "Fire blight of apple and pear", *Diseases of Fruit Crops* (J. Kumar *et al.*, eds.), Vol. 3, pp. 32-65, § 2-1 at p. 32 and § 2-9-2 at p. 49; Exhibit USA-44, submitted by the United States to the Panel.

Article 5.1 should be evaluated solely against the scientific evidence available at the time of the risk assessment, to the exclusion of subsequent information. Resolution of such hypothetical claims would not serve "to secure a positive solution" to this dispute. [404]

216.   Accordingly, we uphold the Panel's finding, in paragraph 8.290 of the Panel Report, that Japan's 1999 Pest Risk Analysis does not satisfy the definition of "risk assessment" set out in paragraph 4 of Annex A to the *SPS Agreement* because it (i) fails to "evaluate the likelihood of entry, establishment or spread of" the plant disease at issue, and (ii) fails to conduct such an evaluation "according to the SPS measures which might be applied". Furthermore, as the 1999 PRA is not a "risk assessment" within the meaning of the *SPS Agreement*, it follows, as the Panel found, in paragraphs 8.291 and 9.1(c) of the Panel Report, that Japan's phytosanitary measure at issue is not "based on" a risk assessment, as required by Article 5.1 of the *SPS Agreement*.

X.   ARTICLE 11 OF THE DSU

217.   Japan raises two challenges under Article 11 of the DSU related to the Panel's fact-finding: one relates to the Panel's analysis under Article 2.2 of the *SPS Agreement*, and the other relates to the Panel's analysis under Article 5.1 of that Agreement. In Section IV of this Report, we found that the Article 11 challenge relating to the Panel's analysis under Article 5.1 was not sufficiently identified in Japan's Notice of Appeal to place the United States on notice thereof. [405] We found that the challenge relating to Article 5.1 was not properly before us, and we therefore declined to rule on it. We thus examine below only Japan's challenge to the Panel's fact-finding under Article 2.2 of the *SPS Agreement*.

218.   With respect to Article 2.2 of the *SPS Agreement*, Japan challenges the Panel's analysis of the likelihood that the pathway of transmission for fire blight from apple fruit to other plants would be completed. In particular, Japan contests the Panel's finding that "it has not been established with sufficient scientific evidence that the last stage of the pathway (i.e. the transmission of fire blight to a host plant) would likely be completed." [406] The Panel made this finding of fact on the last stage of the pathway with respect to apple fruit, which includes mature, symptomless apples as well as apples that are not mature and symptomless. According to Japan, the Panel, in its analysis, made certain errors when evaluating the relevant scientific evidence, each of which constitutes a failure on the part of the Panel to "make an objective assessment of the facts of the case" under Article 11 of the DSU. The errors alleged by Japan are the following:

---

[404]   Article 3.7 of the DSU.
[405]   See *supra*, paras. 127-128.
[406]   Panel Report, para. 8.168.

(i) that the Panel made a "material" factual error in its characterization of the experimental evidence underlying the Panel's conclusion that fire blight was not likely to be transmitted to other plants[407];

(ii) that the Panel arrived at a conclusion that covered infected apple fruit, when the evidence before it "centered around" mature, symptomless apple fruit[408];

(iii) that the Panel failed to take into account the "precautionary principle", or the caution emphasized by the Panel's experts, in arriving at its conclusion on the likelihood of completion of the pathway[409]; and

(iv) that the Panel's conclusion on the likelihood of completion of the pathway is inconsistent with the Panel's recognition that the risk identified by the experts was not merely a "theoretical risk".[410]

219. The United States disagrees with Japan's Article 11 challenge to the extent that it applies to mature, symptomless apples, and contends that the Panel had no authority to make findings on apple fruit other than mature, symptomless apples. The United States argues that Japan essentially challenges the Panel's characterization and weighing of the evidence, effectively seeking to compel a Panel finding on completion of the pathway where the record contains no evidence to support such a finding. In the light of the "high standard" that must be met to succeed on a claim under Article 11, the United States submits that Japan's claim should be rejected with respect to mature, symptomless apples.[411]

220. We begin by noting that Article 11 of the DSU requires that a panel, *inter alia*:

> … make an objective assessment of the matter before it, including an objective assessment of the facts of the case and the applicability of and conformity with the relevant covered agreements, and make such other findings as will assist the DSB in making the recommendations or in giving the rulings provided for in the covered agreements.

221. In the first appeal presenting an Article 11 challenge to a Panel's fact-finding[412], *EC – Hormones*, the Appellate Body identified the "duty to make an objective assessment of the facts [as], among other things, an obligation to

---

[407] Japan's appellant's submission, paras. 52-54.

[408] *Ibid.*, para. 51.

[409] *Ibid.*, paras. 64-70.

[410] *Ibid.*, paras. 60-63.

[411] United States' appellee's submission, para. 10.

[412] Prior to *EC – Hormones*, an Article 11 claim was raised on appeal in *US – Wool Shirts and Blouses*, but that claim addressed solely "whether Article 11 of the *DSU* entitles a complaining party to a finding on each of the legal claims it makes to a panel". (Appellate Body Report, p. 17, DSR 1997:I, 323, at 338) As such, the claim did not challenge the panel's "assessment of the facts of the case". In addition, in *Canada – Periodicals*, the appellant raised Article 11 when challenging the panel's reliance on a "hypothetical example" to make a determination of "like products" under Article III:2 of the GATT 1994. (Appellate Body Report, p. 5, DSR 1997:I, 449, at 452) The Appellate Body, however, made no ruling as to Article 11. (*Ibid.*, pp. 20-23, DSR 1997:I, 449, at 465-468)

consider the evidence presented to a panel and to make factual findings on the basis of that evidence."[413] In *EC – Hormones*, the Appellate Body observed further that the:

> [d]etermination of the credibility and weight properly to be ascribed to (that is, the appreciation of) a given piece of evidence is part and parcel of the fact finding process and is, in principle, left to the discretion of a panel as the trier of facts.[414]

Since *EC – Hormones*, the Appellate Body has consistently emphasized that, within the bounds of their obligation under Article 11 to make an objective assessment of the facts of the case, panels enjoy a "margin of discretion" as triers of fact.[415] Panels are thus "not required to accord to factual evidence of the parties the same meaning and weight as do the parties"[416] and may properly "determine that certain elements of evidence should be accorded more weight than other elements".[417]

222. Consistent with this margin of discretion, the Appellate Body has recognized that "not every error in the appreciation of the evidence (although it may give rise to a question of law) may be characterized as a failure to make an objective assessment of the facts."[418] When addressing claims under Article 11 of the DSU, the Appellate Body does not "second-guess the Panel in appreciating either the evidentiary value of ... studies or the consequences, if any, of alleged defects in [the evidence]".[419] Indeed:

> [i]n assessing the panel's appreciation of the evidence, we cannot base a finding of inconsistency under Article 11 simply on the conclusion that we might have reached a different factual finding from the one the panel reached. Rather, we must be satisfied that the panel has exceeded the bounds of its discretion, as the trier of facts, in its appreciation of the evidence.[420]

Where parties challenging a panel's fact-finding under Article 11 have failed to establish that a panel exceeded the bounds of its discretion as the trier of facts, the Appellate Body has not "interfere[d]" with the findings of the panel.[421]

---

[413] Appellate Body Report, para. 133.
[414] *Ibid.*, para. 132.
[415] Appellate Body Report, *EC – Asbestos*, para. 161. See also, for example, Appellate Body Report, *EC – Tube or Pipe Fittings*, para. 125; Appellate Body Report, *EC – Bed Linen (Article 21.5 – India)*, paras. 170, 177, and 181; Appellate Body Report, *EC – Sardines*, para. 299; Appellate Body Report, *Korea – Alcoholic Beverages*, paras. 161-162; Appellate Body Report, *Japan – Agricultural Products II*, paras. 141-142; Appellate Body Report, *US – Wheat Gluten*, para. 151; Appellate Body Report, *Australia – Salmon*, para. 266; and Appellate Body Report, *Korea – Dairy*, para. 138.
[416] Appellate Body Report, *Australia – Salmon*, para. 267.
[417] Appellate Body Report, *EC – Asbestos*, para. 161.
[418] Appellate Body Report, *EC – Hormones*, para. 133.
[419] Appellate Body Report, *EC – Asbestos*, para. 177, quoting Appellate Body Report, *Korea – Alcoholic Beverages*, para. 161.
[420] Appellate Body Report, *EC – Asbestos*, para. 159, quoting Appellate Body Report, *US – Wheat Gluten*, para. 151.
[421] Appellate Body Report, *EC – Bed Linen (Article 21.5 – India)*, para. 170; Appellate Body Report, *US – Carbon Steel*, para. 142, quoting Appellate Body Report, *US – Wheat Gluten*, para. 151.

A.   The Panel's Characterization of Experimental Evidence

223.   Japan first challenges a "factual error" in one of the statements offered as support for the Panel's finding on the completion of the last stage of the pathway for apple fruit.[422] Japan points to the following statement of the Panel:

> We note that experiments trying to reproduce the conditions applicable to discarded apples have not led to any visible contamination, even when ooze was reported to exist.[423] (footnote omitted)

According to Japan, the experiments referred to by the Panel used inoculated apples, not naturally infected apples. Japan advances that ooze has not been reported in inoculated apples.[424] In Japan's submission, therefore, the above statement is an erroneous characterization of the underlying scientific studies.[425]

224.   We observe that the Panel made this statement in support of its finding of fact that it has not been established with sufficient scientific evidence that the last stage of the pathway (that is, the transmission of fire blight from imported apples to a host plant) would likely be completed.[426] The Panel also formulated this finding of fact in these terms:

> [A]ssuming that [a situation of infected apples or infested apples] would arise, the entry, establishment or spread of the disease as a result of the presence of these bacteria in or on apple fruit would require the completion of an additional sequence of events which is deemed unlikely, and which has not even been experimentally established to date.[427]

In addition to the studies cited by the Panel, the characterization of which Japan contests, the Panel referenced the following evidence to substantiate this finding of fact: (i) the "number of cumulative conditions" identified by the experts for a successful completion of the pathway[428]; (ii) the observation by the experts that contamination by birds had not been established[429]; (iii) to the extent that the experts found "short distance communication" to be possible through rain or bees, this finding "related to contamination at the flowering stage, not to contamination from apple fruit"[430]; and (iv) "[t]he evidence submitted by Japan was essentially circumstantial or deemed unconvincing by the experts."[431] In the light of the other factual material relied upon by the Panel, including its express consideration and discounting of scientific evidence submitted by Japan, we

---

[422]   Japan's appellant's submission, para. 52.
[423]   Panel Report, para. 8.166.
[424]   Japan's appellant's submission, para. 52.
[425]   *Ibid.*
[426]   Panel Report, para. 8.168.
[427]   *Ibid.*, para. 8.171(d).
[428]   *Ibid.*, para. 8.166, quoting *ibid.*, paras. 6.70 (Dr. Hayward) and 6.71 (Dr. Smith).
[429]   *Ibid.*, para. 8.166, citing paras. 241 (Dr. Smith) and 263 (Dr. Geider) of Annex 3 thereto.
[430]   Panel Report, para. 8.166.
[431]   *Ibid.*, para. 8.167.

cannot find that the Panel has exceeded its "margin of discretion"[432] in evaluating the relevant evidence before it, to call into question the Panel's finding in relation to the last stage of the pathway. Accordingly, Japan has failed to establish that the Panel did not satisfy the obligations of Article 11 so as to justify our interference with a panel's finding of fact.

B.   Evidence "Centered Around" Mature, Symptomless Apple Fruit

225.   We turn now to the next aspect of Japan's claim under Article 11 of the DSU—that the Panel acted inconsistently with its obligations thereunder in making findings that covered the completion of the pathway for transmission of fire blight by "infected" apple fruit, because the evidence before the Panel "centered around" the pathway with respect to mature, symptomless fruit.[433] In other words, Japan submits that there is a lack of connection between the evidence considered by the Panel and its findings on the completion of the last stage of the pathway for transmission of fire blight.

226.   As we have just observed, the Panel found that the additional sequence of steps required for completion of the pathway from apple fruit to other host plants would be unlikely to occur.[434] The finding of the Panel covered both the pathway for mature, symptomless apples and that for apples other than mature, symptomless apple fruit. In our view, the Panel did not err in making this finding. However, the Panel's reasoning was perhaps not sufficiently explicit, with the result that Japan deduced that the Panel had failed to make an objective assessment of the facts before it on completion of the last stage of the pathway.

227.   Specifically, it might have been helpful had the Panel been more precise about the scope of its factual analysis. We recall that the Panel made the following findings: (i) infection of mature, symptomless apples has not been established; (ii) the presence of endophytic bacteria in mature, symptomless apples is not generally established; (iii) the presence of epiphytic bacteria in mature, symptomless apples is not excluded, but is considered to be extremely rare; and (iv) infection or infestation of apples other than mature, symptomless apple fruit is not contested.[435] These findings imply that the factual analysis as regards the completion of the last stage of the pathway with respect to mature, symptomless apples does not need to include the hypothesis of the importation of infected apples to Japan, as, according to the Panel, "infection of mature, symptomless apples has not been established".[436] By contrast, the factual analysis concerning the completion of the last stage of the pathway with respect to apples other than mature, symptomless apple fruit, *is* required to address the hypothesis of the importation of infected apples to Japan, as, in the view of the Panel, infection of immature apple fruit is not contested.

---

[432]   Appellate Body Report, *EC – Sardines*, para. 299, quoting Appellate Body Report, *EC – Asbestos*, para. 161.

[433]   Japan's appellant's submission, para. 51.

[434]   *Supra*, para. 224, quoting Panel Report, para. 8.171(d).

[435]   Panel Report, para 8.1 / 1.

[436]   *Ibid.*, para 8.171(a).

228.   The Panel could also have been more precise about the respective responsibilities of the parties for providing proof of a fact. In connection with the *prima facie* case it had to establish, the United States made allegations of fact that the last stage of the pathway would not be completed as regards mature, symptomless apples. [437] The United States was responsible for proving these allegations of fact by reason of the principle set out in *US – Wool Shirts and Blouses* that the party "who asserts a fact … is responsible for providing proof thereof." [438] For its part, Japan, in the context of its attempts to counter the case put forward by the United States, made allegations of fact relating to the completion of the last stage of the pathway with respect to infected apples. [439] Given the Panel's finding of fact that it is unlikely that mature, symptomless apples would be infected, it can be reasonably assumed that any infected apples exported to Japan would be apples other than mature, symptomless apple fruit. Under the principle set out in *US – Wool Shirts and Blouses*, it was thus for Japan, and not the United States, to provide proof of these allegations of fact relating to infected apples.

229.   Having said that the Panel could have been clearer on these two aspects of its reasoning, we nevertheless disagree with Japan that the Panel acted inconsistently with its obligations under Article 11 of the DSU in making a finding that covered the completion of the pathway for transmission of fire blight by "infected" apple fruit, even though the evidence before the Panel "centered around" the pathway with respect to mature, symptomless apple fruit.

230.   The Panel agreed with the United States that, as regards mature, symptomless apples, the completion of the last stage of the transmission of fire blight is unlikely. [440] The Panel referred to various pieces of evidence in support of this conclusion. [441] The evidence identified focused on mature, symptomless apples and, therefore, supported the finding that completion of the last stage of the transmission of fire blight was unlikely, to the extent that this finding concerns mature, symptomless apples.

231.   As regards apples other than mature, symptomless apple fruit, the Panel assumed, correctly, that Japan had the responsibility of providing proof of its allegations of fact, namely that fire blight could be transmitted from an infected apple to a host plant. We understand the Panel to have dealt with these allegations of fact from Japan when it said that "[t]he evidence submitted by Japan was essentially circumstantial or deemed unconvincing by the experts", and that "Japan did not submit sufficient scientific evidence in support of its allegation that the last step of the pathway had been completed or was likely to be completed." [442] We understand the Panel's conclusions to cover infected apples, as Japan made allegations of fact and brought evidence on such

---

[437]   See, for example, Panel Report, paras. 4.82(d) and 4.83.
[438]   Appellate Body Report, p. 14, DSR 1997:I, 323, at 335.
[439]   See, for example, Panel Report, para. 4.84.
[440]   Panel Report, para. 8.171.
[441]   *Ibid.*, para. 8.166.
[442]   *Ibid.*, para. 8.167.

apples.[443] Accordingly, we see no lack of connection between the overall evidence that the Panel considered and the findings it made with respect to the last stage of the pathway for transmission of fire blight. Therefore, we are of the view that the Panel did not act inconsistently with its obligations under Article 11 of the DSU.

C.   Experts' Statements of Caution

232.   Japan's third challenge under Article 11 of the DSU is premised on the Panel's alleged failure to take into account adequately the "precautionary principle". Japan bases this challenge on the fact that the Panel did not take into account "the need of caution emphasized by the experts" with respect to the phytosanitary measure aimed at preventing the entry of fire blight into Japan.[444] Based on what Japan understands to be the experts' recognition that the risk of harm from the introduction of fire blight results in a "general need [for] prudence", Japan argues that the Panel "should have recognized the risk of completion of the pathway from infected apple fruit."[445]

233.   In *EC – Hormones*, the Appellate Body noted that the "precautionary principle" had not yet attained "authoritative formulation" outside the field of international environmental law[446], but that it remained relevant in the context of the *SPS Agreement*, particularly as recognized in certain provisions of that Agreement.[447] However, the Appellate Body found that the "precautionary principle" did not release Members from their WTO obligations and, as such, did not "override the provisions of Articles 5.1 and 5.2 of the *SPS Agreement*."[448]

234.   Japan does not argue that the Panel should have applied the "precautionary principle" as a principle separate and distinct from the provisions of the *SPS Agreement*. Nor does Japan argue that the "precautionary principle" should have been employed by the Panel as part of its interpretive analysis of the requirements of the *SPS Agreement*. Rather, we understand Japan to contend that the "precautionary principle" was embodied in the opinions of the experts cautioning against elimination of phytosanitary measures protecting Japan from fire blight; and that, accordingly, such caution "should have been given greater weight in the conclusion of the Panel on completion of the pathway."[449] Japan's argument, therefore, is aimed solely at the Panel's consideration of the evidence before it.

235.   As an initial matter, we note that Japan relies primarily on statements from two experts and on the fact that the other experts did not object to these views.[450] The first expert cited by Japan observed that:

---

[443]   *Ibid.*, para. 4.84.
[444]   Japan's appellant's submission, paras. 64 and 70.
[445]   *Ibid.*, paras. 68-69.
[446]   Appellate Body Report, para. 123.
[447]   *Ibid.*, para. 124.
[448]   *Ibid.*, para. 125.
[449]   Japan's appellant's submission, para. 69.
[450]   *Ibid.*, paras. 67-68.

> ... when the phytosanitary system is changed it should be changed under circumstances that retain some degree of control on what is happening and not in a single step that *removes control altogether*.[451] (emphasis added)

The second expert cited by Japan observed as follows:

> [A] decision to *remove most restrictions* for importation of apples from fire blight countries should consider that the Japanese apple production is highly sophisticated following a demand for high quality apples. Import of any grade of apple quality to Japan such as low quality at a cheap price could undermine the control of disease problems regardless to the low risk to distribute fire blight with apples.[452] (emphasis added)

236.   The concerns articulated by these experts thus address the consequences associated with eliminating *all* or *most* controls over imports, combined with the importation of poor-grade apples. These concerns do *not* speak about whether the pathway for transmission of fire blight could be completed. Indeed, the same experts cited by Japan as promoting a cautious approach[453], Dr. Ian Smith and Dr. Klaus Geider, also expressed the opinion before the Panel that the completion of the pathway was unlikely.[454] It is therefore difficult to see how the Panel's conclusion that completion of the last stage of the pathway for apple fruit (whether "mature, symptomless" or otherwise) would be unlikely, is necessarily inconsistent with or undermined by the caution expressed by the experts.

237.   Furthermore, the Panel itself made reference to the experts' note of caution:

> [W]e note that even if the scientific evidence before us demonstrates that apple fruit is highly unlikely to be a pathway for entry, establishment and spread of fire blight within Japan, it does suggest that some slight risk of contamination cannot be totally excluded. ... [N]one of the experts were comfortable with the notion of eliminating "in one step" all phytosanitary controls, taking into account Japan's island environment and climate.[455] (footnote omitted)

As such, contrary to Japan's assertion, the Panel did explicitly "tak[e] into account"[456] the experts' cautionary statements, but understood properly that those statements focused on an issue different from the likelihood of completion of the last stage of the pathway for transmission of fire blight from apple fruit. Accordingly, the Panel did not err in refusing to "recognize[] the risk of

---

[451]   *Ibid.*, para. 67, quoting Annex 3 to the Panel Report, para. 423 (Dr. Smith).

[452]   Japan's appellant's submission, para. 67, quoting Dr. Geider's written response to questions posed by the Panel, 10 December 2002, p. 8. See also, Panel Report, para. 6.175.

[453]   Japan's appellant's submission, para. 67.

[454]   Panel Report, para. 6.71, and paras. 241 (Dr. Smith) and 263 (Dr. Geider) of Annex 3 thereto.

[455]   *Ibid.*, para. 8.173, citing paras. 386, 389, 409, 411, 413-414, 419, 423-424, 426, and 429 of Annex 3 thereto.

[456]   Japan's appellant's submission, para. 70.

completion of the pathway from infected apple fruit"[457] on the basis of the experts' statements of caution.

238. In any event, we note that Japan essentially disagrees with the Panel's appreciation of the evidence, and in particular, its appreciation of the experts' expressions of caution. As Japan states in its appellant's submission, "[t]he impact of these expressions of scientific caution, clearly on the record, *should have been given greater weight* in the conclusion of the Panel on completion of the pathway."[458] In *EC – Sardines* and in *EC – Hormones*, the Appellate Body said that:

> [d]etermination of the credibility and weight properly to be ascribed to (that is, the appreciation of) a given piece of evidence is part and parcel of the fact finding process and is, in principle, left to the discretion of a panel as the trier of facts.[459]

Although a panel's discretion is necessarily circumscribed by its duty to render an objective assessment of the facts of the case, Japan has proffered no argument challenging the objectivity of the Panel's assessment. Therefore, in our view, even if the Panel did not give as much weight as Japan would have liked to the experts' statements of caution with respect to modifications to Japan's phytosanitary measure, Japan has failed to establish that, in doing so, the Panel exceeded the bounds of its discretion as the trier of facts.

D. Completion of the Pathway and "Theoretical Risk"

239. Japan's final Article 11 claim alleges an inconsistency in the Panel's fact-finding that renders its analysis of the pathway for transmission of fire blight through apple fruit inconsistent with its obligation to make an "objective assessment of the facts of the case". The Panel noted that "none of the experts were comfortable with the notion of eliminating 'in one step' all phytosanitary controls, taking into account Japan's island environment and climate."[460] The United States had argued that the experts' prudence in this regard amounted to a "theoretical risk", which, as the Appellate Body observed in *EC – Hormones*, was not intended to be the subject of a risk assessment under the *SPS Agreement*.[461] The Panel disagreed with the United States, saying:

> We do not agree with the United States that the scientific prudence displayed by the experts should be completely assimilated to a "theoretical risk" within the meaning given to that terms by the Appellate Body in *EC – Hormones*. On the other hand, we can

---

[457] *Ibid.*, para. 69.
[458] *Ibid.* (emphasis added; footnote omitted)
[459] Appellate Body Report, *EC – Sardines*, para. 300; Appellate Body Report, *EC – Hormones*, para. 132.
[460] Panel Report, para. 8.173, quoting Annex 3 thereto, para. 419, and citing paras. 386, 389, 409, 411, 413-414, 423-424, 426 and 429 thereof.
[461] *Ibid.*, para. 8.175.

only note that Japan did not submit "sufficient scientific evidence" in support of its allegation that the pathway could be completed.[462]

Japan contends that the Panel's rejection of the United States' argument that the experts' prudence constituted a "'theoretical risk' implies that the risk from infected apple fruit is *real*, and that the entire pathway could be completed".[463] As such, in Japan's view, this implicit finding is incompatible with the Panel's ultimate finding that the pathway from apple fruit was unlikely to be completed.[464]

240.   The Panel made the finding of fact that "scientific evidence suggests a negligible risk of possible transmission of fire blight through apple fruit."[465] On the basis of this finding of fact, the Panel concluded that the measure is "clearly disproportionate to the risk identified"[466] and, consequently, that the measure is maintained without sufficient scientific evidence. The conclusion of the Panel that the measure is maintained without sufficient scientific evidence rests on the finding of fact of "a negligible risk of possible transmission of fire blight through apple fruit"[467]; it has no relation to the Panel's rejection of the United States' argument that the experts' prudence constituted a "theoretical risk".

241.   The comments of the Panel in response to the argument of the United States on "theoretical risk" should be viewed in their appropriate context. In *EC – Hormones*, the Appellate Body referred to the notion of "theoretical uncertainty" in the context of Article 5.1 of the *SPS Agreement*. The Appellate Body indicated that Article 5.1 does not address theoretical uncertainty, that is to say, "uncertainty that theoretically always remains since science can *never* provide *absolute* certainty that a given substance will not *ever* have adverse health effects."[468] We understand that the "scientific prudence" displayed by the experts in this case related to the risks that might arise from radical changes in Japan's current system of phytosanitary controls, taking into account Japan's island environment and climate.[469] The scientific prudence displayed by the experts did not relate to the "theoretical uncertainty" that is inherent in the scientific method and which stems from the intrinsic limits of experiments, methodologies, or instruments deployed by scientists to explain a given phenomenon. Therefore, we agree with the Panel that the scientific prudence displayed by the experts should not be "completely assimilated" to the "theoretical uncertainty" that the Appellate Body discussed in *EC – Hormones* as

---

[462]   *Ibid.*

[463]   Japan's appellant's submission, para. 61 (original italics), quoting Panel Report, para. 8.175.

[464]   Japan's appellant's submission, paras. 60-61.

[465]   Panel Report, para. 8.169.

[466]   *Ibid.*, para. 8.198.

[467]   *Ibid.*, para. 8.169.

[468]   Appellate Body Report, *EC – Hormones*, para. 186. (original italics)

[469]   We find support for this understanding of "scientific prudence" in the Panel's references to the experts' views on the removal of controls, which references immediately precede the Panel's finding that the experts' "scientific prudence" could not be "completely assimilated" to a "theoretical risk". (See Panel Report, paras. 8.173-8.174) These statements of the experts, therefore, are the same as those emphasized by Japan in our earlier discussion as statements of caution that should have been given greater weight in the Panel's analysis. (See *supra*, paras. 235-236)

being beyond the purview of risks to be addressed by measures subject to the *SPS Agreement*. Nevertheless, contrary to Japan's understanding, that scientific prudence does not undermine the finding of negligibility of the risk of possible transmission of fire blight through apple fruit: indeed, the experts' scientific prudence is related to a different question, namely, the hypothetical scenario of future changes in Japan's regulatory environment.[470] Accordingly, we disagree with Japan that the Panel's rejection of the United States' argument on "'theoretical risk' implies that the risk from infected apple fruit is *real*, and that the entire pathway could be completed".[471] In our view, the Panel, in rejecting the United States' argument on "theoretical risk", while at the same time finding that the risk of transmission of fire blight through apple fruit is "negligible"[472], did not act inconsistently with Article 11 of the DSU.

242.   We therefore find that the Panel did not act inconsistently with Article 11 of the DSU, with respect to its analysis of the United States' claim under Article 2.2 of the *SPS Agreement*.

XI.   FINDINGS AND CONCLUSIONS

243.   For the reasons set out in this Report, the Appellate Body:

(a)   *finds* that the Panel had the "authority" to make findings and draw conclusions with respect to all apple fruit from the United States, including immature apples;

(b)   *upholds* the Panel's findings, in paragraphs 8.199 and 9.1(a) of the Panel Report, that Japan's phytosanitary measure at issue is maintained "without sufficient scientific evidence" within the meaning of Article 2.2 of the *SPS Agreement*;

(c)   *upholds* the Panel's findings, in paragraphs 8.222 and 9.1(b) of the Panel Report, that Japan's phytosanitary measure at issue was not imposed in respect of a situation "where relevant scientific evidence is insufficient", and, therefore, that it is not a provisional measure justified under Article 5.7 of the *SPS Agreement*;

(d)   *upholds* the Panel's findings, in paragraphs 8.271, 8.285, and 8.290 of the Panel Report, that Japan's 1999 Pest Risk Analysis does not satisfy the definition of "risk assessment" set out in paragraph 4 of Annex A to the *SPS Agreement* because it (i) fails to "evaluate the likelihood of entry, establishment or spread of" the plant disease at issue, and (ii) fails to conduct such an evaluation "according to the SPS measures which might be applied". Consequently, the Appellate Body *upholds* the Panel's findings, in paragraphs 8.291

---

[470]   We express no view on the changes to Japan's phytosanitary measure that might be required to bring it into conformity with Japan's WTO obligations, nor do we speak to any other issue related to the means of implementation of the possible rulings and recommendations of the DSB in this dispute.

[471]   Japan's appellant's submission, para. 61. (original italics)

[472]   Panel Report, para. 8.169.

and 9.1(c) of the Panel Report, that Japan's phytosanitary measure at issue is not "based on" a risk assessment, as required by Article 5.1 of the *SPS Agreement*;

(e)   *finds* that the Panel did not act inconsistently with Article 11 of the DSU, with respect to its analysis of the United States' claim under Article 2.2 of the *SPS Agreement*; and

(f)   *finds* that the issue of the Panel's compliance with Article 11 of the DSU, with respect to its analysis of the United States' claim under Article 5.1 of the *SPS Agreement*, was not raised by Japan in its Notice of Appeal and therefore is not properly before the Appellate Body in this appeal. Consequently, the Appellate Body does not rule on this issue.

244.   The Appellate Body therefore *recommends* that the Dispute Settlement Body request Japan to bring its measure, found in this Report, and in the Panel Report as upheld by this Report, to be inconsistent with its obligations under the *SPS Agreement*, into conformity with that Agreement.

ANNEX A

WORLD TRADE
ORGANIZATION

WT/DS245/5

28 August 2003

(03-4543)

Original:

JAPAN – MEASURES AFFECTING THE IMPORTATION OF APPLES

Notification of an Appeal by Japan
under paragraph 4 of Article 16 of the Understanding on Rules
and Procedures Governing the Settlement of Disputes (DSU)

The following notification, dated 28 August 2003, sent by Japan to the Dispute Settlement Body (the "DSB"), is circulated to Members. This notification also constitutes the Notice of Appeal, filed on the same day with the Appellate Body, pursuant to the *Working Procedures for Appellate Review*.

Pursuant to Article 16 of the Understanding on Rules and Procedures Governing the Settlement of Disputes ("DSU") and Rule 20 of the Working Procedures for Appellate Review, Japan hereby notifies its decision to appeal to the Appellate Body certain issues of law covered in the Panel Report on Japan-Measures Affecting the Importation of Apples (WT/DS245/R, dated 15th July 2003) and certain legal interpretations developed by the Panel.

Japan seeks review by the Appellate Body of the conclusions of the Panel that Japan's phytosanitary measure on the United States apples is inconsistent with the Agreement on the Application of Sanitary and Phytosanitary Measures ("SPS Agreement"). These findings are in error, and are based on erroneous findings on issues of law and related legal interpretations. The Appeal relates to the following issues:

1.   The Panel erred in law in finding that Japan acted inconsistently with its obligations under Article 2.2 of the SPS Agreement. This finding reflects the Panel's erroneous interpretation of the rule of burden of proof, and the Panel's failure to make an objective assessment of the matter before it under Article 11 of the DSU.

2.   The Panel erred in law in finding that Japan's phytosanitary measure was inconsistent with the requirements under Article 5.7 of the SPS Agreement. This finding is based on an erroneous interpretation of the requirements under Article 5.7.

3.   The Panel erred in law in finding that Japan's phytosanitary measure was not based on a risk assessment within the meaning of Article 5.1 of the SPS Agreement. This finding is based on an erroneous interpretation of the requirements of a risk assessment under Article 5.1.

JAPAN – MEASURES AFFECTING THE IMPORTATION OF APPLES

Report of the Panel

WT/DS245/R

Adopted by the Dispute Settlement Body
on 10 December 2003
as Upheld by the Appellate Body

TABLE OF CONTENTS

I.   INTRODUCTION

1.1   In a communication dated 1 March 2002, the United States requested consultations with Japan pursuant to Articles 1 and 4 of the Understanding on Rules and Procedures Governing the Settlement of Disputes ("DSU"), Article XXIII of the General Agreement on Tariffs and Trade 1994 ("GATT 1994"), Article 11 of the Agreement on the Application of Sanitary and Phytosanitary

Measures ("*SPS Agreement*") and Article 19 of the Agreement on Agriculture, with respect to restrictions imposed by Japan on imports of apples from the United States.[1]

1.2　The United States stated that since 1994, Japan had applied quarantine restrictions on US apples imported into Japan to protect against the introduction of fire blight (*Erwinia amylovora*). These restrictions included, *inter alia*, the prohibition of imported apples from orchards in which any fire blight is detected, the requirement that export orchards be inspected three times yearly for the presence of fire blight, the disqualification of any orchard from exporting to Japan should fire blight be detected within a 500-metre buffer zone surrounding such orchard, and a post-harvest treatment of exported apples with chlorine. The United States alleged that Japan's measures were inconsistent with Article XI of GATT 1994; Articles 2.2, 2.3, 5.1, 5.2, 5.3, 5.6, 6.1, 6.2 and 7 and Annex B of the *SPS Agreement*; and Article 14 of the Agreement on Agriculture. Consultations were held on 18 April 2002, but failed to settle the dispute.

1.3　In a communication dated 7 May 2002, the United States requested the Dispute Settlement Body ("DSB") to establish a panel pursuant to Article 6 of the DSU, with standard terms of reference as set out in Article 7.1 of the DSU.[2] The US claims of inconsistency in their Request for the Establishment of a Panel were identical to those set out in their request for consultations, except for additional claims of inconsistency under Article 5.5 of the *SPS Agreement* and Article 4.2 of the Agreement on Agriculture, and omission of the previous claim under Article 14 of the Agreement on Agriculture.

1.4　On 3 June 2002, the DSB established a panel in accordance with Article 6 of the DSU.[3] In accordance with Article 7.1 of the DSU, the terms of reference of the Panel were:

> "To examine, in the light of the relevant provisions of the covered agreements cited by the United States in document WT/DS245/2, the matter referred to the DSB by the United States in that document and to make such findings as will assist the DSB in making the recommendations or in giving the rulings provided for in those agreements."

1.5　On 16 July 2002, the Director-General determined the composition of the Panel as follows:

> Chairman: Mr Michael Cartland
>
> Panelists:　Mr Christian Häberli
>
> 　　　　　Ms Kathy-Ann Brown

1.6　Australia, Brazil, the European Communities, New Zealand and the Separate Customs Territory of Taiwan, Penghu, Kinmen and Matsu reserved their right to participate in the Panel proceedings as third parties.

---

[1]　WT/DS245/1.
[2]　WT/DS245/2.
[3]　WT/DS245/3.

1.7   The Panel met with the parties on 21 and 22 October 2002. It met with third parties on 22 October 2002. The Panel consulted scientific and technical experts and met with them on 13 and 14 January 2003. The Panel held a second meeting with the parties on 16 January 2003.

1.8   On 17 January 2003, the Chairman of the Panel informed the DSB that the Panel had not been able to issue its report within six months. The reasons for that delay were given in document WT/DS245/4.

1.9   The Panel issued its interim report on 20 March 2003. The Final Report was circulated to the parties on 25 June 2003. The report was circulated to Members in all three languages 15 July 2003.

II.   ACTUAL ASPECTS

A.   The Disease at Issue

1.   Fire Blight (Erwinia amylovora)[4]

2.1   *Erwinia amylovora* (*E. amylovora*), the scientific name for the fire blight bacterium, was first reported in the Hudson River Valley of New York State in the United States in 1793. Symptoms of infection of host plants with fire blight depend on the parts infected. Infected flowers droop, wither, and die, becoming dry and darkened in color. Infected shoots and twigs wither, darken, and die; as shoots and twigs wither, they bend downwards resembling a shepherd's crook. Infected leaves take on a curled, scorched appearance.[5] Infected fruit fail to develop fully, turning brown to black, shrivelling, and becoming mummified, frequently remaining attached to the limb. Limbs and trunks of trees may also develop cankers, which, if disease development is severe, may result in plant death.

2.2   The most serious primary infection with fire blight is an over-wintering canker developed in the previous season. Fire blight bacteria overwinter exclusively in infected host plants. In the presence of warm, wet conditions in spring, the disease cycle commences when cankers on infected hosts exude a bacterial-laden ooze or inoculum. This inoculum is transmitted primarily through wind and/or rain and by insects or birds to open flowers on the same or new host plants. *E. amylovora* bacteria multiply externally on the stigmas of these open flowers and enter the plant through stomata (openings through which the plant breathes), nectaries (plant glands that secrete nectar), or wounds. The bacteria may spread within the host plant, causing disease in blossoms and fruiting spurs,

---

[4]   Description compiled from "Report on Pest Risk Analysis concerning Fire Blight Pathogen (*Erwinia amylovora*): Fresh apples produced in the United States of America", Ministry of Agriculture, Forestry and Fisheries, Japan, August 1999 (the "1999 PRA") (Exhibit USA-3 and Exhibit JPN-34) and US First Submission.

[5]   The name "fire blight" was apparently coined in 1817 to describe the sudden browning of leaves associated with *E. amylovora* "as if they had passed through a hot flame and causing a morbid matter to exude from the pores of the bark", Coxe. W. *A View of the Cultivation of Fruit Trees, and the Management of Orchards and Cider, Pears*, M. Carey and Son, Philadelphia, 1817.

twigs, branches, or leaves. New cankers (sunken areas surrounded by cracked bark) can be formed on infected branches or twigs. When bacteria form a canker on the branches, this canker remains as an over-wintering lesion until the next year. Cankers generally cease ooze production during the hot summer months and remain inactive until the following spring when they may reactivate and begin the disease cycle anew.

2.3   Secondary infection can occur during the growing season. The source of the secondary inoculum is bacterial ooze exuding from lesions on shoots, leaves, fruits or branches and which is carried by wind and/or rain, insects or birds.

2.4   Immature apples can be infected with *E. amylovora* through natural openings in the skin (i.e. lenticels) or by diseased branches. The infection of fruit commonly occurs after hail storms in the summer months. Infected fruit exude bacterial ooze, become dry, mummify and remain on the branches.

2.   Host Plants

2.5   The fire blight disease affects numerous host plants of the Rosaceae family, including both cultivated and native wild plants. Fruit tree hosts include apples (genus *Malus*), pears (genus *Pyrus*), quince (genus *Cydonia*), and loquats (genus *Eriobotrya*). Important host plants used in hedges and gardens include genera *Cotoneaster*, *Crataegus* (hawthorn), *Pyracantha* (firethorn), and *Sorbus* (mountain ash), although individual species may not serve as hosts.[6]

3.   Geographical Distribution of Fire Blight

2.6   It is believed that the fire blight bacterium (*E. amylovora*) is native to North America. By the early 1900s, fire blight had been reported in Canada from Ontario to British Columbia, in northern Mexico, and in the United States from the East Coast to California and the Pacific Northwest. Fire blight was reported in New Zealand in 1919, Great Britain in 1957, and Egypt in 1964. The disease has spread across northern and western Europe, although Portugal and Finland remain fire blight-free, and it remains localized in France and Switzerland and restricted to certain spots in Spain, Italy, and Austria. Norway has reported eradication of the disease.[7] Fire blight has spread across the Mediterranean region, including Greece, Turkey, Israel, Lebanon, Iran, and several Central European countries.[8] Latin America and substantial parts of Africa and Asia apparently remain fire blight-free. In 1997, Australia reported the presence of fire blight in the Adelaide and Melbourne Botanical Gardens, but eradication efforts were successful and no further outbreaks have been reported.

---

[6]   European and Mediterranean Plant Protection Organization (EPPO), "Data Sheet on Quarantine Pests: Erwinia amylovora", Quarantine for Europe, 1997, p. 1-2 (Exhibit USA-5).

[7]   At the Panel meeting with the experts on 14 January 2003, Dr Geider noted that there had been a recent report of an outbreak of fire blight in Norway.

[8]   Commonwealth Agriculture Bureau International (CABI), Crop Protection Compendium: Data Sheet on Erwinia amylovora (2002) "Notes on Distribution" (Exhibit USA-6).

4.   Relevant Technical and Scientific Terms

Buffer zone

2.7   An area in which a specific pest does not occur or occurs at a low level and is officially controlled, that either encloses or is adjacent to an infested area, an infested place of production, a pest free area, a pest free place of production or a pest free production site, and in which phytosanitary measures are taken to prevent spread of the pest.

Canker

2.8   A lesion on the bark of a tree or shrub caused by infection. Fire blight cankers on limbs, stem, and trunks appear as sunken, discoloured areas that often exhibit deep cracks in the bark at the margins of the canker. A hold-over canker is one in which the pathogen may survive the winter and, if survival occurs, from which the inoculum for primary infections the following spring originate.

Disease (of plant)

2.9   A disorder of structure or function in a plant of such a degree as to produce or threaten to produce detectable illness or disorder; a definable variety of such a disorder, usually with specific signs or symptoms.

Endophytic and epiphytic

2.10   With respect to *E. amylovora*, the term **endophytic** is used when the bacterium occurs inside a plant or apple fruit in a non-pathogenic relationship. With respect to *E. amylovora*, the term **epiphytic** is used when the bacterium occurs on the outer surface of a plant or fruit in a non-pathogenic relationship.

Entry, establishment and spread (of a pest)

2.11   Entry refers to the movement of a pest into an area where it is not yet present, or present but not widely distributed and being officially controlled. Establishment means the perpetuation, for the foreseeable future, of a pest within an area after entry. Spread refers to the expansion of the geographical distribution of a pest within an area.

Infection

2.12   When an organism (e.g., *E. amylovora*) has entered into a host plant (or fruit) establishing a permanent or temporary pathogenic relationship with the host.

Infestation

2.13   Refers to the presence of the bacteria on the surface of a plant without any implication that infection has occurred.[9]

---

[9]   The Panel has followed the scientific definition of bacterial infestation offered by the experts consulted by the Panel. See Anne 3, para. 67. A general definition of infestation is to be found in *International Standards for Phytosanitary Measures No.5: Glossary of Phytosanitary Terms*, FAO,

Inoculum

2.14 Material consisting of or containing bacteria to be introduced into or transferred to a host or medium. Inoculation is the introduction of inoculum into a host or into a culture medium. Inoculum can also refer to potentially infective material available in soil, air or water and which by chance results in the natural inoculation of a host.

Pathogen

2.15 Micro-organism causing disease.

Vector

2.16 An organism able to transport and transmit a pathogen.

B.   Japan's Fire Blight Measures

2.17 The legislation of Japan relevant to this dispute is:

- Plant Protection Law No. 151 enacted on 4 May 1950 (and specifically Article 7 thereof);

- Plant Protection Law Enforcement Regulations enacted on 30 June 1950 (and specifically Article 9 and Annexed table 2 thereof);

- Ministry of Agriculture, Forestry and Fisheries (MAFF) Notification No. 354 dated 10 March 1997; and

- MAFF "Detailed Rules for Plant Quarantine Enforcement Regulation Concerning Fresh Fruit of Apple Produced in the United States of America " dated 1 April 1997.

2.18 Under the Plant Protection Law and the Enforcement Regulations, importation of host plants of 15 quarantine pests, including fire blight bacteria and pests of rice plant not found in Japan, is prohibited.[10] The legislation, however, permits Japan to decide, on a case-by-case basis, to lift the import prohibition with respect to plants and products according to certain criteria that have been established by past practice. These criteria are:

- Lifting is subject to a proposal of an alternative measure by a foreign government;

- the level of protection required of the proposed measure is that equivalent to import prohibition; and

- the exporting government bears the burden of proving that the proposed measure achieves the required level of protection.

2.19 Paragraph 25 of the Annexed List to Table 2 of the Plant Protection Law Enforcement Regulations sets out conditions under which US apples may be

---

Rome 2002. "Presence in a commodity of a living pest of the plant or plant product concerned. Infestation included infection."

[10] Article 7, para. 1, item 1 of the Law (Exhibits JPN-20 and USA-8) and Article 9, item 1 and Annexed Table 2 of the Enforcement Regulation (Exhibits JPN-21 and USA-9).

imported into Japan: "Fresh fruit of apple which are shipped from the United States of America directly to Japan without calling at any port and which conform to the standards established by the Ministry of Agriculture, Forestry and Fisheries".[11] The relevant standards are currently set by MAFF Notification No. 354[12] and the related Detailed Rules.[13] These are:

(i)   Fruit must be produced in designated fire blight-free orchards. Designation of a fire blight-free area as an export orchard is made by the United States Department of Agriculture (USDA) upon application by the orchard owner. Any detection of a blighted tree in this area by inspection will disqualify the orchard. Currently, the designation is made for orchards in the States of Washington and Oregon;[14]

(ii)   the export orchard must be free of plants infected with fire blight and free of host plants of fire blight (other than apples), whether or not infected;

(iii)   the fire blight-free orchard must be surrounded by a 500-meter buffer zone. Detection of a blighted tree or plant in this zone will disqualify the export orchard;

(iv)   the fire blight-free orchard and surrounding buffer zone must be inspected at least three times annually. US officials will visually inspect twice, at the blossom and the fruitlet stages, the export area and the buffer zone for any symptom of fire blight. Japanese and US officials will jointly conduct visual inspection of these sites at harvest time. Additional inspections are required following any strong storm (such as a hail storm);

---

[11]   Ministerial Ordinance No. 73: Plant Protection Law Enforcement Regulations, Annexed List, para. 25 (Exhibit JPN-21 and Exhibit USA-9). The United States contends that paragraph 25 of the Annexed List to Table 2 of the Plant Protection Law Enforcement Regulations limits the importation of fresh fruit of apple from the United States to Golden Delicious and Red Delicious apple varieties. The Panel, however, notes that there is disagreement between the parties as to the English translation of the aforementioned paragraph 25. The English translation of paragraph 25 provided by Japan makes no mention of the Golden Delicious and Red Delicious variety requirement.

[12]   MAFF Notification No. 354, 10 March 1997, (Exhibit USA-10 and Exhibit JPN-22). Notification No. 354 replaced an earlier Notification No. 1184, which first put into place the Japanese fire blight restrictions. See MAFF Notification No. 1184, 22 August 1994, (Exhibit USA-11).

[13]   MAFF Detailed Rules for US Apples, 1 April 1997, (US translation, Exhibit USA-12 and Exhibit JPN-23). The 1997 Detailed Rules amended but did not replace in full the 22 August 1994 Detailed Rules, which implemented MAFF Notification No. 1184. It is therefore necessary to read the 1994 Detailed Rules in conjunction with the 1997 Detailed Rules in order to understand the full scope of the Japanese fire blight measures. See MAFF Detailed Rules for US Apples, 22 August 1994, (US translation, Exhibit USA-13).

[14]   Japan argues that the current phytosanitary requirements against fire blight can be applicable to apple fruit produced in other states, but that United States has not submitted documentation on the status of other quarantine pests for states other than Washington and Oregon. As such, Japan argues that this is a procedural matter. Japan, Response to Questions from the Panel, 13 November, 2002, Question 47.

(v)   harvested apples must be treated with surface disinfection by soaking in sodium hypochlorite solution (100 ppm or more effective chlorine concentration) for one minute or longer;

(vi)   containers for harvesting must be disinfected by a chlorine treatment;

(vii)   the interior of the packing facility must be disinfected by a chlorine treatment;

(viii) fruit destined for Japan must be kept separated post-harvest from other fruit;

(ix)   US plant protection officials must certify or declare that fruit are free of quarantine pests, "are not infested/infected with . . . fire blight", and were treated with chlorine; and

(x)   Japanese officials must confirm that the US official has made the necessary certification and that the chlorine treatment and orchard designations were properly made. Japanese officials must also inspect both the disinfestation and packing facilities.

C.   International Standards, Guidelines and Recommendations

2.20   In their submissions, the parties considered certain international standards developed by the Interim Commission on Phytosanitary Measures of the International Plant Protection Convention ("IPPC") as relevant to the dispute. The *SPS Agreement* makes reference, in a number of provisions, to "relevant international standards, guidelines and recommendations". Annex A:3(c) of the *SPS Agreement* states that the international standards, guidelines and recommendations relevant for plant health are those developed under the auspices of the IPPC in cooperation with regional organizations operating within the framework of the IPPC.

1.   The IPPC

2.21   The IPPC is an international treaty deposited and administered by the Food and Agriculture Organization of the United Nations (FAO) but implemented through the cooperation of member governments and regional plant protection organizations. The IPPC currently has 120 contracting parties.

2.22   The first text of the IPPC was drafted in 1929 and came into force in 1952, adopted by the FAO Conference one year prior to that. Amendments were adopted by the FAO in 1979 and the revised text came into force in 1991. In response to the role of the IPPC in the context of the Uruguay Round and the negotiation of the *SPS Agreement*, the FAO established a Secretariat for the IPPC in 1992, followed by the formation of the Committee of Experts on Phytosanitary Measures (CEPM) in 1993. Negotiations for amendments to the IPPC, in order to reflect contemporary changes, particularly in light of the *SPS Agreement*, started in 1995 and were finalized in 1997 when the FAO Conference adopted the New Revised Text of the IPPC. The New Revised Text makes provision for the formation of a Commission on Phytosanitary Measures. The amended IPPC will come into force upon ratification by two thirds of its contracting parties.

2.23   The purpose of the IPPC is to secure common and effective action to prevent the spread and introduction of pests of plants and plant products, and to promote appropriate measures for their control. An important role of the IPPC is that of developing International Standards for Phytosanitary Measures (ISPM). National plant protection organizations or regional plant protection organizations may submit draft standards to the Secretariat of the IPPC. These drafts are reviewed, edited, and referred by the Secretariat to the CEPM. Alternatively, the IPPC Secretariat may form an international working group or enlist experts to help draft a standard. The CEPM considers the proposals and recommends action. ISPMs are adopted by the Interim Commission on Phytosantiary Measures following a procedure that includes country consultation.

2.   *International Standards for Phytosanitary Measures (ISPMs)*

2.24   Two ISPMs that have been referred to in this dispute are ISPM 2 on Guidelines for Pest Risk Analysis, adopted in 1996, and ISPM 11 on Pest Risk Analysis for Quarantine Pests, adopted in 2001.[15]

2.25   ISPM 2 provides general guidelines for pest risk analysis (PRA) whereas ISPM 11 establishes guidelines for conducting a risk analysis for *quarantine* pests.[16] The former does not replace the latter, therefore they have been designated by the IPPC as *different* international standards. However, the two standards are related and present the same general framework for conducting a pest risk assessment, although ISPM 11 outlines the analytical items in greater detail than ISPM 2.

2.26   Both ISPM 2 and ISPM 11 describe the PRA process as consisting of three stages. Stage one involves (a) the identification of a pathway, usually an imported product, that may allow the introduction and/or spread of quarantine pests, and (b) the identification of a pest that may qualify as a quarantine pest. Stage two considers the identified pests individually and examines, for each one, whether the criteria for quarantine pest status are satisfied, that is, that the pest is of "potential economic importance to the area endangered thereby and not yet present there, or present but not widely distributed and being officially controlled". Based on the information gathered under stages one and two, stage three determines the appropriate phytosanitary measure(s) to be adopted. The

---

[15]   *International Standard for Phytosanitary Measures No.2: Guidelines for Pest Risk Analysis,* FAO, Rome 1996 (Exhibit JPN-30), and *International Standard for Phytosanitary Measures No.11: Pest Risk Analysis for Quarantine Pests,* FAO, Rome 2001 (Exhibit USA-15).

[16]   The IPPC defines a quarantine pest as: a pest of potential economic importance to the area endangered thereby and not yet present there, or present but not widely distributed and being officially controlled. *International Standards for Phytosanitary Measures No.5: Glossary of Phytosanitary Terms,* p.14, FAO, Rome 2002.

three stages are summarized in both PRA Guidelines as: "initiating the process for analysing risk", "assessing pest risk" and "managing pest risk", respectively.

2.27   In ISPM 2, the process for pest risk assessment is broadly divided into five interrelated steps: consideration of geographical and regulatory criteria; economic importance criteria; spread potential after establishment; potential economic importance; and introduction potential. The 1996 guidelines provide a partial checklist of factors that might affect entry and establishment of a pest.

2.28   In ISPM 11, the process for pest risk assessment is set out in more detail. The PRA process can be broadly divided into three interrelated steps: pest categorization, assessment of the probability of introduction and spread, and an assessment of potential economic consequences (including environmental impacts). Pest introduction is comprised of both entry and establishment. Assessing the probability of introduction requires an analysis of each of the pathways with which a pest may be associated from its origin to its establishment in the PRA area. The 2001 guidelines identify the following broad issues which should be considered and provides detailed guidance under each heading:

(a)   Probability of the pest being associated with the pathway at origin;

(b)   probability of survival during transport or storage;

(c)   probability of pest surviving existing pest management procedures;

(d)   probability of transfer to a suitable host;

(e)   probability of establishment;

(f)   availability of suitable hosts, alternate hosts and vectors in the PRA area;

(g)   suitability of environment;

(h)   cultural practices and control measures;

(i)   other characteristics of the pest affecting the probability of establishment; and

(j)   probability of spread after establishment.

2.29   ISPM 2 states that pest risk management should be proportional to the risk identified in the assessment of risk. Pest risk management options identified in the 1996 guidelines are:

(a)   Inclusion in list of prohibited pests;

(b)   phytosanitary inspection and certification prior to export;

(c)   definition of requirements to be satisfied before export (e.g. treatment, origin from pest-free area, growing season inspection, certification scheme);

(d)   inspection at entry;

(e)   treatment at point of entry, inspection station or, if appropriate, at place of destination;

(f)   detention in post-entry quarantine;

(g) post-entry measures (restrictions on use of product, control measures); and

(h) prohibition of entry of specific products from specific origins.

2.30 Pest risk management options may also concern ways of reducing risk of damage. ISPM 2 states that the efficacy and impact of the various options in reducing risk to an acceptable level should be evaluated in terms of the following factors:

(a) Biological effectiveness;

(b) cost/benefit of implementation;

(c) impact on existing regulations;

(d) commercial impact;

(e) social impact;

(f) phytosanitary policy considerations;

(g) time to implement a new regulation;

(h) efficacy of option against other quarantine pests; and

(i) environmental impact.

2.31 ISPM 11 identifies risk management options in more detail. The 2001 guidelines specifically state that zero-risk is not a reasonable option, and that the guiding principle for risk management should be to manage risk to achieve the required degree of safety that can be justified and is feasible within the limits of available options and resources. As such, pest risk management (in the analytical sense) is the process of identifying ways to react to a perceived risk, evaluating the efficacy of these actions, and identifying the most appropriate options. The uncertainties noted in the assessments of economic consequences and probability of introduction should also be considered and included in the selection of a pest management option.[17] The ISPM lists examples of measures classified into broad categories that relate to the pest status of the pathway in the country of origin. These include measures:

(a) Applied to the consignment;

(b) applied to prevent or reduce original infestation in the crop;

(c) to ensure the area or place or site of production or crop is free from the pest;

(d) for other types of pathways (such as to curb natural spread);

(e) within the importing country;

(f) concerning the prohibition of commodities; and

(g) phytosanitary certificates and other compliance measures.

---

[17] Op. cit., ISPM 11, para 3.

2.32   Another ISPM referred to by Japan in this dispute was ISPM 10 on Requirements for the Establishment of Pest Free Places of Production and Pest Free Production Sites.[18]

III.   CLAIMS OF THE PARTIES

3.1   The **United States** claimed that Japan prohibited the importation of apple fruit unless such apples were produced, treated, and imported in accordance with Japan's highly-restrictive fire blight measures. The United States did not question that fire blight was a plant disease of serious biological and economic consequences nor Japan's right to enact measures to protect against the risks arising from transmission of fire blight disease within its territory. However, the United States claimed that Japan's measures on the importation of apple fruit were not consistent with Japan's obligations under the *SPS Agreement* in that:

- Japan had failed to ensure that its fire blight measures were not maintained without sufficient scientific evidence and these measures were therefore inconsistent with Article 2.2 of the SPS Agreement;

- Japan had failed to ensure that its fire blight measures were based on an assessment of the risks to plant life or health and therefore these measures were inconsistent with Article 5.1 of the SPS Agreement;

- In its assessment of risks, Japan had failed to take into account available scientific evidence, relevant ecological and environmental conditions, and quarantine or other treatment and therefore had acted inconsistently with Article 5.2 of the SPS Agreement;

- Japan had failed to ensure that its fire blight measures were not more trade-restrictive than required to achieve its appropriate level of phytosanitary protection, taking into account technical and economic feasibility, and these measures were therefore inconsistent with Article 5.6 of the SPS Agreement;

- Japan had failed to notify changes in and information on its fire blight measures and therefore had acted inconsistently with Article 7 and Annex B of the SPS Agreement.

The United States further claimed that Japan had acted inconsistently with its obligations under Article XI of GATT 1994 and under Article 4.2 of the Agreement on Agriculture.

3.2   **Japan** argued that the United States had not established a prima facie case in respect of the claims it had made. Japan claimed its measure was fully

---

[18]   *International Standard for Phytosanitary Measures No.10: Requirements for the Establishment of Pest Free Places of Production and Pest Free Production Sites*, FAO, Rome 1999 (Exhibit JPN-24).

consistent with Articles 2.2, 5.1, 5.2, 5.6, 7, and Annex B of the *SPS Agreement*, Article XI of GATT of 1994, and Article 4.2 of the Agreement on Agriculture. Alternatively, Japan claimed that the measure was a provisional measure in conformity with Article 5.7 of the *SPS Agreement* and was otherwise consistent with Articles 5.1, 5.2, 5.6, 7, and Annex B of the *SPS Agreement*, Article XI of GATT of 1994, and Article 4.2 of the Agreement on Agriculture.

IV. ARGUMENTS OF THE PARTIES

A. *The Scope of the Dispute*

1. Relevant Provisions

4.1   **Japan** observed that in the request for the establishment of a panel, the United States made claims additional to those that it had set out in the request for consultations on Japan's measures on the importation of apples.[19] The additional claims of inconsistency concerned Article 5.5 of the *SPS Agreement* and Article 4.2 of the Agreement on Agriculture. Japan noted that no bilateral consultation had taken place in respect of Article 4.2 of the Agreement on Agriculture or Article 5.5 of the *SPS Agreement*. Article 4.5 of the DSU expressly provides that Members should attempt to obtain satisfactory adjustment before resorting to further action. Since the United States had made no attempt to discuss these two provisions with Japan, and further, the United States had not made any claim under these provisions in its written submissions, Japan asked that these provisions not be included in the terms of reference for the Panel and that they be removed from the scope of the proceedings of the Panel.[20]

4.2   The **United States** argued that there was no requirement in the DSU to consult on a particular claim in order to include that claim in a Panel request and to have such a claim form part of the Panel's terms of reference. The purpose of consultations was to provide a better understanding of the facts and circumstances of a dispute; logically, then, a party might identify new claims in the course of consultations.[21] The United States further noted that the Panel had been established by the DSB with standard terms of reference pursuant to DSU Article 7.1. Both Article 4.2 of the Agreement on Agriculture and Article 5.5 of the *SPS Agreement* were named in the US panel request and both were within the Panel's terms of reference. As the Panel was not able to alter its terms of reference, there was no basis for Japan's request to "remove" them from the scope of the proceedings.

4.3   In its first submission, **Japan** argued that the United States had failed to substantiate its claims under Article XI of GATT 1994, Article 4.2 of the Agreement on Agriculture and Articles 2.3, 5.3, 5.5, 6.1 or 6.2 of the *SPS Agreement*. It requested, therefore, that the Panel remove these provisions from the scope of the proceedings. In its second submission, Japan noted that the

---

[19]   WT/DS245/2 and WT/DS245/1, respectively.
[20]   Letter to the Panel from Japan, 6 June 2002.
[21]   Reply of the United States to the Request by Japan for Preliminary Rulings, 16 October 2002.

United States had raised Article XI of GATT 1994 and Article 4.2 of the Agreement on Agriculture during the course of the first substantive meeting of the Panel, but had still failed to make a specific case on the basis of other provisions. As such, Japan requested that the Panel should not consider the merit of any of the provisions that the United States had not addressed, namely, Articles 2.3, 5.3, 5.5, 6.1 or 6.2 of the *SPS Agreement*.

4.4   The **United States** recalled that the Appellate Body had stated that: "[t]here is no requirement in the DSU or in GATT practice for arguments on all claims relating to the matter referred to the DSB to be set out in a complaining party's first written submission to the panel".[22] Furthermore, in *Chile – Price Band System*, the Appellate Body had reaffirmed that the question of whether or not a complaining party has articulated a claim under a provision within the panel's terms of reference cannot be determined from the first written submission alone, but had to be examined on the basis of the complaining party's answers to panel questions and its rebuttal submission.[23]

4.5   The United States further noted that the European Communities had raised concerns whether or not the United States had presented a prima facie case that Japan had violated certain provisions not covered in the US first written submission, and that by that not stating all its claims in a first written submission the United States could prevent the respondent from using all stages of the panel proceeding to defend itself.[24] As the European Communities acknowledged, there is no requirement in the DSU that a complaining party set out its arguments on all of its claims in its first written submission. Hence the United States argued that the Panel should defer its examination of whether arguments had been made and whether these arguments were sufficient to satisfy a prima facie case until the conclusion of all submissions. Furthermore, there would be no prejudice to a respondent's rights of defence so long as the complainant's arguments were made clear in the course of the proceedings and the responding party was given sufficient opportunity to respond. The United States recalled that it had advanced argumentation in its oral statement to the Panel on Article 4.2 of the Agreement on Agriculture and Article XI of GATT 1994, and Japan had had ample opportunity to respond to those arguments.[25]

2.   Objection to Submitted Evidence

4.6   **Japan** noted that in its first written submission, the United States included as exhibits communications from Dr Tom van der Zwet, formerly of the Appalachian Fruit Research Station in West Virginia, and a letter by Professor Sherman Thomson of Utah State University.[26] The declaration by Dr van der

---

[22]   Appellate Body Report in *EC – Bananas III*, para. 145; also Appellate Body Report in *Chile – Price Band System*, para. 158.

[23]   Appellate Body Report in *Chile – Price Band System*, paras. 154-57, 159-62.

[24]   Oral Statement of the European Communities in the Panel meeting with third parties, paras. 3-6.

[25]   Letter from the United States to the Panel on Arguments raised by Australia and the European Communities, 1 November 2002.

[26]   Exhibits USA-18 and USA-19, respectively.

Zwet and the letter of Professor Thomson contained clarifications as to a scientific paper they had jointly published in 1990 entitled "Population of *Erwinia amylovora* on External and Internal Apple Fruit Tissues".[27] Japan stated that it had seen these pieces of evidence for the first time in the US first submission. Efforts to collect new scientific evidence should, first and foremost, be made for the purpose of resolution of the matter through good faith consultations, if necessary, under GATT Articles XXII and XXIII, and Article 4 of the DSU. Japan maintained that the United States should have, and could have, made efforts to obtain and share these pieces of evidence prior to the bilateral consultations, rather than seeking to clarify the scientific evidence after completion of the bilateral consultations. In its view, the United States should have shared this information, at the latest, during the Article 4 DSU consultations held on 18 April 2002. In light of these serious procedural and substantive flaws, Japan requested the Panel to remove the two communications from the proceedings.

4.7   The **United States** noted that the 60-day consultation period ended on 30 April 2002 and that it had requested the establishment of a panel on 7 May 2002, whereas the declaration of Dr van der Zwet was dated 16 July 2002, and the letter of Professor Thomson was dated 23 August 2002. Japan had been made aware of the content of these communications as of the US first submission. Japan's contention that it would be denied an opportunity to settle the matter in good faith through bilateral consultations should the Panel utilize these communications in its findings was erroneous. The dispute settlement procedures envisioned the development of mutually satisfactory solutions at any stage during a dispute; that opportunity remained open to Japan, should it choose to pursue it.[28]

4.8   The United States further argued that Australia's suggestion that the defending party had to be allowed the opportunity to reassess risk if the complaining party learnt of new scientific evidence would upset the balance of rights and obligations of WTO Members under the covered agreements.[29] Nothing in the *SPS Agreement* required that the United States, which had unsuccessfully pursued cooperate efforts to obtain a relaxation of Japan's fire blight measures, had to forego dispute settlement when Japan was not in compliance with its WTO obligations. Furthermore, nothing prevented Japan from reassessing the risk pursuant to Article 5 of the *SPS Agreement* in light of the scientific evidence provided by Drs van der Zwet and Thomson. Japan was familiar with the 1990 paper by van der Zwet *et al.*, and aware of its ambiguities and inconsistencies. Nonetheless, Japan had not sought to clarify issues with the authors in the 12 years since the paper had been published. It was Japan that "should have, and could have, obtained" clarification of the 1990 paper long before because of Japan's obligation under Article 2.2 of the *SPS Agreement* to

---

[27] T. van der Zwet *et al.* (1990) "Population of *Erwinia amylovora* on External and Internal Apple Fruit Tissues", *Plant Disease* 74, pp. 711-16 (Exhibit JPN-7, Exhibit USA-17).
[28] DSU, Article 3.7.
[29] Oral statement of Australia in the Panel meeting with third parties, para. 10.

ensure that its measure was not maintained without sufficient scientific evidence, but Japan appeared to have been relying on an inaccurate reading of the 1990 paper as a basis for its fire blight measures.

4.9   In **Japan's** view, due process required that an expert's opinion be subjected to cross-examination; this was of paramount importance when the opinion related to the central issue of the dispute. Since the WTO dispute settlement procedure was not designed to hear witnesses, however, the parties and the Panel relied on documentary evidence. In order to ensure objectivity, an implicit assumption of the dispute resolution process was that parties should not introduce evidence in an unfair manner. Moreover, while the United States insisted that Japan should have inquired with the authors of van der Zwet *et al.* (1990) for clarification, Japan was not in a position to do so because the conclusion of the article clearly indicated potential *E. amylovora* inside mature, symptomless apple fruit.

4.10   The **United States** recalled that the Panel's working procedures required the parties to "submit all factual evidence to the Panel no later than during the first substantive meeting, except with respect to evidence necessary for purposes of rebuttals or answers to questions".[30] The United States had complied with these procedures. The working procedures and the DSU also provided Japan with ample opportunity to comment on these two communications contained in the US first submission. Furthermore, the United States argued that the Panel *itself* was charged under Article 11 of the DSU with making an "objective assessment of the matter". Thus, the Panel could weigh the evidentiary value of these communications in light of the original 1990 paper, comments by Japan, and the expert advice provided by the scientific experts consulted by the Panel.

4.11   **Japan** contended that fairness in this case required that the findings of an already published paper should be revised or qualified *only* by another published paper. Furthermore, the United States had admitted in the first substantive meeting of the Panel that the US Government had drafted the communications first. As such, the letters focused only on what the United States wanted the authors to state and there was no assurance of the objectivity of these unpublished, private communications. These documents only indicated to what extent the authors were prepared to support the US Government and scientific objectivity could never be achieved by reading these documents.

4.12   The **United States** explained that it had contacted Dr van der Zwet and posed specific questions to him by telephone and e-mail communications. His oral answers had been recorded in writing, and returned to Dr van der Zwet, asking for his review. Dr van der Zwet had made changes to further clarify his answers, and had agreed that his answers could be made public. The United States had submitted specific questions to Professor Thomson by e-mail. Dr Thomson had agreed that his answers could be made public. The respective author had signed each document.

---

[30]   Panel Working Procedures, para. 11, 5 August 2002, Annex 1.

4.13   The United States noted, furthermore, that Japan itself did not practice the purported evidentiary rule mandated by "due process" and "fairness". Japan had also presented unpublished evidence, which had not been subjected to any cross-examination."[31] The United States did *not* object to Japan's introduction of previously unpublished evidence in its first written submission, and was examining this evidence.

4.14   **Japan** was concerned by the US rejection of the notion of procedural fairness and objectivity in the dispute settlement process. Procedural fairness had paramount importance in any dispute and genuine concerns had been expressed in this case, as demonstrated by the third party submission of the European Communities. In this context, Japan stated that it was prepared to withdraw the unpublished evidence that it had cited in its first submission. Japan emphasized that scientific information which had not been available or accessible to Japan could not be taken into consideration for determining whether or not the scientific evidence underlying its measure was sufficient under Article 2.2, as the European Communities and Australia pointed out in their oral statements at the third party meeting.

4.15   In a letter to the parties on 15 January 2003, the **Panel** referred to Japan's request for a preliminary ruling concerning the admissibility of the declaration from Dr van der Zwet (USA-18) and the letter from Professor Thomson (USA-19) submitted by the United States with its first written submission.[32] The Panel noted that, as a matter of principle, the parties were entitled to submit evidence in support of their arguments. Having considered the arguments of the parties, the Panel was not convinced that, in this particular instance, it should exclude the aforementioned exhibits from the proceedings *a priori*. This decision was without prejudice to the weight, if any, that the Panel might ultimately ascribe to these documents, including in light of Japan's comments.

4.16   Subsequent to the Panel's ruling, **Japan** requested that the Panel take fully into consideration its position on this matter, and the question of how these exhibits had been obtained, when determining what weight, if any, should be given to them. Japan contended that the weight given to these exhibits should be, at best, "negligible".

B.   The Measure (or measures) at Issue

4.17   The **United States** observed that Japan prohibited the importation of US apples unless they were produced, harvested and imported according to Japan's

---

[31]   "Communication" of Dr J.P. Paulin to Biosecurity Australia as reported in Australia's "Draft Import Risk Analysis on the Importation of Apples (*Malus x domestica* Borkh) from New Zealand"; (First Written Submission of Japan, para. 124); reference for economic losses from fire blight outbreak in Melbourne, Australia, based on unpublished, anonymous "personal communication" (Exhibit JPN-10, para. 25); unpublished, anonymous paper entitled "Verification of Roberts *et al.* (1998) for probability of introduction and establishment of *Erwinia amylovora*" (Exhibit JPN-16); and unpublished, anonymous document entitled "Occurrence Level of Fire Blight in 2000 When the Japan-U.S. Joint Experiment was Carried Out" (Exhibit JPN-33).

[32]   Panel letter to the Parties, 15 January 2003.

fire blight restrictions. Japan currently imposed nine requirements (related to fire blight) that had to be satisfied in order to import US apples.[33] All nine of these requirements had to be met before imports were permitted. The United States contended that Japan's prohibition on imports of US apples unless all of these requirements had been met was inconsistent with Japan's obligations. Moreover, each of the requirements could be considered a separate phytosanitary measure within the meaning of the *SPS Agreement*. As defined in Annex A (and as relevant to this dispute), an SPS measure was "[a]ny measure applied ... to protect ... plant life or health from risks arising from the entry, establishment or spread of pests, diseases, ... or disease-causing organisms" and such "measures include all relevant laws, decrees, regulations, requirements and procedures including, *inter alia*, end product criteria; processes and production methods; testing, inspection, certification and approval procedures; [and] quarantine requirements".[34] Thus, each of the nine requirements and procedures necessary for importation of US apples was a phytosanitary measure, and each requirement was inconsistent with Japan's obligations under Article 2.2 of the *SPS Agreement*.

4.18   The United States indicated that it did not contest that fire blight was a plant disease of serious biological and economic consequences, and it recognized Japan's right to enact measures to protect against the risks arising from transmission of fire blight disease within its territory. However, the United States argued that Japan could not restrict the importation of apples without scientific evidence that exported apples could transmit the disease.

4.19   **Japan** described its requirements on US apples as a "systemic approach"[35] comprised of measures at various stages which extended from blossom to shipment. The "systemic approach" as a whole was the minimum necessary set of requirements to achieve Japan's appropriate level of protection. Although the requirements were technically independent, they were inseparable and integral parts of a single "measure". Some of the components were interrelated. For example, the inspection and buffer zone requirements were necessary to ensure that the requirement of a disease-free orchard was met. The certification and confirmation requirements were logical procedural steps to ensure that the other requirements had been met. For these reasons, Japan argued that its requirements should be considered as one measure, necessary to protect Japan from fire blight.

4.20   Japan argued that since the degree of prevalence of the disease at production sites, the States of Washington and Oregon, varied from year to year, preventive measures should be such that would provide security even during severe outbreaks, in order to effectively prevent the introduction of fire blight into Japan.

4.21   The **United States** claimed that each of Japan's fire blight restrictions (or requirements) could be considered to be maintained without sufficient scientific

---

[33]   Answers of the United States to Additional Questions from the Panel, 28 January 2003, para. 1.
[34]   *SPS Agreement*, Annex A, para. 1.
[35]   More usually referred to as a "systems approach".

evidence because there was no scientific evidence that harvested, mature US apples, the exported commodity, could serve as a pathway for introduction of fire blight to Japan. Where there was not scientific evidence that each and every step in any hypothetical pathway would be completed, there was no scientific evidence that the pathway would be completed and that exported apple fruit could serve to introduce the disease to Japan. The imposition of any of the Japanese fire blight restrictions (or requirements) on such apple fruit was therefore inconsistent with Japan's obligations under Article 2.2 because there was not "sufficient scientific evidence" to support any measure other than restricting importation to the exported commodity.

4.22   **Japan** countered that Article 2.2 of the *SPS Agreement* provided "Members shall ensure that any … phytosanitary measure … is not maintained without sufficient scientific evidence …" Therefore, it was the measure, not each step of the pathway, that had to be supported by scientific evidence. Japan nevertheless recalled that it had submitted relevant scientific evidence included in scientific literature, international standards and SPS measures of other Members, for each component of the measure in question.

4.23   The **United States** responded that it did not agree that the legal requirement of "sufficient scientific evidence" under Article 2.2 related to "each step of the pathway" identified by Japan rather than to Japan's fire blight measures. However, for Japan to maintain any fire blight measure on imported US apple fruit consistent with Article 2.2, and for Japan to base any fire blight measures on imported US apple fruit on an assessment of risks within the meaning of Article 5.1 and Annex A, the imported commodity had to pose a risk to plant life or health within Japan; there had to be a probability or likelihood of introduction of fire blight via that imported commodity.

4.24   The United States contended that the scientific experts had confirmed that there was no scientific evidence that trade in apple fruit had ever spread fire blight. The experts also confirmed, through their answers to specific questions on the content of the scientific evidence, that there was no scientific evidence that any hypothetical pathway via the imported commodity would be completed because there was no evidence that at least one step in each such hypothetical pathway would be completed. Thus, there was no probability or likelihood of introduction of fire blight via imported US apple fruit, and such fruit did not pose a risk to plant life or health within Japan.

1.   Fire Blight Status of Japan

4.25   The **United States** noted that Japan claimed to be free of fire blight, despite scientific reports in the Japanese literature that documented the occurrence and identification of the pathogen in Japan. Despite substantial evidence to the contrary, for the purposes of this dispute the United States was prepared to assume that Japan was, as it claimed, free of fire blight and fire blight bacteria.

4.26   **Japan** did not dispute that reports of fire blight disease in Japan had been made periodically since the start of the twentieth century. However, these reports were considered unreliable by later studies, and the prevailing academic view did not support the conclusions of these earlier studies.[36] Japan further maintained that had the earlier discoveries been of fire blight, the disease – given its known propagation ability - would by now have spread throughout Japan. Japan also indicated that a plant pathogenic bacterium closely related to *E. amylovora* was reported in the 1990s to cause a fire blight-like disease of pear on Hokkaido. The disease, bacterial shoot blight of pear, had been eradicated from Hokkaido after a five-year programme in the early 1990s.

2.   History of the Dispute

4.27   The **United States** indicated that it had first requested market access for apples in November 1982. It had provided Japan with scientific evidence that fire blight was not transmitted on apple fruit as early as 1983.[37]

4.28   **Japan** noted that its Plant Protection Law of May 1950 and its Enforcement Regulation of June 1950 prohibited the import of host plants of 15 quarantine pests, including fire blight bacteria and pests of rice plant not found in Japan. Japan could decide, on a case-by-case basis, to lift the import prohibition with respect to plants and products on the basis of an alternative measure proposed by the government of a supplying country, if the level of protection provided by the alternative measure was equivalent to the import prohibition. The exporting government bore the burden of proving that the proposed measure achieved the required level of protection. The current phytosanitary requirements were one such "alternative measure" proposed by the United States. In April 1991, the United States first proposed a set of phytosanitary measures for consideration by Japan, and submitted a subsequent proposal in March 1994. On the basis of these proposals, and through subsequent bilateral discussions between the phytosanitary authorities, on 22 August 1994 Japan adopted the present phytosanitary requirements for fire blight required for importation of apples from the United States. These requirements constituted the measure in dispute.

4.29   The **United States** noted that New Zealand had also sought the lifting of Japan's prohibition on the importation of apples linked to fire blight. New Zealand's efforts had resulted in a bilateral agreement which predated that of the United States with Japan, and which contained the present restrictions. The United States had acquiesced to the fire blight measures imposed by Japan in 1994 as an alternative to an outright ban on imported apple fruit. However, the United States maintained that it had accepted these measures reluctantly, recognizing that the scientific evidence did not support the restrictions. The United States argued that it had subsequently undertaken an active, prolonged, good-faith effort to work with Japan to resolve the dispute on a technical level. This included presenting and explaining at numerous bilateral meetings the

---

[36]   A. Mizuno *et al.* (2002, original in Japanese), "Examination of Alleged Occurrence of Fire Blight in Japan", *Research Bulletin of the Plant Protection Service Japan* 39, (Exhibit JPN-13)
[37]   Chronology of US Efforts to Resolve the Dispute Bilaterally (Exhibit USA-1).

scientific evidence that mature apple fruit were not a pathway for fire blight to Japan and proposing alternative measures for Japan's consideration. The United States had even conducted joint research with Japan in 2000, even though it was aware that this research duplicated numerous previous scientific studies that had evaluated the incidence of endophytic and epiphytic bacteria on, or in, mature apple fruit.

4.30   **Japan** argued that the United States had created confusion by submitting inconsistent proposals, and had not presented convincing new evidence sufficient to justify any relaxation in Japan's phytosanitary measure.

4.31   Japan indicated that the table below chronicled the bilateral contacts and proposals made by both parties in relation to Japan's phytosanitary measure.

Table - Bilateral Contacts and Proposals between the United States and Japan regarding Fire Blight-Related Restrictions on Apple Fruit, 1995-2002

Date	Proposal
February 1995	US proposal to narrow the width of the buffer zone from 500 meters to 400 meters.
November 1996	US proposal (1) to narrow the width of the buffer zone to 10 meters, (2) to reduce the number of site inspection routines from three to one only at the harvest time, and (3) continued chlorine treatment. Japan rejected the US proposal in December 1996.
September 1998	US proposal to (1) abolish the buffer zone requirement and (2) relax site inspection routines from three times to one harvest inspection, and (3) presentation of new evidence by Roberts *et al.* (1998).[38] Japan did not accept the methods and results of the Roberts study, nor the US proposal.
August 1999	US proposal (1) a 10-meter wide buffer zone, (2) inspection once at harvest time, and (3) exportation only from orchards where the rate of fire blight occurrence was not over 1%, except for apples from infected trees and the 10-meter area surrounding them.
October 1999	Japan proposed a joint study with the US of two experiments, one on the width of the buffer zone and the other on the number of inspections.
April to December 2000	Joint US-Japanese experiments in Washington State during the 2000 growing season.
February 2001	US communicated to Japan the results of the joint experiments. Japan stated that, *inter alia*, the experiment on the width of the buffer zone was insufficient because it had failed to generate scientific evidence indicating the level of risk during seasons of severe fire blight outbreaks. The inspection routines experiment had not been performed as per Japan's proposal, as the United States was unable to find suitable orchards for the experiment. The United States had instead designed and performed an experiment using artificially inoculated apple twigs.

---

[38]   R.G. Roberts *et al.* (1998), "The potential for spread of Erwinia amylovora and fire blight via commercial apple fruit; a critical review and risk assessment", *Crop Protection 17*, pp. 19-28 (Exhibit JPN-5, Exhibit USA-4).

Date	Proposal
October 2001	Bilateral meeting, but no agreement as to how to evaluate the results of the 2000 experiment. Japan requested the United States to provide additional information on five supplementary issues.
March 2002	US request for consultations under the DSU with respect to Japan's apple import restrictions.

C.   Application of the SPS Agreement

4.32   The **United States** argued that Japan's measures were phytosanitary measures as defined by the *SPS Agreement* in Annex A.

4.33   **Japan** did not dispute that the measure at issue was covered by the *SPS Agreement*.

D.   Burden of Proof

4.34   The **United States** recognized that in this dispute it bore the burden of proof of establishing that Japan's fire blight measures were: (i) maintained without sufficient scientific evidence; (ii) were not based on a risk assessment appropriate to the circumstances; (iii) were not the least trade restrictive necessary to achieve Japan's appropriate level of protection; and (iv) had not been notified in accordance with Article 7 and Annex B of the *SPS Agreement*. As the scientific evidence submitted by the United States demonstrated that mature, symptomless apples had not disseminated fire blight and did not serve as a vector for the introduction of the disease, the lack of any justification for Japan's measure was evident. The United States believed that it had met its burden of proof under the *SPS Agreement*.

4.35   **Japan** considered the issue of the burden of proof - who bore it and how - was central to determine whether or not the scientific evidence underlying Japan's measure was "sufficient" under Article 2.2. In its first submission, the United States had attempted to demonstrate "insufficiency" with information contradicting Japan's scientific evidence. The submission of contradictory information did not by itself demonstrate that Japan's scientific evidence was insufficient. It only implied that there were various conditions that affected the presence or absence of the bacteria in the fruit, and that the risk of dissemination might not manifest itself under certain conditions. Unless those conditions were clearly established, Japan could not know when mature, symptomless apples were safe. The studies the United States cited merely demonstrated that risks might not be present in certain, limited circumstances, not that the risk may never be present or that risk management was unnecessary.

4.36   Japan argued that the proof required of a complaining party was that the defendant's scientific evidence for the perception, identification and evaluation of the risk was conclusively refuted, or the evidence was irrelevant to the introduction or maintenance of the risk management measure in question. In order for an exporting country to establish a prima facie case under Article 2.2, it had to positively prove "insufficiency" of scientific evidence in this sense. Japan contended that this interpretation was consistent with the notion of judicial equity, which emphasized the burden of proof of the United States as the party that naturally[39] possessed a large amount of evidence on the bacteria (*E. amylovora*). Furthermore, the objective of Japan's measure was to manage the risk according to its appropriate level of protection. In order to control that risk and to enable importation, Japan had to rely on the exporting country's proposals and cooperation, as they possessed the information required to evaluate the risk.

4.37   The **United States** recalled that Japan had an *obligation* under Article 2.2 not to maintain a measure without sufficient scientific evidence. The assignment of the burden of proof in dispute settlement could not alter this obligation. In *Japan –Agricultural Products II*, the United States had argued that it would be impossible to prove that no scientific evidence supporting a measure existed because it was impossible to prove a negative. The Appellate Body had noted that, in the context of an argument that there was no scientific evidence supporting a measure under Article 2.2:

> "[It is] sufficient . . . to raise a presumption that there are no relevant studies or reports. Raising [such] a presumption . . . is not an impossible burden. The United States could have requested Japan, pursuant to Article 5.8 of the *SPS Agreement*, to provide 'an explanation of the reasons' for its varietal testing requirement, in particular, as it applies to [several products]. Japan would, in that case, be obliged to provide such an explanation. The failure of Japan to bring forward scientific studies or reports in support of its [measure] would have been a strong indication that there are no such studies or reports. The United States could also have asked the Panel's experts specific questions as to the existence of relevant scientific studies or reports or it could have submitted to the Panel the opinion of experts consulted by it on this issue."[40]

4.38   From this it was clear that while the burden of presenting facts and arguments establishing a presumption of an absence of evidence lay with the United States, this burden was not, in light of the nature of the obligation, a high one. The United States had not simply brought forward evidence that contradicted the evidence that Japan cited (although the evidence, properly read, did significantly contradict Japan 's reading of it). Rather, it had brought forward scientific evidence that: (1) there was *no* scientific evidence that mature apple fruit had ever transmitted *E. amylovora* and introduced the disease; (2) there was *no* scientific evidence that mature apple fruit harvested from an orchard might be infected with *E. amylovora*; (3) there was *no* scientific evidence that mature apple fruit harvested from an orchard might be endophytically contaminated with *E. amylovora*; and (4) there was *no* scientific evidence that a vector existed to transfer any hypothetically surviving *E. amylovora* on a discarded mature apple fruit within Japan to a susceptible plant host.

---

[39]   By virtue of the presence of *E. amylovora* on the territory of the United States.
[40]   Appellate Body Report in *Japan – Agricultural Products II*, para. 137.

4.39   The United States further observed that Japan had the same access to the scientific evidence as any other WTO Member. Further, Japan could not credibly fault the US creation of, and provision of, relevant scientific evidence over the course of the past 15 years. Over that time, the United States had conducted a comprehensive review of the fire blight literature and four experiments, including even the repetition of a study documenting the absence of endophytic bacteria in mature fruit, simply to obtain the evidence in the presence of Japanese scientists. That Japan continued to deny the affirmative scientific evidence of a lack of risk from mature apple fruit supported a conclusion not that Japan lacked the ability to obtain evidence, but that it did not wish to obtain it.

4.40   **Japan** argued that the US arguments reflected its risk-taking approach. The United States had nothing to lose if fire blight were disseminated into Japan or any other country. As such, the US approach was not objective. The United States would immediately recognize the risk posed by apple fruit if it was required to guarantee that the apples would not disseminate the disease. Japan noted that Dr Paulin, in commenting on Australia's draft risk assessment for fire blight, had clearly stated that the risk is "different from zero".[41] As such, one could not deny that the risk was genuine. Risk-taking could not be confused with objectivity. For countries with fire blight, the available evidence might imply too small a risk to worry about. But for countries free of the disease, the same evidence and the same risk could be significant. Therefore even if some evidence did not appear to be "sufficient" according to the "mainstream opinion", it had to be evaluated in light of Member's right to act in a discretionary manner and to ensure its level of protection.

4.41   Japan maintained that it's interpretation was consistent with the Appellate Body's ruling in *EC – Hormones* on Article 5.1. The Appellate Body had stated:

> "[E]qually responsible and representative governments may act in good faith on the basis of what, at a given time, may be a divergent opinion coming from qualified and respected sources. By itself, this does not necessarily signal the absence of a reasonable relationship between the SPS measure and the risk assessment, especially where the risk involved is life-threatening in character and is perceived to constitute a clear and imminent threat to public health and safety. Determination of the presence or absence of that relationship can only be done on a case-by-case basis, after account is taken of all considerations rationally bearing upon the issue of potential adverse health effects.[42] "

This ruling clarified that refutation by a mainstream opinion might not be enough to establish a prima facie case under Article 5.1, which could be considered substantiation of Article 2.2.

---

[41]   J.P. Paulin, Communication, Biosecurity Australia, Draft Import Risk Analysis on the Importation of Apples (*Malus x domestica* Borkh) from New Zealand (2000), (Exhibit NZL-4).
[42]   Appellate Body Report in *EC - Hormones*, para. 194.

4.42   Furthermore, Japan considered that an Article 2.2 case inevitably raised issues relating to the appropriate level of protection of the importing Member, which was also addressed in Article 4 on equivalence. In order to understand the *SPS Agreement* in a coherent manner, Article 2.2 had thus to be interpreted in light of Article 4. An importing Member applied a measure designed to achieve its appropriate level of protection; when an exporting Member questioned the sufficiency of the scientific evidence relating to this measure, the exporting Member had to objectively demonstrate that the appropriate level of protection of the importing Member would be achieved by an alternative SPS measure. Otherwise, the importing Member would be compelled to abolish the measure without any assurance of achieving its appropriate level of protection. As a result, the appropriate level of protection of the importing Member would be undermined and the object and purpose of the SPS measure to protect human, animal or plant life or health, while promoting international trade, would not be achieved. Therefore, Japan argued, it could not be concluded that an exporting Member had established a prima facie case of inconsistency with Article 2.2 when it had only shown that the risk might not exist under certain limited circumstances.

4.43   The **United States** argued that Japan had mischaracterized the relationship between Article 2.2 and Article 4. Article 4, which required a Member to accept a measure as equivalent to its own measure if the exporting Member objectively demonstrated that the measure achieved the importing Member's appropriate level of protection, presupposed that the measure imposed by the importing Member was maintained with sufficient scientific evidence. Article 4 could not be read in such a way that an importing Member could escape this basic obligation under Article 2.2. Thus, while Article 4 could provide a particular avenue for the United States to seek recognition of its measure as equivalent to a Japanese measure complying with Article 2.2, Japan had to have sufficient scientific evidence to maintain its measure under Article 2.2 in the first instance. Japan's appropriate level of protection had no part to play in this analysis.

4.44   **Japan** observed that under Article 4, it would be obligated to accept apples on the basis of the "mature, symptomless" criteria if, and only if, the United States objectively demonstrated that Japan's current phytosanitary requirements and the "mature, symptomless" criteria were equivalent. If the only proof required of the United States under Article 2.2 was evidence that the risk may not exist under certain, limited circumstances, it would be clearly inconsistent with Article 4. The exporting country would not have to provide evidence of equivalence, but would be able to prevail by merely contradicting the importing country's evidence. Japan argued that should this approach be allowed, the exporting country would always be able to amend or abolish the SPS measure of the importing country, by supplying such non-conclusive evidence. Such proof evidently did not objectively demonstrate that the "mature, symptomless" criteria were the equivalent of Japan's appropriate level of protection, which it described as equivalent to an import prohibition. The consequences for the importing country could be disastrous; as Japan would be forced to accept a level of protection provided by a measure that had not been objectively demonstrated to be equivalent to that of its current measure and would be thus subject to a higher level of risk.

4.45   In this connection, Japan requested the Panel to consider carefully whether the "mature, symptomless" criteria would objectively achieve Japan's level of protection. This was the only assurance of protection from fire blight that the United States argued was necessary. If the Panel was not convinced by the assurance of this criteria, Japan argued that the case under Article 2.2 had to be dismissed, because the burden of proof lay with the United States.

4.46   The **United States** claimed that Japan was attempting to import into the analysis of the US claim under Article 2.2, the concept of the appropriate level of protection from Article 5.6. A Member's appropriate level of protection formed an integral part of its commitments under Article 5.6 to ensure that any phytosanitary measure was no more trade-restrictive than required, taking into account technical and economic feasibility, to achieve its appropriate level of protection. As a result, in dispute settlement cases, a complaining Member could make a prima facie case by showing, *inter alia*, that an alternative measure achieved the importing Member's appropriate level of protection. In this case, there was no basis for importing this concept into the US claim under Article 2.2 that Japan's fire blight measures were maintained without sufficient scientific evidence.

4.47   The United States argued that, to make its prima facie showing, it may demonstrate that there was no "rational or objective relationship" between the SPS measure imposed on the exported commodity and the scientific evidence of a risk to plant life or health within Japan posed by such commodity. The United States had satisfied its burden by demonstrating (as confirmed by the scientific experts) that there was no scientific evidence that the exported commodity (harvested, mature apple fruit) posed a risk to plant life or health within Japan. Japan's appropriate level of protection played no part in this analysis.

E.   *Article 2.2*

1.   General

4.48   The **United States** argued that the Japanese fire blight measures were inconsistent with Article 2.2 of the *SPS Agreement* because they were maintained without sufficient scientific evidence. The obligation not to maintain an SPS measure "without sufficient scientific evidence" had been at the centre of the *Japan – Agricultural Products II* dispute.[43] Both the Panel and Appellate Body had read this phrase in light of the ordinary meaning of the word "sufficient" ("of a quantity, extent, or scope adequate to a certain purpose or object"), and in the context of Article 5.1 (there must be a rational relationship between a risk assessment and an SPS measure), Article 3.3 (a scientific justification for an SPS measure exists if there is a rational relationship between

---

[43]   Panel report and Appellate Body Report in *Japan – Agricultural Products II.*

the SPS measure and available scientific evidence), and Article 5.7 (providing a qualified exemption from Article 2.2 for provisional SPS measures where "relevant" scientific evidence is insufficient).[44] The Appellate Body had affirmed the conclusion of the Panel that the obligation in Article 2.2 not to maintain an SPS measure "without sufficient scientific evidence" required that "there be a rational or objective relationship between the SPS measure and the scientific evidence". Furthermore, "[w]hether there is a rational relationship between an SPS measure and the scientific evidence is to be determined on a case-by-case basis and will depend upon the particular circumstances of the case, including the characteristics of the measure at issue and the quality and quantity of the scientific evidence."[45]

4.49   The United States maintained that there was *no* scientific evidence of *any* quality that the imported commodity - mature apple fruit - had ever transmitted the disease or was a pathway for introduction of fire blight.[46] Thus, the first and most fundamental characteristic of the fire blight measures, their application to mature apple fruit, was not supported by any scientific evidence. To the contrary, all of the scientific evidence showed that mature, symptomless apple fruit had never transmitted and were not a pathway for the disease. There could be no rational or objective relationship between the Japanese fire blight measures and the scientific evidence because the measures were directed at a commodity for which there was no evidence of risk to plant life or health within Japan. Thus, there was no evidence, let alone sufficient evidence, for Japan to maintain its fire blight measures, and Japan was acting inconsistently with Article 2.2 of the *SPS Agreement*.

4.50   **Japan** argued that a variety of published literature on the ecology, properties and survivability of *E. amylovora* established that the bacteria were evidently capable of long-term survival inside, or on the surface, of what the United States termed "mature, symptomless" apple fruit. The fact that bacteria could exist and survive inside mature, symptomless apple fruit meant that the fruit could cause fire blight symptoms later on. For Japan, the implication was profound: apple fruit could be contaminated and yet be found fit for exportation.

---

[44]   *Ibid.*, paras. 73-80.

[45]   *Ibid.*, para. 84.

[46]   Under US law, exported apple fruit must be of a Federal or State grade that meets a minimum quality established by regulation. *US Export Apple Act*, 7 U.S.C. § 581. Exported US apples must currently satisfy at least the requirements for the "U.S. No. 1" grade, 7 C.F.R. § 33.10 (minimum requirements for export apples), pursuant to which apples must be:

"[M]ature but not overripe, carefully hand-picked, clean, fairly well-formed; free from decay, internal browning, internal breakdown, bitter pit, Jonathan spot, scald, freezing injury . . . and broken skin or bruises except those which are incident to proper handling and packing. The apples are also free from damage caused by . . . sunburn or sprayburn, limb rubs, hail, drought spots, scars, stem or calyx cracks, disease, insects, [or] damage by other means . . . "

United States Standards for Grades of Apples, 7 C.F.R. § 51.302 (requirements for US No. 1 same as for "U.S. Fancy", except for "color, russeting, and invisible water core"). Individual states may have standards that exceed the federal standards for grades. See, e.g., *Washington Administrative Code 16-403-140* ("Washington State standard apple grades for extra fancy or fancy shall be equivalent to or better than the U.S. standards for grades of apples ....").

Once introduced into Japan, fire blight would have ample potential for growth and infection and lead to major negative, irreversible consequences.

4.51   Furthermore, Japan contended that the US argument raised the two questions of: (i) the ambiguity/subjectivity of the criteria: and (ii) the practicality of maintaining the appropriate quality, the very two issues crystallized through the Panel process. When asked under which definition of "maturity" they believed that mature apple fruit would not disseminate the disease, Japan was of the view that the experts had not been able to respond clearly. Moreover, Dr Geider and Dr Smith in particular, had expressly admitted that "immature" and "mature" were not two clearly separate phenomena and that maturation was a "continuous process". Indeed, van der Zwet's *et al.* (1990) description of apple fruit as "mature" and the later disavowal of the description by Dr van der Zwet and Professor Thomson were clear scientific evidence that even experienced researchers might err. In this connection, Japan emphasized that neither Dr van der Zwet's declaration nor Professor Thomson's letter clearly explained that the tested apples had been physiologically immature. The 1990 study thus indicated that apple fruit at physiological maturity might still be subject to bacterial infestation/infection. There was also what Japan believed to be agreement among the experts that the "symptoms" (which must be recognized by the human eye) would be the key indicator of the risk, and that the symptoms might not be always detected.

4.52   In Japan's view, each of the current requirements, such as the designation of a fire blight-free area, the necessity and width of a buffer zone, the frequency and timing of field inspections and surface disinfection, were reasonably supported by scientific evidence contained in relevant literature, similar measures taken by other countries and international standards, and there was a "rational or objective relationship" between the measure and the evidence.

2.   Nature of the Scientific Evidence

4.53   The **United States** argued that what at times might appear to be a highly technical dispute in fact revolved around a simple biological reality: mature apple fruit were not part of the disease cycle for fire blight bacteria. As a result, there was no scientific evidence that mature apple fruit had ever transmitted or could serve as a pathway for the fire blight disease. As imports of mature apple fruit did not pose a risk to plant life or health within Japan, restricting importation of apples to mature fruit (the exported commodity) was a measure that was reasonably available and that achieved Japan's appropriate level of protection.

4.54   **Japan** maintained that a risk generally meant a negative, stochastic event, the likelihood of which had to be assessed on the basis of previous observations. The United States erred because it limited the scope of "observations" too narrowly, only to "direct" evidence establishing a pathway. There was nothing in the *SPS Agreement* which limited the kind of evidence under Article 2.2 only to "direct" evidence; the Article only referred to "scientific evidence". Moreover, in phytosanitary protection, there might not be any such "direct" evidence. Risk still existed even though there was no "direct" evidence for any pathway and, in order to assess the risk, the scope of investigation had to be expanded to include various "indirect" observations. Coupled with inherent difficulties in identifying a definite cause of the spread, it was very unlikely that anyone would be able to uncover a piece of direct evidence. The risk of a pathway needed to be assessed on the basis of indirect observations. Discarding these pieces of indirect evidence was not scientific.

4.55   The **United States** claimed that Japan had not been able to identify any scientific evidence that imports of apple fruit posed a risk of introduction of fire blight to Japan. Scientific evidence that apple fruit posed a risk of introduction of fire blight to Japan could have consisted of: (1) evidence that fruit had, in fact, introduced the disease to other areas and; (2) evidence that fruit were a pathway for introduction. On the first point, Japan had failed to identify evidence that imports of apple fruit had ever transmitted *E. amylovora* to a new area. On the second point, Japan had neither identified each step necessary for imported apple fruit to serve as a hypothetical pathway (for example, the five steps identified by the International Plant Protection Convention)[47] nor cited the scientific evidence on which it relied to establish that each step of the hypothetical pathway would be completed. Japan had not identified evidence establishing a likelihood that apple fruit could introduce fire blight to Japan because there *was* no such evidence. The United States believed that the scientific experts had unanimously stated that there was no scientific evidence that trade in apple fruit had ever been the means of introducing fire blight into a new area. The experts had also unanimously confirmed that there was no scientific evidence that any hypothetical pathway would be completed.

4.56   **Japan** argued that a distinction had to be made between "direct" and "indirect" scientific evidence. "Direct" evidence was a conclusive scientific discovery, for example that *E. amylovora* and fire blight, had been transmitted via apple fruit. "Indirect" evidence showed the ability of contaminated apple fruit to go through each of the steps necessary for it to eventually cause fire blight in the importing country. If the US interpretation were correct, importing Members would be allowed to protect only against the known, established dissemination pathways, and no other measure could be taken. Following this line of argumentation, Japan believed that it would be stripped of any phytosanitary protection against the disease, because the exact pathway of trans-oceanic dissemination of the disease had not been fully established. For example, there was no *direct* evidence establishing a pathway through "immature, symptomful" apple fruit. It was, however, unreasonable that Japan would be forced to accept shipments of blighted apples under the *SPS Agreement* simply because there was no "direct" evidence establishing a pathway.

4.57   The **United States** claimed that the Panel should look not at whether evidence was direct or indirect but whether it was scientific.[48] Article 2.2 of the

---

[47]   Op. cit., ISPM 11, paras. 2.2.1.1-2.2.1.5.
[48]   The United States noted that in its First Submission it had stated: "The evidence Japan cites is circumstantial, not direct or scientific evidence, and Japan makes no assessment of the relative

SPS Agreement stated that a Member shall ensure that an SPS measure is not maintained "without sufficient scientific evidence". The term "scientific evidence" was not defined in the *SPS Agreement* but could be interpreted according to the ordinary meaning of the words in their context, in light of the object and purpose of the Agreement. "Evidence" was defined as "something serving as a proof".[49] "Scientific" was defined as "[o]f, pertaining to, or of the nature of science; based on, regulated by, or engaged in the application of science ... ; valid according to the objective principles of the scientific method".[50] The "scientific method" was defined as "a method of procedure that has characterized natural science since the 17th Century, consisting in systematic observation, testing, and modification of hypotheses".[51] Thus, "scientific evidence" should be understood as something serving as proof that was valid according to the objective principles of the scientific method, understood as systematic observation, testing, and modification of hypotheses. The United States did not assert that evidence sufficient for Japan to maintain its fire blight measures had to be direct or that it may not be indirect, but under Article 2.2 such evidence had to be scientific, i.e., valid according to the objective principles of the scientific method.

4.58 **Japan** recalled that the United States claimed that Japan's current phytosanitary requirements had been without sufficient scientific evidence from as early as 1994, and that Japan had been in violation of the *SPS Agreement* when the instrument entered into force in 1995. However, the current measure had been introduced on the basis of agreement between the two governments, in order to allow importation of American apples, while preventing introduction of *E. amylovora* with the security equivalent of import prohibition. It was unreasonable for the United States to now claim that the evidence was insufficient from the beginning.

4.59 The **United States** observed that it had acquiesced to the fire blight measures imposed by Japan in 1994 as preferable to an outright ban on imported apple fruit, although it had recognized that the scientific evidence did not support the restrictions imposed by Japan. It had never accepted the consistency of these measures with Japan's WTO obligations.

4.60 **Japan** stated that it was only in the course of the proceeding that it had access to new information which might warrant a new risk assessment in light of the potential insufficiency of the previous evidence. Sufficiency of the evidence was without question until, at the earliest, the date of the first US submission.

---

effectiveness of this measure on reducing the likelihood of entry or overall disease risk" when discussing the evidence that Japan cited to support its requirement that containers for harvesting be treated with chlorine. The United States clarified that if use of the word "direct" in this passage had led to the repeated invocation of "indirect" and "direct", by Japan, it regretted the imposition on the Panel's time and would be content to argue simply that "circumstantial" evidence was not "scientific" evidence.

[49] *The New Shorter Oxford English Dictionary*, vol. 1, p. 867, Oxford University Press, 1993.
[50] *Ibid.*, p. 2717.
[51] *Ibid.*

4.61 The **United States** noted that Australia had also argued that a complaining party may not "claim inconsistency [with Article 2.2] on the basis that the measure is not based on sufficient scientific evidence, if the claims relating to the *sufficiency* of evidence include evidence that was not available to the respondent party at the time of the initiation of the WTO complaint".[52] Australia had further argued that "a WTO member apprised of new scientific evidence must be allowed the opportunity to reassess the risk in terms of the relevance of the evidence to the factors enumerated in Article 5.2 of the *SPS Agreement*". However, the United States argued that a rule that factual evidence not available at the initiation of the dispute settlement proceeding could not be considered by a panel would bar evidence that could be relevant to the Panel's factual determinations. Australia appeared to argue that a claim that scientific evidence was insufficient could not rest on scientific evidence produced after the claim was made. However, the situation Australia posited did not arise in this dispute. The US claim that the Japanese fire blight measures were maintained without sufficient scientific evidence did not rest or even rely on Dr van der Zwet's declaration or Professor Thomson's letter. Rather, Japan's fire blight measures were inconsistent with Article 2.2 because there had never been any scientific evidence that mature apple fruit transmitted the fire blight disease.

4.62 **Japan** claimed that of the new information the United States had sought to introduce in this proceeding, it did not consider the documents signed by Dr van der Zwet or by Professor Thomson to offer any serious scientific information or new evidence which would warrant a new risk assessment. Nor would the sufficiency of the evidence be challenged by these documents. Japan considered that the only new pieces of evidence were Roberts (2002) and Taylor *et al.* (2002).[53] In its analysis, these pieces of evidence were not yet sufficient to warrant revision of the current phytosanitary requirements. However, Japan invited the United States to supplement Roberts (2002) with answers to five additional questions. Together, they could then be considered in a formal, new pest risk analysis to judge whether the current phytosanitary requirements needed to be revised.

3. Transmission of the Disease

4.63 The **United States** underlined that the scientific literature revealed no evidence that mature, symptomless apple fruit had ever transmitted fire blight disease. The scientific evidence established that such fruit had never transmitted and did not play a role in the transmission of fire blight. According to the United States, the scientific experts had unanimously stated that there was no scientific evidence that trade in apple fruit had ever been the means of introducing fire

---

[52] Australian Statement at the third party session with the Panel, 22 October 2002, para. 10.

[53] R.G. Roberts (2002), "Evaluation of Buffer Zone Size on the Incidence of *Erwinia Amylovora* in Mature Apple Fruit and Associated Phytosanitary Risk", *Acta Horticulture* 590: 47-53 (Exhibit USA-16); and R.K. Taylor *et al.* (2002), "The Viability and Persistence of *Erwinia amylovora* in Apples Discarded in an Orchard Environment", 590: 153-55. Paper at 9th International Workshop on Fire Blight, Napier New Zealand, 8-12 October 2001 (Exhibit USA-20).

blight into a new area. The United States quoted a number of studies in support of this conclusion including:

> Thomson (2000): "[I]t has never been demonstrated that mature fruit are involved in dissemination of *Erwinia amylovora* and serve as a source of new infections in orchards. It would be extremely unlikely that contaminated fruit could be responsible for establishing new outbreaks of fire blight."[54]

> Roberts *et al.* (1998): "Using published data on the incidence of *E. amylovora* on mature, symptomless apple fruit and several conservative assumptions, we have estimated the risk of establishing new outbreaks of fire blight in previously blight-free areas, and found this risk to be extremely low. We have found no evidence in the scientific literature that apple fruit in commercial shipments, whether contaminated with *E. amylovora* or not, have provided inoculum for an outbreak of fire blight."[55]

> European and Mediterranean Plant Protection Organization (1997): "[T]he risk of [fire blight] transmission on fruit is considered insignificant in current trade practice."[56]

> Thomson (1992): "The presence of *E. amylovora* on or in healthy fruit *has not been shown* to be a source of inoculum in fruit orchards. ... It seems very remote that contaminated fruit could be responsible for establishing new outbreaks."[57]

> Roberts *et al.* (1989): "[H]ealthy, mature apple fruit, even when harvested from blighted trees, are unlikely to harbour *E. amylovora* populations and therefore are unlikely to pose a phytosanitary risk to areas free from fire blight."[58]

> Dueck (1974): "[T]he risk of disseminating fire blight bacteria on symptomless mature apples is considered negligible."[59]

4.64   In the absence of any affirmative evidence, the scientific literature described the risk of transmitting fire blight disease through mature, symptomless apple fruit as "negligible", "unlikely", "very remote", "insignificant", "extremely low", or "extremely unlikely". The United States

---

[54]   S.V. Thomson, Epidemiology of Fire Blight, in Fire Blight: The Disease and Its Causative Agent, *Erwinia Amylovora*, at 17 (J.L. Vanneste, ed.) (2000) (citing additional sources concluding that fruit do not transmit the disease) (Exhibit USA- 2).

[55]   Op. cit., Roberts, et. al. (1998), pp. 19-28.

[56]   EPPO, "Data Sheet on Quarantine Pests: Erwinia amylovora", *Quarantine for Europe*, at 5: Means of Movement and Dispersal (Exhibit USA-5). The EPPO goes on to "recommend[] countries *at high risk* to prohibit importation of host *plants for planting*" but does *not* recommend any restrictions on importation of fruit. (emphasis added).

[57]   S.V. Thomson (1992), "Fire blight of apple and pear", *Plant Diseases of International Importance*, vol. 3: Diseases of Fruit Crops 32-65 (J. Kumar et al., eds.).

[58]   R.G. Roberts *et al.* (1989) "Evaluation of Mature Apple Fruit from Washington State for the Presence of Erwinia amylovora", *Plant Disease* 73: 917-21, at 920 (Exhibit USA–28).

[59]   J. Dueck (1974), "Survival of Erwinia amylovora in association with mature apple fruit", *Canadian Journal of Plant Science* 54: pp. 349-51, at 351 (Exhibit USA–42).

noted that in describing the risk of transmission as "negligible" rather than "zero", the scientific reports merely reflected "the uncertainty that theoretically always remains [that an event may occur] since science can never provide absolute certainty" that an event may never occur.[60]

4.65   **Japan** questioned the conclusions of the United States, stating that there was no ecological study that was available on the possible dissemination of fire blight via apple fruit. As a matter of common sense, it could be easily envisaged that *E. amylovora,* surviving either inside or outside apple fruit, could be transmitted to nearby host plants, either by way of rain, wind, insects, etc. Once such fruit was introduced into Japan, the bacteria would be exposed to its environment at all stages of distribution, storage, consumption and disposal of the fruit, causing a real risk of dissemination.[61]

4.66   Japan further argued that the scientific evidence did not document *any* cause of trans-oceanic dissemination. The absence of evidence attributing the cause to fruit did not demonstrate that the bacteria could have been transmitted only via budwood or nursery stock. Furthermore, the previous experiences of long-distance, trans-oceanic dissemination showed that *E. amylovora* was capable of propagating into a new environment outside of its favoured host of budwood and nursery stock. Put in the context of van der Zwet *et al,* (1990) and Goodman (1954)[62], which found endophytic *E. amylovora* in apple fruit, these two pieces of evidence reinforced each other and suggested a risk that endophytic *E. amylovora* in fruit could survive trans-oceanic shipment and later cause fire blight in foreign destinations.

4.67   With respect to the latter point, the **United States** explained that the van der Zwet *et al.* (1990) paper had not isolated endophytic (internal) *E. amylovora* from any harvested mature apple fruit, the exported commodity. In fact, according to the United States, the scientific experts had unanimously stated that there was no scientific evidence that harvested mature apple fruit would harbour internal populations of fire blight bacteria. The United States also argued that Japan had ignored the subsequent conclusions of the authors of the 1990 paper to the contrary - conclusions based not on speculation, but on reviews of the scientific literature. Professor Thomson had written in 1992 that: "The presence of *E. amylovora* on or in healthy fruit has not been shown to be a source of inoculum in fruit orchards. ... It seems very remote that contaminated fruit could be responsible for establishing new outbreaks." Dr van der Zwet co-authored the Roberts *et al.* (1998) paper cited in paragraph 4.63 above that

---

[60]   Appellate Body Report in *EC – Hormones*, para. 186, Panel Report, *EC – Hormones*, paras. 8.152-8.153. As both the Panel and the Appellate Body concluded in *EC – Hormones*, theoretical uncertainty is not the kind of risk which a risk assessment and, therefore, an SPS measure, is to address. Thus for the United States, the scientific conclusion that mature, symptomless apple fruit posed a "negligible" or "insignificant" risk of transmitting the disease reflected the scientific evidence that exported apples had *never* transmitted fire blight and were *not* a pathway for the disease.
[61]   Probability of fire blight dissemination via mature, apparently healthy apple fruit (Exhibit JPN-14).
[62]   R.N. Goodman (1954), Apple fruit a source of overwintering fireblight inoculum, *Plant Disease Reporter.* 38: 414.

concluded: "We have found no evidence in the scientific literature that apple fruit in commercial shipments, whether contaminated with *E. amylovora* or not, have provided inoculum for an outbreak of fire blight." And Professor Thomson in 2000 wrote again: "[I]t has never been demonstrated that mature fruit are involved in dissemination of *E. amylovora* and serve as a source of new infection in orchards."[63] Japan apparently rested much of its case on a conjectural statement by two authors, both of whom had published subsequent work explicitly drawing the opposite conclusion.

4.68   **Japan** recalled its contention that the United States apparently believed that any "scientific" evidence must be "direct" evidence. If an event occurred infrequently and was difficult to simulate, a scientific analysis would depend on indirect or circumstantial evidence. Trans-oceanic dissemination of fire blight was one of these infrequent phenomena. However, such transmission had occurred four times during the 200-year history of fire blight: (i) from the United States to New Zealand in 1919; (ii) from the United States to the United Kingdom in 1957; (iii) from the United States to Egypt in 1962; and (iv) from the mainland United States to Hawaii in 1965. In these cases, transmission pathways had been variously discussed, but not definitely identified. The observation of only four cases could not establish that the likelihood of dissemination through apple fruit was scientifically "negligible". The likelihood of such dissemination had to be inferred from available, often indirect, evidence such as the known properties of *E. amylovora* and apple fruit, as well as past studies and real experiences.

4.69   The **United States** countered that none of these alleged instances of dissemination involved apple fruit. According to the United States, the experts had unanimously stated that there was no scientific evidence that trade in apple fruit had ever been the means of introducing fire blight into a new area. The experts had also agreed that the scientific evidence indicated that the long-range means of transmission of fire blight was through movement of infected plants. In the scientific literature, the introduction of fire blight to New Zealand and Egypt had been linked to movement of infected propagative material (nursery stock) and not to trade in apple fruit.

4.70   **Japan** noted that there were two incidents of trans-oceanic dissemination that did not involve budwood or nursery stock. The dissemination of fire blight to the United Kingdom in 1957 was attributed by some literature to contamination of cargo crates by the bacteria. The transmission of fire blight to Hawaii in 1965 had been attributed by one report to blighted pear fruit. This implied that human acts of transporting fruit over an ocean could cause dispersion of fire blight to a distant location. This was the exact dissemination route - albeit through different fruit - that Japan was concerned about. Drs van der Zwet and Thomson had clearly perceived the risk of long-distance dissemination via fruit from these two pieces of evidence:

---

[63]   S.V. Thomson (2000), "Epidemiology of Fire Blight", in *Fire Blight: The Disease and Its Causative Agent, Erwinia amylovora*, at 17 (J.L. Vanneste, ed.), (Exhibit USA-2).

"[t]he positive discovery of endophytic *E. amylovora* from 14 apples of two cultivars in Utah requires caution and may partially explain the observations of fruit blight symptoms on pear shipments to Hawaii and England."[64]

4.71   The **United States** observed that although Japan conceded that the dissemination of fire blight to Great Britain did not appear to be associated with apple fruit, nonetheless, Japan believed it "*impl[ies]* that human acts of transporting *fruit* over an ocean can cause dispersion of fire blight to a distant location". Japan apparently believed that the introduction had been demonstrated to be linked to contaminated pear fruit boxes from the United States. Taken at face value, Japan was suggesting an implication from evidence that, Japan itself admitted, did not relate to apple fruit. Whether or not an implication could rise to the level of scientific evidence, the implication was robbed of foundation when one examined the literature related to the spread of fire blight to Great Britain. The literature made clear that contamination of bins was only one theory on the source of inoculum; equally probable was that the disease was introduced on infected nursery stock (Great Britain Ministry of Agriculture, Fisheries and Food (1969), Lelliot (1959)). Both of these primary accounts on the introduction of fire blight to Great Britain explicitly *rejected* that dissemination could be linked to fruit. The US also argued that the experts had noted that the suggestion in the literature that contaminated fruit crates may have been responsible for spread of fire blight to the United Kingdom seemed to be based entirely on circumstantial evidence. Dr Hayward had commented that "Overall there is little evidence to support the [Japanese] statement that the pest has a remarkable degree of survival ability outside the favourable host of the wood".[65]

4.72   Furthermore, the US review of the research literature confirmed that *E. amylovora* was not, in fact, found in Hawaii. The only reference given for Japan's assertion that fire blight was disseminated to Hawaii was a University of California newsletter that anecdotally related an incidence of infected Californian pear fruit arriving in Hawaii. Despite this anecdotal report, and in spite of the movement of other fruit to Hawaii over decades, fire blight had never been recorded as occurring and was not known to occur in Hawaii. Indeed, the United States claimed that Hawaii was an excellent example of how unrestricted trade in mature, symptomless apple fruit did not spread fire blight. Although a number of fire blight host plants were found in Hawaii (as well as the bird that Japan claimed might hypothetically vector epiphytic bacteria from a discarded fruit to a susceptible plant host), Hawaii imported about 20 million apples annually from the US mainland without any restrictions due to fire blight and there had been no introduction of fire blight to Hawaii.

4.73   **Japan** maintained that the significance of the history was unmistakable: the bacteria had the ability to spread not only through the favoured, insulated medium of budwood and nursery stock, but through other, possibly less favorable media (*inter alia*, cargo crates and fruits) as well. Japan also noted

---

[64]   Op. cit., van der Zwet *et al.* (1990).
[65]   Para. 6.36.

what it termed overall confirmation by the experts of the presence of a real "risk" (which included completion of the pathway) of dissemination of the disease from apple fruit.

4.74   The **United States** argued that the scientific evidence was further borne out by real world experience. Although fire blight was geographically dispersed in the United States, the United States had exported 10,505,500 metric tons of apple fruit over the last 35 years (assuming 88 apples per 42 lb. box, approximately 48.5 billion apples) without a single instance of fire blight being spread through exports of US apple fruit in that time. Indeed, billions of fruit had been shipped world-wide without a single documented instance of fire blight transmission via exported apple fruit.

4.75   The United States underlined that only a tiny portion of these exports were made under conditions as stringent as those set by Japan.[66] In fact, of 66 fire blight-free countries, 58 imposed no fire blight-related restrictions on imported fruit. Over the past 35 years, the United States had exported 4,794,495 metric tons of apple fruit, or approximately 22.1 billion apples, to ten fire blight-free markets (Chinese Taipei, Hong Kong, Indonesia, Saudi Arabia, Thailand, the United Arab Emirates, Malaysia, Venezuela, the Philippines, and Colombia). None of these markets imposed measures similar to the Japanese requirements, and none of these areas had reported transmission of fire blight through imports of US apple fruit. Thus, although nearly all trade in apple fruit occurred without any restrictions for fire blight, there was no evidence that fire blight had ever spread through exported apples.

4.76   **Japan** remarked that eight of the markets identified by the United States were in tropical regions while the other two countries (Saudi Arabia and the United Arab Emirates) were in a desert region. None had the temperate climate of Japan. Moreover, with the exception of Chinese Taipei, none of the others had any significant apple production. Clearly, none had the favourable conditions for the introduction and establishment of *E. amylovora*. Furthermore, Hawaii's climate was not as favourable to fire blight as that of Japan. Since these US figure on apple exports were in the order of billions, any incremental risk caused by one additional apple might be very low. However, what was in dispute was a phytosanitary mechanism that would possibly affect the phytosanitary quality of all of these billions of apples for years to come. So however minute the risk might be for one additional apple, the risk posed by billions of apples would be significantly higher.

4.77   The **United States** argued that Japan had provided no citation nor any explanation for its assertion that only countries with temperate climates were at risk for introduction of fire blight. It appeared that several countries without temperate climates nonetheless had fire blight, including Cyprus, Iran, Israel, Jordan, Lebanon, Egypt, Bermuda, Guatemala, and Mexico. Japan had also not explained why only apple production should be relevant as to whether or not fire

---

[66]   The United States included a Table Detailing Fire Blight Measures on Imported Apples in Fire Blight-Free Areas (Exhibit USA-14).

blight might be introduced into an area as there were numerous other host plants for fire blight.

4.78   **Japan** contended that the alleged absence of measures similar to those of Japan merely reflected the level of protection of these markets against the risk of fire blight. Compared to Japan, these countries and territories had hostile environments for the propagation of fire blight, and they could afford to have a policy more tolerant of the risk.

4.79   The **United States** argued that Japan had simply *assumed* that the application of different measures reflected a lower level of protection in these countries, rather than a recognition by these countries that their equally stringent level of protection could be met through minimal or no SPS measures. This assumption by Japan was not supported by citation to any correspondence, documents, or public statements by these countries explaining their appropriate level of protection. Furthermore, Japan had failed to address the larger point that many more billions of apple fruit had been traded between other countries, with and without fire blight, than reflected in US export statistics. Nonetheless, as the United States believed the experts had unanimously confirmed, there was no evidence from anywhere in the world that fire blight had been introduced or spread through trade in apple fruit.

4.80   **Japan** stated that it had ideal climatic and geographic conditions for wide-scale spread and occurrence of fire blight. It was rich in susceptible hosts of *E. amylovora* - with commercial production of apples and pears valued at over 100 billion yen (more than US$800 million) annually and significant populations of horticultural hosts such as hawthorn, firethorn and mountain ash in both urban and rural areas. Japan's temperate warm and humid climate would be hospitable for the bacteria and Japan believed that the consequences of fire blight entry would be recurrent and irreversible. It would be virtually impossible to eradicate the disease once it was hosted in Japan's hospitable environment. The economic damage reported from fire blight outbreaks in other parts of the world would be more severe in Japan because of its host populations and temperate climate.[67] Indeed, out of a very limited number of fire blight-free countries in the temperate region, two of them (Australia and the Republic of Korea) prohibited the importation of apple fruit from fire blight-occurring countries entirely.

4.81   The **United States** noted that Japan had apparently dismissed the possibility that the disease could be eradicated before spread, despite evidence to the contrary from Australia and Norway. Japan also did not evaluate whether the disease, once established, could be prevented from spreading – even though Japan admitted the existence of evidence that Europe has successfully done so.

---

[67]   Damages on apples in Michigan in 1991 were estimated to be US $3.8 million; during the 1982-84 outbreak in Egypt, 95% of the Le Conte variety of pear was lost; damages on pear in California in 1976 were estimated to be US$4.7 million (Exhibit JPN-10 gives further examples of economic losses from fire blight outbreaks).

4. Pathway for Transmission of the Disease

4.82   The **United States** argued that not only was there no evidence that mature, symptomless fruit had ever spread fire blight, but there was also no evidence that mature fruit could be a pathway for the spread of the bacteria. The scientific evidence indicated that:

(a)   Fire blight bacteria were not associated internally with the exported commodity (mature, symptomless apple fruit);

(b)   fire blight bacteria were rarely associated externally with the exported commodity, even when harvested from blighted trees and orchards;

(c)   even if a mature, symptomless apple had been externally contaminated with bacteria, such bacteria were unlikely to survive normal commercial handling, storage, and transport of fruit; and

(d)   even if the imported commodity had been externally contaminated with bacteria, there was no dispersal mechanism or vector to allow movement of such bacteria from the fruit to a suitable host.[68]

4.83   Because the chain of transmission – from association of bacteria with fruit, to bacterial survival of handling, storage, and transport, to vectoring of bacteria to a suitable host - was never completed, imports of apple fruit were not a means of, and could not result in, transmission of fire blight bacteria to Japan. Thus, as mature, symptomless apple fruit were not a pathway for the fire blight disease, there was no scientific basis to restrict imports of such fruit.

4.84   **Japan** contended that a pathway to apple trees from infected apple fruit might or might not be direct. One could easily envisage complex, intertwined potential pathways from imported fruit to an orchard, or to other host plants for fire blight bacteria. Japan recalled that some authors believed the transmission of the disease to the United Kingdom was due to contaminated cargo crates destined to fruit orchards. Japan failed to understand how dissemination from cargo crates to orchards would be any more likely than dissemination from fruit to suburban host plants. It was scientifically sound to envisage, consider and evaluate a variety of potential routes of propagation from fruit to other host plants in the environment. Japan noted what it termed the overall confirmation by the experts of the presence of a real "risk" (which included completion of the pathway) of the dissemination of the disease from apple fruit. When asked if the bacteria inside an infected apple fruit, inadvertently or erroneously found fit for export, would survive the storage and other handling process, Japan believed the experts had unanimously acknowledged that there was a real risk of dissemination. In particular, Japan was of the view that Dr Smith had clearly stated that the risk had to be managed. In Japan's view, the experts could not have been referring to mere theoretical uncertainty, because such a risk could not be "managed". According to Japan, since the experts had acknowledged that

---

[68]   The United States also noted that there are additional conditions, such as discard near a fire blight host that is in a state receptive to infection, that also must be satisfied in order for exported fruit to transmit the disease to an importing country. See Roberts, *et al.* (1998), pp. 19-28, at 24.

there was a real risk of dissemination, they had admitted that the pathway would be complete. Although the experts had recognized that the risk arising from "mature, symptomless" apple fruit would be negligible, that risk would be negligible only, as Japan believed that Dr Smith had stated, when phytosanitary requirements are met.

4.85   The **United States** argued that Japan had presented at least three different hypothetical pathways in the course of the proceeding. These shifting arguments made the Panel's analytical task slightly more complex, but not more difficult as none of these hypothetical pathways was supported by scientific evidence that established that the exported commodity presented a probability or likelihood of introduction of fire blight to Japan. The first hypothetical pathway was identified in Japan's first written submission: in this two-step pathway, (1) mature apple fruit were either infected or endophytically contaminated and (2) such fruit then somehow transmitted *E. amylovora* and fire blight. According to the United States, it had demonstrated, and the experts had confirmed, that the first step in this pathway was not supported by any scientific evidence and that none of the alleged four instances of trans-oceanic dissemination of fire blight cited by Japan as "indirect" evidence provided any scientific evidence to establish a probability or likelihood that imported mature apple fruit (as opposed to imported fire blight host plants) could introduce fire blight to Japan.

4.86   The second hypothetical pathway that Japan identified was the importation of "mature, apparently healthy, but infected" apple fruit. According to the United States, it had demonstrated, and the scientific experts had confirmed, that there was no scientific evidence that harvested mature apple fruit would be infected with fire blight, no scientific evidence that mature apple fruit would harbour endophytic (internal) populations of bacteria, and no scientific evidence that a harvested fruit with epiphytic bacteria in the calyx would become infected. Thus, there was no scientific evidence to support the third step in Japan's hypothetical pathway, that imported apple fruit would result in the presence of a "mature, apparently healthy but infected fruit" within Japan. Japan's hypothetical pathway was severed at this point, establishing that there was no scientific evidence that the pathway would be completed. Thus, there was no probability or likelihood of introduction of fire blight to Japan via imported US apples.

4.87   Japan had presented a third hypothetical pathway when it had asked the scientific experts to assume that an infected fruit would be imported. However, as the United States believed the experts had confirmed, the scientific evidence established that harvested fruit were horticulturally mature and such fruit were not infected; thus, an infected fruit arriving in Japan would have to be immature and would not pass through normal commercial processes of picking, sorting, storage, inspection, and export. (Indeed, Japan had conceded that exported US apples are mature and apparently healthy.) As a result, the United States was of the opinion that Japan's discussion with the experts had not demonstrated any risk posed by the exported commodity (harvested mature apple fruit) but rather had been based solely on the risk posed by something other than that commodity (infected, immature apple fruit). Under the *SPS Agreement*, a phytosanitary measure imposed on an exported commodity had to be based on a risk to plant life or health within Japan posed by that exported commodity. Because the scientific evidence established that a harvested fruit would be horticulturally mature, and therefore not infected, exported US apples did not pose a risk of introducing fire blight to Japan, even according to this alternative hypothetical pathway that Japan had presented to the experts.

4.88   Thus, the United States contended that there was no scientific evidence that any of the hypothetical pathways identified by Japan would be completed and that fire blight could be introduced into Japan via imported US apple fruit. Under Article 2.2, for there to be "sufficient scientific evidence" to maintain a fire blight measure on imported apple fruit, there had to be a "rational or objective relationship" between the scientific evidence of a risk to plant life or health within Japan posed by imported apple fruit and that fire blight measure. Where there was no scientific evidence that mature apple fruit had ever transmitted fire blight and where there was no scientific evidence that any hypothetical pathway involving mature apple fruit would be completed, the exported commodity posed no risk to plant life or health within Japan. As a result, no measure could be imposed on imported apple fruit consistent with the *SPS Agreement* to protect against introduction of fire blight, except restricting importation to the exported commodity: mature (and therefore symptomless) apple fruit.

4.89   **Japan** countered that ISPM 2 on Guidelines for Pest Risk Analysis (the 1996 Guidelines) did not require each step of a pathway to be supported by scientific evidence. On the contrary, the Guidelines stated that "[p]otential pathways which may not currently exist should be assessed if known.".

5.   Endophytic (internal) Bacteria and Mature Apple Fruit

4.90   The **United States** claimed that numerous studies had indicated that mature, symptomless apple fruit did not harbour endophytic populations of the bacteria.[69] In particular:

> Roberts (2002): "This report on the joint Japanese-US research was the largest investigation to date of whether mature, symptomless apple fruit harboured the bacterium internally. 30,900 fruit from two sites in Washington State, USA, had been harvested at 0, 10, 25, 50, 100, or 300 meters from a source of fire blight inoculum. Nine hundred fruit had been analyzed at harvest for internal populations, and no bacteria had been detected, even from trees with or directly adjacent to fire blight. Thirty thousand fruit had been placed in commercial cold storage for 2-3 months (depending on date of harvest). None of these 30,000 fruit had developed

---

[69]   The United States noted that in most studies that tested mature, symptomless fruit for internal and/or external bacterial populations, the experimental designs were purposely biased in favor of positive detection because fruit were not randomly selected but were frequently harvested from blighted trees and orchards, and often were harvested directly from blighted spurs or shoots. Nonetheless, these studies had not detected internal populations of bacteria in mature, symptomless apple fruit and had very rarely detected external populations of bacteria on such fruit.

external disease symptoms. Of the 30,000 fruit, 1,500 had been sliced open, and no internal disease symptoms were present. Of the 1,500 sliced fruit, the internal surfaces of 500 had been streaked and plated onto selective media, and no fire blight bacteria had been isolated from any fruit."[70]

Van der Zwet *et al.* (1990): "One relevant experiment had harvested immature, mature, and some possibly mature fruit from four different geographic locations, and no internal bacteria had been detected from any of the mature fruit (80 fruit from West Virginia, USA) or possibly mature fruit (40 fruit from Washington, USA, 40 fruit from Utah, USA, and 80 fruit from Ontario, Canada), even when harvested from blighted trees."[71]

Roberts *et al.* (1989): "No internal fire blight bacteria had been detected in 1,555 mature, symptomless apple fruit harvested over two years from blighted (in some cases, severely blighted) trees of seven apple cultivars grown at five locations in Washington, USA."[72]

Dueck (1974): "No internal bacteria had been isolated from any of 60 mature, symptomless apple fruit harvested in Ontario, Canada, from severely infected trees. The report concluded: "*Mature apples* are highly resistant to infection. Only when forcibly introduced into the cortex were fruit infected. . . . [U]nder orchard conditions apples, particularly from resistant cultivars, are not infected."[73]

The United States believed that the scientific experts had unanimously confirmed that there was no scientific evidence that harvested mature apple fruit would harbour populations of fire blight bacteria.

4.91   The United States observed that these results were not surprising as they reflected the biology of the disease. Blossoms that became infected tended to abort their fruit and any fruit that become infected (either through movement of the bacteria through internal tissues from a canker to the fruit or through external wounding of the fruit) did not develop normally. Instead, they turned brown to black, shrivelled and, like the blossoms, remained attached to the spur, taking on a mummified appearance. Thus, while immature apple fruit might contain detectable levels of internal fire blight bacteria without yet having developed disease symptoms by the time of harvest, mature, symptomless apple fruit would not harbour internal populations of fire blight bacteria.

4.92   **Japan** argued that a variety of published literature on the ecology, properties and survivability of *E. amylovora* established that: (1) the bacteria were able to grow at a temperature of 3-5 degrees to 37 degrees Celsius; (2) the bacteria were facultative anaerobae; and (3) they had the ability to utilize as carbon sources glucose, fructose, or L-arabinose. The bacteria were evidently

---

[70]   Op. cit., Roberts (2002).
[71]   Op. cit., van der Zwet *et al.* (1990).
[72]   Op. cit., Roberts *et al.* (1989).
[73]   Op. cit., Dueck (1974).

capable of survival inside or on the surface of apple fruit. In addition, van der Zwet *et al.* (1990) reported that:

(a)   Mature Rome Beauty apples of West Virginia had developed internal fruit blight symptoms after 37 to 121 days in cold storage, "presumably from endophytic bacteria"; and

(b)   up to 21% of symptomless Red Rome fruit harvested in July and August in the State of West Virginia had endophytic bacteria; and

(c)   in a geographic survey, *E. amylovora* had been detected from the inside of 14 *symptomless* apple fruit sampled in July, August and September in the State of Utah.

4.93   Japan claimed that the United States had attempted to discount all of these findings. First, the United States dismissed (b) and (c) above, as studies on "immature fruit". For this purpose, the United States had sought clarification from Dr van der Zwet and Professor Thomson if these were made on mature fruit. However, Professor Thomson had observed in Thomson (2000) that, "[v]an der Zwet *et al.* (1990) recovered *E. amylovora* from inside mature apple fruit".[74] Moreover, in an earlier report of the same geographical survey, the authors had summarized the characteristics of the tested apples as "[m]ature, apparently healthy" apples. Furthermore, Roberts *et al.* (1998), co-authored by Dr van der Zwet, stated clearly that apple fruit harvested in Utah, West Virginia, Washington and Ontario in table 4 of van der Zwet *et al.* (1990) were mature and symptomless.

4.94   The **United States** recognized that van der Zwet (1990) had been the source of some confusion as it reported on numerous different experiments conducted in different locations without distinguishing between immature and mature fruit. However, the "Geographic Survey" experimental data, especially as later clarified by two lead authors of the paper, supported the position that mature, symptomless apples did *not* harbour internal populations of the bacterium.[75] The United States argued that the Roberts *et al.* (1998) and Thomson (2000) papers were review papers and therefore were intended to survey the literature. Inaccurate reports on the findings in van der Zwet *et al.* (1990) could not be used to establish a fact not supported by that paper, especially when efforts had been made to correct the errors of interpretation that had arisen from this work. Thomson (2000) had written: "Van der Zwet *et al.* (1990) recovered *E. amylovora* from inside mature apple fruit only when it was grown within 60 cm of visible fire blight infections." These results, however, were presented in table 3 in van der Zwet *et al.* (1990), which had clearly indicated that the fruit in question were harvested in July and August 1986 and were therefore immature apple fruit. Thus, Thomson (2000) did not provide support for Japan's assertion that van der Zwet *et al.* (1990) recovered

[74]   Op. cit., Thompson (2000).
[75]   Van der Zwet Declaration, 16 July 2002 (Exhibit USA-18) and letter from S.V. Thomson, Utah State University, to R.G. Roberts, US Department of Agriculture, 23 August 2002 (Exhibit USA-19).

endophytic *E. amylovora* from inside mature apple fruit. Dr van der Zwet himself had confirmed the immature status of these fruit in his declaration.[76]

4.95   **Japan** also stated that the United States had discounted the internal fruit blight symptoms which mature Rome Beauty apples had developed in cold storage, presumably from endophytic bacteria, by citing the article's observation that "[i]nternal fruit blight symptoms were difficult to distinguish from other fruit rots". However, the article continued: "[r]andom sampling from the surface of blighted fruit in storage resulted in recovery of *E. amylovora*". The article concluded: "[a] few uninoculated fruit of Rome Beauty stored at 1 C developed fire blight. Thus, asymptomatic fruit of a susceptible cultivar, harvested from blighted trees, may develop fire blight during commercial storage."[77] The authors explicitly stated that the developed symptoms were "fire blight".

4.96   The **United States** replied that in the 1990 paper, Dr van der Zwet had clearly stated that he could not reliably differentiate the internal decay symptoms present in the fruit as being fire blight or fungal decay. Therefore, his diagnosis of fire blight in stored fruit - in his words, "presumably" caused by endophytic bacteria – would have been validated *only* if: (1) the fruit had been assayed for the presence of endophytic bacteria before storage and such bacteria had been recovered; and (2) the internal rots had been assayed microbiologically and *E. amylovora* had been isolated. Neither condition had been satisfied according to the methods and experimental results described in the paper.

4.97   **Japan** claimed that despite attempts to revise van der Zwet *et al.* (1990), the United States had failed to deny: (1) the expression of fire blight in "mature, symptomless" apple fruit, presumably from endophytic bacteria; (2) recovery of the bacteria from core sections of apples harvested in July and August, some of which were mature; and (3) recovery of the bacteria from inside mature, apparently healthy apples harvested in July, August or September. Van der Zwet *et al.* (1990) had shown that mature apple fruit harboured the risk of endophytic *E. amylovora*. While disagreeing with this objective evaluation of the evidence, the United States admitted that the bacteria might exist inside close-to-mature apple fruit. The only way that the US claim could be compatible with the observed occurrence inside close-to-mature apple fruit would be if the bacteria disappeared during the critical few days or weeks before maturation. However, the United States had not provided a theory, much less evidence, to explain the implied disappearance of the bacteria.

4.98   The **United States** argued that in clarifying that no endophytic bacteria had been recovered from any mature fruit in any of the experiments reported in the van der Zwet *et al.* (1990) paper, the authors had merely confirmed what a careful reading of the 1990 paper suggested. The only fruit expressly described in the 1990 paper as "mature" had been those in the storage experiment reported in table 2; as the scientific experts had noted, endophytic bacteria had not been recovered from these "mature" fruit (the fruit were not even tested for internal bacteria) and thus the suspected symptoms were not confirmed as fire blight.

---

[76]   Op. cit. (Exhibit USA-18).
[77]   Op. cit., van der Zwet *et al.* (1990).

None of the fruit involved in the geographic experiment reported in table 4 were described as "mature" in the 1990 paper, and the authors had confirmed that no endophytic bacteria had been recovered from any mature or possibly mature fruit in that experiment. Thus, the 1990 paper itself did not claim that internal bacteria had been isolated from any "mature" fruit; the authors' recent statements merely confirmed that fact.

4.99   Furthermore, **Japan** argued that there was ambiguity in the concept of "maturity". "Maturity" and *"immaturity"* were part of a continuum. As such, maturity was inherently a subjective concept and could allow a variety of interpretations. Professor Thomson had determined "maturity" in terms of "commercial" maturity, or harvest dates. By doing so, in his letter of "clarification" the author pushed back the "maturity" dates so that the Utah apples tested positive in the survey would became "immature". All of those apple fruit could well have been mature under the "physiological" maturity criteria, because physiological maturity supposedly preceded commercial maturity. Furthermore, Japan strongly suspected that the authors of van der Zwet *et al.* (1990) might have considered that the apple fruit tested in the study were "physiologically mature" on the basis of the colour, firmness of the tissue, and other features they witnessed. Otherwise, it was inconceivable that the authors continued repeatedly in later publications to characterize the apples as being "mature".[78] Japan maintained that there was no evidence to show that "physiologically mature" apple fruit would further undergo a decisive process in which all endophytic bacteria would be eliminated by the time of the harvest. Any endophytic bacteria which had been found inside "physiologically" mature apple fruit were therefore likely to survive until "commercial" maturity in light of the ecology and other known properties of the bacteria and apple fruit. The "symptomless" criterion was even more difficult to manage, because there would be no objective yardstick. Japan noted that in Roberts *et al.* (1989), a study that failed to recover the fire blight bacteria from inside mature, symptomless apples, sampling was not randomized. Japan further noted that there was what it believed was agreement among the experts that the "symptom" (which must be recognized by the human eye) would be the key indicator of the risk, and that it might not be always detected. Indeed, the ambiguity/subjectivity, confirmed by the experts, was further compounded by the less-than-satisfactory practices surrounding the export of American apples. Although the United States alleged that "any infected, immature fruit would not pass through normal harvesting, sorting, and storage procedures developed and applied by growers, distributors, and exporters, and ... any infected, immature fruit would not pass through grading and inspection procedures by Federal-State inspectors, including application of the standards of the U.S. Apple Export Act", there was clear evidence to the contrary showing that the none of the safeguards (including inspection by Federal-State inspectors) worked.[79]

---

[78]   Op. cit., Thomson (2000) and Roberts *et al.* (1998).
[79]   Comments of Japan on the US answers to additional questions from the Panel, 31 January 2003, para. 7.

4.100 The **United States** contended that *E. amylovora* did not exist in mature fruit because immature fruit that became infected with fire blight would not develop to maturity, as previously described. Furthermore, there was a long-established scientific, commercial and horticultural basis for the use of the concepts of physiological and commercial maturity.[80] The United States believed the scientific experts had confirmed both of these points.

4.101 **Japan** recalled that no study had ever been conducted concerning (latent) infection of *E. amylovora* through the pedicel of apple fruit. Starting in 2002, therefore, Tsukamoto *et al.* had conducted experiments to clarify the ability of *E. amylovora* to invade and multiply through the pedicel.[81] The study provided preliminary evidence that *E. amylovora* could move and multiply in the system of the pedicel in apple fruit. Japan was of the view that the cause of the internal browning of apple fruit in this experiment was worthy of further investigation.

4.102 The **United States** commented that Japan's unsuccessful attempt to recover endophytic bacteria from apple fruit by cutting open the pedicels and inoculating them with high numbers of bacteria could not be considered an effort to obtain additional necessary information to justify its fire blight restrictions. The preliminary results reported that *E. amylovora* had *not* been found, and the browning of the fruit could have many causes. The study did not provide additional information with respect to steps in Japan's hypothetical pathway – which the experts had concluded would not be completed.

6. *Epiphytic Bacteria and Mature Apple Fruit*

4.103 The **United States** claimed that a review of the scientific literature suggested that the epiphytic presence of fire blight bacteria on mature, symptomless apple fruit at harvest was extremely rare. In those few instances when external bacteria had been detected, the fruit had been harvested from or within 10 meters of an infected tree in severely infected orchards. Thus, in most cases, mature, symptomless apples, even when harvested from infected trees or orchards, would not be externally contaminated with fire blight bacteria. The following authors had provided relevant evidence:

> Thomson (2000): "Populations of *E. amylovora* are rare on mature fruit and when present are probably due to deposition from a nearby source of active inoculum. In every case where *E. amylovora* has been detected on fruit, it has been from orchards with high levels of fire blight infection."[82]

---

[80] See, *e.g.*, A.E. Watada et al. (1984), Terminology for the Description of Developmental Stages of Horticultural Crops, *Hort Science* 19: 20-21 (Exhibit USA-41).
[81] T. Tsukamoto *et al.* (2003), "Invasion, Multiplication and Movement of *Erwinia Amylovora* in pedicel tissues of apple fruit", unpublished (Exhibits JPN-39 and JPN-42).
[82] Op. cit., Thomson (2000).

Hale and Taylor (1999): "No epiphytic fire blight bacteria were isolated from calyxes (the opposite end of the fruit from the stem) of 150 mature fruit harvested from an infected orchard."[83]

Hale *et al.* (1996): "No epiphytic fire blight bacteria were found on the calyxes and surfaces of 173 mature, symptomless apple fruit harvested from infected trees in New Zealand."[84]

Clark *et al.* (1993): "No epiphytic fire blight bacteria were detected on calyxes of 750 mature, symptomless apple fruit even from within 20 cm of inoculated blight sources (flowers) showing disease symptoms."[85]

van der Zwet *et al.* (1991): "No epiphytic fire blight bacteria were detected on surfaces or calyxes of apple fruit from six susceptible cultivars from blighted orchards in West Virginia, USA."[86]

van der Zwet *et al.* (1990): "No epiphytic bacteria were recovered from 80 mature, symptomless apple fruit from West Virginia, USA, 40 possibly mature fruit from Washington, USA, and 80 possibly mature fruit from Ontario, Canada; of 40 possibly mature fruit from Utah, USA, harvested in a severely blighted orchard, only 1 contained epiphytic bacteria in the calyx. No epiphytic bacteria were detected after storage on any of 160 mature, symptomless fruit from Washington State, USA. Epiphytic bacteria were recovered after storage from 5 of 175 mature, presumably symptomless fruit harvested within 10 meters of infection in severely blighted orchards in West Virginia, USA."[87]

Roberts *et al.* (1989): "No epiphytic fire blight bacteria were detected on the surfaces of 1,555 mature, symptomless apple fruit harvested from blighted (in some cases, severely blighted) trees of seven apple cultivars grown at five locations in Washington, USA."[88]

Sholberg (1988): "Epiphytic bacteria were detected on approximately 18-54 (the actual number was not given) of 54 mature, presumably symptomless apples harvested from a severely blighted orchard (including severely infected pear trees)."[89]

---

[83] C.N. Hale and R.K. Taylor (1999), "Effect of Cold Storage on Survival of *Erwinia amylovora* in Apple Calyxes", *Acta Horticulturae* 489, pp. 139-43 (infected orchard had less than five strikes per tree).

[84] C.N. Hale *et al.* (1996), "Ecology and epidemiology of fire blight in New Zealand", *Acta Horticulturae* 411, pp. 79-85.

[85] R.G. Clark *et al.* (1993), "A DNA Approach to Erwinia amylovora Detection in Large Scale Apple Testing and in Epidemiological Studies", *Acta Horticulturae* 338, pp. 59-66 (Exhibit JPN-25).

[86] van der Zwet *et al.* (1991), "Evaluation of calyx tissues of several apple cultivars for the presence of Erwinia amylovora", *Phytopathology* 81, p. 1194 (no indication of numbers of fruit tested).

[87] Op. cit., van der Zwet *et al.* (1990).

[88] Op. cit., Roberts *et al.* (1989).

[89] P.L. Sholberg *et al.* (1988), "Occurrence of Erwinia amylovora of pome fruit in British Columbia in 1985 and its elimination from the apple surface", *Canadian Journal of Plant Pathology* 10: 178-82, 180 tbl. 2 (Exhibit JPN-37). Epiphytic bacteria detected from fruit harvested from "severely damaged" orchard in which "[a]lmost every . . . apple tree was infected" after August hail storm).

> Hale *et al.* (1987): "Epiphytic bacteria were detected in the calyxes of 3 out of 2,100 mature, symptomless fruit harvested in New Zealand, and only from severely infected trees in a severely blighted orchard; no isolations were made from fruit harvested from moderately blighted orchards."[90]

> Dueck (1974): "No external bacteria were isolated from any of 60 mature, symptomless apple fruit harvested in Ontario, Canada, from severely infected trees. The report concluded: "Furthermore, apples from severely infected trees of a susceptible cultivar, having been exposed to high levels of inoculum during the growing season, were free of the bacterium at harvest time".[91]

The United States believed that the scientific experts had unanimously agreed that epiphytic calyx populations on mature apple fruit would only rarely occur when fruit were harvested from orchards with severe fire blight and with nearby active sources of inoculum.

4.104 **Japan** agreed that epiphytic bacteria sometimes existed on the surface including the calyx – a part that was difficult to disinfect – of "mature, symptomless" apple fruit. However, Japan did not agree with the conclusion that the external presence of the bacteria was extremely rare. Sholberg *et al.* (1988), for example, clearly stated that "*E. amylovora* may be present on symptomless fruit at harvest under certain conditions".[92]

4.105 The **United States** argued that the rarity of external contamination of mature, symptomless apple fruit was a logical consequence of the biology of the fire blight bacteria and the disease cycle. Bacteria were most prevalent in infected hosts during the spring, when blossoms were present. The bacterial inoculum that exuded in warm, wet conditions from infected shoots, cankers, infected fruit and blossoms might infect new hosts via blossoms as well as other natural plant openings. However, as conditions in the orchard became less hospitable (hotter and drier) and the opportunities for new infections (and, hence, the bacterium's reproductive chances through blossoms and other openings) diminished during the apple fruit growing season, the bacteria showed a marked decline in population counts, becoming extremely rare on fruit by the time of harvest. The scientific evidence indicated that bacteria on the surface of fruit died within a short time. Thus, on those rare instances in which external populations had been detected, this was probably due to deposition from a nearby source of active fire blight.

Although the precise number of positive fruit was not given, the United States had calculated (based on the experimental methods used) that 18-54 fruit could have been positive.

[90] C.N. Hale *et al.* (1987), "Occurrence of Erwinia amylovora on apple fruit in New Zealand", *Acta Horticulturae* 217, pp. 33- 40, at 37 (fruit harvested from severely blighted, lightly infected, and fire blight-free orchards) (Exhibit JPN-8).

[91] Op. cit., Dueck (1974).

[92] Op. cit., Sholberg *et al.* (1988).

7. Scientific Evidence and the Steps in Japan's Systems Approach

4.106 The **United States** argued that the Japanese prohibition on the importation of US apples unless all nine fire blight requirements or restrictions were met was not supported by scientific evidence. In addition, as mature, symptomless apple fruit were not a pathway for the disease, imported US apple fruit did not pose a phytosanitary risk to plant life or health within Japan, and each of the specific restrictions imposed by the Japanese measures had no basis in science.

4.107 **Japan** countered that its plant quarantine measure against fire blight was a "systemic approach", which ensured conditions that would not allow the presence of fire blight bacteria either outside or inside of apple fruit shipped to Japan. This approach was consistent with the relevant international standards of the IPPC and each component of the systems approach was supported by scientific evidence.

(i) Prohibition of Imported Apples from Orchards in which any Fire Blight is Detected

4.108 The **United States** noted that Japan prohibited any fruit from a "designated" export orchard in which fire blight had been detected. Japan deemed any occurrence of fire blight, no matter how severe or light, in an orchard to pose an unacceptable risk of transmitting fire blight on any fruit from that orchard. Depending on the size of the orchard, Japan's orchard freedom requirement could prohibit fruit from being exported that was harvested tens, hundreds, or thousands of meters away from a single, lightly infected fire blight host (for example, an apple tree with a single, inactive canker) that might have exhibited symptoms many months before harvest (for example, one blighted blossom or shoot). Such an indeterminate restriction bore no rational or objective relationship to the scientific evidence.

4.109 **Japan** argued that designation of a fire blight-free area was an essential element of its "systemic approach". Japan's requirement was in line with the Requirements for the Establishment of Pest Free Places of Production and Pest Free Production Sites of the IPPC (ISPM 10). This standard defined a "pest free place of production" as:

> "[A] place of production in which a specific pest does not occur as demonstrated by scientific evidence and in which, where appropriate, this condition is being officially maintained for a defined period."[93]

The IPPC requirements further provided that:

> "[The pest free place of production] provides a means for an exporting country, if so required by an importing country, to

---

[93] *International Standard for Phytosanitary Measures No.10: Requirements for the Establishment of Pest Free Places of Production and Pest Free Production Sites*, FAO, Rome 1999 (Exhibit JPN-24).

ensure that consignments of plants, plant products or other regulated articles produced on, and/or moved from, the place of production are free from the pest concerned."[94]

4.110 Japan observed that the efficacy of the fire blight-free area was demonstrated by a variety of scientific studies that reported the relative absence of endophytic and epiphytic bacteria in symptomless apples that were harvested from blight-free orchards.[95] This was particularly the case in Europe, where many countries favoured a fire blight-free area and a number of countries required the growing of host plants in fire blight-free areas.[96] The distance between a harvested apple and an infected fire blight host depended on the scale of the orchard; variation in this distance would occur whenever a pest free area was designated.

4.111 The **United States** contended that the use of pest-free places of production or pest-free production sites might be appropriately used to manage the risk identified with a particular pathway. However, the scientific evidence demonstrated that mature apple fruit did not serve as a pathway for the introduction of fire blight. Thus, the conditions for establishing pest free places of production or production sites were not relevant to ensuring that imported fruit were disease-free and did not transmit fire blight. The United States also noted that under US law and regulations, exported apple fruit must be disease-free (symptomless).[97] Thus, even if fire blight disease was present in a production site or area, exported mature apple fruit did not facilitate the introduction of *E. amylovora* to new areas.

4.112 **Japan** noted that the experts advising the Panel had all agreed that it would be reasonable to require that imported apples come from a fire blight-free orchard.

4.113 The **United States** observed that certain experts had expressed views on what restrictions might be "reasonable" within the context of attempting to forge a "compromise" between the parties' views, to provide "transition time" for Japan to phase-in relaxed measures, to avoid "squeez[ing] Japan" into eliminating its fire blight measures, and to propose measures that Japan might adopt until Japan had "confidence" to liberalize further. These comments were made in the context of Japan's follow-up questions at the experts' session, which were phrased in terms of what would be "reasonable" and not in terms of "what is the content of the scientific evidence". Thus, Japan had invited the experts to comment on matters beyond their expertise and mandate – that was, to provide scientific and technical advice on the scientific evidence relating to fire blight and exported apple fruit.

---

[94]   *Ibid.*
[95]   See, e.g., Hale *et al.* (1987), van der Zwet *et al.* (1990), Clark, *et al.* (1993).
[96]   EPPO Standards; Phytosanitary Procedures, *Erwinia amylovora,* Sampling and Test Methods (1992) (Exhibit JPN-26).
[97]   See footnote 46.

(ii)   Prohibition of Imported Apples from any Orchard should Fire Blight be Detected within a 500-Meter Buffer Zone Surrounding the Orchard

4.114 The **United States** recalled that the Japanese fire blight measures established that a "designated" export orchard had to be surrounded by a 500-meter buffer zone. If any fire blight was detected in the 500-meter buffer zone, no fruit from the designated export orchard could be exported to Japan. Given that there was no scientific evidence that mature, symptomless apple fruit were a pathway for the introduction of fire blight, even if the fruit were picked from highly infected trees, there was obviously no evidence to support a requirement for such a buffer zone. According to the Unites States, the scientific experts had confirmed that buffer zones surrounding orchards, which might be appropriate in fire blight-eradication efforts and in measures to ensure fire blight-freedom for nurseries of fire blight host plants, were not relevant with respect to contamination of mature apple fruit.

4.115 **Japan** stated that the necessity of establishing a buffer zone was recognized by ISPM 10.[98] If a blighted tree were found in the buffer zone, the designation as a pest-free place of production would be cancelled. Following the IPPC recommendations, Japan considered that the width of the buffer zone had to be determined on the basis of the distance over which the pest was likely to spread naturally during the course of the growing season. The requirement of a 500-meter buffer zone was supported by the scientific evidence, *inter alia*: (1) *E. amylovora* had been isolated in a monitoring survey in Belgium at a point 250 meters away from the inoculum source in wet weather, and was detected 1 kilometer away by the indirect immunofluorescence method; and (2) a large-scale experiment over five seasons in New Zealand had not detected the bacteria at the calyx end of 60,000 apples when the orchards were surrounded by a 500-meter buffer zone.[99]

4.116 Japan further observed that international practice since the 1970s also supported the introduction of a buffer zone of this size. For example, EPPO's quarantine requirements for *E. amylovora* provided that "countries which consider themselves to be at high risk can specify that the [pest-free seedling] field, as well as the surrounding zone of radius of at least 250 meters, must be inspected at least once in July/August and once in September/October and that spot checks should be carried out in the surrounding zone of radius of at least 1 kilometer in places where host plants are grown, at least once in July/October".[100] Germany required that if an infection of fire blight was found, "diseased plant material and plants surrounding these places are destroyed

---

[98]   "Where the biology of the pest is such that it is likely to enter the place of production or production site from adjacent areas, it is necessary to define a buffer zone around the place of production or production site within which appropriate phytosanitary measures are applied." Op. cit., ISPM 10, para. 1.1.

[99]   J. van Vaerenbergh *et al.* (1987), "Monitoring fireblight for official phytosanitary legislation in Belgium", *EPPO Bulletin* 17, pp. 195-203, at 198 and Clark *et al.* (1993), p. 62.

[100]   EPPO, *supra* n. 85.

immediately over a radius of 500 meters".[101] In the Netherlands, host plants of *E. amylovora* within 500 meters around the nuclear stock plots and the multiplication fields of source-material were removed.[102] These practices reflected recognition of a risk of spread of the disease within the range of several hundred meters.

4.117 The **United States** argued that none of the examples cited by Japan was pertinent. Obviously, a report of 250-meter dispersal did not support a 500-meter buffer requirement. More importantly, the report referenced by Japan contained serious flaws and was of limited (if any) relevance to bacterial presence in, or on, mature, symptomless apple fruit. In particular, the study by J. van Vaerenbergh *et al.* (1987), was based on a test that detected dead as well as live bacteria and had failed to confirm that the "dispersed" bacteria were of the same strain as the bacteria found on the source (and therefore not from some *other* fire blight host in the area). Furthermore, the EPPO requirements were part of a fire blight eradication programme, not a programme to address any risk of fire blight transmission on imported fruit. The risk of transmission of fire blight was known to be much greater for plants than for mature, symptomless fruit, and trade in plants required significantly different measures than trade in fruit.[103]

4.118 **Japan** maintained that dead cells were unlikely to stay responsive to test techniques for a long period of time, and no such other sources had been identified in the survey; therefore it was reasonable to assume that live bacteria from the source were detected in the survey. Japan also argued that the buffer zone requirement of EPPO was for the purpose of ensuring that host plants were grown in a disease-free environment – which was exactly the purpose of its "systemic approach".

(iii)   Inspection of Orchards Three Times Yearly

4.119 The **United States** recalled that along with the requirements that an orchard and a 500-meter buffer zone surrounding such orchard be free of fire blight, Japan required that the orchard and buffer zone be inspected at least three times yearly, at the blossom, fruitlet (small fruit), and harvest seasons. Further inspections could be required following strong storms, such as hailstorms. However, the scientific evidence indicated that fire blight bacteria had only rarely been detected on the outside of mature, symptomless apple fruit harvested from, or within 10 meters of, severely infected trees in severely blighted orchards. Only a harvest season inspection that detected severely blighted orchards might be relevant to the likelihood that there could be fire blight bacteria on the surface of mature, symptomless apple fruit. However, even that

---

[101] W. Zeller (1987), Present Status of Fireblight in the Federal Republic of Germany, *EPPO Bulletin* 17, pp. 223-224 (Exhibit JPN-27).

[102] C.A.R. Meijneke (1979), "Prevention and Control of Fireblight", *EPPO Bulletin* 9(1), pp. 53-62 (Exhibit JPN-19).

[103] EPPO recommends "countries at high risk to prohibit importation of host plants for planting" but does *not* recommend restrictions on importation of fruit, *supra* n. 5.

inspection was unnecessary because there was no scientific evidence that mature, symptomless apple fruit transmitted the bacteria.

4.120 **Japan** claimed that field inspections were necessary to ensure the efficacy of the "systemic approach". The IPPC requirements provided:

> "The verification of pest free status is done by [national plant protection authorities] personnel ... who undertake specific surveys to assess the pest free status of the place of production ... (and the buffer zone, if required). These most often take the form of field inspections ... Pest free status may be verified by a stated number or frequency of inspections or tests (e.g., three inspections at monthly intervals) ... Monitoring surveys should be conducted at adequate frequency over one or more growing seasons [in the buffer zone]."[104]

It was not feasible to confirm the absence of fire blight symptoms in each tree in an orchard, and there was always a risk that detection errors might occur. Inspection at blossom stage was appropriate because this was when trees were most susceptible to fire blight infection, whereas it was at fruitlet stage that the symptoms were most readily detectable. According to the relevant literature: (1) the flower had the highest susceptibility to fire blight; (2) the shoots and leaves were actively growing at the fruitlet stage and the symptoms of fire blight were easily observed; and (3) the activity of *E. amylovora* was high during these two stages. Moreover, the typical symptom of fire blight (exudation of bacterial ooze) appeared during these seasons.

4.121 The **United States** observed that the blossom and fruitlet surveys would not reveal some instances of harvest season fire blight because fire blight bacteria might infect new hosts after the small fruit season or the disease might express itself in an already infected host.

4.122 **Japan** considered that a third inspection at the harvest stage was required exactly because infection could still occur after the fruitlet stage, as the mechanism of invasion of *E. amylovora* inside apple fruit was not known, and bacteria survived inside the fruit or at the calyx end.

4.123 The **United States** argued that detecting all instances of fire blight in an orchard was irrelevant to the question of whether bacteria would be present on mature, symptomless apple fruit. There was no scientific evidence that the presence of fire blight at the blossom or fruitlet stages affected the likelihood that fire blight bacteria would be found on mature, symptomless apple fruit. Thus, the three inspections requirement bore no rational or objective relation to the scientific evidence.

4.124 **Japan** maintained that three inspections were the minimum requirement in order to confirm that fire blight had not occurred in export orchards throughout the season, and the timing of these inspections was set at the three stages most suitable for detection of symptoms. The US argument erred in its refusal to acknowledge detection errors. In addition, it was probable for the

---

[104] Op. cit., ISPM 10, para. 2.2.3.

symptoms at early stages to be pruned out, so only one inspection at harvest stage could never ensure the fire blight-free status of the orchard.

(iv) Prohibition of Imported Apples Unless Treated with Chlorine

4.125 The **United States** recalled that Japan prohibited the importation of any apple fruit that had not been treated by immersing the fruit for one minute in a tank containing 100 parts per million free chlorine. While there was scientific evidence relating to the effect of chlorine on populations of fire blight bacteria, there was not a rational or objective relationship between Japan's chlorine treatment requirement and the scientific evidence that mature, symptomless apple fruit were not a pathway for the fire blight disease.

4.126 **Japan** argued that the surface of harvested apple fruit could be infected by *E. amylovora*, after harvest during the transportation, washing, selection and other steps. As previously noted, numerous studies had detected the bacteria on the surface of apples.[105] Therefore, the surface of harvested apple fruit needed to be sterilized.

4.127 The **United States** did not contend that there was not scientific evidence of the efficacy of a chlorine treatment in reducing external bacterial populations. This evidence, however, did not support any measures on harvested mature, symptomless apple fruit since there was no evidence that mature, symptomless apple fruit transmitted the fire blight disease.

4.128 **Japan** observed that the United States accepted the efficacy of the chlorine treatment and the existence of scientific reports that detected epiphytic bacteria. Nevertheless, the United States rejected disinfection because apples had not been shown (presumably by direct or documented evidence) to be a pathway. In Japan's view, this conclusion was the outcome of an erroneous interpretation of the burden of proof.

(v) Prohibition of Imported Apples from US States other than Washington or Oregon

4.129 The **United States** recalled that Japan prohibited the importation of US fruit other than fruit produced in designated export orchards within the States of Washington or Oregon. The US requests that Japan expand the list of states eligible to export apple fruit had been to no avail. The United States argued that Japan had presented no evidence to support its limitation of imported US apples to Washington or Oregon fruit.

4.130 **Japan** contended that there was nothing arbitrary about permitting only the orchards in the States of Washington and Oregon to export apples to Japan. The reasons were that (1) the US initial request was only for these states, and (2) the United States had submitted a proposal of phytosanitary measures that would

---

[105] Op. cit., van der Zwet *et al.* (1990); Sholberg *et al.* (1988).

prevent the introduction of *E. amylovora* into Japan only for apple fruit produced in Washington and Oregon.

4.131 The **United States** claimed that the scientific evidence established that mature, symptomless apple fruit - regardless of origin - were not a pathway for the disease. As there was no scientific evidence that mature, symptomless apple fruit transmitted the disease, the prohibition of US apples from states other than Washington or Oregon was not rationally or objectively related to the scientific evidence.

4.132 **Japan** noted that the current phytosanitary requirements regarding fire blight were applicable to apple fruit produced in other states, and it was possible to import those apple fruit under the same conditions. However, the United States had not submitted documentation that described the status of other quarantine pests in states other than Washington and Oregon. Consequently, the existence of other quarantine pests in other states was not known. If the United States could certify the absence of other pests, or if it proposed a measure that was suitable for preventing the introduction of these pests, Japan would accept shipments of apples from other states under the same conditions as for Washington and Oregon.

> (vi)   Prohibition of Imported Apples unless Other Production, Harvesting, and Importation Requirements Are Met

4.133 The **United States** recalled that Japan prohibited the importation of US apples unless other harvesting, production, and importation requirements were also met. These included the chlorine treatment of containers for harvesting, chlorine treatment of the packing site, and post-harvest separation of apples for export to Japan from apples for other destinations. None of these requirements bore a rational or objective relation to the scientific evidence. According to the United States, the scientific experts had not identified any scientific evidence that contamination of mature apple fruit after harvest would occur through harvesting, packing storage, or transport.

4.134 **Japan** claimed that the chlorine treatment of containers was necessary to avoid contamination of fruit by contaminated harvest containers. As fruit containers (cargo crates) were suspected to be the cause of introduction of fire blight into the United Kingdom, the sterilization of containers for harvest was necessary to prevent introduction of *E. amylovora*. Chlorine treatment of the packing site was a safety measure to prevent contamination of fruit by packing line equipment.

4.135 The **United States** noted that the chlorine treatment of containers for harvesting was apparently based on a scientific study that presented circumstantial, not scientific, evidence that contaminated fruit boxes could have been a source of inoculum.[106] This same study also stated that the likelihood that fire blight was transmitted via infected fruit "is very slight and can probably be

---

[106]   R. A. Lelliot (1959), "Fire Blight of Pears in England", *Agriculture* 65, pp. 564-568.

ignored".[107] According to the United States, the experts had agreed that there was no scientific evidence that fruit cargo crates might spread fire blight. The United States was of the view that Dr Smith had remarked that even the idea that *E. amylovora* could survive on crates as ooze for any significant time is quite conjectural (let alone be transmitted from them).

4.136 The United States argued that Japan simply had not presented any supporting evidence of contamination in the packing facility.[108] The same was true with respect to Japan's requirement that apples destined for Japan be kept separated from fruit for other destinations. The United States was not aware of any evidence that supported these measures, hence there could be no rational relationship between these requirements and evidence which did not exist.

4.137 **Japan** contended that separation of fresh apple fruit for Japan from other fruit was necessary to prevent the former from being contaminated by *E. amylovora* after harvest. Japan argued that the US counter-argument rested solely on its rejection of any evidence other than "direct" evidence, a position for that there was no textual support in the *SPS Agreement*.

F.   Article 5.1

1.   General

4.138 The **United States** claimed that Japan's fire blight measures were not "based on" a risk assessment within the meaning of Article 5.1 and Annex A and therefore were inconsistent with Article 5.1 of the *SPS Agreement*. As the Appellate Body had noted in *Australia - Salmon*, to be consistent with Article 5.1 a risk assessment had to: "(1) identify the diseases whose entry, establishment or spread a Member wants to prevent within its territory, as well as the potential biological and economic consequences associated with the entry, establishment or spread of these diseases; (2) evaluate the likelihood of entry, establishment or spread of these diseases, as well as the associated potential biological and economic consequences; and (3) evaluate the likelihood of entry, establishment or spread of these diseases according to the SPS measures which might be applied."[109]

4.139 **Japan** maintained that in line with its obligations under this provision, it had performed two full pest risk analyses: the first in 1996 and a second in 1999.[110] The 1999 PRA in particular had been performed specifically on US apples and was fully consistent with the International Standards for Phytosanitary Measures No. 2: Guidelines for Pest Risk Analysis (hereinafter "ISPM 2" or the "1996 Guidelines").[111]

---

[107]   *Ibid.*
[108]   US first submission, para. 62.
[109]   Appellate Body Report in *Australia – Salmon*, para. 121.
[110]   "Pest Risk Analysis concerning Fire Blight Pathogen (*Erwinia amylovora*), Ministry of Agriculture, Forestry and Fisheries, Japan, 1996 (the "1996 PRA") (Exhibit JPN-31); and the 1999 PRA, op. cit.
[111]   Op. cit., ISPM 2.

2. Evaluation of the Likelihood of Entry, Establishment or Spread

4.140 The **United States** did not contend that Japan's 1999 PRA had not fulfilled the first requirement under Article 5.1 - it had identified fire blight as the disease whose entry, establishment or spread Japan wanted to prevent within its territory as well as potential associated biological and economic consequences. However, the 1999 PRA had not fulfilled either of the two remaining requirements. Japan had failed to focus on the scientific evidence relating to the importation of apple fruit, making only general statements of possibility rather than an assessment of the likelihood, or probability, of entry, establishment or spread. The Appellate Body in *Australia – Salmon* had stated that "for a risk assessment to fall within the meaning of Article 5.1 and the first definition in paragraph 4 of Annex A, it was not sufficient that [it] conclude that there is a possibility of entry, establishment, or spread of diseases". Further, the Appellate Body in *Australia – Salmon* had concluded that the second requirement for a risk assessment under Article 5.1 would not be met when the assessment made "general and vague statements of mere possibility of adverse effects occurring; statements which constitute neither a quantitative nor a qualitative assessment of probability."[112]

4.141 **Japan** considered that the 1999 PRA was based on plain, undisputable logic. No one could challenge the likelihood of dissemination of the disease once it was introduced into the country. The 1999 PRA had addressed not a theoretical possibility but the likelihood of the introduction and spread of fire blight through apple fruit. The Appellate Body had clearly established that risk assessments did not have to take the form of a quantitative analysis. Furthermore, it appeared to Japan that the United States was faulting the 1999 PRA because the analysis had not reached the conclusion the United States desired to see – that "mature, symptomless" apples did not disseminate the disease. No case could, however, be established against a risk assessment on such a basis.

4.142 The **United States** contended that the fact that the Japanese Pest Risk Analysis had not evaluated the likelihood or probability of entry was evident from its fundamental failure to identify and discuss those scientific studies that were relevant to the apples to be imported. A proper focus on studies relevant to mature, symptomless fruit would have allowed Japan to begin to assess the probability of imported US apples being infected or infested with fire blight bacteria. Instead, Japan presented the results of studies on, *inter alia*, immature fruit, visibly infected or damaged fruit, artificially wounded and inoculated fruit in storage, visibly infected fruit left on trees, apple leaves, and pear fruit. Indeed, the 1999 PRA had explicitly dismissed certain evidence on the basis that it related "only" to "symptomless" or "healthy looking" fruit that is "mature."[113] However, this was the very fruit that the United States sought to export to Japan and for which Japan had to assess risk.

---

[112] Appellate Body Report in *Australia - Salmon,* paras. 123 and 129.
[113] Op. cit., the 1999 PRA, para. 1-1, p. 6.

4.143 **Japan** observed that the 1999 PRA had taken into account all available evidence that related not only to apple trees but mature and immature, visibly blighted and symptomless apple fruit - including van der Zwet *et al.* (1990).[114]

4.144 The **United States** also argued that Japan's 1999 PRA had not evaluated the likelihood of entry because it failed to describe fully the steps that had to be completed for entry of the bacteria. The International Standards for Phytosanitary Measures No. 11: Pest Risk Analysis for Quarantine Pests (hereinafter "ISPM 11" or the "2001 Guidelines") laid out the steps that comprised an evaluation of the probability of entry: (1) identification of relevant pathways; (2) the probability of the pest being associated with the pathway at origin; (3) the probability of survival of the pest during transport or storage; (4) the probability of the pest surviving existing pest management procedures; and (5) the probability of transfer of the pest to a suitable host.[115]

4.145 **Japan** observed that its 1999 PRA had been undertaken before the adoption of ISPM 11, and could therefore be based only on the 1996 Guidelines. However, the 2001 Guidelines were developed from the 1996 Guidelines, and both had substantially the same framework. For this reason, Japan had not considered it necessary to review the 1999 PRA after the adoption of the 2001 Guidelines. Moreover, Article 5.1 provided "Members shall ensure that their … phytosanitary measures are based on an assessment…of the risks to …plant life or health, taking into account risk assessment techniques developed by the relevant international organizations." Therefore, the obligation of an importing Member was to "take into account", not to "strictly follow", such risk assessment techniques.

4.146 The **United States** argued that since there was no scientific evidence that apple fruit had ever introduced or spread fire blight, apple fruit might then only pose a risk of introduction of fire blight to Japan if there was scientific evidence that fruit were a pathway for introduction. Japan had not identified each step necessary for imported apple fruit to serve as a hypothetical pathway. Neither had Japan cited scientific evidence to establish that each step of the hypothetical pathway would be completed – understandably, since there was not scientific evidence to support each step.

4.147 The United States claimed that identification of each step necessary for imported apple fruit to serve as a hypothetical pathway was not difficult using the five steps identified in ISPM 11, above. Applying these evaluative steps to the case of *E. amylovora* and apple fruit, it was possible to identify the actual steps that had to be completed for imported apple fruit to serve as a pathway for the disease. These steps were: (1) apple fruit had to be externally or internally contaminated with fire blight bacteria; (2) the bacteria had to survive harvest, commercial handling, and storage conditions; (3) the bacteria had to survive transport (including cool storage), handling, and discard conditions (including consumption); (4) the apple fruit had to be discarded near a host plant; (5) the host had to be at a receptive stage (i.e., able to be infected); (6) the bacteria had

---

[114] Op. cit.
[115] Op. cit., ISPM 11.

to be transferred from the discarded, contaminated fruit to a susceptible host; and (7) suitable conditions had to exist for infection to occur and fire blight to develop.[116]

4.148 **Japan** contended that the 1999 PRA had identified the steps in the pathway necessary for fire blight to be disseminated via mature, apparently healthy apple fruit imported from the United States. The steps in the pathway of dissemination by bacterial ooze, and the relevant scientific evidence relating to these steps were:

(i)   Mature, apparently healthy apple fruit that had *E. amylovora* inside or in the calyx were harvested in the United States (van der Zwet *et al.* 1990, Hale *et al.* 1987).

(ii)   *E. amylovora* inside or in the calyx of mature, apparently healthy apple fruit survived through cold storage and transport (van der Zwet *et al.* 1990).

(iii)   Mature, apparently healthy apple fruit were imported and sold in retail shops in Japan.

(iv)   Either internal fruit blight was discovered in households etc., and infected apple fruit were discarded as garbage, and were transported by large birds (crows, etc.) from garbage dumps to hedges, roadside trees such as hawthorn, cotoneaster, etc. or to orchards near cities (often garbage dumps were located near hedges or roadside trees in many cases); OR

(v)   People went to the suburbs for leisure bringing apple fruit, and apple fruit with blighted cores were discarded after eating.

(vi)   Under the warm and humid weather conditions of Japan, bacterial ooze exuded from discarded apple fruit in the fields (Thomson 1992, Smith *et al.* 1986).

(vii)   Bacterial ooze adhered to the beaks or legs of small birds (Schroth *et al.* 1974, Seidal *et al.* 1994); AND/OR bacterial ooze adhered to the mouths and legs of insects (flies, ants, etc.). (Thomson *et al.* 1992, van der Zwet and Keil 1979); AND/OR wind and rain dispersed aerosol that contained bacterial ooze (van der Zwet. 1994).

(viii) Fire blight bacteria, which existed in bacterial ooze adhering to small birds or insects, or in aerosol, invaded into susceptible organs (flowers etc.) or scars of pear or apple trees in commercial orchards, and the pear or apple trees became a primary inoculum source; AND/OR the fire blight bacteria invaded into susceptible organs (flowers etc.) or scars of susceptible host plants (hedges, road trees, etc.), and the plants became primary inoculum sources (Thomson 1992, van der Zwet 1994, Schroth *et al.* 1974).

---

[116] These steps are closely related to the linear model presented in Roberts *et al.* (1998), but break out two of the nodes in that model into sub-parts. See Roberts *et al.* (1998), pp. 19-28, at 24-25.

4.149 Japan also maintained that the 1996 Guidelines did not require each step of a pathway to be supported by scientific evidence. On the contrary, the Guidelines stated that "[p]otential pathways which may not currently exist should be assessed if known".

4.150 The **United States** argued that it had reviewed Japan's 1999 PRA and had not been able to find a description of any hypothetical pathway that identified the various steps that would need to be completed in order for imported apple fruit to serve as a pathway. The United States maintained that, in fact, the scientific evidence demonstrated that steps in this hypothetical pathway would not be completed. For example, the United States believed that the scientific experts had confirmed that there was no scientific evidence that endophytic (internal) fire blight bacteria had been recovered from mature apple fruit harvested from an orchard. Nor, as the United States believed the scientific experts had unanimously confirmed, was there any scientific evidence that "mature, apparently healthy but infected fruit" (steps (iv), (v) and (vi)) existed; rather, this appeared to be a conjectural creation by Japan. The citation to van der Zwet *et al.* (1990) did not provide "[e]vidence of *E. amylovora* infection with apple fruit" (or, more precisely, with "mature" apple fruit, the hypothetical pathway) because there was no experiment reported in that paper establishing that *E. amylovora* was the cause of fire blight infection in any mature, harvested fruit. While Hale *et al.* (1987) recovered epiphytic bacteria from the calyxes of a small number of fruit harvested from a severely blighted orchard (but recovered no bacteria from any fruit harvested from moderately blighted orchards), the paper provided no evidence that epiphytic bacteria could infect a harvested, mature fruit or that there could exist any "mature, apparently healthy, but infected fruit". Moreover, the United States believed that the scientific experts had unanimously stated that there was no scientific evidence that any epiphytic calyx populations can infect a mature apple fruit. Finally, the cited studies by Thomson (1992) and Smith *et al.* (1986) related to cankers and to infected, immature fruit and thus did not provide any evidence that a harvested mature fruit might be infected or that "mature, apparently healthy but infected" fruit existed.

4.151 **Japan** contested the US conclusion that the external presence of the bacteria was "extremely rare". Sholberg *et al.* (1988), for example, clearly stated that "*E. amylovora* might be present on symptomless fruit at harvest under certain conditions" and van der Zwet *et al.* (1990) had shown that mature apple fruit harbor risk of endophytic *E. amylovora*. Japan noted that the United States admitted that the bacteria might exist inside close-to-mature apple fruit. The only way that the US claim could be compatible with the observed occurrence inside close-to-mature apple fruit was if the bacteria would disappear in the critical few days or weeks of maturing. However, the United States did not even provide a theory, not to mention evidence, to explain the disappearance.

4.152 The **United States** indicated that even in the rare instance in which mature, symptomless fruit might be externally contaminated, such external populations of fire blight would die off rapidly because the bacteria were vulnerable to environmental conditions and not suited to external survival (other than on stigmas of developing flowers). The 1999 PRA did not present any evidence relating to the probability of survival of fire blight bacteria during commercial handling, storage, and transport (steps 2, 3, and 4 of the 2001 Guidelines for evaluating the probability of entry). Rather, the scientific evidence established that any surviving epiphytic bacteria were extremely unlikely to survive harvest, commercial handling, storage, transport, retail distribution, consumption and discard. In fact, the effect of cool storage alone (for example, through the 55-day mandatory cold treatment Japan required on US apples for codling moth) made probability of survival of any epiphytic bacteria very unlikely.[117] Furthermore, as the United States believed the scientific experts had unanimously confirmed, there was simply no scientific evidence of the existence of a vector or the probability of the transfer of any hypothetically surviving bacteria from a discarded fruit to a susceptible host (step 5 of the 2001 Guidelines). Thus, the scientific evidence established that apple fruit did not serve as a pathway because the necessary steps would not be completed.

4.153 **Japan** countered that the storage experiment of van der Zwet *et al.* (1990) had shown that mature Rome Beauty apples of West Virginia had developed internal fruit blight symptoms after 37 to 121 days in cold storage, "presumably from endophytic bacteria". The study concluded "A few uninoculated fruit of Rome Beauty stored at 1° C developed fire blight. Thus, asymptomatic fruit of a susceptible cultivar, harvested from blighted trees, may develop fire blight during commercial storage." While the 1999 PRA had not explicitly referred to this article, the analysis did take it into account in examining the section entitled "probability of introduction into Japan by normal transport method". Furthermore, the 1999 PRA considered that latent *E. amylovora* inside apparently healthy apple fruit could not be discovered by visual inspection. Neither could *E. amylovora* inside apple fruit be disinfected by the surface chlorine treatment nor be eliminated by "normal commercial fruit handling (such as removal of trash, sorting, rinsing, grading, and packing)".

4.154 In addition, Japan indicated that the 1999 PRA had discussed the issue of transfer to a suitable host and concluded that "In the course of the distribution, processing and consumption, some [fresh fruit] can be released to the natural environment as leftovers, waste or useless materials".[118] As a matter of common sense, it could easily be envisaged that surviving *E. amylovora*, either inside or outside apple fruit, could be transmitted to nearby host plants, either by way of rain, wind, insects, etc. Once such fruit were introduced into Japan, bacteria would be exposed to the environment at all stages of distribution, storage, consumption and disposal of the fruit, causing a real risk of dissemination. Japan

---

[117] In its first submission, the United States made reference to a large-scale study (Hale and Taylor (1999) that had examined the survival of fire blight bacteria on fruit subject to normal commercial cooling and storing by surface-inoculating fruit with varying numbers of bacteria and measuring surviving bacteria after storage. Under both "commercial conditions" and "laboratory conditions", the study had found that, of 570 inoculated fruit, bacteria had been eliminated on all but two fruit after storage for 25 days at cool temperatures and 14 days at room temperature. Bacteria were only isolated from some of the fruit that had been inoculated with extremely large numbers of bacteria - levels far higher than those that have been found on harvested mature, symptomless fruit.

[118] Op. cit., the 1999 PRA.

considered that one should envisage complex, intertwined potential pathways from imported fruit to an orchard, as suggested by the 2001 Guidelines. Japan noted that the 2001 Guidelines stated that "[p]otential pathways, which may not currently exist, should be assessed", and that "[e]stimation of the probability of introduction of a pest ... involves many uncertainties ... this estimation is an extrapolation from the situation where the pest occurs to the hypothetical situation."

4.155 The **United States** noted that there was no scientific evidence of any vector to transfer any hypothetically surviving bacteria from a discarded fruit to a susceptible host.[119] Japan's citation to van der Zwet & Keil (1979) was inapt as the "[e]vidence of *Erwinia amylovora* dissemination by insects, birds, wind, and rain" referred to dissemination of bacteria from diseased host plants. There was no evidence that "insects, birds, wind and rain" would transfer bacteria from epiphytically contaminated and discarded fruit; in fact, the scientific evidence confirmed that there was no vectoring of epiphytic bacteria from contaminated, discarded fruit. Thus, the last step in Japan's hypothetical pathway was also not supported by any scientific evidence.

4.156 **Japan** argued that bacterial ooze could adhere to birds feeding on apple fruit discarded by Japanese people in urban and rural areas, or to insects, or in aerosol and invade the susceptible organs (flowers, etc) or scars of pear or apple trees in commercial orchards or other host plants. In this context, Japan recalled the statement of Dr Geider at the expert meeting that there was no minimum number of bacteria necessary for multiplication.

4.157 The **United States** made clear that it was not disputing the existence of vectors for bacterial ooze within Japan, but as the scientific experts had confirmed, that there was no scientific evidence that imported apple fruit would be blighted and produce bacterial ooze. Therefore, Japan's hypothetical pathway would not be completed.

4.158 Furthermore, the United States argued that Japan had presented no evaluation of the likelihood or probability of establishment and spread of fire blight. ISPM 11 laid out factors to consider in evaluating the probabilities of both establishment and spread. As regards the probability of establishment, factors included the availability, quantity, and distribution of hosts in the pest risk analysis area, the environmental suitability of the pest risk analysis area, the reproductive strategy of the pest, its potential for adaptation, the method of pest survival, and cultural practices and control measures in the pest risk analysis area.[120] As regards the probability of spread, factors included the suitability of the natural environment for natural spread of the pest, the presence of natural barriers, the potential for movement with commodities or conveyances, the

---

[119] The US review of the scientific literature had revealed no report of a vector or mechanism by which any fire blight bacteria on or in apple fruit had been transmitted to a susceptible host. According to the Roberts *et al.* (1998) review study "There are no specific pathways recorded that document movement of *E. amylovora* from fruit, either imported or domestic in origin, to susceptible host tissues in an orchard or nursery".

[120] Op. cit., ISPM 11, para. 2.2.2.

intended use of the commodity, potential vectors of the pest in the pest risk analysis area, and potential natural enemies of the pest in the pest risk analysis area.[121]

4.159 The United States noted that Japan had presented evidence relating to some of these factors, but its conclusions on possibilities again fell short of an evaluation of probabilities, particularly as Japan had not considered important contrary evidence. Japan had not identified the probable means by which the fire blight bacteria would enter and therefore the likely place of establishment (that is, the city, country, growing regions, or elsewhere). Japan had also apparently dismissed the possibility that the disease could be eradicated before spread, despite contrary evidence from Australia and Norway. Japan also had not evaluated whether the disease, once established, could be prevented from spreading, despite admitting the existence of evidence that Europe had successfully done so. The failure to evaluate this evidence was all the more striking given that EPPO recommended that European nations at high risk of fire blight introduction restrict the importation of host plants for planting but not the importation of fruit of fire blight hosts.

4.160 **Japan** countered that although the United States pointed out the desirability of further evidence, it had failed to demonstrate how the perceived need could constitute a case of inconsistency with the text of Article 5.1. According to the overly strict US interpretation of Article 5.1, many pest risk analyses implemented by other countries, including the United States, could be inconsistent with this Article. Such a situation, however, had not been foreseen by the *SPS Agreement*.

4.161 Japan considered that the pathway with "mature, apparently healthy but infected fruit" and/or "bacterial ooze" was the most probable one, but did not preclude other possibilities, including a pathway which began with a small colony of the bacteria in apple fruit. As Japan believed that Dr Geider had noted, that there was no definite minimum number of bacteria that would be necessary to multiply and disseminate the disease. The United States did not understand the fact that the 1999 PRA could take into account only 1996 Guidelines. Japan also considered that the suggested possibility of eradication of fire blight was merely illusory. Introduction of the disease into Australia had been a very limited incident with only three trees infected. Moreover the fact that fire blight had been found not in orchards but at botanical gardens in an urban area contributed to its successful eradication. Japan was not aware of the details of the eradication in Norway, but its cooler climatic conditions could have been the main cause of successful eradication. With respect to the situation in Europe, Japan was of the view that Europe was suffering from an expansion of the disease on a massive scale, due to its failure to take appropriate measures. In France, for example, the "protected zone" (or the fire blight-free area) had diminished in size from the eastern half of the country in 1997 to only the island of Corsica today.

---

[121] Op. cit., ISPM 11, para. 2.2.3.

3.   Evaluation of Risk According to the Measure which Might be Applied

4.162 The **United States** recalled that with respect to the third requirement of a risk assessment within the meaning of Article 5.1 and Annex A, Japan had to evaluate the likelihood of entry, establishment or spread of fire blight disease according to the SPS measures which might be applied.[122] As the Appellate Body had noted in *Australia – Salmon*, a risk assessment that "identifies such measures but does not, in any substantial way, evaluate or assess their relative effectiveness in reducing the overall disease risk" did not "fulfil the third requirement" for a risk assessment, "i.e., it does not contain the required evaluation of the likelihood of entry, establishment, or spread of the diseases of concern according to the SPS measures which might be applied".[123] The Japanese analysis of certain SPS measures which might be applied had not met this requirement. Japan had identified some SPS measures which might be applied to US apples in that it had named those measures it already applied. However, the 1999 PRA had not evaluated the "relative" effectiveness of any of these measures in reducing the overall disease risk.

4.163 The United States claimed that the 1999 PRA had also failed to consider the SPS measures "which might be applied", rather than those measures which it had already applied. The United States had informed Japan that measures on mature, symptomless apples were not necessary because these fruit did not serve as a pathway for the disease; the United States had even proposed compromise alternative measures to Japan. Japan, however, had failed to consider these alternative measures, although no other fire blight-free countries imposed the same fire blight measures as Japan - indeed, the vast majority imposed no fire blight measures on imported fruit at all. Thus, Japan's assessment of risk did not meet the third requirement of a risk assessment within the meaning of Article 5.1 and Annex A of the *SPS Agreement*.

4.164 **Japan** stressed that its phytosanitary requirements were based on the proposals of the exporting government. Indeed, Japan had considered a variety of US proposed "compromises" during bilateral and technical meetings, and had proposed in 1999 to perform a joint study to generate data supporting modification of the measure. Unfortunately, the 2000 study had not been implemented the way Japan had hoped and had not generated data that would have warranted modification of the conclusion of the 1999 PRA. The United States had officially proposed the "mature, symptomless" criteria for the first time only at the bilateral consultations in April 2002. Until then, the United States had only proposed to narrow the width of the buffer zone and to reduce the number of field inspections. Japan also considered that when a country planned to introduce a new measure, the efficacy and impact of more options should be taken into account. However, when a measure was already in effect, the analysis and evaluation would inevitably focus on the current measure.

---

[122] Appellate Body Report in *Australia–Salmon*, para. 121.
[123] *Ibid.*, paras. 133-34.

4.165 The **United States** noted Japan's suggestion that it could not have considered the "mature, symptomless" criteria in its risk assessment because these were not officially proposed until the 2002 WTO consultations. However, Japan had been well aware of these criteria, which first appeared in the fire blight literature in 1924 and which had been repeated often in the literature through the last three decades. Japan had expressly refused to consider scientific evidence stating that "there are some reports that the possibility of fire blight transmission by fresh apple fruit can be denied or neglected[,] [h]owever, in these reports, they only stated that 'symptomless, mature fruit' (McLarty 1922, Dueck 1974), 'healthy looking mature fruit' (Roberts *et al.* 1989), 'fruit harvested from symptomless orchards with[out] fire blight' (van der Zwet *et al.* 1990) are safe". This rendered Japan's evaluation of the likelihood of entry inadequate and its assessment of the risks of entry, establishment or spread of fire blight inconsistent with Article 5.1.

4. *Measures Based on an Assessment of the Risks*

4.166 The **United States** further considered that Japan's requirements on US apples were inconsistent with Article 5.1 because the 1999 PRA results did not "sufficiently warrant" - i.e reasonably support - the SPS measure.[124] As indicated by ISPM 11, the probability of entry of a pest was linked to the probability of the pest being associated with the pathway at origin, considering, for example, the prevalence of the pest in the source area, the occurrence of the pest in a life-stage that would be associated with commodities, seasonal timing, and commercial procedures applied at the place of origin, such as handling, culling, roguing, and grading. Thus, to support measures on the importation of apples, Japan's PRA had to have examined whether the exported commodity (mature, symptomless apple fruit) might serve as a pathway for the disease. Japan had merely presented a list of scientific studies on the presence of fire blight bacteria on apples without any evaluation of the relevance of the studies for the apples to be imported. Such an unreasoned recitation of evidence could not "reasonably support" the SPS measures Japan had imposed. Thus, the resulting analysis of the risk posed by imported apples did not "sufficiently warrant" or "reasonably support" the Japanese fire blight measures.

4.167 **Japan** stated that fire blight was often prevalent in the States of Washington and Oregon, and the 1999 PRA noted that van der Zwet *et al.* (1990) had detected *E. amylovora* inside mature, symptomless apples. While it did not estimate numerical probabilities of contamination by the bacteria, the PRA qualitatively evaluated the probability.

4.168 Japan maintained that the 1999 PRA covered the path of analysis required by the 1996 and 2001 Guidelines. The only issue which remained was how "new evidence" would impact on the consistency of the 1999 PRA with Article 5.1. Japan believed that conformity of a risk assessment under Article 5.1 should be assessed in light of information available at the time of conducting the risk

---

[124] Appellate Body Report in *EC – Hormones*, para. 193.

assessment. Once a risk assessment was fully completed consistent with the *SPS Agreement*, the party concerned had fulfilled its obligation, and it should not be held in violation of the Agreement retroactively because of the subsequent discovery of new evidence. Article 5.1 should not be interpreted to require a full, formal risk assessment immediately each time a new piece of evidence became available. The importing Member should be given an opportunity to consider whether or not the new information would warrant a new risk assessment. In this context, Japan had taken into account new data submitted by the United States and by New Zealand during the proceedings, and concluded that they were not yet sufficient to warrant a modification of the current phytosanitary requirements.

4.169 The **United States** considered that, in general, the consistency of a measure with a Member's WTO obligations should be judged as of the time of establishment of the dispute settlement panel (assuming that the same measure was the subject of consultations). It disagreed with Australia's argument that a Member that learnt of new scientific evidence must be allowed the opportunity to reassess risk in accordance with the factors in Article 5.2 of the *SPS Agreement*.[125] This would imply that an exporting Member could not pursue dispute settlement until the importing Member had been given an opportunity to reassess risk. Such a rule would upset the balance of rights and obligations of WTO Members. Nothing in the *SPS Agreement* required the United States, which had unsuccessfully attempted to work with Japan to relax its current fire blight measures for nearly eight years, to forego dispute settlement when Japan was not in compliance with its WTO obligations. However, nothing prevented Japan from reassessing risk pursuant to Article 5 of the *SPS Agreement* in light of the scientific evidence while dispute settlement proceedings were ongoing.

4.170 Furthermore, the United States stressed that the timing of availability of any scientific evidence presented in this dispute should not alter the outcome of the Panel's analysis of any legal claim. As the experts had confirmed, there had never been any scientific evidence that mature apple fruit (the exported commodity) had ever transmitted fire blight or could serve as a pathway for introduction of fire blight to Japan. All of the most recent scientific evidence merely served to confirm further this point. Japan's measure was based on nothing more than theoretical uncertainties, such as, what if an infected, immature fruit were somehow imported along with the exported commodity – even though the experts had stated such fruit would not be harvested because they were immature and had symptoms of fire blight. According to the Appellate Body in *EC – Hormones*, such theoretical uncertainties were not the type of risk which a risk assessment, and therefore any Japanese fire blight measure, were to address.[126]

4.171 The United States recalled that in *Australia – Salmon*, the Appellate Body had confirmed the relationship between Articles 5.1 and 2.2, stating that by maintaining an SPS measure "in violation of Article 5.1, Australia had, by

---

[125] Australian Statement at the Third Party Session with the Panel, 22 October 2002, para. 10.
[126] Appellate Body Report in *EC – Hormones*, para. 186.

implication, also acted inconsistently with Article 2.2 of the *SPS Agreement*".[127] Thus, to the extent that the Panel found that Japan had maintained the fire blight measures without basing them on a risk assessment under Article 5.1, the Panel should also conclude that Japan had acted inconsistently with Article 2.2. Nevertheless, the United States requested that the Panel find that Japan had breached Article 2.2 independently of its breach of Article 5.1. An independent finding under Article 2.2 would assist the parties in achieving a satisfactory settlement, and avoid the potential for further litigation, by making clear that Japan's breach could not be cured through mere redrafting of an analysis not based on scientific evidence.

G.   Article 5.2

4.172   The **United States** claimed that Japan's 1999 PRA was flawed because it did not "take into account" certain information identified in Article 5.2 of the *SPS Agreement*. Article 5.2 sets out certain information that must be taken into account when conducting a risk assessment, including "available scientific evidence; . . . relevant ecological and environmental conditions; and quarantine or other treatment". Although the 1999 PRA presented some information relating to fire blight, it had failed to take into account certain key pieces of information. First, Japan had failed to take into account available scientific evidence that mature, symptomless apple fruit did not serve to transmit the fire blight disease. As previously noted, in its 1999 PRA Japan had identified, but expressly disregarded, literature that concluded that "mature, symptomless" fruit did not transmit fire blight on the grounds that such reports referred *only* to "mature, symptomless" fruit.

4.173   **Japan** contended that it had taken into consideration the scientific evidence then available in both its 1996 and 1999 PRAs. Japan considered that the US complaint was about the conclusion the analysis had drawn, rather than Japan's failure to evaluate the evidence. Japan had fully reviewed the evidence about *E.amylovora* in mature, symptomless apple fruit.

4.174   The **United States** further argued that Japan had failed to take into account relevant ecological and environmental conditions in the States of Washington and Oregon. Japan expressly limited the importation of US apples to fruit harvested from orchards in Washington and Oregon, but failed to consider the available scientific evidence relating to mature, symptomless apples harvested from Washington. Not a single mature, symptomless Washington apple fruit had ever tested positive for internal or external fire blight bacteria, even when harvested from infected trees.

4.175   **Japan** observed that both Washington and Oregon suffered from significant fire blight outbreaks in 1985, 1988, 1993, 1994, 1997 and 1998, and the incidence of the disease in these states was not generally low.[128] Japan

---

[127]   Appellate Body Report in *Australia – Salmon*, para. 138.
[128]   Occurrence Level of Fire Blight in 2000 when the Japan-US Joint Experiment was Carried Out (Exhibit JPN-33).

recalled that two joint US-Japan experiments had been planned for 2000, one on the width of the buffer zone and another on the number of field inspections. Japan considered the buffer zone width experiment to be a joint experiment, and accepted the results of the experiment as data for a non-severe fire blight year in the State of Washington. However, Japan did not consider that the ecology of fire blight (in this case, the scattering distance of the bacteria) had been wholly revealed by the result. Japan considered that the US design of the second experiment on field inspections was illogical and it could not accept the results. At a technical meeting held in October 2001, Japan had invited the United States to provide additional information on five items:

(i)   The situations of occurrence of fire blight in the States of Washington and Oregon;

(ii)   the difference between the two states and other states in terms of the occurrence of fire blight;

(iii)   the forecasting systems of fire blight in the States of Washington and Oregon;

(iv)   the mechanism by which *E. amylovora* invaded inside apple fruit; and

(v)   the spreading mechanism of fire blight in the State of Washington, especially the scattering distance of *E. amylovora*.

4.176 On fire blight outbreaks since 1985, the **United States** argued that the data Japan had presented were not *actual* data on fire blight incidence but were merely the *predicted* fire blight incidences calculated by an often inaccurate computer forecasting model (CougarBlight). In response to items (i) and (ii), the United States replied that the occurrence of fire blight in Oregon, Washington, and the rest of the United States were not systematically recorded because the disease was endemic and not under official control. Therefore, this data was unavailable. For item (iii), there were no official, mandated forecasting systems for fire blight outbreak. CougarBlight and MaryBlight were two computer-forecasting programmes that were commonly used, and Japan was well aware of them. For item (iv), the United States had not provided data on a mechanism by which *E. amylovora* could "invade inside apple fruit" because it did not invade inside mature apple fruit harvested from orchards, as amply demonstrated by the scientific evidence. Thus, Japan was requesting the United States to provide hypothetical data on a non-existent phenomenon. For item (v), the United States was unaware of any means of spreading fire blight inside Washington State that had not been documented elsewhere for other areas: wind-driven rain, some insects, infected nursery stock, and contaminated pruning tools. The United States further noted that the request for this extra data had come two years after Japan proposed the joint experiments and approximately ten months after the results of these same experiments became available. The request also was made despite the ample scientific evidence that mature apple fruit do not transmit fire blight. Finally, the United States noted that the requested data was for two years when the environmental conditions were conducive to fire blight development and severe blight occurred in the growing areas in central Washington (Roberts *et al.* (1989)). Nonetheless, no fire blight bacteria were detected inside mature fruit and no fire blight disease developed in any fruit during the period of cold storage.

4.177 **Japan** indicated that it was not satisfied with the US replies. It had requested the information in items (i) and (ii) because if the situations of occurrence of fire blight in Washington and Oregon were substantially different from those of other states and the level of occurrence in 2000 was about average in the Pacific Northwest, these data would be helpful to evaluate the results of the 2000 experiment. Japan considered that it was negligent on the part of an exporting country, such as the United States, not to have data on the occurrence situation of a pest of serious concern to the importing country, Japan. The intent behind item (iii) was to ascertain if fire blight was adequately forecasted in Washington and Oregon, so that the inspections could be reduced during a low fire blight year. However the reply of the United States showed that fire blight in Washington and Oregon was not monitored at all. Item (iv) was also important as knowledge about how *E. amylovora* invaded into fruit (only via infected pollens, or through pedicel from infected branches, etc.) affected the timing of the orchard inspections. Finally, data on the spreading mechanism of fire blight in Washington and Oregon States and especially the scattering distance of *E. amylovora* (item (v)) had a bearing on the width of the buffer zone. The reply of the United States confirmed that the findings of J. Van Vaerenbergh *et al.* (1987) were relevant to both states.[129]

4.178 Japan further stated that obviously its access to information on the relevant ecological and environmental conditions in the States of Washington and Oregon was limited. In light of judicial equity, the exporting Member should positively demonstrate such information that was solely or generally available in that exporting Member. This understanding of the *SPS Agreement* was consistent with Article 6.3, which put the burden of proof on an exporting Member to provide objective demonstration of any pest- or disease-free areas or areas of low pest or disease prevalence.

4.179 The **United States** claimed that Japan had also failed to take into account quarantine or other treatments. While Japan had recognized in the 1999 PRA that the chlorine treatment it currently required was adequate "to sterilize fire blight bacteria that may have attached to the surface of fresh apple fruits", Japan had not considered the scientific evidence that chlorine treatment by itself mitigated any possibility that bacteria could be found externally on mature, symptomless apple fruit. Thus, by failing to take into account available scientific evidence, relevant ecological and environmental conditions, and quarantine or other treatments, the United States maintained that Japan had acted inconsistently with Article 5.2.

4.180 **Japan** argued that studies showed that *E. amylovora* existed both inside and outside mature apple fruit and it was evident that the bacteria inside apple fruit could not be eliminated by the chlorine treatment.

---

[129] "In or shortly after periods of rain, the pathogen could be isolated at a maximum distance of 250m from the hawthorn hedge and detected by up to 1km.", Vaerenbergh, *et al.* (1987), op. cit.

H.   Article 5.6

4.181 The **United States** claimed that Japan had acted inconsistently with Article 5.6 of the *SPS Agreement* because Japan's fire blight measures were more trade-restrictive than required to achieve Japan's appropriate level of phytosanitary protection. The Panel and Appellate Body had found in *Australia – Salmon* that there were three elements necessary "to establish a violation of Article 5.6". First, there had to be another measure that "is reasonably available taking into account technical and economic feasibility". Second, the measure had to achieve "the Member's appropriate level of sanitary or phytosanitary protection". Third, the measure had to be "significantly less restrictive to trade than the SPS measure contested". If any one of the three elements was not met, "the measure in dispute would be consistent with Article 5.6".[130] The United States contended that restricting importation to mature, symptomless apple fruit was an alternative measure that was reasonably available, achieved Japan's appropriate level of protection (ALOP), and was significantly less restrictive to trade than Japan's fire blight measures.

4.182 **Japan** argued that the United States had not established that exportation of "mature, symptomless" apple fruit to Japan would achieve Japan's appropriate level of protection, which was to prevent introduction of *E. amylovora* with the security equivalent of import prohibition. The alternative proposed by the United States was: (1) not based on scientific evidence; (2) not supported by real life experience; (3) not practical to implement; and (4) not scientifically sound. As the measure proposed by the United States did not meet Japan's ALOP, Japan was acting consistently with Article 5.6.

4.183 The **United States** claimed that restricting the importation of apples to mature, symptomless apple fruit was a reasonably available measure that was already in use. US law and regulations currently imposed the requirement that exported apples be mature and be free from decay, broken skin or bruises, or damage caused by disease or any other means.[131] In addition, almost all (60 of 66) fire blight-free areas in the world allowed US apples meeting US export standards to be imported without any production restrictions or post-harvest

---

[130] Appellate Body Report in *Australia – Salmon*, para. 194; see also Panel Report in *Australia – Salmon*, para. 8.167.

[131] Under the US Export Apple Act, exported apple fruit had to be of a Federal or State grade that met a minimum quality established by regulation. Those regulations (7 C.F.R. § 33.10) currently required exported US apples to satisfy at least the requirements for the "U.S. No. 1" grade, pursuant to which apples had to be: mature but not overripe, carefully hand-picked, clean, fairly well-formed; free from decay, internal browning, internal breakdown, bitter pit, Jonathan spot, scald, freezing injury and broken skin or bruises except those which were incident to proper handling and packing. The apples were also free from damage caused by sunburn or sprayburn, limb rubs, hail, drought spots, scars, stem or calyx cracks, disease, insects, [or] damage by other means". Thus, US law and regulations required that exported fruit be mature (and also free from any disease symptoms). Apple fruit for export were inspected by Federal-State inspectors for compliance with the requirements of the US Export Apple Act, the applicable grade standard, and any additional phytosanitary requirements of the export market. Upon completion of the inspection, including sampling of the shipment and visual inspection for pests and/or disease, an export certificate was issued as to the quality/condition of the apples and a separate phytosanitary certificate was issued as to freedom of quarantine pests/disease and a statement as to the required treatment.

treatments. These regions were, effectively, imposing only a mature, symptomless fruit measure on imported US apples.

4.184 The United States noted that compliance with the US Export Apple Act did not require inspection of apple orchards, and there was no state regulation or requirement that required orchard inspections. As the scientific evidence demonstrated that harvested fruit would be mature and symptomless, regardless of whether they were harvested from orchards with fire blight or without, orchard inspections for fire blight were neither necessary nor relevant to ensure that exported apple fruit would be mature and symptomless.

4.185 **Japan** noted that the experts appointed by the Panel had unanimously acknowledged that it would be reasonable to establish a fire blight-free orchard, to implement field inspection(s) and to require certification that the apple fruit were indeed produced in a fire blight-free area, in order to achieve Japan's appropriate level of protection.

4.186 The **United States** stated that it was not arguing that compliance with the US Export Apple Act as such would constitute the alternative measure that was reasonably available, although compliance with US law did achieve Japan's appropriate level of protection. Rather, consistent with Article 2.2, Japan could require that imported apple fruit be restricted to mature apple fruit. Such a measure was reasonably available, achieved Japan's appropriate level of protection, and was significantly less restrictive to trade than Japan's current fire blight measures. The United States also commented that Japan's assertion that the experts had agreed that a fire blight-free orchard would be reasonable, misrepresented both the context and the content of the experts' answers at the expert session. In discussing certain measures as candidates for a "compromise", the experts were no longer commenting on matters within their expertise or mandate to provide scientific and technical advice on the scientific evidence relating to fire blight and exported apple fruit.

4.187 **Japan** stated that the United States had not defined exactly what "mature, symptomless" fruit would mean. Nor had the United States defined specific means to produce, select and export only such apple fruit. In *Japan – Agricultural Products II*, the Appellate Body had held that, under the prima facie rule, a measure should be argued and proven by the complaining party, and the Panel was not allowed to compare the existing measure with another hypothetical measure that the complaining party did not prove to be equally effective. In this case, there was no evidence provided by the United States that there was indeed an alternative "measure" which would ensure that apple fruit shipped to Japan were of adequate quality. Consequently, Japan requested the Panel to consider not the hypothetical or ideal "mature, symptomless" criteria, which the United States did not prove actually existed, but the ambiguous nature of the "mature, symptomless" criteria as presented in this proceeding. Japan maintained that the United States had not met its burden of proof that such apples would indeed meet Japan's level of protection.

4.188 The **United States** described the normal procedures for apples destined to markets other than Japan. Apples were harvested when the growers and consultants had determined that the variety within the local growing location had reached optimum level of maturity for the various marketing seasons; *i.e.*, early, mid-season, and late season.[132] Apples were harvested into bulk bins and typically were delivered to cold storage facilities the same day as harvested, or the following day (after overnight cooling in the orchard). Upon delivery to the cold storage/packing facility, the field-run apples were placed in either regular cold storage rooms or in controlled atmosphere ("CA") rooms. Temperatures were maintained at, or near, 32 degrees F. In CA rooms, the oxygen was also maintained between 1% and 5%. Due to the ability to preserve fruit condition for 12 months or more under CA conditions, the duration of storage was determined by the marketing plan of the growers and packing facilities and varied from several days to several months. As the fruit was needed for the market, it was removed from storage, separated from leaves and other debris, and washed, sized, sorted, and graded by packing facility personnel.[133] Following grading the fruit was placed in the packages or containers that were used for shipment and the shipping cartons were properly labeled as to variety, grade, size, responsibility, origin, etc.

4.189 Prior to export, the apples were inspected by the Federal-State inspectors (eg., Washington State Department of Agriculture inspectors working under cooperative agreements with US Department of Agriculture, Agricultural Marketing Service ("USDA-AMS") and Animal Plant Health Inspection Service ("USDA-APHIS")). The apples were inspected for compliance with the applicable grade standard, the requirements of the US Export Apple Act, and the phytosanitary requirements of the receiving foreign country. The phytosanitary inspection included sampling of the shipment, visual inspection for pests and/or disease, and when applicable, certification of treatment. Upon completion of the inspection, an export certificate was issued as to the quality and condition of the apples. A separate phytosanitary certificate was issued as to freedom of quarantine pests or disease and a statement as to the required treatment.

4.190 The United States explained that given the multiple human and machine-based examinations that each fruit was subjected to, and the strict grade requirements that categorically excluded immature fruit, it was extremely unlikely that an immature fruit would be included in a carton of mature, export-quality apple fruit. The harvest process involved careful and repeated assessment of the maturity of apple fruit utilizing numerous objective criteria. Any very small apples (those most likely to be immature) were eliminated from fresh market packs for commercial reasons; *i.e.*, they were not saleable. Apples were held in cold storage for a period of several days to several months (the vast

---

[132] For example, according to the Washington State Apple Commission, in mid-August, apple growers started testing the maturity of their apples to accurately predict when to harvest their crop to put in controlled atmosphere rooms so the apples are mature, but not too ripe. Firmness, skin color, seed color, sugar level and flesh chlorophyll were tested.

[133] Sometimes apples were pre-sorted and pre-sized, but not packaged, and returned to cold storage in field bins. When needed to fill an order for market, the particular variety, grade, and size of apples was taken from cold storage, given a final washing, sorting/grading, and was then placed in the shipping container and labelled.

majority being held for months), during which time the apples continued to ripen, although at a greatly reduced rate. Any immature fruit that had inadvertently been harvested would likely show shrivelling and might also show signs of chilling injury (depending upon storage temperature), making such a fruit more easily detectable during the subsequent sorting and grading operations. According to the United States, the scientific experts had confirmed that harvested fruit were mature and therefore not infected; any immature, infected fruit would not be exported.

4.191 **Japan** noted that a risk of accidental contamination or erroneous grading was very real, as had been recognized by the experts appointed by the Panel, given the obvious possibility of human errors. While the degree of the risk was open to discussions, the experts had acknowledged that a phytosanitary measure should be in place to manage that risk. In this context, Japan indicated that in November 2002, Chinese Taipei had discovered codling moth larva in apple fruit shipped from the State of Washington. Apparently, the commercial screening had not been rigorous enough to detect the codling moth larvae holes. This was exactly one of the risks which Japan's measures were necessary to protect against. In other words, the United States was proposing to replace the current phytosanitary requirements with something (i) the efficacy of which had been demonstrated to be questionable and was not known and (ii) the quality of which the United States did not guarantee. It would be a grave mistake to assume the proposal would achieve Japan's appropriate level of protection or would provide security at a level comparable to that of the current requirements.

4.192 The **United States** noted that Japan evidently relied on the export of mature, symptomless fruit. Japan had stated that "[t]hese pieces of evidence demonstrate that a phytosanitary measure is needed to counter the risk of dissemination arising from the ambiguity of the mature, symptomless criteria and that the accidental or intentional failure on the part of American growers/shippers to ship apple fruit of the adequate quality". However, Japan's fire blight measures did not counter the unestablished and hypothetical risk of accidental or intentional shipment of immature, infected fruit. Even under the measures Japan had had in place for the past eight years, a US grower or shipper complying with all of the Japanese fire blight measures hypothetically might still accidentally, or intentionally, include an immature, infected fruit in a bin containing fruit intended for export to Japan – or in a container with any other product being exported to Japan. Japan's fire blight measures would not protect against the risk of that occurring. However, as Japan had implicitly acknowledged by implementing the current measures, Japan was protected against hypothetical risks such as these precisely because the exported commodity was the exported commodity.

4.193 The United States claimed that the scientific evidence established that a harvested fruit would be horticulturally mature, and that the experts had confirmed that mature apples were not infected. (Despite Japan's insistence over the subjectivity of the "mature, symptomless" criteria, Japan had not provided any scientific evidence that the terms "mature" and "symptomless" were not objective concepts.) Horticultural maturity was measured according to objective criteria, and growers, distributors, and exporters applied such criteria to ensure product that was commercially saleable and of high quality. US grading standards and law, enforced by Federal-State inspectors, required exported apples to be mature and symptomless. Therefore, the scientific evidence indicated that exported US apples were not infected and did not pose a risk of introducing fire blight to Japan.

4.194 **Japan** contended that when the experts had stated that there was no scientific evidence of "mature, harvested" apple fruit disseminating fire blight disease, they had made clear that "mature, symptomless", "mature" or "mature, harvested" apple fruit were concepts open to a variety of interpretations. Similarly, they acknowledged that "symptoms" might not be detectable in diverse circumstances. In sum, what the experts had confirmed was that an ideal mature, symptomless apple fruit would bear only a very low degree of risk. In real life, however, there were a host of possibilities between immature, blighted apple fruit and ideally mature, symptomless apple fruit, and the experts acknowledged that maturation was a continuous process. Moreover, according to Japan, the experts had unanimously acknowledged that there was a real risk of dissemination from the bacteria inside an infected apple fruit, inadvertently or erroneously found fit for export. In particular, Japan believed that Dr Smith had clearly stated that the risk had to be "managed".

4.195 Japan further argued that the concept of "maturity" was easily manipulated. Referring to the declaration of Dr van der Zwet and the letter from Professor Thomson, Japan observed that it had taken two separate negotiations with these authors for them to claim that what they had previously written was not true. Nevertheless, the experts were not certain under which concept, physiological or commercial maturity, the tested apples had been "immature". Consequently, the "mature, symptomless" criteria were based on subjective, relative concepts that did not provide sufficient certainty to serve as the basis for phytosanitary measures. The Organization of Economic Co-operation and Development (OECD) Guidelines provided "objective tests for determining ripeness of fruit", but for the purpose of standardizing marketing practices, for consumer convenience. These Guidelines were not based on bacteriological principles and did not take into account phytosanitary concerns.[134] Moreover, it would be extremely difficult to enforce the OECD Guidelines on every apple fruit shipped to Japan so as to ensure that security was maintained.

4.196 Japan argued that the "mature, apparently healthy" apple fruit criteria could offer security only when the mechanism by which the bacteria did not exist in such fruit was identified. An appropriate test method of determining ripeness of apple fruit could then be developed taking into account the mechanism.

4.197 The **United States** explained that the OECD guidelines specified several methods and instruments that could be used for the determination of horticultural (or commercial) maturity of apple fruit. Of the four methods given in the OECD

---

[134] *OECD Scheme for the Application of International Standards for Fruit and Vegetables* (1998) Guidance on Objective Tests for Determining the Ripeness of Fruit.

guidelines, three were routinely used by growers, fieldmen, and packinghouse personnel in the United States to determine correct harvest maturity: firmness, soluble solids, and starch.[135]

4.198 According to the United States, the fact that Japan's fire blight measures were more trade-restrictive than necessary was also evident from the range of other possible measures that were less trade-restrictive and that would more than achieve Japan's appropriate level of protection. Japan could, for example, require a phytosanitary certificate of fire blight freedom for the exported commodity (mature apple fruit). Other examples of such alternatives included: (1) requiring that imported mature, symptomless fruit be harvested in Washington or Oregon; (2) requiring that imported mature, symptomless fruit be harvested at least 10 meters from a source of inoculum; or (3) requiring that mature, symptomless fruit be treated with chlorine. As the scientific evidence established that billions of exported apple fruit had never transmitted fire blight and mature, symptomless fruit were not a pathway for the disease, any of these less trade-restrictive measures would more than achieve Japan's appropriate level of protection - although, for the same reason, they also would be more trade-restrictive than necessary. Only a requirement that exported US apples be mature and symptomless could be considered as necessary given the scientific evidence.

4.199 Restricting importation of US apples to mature, symptomless fruit would also be significantly less restrictive to trade than the current Japanese fire blight measures. The United States recalled that one comprehensive scientific study had estimated that only 1% of US apples were harvested from orchards that satisfied all of Japan's fire blight measures. Under the US proposed alternative measure, by definition, all US exports would qualify for export to Japan.[136]

4.200 **Japan** emphasized that the burden to prove that the real risk arising from the ambiguity of the "mature, symptomless" criteria was negligible lay with the United States. In this respect, the United States' only evidence was the statistics of successful shipments with Saudi Arabia, the United Arab Emirates and six other countries. This evidence had been fully refuted by Japan. None of these countries of the desert or tropical regions had a climate comparable to that of Japan. To the contrary, Japan had submitted direct evidence of failure in ensuring adequate quality of apples by Washington apple growers and shippers. Consequently, the United States had not met its burden of proof that such apples would indeed meet Japan's level of protection.

I. Article 5.7

4.201 The **United States** noted that Japan had invoked Article 5.7 as an alternative defence, but it did not believe that Japan had met the necessary

---

[135] As reflected in the OECD guidelines, fruit samples were evaluated sequentially during the pre-harvest and harvest period to determine the point at which the fruit exhibited a combination of firmness, soluble solids, and starch index values that were optimum for the proposed use of the fruit, which could include immediate sale on the fresh market, regular atmosphere cold storage, or short- to long-term controlled atmosphere storage.
[136] Op. cit., Roberts et al. (1998).

requirements under that provision. As noted by the Panel and Appellate Body in *Japan - Agricultural Products II*, Article 5.7 set out four requirements that had to be met in order to adopt a provisional SPS measure exempt from Article 2.2. Pursuant to the first sentence of Article 5.7, the provisionally adopted measure could be imposed only "[i]n cases where relevant scientific evidence is insufficient" and had to be adopted "on the basis of available pertinent information". Pursuant to the second sentence of Article 5.7, the provisional measure could not be maintained unless the adopting Member "seek[s] to obtain the additional information necessary for a more objective assessment of risk" and "review[s] the . . . measure within a reasonable period of time". The four requirements "are clearly cumulative in nature" and "[w]henever *one* of these four requirements is not met, the measure at issue is inconsistent with Article 5.7".[137]

4.202 **Japan** stated that, should the Panel find that Japan's measure was maintained "without sufficient scientific evidence" in the sense of Article 2.2, it argued in the alternative that its measure was a provisional measure consistent with Article 5.7. Japan maintained that this alternative argument was necessary only in the event that the Panel should: (1) reject Japan's interpretation of the burden of proof; (2) accept the interpretation but find satisfactory the "mature, symptomless" criteria; or (3) otherwise find that the scientific evidence had become insufficient.

4.203 Japan understood the initial US claim to be that there was, allegedly, no longer sufficient scientific evidence for Japan's phytosanitary requirements in light of information which had become available some time after 1994. However, the United States had failed to identify specifically when they believed the scientific evidence underlying Japan's measure became insufficient.

4.204 The **United States** argued that it was not claiming that the scientific evidence suddenly became insufficient to support Japan's fire blight measures at some point after 1994. There had never been scientific evidence that mature apple fruit transmitted the disease. This evidence predated the entry into force of Japan's fire blight measures in 1994 and continued to be the same. Thus, Japan had been acting inconsistently with its commitment under Article 2.2 not to maintain its fire blight measures without sufficient scientific evidence since the entry into force of the *SPS Agreement* in 1995.

4.205 **Japan** recalled that its current phytosanitary requirements were introduced on the basis of an agreement between the two governments, in order to allow importation of US apple fruit while preserving Japan's appropriate level of protection. The measures had been developed on the basis of proposals from the United States, hence it was unreasonable for the United States to now claim that the evidence had been insufficient from the beginning. Nonetheless, Japan clarified that, should the Panel find the scientific evidence insufficient to support Japan's measure under Article 2.2, the measure could be considered to be a

---

[137] Appellate Body Report in *Japan – Agricultural Products II*, para. 89.

provisional measure in the context of Article 5.7 since the date of entry into force of the *SPS Agreement*.

4.206 The **United States** reiterated that it had acquiesced to the fire blight measures in 1994 as preferable to an outright ban on imported apple fruit, although it had recognized that the scientific evidence did not support the restrictions imposed by Japan. It had never accepted the consistency of these measures with Japan's WTO obligations.

4.207 The United States argued that the Panel's analysis of Japan's alternative defence could begin and end with the first requirement that the provisional measure be imposed only "[i]n cases where relevant scientific evidence is insufficient". This required that, at the time the provisional measure was adopted, the information necessary for an objective assessment of risk was lacking. If there had been sufficient information to conduct a risk assessment and that information supported a measure, there would be no need to adopt a measure "provisionally", since it could be adopted "based on" the risk assessment pursuant to Article 5.1. Likewise, if there were sufficient information to conduct a risk assessment and that assessment indicated that a measure was *not* justified, a Member which would not be able to adopt a measure under Article 5.1 should not then be free to adopt a measure "provisionally" under Article 5.7. Otherwise, the obligation in Article 5.1 would become meaningless.

4.208 The United States contended that "sufficiency" in the first sentence of Article 5.7 should be understood to relate to the information available for a risk assessment. This was also supported by the language of the second clause of that sentence. "In cases where relevant scientific evidence is insufficient", provisional measures could be adopted "on the basis of available pertinent information including that from the relevant international organizations as well as from ... phytosanitary measures applied by other Members". It would not be necessary to adopt a measure "on the basis of" such "available pertinent information" if the measure could be "based on" a risk assessment (which presupposed that there was sufficient scientific information to conduct the risk assessment). Thus, the phrase "[i]n cases where relevant scientific evidence is insufficient" indicated that a provisional measure could be taken only where some piece of scientific evidence bearing on or pertinent to a more objective assessment of risk was unavailable. Japan had not demonstrated that the relevant scientific evidence was insufficient.

4.209 **Japan** recalled that Article 5.7 did not define what a "provisional measure" was, but conferred on an importing Member a right to "provisionally" adopt an SPS measure, subject to the conditions therein. The text of the Article suggested that a "provisional" measure was one that would meet the two requirements in the first sentence of the Article, namely: (i) the measure was imposed in respect of a situation where "relevant scientific information is insufficient"; and (ii) the measure was adopted "on the basis of available pertinent information". Indeed, the Appellate Body in *Japan – Agricultural Products II* appeared to concur with this interpretation when it stated, "even if the varietal testing requirement were considered to be a provisional measure adopted in accordance with the first sentence of Article 5.7 ...".[138] Nonetheless, even if the Panel were to conclude that "provisionality" related to the length of time, Japan's measure was "provisional" because only eight years had passed since the introduction of the current SPS measure.

4.210 The **United States** contended that the scientific evidence in this case was more than sufficient to establish that imported mature apple fruit did not pose a risk to plant life or health within Japan. The scientific evidence established that exported fruit had not resulted in introduction of fire blight to new areas, despite billions of fruit traded. Major reviews of the scientific evidence related to the epidemiology of the disease had either not considered it necessary to describe the insignificant risk posed by trade in fruit or had explicitly concluded that fruit were not implicated in spread of the disease. The scientific evidence also established that mature apple fruit were not a pathway for the disease. According to the United States, the experts had confirmed that any hypothetical pathway would not be completed because for every such pathway there was at least one step for which there was no scientific evidence in support. This was not a case where the relevant scientific evidence was insufficient; the evidence was more than sufficient to establish that imported apple fruit had never transmitted and were not a means of introduction of fire blight to Japan. As a result, the first requirement under Article 5.7 was not satisfied, and Japan could not adopt provisional measures pursuant to that provision.

4.211 **Japan** believed that considerable scientific evidence existed to support its measure to control the risk of fire blight in US apples. If the Panel were to find that this evidence was not sufficient under Article 2.2, it was nonetheless "available pertinent information" in the context of Article 5.7. These pieces of evidence demonstrated that a phytosanitary measure was needed to counter the risk of dissemination of fire blight via imported US apples.

4.212 The **United States** claimed that Japan had not identified specific "available pertinent information", but instead made vague references to "foreign SPS measures and a range of literature". Even if one were to consider the information that Japan had put forward with respect to Article 2.2 as "available pertinent information", this would not support the measure. None of this information even suggested that mature apple fruit could serve as a pathway for fire blight. Furthermore, foreign fire blight measures in the vast majority of cases either supported the opposite conclusion (they were non-existent or minimal and had nevertheless not resulted in fire blight transmission) or related to the prevention of fire blight spread on host plants (rather than on fruit), such as the buffer zone measures.[139] Speculation was not enough to justify application of a "provisional" measure under Article 5.7. If speculation were sufficient, Members would not need to conduct risk assessments, nor would they need to maintain measures with sufficient scientific evidence; Article 5.7 would simply swallow the rest of the *SPS Agreement*.

---

[138] *Ibid.*, para. 94.
[139] Exhibit USA-14 details fire blight measures imposed on imported apples in fire blight-free areas.

4.213 **Japan** argued that it was evident that its measure was based on available information, including the SPS measures of other Members and a range of literature. Evidence which supported its position included:

(i)   Recovery of the bacteria in van der Zwet *et al.* (1990) and Hale *et al.* (1987) from apparently healthy apple fruit at the very late stage of development ("mature/immature");

(ii)   ambiguity of "maturity" as confirmed by the experts;

(iii)   critical importance of the "symptomless" status as confirmed by the experts;

(iv)   failure in the export practice of Washington apple growers/shippers as demonstrated by the codling moth incident;

(v)   overall confirmation by the experts of the presence of a real "risk" (which included completion of the pathway) of dissemination of the disease from apple fruit;

(vi)   unknown fate of the bacteria inside the apple fruit;

(vii)   relevant scientific evidence for each component of the measure in question, included in scientific literature, international standards and SPS measures of other Members; and

(viii)   several scientific articles supporting each step of the pathway.

4.214 In reply, the **United States** claimed that even a cursory review of Japan's evidence revealed that it did not relate to the steps in Japan's hypothetical pathway. Likewise, the "evidence" did not constitute "pertinent available information" within the meaning of the first sentence of Article 5.7 because it was, in certain instances, nothing more than speculative (items (i) to (vi)) and, in others, not "pertinent" to the exported commodity (items (vii) and (viii)).

4.215 The United States contended that Japan had also failed to meet the requirements of the second sentence of Article 5.7, to "seek to obtain the additional information necessary for a more objective assessment of risk".

4.216 **Japan** recalled that the Appellate Body in *Japan – Agricultural Products II*, had stated that "Article 5.7 does not specify what actual results must be achieved; the obligation is to 'seek to obtain' additional information".[140] Japan had proposed, and implemented part of, a joint study by experts of both countries in 2000 for the purpose of verifying if the current measure could be replaced with another measure maintaining the same level of protection. Japan was also seeking additional information on five items from the United States for the purpose of a "more objective assessment of the risk", as had been noted in paragraph 4.175, above.

4.217 The **United States** argued that Japan's actions in connection with the joint study actually confirmed that it had not been seeking such additional information. Notwithstanding the clear confirmation through this study of results which had been presented to Japan over the previous twelve years, Japan had

---

[140]   Appellate Body Report in *Japan – Agricultural Products II*, para. 92.

waited eight months after the results became known to inform the United States of the alleged flaws in a study it had proposed and previously agreed to, and asked five questions to which it knew the answers. Japan had waited until the 2001 harvest season was under way to comment, at which point it was too late to change its measure to allow shipment of that crop, ensuring at least another year without significant US apple imports. This, the United States maintained, was evidence that Japan had affirmatively avoided relevant additional information. Furthermore, the United States claimed that even if Japan's participation in the joint study could be considered an effort to obtain additional information with respect to the presence of *E. amylovora* in mature apple fruit, it provided no information with respect to other elements of the pathway. Here as well, Japan's refusal to acknowledge information submitted to it over the previous 12 years supported the conclusion that it was not seeking this information, but avoiding it.

4.218 The United States claimed that Japan had also failed to meet the requirement of the final element of Article 5.7, that it "review ... the ... measure within a reasonable period of time". In *Japan – Agricultural Products II*, the Panel had correctly concluded that Japan could not meet this requirement if it was not even seeking the relevant information.[141] Japan in its 1996 and 1999 pest risk assessments had never examined, let alone sought, information and evidence on critical elements of the pathway for transmission of fire blight, nor had Japan done so since. Under these circumstances, it was clear that Japan had not reviewed the measure in the nearly eight years since 1995, notwithstanding the periodic restatements (in response to US prodding) of its speculation that mature apple fruit posed a risk of transmitting fire blight.

4.219 **Japan** stated that the Appellate Body had held that "[i]n our view, what constitutes a 'reasonable period of time' has to be established on a case-by-case basis and depends on the specific circumstances of each case, including the difficulty of obtaining the additional information necessary for the review *and* the characteristics of the provisional SPS measure".[142] The current SPS measure had first been introduced in August 1994, and only eight years had passed since then. A full review had been made of the measure at the time of the 1996 PRA, and again in 1999, satisfying the requirement of a review in the second sentence. Japan further noted that new information for a further review would not be forthcoming unless the United States cooperated, and the process of generating information naturally took time, as was evident from the history of the two experiments conducted in 2000. Japan also noted that it faced difficulties in obtaining additional information through ecological studies. Japan was unable to perform such studies independently as it did not have native fire blight bacteria. As such, cooperation from the United States was essential.

4.220 The **United States** did not believe that a provisional measure needed to be so identified at the time it was adopted, as Article 5.7 did not provide for such a requirement. However, subsequent actions by the Member adopting the measure could demonstrate that a provisionally adopted measure that satisfied

---

[141] Panel Report in *Japan – Agricultural Products II*, para. 8.58.
[142] Appellate Body Report in *Japan – Agricultural Products II*, para. 93.

the requirements of the first sentence might not continue to benefit from the qualified exemption under Article 5.7.

4.221 **Japan** agreed that there was no requirement under Article 5.7 for a Member to label its measure as "provisional". The Article allowed the Member to adopt the measure "provisionally" until such time when a more objective risk assessment was performed and a new measure was introduced within a reasonable period of time, if necessary, as a result of the risk assessment. While Japan's phytosanitary requirements were not formally labelled as a "provisional regulation", the regulations establishing these requirements were in the form of a Ministerial Ordinance or other less authoritative documents, which could easily be amended.

J.   Article 7 (annex b)

4.222 The **United States** claimed that despite years of bilateral discussions with Japan on its fire blight measures, Japan had not complied with its basic notification obligations under Article 7 and Annex B of the *SPS Agreement*. Japan had substantively changed its fire blight measures since the entry into force of the *SPS Agreement* in 1995, but it had failed to notify these changes. This made it significantly more difficult for WTO Members to understand exactly what measures Japan had imposed to address fire blight. Specifically, Japan appeared to have amended or introduced MAFF Notification No. 354 on 10 March 1997, which set the requirements for imports of US apples, and MAFF "Detailed Rules for U.S. Apples" on 1 April 1997, which implemented Notification No. 354, without notifying WTO Members. By failing to notify the changes made to its fire blight measures through these two instruments, Japan had acted inconsistently with Article 7 and Annex B, paragraphs 5 and 7, of the *SPS Agreement*.

4.223 **Japan** countered that it had not substantively changed its fire blight measures since the entry into force of the *SPS Agreement* in 1995. Japan had notified that it would designate *E. amylovora* as one of the diseases that triggered import prohibition as from 1 April 1997, in accordance with the provisions of Article 7 and Annex B.[143] This change of the regulatory status of *E. amylovora* did not affect in any way the measure at issue, which had already been in place. The bacterium had already been placed in a high-risk category at the time of the introduction of the phytosanitary measure. No Member made any comments regarding the designation by the deadline set out in the notification of 17 February 1997. The amendments to the Notification and the Detailed Rules in 1997 were technical re-phrasing of the regulations reflecting the designation of the bacterium, and did not modify, in any way, the phytosanitary requirements against fire blight. The obligation of a Member under Article 7 of the *SPS Agreement* was to notify "changes" in its phytosanitary "measures". Japan argued that it was thus fully compliant with the provisions of Article 7 and Annex B.

---

[143]   G/SPS/N/JPN/19, 17 December 1996.

K.   Article XI of GATT

4.224 The **United States** claimed that Japan had acted inconsistently with its obligations under Article XI of GATT 1994. GATT Article XI prohibited Members from using prohibitions or restrictions on imports other than duties, taxes, or charges. The Japanese fire blight measures prohibited the importation of apples from the United States unless produced, harvested, and imported according to Japan's fire blight restrictions. Thus, Japan had acted inconsistently with GATT Article XI.

4.225 In respect of Article XI of GATT 1994, **Japan** countered that it had established that its measure was consistent with the *SPS Agreement*, and invoked Article 2.4 of the *SPS Agreement*.[144]

L.   Article 4.2 of the Agreement on Agriculture

4.226 The **United States** claimed that Japan had also acted inconsistently with its obligations under Article 4.2 of the Agreement on Agriculture. Article 4.2 of the Agreement on Agriculture prohibited Members from maintaining, resorting to, or reverting to any prohibited measures, such as quantitative import restrictions, that impeded market access. The Japanese fire blight measures prohibited the importation of apples from the United States unless produced, harvested, and imported according to Japan's fire blight restrictions. Thus, Japan had acted inconsistently with Article 4.2 of the Agreement on Agriculture.

4.227 In respect of Article 4.2 of the Agreement on Agriculture, **Japan** argued that the measure in question was not a measure which had been "required to be converted into ordinary customs duties", and therefore was not prohibited under that article.[145]

V.   SUMMARY OF THIRD PARTY SUBMISSIONS

A.   Australia

5.1   Australia noted that fire blight was a serious disease of apples and pears, in terms of the potential biological and economic consequences. Australia and Japan were among the very few fire blight disease-free countries where it was possible to grow apples and pears on a commercially significant basis. In accordance with the *SPS Agreement*, WTO Members were entitled to take measures that might be necessary to prevent the entry, establishment or spread of exotic disease or pests. Those rights did not require positive proof that the disease or pest in question would be introduced through an imported product. Rather, a WTO Member maintained the right to take measures to guard against the *likelihood* of disease or pest transmission through an imported product.

---

[144] See also Japan's procedural argument, paras 4.1-4.3.
[145] *Ibid.*

1. Burden of Proof

5.2   In Australia's opinion, the adopted reports of several relevant WTO disputes had clarified that the burden of proof rested on the complainant party and that assertions, in the case of the *SPS Agreement*, had to be supported by relevant and reliable scientific evidence. The Appellate Body in *EC – Hormones* had acknowledged the importance of correctly allocating the burden of proof in SPS disputes, which raised "multiple and complex issues of fact".[146] The Appellate Body had stated that the complaining party bore the initial burden of proof to establish a prima facie case of inconsistency with an identified provision of the *SPS Agreement*. The Appellate Body had reiterated that:

> "a prima facie case is one which, in the absence of effective refutation by the defending party, requires a panel, as a matter of law, to rule in favour of the complaining party presenting the prima facie case".[147]

2. Standard for Developing a prima facie Presumption

5.3   Australia considered that when developing a prima facie case, all assertions must be documented and relate to relevant legal tests including the *likelihood* of entry, establishment or spread. Scientific evidence to support a prima facie presumption should be valid scientific evidence, based on scientific principles, including scientific studies. In Australia's view, it was insufficient to assert that there was *no* evidence of entry, establishment or spread of the disease in question associated with the import of the product at issue, or according to a measure which might be applied.

5.4   In the case before the Panel, it was Australia's assertion that the United States bore the burden of establishing a prima facie case that there was not a rational or objective relationship between Japan's measures and the scientific evidence. In doing so, it was Australia's contention that the United States could not rest its case on assertions about the quality and quantity of scientific evidence relied upon by Japan. The arguments of the United States had to be supported by scientific evidence.

3. Conflicting Scientific Evidence and Opinion

5.5   According to Australia, scientific evidence need not be monolithic in character and that conflicting scientific evidence was not unusual; in fact, it was rare for scientific opinion to be unanimous. As such, minority scientific opinion, based on valid scientific data, could not be discounted as evidence. The Appellate Body in *EC – Hormones*, recognizing the realities of conflicting scientific evidence, had considered that a risk assessment need not come to a "monolithic conclusion" that coincided with the scientific conclusion or view

---

[146]   Appellate Body Report in *EC - Hormones*, para. 97.

[147]   *Ibid.*, para. 104.

implicit in the SPS measure.[148] Nor had a risk assessment to embody only the majority scientific view. Further, the Appellate Body had emphasized the need for a practical or "real world" approach to risk. A risk assessment was not confined to an examination of only those factors susceptible to quantitative analysis by empirical or experimental laboratory methods.[149]

5.6   In the case before the Panel, Australia argued that even when limited to mature and symptomless apples, the available science showed there was no monolithic opinion on the risk of transmission of fire blight through fruit. In reply to a question from the Panel, Australia provided its understanding of the conflicting views regarding the presence or absence of infestation and of infection of fruit with fire blight. Australia identified the following studies as supporting a view of infestation (surface colonization) of fruit with *E. amylovora:*

Hale *et al.* (1987)	Isolated viable *E. amylovora* from 3% of harvested mature apples from a severely infected orchard (natural infection).
Sholberg *et al.* (1988)	Isolated viable *E. amylovora* from 100% of fruit harvested in September (coinciding with commercial harvest) from symptomless apple trees grown adjacent to blighted pear trees.
	Isolated an average of $10^{3.3}$ colony-forming units (cfu) per ml of viable *E. amylovora* at harvest, from naturally contaminated, blemish free and apparently healthy fruit from an orchard severely damaged by fire blight after a hail storm.
van der Zwet *et al.* (1990)	Isolated viable *E. amylovora* from the calyx, stem-end and surface of apples, some harvested in September, from naturally infected orchards in West Virginia and Utah.
	In West Virginia, 5% (2/40) of healthy Delicious variety fruit harvested 30 km away from infected orchards (see Methods section -Geographic survey) had calyx infestation. The population of *E. amylovora* exceeded 1000 cfu per fruit.
	Mature, symptomless, non-disinfested fruit (4%) developed blight symptoms following injury (fruit injury experiment).
	Australia understood that the maturity of the fruit used in the experiments was either: (i) "mature" (harvest date inferred as mid-October); (ii) "collected at harvest" (i.e. September – the use of the word "harvest" supported an assumption of maturity); (iii) "developing fruit" (use of the word "developing" supported the assumption that the fruit was not mature); (iv) "harvested in August and September" (use of the word "harvested" supported an assumption of maturity); and (v) "sampled in late July, August and September" (the apparent avoidance of the terms "harvest" and "developing" supported the assumption these fruit were of mixed maturity).

---

[148]   *Ibid.*, para. 194.
[149]   *Ibid.*, para. 187.

On the other hand, Australia understood the following studies to support a conclusion of non-infestation of mature apple fruit:

Dueck (1974)	Did not isolate *E. amylovora* from external tissues of 60 mature apples harvested from severely infected trees (natural infection).
Hale *et al.* (1987)	Did not isolate *E. amylovora* from 1300 mature apples harvested from two lightly (naturally) infected and three symptomless orchards.
Clark *et al.* (1993)	A DNA hybridization method did not detect *E. amylovora* in calyxes of either immature or mature apples harvested from within 20 cm of the inoculum source, in a season not conducive for spread of fire blight.
Hale *et al.* (1996)	*E. amylovora* was not detected either in the calyxes or on the surfaces of mature 173 fruit harvested (even) within 5 cm of inoculum sites, approximately 4 months after artificial inoculation.

With respect to the infection (internal colonization) of mature fruit with *E. amylovora*, Australia noted that the following studies supported a positive finding:

Goodman (1954)	Recovered viable *E. amylovora* from the tissues "directly beneath the skin" of several apples that were retained on trees until February. These trees had been severely affected during the previous growing season. The report stated that the fruit had moist flesh, indicating that they were not mummified and therefore supporting the conclusion that they had developed normally.
van der Zwet *et al.* (1990)	One per cent mature (harvested in October) surface sterilized fruit from a disease free tree developed blight in storage. Australia noted that the results of this experiment were confirmed by diagnostic tests conducted on a random sample of blighted fruit. Recovered viable *E. amylovora* from the internal tissue of mature Rome Beauty and Delicious variety apples, grown in blighted orchards in Utah. According to the Methods section Delicious fruit (for the "blighted category") were collected from healthy trees located 1-2 m from severely blighted Jonathan trees.
Anderson (1952)	Isolated viable *E. amylovora* from mature pears that had been artificially inoculated and held in cold storage for several months. This demonstrated that *E. amylovora* could survive in mature pear fruit.

McLarty (1924), (1925) and (1926)	Isolated viable *E. amylovora* from apples that had been artificially inoculated on the tree when they were immature, allowed to mature and then held in storage for several months. This demonstrated that *E. amylovora* could withstand the physiological changes in fruit as it matured.

5.7   In contrast, Australia indicated that the following studies supported a negative finding of internal *E. amylovora* in mature apple fruit.

Dueck (1974)	Did not isolate viable *E. amylovora* from internal tissues of 60 mature apples harvested from severely infected trees (natural infection).
Roberts *et al.* (1989)	*E. amylovora* was not recovered from core tissues of 1,555 symptomless fruit harvested from blighted trees and cold stored. The authors clearly indicated that the fruit they had used in their experiments were mature. The harvest dates ranged from late August through to late September. Washington is at a higher latitude and therefore fruit grown in West Virginia or Utah was expected to mature earlier or at a similar time, subject to varietal differences.
Roberts (2002)	*E. amylovora* symptoms were not observed on core tissues of 1,500 symptomless fruit harvested from blighted trees (exposed to natural and artificial inoculum). Diagnostic tests on 500 of these fruit also proved negative. Australia noted that environmental conditions during the experiments reported in this work were apparently not conducive for the disease. Roberts *et al* (1989) in the discussion section noted the implications of humid weather in Washington for the recovery of *E. amylovora* from fruit.
van der Zwet *et al.* (1990)	*E. amylovora* was not recovered from the internal tissue of mature apples grown in Washington, West Virginia and Ontario.

5.8   In accordance with these results, it was Australia's view that the Panel should reaffirm the principle that where there was conflicting science, governments could, in good faith, rely on science that provided the appropriate level of protection the importing Member deemed necessary.

4.   The Product at Issue

5.9   Australia deemed it necessary to clearly identify the product at issue and to ensure that claims, counterclaims, arguments and evidence related to the identical product. In this context, Australia recalled that in *Australia – Salmon*, the Appellate Body had found that the SPS measure at issue in the dispute could only be the measure that was actually applied *to the product at issue*.[150] (emphasis added) The United States in its request for a panel had identified the product at issue as "apples". As such, evidence submitted only in relation to mature, symptomless apples would not be applicable to the first two tests of Article 5.1 in establishing whether Japan's risk assessment met the criteria for a

---

[150]   *Ibid.*, para 103.

proper risk assessment.[151] Because the United States had not limited the product coverage of its complaint to mature, symptomless apples, it was Australia's contention that a risk assessment would need to include an identification of the disease in apples of US origin, as well as the likelihood of entry, establishment or spread from all apples of US origin, not just mature, symptomless apples.

B.   Brazil

5.10   As a country with fire blight-free status that permitted the importation of US apples, under the conditions set out below, Brazil had a special interest in this dispute. As one of the world's major exporters of agricultural products, Brazil was also interested in ensuring that the *SPS Agreement* was interpreted and implemented correctly.

1.   Issues in Relation to the SPS Agreement

5.11   Brazil noted that the United States claimed that Japan had acted inconsistently with Article 2.2 of the *SPS Agreement* because its measures were "maintained without sufficient scientific evidence". Article 2.2 of the *SPS Agreement* states the general obligation of providing sufficient scientific justification to underpin measures implemented by a Member. It also states that sanitary and phytosanitary measures should be "based on scientific principles" and be "applied to the extent necessary to protect human, animal or plant life or health". In Brazil's view, these three obligations should be taken into account together when determining whether or not a country was acting in consistency with Article 2.2.

5.12   The intent of the *SPS Agreement* was to protect human, animal, and plant health and life from risks arising from trade in agricultural products while avoiding unnecessary restrictions to trade. For that reason, a sanitary measure should not only be based on scientific criteria but also be applied only to the "extent necessary to protect human, animal or plant life or health. In other words, the measure should be the least restrictive to trade as possible. This obligation was reiterated in Article 5.6.

5.13   The best way for a country to comply with this requirement was to base its SPS measures, to the extent possible, on international standards, guidelines, and recommendations. This was the desirable scenario for Brazil. When countries based their measures on internationally agreed standards, guidelines, and recommendations, they minimized potential conflicts and reduced negative impacts to trade.

5.14   However, Brazil realized that countries faced situations where they had to adopt measures that diverted from the international standard, guideline, or recommendation. Where specific circumstances related to the product and the

---

[151]   The first two tests to which Australia referred were the first two of three tests established in paragraph 121 of the Appellate Body report in *Australia - Salmon:* identification of the disease and an evaluation of the likelihood of entry, establishment or spread, as well as the associated consequences.

pest required a different measure, countries should base their measure on an appropriate risk assessment, that took into account "risk assessment techniques developed by the relevant international organizations", such as the IPPC. The IPCC had developed objective criteria for pest risk assessments which, in Brazil's view, helped countries to comply with their obligations under Articles 2.2, 5.1, 5.2 and 5.6 of the *SPS Agreement*.

5.15   In this connection, Brazil recalled the findings of the Appellate Body in *Australia - Salmon* that a risk assessment within the meaning of Article 5.1 had to:

(i)   Identify the diseases whose entry, establishment or spread a Member wants to prevent within its territory, as well as the potential biological and economic consequences associated with the entry, establishment or spread of these diseases;

(ii)   evaluate the likelihood of entry, establishment or spread of these diseases, as well as the associated potential biological and economic consequences; and

(iii)   evaluate the likelihood of entry, establishment or spread of these diseases according to the SPS measures which might be applied.

5.16   Although the United States had not raised the question of equivalence of sanitary and phytosanitary measures, for Brazil there seemed to be a close link between the US claims and the implementation of Article 4 of the *SPS Agreement*. Article 4 stated that "Members shall accept the sanitary or phytosanitary measures of other Members as equivalent even if this measure differs from their own or from those used by other Members trading in the same product". Article 4 also indicated that in order for SPS measures to be considered equivalent, the exporting country had to objectively demonstrate that the alternative measure achieved the appropriate level of protection (ALOP) of the importing country, that is, that its measure produced the same effect in terms of achieving the ALOP of the importing country. In this case, even if the Japanese measures related to the import of US apples were consistent with the requirements of Article 2.2, Japan should have given full consideration to the question of equivalence of the US sanitary measures. Brazil attached great importance to the implementation of Article 4, which was a useful tool for countries, especially developing country Members, to implement their obligations under the *SPS Agreement*.

5.17   Japan had submitted, as an alternative defence, that its measures were justifiable under Article 5.7 of the *SPS Agreement*. Brazil advocated a strict interpretation of Article 5.7 to prevent its use as a disguised barrier to trade. For a measure to be considered consistent with Article 5.7, four requirements must be met fully and concurrently:

(a)   "Relevant scientific information is insufficient";

(b)   the measure is adopted "on the basis of available pertinent information, including that from the relevant international organizations as well as from sanitary and phytosanitary measures applied by other Members", (which meant that all information relevant to the case should be taken into account);

(c)   the country that applies the measure should seek to obtain "additional information necessary for a more objective assessment of risk"; and

(d)   the country that applies the measure should also seek to review the measure accordingly within a reasonable period of time.

2.   Brazilian Phytosanitary Measures on US Apples[152]

5.18   Although Brazil was fire blight-free, Brazilian legislation required only that the US phytosanitary authorities certify that apples exported to Brazil be produced in fire blight-free areas or receive post-harvest treatment. Brazil stated that its sanitary measure was based on the available scientific information and was applied only to the extent necessary to protect its territory from the entry and dissemination of the fire blight pest.

5.19   In specific terms, Instrução Normativa (Instruction Norm) No. 4/2001 of 11 January 2001, established specific sanitary requirements for some pests, including *E. amylovora* affecting apples produced in the United States. This regulation covered two situations where US apples could be exported to Brazil:

(a)   Apples coming from non fire blight-free areas had to receive a post harvest treatment before being exported. US phytosanitary authorities had to certify that: "The shipment was treated with TCM n° 14 to eliminate fire blight, under official supervision attesting the treatment's efficacy for the pest". TCM no. 14 required that apples were submitted to an immersion bath with a chlorine solution at the concentration of 100 ppm for 1 minute, with a view to eliminate fire blight.

(b)   US phytosanitary authorities must certify that: "The product was cultivated in an area recognized by the phytosanitary authorities of the importing country as free of fire blight, according with COSAVE Standard 3.2 - Requirements for establishing pest free areas".

5.20   The Brazilian phytosanitary authorities had engaged in bilateral negotiations with their US counterparts with a view to determining the areas considered free of fire blight. After those areas had been established, the only measure affecting the importation of US apples from pest-free areas was a phytosanitary certificate attesting that the product came from one of the free areas. Apples were not required to undergo any further treatment or quarantine procedure. Brazil considered its measures on US apples to be in conformity with Article 6 of the *SPS Agreement*.

---

[152]   Reply from Brazil to a question from the Panel, 13 November 2002.

5.21   Brazilian requirements for the importation of apples from fire blight-free countries were essentially the same. The phytosanitary authorities of the exporting country had to certify that the pest was not present in the country.

C.   European Communities

5.22   The European Communities stated that it was intervening as a third party because of systemic interests related to the interpretation and application of the *SPS Agreement*.

1.   Procedural Issues

5.23   Japan, as the respondent party, had raised issues of general procedural interest for the European Communities, especially in the context of relying on available scientific evidence to support protection measures.

5.24   The European Communities noted that the United States had failed to state its claims with regard to a number of articles that it had mentioned in the request for the establishment of the Panel. The European Communities was of the view that the comprehensive identification of all the claims at the earliest possible point in the procedure was of great importance for the correct development of dispute settlement.[153] The Appellate Body had made it clear on several occasions that a Panel could not rule in favour of a complaining party "which has not established a prima facie case of inconsistency based on specific legal claims asserted by it".[154.] A panel could not make a case for the complainant. The issue of whether the United States had failed to appropriately state all of its claims raised the further concern of whether the United States had been able to submit a prima facie case that Japan had violated certain provisions.

5.25   The European Communities was of the view that the practice of not stating all claims in the first written submission prevented the respondent from using all the various stages of the Panel procedure to properly defend itself. This practice also prevented third parties from being aware of the substance of certain claims at issue and making any pertinent contribution. Furthermore the fact that the United States had deliberately chosen not to advance arguments on all claims

---

[153]   The European Communities recalled that in *Chile – Price Band System* dispute, the Appellate Body made reference to its earlier case law that "there is no requirement in the DSU or in GATT practice for arguments on all claims relating to the matter referred to the DSB to be set out in a complaining party's first written submission to the panel." However, the Appellate Body had further specified that: "The requirements of due process and orderly procedure dictate that claims must be made explicitly in WTO dispute settlement. Only in this way will the panel, other parties, and third parties understand that a specific claim has been made, be aware of its dimensions, and have an adequate opportunity to address and respond to it. WTO Members must not be left to wonder what specific claims have been made against them in dispute settlement. As we said in *India – Patents*: 'All parties engaged in dispute settlement under the DSU must be fully forthcoming *from the very beginning* both as to the claims involved in a dispute and as to the facts relating to those claims. Claims must be stated clearly' (Appellate Body Report in *India - Patents*, para. 94). (emphasis added), Appellate Body Report in *Chile – Price Band System*, paras. 158 and 164.

[154]   Appellate Body Report in *Japan – Agricultural Products II*, para. 129. See also Appellate Body Report in *Brazil – Aircraft*, para. 194.

in this case, and then to defend itself against Japan's request to strike out certain claims by defining this request as "premature", showed a clear disrespect for the rights of the respondent and for the interests of third parties. The European Communities considered this attitude to be contrary to Article 10 of the DSU.

5.26   The European Communities took note of Japan's argument that the United States had not properly identified its claim because it had not indicated from which point in time the measures applied by Japan should be considered as incompatible with the obligations under the *SPS Agreement*.[155] Japan further argued that unless the relevant point in time was identified, the possibility opened by Article 5.7 could not be properly used, as it would be impossible for Japan to determine the "reasonable period of time".

5.27   The European Communities considered that to be in line with the obligations under Article 2.2 of the *SPS Agreement,* "sufficient scientific evidence" had to support any sanitary or phytosanitary measure at any point in time. This meant that in cases where scientific evidence available at the time of the introduction of the measure had been sufficient to justify the measure but had later been overturned by new scientific evidence, the measure could no longer be maintained. However, in order to establish a prima facie case of violation of Article 2.2 and to allow the correspondent to construct a defence, the European Communities was of the view that the United States should have specified the point in time at which it considered that the Japanese measures at issue had become "maintained without sufficient scientific evidence". This was particularly true because the United States was not contesting the very adoption of the measures under Article 2.2 but only their maintenance.

5.28   The European Communities noted Japan's objection to the use, by the complainant, of evidence, which had not been published, and which had been submitted to the respondent for the first time with the complainant's submission. The European Communities viewed the issue raised by Japan as more than merely procedural. The nature of the evidence to be considered "sufficient" under Article 2.2 of the *SPS Agreement* required that this be "public" and certainly "scientific", i.e. reached through verified expert knowledge. The European Communities argued that the United States could not use arguments related to the submission of evidence to shift the burden of proof under Article 2.2 of the *SPS Agreement.*

2.   *Legal Arguments on Articles 2.2, 5.1 and 5.7*

5.29   Article 2.2 of the *SPS Agreement* creates an obligation for the Member to ensure that sanitary or phytosanitary measures are "not maintained without sufficient scientific evidence", apart from cases of application of Article 5.7 of the Agreement. In this context, the European Communities recalled that obviously it was possible that there could be different scientific opinions about the need to protect plant life. Certain scientific studies could conclude that there were risks of spreading a plant disease while other studies could come to the

---

[155]   Japan first submission, paras. 18-28.

opposite conclusion. As such, "scientific evidence" was the total of the available evidence.[156]

5.30   The European Communities argued that the crucial notion in that context was "sufficient". The Appellate Body had found that there had to be a "sufficient or adequate relationship between two elements, *in casu*, between the SPS measure and the scientific evidence". This relationship was also qualified as "rational or objective" and had to be determined in each individual case according to its particular circumstances, including the characteristics of the measure and the quality and quantity of scientific evidence.[157]

5.31   In this context, the distribution of the burden of proof was important. In order to establish an inconsistency of Japan's measures with the obligations of Article 2.2, it was for the United States to show in the first place, that these measures were not supported by sufficient scientific evidence. To do so, the United States might use any evidence available, including new scientific evidence, which was available at the time when the measures were initially introduced. However, the notion of evidence in Article 2.2 could not be understood to include scientific information that was not available or accessible to the party imposing the SPS measures. Therefore private or unpublished scientific evidence, of which the party had no knowledge, could not be taken into account when establishing whether the scientific evidence on which the SPS measure was based was (still) sufficient. The European Communities argued that this interpretation of the notion of "evidence" as meaning "*available* evidence" was in line with the provisions on risk assessment as Article 5.2 that obliged Members to take into account "*available* scientific evidence".

5.32   The European Communities recalled that Article 5.1 of the *SPS Agreement* obliged Members to ensure that their SPS measures were based on an assessment of the risks. There were at least three conditions for a risk assessment to be in line with Article 5.1. The risk assessment had to "identify" the diseases that the Member wanted to prevent and had to identify their biological and economic consequences. The risk assessment had also to evaluate the likelihood of the entry, establishment or spread of the disease in the territory of the Member and the potential biological and economic consequences. Finally, the same likelihood and consequences had to be evaluated according to the SPS measures which may be applied.[158]

5.33   In the present case, Japan had clearly identified the disease. With regard to the likelihood of entry, establishment or spread of the disease within Japan it was established jurisprudence that the risk assessment must not only establish a *possibility* but the *"likelihood, i.e. probability"* of such entry, establishment or

[156]   In *Japan – Agricultural Products II*, the Appellate Body referred to its report in *EC - Hormones* with regard to the existence of "mainstream" scientific opinion" and "divergent opinion coming from qualified and respected sources". For the European Communities, both were "scientific evidence" in the sense of Article 2.2 of the *SPS Agreement*.

[157]   Appellate Body Report in *Japan – Agricultural Products II*, para.73 and para.84.

[158]   Appellate Body Report in *Australia - Salmon*, para.121; Appellate Body Report, *Japan – Agricultural Products II*, para. 112.

spread.[159] Such risk assessment must refer to the likely consequences of the imports to which SPS measures might be applied. In the present case, therefore, the risk assessment carried out by Japan must concern apples as imported from the United States. Finally, the risk assessment carried out by Japan must have evaluated the likelihood of entry, establishment or spread of the disease through the importation of US apples in the hypothesis of the SPS measures being applied. In this regard, it was to be noted that a reasonable relationship between the risk assessment and the SPS measure must exist. However, that did not mean that the risk assessment had to come to a monolithic conclusion that coincided with the scientific conclusion or view implicit in the SPS measure. It might well be that in a given case there were divergent views of qualified scientists about a particular issue, indicating a state of scientific uncertainty. It was also possible for Members to act in good faith on the basis of what, at a given time, might be a divergent opinion coming from qualified and respected sources.[160]

5.34   The European Communities noted that Japan had submitted that if the Panel were to find that the evidence it had relied on was insufficient, thus causing a violation of Article 2.2, Japan's measures would still be justified under Article 5.7 of the *SPS Agreement* and could be maintained provisionally. In light of this alternative defence under Article 5.7, the European Communities restated its view that the precautionary principle had become a full-fledged and general principle of international law.[161] In addition, according to the Appellate Body, Article 5.7, together with other provisions of the *SPS Agreement*, reflected the precautionary principle.[162]

5.35   In *EC – Hormones*, the Appellate Body had usefully clarified some of the aspects related to the interpretation and application of the precautionary principle under the *SPS Agreement*. In particular, the Appellate Body had concurred with the European Communities that Article 5.7 did not exhaust the relevance of the principle. Thus, when reflected in the sixth paragraph of the preamble and in Article 3.3 of the Agreement, it granted Members the right to establish their own chosen level of protection. With regard to the specifics of Article 5.7, it was clear to the European Communities that a precautionary SPS measure had still to be

---

[159]   Appellate Body Report in *Australia - Salmon*, para. 123.

[160]   Appellate Body Report in *EC – Hormones*, para. 194.

[161]   According to the European Communities, at international level, the precautionary principle had first been recognized in the World Charter for Nature, adopted by the UN General Assembly in 1982 and had subsequently been incorporated into various international conventions on the protection of the environment. At the beginning of nineties, the Rio Declaration that concluded the 1992 Rio Conference on the Environment and Development, codified an application of this principle in its Principle 15, which stated that: "in order to protect the environment, the precautionary approach shall be widely applied by States according to their capability. Where there are threats of serious or irreversible damage, lack of full scientific certainty shall not be used as a reason for postponing cost-effective measures to prevent environmental degradation." Since then, the United Nations Framework Convention on Climate Change and the Convention of Biological Diversity had both referred to the Precautionary Principle. On 28 January 2000, at the Conference of the Parties to the Convention on Biological Diversity, the Protocol on Biosafety concerning the safe transfer, handling and use of living modified organisms resulting from modern biotechnology confirmed the key function of the precautionary principle.

[162]   Appellate Body Report in *EC – Hormones*, para. 124.

based on an assessment of the available pertinent information with regard to the risks posed by substances, diseases or organisms present in a given good. There was no requirement to conduct a quantitative analysis or to embody the view of the majority of the scientific community (assuming that there was some available scientific evidence to take into account). A Member might well act in good faith on the basis of non-quantifiable data of a factual or qualitative nature, as well as of a divergent opinion coming from qualified and respected sources, or any new pertinent information that might become available.[163]

5.36 In *Japan – Agricultural Products II*, the Appellate Body had further clarified four cumulative conditions for the application of Article 5.7. The measure had to be: (1) imposed in respect of a situation where relevant scientific information was insufficient; and (2) adopted on the basis of available pertinent information. Such a provisional measure might not be maintained unless the Member which had adopted the measure; (3) sought to obtain the additional information necessary for a more objective assessment; and (4) reviewed the measure accordingly within a reasonable period of time. These four requirements were cumulative and equally important for the purpose of determining compliance with the provisions of Article 5.7. Whenever one of these four requirements was not met, according to the ruling of the Appellate Body, the measure was inconsistent with Article 5.7.[164] It was furthermore the view of the European Communities that the "provisional" nature of the measures adopted on the basis of Article 5.7 did not refer to a time limit but to the development of scientific knowledge.[165]

5.37 The European Communities further submitted that the application of the precautionary principle under Article 5.7 of the *SPS Agreement* should also take into account the following criteria which it believed to be fully consistent with the Article 5.7 as interpreted by the Appellate Body.[166]

5.38 Firstly, the SPS measures envisaged should be proportionate and no more trade restrictive than was required to achieve the level of protection deemed to be appropriate by the Member that applied them. Precautionary measures should not, however, be assessed only against reduction of immediate risks. It was, in fact, in situations in which the adverse effects did not emerge until long after exposure that the cause-effect relationships were more difficult to prove scientifically and that – for this reason – the precautionary principle often had to be invoked. In this case, the potential long-term effects had to be taken into account in evaluating the proportionality of the measures.

5.39 Secondly, the measures should not be discriminatory in their application. Measures taken under the precautionary principle should be designed to achieve an equivalent level of protection without arbitrarily invoking the geographical

[163] *Ibid.*, paras. 172, 124, 187 and 194.
[164] Appellate Body Report in *Japan – Agricultural Products II*, para. 89.
[165] See *Communication of the European Commission on the Precautionary Principle*, WT/CTE/W/147, G/TBT/W/137, of 27 June 2000.
[166] These criteria have also be described in greater details in the *Communication of the European Commission on the Precautionary Principle*, cited above, heading 6.3.

origin or the nature of the production process to apply different treatments in an arbitrary manner. This was in line with the general obligation expressed in Article 2.3 of the *SPS Agreement*.

5.40   The goal should be to achieve consistency between measures adopted in similar circumstances or using similar approaches. Of course, the comparability between two different situations should be assessed on the basis of the available pertinent information in each case.

5.41   The measures adopted presupposed examination of the benefits and costs, economic and non-economic, as appropriate, of action and lack of action. This examination must consider whether, on the basis of the available pertinent information, another measure was reasonably available that achieved the appropriate level of protection and was significantly less restrictive on trade.

5.42   The measures, although provisional, might be maintained as long as a more complete risk assessment could not be conducted because the scientific data remained incomplete, imprecise or inconclusive and as long as the risk was considered to be too high relative to the chosen level of protection. However, maintenance of the measures should depend on the development of scientific knowledge. Therefore, the regulatory authorities should re-evaluate the data and the measure once new scientific information was obtained.

D.   New Zealand

5.43   New Zealand's participation as a third party reflected its "substantial interest" in the issues of principle arising from Japan's fire blight measures that restrict the import of apples. As a nation whose economy relies heavily on agricultural exports, the proper implementation of the *SPS Agreement* was of fundamental importance to New Zealand. New Zealand considered that the fire blight measures imposed by Japan were inconsistent with Japan's obligations under the *SPS Agreement*. Japan's measures also had significant practical consequences for New Zealand, since they made exports of New Zealand apples to Japan uneconomic.

1.   Scientific Evidence Relating to Fire Blight

5.44   Scientific evidence plays a fundamental role in the framework established by the *SPS Agreement*. The *SPS Agreement* underlined the importance of sanitary or phytosanitary measures being objectively justifiable, and emphasised the need to apply scientific principles and scientific evidence in the development of measures. Japan's fire blight measures on fresh apple imports were not supported by scientific evidence and were inconsistent with the requirements of the *SPS Agreement*.

5.45   Japan had explained that it was seeking to protect itself against the introduction of fire blight via apple fruit imports. Available scientific evidence had demonstrated, however, that mature apple fruit had never been shown to cause the introduction of fire blight and that mature apple fruit were not a pathway for fire blight.

5.46   The absence of a pathway via mature apple fruit was shown in the first instance by the complete lack of evidence that fire blight had ever been introduced into an area by mature apple fruit from anywhere in the world, taking into account both incidents of trans-oceanic and continental dissemination of fire blight.

5.47   In the case of New Zealand, the method of introduction (entry and establishment) of *E. amylovora* into New Zealand was not known, although one group of scientists believed that fire blight was imported into New Zealand on nursery stock.[167] The method of introduction of *E. amylovora* into the United Kingdom was also not known. It might have been introduced on infected plant material or on contaminated fruit crates, but this had never been proved.[168] In the case of Hawaii, *E. amylovora* had been isolated in Hawaii in 1965 from rotten pears imported from the United States. Although the bacteria entered Hawaii at that time, it was not associated with apple fruit, and it did not establish on host plants in Hawaii. In the absence of establishment, it could not be claimed that fire blight had been introduced to Hawaii. Finally, in the case of Egypt, fire blight had been reported to occur in Egypt in 1964.[169] While El-Helaly *et al.* had not directly addressed the question of the source of introduction of the disease, however, they did suggest that it was most likely to have been introduced on imported nursery stock from European countries where the disease had long been established.

5.48   New Zealand stressed that scientific research using molecular techniques into the spread of fire blight disease in Europe had concluded that despite the uncontrolled trade in apple fruit into and within the European Union, introduction of fire blight had been via sequential spread or the importation of infected planting material - but not by apple fruit.[170] In this regard New Zealand also noted that a paper published by Jock *et al.* (2002) had demonstrated that, despite barely controlled trade in fire blight host plants and plant products, the

---

[167]   New Zealand referred to publications by A.H. Cockayne (1920), "Fire Blight: A Serious Disease of Fruit Trees", *New Zealand Journal of Agriculture* No. 20, pp. 156-157; J.A. Campbell (1920), "The Orchard: The Outbreak of Fire Blight", *New Zealand Journal of Agriculture* No. 20, pp. 181-182; J.D. Atkinson (1971), "Diseases of Tree Fruits", *New Zealand Department of Scientific And Industrial Research Information Series* 81; and W.G Bonn and T. van der Zwet (2000), "Distribution and Economic Importance", in *Fire Blight; The Disease and its Causative Agent – Erwinia amylovora*, Ed. J.L. Vanneste, CAB International.

[168]   R.A. Lelliott (1959), Fire Blight of Pears in England, *Agriculture* 65 pp. 564-568; T. van der Zwet, and H.L. Keil (1979), "Fire Blight – A Bacterial Disease of Rosaceous Plants", US Department of Agriculture Handbook No. 510, p. 12; and Bonn & van der Zwet (2000) *Fire Blight: the Disease and its Causative Agent, Erwinia amylovora*, at. 37-53 (J. L. Vanneste ed.).

[169]   El-Helaly, A.F., Abo-El-Daheb, M.K., El-Goorani, M.A. (1964), "The Occurrence of Fire Blight Disease of Pear in Egypt", *Phytopathologia Mediterranea* No.3, pp. 156-163.

[170]   López, M.M., Gorris, M.T., Llop, P., Cambra, M., Borruel, M., Plaza, B.; Roselló, M., García, P, Palomo, J.L., and Berra, D. (1999). Fire blight in Spain: situation and monitoring. *Acta Horticulturae* 489, 187-191; Zhang, Y., and Geider, K. (1997). Differentiation of Erwinia amylovora strains by pulsed-field gel electrophoresis. *Applied and Environmental Microbiology* 63(11) 4421-4426.

---

spread of fire blight around Europe was normally sequential by vectors such as insects, birds and wind.[171]

5.49   New Zealand stated that scientific experts who had studied the likelihood that fire blight would be introduced via the importation of mature apple fruit had concluded that the risk that such an event would occur was so low as to be negligible. Scientific research into four key steps of the chain of events making up the disease pathway justified this conclusion of negligible risk:

(i)   Fire blight bacteria did not occur internally in mature apples.

(ii)   The incidence of bacteria on the surface, including in the calyx, of mature apples was very rare.

(iii)   Normal post-harvest handling practices for apples exported to Japan (including cold storage) had been shown to further reduce the likelihood of fire blight bacteria being present on mature apples imports, which had already been shown to be extremely unlikely.

(iv)   Scientific evidence also supported the view that there was no vector to transfer bacteria from a mature apple to a receptive host plant. This, therefore, indicated that there was a complete break in the transmission pathway at this point.

5.50   Mature apples were the only type of apples exported. Immature fruit were not harvested or exported, as fruit harvested when immature would not ripen and would be unmarketable. In addition, mature apples were, by their nature, symptomless since infected blossom clusters or fruitlets developed abnormally, and aborted or shrivelled on the branch.

2.   Inconsistency of Japan's Fire Blight Measures with the SPS Agreement

5.51   New Zealand considered that Japan's fire blight measures were inconsistent with Japan's obligations under Articles 2.2, 5.1, 5.2 and 5.6 of the *SPS Agreement*. In accordance with the normal rules on burden of proof that were confirmed in the SPS context by the Appellate Body in *EC - Hormones*, the United States was required to establish a prima facie case that Japan's measure was inconsistent with the *SPS Agreement*. It was then for Japan to present scientific evidence satisfactory to rebut the presumption established by the United States.

5.52   According to Article 2.2 of the *SPS Agreement*, Japan shall not maintain SPS measures without sufficient scientific evidence. In *Japan – Agricultural Products II*, the Appellate Body stated that this meant there had to be a rational relationship between the scientific evidence and the SPS measures being maintained. In the view of New Zealand, the points made by Japan fell well short

---

[171]   Jock, S., Donat, V. Lopez, M.M., Bazzi, C., and Geider, K. (2002), "Following spread of fire blight in Western, Central and Southern Europe by molecular differentiation of *Erwinia amylovora* strains with PFGE analysis", *Environmental Micobiology* 4(2), pp. 106-114.

of objective, scientific support for the application of fire blight measures to mature apple fruit. Japan's fire blight measures bore no rational relationship to the scientific evidence since they regulated the importation of a commodity that the scientific evidence had shown was not a pathway for the introduction of fire blight - the disease Japan aimed to protect itself against.

5.53   This case was also not one where Japan could rely on Article 5.7 of the *SPS Agreement* to justify the imposition of its fire blight restrictions as provisional measures. Scientific evidence about the introduction of fire blight caused by imports of mature apples was not insufficient. In fact, a significant quantity of scientific research had been conducted to investigate the sources of introduction of fire blight to new areas, and to assess the nsk that mature apple imports would result in introduction of fire blight. None of this research had demonstrated a link between mature apples and introduction of fire blight.

5.54   Under Article 5.1 of the Agreement, Japan had to base its fire blight measures on a nsk assessment. Neither Japan's 1996 nor its 1999 Pest Risk Analyses (PRAs) on fire blight constituted a "risk assessment" as required by Article 5 1 in the opinion of New Zealand. Although Japan had fulfilled the first requirement of a risk assessment in that it has identified fire blight as the disease it wanted to prevent within its territory, Japan had neither evaluated the likelihood of entry, establishment or spread of the disease nor had it evaluated those matters according to the SPS measures which might be applied. Japan's attempts at risk assessment were not characterised by a systematic scientific approach. Japan had not considered many of the elements critical to a proper risk assessment of the introduction and spread of fire blight. Much of Japan's analysis related solely to the *possibility* of fire blight bacteria arriving in the country, rather than to the *probability* of entry, establishment and spread of the disease. Furthermore Japan had not evaluated the relative effectiveness of each of its SPS measures in reducing the overall risk purportedly presented by mature apples. Japan had also not considered any alternative measures other than those that it already imposed on the importation of apple fruit.

5.55   Article 5.2 required certain matters to be taken into account in the assessment of risk. In New Zealand's view, Japan had acted inconsistently with Article 5 2 by not taking into account all available scientific evidence.

5.56   Finally, contrary to Japan's obligations under Article 5.6, Japan's fire blight measures were patently more trade-restrictive than required. The only measure required to achieve the level of protection desired by Japan - that was, the prevention of any cases of entry and establishment of fire blight bacteria or disease - was to restrict imports of apples to mature apple fruit.

> ### 3.   *Chronology of Bilateral Discussion between New Zealand and Japan*

5.57   In reply to a question from the Panel, New Zealand prepared a chronology and description of bilateral discussions leading to Japan's granting access to New

Zealand apples with restrictive conditions in May 1993.[172] The chronology charted communications between the Ministry of Agriculture, Fisheries and Food of Japan (MAFF) and New Zealand as going back to October 1983. According to the chronology, New Zealand first made a proposal to Japan's MAFF on fire blight in August 1987. Bilateral discussions between New Zealand and Japan over technical quarantine issues related to fire blight continued until May 1993, when apples from New Zealand were granted access in accordance with certain restrictive conditions, similar to those imposed on US apples.

4.   Apple Maturity and Trade

5.58   Responding to a question from the Panel on apple maturity and export, New Zealand noted that its pipfruit industry was primarily an export industry. New Zealand exporters had found it essential to develop comprehensive, objective maturity parameters for determining optimum harvest timing in order to ensure that fruit had sufficient storage potential to withstand many weeks of storage, shipping and distribution to offshore markets. Fruit that was harvested in an immature state would develop storage disorders (e.g. bitter pit, superficial scald) and had a high tendency to shrivel. More importantly, they would not develop the organoleptic characteristics required in the market.

5.59   Many years of research and refinement by the pipfruit industry had resulted in the development of objective maturity management specifications for each variety of apple. These specifications were based on a range of parameters including starch levels, fruit firmness, percentage of soluble solids, titratable acid, background and foreground colour and length of harvest period. The specifications that defined when harvest should commence and when it should finish were specific to each variety and would combine a range of parameters from the list above. In addition, the specifications were developed specifically for New Zealand conditions, in order to ensure objectivity in the maturity assessment process. The maturity parameters taken into account by the New Zealand pipfruit industry were set out in Enzafruit's 2002 *Best Practice Guidelines – Harvest Management*.[173] The *Best Practice Guidelines* included protocols for the measurement of each parameter. The maturity management specifications and parameters currently applied by New Zealand growers and exporters had been developed over the course of at least two decades specifically for New Zealand conditions. For example, starch pattern indices charts set out specific North Island and South Island optimum starch content parameters for each variety of apple to be exported. Development of New Zealand-specific specifications had been particularly valuable to ensure objectivity in the maturity assessment process. The *Best Practice Guidelines* were consistent with the overall framework, and used the same testing technologies, as set out in the OECD Guidelines.[174]

---

[172] Exhibit NZL-12.

[173] Exhibit NZL-13.

[174] New Zealand had also been actively involved in the OECD Scheme for the Application of International Standards for Fruit and Vegetables – including in the development of the Guidance on

5.60   Until 2000, all apples exported from New Zealand were required to comply with the maturity management specifications contained in the *Best Practice Guidelines* in order to obtain phytosanitary certification for export from the NZ Ministry of Agriculture and Forestry. In 2000, New Zealand's pipfruit industry was deregulated, allowing additional exporters to enter the market. Since then, the *Best Practice Guidelines* continued to be applied by New Zealand growers as a matter of practice. New Zealand exporters, including Enzafruit, conducted random testing of consignments to ensure that the apples sold to them by New Zealand growers and supply centres (eg. pack houses and cool stores) met the optimum maturity management specifications set out in the *Best Practice Guidelines*.

E.   Separate Customs Territory of Taiwan, Penghu, Kinmen and Matsu

5.61   As a WTO Member free of fire blight and as a significant importer of US apples, the Separate Customs Territory of Taiwan, Penghu, Kinmen and Matsu (Chinese Taipei) had a substantial trade interest in the dispute before the Panel. For Chinese Taipei, the key issue in this dispute was the pathway of the fire blight bacterium and the proper risk assessment to be performed in relation to it. The *SPS Agreement* provided an outline of procedures to be followed by Members undertaking risk assessments. These procedures had been explained and elaborated in dispute-settlement decisions. According to the Appellate Body in *Australia – Salmon*, Members adopting a specific SPS measure had to evaluate the likelihood of entry, establishment or spread of the disease in question on *all* kinds of alternative measures. In this context, it appeared to Chinese Taipei that Japan should have performed a risk assessment on all kinds of possible measures, which might include those proposed by the United States.

5.62   Chinese Taipei noted that Article 4 of the *SPS Agreement* had been invoked in this dispute. Article 4, embodied the so-called "equivalence principle", which mandated that when Members applied different SPS measures that achieved the same level of protection, these measures should be regarded as equivalent.

5.63   With respect to the burden of proof in this case, Chinese Taipei noted that the initial burden of proof lay with the complaining party, which had to establish a prima facie case of a violation. The United States had to meet its burden of proof by establishing a prima facie case of a violation and, if it did so, then Japan should come forward with sufficient facts and arguments so as to rebut the prima facie case made by the United States. In particular, Japan had to demonstrate that its measures were :

    (a)   Applied only to the extent necessary to protect human, animal or plant life or health;

Objective Tests for Determining Ripeness of Fruit. New Zealand's experience in developing its own maturity management specifications for exports of New Zealand pipfruit was of considerable value in the process of developing generic OECD Guidelines on maturity and ripeness.

(b)   based on scientific principles and not maintained without sufficient scientific evidence;

(c)   based on an assessment, as appropriate to the circumstances, of the risks to human, animal or plant life or health; and

(d)   based on risk assessment techniques developed by the relevant international organization.

5.64   Chinese Taipei recalled that the United States had compiled a large amount of scientific information to demonstrate that "mature, symptomless apples rarely become the pathway for transmitting fire blight bacteria" and that "restricting the importation of apples to mature, symptomless apples was a reasonably available measure which would achieve Japan's appropriate level of protection". The United States further demonstrated that its laws and regulations already imposed a requirement that exported apples be mature and be free from decay, broken skin or bruises, or damage caused by disease or other problems. In the view of Chinese Taipei, the United States had met its obligation in providing scientific evidences to establish a prima facie case. It was thus incumbent upon Japan to demonstrate that it had taken the US measure into consideration and, if it rejected the US position, to provide a scientifically sound basis for doing so.

5.65   According to Article 5.7 of the *SPS Agreement*, Members may provisionally adopt sanitary and phytosanitary measures where relevant scientific evidence is insufficient. In this way, the "precautionary principle" had been embodied in the Agreement, at least in a limited way. However, Chinese Taipei noted that any sanitary and phytosanitary measures instituted pursuant to Article 5.7 must be temporary in nature, and that these measures should be reviewed within a reasonable period of time while the Member imposing them sought to obtain the additional information necessary for a proper risk assessment. As each sanitary and phytosanitary measure was employed to address a different need under different circumstances, and relevant scientific evidence differed greatly, Chinese Taipei suggested that the best course was to adopt a case-by-case approach in order to determine the appropriate length of the reasonable period of time pursuant to Article 5.7 and the sufficiency of the development of scientific information.

5.66   According to the results obtained from the joint Japan-US experiments on fire blight in 2000, no fire blight bacteria had been detected on the surface of mature, symptomless apples. The experiment had been conducted in the US State of Washington for one year. Chinese Taipei affirmed and supported this scientific research undertaken jointly by Japan and the United States and encouraged the parties to the dispute to perform further scientific research in order to resolve their differences outstanding. The United States could repeat the experiments it had performed in other apple production areas where the climate and fire blight severity were different from Washington State, and they could do so for more than one year. Chinese Taipei argued that this action would provide more representative results and clarify the misgivings of Japan on the aforementioned joint scientific experiment. They were further of the view that it might be premature to rule that Japan had exhausted its recourse to Article 5.7.

1.   Chinese Taipei's Measures on US Apples

5.67   In its first written submission, the United States had indicated that Chinese Taipei was its leading export market for apples, with no reported transmission of fire blight despite the lack of measures barring or impeding imports to guard against fire blight. According to Chinese Taipei's quarantine regulations, the importation of host plants or plant parts (excluding seeds) had to be accompanied by a phytosanitary certificate issued by the plant quarantine authority of the exporting country, stating that the plants or plant parts had been thoroughly inspected and found free from fire blight bacteria. Otherwise, the plants or plant parts would be destroyed or returned. Moreover, apples could be imported into Taiwan only after plant quarantine officers had inspected them upon arrival.

5.68   In conclusion, Chinese Taipei considered that Japan was obliged to perform a risk assessment on all possible kinds of alternative measures. However, it was incumbent on the exporting Member to demonstrate sufficient science-based and technical information supporting proposed alternative measures or criticism of proposed measures. Finally, as the "precautionary principle" was embodied in Article 5.7 of the *SPS Agreement*, and the relevant scientific evidence differed greatly under different circumstances, Chinese Taipei suggested that the Panel adopt a case-by-case approach to determining the length of the reasonable period of time pursuant to Article 5.7 and the sufficiency of the development of scientific information.

VI.   PANEL'S CONSULTATION WITH SCIENTIFIC EXPERTS

A.   Panel's Procedures

6.1   The Panel recalled that paragraph 2 of Article 11 of the *SPS Agreement* provided that:

> "In a dispute under this Agreement involving scientific or technical issues, a panel should seek advice from experts chosen by the panel in consultation with the parties to the dispute. To this end, the panel may, when it deems it appropriate, establish an advisory technical experts group, or consult the relevant international organizations, at the request of either party to the dispute or on its own initiative."

6.2   Noting that this Panel involved scientific or technical issues, the Panel consulted with parties regarding the need for expert advice. Neither party objected to the Panel's intention to seek expert advice. On 10 September 2002, the Panel wrote to the International Plant Protection Convention and to the parties to request the names of suitably qualified scientific experts. After consultation with the parties, the Panel communicated the following working procedures for consultations with scientific and technical experts on 18 October 2002:

Nature of advice

1.   On the basis of the first submissions from both parties, the Panel will determine the areas in which it intends to seek expert advice.

Selection of experts and questions to experts

2.   The Panel will seek expert advice from individual experts.

3.   The Panel will solicit suggestions of possible experts from the Secretariat of the International Plant Protection Convention (IPPC), and, subsequently, from the parties. The parties are asked not to engage in direct contact with the individuals suggested.

4.   The Secretariat will seek a brief curriculum vitae from each individual suggested. These curricula vitae will be provided to the parties. Parties will have the opportunity to comment on and to make known any compelling objections to any particular expert under consideration.

5.   The number of experts the Panel selects will be determined in light of the number and types of issues on which advice will be sought, as well as by the different areas on which each expert can provide expertise.

6.   Experts will be appointed on the basis of their qualifications and the need for specialized scientific expertise.

7.   The Panel will inform the parties of the experts it has selected.

8.   The Panel will prepare specific questions for the experts. Parties will have the opportunity to comment on the proposed questions, or suggest additional ones, before the questions are sent to the experts.

9.   The experts will be provided with all relevant parts of the parties' submissions on a confidential basis.

10.   The experts will be requested to provide responses in writing. Copies of these written responses will be provided to the parties. The parties will have the opportunity to comment in writing on the responses from the experts.

Meeting with experts

11.   The Panel intends to schedule a meeting with experts prior to the second substantive meeting. A date for the meeting will be agreed in consultation with parties. Prior to said meeting, the Panel would ensure that: (i) the parties' comments on the experts' responses would be provided to the experts; (ii) the experts would individually be provided with their colleagues' (the other experts) responses to the Panel's questions.

12.   Parties are free to include scientific experts in their delegations and may, of course, submit scientific evidence.

6.3   The experts were invited to meet with the Panel and the parties to discuss their written responses to the questions and to provide further information on 13 and 14 January 2003. A summary of the information provided by the experts in writing is presented below. A transcript of the meeting with the experts is included in Annex 3.

6.4   The experts advising the Panel were:

Dr Klaus Geider, Professor of Molecular Genetics and Phytopathology, Max-Planck-Institut für Zellbiologie, University of Heidelberg, Ladenburg, Germany;

Dr Chris Hale, Science Capability Leader, Insect Group (Plant Health and Fire Blight) HortResearch, Auckland, New Zealand;

Dr Chris Hayward, Consultant on Bacterial Plant Diseases, Indooroopilly, Queensland, Australia; and,

Dr Ian Smith, Director-General, European and Mediterranean Plant Protection Organization, Paris, France.

B.   Summary of the Written Responses by the Experts to the Panel's Questions

Maturation of fruit

Question 1: Is there a commonly accepted definition or criterion (biological, physiological, commercial, etc.) for determining if an apple fruit is mature?

If yes, is this definition accepted by farmers, packers, traders, inspection agents and consumers in determining apple maturity?

If no, is maturity an inherently subjective concept, decided by local farmers? Is there a distinction between physiological and commercial maturity? Please explain.

6.5   **Dr Hale** replied that there were accepted definitions for determining if an apple fruit was mature. He defined physiological and commercial maturity as:

- *Physiological maturity - point at which picked apples will ripen. If this point has not been reached at harvest then fruit will not ripen and product will shrivel and be unacceptable.*

- *Commercial maturity - start of the ripening process. The ripening process will then continue and provide a product that is consumer-acceptable.*

- *Commercial maturity was usually determined by exporting companies. However, the definition of commercial maturity had to be accepted by other participants in the apple industry, i.e. growers, packers, traders, inspection agents, and finally consumers, or else the product would be* unsaleable. Maturity assessments included colour, starch index, soluble solids content, flesh firmness, acidity, and ethylene production rate.

6.6   **Dr Hayward** stated that there were objective methods for the determination of the maturity of apple fruit that formed the basis of the Organization of Economic Cooperation and Development's (OECD) international standards. Immature fruit will not ripen when picked and would be unmarketable. He classified fruit as physiologically mature when they were at the stage of development where, if they are detached, they continue to develop and ripen. Commercial maturity followed physiological maturity, and commercial mature fruit have the attributes favoured by customers.

Question 2: With respect to the maturation of apple fruit:

   (a)   *If an apple fruit is naturally (rather than experimentally) infected with fire blight, can it develop into a healthy-looking mature fruit?*

6.7   **Dr Geider** replied that dormant persistence of *E. amylovora* in fruits was not documented and was difficult to demonstrate. When natural infections occurred at an advanced growth stage in apples, the apples began to rot and ooze (exudate) appeared. An infected apple growing into a healthy-looking fruit while colonized by *E. amylovora* had never been described in the scientific research literature.

6.8   **Dr Hale** stated that it was important to make a distinction between infected and infested fruit. Infected fruit were diseased whereas infested fruit were contaminated with *E. amylovora* but not diseased. Naturally infected fruit would be small, shrivelled, might show some lesions, and would not mature. Consequently, they were highly unlikely to develop into "healthy-looking fruit".

6.9   **Dr Hayward** replied that natural infection of an apple fruit would be the result of infection of flowers through natural openings including stigmas and anthers, stomata on the styles, fruit surfaces and sepals, hydathodes and the specialised stomata termed nectarthodes located in the hypanthium (floral cup) (Thomson, 2000). Disease progression depended on several factors such as rainfall (affecting the mobility of the inoculum) and the size of the inoculum dose. If the level of inoculum were high and the conditions conducive the flower would wither and die. If the level of the inoculum were lower it would usually decline and not create infections (Thomson, 2000). If the inoculum was at an intermediate level the fruitlet would either abort or develop into an infected fruit. If the infection remained confined to the calyx (the dried-up flower part), a healthy-looking mature fruit would develop.

6.10   **Dr Smith** defined "infection" as meaning not just the presence of bacteria, but an active process of pathogenesis. On the basis of this definition, a diseased fruit could not develop into a healthy-looking mature fruit. *E. amylovora* was not reported to cause latent infections of fruits. Fruits were susceptible when they were young and ceased to be so as they matured. Nor was *E. amylovora* reported naturally to cause storage rot of fruits. A fruit naturally carrying bacteria can develop into a healthy-looking mature fruit if these bacteria do not infect the fruit; in fact, failing to infect, the bacteria would probably die long before the fruit matures.

   (b)   *How long does it take for an infected apple fruit to develop visible symptoms of fire blight?*

6.11 **Dr Geider** stated that immature apples were rarely used for experiments relating to fire blight because they often did not show clear fire blight symptoms after inoculation.

6.12 **Dr Hale** stated that if natural infection took place at the flowering stage, fruit were unlikely to develop but instead to shrivel and blacken. For immature fruit, visible signs would depend on the severity of natural infection at flowering, weather conditions, and injury, e.g. from hailstorms. Artificially inoculated immature fruit took 3-4 days to show symptoms. Mature fruit were difficult to infect and were unlikely to develop symptoms unless inoculated with high concentrations of *E. amylovora* and kept in conditions highly conducive to multiplication of the bacteria.

6.13 **Dr Hayward** replied that the length of time it took for an infected apple fruit to develop symptoms would depend on many factors: the resistance of the host; the conduciveness of the environment (especially temperature, rainfall and humidity), the route of inoculation and the inoculum dosage. He was unable to find any data about natural infections of apples through wounds and the length of time it might take for symptoms to develop.

6.14 **Dr Smith** stated that young fruits rapidly became infected after inoculum reached their surface, especially if they were wounded, and the infection proceeded through the tissues of the fruit within days. The fruits were shrivelled and destroyed within very few weeks.

   (c)   Can healthy-looking apple fruit carry fire blight bacteria (either internally or externally)? Is there any relevant evidence in this respect regarding fruit harvested from an orchard, as opposed to experimentally inoculated apple fruit?

6.15 **Dr Geider** replied that the persistence of *E. amylovora* within healthy fruits had not been documented. Surface contamination could not be excluded and might be caused naturally by insects (Hildebrand *et al.*, 2000) or by handling during or post harvest.

6.16 **Dr Hale** noted that healthy-looking apple fruit from heavily infected orchards had been shown to carry *E. amylovora* infestations on the calyx tissues (Hale *et al.*,1987). Calyx infestation was likely to be due to low level infestation at flowering which did not result in infection. Bacteria might then survive, presumably at low levels, on the calyx. Other reports of *E. amylovora* associated with the surface of mature fruit (Dueck 1974; Dueck & Morand 1975; Sholberg *et al.* 1988; Roberts *et al.* 1989) were likely to be as a result of deposition of *E. amylovora* from nearby sources of inoculum. Fruit from an orchard in which flowers were artificially inoculated with *E. amylovora* were shown by Hale *et al.* (1996) to be free of calyx infestation at harvest.

6.17 **Dr Hayward** stated that healthy-looking apple fruit from naturally infected trees did not contain detectable populations of *E. amylovora* in the calyx, stem, peel or cortex (Dueck, 1974). Roberts *et al.* (1989) did not find *E. amylovora* in core tissues or aqueous sonicates from 1,555 mature, symptomless fruit harvested from blighted trees of seven apple cultivars grown at five locations in Washington State. Roberts (in press, 2002) found no internal populations of *E. amylovora* in any of 900 fruit analyzed directly after harvest, even when harvested from trees with or directly adjacent to fire blight. *E. amylovora* was not detected in washings from fruit from orchards with 1-2 infections per tree, and was found on less than 1% of fruit from an orchard severely affected by the disease (Hale *et al.*, 1987). Clark *et al.* (1993) did not detect *E. amylovora* in calyxes of either immature or mature apple fruit, even from within 20 cm of inoculated blight sources (flowers), in a season not conducive to the spread of the disease during flowering. Dr Hayward stated that although the evidence was not monolithic, the conclusion he drew from several independent studies was that *E. amylovora* did not occur as an endophyte in healthy-looking mature fruit and the presence of *E. amylovora* as an epiphyte on fruit surfaces was a rare event.

6.18   **Dr Smith** answered that any surface in an infested orchard could carry fire blight bacteria which were splashed onto it by rain. There was disagreement about how long such populations might survive under various conditions, and whether they could be considered as real "epiphytic populations" (implying that they persist and even reproduce at a low level over quite long periods of weeks or months) or merely transient contaminants (disappearing within days). On fruits, the critical question was not whether, but how long, such bacteria could be carried externally.

6.19   Dr Smith noted that, in theory, mature fruits could carry bacteria but this was unlikely because contaminant inoculum was not normally available at the time when the fruits were mature and because superficial populations mostly did not persist. There was evidence that bacteria persisted longer in the calyx (a relatively protected site different from the surface but not strictly internal to the fruit) than on the surface. Bacteria carried "internally" could in theory be "endophytic", persisting inside the tissues of the fruit and reproducing at a low level without infecting the fruit. However, Dr Smith knew of no evidence that demonstrated that *E. amylovora* could survive endophytically in apple fruit in this way. Internal bacteria could also in theory cause a limited rot in the core of the apple, not externally visible. Although there were scattered suggestions in the literature that this could very occasionally occur, given the level of detail at which the observations were described, it was not certain that these symptoms really concerned fire blight, whether these observations concerned apple (as opposed to pear) fruit, or mature fruit. In any case, such observations were rare and of marginal significance, had not been systematically studied, and were not taken into practical account in fire blight epidemiology.

> (d)   *Is there any evidence or probability that mature apple fruit have ever been the means of introduction of fire blight in an area previously free of the disease?*

6.20   **Dr Geider** stressed that the establishment of fire blight in orchards not adjacent to plants with fire blight was a rare event. There was no evidence that trade in fruit had caused the establishment of the disease in any area. In Europe, the fire blight outbreaks in Northern Italy and Central Spain could be attributed to trade in plants from tree nurseries. The spread of the disease to all other European countries most likely occurred by sequential spread.

6.21   **Dr Hale** stated that there was no evidence to suggest that mature apple fruit have ever been the means of introduction (entry, establishment and spread) of fire blight into an area free of the disease.

6.22   **Dr Hayward** could find no evidence that mature apple fruit had ever been the means of introduction of fire blight to an area previously free of the disease.

6.23   **Dr Smith** replied that there was no evidence that mature apple fruit have ever been the means of introduction of fire blight in an area previously free of the disease. Fire blight has been introduced into many countries, and areas within countries, and there was no case in which it was probable that mature apple fruit were the pathway.

Geographic spread of fire blight

Question 3: Based on the scientific evidence available today, can you advise the Panel of the means by which fire blight is transmitted? Has there been a clarification of the science over the years regarding the transmission of fire blight? Please address the following specific questions:

6.24   **Dr Hale** stated that populations of *E. amylovora* could multiply to high numbers in an *epiphytic* phase on some floral parts (Johnson & Stockwell 1998). *Endophytic* populations of *E. amylovora* had been found in healthy buds. However, there had been no success in reactivating these bacteria to cause disease. Infection events originating from endophytic bacteria may be infrequent and were not responsible for major epidemics of fire blight. It was often difficult or impossible to determine the origin of inoculum in fire blight outbreaks. Bees were a major factor involved in the secondary local spread of fire blight from inoculum sources during pollination.

6.25   Dr Hale further stated that long-term survival of *E. amylovora* in the soil was unlikely. It was also unlikely that *E. amylovora* in soil would be splashed on to flowers and shoot tips (Thomson, 2000). Fruit tended to decompose rapidly on the soil surface and those remaining fruit hanging in trees usually did not show oozing or release of bacteria in the spring (Thomson, 2000). *E. amylovora* was rarely found on mature fruit and was then probably due to deposition from nearby active sources of inoculum (Thomson, 2000). In every instance where *E. amylovora* had been detected on fruit, it had been on fruit from orchards with high levels of fire blight infection or located near to severely infected orchards. It had never been demonstrated that mature fruit were involved in the dissemination of *E. amylovora* and served as a source of new infections. Consequently it was considered to be extremely unlikely that contaminated fruit could be responsible for establishing new outbreaks of fire blight.

6.26   **Dr Hayward** replied that wind-driven rain and pollinating insects were the most important vectors in transmission to flowers. Transmission over long distances, e.g. by migrating birds such as starlings, on contaminated fruit boxes, on fruit, or in the form of fire blight strands perhaps capable of long range aerial dispersal, were not amenable to experimental study and the evidence, if there was any, was circumstantial. The application of DNA-based methods to distribution of strains of *E. amylovora* (PFGE pattern analysis) had been a notable recent advance. This was a powerful tool regarded by many as the gold standard for epidemiological studies and enabled common sources of infection to be determined in disease outbreaks.

> (a)   *Please comment on the scientific literature on how fire blight has spread so fast globally. Is there scientific evidence to believe that this spread may be related to the movement of mature apple fruit?*

6.27   **Dr Geider** noted that the disease remained confined to North America until the beginning of the last century. In the early 20th century, fire blight was first reported to have occurred in Japan (see questions 35 and 36). In 1919 fire blight was reported in New Zealand. Fire blight in Europe was first detected in England (1956), then in Egypt (1962) and from these two countries presumably spread to Central and Western Europe and to Eastern Europe, respectively. In Australia, *E. amylovora* was identified in 1997 as affecting a few plants in the Melbourne Botanic Gardens. After eradication of all fire blight host plants in the gardens and neighbouring areas, the pathogen was eradicated. Disease symptoms resembling fire blight have also been reported from Korea.

6.28   **Dr Hale** stated that fire blight had taken 220 years to spread from New York State, USA in 1780, to its latest geographic locations (Bonn & van der Zwet, 2000). There was no scientific evidence to suggest that the spread might be related to the movement of mature apple fruit. On the contrary, most of the available evidence suggested that the major spread had been through the movement of planting material. New high yielding cultivars tended to be very susceptible and high intensity plantings of these new cultivars had exacerbated the more rapid spread of fire blight over the last 30 years. Spread of the disease to Europe and the Eastern Mediterranean was thought to have been due to its introduction into the United Kingdom and Egypt, followed by incremental short-distance spread due to birds, wind-driven rain, aerosols, and the importation of infected budwood or trees.

6.29   **Dr Hayward** answered that the global spread of fire blight, particularly since the late 1950s through to the 1990s in Europe and the Mediterranean, seemed most likely to be attributable to a combination of sequential spread and the importation of contaminated plants by nurseries. Dr Hayward could find no evidence that this spread might be related to the movement of mature apple fruit.

6.30   **Dr Smith** observed that it had been a long time before fire blight first spread outside North America, and it had been ten years before fire blight had moved outside the first country of infection in Europe. Even 20 years after its first appearance in the UK, fire blight was still limited to areas along the North Sea and the Baltic. In fact, fire blight had progressed southwards rather slowly. The later focus of fire blight in the eastern Mediterranean had spread more rapidly. By comparison, citrus leaf miner (*Phyllocnistis citrella*) had spread to the whole Mediterranean basin within two years and glasshouse pests like *Frankliniella occidentalis* and *Liriomyza spp.* had spread around the world in 20 years. Because fire blight did not spread very fast compared with many other plant diseases, it had been possible to contain it.

6.31   Dr Smith further stated that fire blight spread very effectively over short distances, but that it did not spread readily over long distances. Though it was only conjecture that fire blight had initially been spread in Europe by migrating birds, this explanation was at least consistent with the geographical spread. The geographical pattern was in no way consistent with spread on fruits, and this pathway was inherently much less probable. The new appearance of fire blight at long distances from existing outbreaks could readily be attributed to the illegal import of infected planting material. Not only was there no evidence that fruits had ever introduced fire blight to an area, but there was also no necessity to invoke such an improbable pathway since there were much more probable alternatives.

> *(b)   Several sources report that it was suspected that plant materials or fruit bins contaminated with fire blight bacteria were responsible for the introduction of the disease into the United Kingdom. Please comment on the extent to which this hypothesis has been confirmed or experimentally tested in the UK case and any of the other cases of trans-oceanic dissemination of fire blight.*

6.32   **Dr Geider** answered that the precise source for distribution of fire blight into a "primary" fire blight region such as New Zealand, England or Egypt could not be traced back. His studies of PFGE pattern in Europe and the Mediterranean region indicated a sequential spread from England and Egypt into neighbouring countries. However, the subsequent introduction of fire blight into Northern Italy and Central Spain through human activities was an exception that could be traced back to trade in nursery plants.

6.33   **Dr Hale** was not aware of any conclusive evidence regarding the method of introduction of fire blight into the United Kingdom. Suggestions that the disease might have been introduced on infected plant material or on contaminated fruit crates had never been proved. Lelliott (1959) stated that it is not known how fire blight entered the United Kingdom, but he also noted that "the chance that it was introduced with infected fruit is very slight and can probably be ignored". It was possible that bacteria could have survived on contaminated fruit crates, but this was probably unlikely as there was no scientific proof that the crates were contaminated or that contaminated crates could represent a source of infection.

6.34   **Dr Hayward** stated that apparently there had been no tests of the hypotheses that fruit bins or plant materials were the source of the first fire blight outbreak in the United Kingdom in 1957. Experiments (Keck *et al.* 1996) showing survival of *E. amylovora* on pieces of wood and plastic in petri dishes do not relate to conditions under which fruit crates are stored and transported. Dried bacterial ooze on crate surfaces would be subject to the effects of desiccation, diurnal temperature variation when not kept in cold storage, and probably to the deleterious effects of exposure to UV radiation.

6.35   **Dr Smith** replied that planting material was the one commodity for which there was almost direct evidence of a human-mediated international pathway. In Europe, infected plants were known to have been moved in trade, though not directly in relation to an outbreak. Also, several localized outbreaks (e.g. in Poland, in Romania) could be related to known imported planting material, although it could not be proved that any particular imported plant was the culprit. Thus, it was perfectly plausible that the original outbreak in the United Kingdom was connected with the illegal import of planting material. The explanation involving fruit crates seemed to be based entirely on circumstantial evidence and did not appear inherently very probable. Ooze on imported fruit crates would not come from fruits since the only fruits which could release ooze would be immature (not harvested) ones. It would have to come from shoot cankers. Although this idea had been presented in the literature because of an old British suggestion on the subject, no European country had judged it necessary to establish phytosanitary measures for crates (such as the Japanese requirement of chlorine treatment of containers for harvesting).

> (c)   *Please comment on Japan's conclusions in its first submission, paragraph 73, that "... these incidents suggest a remarkable degree of (1) the survival ability of the bacteria outside the favorable host of the wood ...".*

6.36   **Dr Hayward** stated that there was little evidence to support this statement. *E. amylovora* was a poor survivor in non-sterile soil – perhaps a reflection of its inability to compete with soil microflora. *E. amylovora* does not produce desiccation-resistant and UV-resistant cells. It was more likely to be able to survive when present as aggregates embedded in a polysaccharide matrix of either bacterial or plant origin, as in bacterial ooze or fire blight strands, but there had been a lack of investigation.

> (d)   *Would you characterize the likelihood of dissemination through trade in apple fruit as negligible based on historic and scientific evidence? Please comment in particular on any evidence of transmission of the disease in the past.*

6.37   **Dr Geider** stated that the dissemination of fire blight with apples could not be scientifically totally excluded, but it appeared extremely unlikely either that it had occurred or could occur. In his research work, he had discovered an ordered occurrence of PFGE pattern types in Europe and the Mediterranean region without there being any observed mixing of pattern types - despite the essentially uncontrolled trade of fruits and plants in most European countries. If fruit trade had distributed the disease frequently, the East European pattern type Pt2 would also be found in Central and Western Europe.

6.38   **Dr Hale** considered the likelihood of dissemination through trade in apple fruit to be highly unlikely based on the lack of historic and scientific evidence. Historically, large volumes of apple fruit had been traded world-wide from countries with fire blight and there was no scientific evidence that apple fruit had been the means by which fire blight had been introduced into countries without the disease.

6.39   **Dr Hayward** argued that the historic and scientific evidence suggested that the likelihood of fruit being a pathway for introduction of fire blight was negligible. Compelling evidence of nursery stock as a pathway came from observations from Spain and Egypt.

6.40   **Dr Smith** replied that there was a very small probability that healthy mature fruit could still externally carry living bacteria after shipping. There was then a very much smaller probability that these bacteria could be transmitted to and infect host plants. In combination, the likelihood was negligible.

Question 4: Please confirm whether or not EPPO recommends countries at high risk to prohibit importation of host plants for planting, with an exception to be made for importation during the winter months (Exhibit USA-5). EPPO does not recommend that importation of fruits be prohibited, and states "it is widely accepted that fruits present an insignificant risk in practice". Please comment on this statement.

   (a)   Are the specific quarantine requirements recommended by EPPO (Japan's first submission, paragraph 162), applicable to seedlings, nursery stock or apple orchards? Are they significant with respect to import requirements on mature apples?

6.41   **Dr Geider** opined that while there was evidence that a primary source of long distance distribution could be the importation of latently infected host plants, fire blight had not often been distributed that way. However, based on research work in Northern Italy and Central Spain, he was of the view that the most likely method of introduction of fire blight had been plant importation, as the pattern type from those regions (Pt3) had not been found in countries adjacent to the affected regions. There was also a possibility that pattern Pt2 in Southern Italy could have been introduced with plants, since insects would not easily have been able to cover the maritime distance from Egypt or Greece to Italy. Birds could also be associated with the distribution of these *E. amylovora* strains and such remote places as the Greek islands or oases in Israel could have received fire blight this way.

6.42   Dr Geider further was of the view that inspection of imported plants was the most effective way to prevent new outbreaks of fire blight. He did not think that buffer zone regulations were necessary for the importation of mature apples, since these fruits had an extremely low risk of fire blight distribution. However, he cautioned that apples should not be exported if they were picked from a fire-blighted orchard so as to avoid the probably very low risk of accidental contamination.

6.43   **Dr Hale** considered the EPPO recommendations to have been specifically designed for planting material - considered to be the major source of the disease and a major factor in the spread of the disease. Fruit were considered by EPPO to be insignificant in the transmission of fire blight and consequently the quarantine requirements for planting material were not relevant in the context of fruit import/exports.

6.44   **Dr Hayward** noted that the specific quarantine requirements recommended by EPPO applied to seedling and nursery stock rather than to apple orchards. As such, these quarantine requirements were eradication measures to be adopted when a pest incursion had occurred.

6.45   **Dr Smith** stated that the EPPO requirements covered plants for planting; fruit orchards were not considered relevant since no plants for planting were moved from them, and no requirements were recommended for fruits. Since the EPPO requirements were considered adequate for "plants for planting" from a nursery, which presented a much higher risk than fruits, it followed that they could be considered much more than sufficient for the lesser risk presented by fruits.

> (b)   *Please comment on Japan's statement (paragraph 97, Japan's first submission) that "as a result" of the decision by EPPO "not to control shipments of fruit, fire blight disease is rapidly expanding inside Europe"*

6.46   **Dr Geider** reasoned that on the basis of the ordered PFGE pattern type in Europe, it was "pure speculation" to connect uncontrolled fruit shipments with disease expansion. There was no indication that the disease moved with trade in apples.

6.47   **Dr Hale** stated that there was no evidence that EPPO's decision not to control shipments of fruit was the cause of fire blight's spread inside Europe, and the shrinking of the protected zone, particularly in France. Evidence suggested that the disease was mainly transmitted over long distances by the movement of latently infected planting material or planting material with undetected cankers. Aerosols might also have played an important role in the rapid long distance spread in Europe. There was no evidence that the movement of fruit throughout Europe had played a role in spread of the disease.

6.48   **Dr Hayward** noted that the EPPO decision not to control shipments of fruit was based on their judgement that fruit were not a pathway for the introduction of fire blight. The evidence suggested that expansion of the distribution of fire blight in Europe was most likely a function of sequential transmission combined with distribution of latently infected nursery stock.

6.49   **Dr Smith** stated that apple fruit were traded freely between, and within, European countries and especially within the European Union - despite the very great interest of certain countries in protecting themselves from the introduction of fire blight. The 1971 EPPO meeting considering recommendations on regulations to address the risk of fire blight spread had concluded "that because the risk involved in the importation of fruits is negligible, they would not need to be subjected to special requirements". EPPO recommendations were not mandatory. Each country decided what measures it would apply (jointly in the case of the European Union). A survey of the present regulations of EPPO member countries showed that no member country maintained restrictions on apple fruit with respect to fire blight. Dr Smith considered that Japan's suggestion did not reflect the truth of the matter. The European countries then and now take science-based and well considered decisions on pest risk management, and that it was absurd to suggest that the national plant protection organizations of all these countries had been so negligent as to not take account of a pathway if it might really allow the "rapid expansion" of fire blight. Dr Smith added that apple and pear fruits had never been subject to phytosanitary restrictions within Europe, and that in more recent times the EU had established its Single Market. It would not have been an easy matter in practice to prohibit, use phytosanitary certificates for, or treat or inspect fruits, on a European scale and such considerations must also have applied.

Question 5: Please comment on any evidence available regarding the distribution of E. amylovora strains and the conclusions which may be drawn as to the pathway for the spread of infection.

6.50   **Dr Geider** replied that his research work on PFGE pattern types gave some information regarding the spread of fire blight in the last century. The only PFGE pattern type found in New Zealand (Pt1), was also present in some strains from North America, England, Central Europe and transiently from Australia. This meant that the source of fire blight in New Zealand could not be traced back with the current data. It was likely that pattern type Pt1 in Central Europe was introduced from England. Pt1 in Australia could not be connected to a definable event, but given the large numbers of tourists (1.5 million people per year) visiting the Melbourne Botanical Gardens, it could have been a human source. Taking into account the strict Australian quarantine measures at airports, dissemination by fruit was very unlikely. One hypothesis was that somebody had used a contaminated knife to take plant samples in the Melbourne Botanical Gardens.

6.51   Dr Geider noted that the PFGE pattern types in Europe were well ordered. It could be assumed that the disease had been established before 1956 in England through the introduction of infected plants. The repeated speculation about the introduction of fire blight in England (no fire blight in Scotland) by contaminated wood such as crates from New Zealand could not be ruled out, but the existence of the two major pattern types Pt1 and Pt4 pointed to at least two introductions of fire blight. Dr Geider had identified the two pattern types as those of strains typically found in Canada. As such, contaminated plants from Canada (or adjacent US regions with fire blight) were one likely source. Contaminated plant material from New Zealand had also been suggested as another potential source of the infection and this hypothesis was supported by molecular analysis that the PFGE pattern type Pt1, exclusively found in New Zealand, was recovered in many but not all English *E. amylovora* strains. A second introduction of fire blight to England could have occurred with strains of another pattern type such as Pt4.[175]

6.52   The pattern type Pt2 from Egypt had only been found once in a strain claimed to be isolated in California (Zhang and Geider, 1997). A connection could not be recovered, but its origin in North America could be assumed. Pattern type Pt2 from Egypt could easily be distinguished from the other European patterns and had spread sequentially to neighbouring countries including Northeast Turkey, Iran, Greece and the Balkans. It had now reached

---

[175]   A divergence of pattern types could be another explanation for different pattern types found in England.

Hungary, and was close to the area with Pt1 in Austria. The sequential spread could be explained by carriage of the pathogen by bees and other blossom-visiting insects. Any contribution of fruits to the further spread of the disease was unlikely. The *E. amylovora* pattern types in North America were diverse (typical given the long persistence of the disease in the continent) and contained the pattern types Pt1, Pt2 and Pt4 that had been found in Europe.

6.53   The pattern type Pt3 from Northern Italy and Central Spain could be associated with plant imports from Belgium with the same pattern type. There were some exceptions from the main pattern types such as Pt5 (found in Bulgaria and Israel) or Pt6 in the area of Ravenna/Italy. Other variations of *E. amylovora* were occasionally detected and showed a low level of spontaneous changes in the bacterial genome. No efforts had been made to follow further spread of peculiar pattern types.

6.54   Dr Geider noted that it was puzzling why the Southern hemisphere was still free of fire blight, although plant and fruit imports were not controlled stringently in Chile, Brazil, Argentine or South Africa. In contrast, Egypt, with a relatively hot climate unsuitable for good growth and survival of *E. amylovora*, had become infected - most probably by contaminated plants. There was a low to moderate risk of fire blight distribution from trade in living host plants; however, there was little risk associated with other plant materials.

6.55   **Dr Hale** recalled that Jock *et al.* (2002) had presented evidence for the distribution of *E. amylovora* strains in Europe and concluded that despite barely-controlled trade in fire blight host plants and associated products (fruit), the patterns of distribution of strains indicated sequential spread from areas with fire blight into previously fire blight-free areas. There was no evidence that implicated fruit as a means of transmission of fire blight through Europe.

6.56   **Dr Hayward** noted that both Jock *et al.* (2002) and also Zhang and Geider (1997) had examined the genetic diversity of strains of fire blight from all countries including the United States - universally accepted as the centre of origin of fire blight disease on apples and pears. Some North American strains were highly divergent in pattern from any of those occurring elsewhere; patterns of other American strains resembled those from strains in other parts of the world. Patterns Pt1 and Pt4 were found in strains from England, perhaps suggesting multiple introductions; Pt1 was also found in central Europe and eastern France. Strains from Egypt, Greece and Turkey had the same pattern (Pt2). *E. amylovora* showed greatest genetic diversity at its centre of origin (USA). Jock *et al.* (2002) concluded that the appearance of Pt3 in northern Italy and central Spain could be explained by the importation of contaminated plants by nurseries.

Question 6: Can the source of a fire blight infection be identified (eg, by DNA or other test)? If, for example, an outbreak were to occur in a country following importation of apple fruit from all sources, could the source of the contaminated fruit be traced back?

6.57   **Dr Geider** noted that using PFGE analysis, it was possible to establish a general relationship between *E. amylovora* strains. For example, diseased young apple trees in Southern Germany, imported from northern Italy, displayed the typical Central European pattern type Pt1 from the surrounding area in Germany rather that the pattern type Pt3 found in Italy (Jock *et al.*, 2002). In other cases, such as the recent appearance of fire blight in central Spain, the infection could be traced back to plant imports from Belgium. The establishment of fire blight with Pt3 in northern Italy could be explained by a similar incident, although not proved due to the lack of documentation on trade in plants in Italy. Researchers were still working on more precise tools to describe individual strains from fire blight areas.

6.58   **Dr Hale** answered that there was no evidence of apple fruit being the source of an outbreak of fire blight. It might be possible to determine the source of *E. amylovora* strains involved in future outbreaks of the disease if a detailed molecular analysis was carried out on a large number of strains from sources world-wide (similar to that of Jock *et al.*, 2002), using agreed technologies, and if the current pattern of distribution of the *E. amylovora* strains could be categorically stated. At present, it was only possible to assign major pattern types to particular areas/regions/countries. However, Zhang & Geider (1997) had reported that there were peculiar properties of individual strains that could be useful in tracing epidemic outbreaks.

6.59   **Dr Hayward** stated that the PFGE typing procedure could enable determination of common sources in particular outbreaks (such as the situation in northern Spain (Lopez *et al.*, 1999) and probably also in Egypt).

6.60   **Dr Smith** stated that the source of a fire blight infection could not be identified with certainty, though DNA and other tests might give strong indications. *E. amylovora* had been categorized into strongly differentiated strains in only a few cases. Most isolates were not so distinctly identifiable, though conclusions could be drawn from comparisons based on many isolates.

Potential pathways for fire blight transmission

Transmission of fire blight via apple fruit

Question 7: Please comment on Japan's statement (paragraph 70, Japanese first submission) that "No ecological study is available on possible dissemination of fire blight via apple fruit".

6.61   **Dr Geider** replied that the statement was unrealistic. There were generally accepted methods of fire blight dissemination. Long distance spread was mostly caused via latently infected fire blight host plants in commercial trade. The most common method of short distance spread was caused by blossom-visiting bees and similar insects. Contaminated tools could distribute the disease in an orchard through pruning activities. "Strands" formed from ooze on branches could be distributed by wind to other trees, even over intermediate distances. In addition, animals, especially birds, which had been contaminated with ooze from fire-blighted plants might also occasionally be responsible for intermediate distance spread. Sequential fire blight distribution was dominant as the pattern of fire blight infection. New establishment of the disease by other than sequential distribution was so rare that it was not possible to conduct ecological studies.

6.62   **Dr Hale** observed that Taylor *et al.* (2003) had studied apple fruit infested with a marked strain of *E. amylovora* discarded in an orchard at flowering with conditions conducive to fire blight infection. Their results had shown that host plants did not become infected and that no *E. amylovora* could be detected on either leaves or flowers when tested by PCR. Hale *et al.* (1996) had presented results from studies on the ecology of the possible dissemination of *E. amylovora* via apple fruit that had been infested (calyx) or contaminated (surface) and placed adjacent to flowers in apple trees. There had been no movement of *E. amylovora* from the inoculum source to blossoms and no symptoms had developed in the trees during the season. No *E. amylovora* had been detected in calyxes or on surfaces of either immature or mature fruit even from within 5 cm of the inoculum source. However, there was no information available on the use of naturally infested or naturally contaminated fruit for such experiments.

6.63   **Dr Hayward** noted the definition of ecology as "the study of relationships of organisms or groups of organisms to their environments, both animate and inanimate" (Thain and Hickman, 1994). Much of the research on fire blight had clearly been concerned with the relationship of the pest (*E. amylovora*) to its hosts and their interaction with the environment. With regard to possible transmission of fire blight on fruit, much work had been concerned with survival of the pest on the epidermis or the calyx of fruit (e.g., Hale *et al.*, 1987; Hale *et al.*, 2001; Hale *et al.*, 2002; Roberts 2002). Some of these recent studies had used genetically marked (antibiotic resistant) strains of the pest.

6.64   **Dr Smith** replied that movement of *E. amylovora* on apple fruit did not constitute a significant element in the ecology of the pathogen. Management of the disease in apple orchards did not have to take any account of the possibility that new infections arose from bacteria persisting on harvested fruits, or even dropped or discarded fruits. To that extent, no one had thought it worthwhile to undertake such research. Experiments could be devised in which artificially inoculated fruits were placed in the vicinity of healthy trees, under various conditions. However, significant and reproducible transmission could probably only be achieved by bringing the fruits into an absurdly close vicinity to the susceptible tissues. If individual cases of transmission were obtained under more realistic conditions, it would be impossible to exclude other means of transmission as the cause. Dr Smith stated that it was very hard to do research on very rare events and quoted the paper of Taylor *et al.* (Exhibit USA-20) as a recent example of such a study.

Question 8: Please comment on any scientific studies which seek to quantify the risk or probability of fire blight transmission at any step along potential pathways?

6.65   **Dr Hale** replied that Roberts *et al.* (1998), using published data from many different sources on the incidence of *E. amylovora* on mature, symptomless apple fruit, had sought to estimate the risk of new outbreaks in fire blight-free areas. In this work, estimates of probability had been used at various steps, i.e. probability of calyx infestation in mature, symptomless fruit; probability of surface contamination of mature, symptomless fruit; probability of survival of *E. amylovora* on fruit through cool storage and shipping; probability of survival of *E. amylovora* on fruit through discard; probability of fruit discarded when hosts are receptive and conditions conducive for fire blight development; and probability of transfer of *E. amylovora* from discarded fruit to receptive hosts. However, although there was some qualitative and quantitative ecological information on each of these steps (Hale *et al.*, 1996; Hale & Taylor, 1999; Taylor *et al.*, 2002, 2003), the authors had not quantified the risk or probability of transmission of *E. amylovora* at any of these steps in the potential pathway.

6.66   **Dr Hayward** noted that Roberts *et al.* (1998) and Yamamura *et al.* (2001) had relied on the same published data but used a different approach to quantify the risk or probability of fire blight transmission along potential pathways. Roberts *et al.* (1998) had used a simple linear model to estimate the risk of a pest being introduced and established via commercial shipments of mature apple fruit. The probability of introduction had been estimated using three different levels of phytosanitary stringency prior to export. The authors had claimed that their assumptions were conservative. The study by Yamamura *et al.* (2001) was different in several respects. In particular, three assumptions had been made:

(a)   That a beta distribution approximately described the proportion of infected fruits in the production area of a given consignment;

(b)   that every consignment contained fruits that were drawn at random from the infinite population of the production area; and

(c)   each infected fruit caused infection of fire blight in the importing country by an independent constant probability.

Dr Hayward stated that he was not in a position to judge whether these were valid assumptions – such a judgement required the opinion of a statistician. The author of the first study had revised his estimates taking into account new published information, and also the requirement in the Japanese protocol for a post-harvest chlorine treatment. (Roberts, 2002). According to the author, "These new estimates strongly reinforce the conclusion drawn in the original 1998 PRA that international trade of commercial, export quality apple fruit poses a negligible risk of introducing fire blight to importing countries".

6.67   **Dr Smith** stated that in general it was desirable to try to quantify the probability of movement along a pathway by estimating the probabilities of individual components and calculating their overall product, which could be expressed for example as "once in so many thousand years". This was preferable to the use of imprecise expressions such as "very probable", "fairly probable", "extremely improbable". However, it was commonly the case that some steps on the pathway were subject to greater uncertainty than others. The result was that the improved precision arising from careful and realistic estimates for some steps was cancelled by the massive uncertainty of others.

Question 9: In the light of the IPPC Guidelines for Pest Risk Analysis of 1995 (Exhibit JPN-30) and the IPPC Pest Risk Assessment standard of 2001 (Exhibit USA-15), please describe the sequence of events that would be necessary for E. amylovora on mature apple fruit imported into Japan to be a pathway for the introduction of fire blight? Are you aware of any evidence that this pathway has ever been completed, either experimentally or in natural situations?

6.68 **Dr Geider** stated that the only way to spread fire blight with an apple was through accidental heavy surface contamination (by hand, when harvested from a fire-blighted tree). The apple then had to be touched by a consumer or visited by an insect, who had to then immediately have contact with leaves, or for more impact, with the blossoms of a fire blight host plant which might then develop symptoms. Dr Geider noted that even in his laboratory inoculations, by cutting leaf tips with scissors and inserting bacteria into the wound, not all apple seedlings developed fire blight.

6.69 **Dr Hale** described the sequence of events necessary for *E. amylovora* on mature apple fruit imported into Japan to be a pathway for the introduction of fire blight (i.e. entry, establishment and spread) as follows:

(a)   *E. amylovora* had to be associated with mature, symptomless fruit, i.e. calyx infestation or surface contamination;

(b)   *E. amylovora* had to survive storage and transport;

(c)   *E. amylovora* had to be transferred to a suitable host, which in turn was dependent on the availability of suitable hosts, discard of fruit in the vicinity of host plants, and the presence of a vector for transfer to the host; and

(d)   the establishment of *E. amylovora* on a suitable host, which would be dependent on the numbers of bacteria required for infection, and be related to environmental conditions and the receptiveness of the host.

Dr Hale was not aware of any evidence to suggest that this pathway had ever been completed either experimentally or in natural situations. In fact, the evidence (Hale *et al.*, 1996; Hale & Taylor, 1999; Taylor *et al.*, 2002, 2003) suggested that this pathway had not been completed because:

(e)   *E. amylovora* was not associated with mature, symptomless fruit from orchards without fire blight;

(f)   *E. amylovora* might be associated with mature, symptomless fruit from orchards severely infected with fire blight, but *E. amylovora* populations infesting fruit calyxes tended to decline in cool storage (Hale & Taylor, 1999); and

(g)   *E. amylovora* was not transferred from calyx-infested or surface-contaminated fruit to suitable hosts in conditions conducive to spread of fire blight even when fruit were placed adjacent to flowers and growing shoots (Hale *et al.*, 1996; Taylor *et al.*, 2003).

6.70 **Dr Hayward** stated that for mature apple fruit exported to Japan to be a pathway for the introduction of fire blight the following conditions would have to apply:

(a)   The pest was either in or on the calyx of mature apparently healthy fruit;

(b)   the pest survived cold storage and transport;

(c)   fruit were either dumped prior to retail or discarded by a consumer;

(d)   infected apple fruit were placed in fields; and

(e)   birds, insects, or wind and rain disseminated bacterial ooze from the discarded fruit to pears, apples or ornamental hosts in hedgerows.

Dr Hayward was not aware that this pathway had ever been completed, either experimentally or in natural situations.

6.71 **Dr Smith** answered that the fruits should first be contaminated by *E. amylovora*. This had been experimentally shown to be possible, though at low levels, in orchards with a high level of available inoculum. Such contamination was most likely to be superficial or in the calyx. The bacteria had then to persist as a significant and viable population, first while the fruit was on the tree, then at picking and during storage, and finally during shipping. Some proportion of a lot of contaminated fruits had then to be discarded, as waste from consumption, or as unsold fruits. The waste fruit material would in a few days, or at most weeks, decompose by the action of other micro-organisms and *E. amylovora* would not be expected to survive this process in competition. So the next step had to intervene in the short time while some viable *E. amylovora* remained. Rainsplash would be the simplest mechanism for transmission, but it seemed exceedingly unlikely that fruit waste would be deposited in a suitable location. Otherwise, it had to be supposed that insects, or birds, could feed on the discarded fruit waste and then fly to apple trees. It remained necessary to determine what insects would behave in this way. Birds were conjectured to have carried *E. amylovora* on their feet from infected branches to infect new shoots; however it was less clear whether they might, by feeding on waste fruit, introduce inoculum into a tree. Finally, susceptible tissue had to be available at the time when the fruit waste was discarded (this would most often not be the case, but long storage or inter-hemisphere trade could make it possible). A conceivable short-cut might occur if fruits became internally infected and these fruits were not detected. If this ever happened (which was debatable), then there was a stronger possibility that viable bacteria remained in the fruits during storage and shipping. Thereafter, the pathways joined. If such externally invisible internal infection occurred, the phenomenon was certainly extremely rare, and this had also to be taken into account in evaluating the probability of this pathway. The only element of this pathway that appeared to be confirmed experimentally was the initial superficial contamination of fruits by bacteria. The information on internal infection of fruits was based on very rare casual observations, and the phenomenon had never, to his knowledge, been reproduced experimentally.

Question 10: Are you aware of any studies which report the detection of endophytic bacteria in mature, symptomless apple fruit? Please describe your understanding of the state of knowledge in this regard.

6.72   **Dr Geider** stated that it was difficult to envisage naturally occurring endophytic bacteria within an apple.

6.73   **Dr Hale** replied that bacteria which multiply in internal tissues without causing disease are normally considered to be endophytic (Thomson, 2000). Van der Zwet *et al.* (1990) had recovered *E. amylovora* from inside mature apple fruit only when it was grown within 60 cm of visible fire blight infections. It had never been demonstrated that mature, symptomless fruit were involved in dissemination of endophytic *E. amylovora* and served as a source of new infections in orchards (Thomson, 2000). It would be extremely unlikely that endophytically contaminated fruit could be responsible for establishing new outbreaks of fire blight (Roberts *et al.*, 1989; van der Zwet *et al.*, 1990; Thomson, 1992 b; Hale *et al.*, 1996).

6.74   **Dr Hayward** knew of no studies which reported the detection of endophytic bacteria in mature, symptomless apple fruit – assuming that in the study of van der Zwet *et al.* (1990) positive samples came from immature fruit. If the pest occurred as an endophyte in mature fruit it would enter through the flower. The presence of endophytic bacteria could be sought either in core samples from surface sterilized fruit (Roberts, 2002) or in the calyx (Hale *et al.*, 1987). The latter authors had not found the pest on the epidermis of commercially packed apple fruit and only found it in low numbers from less than 1% of the calyx ends of fruit from an orchard severely affected by the disease. Roberts (2002) had not detected the pest in 900 fruit after harvest, and of 30,000 fruit stored in cold storage for three months none developed fire blight.

6.75   **Dr Smith** replied that he knew of no convincing evidence of endophytic bacteria in symptomless apple fruit. Van der Zwet *et al.* (1990) had referred to endophytic infection but this paper was not convincing in several respects.

Question 11: Regarding bacteria in and/or on mature apple fruit, please explain how the studies by van der Zwet & Beer, (1992, 1995, 1999), Hale (1987) and van der Zwet et al. (1990) differed, and the implications of their results. Have the results of these studies been confirmed by other experiments or studies?

6.76   **Dr Geider** stated much data from experiments were open to personal interpretation and judgement. Evidence of colony hybridization was circumstantial and often flawed because of a population of *Pantoea agglomerans* (*Erwinia herbicola*). Some of the papers about *E. amylovora* in apples gave a general report without documenting any detailed laboratory data. It was unusual for the authors to publish contradictory papers or statements, and it might be advisable to reassay fruits from various sources including fire blighted orchards.

6.77   **Dr Hale** noted that van der Zwet & Beer (1992, 1995, 1999) discussed the infection of immature fruit through lenticels, wounds or infected spurs. Immature fruit infection was most common following hailstorms. Infected apples nearing maturity turned brown, shrivelled, and appeared mummified as they remained attached to the spur. Infected fruit would not be harvested as they would never become mature, symptomless fruit. In Hale *et al.* (1987), *E. amylovora* had not been detected in washings from mature fruit from orchards in which no fire blight symptoms had been seen nor from fruit from orchards with low levels of infection (1-2 infections/tree). *E. amylovora* had been isolated from a small number (<1%) of fruit from a severely infected orchard (75 infections/tree). For both fully mature and packed fruit, i.e. mature, symptomless fruit, *E. amylovora* had only been detected in the calyx and not on the fruit surface. This suggested that *E. amylovora* could survive in the dried remnants of flowers infested at flowering time. Hale *et al.* (1987) had concluded from these results that apple fruit harvested from orchards with no fire blight symptoms during the growing season were unlikely to constitute a means of disseminating the disease. Van der Zwet *et al.* (1990) had not detected *E. amylovora* on or in fruit from two orchards without fire blight. Endophytic populations had been recovered from apples located within 30cm of blighted shoots but not from 60-200cm away. *E. amylovora* had not been detected in core tissues of fruit from apparently healthy trees grown in four regions of North America. The authors had concluded that the dissemination of *E. amylovora* to areas or countries without fire blight was extremely unlikely when mature, symptomless, undamaged fruit were harvested from apparently healthy trees in orchards free of fire blight.

6.78   Dr Hale also stated that van der Zwet *et al.* (1990) had reported that disease developed among surface-disinfested fruit after cold storage. However, internal fruit blight symptoms had been difficult to distinguish from those of other fruit rots. *E. amylovora* had been detected from the surfaces of blighted fruit in storage, mainly from fruit collected at or directly below blighted shoots. The authors stated that after one month of cold storage some of the disinfested fruit had been blighted presumably from endophytic bacteria. However, van der Zwet (Exhibit USA-18) had suggested that it was equally probable that damage to fruit at the time of disinfestation might have allowed surface bacteria to enter fruit tissues. A low incidence of blight had also been observed among stored fruit harvested from apparently healthy trees within 10m of fire blight infected trees, van der Zwet (Exhibit USA-18). *E. amylovora* had been recovered from extremely small numbers of asymptomatic fruit harvested from orchards with fire blight symptoms - suggesting that small populations of bacteria might remain on the old flower parts in the calyx. That *E. amylovora* had not been recovered from mature fruit from resistant cultivars in West Virginia or from Washington State fruit was indicative that mature fruit from symptomless trees were unlikely to be infested with the bacterium.

6.79   Dr Hale noted that all the reports concluded, overall, that mature, symptomless apple fruit harvested from orchards without fire blight symptoms did not harbour *E. amylovora*. He noted that it had now been confirmed that, on the occasions when *E. amylovora* was associated with fruit from symptomless trees, the trees were only 10m from severe blight sources.

6.80   **Dr Hayward** noted that Hale *et al.* (1987) did not use destructive sampling to obtain core samples but relied on surface washing of shoots, flowers and fruits. A later study (Roberts, 2002) had confirmed that *E. amylovora* did not occur as an endophyte in mature, healthy fruit.

6.81   **Dr Smith** answered that the three publications of van der Zwet & Beer were successive versions of a practical guide to integrated disease management for fire blight, and not strictly speaking "studies". They clearly described "fruit blight", using phrases like "immature fruit may become infected", "infected apple and pear fruits turn brown and black, respectively, shrivel, and appear mummified as they remain attached to the spur". The inoculum for these infections had to come initially from the fruit surface, and infected through wounds (hailstorms were cited as a predisposing factor). The description in these three publications was appropriate in the context of practical fire blight management. Fire blight was not important on harvested or stored fruits, and these cases were therefore not referred to at all.

6.82   Dr Smith noted that Hale *et al.* (1987) had been concerned as to whether *E. amylovora* could be detected on the surface of fruits or in the calyx. They showed that the bacterium could be detected, but that this depended on the level of inoculum in the orchard (the more inoculum, the more likely was detection) and on the time of testing (more likely on immature than on mature fruit), and on the part of the fruit (contamination persisted longer in the calyx than on the surface of the fruit). This paper had presented coherent results, and was one of the few demonstrations that *E. amylovora* could in fact be recovered, at low levels, from mature fruits in orchards, or from the calyx (only) of fully mature packed fruits.

6.83   Dr Smith described the paper of van der Zwet *el al.* (1990) as concerned with whether *E. amylovora* could be recovered from outside or inside apple fruit when harvested from the immediate proximity of blighted shoots and then stored, or when artificially inoculated and stored. It was noteworthy because it was the only published paper that recorded the isolation of *E. amylovora* from core sections of fruits – although it was not clear if these were symptomless fruit, and their maturity was not specified. However, the paper of van der Zwet *el al.* (1990) had presented a number of anomalous features. In relation particularly to the experiment reported in Table 2, the fruits which had been disinfested showed much more "disease" than those which had not. This was a very strange result, which the authors failed to comment on or explain. Twenty fruits had been sampled (but it was not clear if they had been destroyed) each month, and it was not clear what fruits remained and what the percentages of disease incidence referred to. Curiously, disease incidence seemed to decline in storage. There was in fact no confirmation that the disease symptoms were due to *E. amylovora*.[176]

---

[176]   A plating procedure for washings from fruit was said to have been performed on sampled fruits but no results were presented. Concerning the results reported in Table 3, data for three years (1984, 1985, 1986) were confounded. It was not clear how the bacteria were extracted (both core segments and wash water were mentioned in Materials and Methods, but the latter case was not mentioned in Table 3). Controls were referred to in 1986, but seem to have been used for the experiments in all three years.

6.84   Dr Smith observed that the experiments reported in the paper of van der Zwet *et al.* (1990) were performed by different scientists at four widely separated locations in several different years. Such a situation was perfectly normal and acceptable, but it did engender potential difficulties in interpreting results when there were contradictions and anomalies, such as in this case. Overall, the study reported in the paper failed to convince. Experiments were said to have been performed and procedures followed, but no results were reported. He wondered whether the research programme had not gone according to plan, and suggested that it might have been better to repeat some of the experiments or design better ones before publishing certain results.

Question 12: Please comment on the information provided in Exhibits USA-18 and USA-19 in the light of other available scientific evidence regarding epiphytic and endophytic bacteria on or in mature, symptomless apple fruit. In your view, is the value of the scientific information provided in these exhibits affected by the fact that they were not published in a scientific journal?

6.85   **Dr Geider** stated that the scientific papers referred to seemed to be a collection (even at the time of publication) of old data enriched with more recent observations. The identification methods were mainly classical and could have been undertaken by visual inspections of fruits for rot - rots which could have been caused by micro-organisms other than *E. amylovora*. The "Plant Disease" paper gave the impression that the fire blight pathogen was found in late season. Young apples could possibly become infected through adverse weather conditions even late in growth and might thus carry the pathogen for some time. However, Dr Geider did not think that they would develop into mature fruits which could be sold at market as the pathogen could not be carried from an infected flower to the late stage of a matured apple. Nevertheless, the letters of Drs van der Zwet and Thomson weakened the conclusions of their 1990 paper. Dr Geider also stated his view that scientific arguments without new data were not so significant in their content as to justify another publication.

6.86   **Dr Hale** stated that the declaration from Dr van der Zwet (Exhibit USA-18) clearly explained the situation relating to epiphytic and endophytic bacteria on or in mature, symptomless fruit discussed in van der Zwet *et al.* (1990):

(i)   In most cases the fruit had definitely been immature.

(ii)   The sources of fruit in the West Virginia experiments had either been from blighted orchards or control orchards within 10m of blighted trees.

(iii)   Only epiphytic bacteria had been isolated from immature fruit from West Virginia orchards. *E. amylovora* had not been isolated from internal tissues.

(iv)   In Utah, *E. amylovora* had been recovered both on and in fruit from blighted orchards.

(v)   No *E. amylovora* had been recovered either on or in fruit from Washington or Ontario.

(vi)   Epiphytic *E. amylovora* had been isolated from the calyx of an immature apple from a symptomless tree from within 10m of severely blighted trees.

(vii)   In stored, mature fruit collected from various distances from blight sources, internal symptoms had been difficult to distinguish from those of other rots. The blight referred to in disinfested fruit might have been due to endophytic *E. amylovora,* but might equally have been due to epiphytic *E. amylovora* entering wounds after handling during the surface disinfestation process.

Professor Thomson's letter (Exhibit USA-19) stated that most fruit had been immature, and that only Delicious fruit harvested on 29 September could have been near maturity. Professor Thomson had also clarified that all positive *E. amylovora* detections had been either in or on immature fruit with a single exception. In this one case, epiphytic bacteria had been detected in the calyx of an apple from a blighted tree in a severely blighted orchard.

6.87   Dr Hale indicated that the information presented in Exhibits USA-18 and USA-19 clarified a number of discussion points presented in van der Zwet *et al.* (1990), and was consistent with results obtained by other research workers (Hale *et al.*, 1996). Although the information provided in these exhibits was not published in a scientific journal, in his view the exhibits were particularly valuable as they clarified a number of important points.

6.88   **Dr Hayward** stated that Dueck (1974), Hale *et al.* (1987) and Roberts (2002) had shown that *E. amylovora* did not occur on the epidermis of mature fruit nor as an endophyte. The first author had not detected *E. amylovora* on the surface of symptomless fruit of naturally infected trees and had concluded that mature fruit presented a negligible risk for the dissemination of fire blight bacteria. Sholberg *et al.* (1988) had sampled fruit from apple trees inter-planted with Bartlett pear (highly susceptible to fire blight) and found that all apple fruit and leaves were contaminated with *E. amylovora* at harvest. Dr Hayward noted that papers published in scientific journals were usually subjected to peer review by two referees and the editor. Papers from a research institute would commonly be required to undergo in-house review before submission - this was also commonly the case with papers submitted by University staff. As such, documents that had not undergone any review process carried lesser weight.

6.89   **Dr Smith** felt it was essential, in discussing van der Zwet *et al.* (1990), to be clear whether the fruits were mature or immature. This was perhaps not a critical point at the time the research had been carried out. Dr Smith could not see any way to resolve this question other than asking the authors, and their replies were more valuable than if they had been in a general discussion on the subject published in a journal because they addressed specific questions.

Question 13: With regard to the citation of the conclusions by Sholberg et al. (1988), can you comment on the "certain conditions" in which E. amylovora may be present on symptomless fruit at harvest? How likely are these conditions to be found in apple fruit exported from the states of Washington and Oregon?

6.90   **Dr Geider** stated that contamination with *E. amylovora* could occur at several stages of fruit development. It was very difficult to judge when, where and why contamination occurred and what would be the next stages of pathogen development, although maturation into a fruit for the market seemed unlikely.

6.91   **Dr Hale** noted that Sholberg *et al.* (1988) had isolated *E. amylovora* from apple and pear leaves at harvest and extrapolated that these "results show that *E. amylovora* may be present on symptomless fruit at harvest under certain conditions". In this study, apple leaves and fruit had been sampled and bulked together for each group of trees; the apple trees were adjacent to fire blighted pear trees and the year of the study had been an extraordinary year for early fire blight. The naturally contaminated fruit used for the surface disinfestation trials had come from an orchard severely damaged by fire blight after a hail storm, resulting in blighted shoots and small fruit exuding bacteria. The "certain conditions" appeared to refer to fruit being sampled from trees adjacent to fire blighted pears in a year particularly conducive to the disease, and naturally contaminated "apparently healthy" fruit from an orchard severely damaged by fire blight. Dr Hale's understanding was that these conditions would be unlikely to occur for apple fruit exported from the States of Washington or Oregon.

6.92   **Dr Hayward** considered the "certain conditions" to which Sholberg *et al.* (1988) referred as the proximity of the apples to a gross infection source (Bartlett pear) during "an extraordinary year for early fire blight development in British Columbia" when the experiment was conducted. Transmission of *E. amylovora* from pear to apple would have been primarily through wind-driven rain. High humidity would have been required for colonization of leaves and fruit. Dr Hayward thought it highly improbable that any grower in Washington or Oregon would grow apples near to a gross infection source such as Bartlett pear. If the climatic conditions were drier and less humid, then secondary transmission would occur less often.

6.93   **Dr Smith** noted that Sholberg *et al.* (1998) had stated that these certain conditions (proximity of blighted pear trees, extraordinary year for early fire blight) were for British Columbia. While he was not competent to comment in detail on the similarity of conditions in Washington or Oregon, at an elementary level he supposed the likelihood to be similar.

Question 14: Please comment on the statistical methods and values assigned by Roberts, et al. (1998) and by Yamamura, et al. (Exhibit JPN-15) Please comment on the significance of the different conclusions reached in these studies.

6.94   **Dr Geider** noted that in most experiments one dealt with standard deviations. In this case, sampling studies had been applied. Sampling studies could be used to claim validation of an extensive survey, but they did not help in the case of accidental contamination. He disagreed with the characterization of extremely high risks for fire blight dissemination. There were numerous examples which demonstrated that localized foci of infection did not expand, such as the recent infection in an orchard of the Biological Research Institute (BBA, Heidelberg-Dossenheim), where apple seedlings had been imported from Belgium. One seedling had developed fire blight (pattern type Pt1), but the others had not, nor had any of the other trees in the orchard. The transient fire blight event in Australia in 1997 was another example.

Discarded fruit

Question 15: Japan's 1999 Pest Risk Analysis at Section 2-2-4-3 considers, inter alia, the case of un-marketed fresh fruits, and indicates that "if they are released as juice, leftovers, waste, useless materials in the fields surrounding ranches or in a natural environment, they can be the source of the disease". What is your view about the likelihood of this pathway, specifically, the likelihood that bacteria surviving on imported apple fruit would survive release as juice, leftovers, waste, or useless materials and serve as a means of transmission of fire blight? Is there any information about the volumes of imported fresh fruit that might be thrown away?

6.95   **Dr Geider** stated that the detection of a pathogen in plant material was difficult at low levels. It could be shown that pollen collected by bees in the neighbourhood of a fire blighted orchard contained *E. amylovora* (Bereswill *et al.*, 1994). In this and the other cases, claims about the amount, the rate of decay and persistence of *E. amylovora* at a low level should be known. It could happen that an apple with *E. amylovora* might release the bacteria into fruit juice. However, commercial apple juice had to be sterilized immediately after pressing. His own data clearly indicated that *E. amylovora* survival in soil-like environments rapidly diminished within days (Hildebrand *et al.*, 2001). Farm material could be contaminated with *E. amylovora* and there might also be some risk with nursery stocks of living fire blight host plants.

6.96   Dr Geider noted that retail stores might dispose of large amounts of fruits, such as apples and pears, if they did not meet their quality standards. However, the scenario of insects visiting rotting fruit in a waste bin or in a garbage dump and carrying away *E. amylovora* cells which would eventually contaminate the nearby flowers of host plants was not realistic. The pathogen would most likely decay immediately in this environment and other bacteria would take over.

6.97   **Dr Hale** replied that there was a hypothetical risk that leftovers or waste material could possibly carry *E. amylovora* and provide a source of inoculum. However, any contaminating bacteria would then require dissemination to susceptible hosts at a receptive stage under climatic conditions conducive to infection. Hale *et al.* (1996) and Taylor *et al.* (2002, 2003) had been unsuccessful in attempts to transmit *E. amylovora* from contaminated, discarded apples to susceptible hosts, e.g. apples and cotoneasters at flowering (most susceptible stage). Discarded fruit had been visited and eaten by birds but had not resulted in transmission of *E. amylovora* to host plants; ants, bees, flies, moths and spiders had not been contaminated and had not transmitted *E. amylovora* to susceptible host plants; rainwater had not been contaminated, and splash had not transmitted *E. amylovora* from infested fruit to flowers or leaves. Dr Hale also stated that if *E. amylovora* did survive on imported apple fruit then it was likely to be affected by the processing into juice, which might include heat treatment.

6.98   **Dr Hayward** had no information about the volumes of imported fresh fruit that might be dumped. He thought it highly unlikely that the *E. amylovora* would survive in juice, leftovers or other waste because these materials were high in fermentable sugar content. The saprophytic relatives of *E. amylovora* (i.e., other members of the Enterobacteriaceae) were profusely distributed in the environment and fermented a wide range of sugars, lowering the pH to a level inimical to other bacteria. Lactic acid bacteria and acetic acid bacteria would also be involved. Many of the saprophytes would have a more rapid growth rate than *E. amylovora*. In compost there would be other interactions including the antibiotic effects of actinomycetes and fungi.

6.99   **Dr Smith** replied that any bacteria which might be present in imported apple fruit would not survive release as juice, leftovers etc. They would very rapidly die out in competition with other micro-organisms. Their best chance of short-term survival would be for the fruits to be simply discarded, without any processing. Longer term survival would, according to available information, be favoured by desiccation, but this applied mainly to dried bacterial ooze. Imported fruits would not carry ooze, and there was no obvious way in which fresh fruits carrying low populations of bacteria could dry out while allowing these bacteria to survive.

Question 16: Is there any evidence available regarding the spread of fire blight infection from discarded, contaminated apple fruit, including in orchards at the most vulnerable phase of the growing cycle? Please comment on the relevance of the study presented as Exhibit USA-20 to Japan's concern about risk from discarded apple fruit.

6.100   **Dr Geider** stated that there was no evidence that fire blight spread from discarded fruit. Since the likelihood was very low, it would be impossible to trace back a fire blight outbreak to that source.

6.101   **Dr Hale** stated that evidence on these questions had been presented as Exhibit USA-20 and in Taylor *et al.* 2003. Spread of *E. amylovora* from inoculated (calyx-infested) apples to susceptible hosts had not been detected over 2 seasons by either culture or PCR tests on rainwater, apple flowers or leaves, nor had it been associated with insects and spiders. The climatic conditions over the sampling period had been conducive to fire blight infection with several moderate and high risk infection events occurring in each season. The results demonstrated that *E. amylovora* present in contaminated apple calyxes was not transferred to susceptible hosts that had been in a receptive stage at flowering. Therefore, should *E. amylovora* exist on exported commercial apple fruit, there was no evidence to suggest that these bacteria would provide inoculum for new fire blight infections. Consequently, there was a discontinuity in the pathway for dissemination of *E. amylovora* from an infected fruit to a susceptible host as there was no demonstrated spread of the fire blight bacterium from the discarded fruit.

6.102   **Dr Hayward** was not aware of any evidence regarding the spread of fire blight infection from discarded contaminated apple fruit, including in orchards at the most vulnerable phase of the growth cycle. Taylor *et al.* (2002, in press) had artificially inoculated apples at the calyx end of the fruit with a genetically marked strain of *E. amylovora*. The infested apples had been hung in apple orchards at blossom time over a 20-day period. Numbers of bacteria had declined 10,000-fold during the time span of the experiment. The genetically marked strain had never been detected on apple flowers or leaves, in rainwater or in trapped insects. The results suggested that *E. amylovora* was not spread from calyx-infested apples to susceptible hosts.[177]

6.103 **Dr Smith** replied that Exhibit USA-20 confirmed the general understanding of fire blight epidemiology, that fallen fruits did not provide a pathway of transmission for new infection. It was useful and relevant that this had been directly demonstrated. Such a study could not prove that such transmission never occured, but, unless reproducible results were obtained, such a study could not prove that transmission would occur, either.

Question 17: In the risk assessment included as Exhibit USA-4, Parameter p(4) is the probability that a fair to good host is at a receptive stage if fire blight contaminated fruit were to be discarded near a host. The author indicates that "We are considering the only receptive stage for the plant as the flowering stage". Please comment on this assumption.

6.104 **Dr Geider** considered the statement as hardly correct since there was very low risk, provided there was a contaminated apple, that insects would carry bacteria such as *E. amylovora* to neighbouring plants (see Hildebrand *et al.*, 2000). The flowering stage was the dominant stage at which infection of a plant took place; injuries, succulent shoots and stomata of leaves were possible but much less common pathways for disease entry.

6.105 **Dr Hale** noted that the authors considered flowering to be the only receptive stage for the purpose of the model because the flowering stage was when the plant was at its most receptive. This was the stage when insects would be most likely to visit discarded fruit and then move to open flowers and stigmas, where the bacteria could multiply (Thomson 2000). The flowering stage was the only stage when injury to tissues was not required in order to result in infection with *E. amylovora*. The infection of leaves and immature fruits, as a result of insects, wind or rain, required damage to the plant surface e.g. hail damage or piercing insects (which were not the types of insects likely to visit decaying fruit).

6.106 **Dr Hayward** stated that the published evidence indicated that the flowering stage was the only receptive stage for transmission to occur through insects or wind-driven rain. If birds such as starlings were involved in long range transmission, as had been proposed, some other route may have been involved but there was no data on this.

6.107 **Dr Smith** stated that fire blight could also enter through wounds, but this was only significant in situations where wounds were especially and unusually

---

[177] Dr Hayward noted that an argument against the validity of these results was that the marked strain might in some way be made less competitive as a result of the genetic modification (selection in culture of a mutant resistant to both rifampicin and nalidixic acid).

frequent (e.g. during pruning, after a storm). These special situations did not invalidate the author's view on the "only receptive stage", since woundings were relatively rare and random.

Question 18: The above exhibit also includes a statement that "... survival in soil is not considered epidemiologically significant". Does this mean that waste is not considered to pose a phytosanitary risk?

6.108 **Dr Geider** responded that *E. amylovora* would decay rapidly in soil (Hildebrand *et al.*, 2001), so there was no risk of dissemination of fire blight from the soil. However, discarded apples might not always be immediately covered with soil and could be accessible for insects. Nevertheless, there remained the question of whether or not *E. amylovora* was associated with the discarded fruits and how long it would persist.

6.109 **Dr Hale** replied that it was possible that decaying apples (waste) could release bacterial cells into the soil, which might then be a reservoir for spread. However, several researchers had considered soil to be of little epidemiological significance (Thomson 2000). Hildebrand *et al.* (2001) had shown that populations of *E. amylovora* declined rapidly in soil, presumably due to predation by degrading micro-organisms. Consequently, they considered that, although soil and waste associated with soil could not totally be overlooked as a source of inoculum, it was unlikely that *E. amylovora* would be transmitted from soil via rain splash or by insect vectors to susceptible flowers or shoot tips.

6.110 **Dr Hayward** stated that it was very unlikely that apple waste was epidemiologically significant because *E. amylovora* was a poor competitor in soil (Hildebrand *et al.*, 2001). Bacterial pathogens of plant foliage were in general poor survivors as free cells in soil. However they often had a significant capacity for survival in seed or when they were embedded in the vascular tissue of their host plants and buried in soil. *E. amylovora* had never been found in seed of apple (van der Zwet 1990) or any other plant. There was no evidence that the fire blight pathogen survived in soil in any "protected site" such as seed or vascular tissue. Apple waste composted or otherwise disposed of into the environment would decompose very quickly and would not be a phytosanitary risk.

6.111 **Dr Smith** noted that great numbers of *E. amylovora* must be washed onto and into the soil every time it rained in an infected orchard. They presumably died out in contact with soil microflora. Fruit wastes probably offered a better environment than soil, but they constituted a very short-lived environment.

Contamination of apple fruit in the orchard

Question 19: Please describe the current state of knowledge regarding the contamination (internal or external) of mature apple fruit in the orchard. In this context, please specifically address the following:

    (a)   Please comment on the contribution of the study provided as Exhibit JPN-8 to knowledge regarding epiphytic contamination of apple fruit.

> *(b)   Please comment on the conclusions of Thomson (2000) in this respect. Are you aware of any other studies which may be relevant regarding contamination (internal or external) of mature apple fruit in the orchard?*

6.112 **Dr Geider** responded that his research work had shown that *E. amylovora* could be detected on insects caught in a fire-blighted orchard (Hildebrand *et al.*, 2000), so it was possible that apples from a "severely blighted" orchard could become surface contaminated. Also ooze droplets and "strands" could contribute to this contamination. He concluded that it was not advisable for phytosanitary reasons to export apples picked in orchards with severe fire blight, although apples might be harmless for disease distribution.

6.113 **Dr Hale** noted that *E. amylovora* had been isolated from calyxes but not from the surfaces of mature apples from a severely infected orchard (75 infections/tree). The calyx infestation was likely to be as a result of infestation at flowering in the severely infected orchard. *E. amylovora* was not isolated from either calyxes or the surfaces of mature apples from three lightly infected orchards (1-2 infections/tree) or from six orchards with no fire blight symptoms. As a result he concluded that fruit from orchards without symptoms was unlikely to constitute a means of disseminating fire blight (Hale *et al.*, 1987).

6.114 Dr Hale agreed with the conclusions of Thomson (2000) that contamination of mature fruit was rare and only occurred when there were active sources of fire blight either in the orchard or close by. Wherever *E. amylovora* had been detected on mature fruit it had been associated with fruit from orchards with high levels of fire blight infection. Thomson's conclusions appeared logical, i.e. it was unlikely that contaminated fruit could be responsible for establishing new outbreaks of fire blight. Also, it had never been demonstrated that mature fruit were involved in the dissemination of *E. amylovora* and served as sources of new infections in orchards. Dr Hale was not aware of any studies on contamination of mature fruit in orchards other than those reviewed by Thomson (2000).

6.115 **Dr Hayward** indicated that the evidence showed that *E. amylovora* was rarely found on the epidermis of apple fruit except under the "certain conditions" of Sholberg *et al.* (1988) where there had been a gross source of infection in close proximity and the climatic conditions had favoured secondary transmission. Hale *et al.* (1987) showed that there was no survival on the epidermis but some in the calyx when the orchard was severely affected by fire blight. Roberts (2002) provided the most recent evidence that *E. amylovora* did not exist in core samples of mature, symptomless apple fruit. Thomson (2000) had assessed the capacity of *E. amylovora* as an epiphyte and concluded that it was not a very successful epiphyte and that populations declined within a few hours or days. The exception was that the pistil surface was a favoured site for epiphytic growth, yet according to Thomson "These colonised flowers do not appear any different from normal flowers and usually develop into healthy fruit" (Thomson, 1986). Dr Hayward knew of no work which disputed Thomson's assessment.

6.116 **Dr Smith** stated that the article of Hale *et al.* (1987) confirmed the basic point that fire blight bacteria could be isolated from fruit surfaces and calyces, mainly of immature fruit, but in rare cases also of mature fruit, especially if the orchard was heavily infected. The conclusions of Thomson (2000) seemed well-reasoned, considered endophytism at length, and did not refer to the possibility that it might concern fruits (except to quote the results of van der Zwet *et al.*, 1990).

Question 20: Please comment on the availability of testing techniques to identify the presence of very low populations of E. amylovora on or in apple tissue. Is there a minimum or threshold level for the number of bacteria necessary for an outbreak of fire blight?

6.117 **Dr Geider** noted that PCR analysis could detect about 100 bacteria in an assay. The absolute number depended on the efficiency of extraction, enrichment and contamination by plant material interfering with PCR. This amount and possibly less could also be applied to slices of immature pears in order to obtain reproducible symptoms. The ecology in nature was certainly different, because in the common spread of fire blight many flowers would be visited by many insects, which might release only a few bacteria and some of them would eventually cause the disease.

6.118 **Dr Hale** noted that molecular techniques utilising PCR for the detection of *E. amylovora* had been developed (Bereswill *et al.*, 1992, 1995; McManus & Jones 1995; Maes *et al.*, 1996).[178] There were some quantitative data that suggested that *E. amylovora* had to colonize the flower and rapidly multiply on stigmas to reach populations $\geq 10^6$ colony forming units at an early stage in flower development (before 4-5 days after bud burst) in order to initiate infection (Thomson 2000; R.K. Taylor unpublished results). The population increase was likely to be dependent on temperature and relative humidity, i.e. conditions must be conducive to the initiation of the infection process. Once pollination and subsequent fertilisation had taken place there were major changes in stigma receptivity and inhibitory compounds produced on the stigma which might prevent colonization and infection as the flower aged. Hale *et al.* (1996) also suggested that populations of *E. amylovora* > 10^5 were necessary to cause flower infection and subsequent symptoms in apple and cotoneaster.

6.119 **Dr Hayward** stated that there was a consensus that the best method to detect low numbers of a bacterium in a particular substrate such as soil or plant material was to combine culture with the polymerase chain reaction (a procedure known as BIO-PCR in which the low population was amplified in a selective liquid medium to numbers detectable using PCR). He had no information on a

---

[178] Taylor et al. (2001) had provided an alternative approach to the development of specific primers for *E. amylovora* and the application of PCR in the detection of *E. amylovora* in plant material. Using this method less than 10 colony forming units of *E. amylovora* were detected in apple tissue samples. However, most PCR techniques detected both living and dead *E. amylovora* cells and consequently some caution was required in interpreting the results, as dead *E. amylovora* cells do not pose a phytosanitary risk.

minimum or threshold level for the number of bacteria necessary for an outbreak of fire blight.

Question 21: What evidence is available regarding the survival of E. amylovora in or on mature apple fruit? Is there any evidence that such internal or external bacteria can be the source of outbreaks of infection? Is there any evidence relating specifically to mature apple fruit harvested from an orchard rather than to experimentally inoculated apple fruit?

6.120 **Dr Geider** noted that survival studies were rare in fire blight research as they were tedious to do, dependent on many storage conditions of the bacteria associated with or without plant material and because of the huge differences of recovery. Apples were rarely used for experimental inoculations because of difficulties in obtaining symptoms.

6.121 **Dr Hale** indicated that *E. amylovora* was not detected on the surface of fruit harvested from either heavily or lightly naturally-infected orchards but that *E. amylovora* did survive in calyxes of a few fruit from severely infected orchards (Hale *et al.*, 1987; Hale & Taylor 1999). However, *E. amylovora* was not detected in these naturally-infested calyxes of mature fruit after a period of cool storage. Hale *et al.* (1996) reported survival of *E. amylovora* in apple calyxes after experimental infestation and Taylor *et al.* (2003) showed that small populations persisted in artificially-infested calyxes of mature fruit after discard of these fruit in an orchard. *E. amylovora* did not appear to survive well on fruit as surface contaminants were likely to be adversely affected by ultraviolet radiation. There was no evidence that either internal or external *E. amylovora* associated with mature apple fruit were sources of outbreaks of fire blight in the field. However, internal *E. amylovora* could possibly cause infection of immature fruit e.g. infection at flowering might cause symptoms on immature fruit.

6.122 **Dr Hayward** stated that *E. amylovora* did not survive on the apple epidermis but had limited capacity to survive in the calyx (Hale *et al.*, 1987; Hale *et al.*, 1999; Taylor *et al.*, 2002). Cool storage reduced survival in the calyx (Hale *et al.*, 1999). Roberts (2002) and Dueck (1974) had shown that *E. amylovora* did not occur as an endophyte in mature, symptomless fruit. Dr Hayward could find no evidence that epiphytic or endophytic populations on/in apple fruit could be the source of outbreaks of infection. In the work of Roberts (2002), Dueck (1974), and Hale *et al.* (1987), apple fruit were harvested from orchards; in the later work of Hale and Taylor a genetically marked strain of *E. amylovora* had been used.

6.123 **Dr Smith** referred to Sholberg *et al.* (1988) who had conducted experiments with artificially infected and naturally infected fruits. Artificially infected fruits stored at 2-4°C showed about a ten-fold decrease in recovery per two months of cold store. Natural inoculum did not survive 5 months, but no detailed time course study had been done. In general, at ambient temperatures, *E. amylovora* was only supposed to survive on plant surfaces for a few days. Since it was not at all clear that *E. amylovora* ever normally existed within mature apple fruit, the possibilities for studying survival under these conditions were limited. Artificial contamination could hardly be used because of the assumptions that would have to be made on where and how the bacteria were introduced. Studies on naturally occurring bacteria in mature fruit would require that a reliable source of such fruits could be found. Dr Smith noted that the issue of whether *E. amylovora* on or in mature fruits can be a source of outbreaks had already been extensively considered in replies to other questions.

Question 22: Section 2-2-4-2 of the 1999 PRA on "Difficulty in detection by import inspection" indicates that "E. amylovora has an extremely high growth potential. Even a small amount of bacteria bursts into growth under certain conditions." Is propagation capacity dependent on the host of the bacteria? Does this apply specifically to mature apple fruit?

6.124 **Dr Geider** opined that fortunately for apple and pear production, the "growth potential" of *E. amylovora* in mature fruits was low to moderate. Fire blight outbreaks required the presence of fire blight in an area and favourable weather conditions. The occasional fast spread in orchards was unrelated to the rare establishment of fire blight in a region without the disease. Nearly all dissemination of fire blight had been shown to be sequential: convincingly seen in the spread from Egypt to Israel, Turkey, the Balkans to Hungary with the same pattern type Pt2 (Jock *et al.*, 2002). How fire blight got to New Zealand, to Egypt or to England was unknown. Distribution to Northern Italy and Central Spain could be associated with plant imports, but not with contaminated fruits.

6.125 **Dr Hale** stated that the propagation capacity of *E. amylovora* was dependent on the host susceptibility and the environmental conditions encountered. The most susceptible host plant parts were flowers, young shoots, and immature fruit. Pears were more susceptible than apples and immature pear fruit were preferred for diagnosis of fire blight because of their susceptibility and rapid symptom development in pathogenicity tests. There was no evidence to suggest that *E. amylovora* would "burst into growth" either in or on mature apple fruit under any conditions. Experience showed that it was difficult to infect mature apples.

6.126 **Dr Hayward** stated that the growth rate of *E. amylovora* varied depending on the environment, whether in artificial medium or in the tissue of a host plant. Temperature, nutrient availability and water activity were among the most important factors, and host plants differed in susceptibility. The propagation capacity (generation time) depended on the resistance or susceptibility of the host, and this applied to apple fruit or any other plant part. The most rapid growth rate would only be attainable in artificial medium where all environmental parameters were optimal for growth. In the natural environment the bacteria would rarely have an "extremely high growth potential."

6.127 **Dr Smith** stated that most bacteria had an extremely high growth potential and small amounts of them would burst into growth under certain conditions, so this statement was in no way remarkable. The fact that different hosts were more or less susceptible to fire blight might be related to how fast bacteria multiply on that host. There was no indication, to Dr Smith's knowledge, that *E. amylovora* multiplied at all on the surface or in the calyx of mature fruits.

Orchard inspections

Question 23: With regard to the timing of inspections to determine whether an orchard is fire blight-free, what is the relevance of the fact that the flower has the highest susceptibility of infection? If it is at the fruitlet stage when symptoms of fire blight are most easily observed, why is inspection at an earlier stage relevant? At a later stage? Are you aware of any studies where infection not detected at the fruitlet stage was detected at harvest? Is there any scientific evidence that early season infections cannot be confirmed as fire blight during a harvest season inspection?

6.128 **Dr Geider** considered that flowers were the most common entry point for fire blight. However, necrosis could be misleading since other bacteria such as Pseudomonads could cause similar symptoms (without affecting other parts of the tree). Even frost damage could result in necrosis. Typical fire blight symptoms such as necrosis and ooze could be best seen on young fruits. Nevertheless, unpredictable events such as hail storms could cause rapid dissemination at all times of the "green season". In his view, the "best" inspection time would be after flowering in June. There was almost no chance of detecting fire blight if there were no visible symptoms of the disease, however, inspections could never prove the absence of fire blight, they could only identify fire blight when it was at an advanced stage. When necrotic branches were pruned (a common practice), there might not be any sign of fire blight at harvest.

6.129 **Dr Hale** indicated that flowers had the greatest susceptibility and usually showed dramatic symptoms, i.e. browning or blackening of flowers. Symptoms at this stage provided an early warning of fire blight problems in an orchard. Most severely infected flowers dropped from the tree. Some flowers which had been lightly infected might continue to develop into fruitlets after pollination. If the infection continued to develop then the fruitlets ceased development, became brown/black, shrivelled, and finally aborted. However, in some instances the fruitlets might remain attached throughout the growing season. Immature fruit might also become infected from shoot tip infection, particularly after hail storms. Infection and symptom expression in the orchard at flowering alerted growers to the fact that some flowers might be infested (rather than infected) and that *E. amylovora* might persist in the dried-up flower parts (the calyx) of the developing fruit. Inspection during the flowering to fruitlet development period was likely to provide similar results. Inspection at a later stage, at harvest, would provide a final check on the fire blight status of the orchard.

6.130 Dr Hale further stated that there were no reports of infestation of fruit detected at harvest that were not detected at the immature fruitlet stage. Hale *et al.* (1987) and Hale & Taylor (1999) had found calyx infestation with *E. amylovora* at harvest, but fire blight symptoms had been very severe in the orchards during the season. Hale & Clark (1990) had detected *E. amylovora* from symptomless immature fruit from two orchards with no detectable blossom symptoms. However, subsequent inspection had found fire blight in alternative hosts in the orchard. There was no evidence to suggest that early season infections causing fire blight symptoms in trees could not be confirmed at harvest, unless infections had been pruned out. Symptoms at harvest suggested that infection had taken place earlier in the season. In fact, Roberts (2002) had shown that fire blight infections on trees at harvest (infections had been left on trees throughout the growing season) could be confirmed as fire blight by isolation and PCR. Thus a single preharvest inspection should address Japan's concern that any fire blight symptoms occurring in an orchard at any time during the season could be confirmed as being caused by *E. amylovora.*

6.131 **Dr Hayward** replied that although the flower had the highest susceptibility to infection there might be no evidence on inspection. Thomson (1986) had shown that natural populations of *E. amylovora* occurred almost exclusively on pistils with populations often reaching one to 10 million colony forming units per healthy flower. "These colonised flowers do not appear any different from normal flowers and usually develop into healthy fruit." Inspection at the flowering stage would not help in detection of this type of infection; complementary cultural studies would be required. It was at the fruitlet stage when symptoms were the most easily observed and inspection at an earlier stage seemed unnecessary. He was not aware of any studies where infection had not been detected at the fruitlet stage, but then detected at harvest. Neither was he aware of any scientific evidence that early season infections could not be confirmed as fire blight during a harvest season inspection.

6.132 **Dr Smith** stated that while he was not really competent to answer the question, he believed that in Europe the recommended inspection times were once in July/August and once during September/October.

Buffer zones

Question 24: What evidence is available regarding the need for, or effectiveness of, buffer zones around orchards with regard to fire blight contamination of mature apple fruit harvested from the orchard? Does this differ from measures that would be appropriate with regard to a fire blight eradication programme?

6.133 **Dr Geider** was of the view that buffer zones to protect mature apples from fire blight was not a reasonable measure, except when used to reduce the risk of late introduction of fire blight. However, even then, almost mature apples might not be affected by the disease.

6.134 **Dr Hale** stated that Japan based its requirement for buffer zones on: (i) the 500-metre eradication countermeasures against *E. amylovora* in Europe (Meijneke 1979; Zeller, 1987); (ii) the 400-metre zone against citrus canker in Japan required by USA for Unshu oranges; and (iii) the fact that van Vaerenbergh and Crepel (1987) showed dispersion of *E. amylovora* for 250 metres in humid weather.

6.135 However, measures for an eradication programme were not necessarily the same as those required for a programme designed to reduce the risk of fire blight transmission on imported, mature, symptomless apple fruit. Clark *et al.* (1993) had reported that since the introduction of buffer zones, *E. amylovora* had not been detected in calyxes of some 60,000 immature fruit tested from inspected orchards. However, most recently Roberts (2002) had shown conclusively that no buffer zone of any size was justified by the existing scientific data, as fruit harvested from blighted trees or adjacent to blighted trees had not harboured *E. amylovora*. In this study 30,900 mature, symptomless fruit had been harvested zero to 300 metres from fire blight inoculum sources. None of the fruit which were subsequently cool-stored had developed fire blight symptoms and none of the sliced fruit had yielded *E. amylovora* - even when harvested from trees directly adjacent to fire blight sources.

6.136 **Dr Hayward** stated that according to ISPM No.5 (1999) "Glossary of Phytosanitary Terms" a buffer zone was: "An area in which a specified pest does not occur or occurs at a low level and is officially controlled, that either encloses or is adjacent to an infested area, an infested place of production, a pest free area, a pest free place of production or a pest free production site, and in which phytosanitary measures are taken to prevent spread of the pest". The literature (e.g. Zeller, 1987; Meijneke, 1979) confirmed that the 500-metre buffer zone was a recommendation for eradication of fire blight, rather than requirement around a production site. Roberts (2002, in press) had obtained results which indicated that a buffer zone of any size provided no phytosanitary security.

6.137 **Dr Smith** stated that in Europe buffer zones were important around nurseries, but the issue did not arise for orchards. In practice, NPPOs found it most practical to eliminate susceptible hosts in these buffer zones. In other words, they inspected for the presence of hosts (which was easier than inspecting or testing hosts for infection). Published results on superficial contamination of apple fruit by *E. amylovora* strongly suggested that the dispersal involved was only over very short distances; it was very unlikely that bacteria carried from a tree in a surrounding zone would make any significant or detectable contribution to surface populations on fruits. Fire blight eradication programmes were trying to prevent infection of shoots (mainly via flowers) which remained in place slowly allowing bacterial development over months or even years, until active cankers finally released inoculum for further spread. Thus, a buffer zone protected the official fire blight-free status of a place.

Question 25: Does the size of a buffer zone for another disease of fruit, eg citrus canker, have any scientific relevance with regard to the size of a buffer zone which might be appropriate to ensure the fire blight –free status of an apple orchard? Please explain.

6.138 **Dr Geider** considered that a reasonable size for a buffer zone for fire blight protection was the distance of bee flight. Some biologists assumed that bees could cover up to 1 km from a bee hive.

6.139 **Dr Hale** noted that Stall (1988) had suggested that citrus canker could potentially be transmitted on citrus fruit, as mature fruit did show symptoms, but there was no authenticated record of this transmission taking place. However, the epidemiology of fire blight was different from that of many bacterial diseases, e.g. citrus canker, as there was no evidence of *E. amylovora* being associated with lesions on mature fruit. *E. amylovora* might be found in infested calyxes, but this was only in fruit from severely infected orchards (Hale *et al.*, 1987). Dispersal of fire blight and citrus canker had some similarities in that they could both be dispersed over short distances by wind and rain, and over long distances by propagating material. However, citrus canker, unlike fire blight, was not dispersed by bees, but could be dispersed in infected cull fruit and processed pulp. Consequently, although fire blight and citrus canker were both bacterial diseases their epidemiologies differed in the important factor that mature citrus fruit could show symptoms of canker and could potentially transmit the disease whereas mature apples harvested from orchards without fire blight symptoms did not harbour *E. amylovora* and had never been implicated in the spread of the disease.

6.140 **Dr Hayward** stated that fire blight and citrus canker were both bacterial diseases affecting the foliage and fruit of their host plants. Like most bacterial diseases affecting foliage and fruit they shared a propensity towards secondary dispersal of inoculum by wind driven rain. Otherwise there were many differences in epidemiology of the two diseases (Goto, 1992); and it was these differences that were important in determining the size of a buffer zone. The zone size recommended for citrus canker had no relevance to fire blight. Insect transmission was a major factor for fire blight but not in citrus canker. The range and diversity of other plants susceptible to fire blight was great, including common hedgerow plants like hawthorn and ornamental shrubs (e.g, Cotoneaster and Pyracantha) whereas the host range of citrus canker was much more limited.

6.141 **Dr Smith** stated that the size of a buffer zone for another fruit disease, eg citrus canker did not necessarily have any scientific relevance with regard to the size of a buffer zone which might be appropriate to ensure the fire blight-free status of an apple orchard as it depended on the biology of each disease. Citrus canker, for example, was a disease in which the pathogen infected shoots and leaves, and also caused limited cankers on the fruits, from which the bacterium could continue to spread by rain splash from fruit to fruit. Insects were not especially associated with spread, and there was no especially receptive stage. All these factors had to be taken into account in deciding on the size of a buffer zone, and a really intimate knowledge of the disease was needed.

Post-harvest treatment of apple fruit

Question 26: Is there evidence available regarding the contamination of mature apple fruit by harvest labour or other means in an orchard where a source of contamination exists? Please comment on the likelihood of contamination by:

  (a) normal harvesting practices;

  (b) pruning operations and contamination of agricultural machines/equipment;

  (c) packing facilities with/without commingling fruit from different orchards;

  (d) storage and/or overseas transport.

6.142 **Dr Geider** stated that since ooze formation was very low at the harvest time for apples, there was little chance of fruit contamination with *E. amylovora*, even when there were some undetected fire blight foci in an orchard. The circumstances listed could contribute to a low increase of hidden fruit contamination if fire blight still resided in a tree. However, there was almost no risk of dissemination of the disease with fruit.

6.143 **Dr Hale** stated that surface contamination of fruit due to pickers moving from tree to tree could be possible in a severely infected orchard. However, fruit for export was highly unlikely to be harvested from heavily infected orchards (pre-harvest inspection would condemn the orchard). Survival of *E. amylovora* on the surface of mature fruit as contaminants was not likely even in heavily infected orchards (Hale *et al.*, 1987).

6.144 He further noted that pruning operations were not carried out when fruit were mature and consequently contamination was unlikely. It was possible that agricultural equipment used in severely infected orchards could become contaminated. However, equipment was unlikely to be moved from severely infected orchards to symptomless orchards under common hygiene practices.

6.145 Dr Hale indicated that there was no evidence to suggest that the contamination of fruit was likely due to packing facilities. Fruit from orchards with no symptoms of fire blight at harvest were unlikely to be contaminated with *E. amylovora*. It was also unlikely that fruit, even from severely infected orchards, would be surface contaminated (Hale *et al.*, 1987) and consequently contamination due to commingling of fruit from different orchards was not likely to be an issue.

6.146 Dr Hale observed that there was no evidence to suggest that there was any likelihood of contamination during post-harvest storage or overseas transport of mature apple fruit. In fact, Hale & Taylor (1999) found that post-harvest cold storage reduced populations of *E. amylovora* in both naturally and artificially-infested calyxes of mature apple fruit. This suggested that bacterial survival was likely to be adversely affected during normal cool storage and transport conditions, thus reducing the likelihood of any possibility of contamination. Normal commercial practice was likely to clearly mark fruit boxes for different destinations and consequently contamination with fruit for other destinations was also unlikely.

6.147 **Dr Hayward** noted his lack of familiarity with normal harvesting practices, pruning operations, etc., but stated that in his search of the fire blight literature he had not found any evidence regarding the contamination of mature apple fruit by harvest labour or other means in an orchard where a source of contamination existed.

6.148 **Dr Smith** replied that any possible level of contamination of mature fruits arising from any of these points would not be of an order of magnitude that would make any significant difference to the ultimate possibility of survival on the fruits and transmission to a susceptible host.

Question 27: If fruit were disinfected prior to packing, in your view would this be sufficient to remove the risk of spread of fire blight from packing facilities? What would be the effect on this risk if the fruit came from orchards free of fire blight; those with low levels of infection?

6.149 **Dr Geider** replied that fruit disinfection was mainly an act of good will. Given the general low risk of distributing fire blight with fruit, disinfection did not make sense as it could lower fruit quality and might even create chlorinated compounds unhealthy for the consumer.

6.150 **Dr Hale** considered that a chlorine wash prior to packing would remove any possible surface contamination of fruit with *E. amylovora*. It might also remove *E. amylovora* from the exposed parts of the calyx (see Exhibit USA-22). However, it would not remove *E. amylovora* located on the unexposed parts of the calyx-end of fruit from severely infected orchards. Evidence suggested that mature, symptomless fruit harvested from orchards with either no fire blight symptoms or only low levels of infection would not harbour *E. amylovora* either on the surface or in the calyx (Hale *et al.*, 1987). Consequently, in the unlikely event of surface contamination from the packing facility, disinfection (disinfestation) prior to packing would remove any hypothetical risk of spread from the facility.

6.151 **Dr Hayward** noted that questions 27-29 referred to disinfection of a fruit prior to packing; purists might argue that one should refer to disinfestation rather than disinfection in this context. For inanimate surfaces the term disinfection was correctly applied. There was substantial literature on the efficacy of post-harvest treatment of fruit and vegetables. There were risks; any treatment involving immersion in an aqueous medium could serve to mobilise or leach inoculum from within protected sites such as stomates, lenticels, etc. The result was that the previously clean majority might be contaminated by the diseased minority. There was also the greater risk of injury to the fruit during post-harvest treatment handling and these injuries allowed entry by many pests. A post-harvest treatment of apple fruit prior to packing might be sufficient to remove the risk of spread of fire blight from packing facilities but whether it was necessary required careful judgement. Apple fruit injured at the time of inoculation with *E. amylovora* were more likely to develop fire blight than those injured before or after inoculation (van der Zwet *et al.*, 1990). If apples were harvested from a disease-free orchard a post-harvest treatment should be avoided, unless required for other reasons. If there was a low level of infection treatment might be necessary.

6.152 **Dr Smith** stated that the risk of cross contamination between fruit batches was not significant. What was most important was clearly to maintain the identity and integrity of the batches, and thus to ensure that fruit from a significantly infected orchard were not mistakenly certified as coming from a fire blight-free orchard.

Question 28: Can you confirm that the calyx of an apple is more difficult to disinfect than other surfaces of the fruit? Can you comment on the efficacy of chlorine wash (or other disinfection processes) on epiphytic bacteria which may exist in the calyx of the apple? Please comment on the relevant evidence available in this regard.

6.153 **Dr Geider** replied that the calyx was difficult to access with disinfectants. The surface of apples could be quite water repellent and therefore less suitable. The efficacy of apple treatment depended on the structure of the apple surface, which could also affect accidental contamination with *E. amylovora*.

6.154 **Dr Hale** noted that calyx disinfestation (i.e. specifically *in* the calyx rather than *on* the calyx) rather than disinfection was what was under consideration. The calyx of mature fruit was, in his experience, very difficult to disinfest of *E. amylovora*. However, viable populations of *E. amylovora* had been reduced in artificially-infested calyxes using periods of cold storage (Hale & Taylor 1999). External fruit surfaces could be easily disinfested of *E. amylovora* using sodium hypochlorite or benzalkonium chloride (Janisciewicz & van der Zwet 1988; Roberts & Reymond 1989).[179]

6.155 **Dr Hayward** noted that there was some evidence that the calyx of fruit was a protected site for the survival of *E. amylovora*, which proliferated as an epiphyte on the stigmatic surfaces (Thomson,1986) and the remnants of these surfaces were enclosed by the calyx. Taylor *et al.* (2002) had looked at the survival of *E. amylovora* in discarded fruit and found that low levels of *E. amylovora* persisted after an initial sharp decline. They commented that the persistence of small populations might be because Braeburn apples had a closed calyx which might provide some protection for *E. amylovora* from adverse environmental conditions and that the calyx region of the apple mainly consisted of dead plant tissue providing little or no nutrient for the growth and survival of *E. amylovora*. Hale and Clark (1990) had used a DNA probe to detect low numbers of *E. amylovora* in calyxes. For both fully mature and packed fruit the pest had been detected in washings only from the calyx end and not from the fruit epidermis - again suggesting that the pathogen was more likely to survive in association with the dried remnants of the flower parts (Hale *et al.*, 1987). Sholberg *et al.* (1988) had compared organic acid treatments (acetic, propionic, etc.) and found they were equally effective. Acetic acid treatment did not cause phytotoxicity. These organic acids were possibly more penetrative than chlorine and might disinfest the calyx more readily. The results of these authors showed that 1M acetic acid was an effective surface sterilant. Chlorine at 100 micrograms per ml (100 ppm) was not effective "... probably because the bacteria at the calyx end of the apple are protected from the action by chlorine by the sepals" (Sholberg *et al.* (1988)).

6.156 **Dr Smith** stated that while he was not really competent to answer the question, it seemed plausible that a water-based disinfectant would penetrate less well to all parts of the calyx cavity.

---

[179] Quoting his own unpublished results, Dr Hale stated that a chlorine (100 ppm) wash had not satisfactorily disinfested *E. amylovora* from the unexposed parts of the calyx of fruit artificially infested by injecting suspensions of *E. amylovora* directly into the calyx. However, in the work reported in Exhibit USA-22, the calyxes had been infested by placing drops of *E. amylovora* suspension on the calyx-end of the fruit and consequently the bacteria were more accessible to the disinfestation treatment as they were on the exposed parts of the calyx.

Question 29: Roberts, et al. (1998) contains a reference to van der Zwet, et al. (1990), regarding the testing of refrigerated, stored fruit. The statement is made that a greater proportion of "surface-sterilized fruit" developed visible fire blight symptoms than "non-surface sterilized" fruit. What kind of treatment was used for surface sterilization? How does this compare with the chlorine wash required by Japan? What is the significance of finding more fire blight on sterilized fruit than non-sterilized?

6.157 **Dr Geider** stated that his experience was with surface sterilization of pears used for fire blight experiments. In the laboratory, this procedure was done to avoid fast fungal growth. However, surface sterilized fruits often developed rot symptoms, and the surface sterilization of pears had been discontinued. It was possible that the removal of the epiphytic micro-organisms opened the fruits to the entry of other micro-organisms. In addition, sterilization might change the surface structure of fruits, which could facilitate access by pathogens. However, the meaning of the phrase "fire blight on surface-sterilized fruits" was unclear and how symptoms were connected with fire blight.

6.158 **Dr Hale** recalled that van der Zwet *et al.* (1990) had surface-sterilized fruit by immersing fruit for three minutes in 0.65% NaOCl and rinsing 3 times in distilled water. The chlorine wash requested by Japan was for fruit to be immersed for 1 min in NaOCl solution containing 100 ppm available chlorine. Internal blight symptoms were difficult to distinguish from those of other fruit rots. Although van der Zwet *et al.* (1990) had speculated that infection was from endophytic *E. amylovora*, the fruit had not been tested to confirm the presence of endophytic bacteria. Dr Hale considered that it was equally probable that the disinfestation process may have resulted in infection of fruit by epiphytic (surface) bacteria. The handling and disinfestation of the fruit could have resulted in injuries that allowed surface bacteria to infect the fruit.

6.159 **Dr Hayward** suggested it was useful to compare the details of the disinfection process used by Sholberg *et al.* (1988) with that of van der Zwet *et al.* (1990). To ensure that Red Delicious apples had been effectively surface-sterilized for experimental purposes, Sholberg *et al.* (1988) used 400 micrograms per ml available chlorine prepared from commercial bleach (5.25% NaOCL) for 2 minutes, whereas the latter authors had treated their apple fruit with 0.65% sodium hypochlorite for 3 minutes followed by three rinses in distilled water (one assumes sterile water but this was not stated). Considerably more disease had developed among the surface-disinfested Rome Beauty fruit than among the non-disinfested ones. It seems likely that these results were due to the slow leaching of the pest from its protected site within the calyx, and possibly also to injury during handling of the fruit, and the dispersal of the inoculum from some of the fruit to all of the fruit. The Japanese protocol proposed immersion in a sodium hypochlorite solution (chlorine level more than 100 ppm) for longer than one minute. However, Sholberg *et al.* (1988) had found 100 ppm chlorine to be inadequate for surface sterilisation.

6.160 **Dr Smith** referenced his reply to Question 11 and observed that the result of this study was strange and unless it was confirmed by further work, this result should not be considered as a convincing basis for any phytosanitary measure.

Question 30: What is the likelihood of bacteria on apple fruit surviving normal commercial, shipping and export procedures? Does this likelihood change if cool storage conditions are not maintained?

6.161 **Dr Geider** replied that in a dry environment, *E. amylovora* would survive more efficiently on apple surfaces. Cool storage could increase survival, whereas moisture and other micro-organisms would add to the decay of the pathogen (Hildebrand *et al.*, 2001).

6.162 **Dr Hale** noted that Hale & Taylor (1999) had shown that cool storage of mature apple fruit reduced the survival of *E. amylovora* in calyxes of artificially infested fruit. Incubation of fruit at 20°C for 14 days after cool storage (to simulate possible retail conditions after export) had not resulted in an increase in the detectable levels of *E. amylovora* in the calyxes. In fact, there had been a further reduction and *E. amylovora* had only survived when calyxes were infested with large numbers of bacteria, i.e. $>10^5$ colony forming units. The number of calyx-infested fruit from a severely infected orchard had been reduced from 2% at harvest to 0% after cool storage. After a further 14 days incubation at 20°C there had still been no detectable *E. amylovora* in the calyxes. Consequently, there appeared to be no evidence for any likely change in survival of *E. amylovora* if cool store conditions were not maintained.

6.163 **Dr Hayward** considered there to be a low likelihood of bacteria on apple fruit surviving normal commercial shipping and export procedures. Sholberg *et al.* (1988) had shown that cold storage alone reduced the number of surface-borne *E. amylovora* on artificially inoculated Red Delicious apples and that it had reduced the number of bacteria on naturally contaminated Newtown apples to levels below detection after storage at 2 C for 5 months. Hale and Taylor (1999) had shown that cool storage of mature, export quality apples in either the laboratory at 0 C +/- 0.5 C or a commercial pack house (2 C +/- 0.5 C) for a period of 25 days had reduced the survival of *E. amylovora* in calyxes of both inoculated and naturally infested fruit, and concluded that cool-stored, mature, export quality fruit were unlikely to be a vector of the fire blight bacterium. Further, Roberts (2002, in press) had found that none of 30,000 fruit in cold storage for 3 months developed fire blight.

6.164 Dr Hayward further stated that the minimum growth temperature for *E. amylovora* was 3-5 C. If apples were stored at an ambient temperature permitting optimal growth (e.g., 18-28 C) then any *E. amylovora* present would presumably be able to proliferate but there was no data to compare with Figure 1 in Sholberg *et al.* (1988) which clearly showed a decline in survival to extinction after six months storage at 2-4 C. Dr Hayward noted that this likelihood would increase at higher ambient temperatures.

6.165 **Dr Smith** noted that superficial bacteria (at least artificially applied) could apparently survive months in cold store, while such populations were said by many authors to die out within days on plant surfaces at ambient temperatures.

Question 31: Is there any evidence regarding the ability of fruit cargo crates to spread fire blight? Is there any evidence that this could be a potential source of contamination if the fruit came from orchards free of fire blight or from orchards with low levels of infection?

6.166 **Dr Geider** replied that there was no evidence that fruit cargo crates distributed fire blight. Fruit from orchards with low disease levels were not at all a risk for dissemination.

6.167 **Dr Hale** stated that it had been suggested by Lelliott (1959) that fire blight might have been introduced into the United Kingdom on contaminated fruit crates and that subsequent spread in the United Kingdom might have been due to the use of recycled contaminated crates from those orchards where the initial fire blight symptoms had been observed. However, this had never been proved (Bonn & van der Zwet 2000). Keck (1996) had reported that under laboratory conditions *E. amylovora* could survive for several months on wood of non-host plants or on plastic (materials which might be used in cargo crates). However, there had been no further investigations to determine if contaminated crates could really represent a source of inoculum for the spread of fire blight. There was no evidence that cargo crates could be a potential source of contamination if mature fruit came from orchards free of fire blight or from orchards with low levels of infection.

6.168 **Dr Hayward** indicated that he had found no evidence regarding the ability of fruit cargo crates to spread fire blight and in his opinion the likelihood was negligible. In the example of the UK outbreak (1957) the other possibility of introduction was on propagating material. One of the two *E. amylovora* strains found in the United Kingdom (Pt1) was present in New Zealand and in parts of central Europe (Jock *et al.*, 2002). There had never been insistence on the crate theory in the United Kingdom (Lelliott, 1959). Furthermore, as fire blight had spread through Europe and the Mediterranean in the past four decades several examples had emerged of its introduction on propagating material, but none of introduction on crates.

6.169 **Dr Smith** responded that there was no direct evidence of the spread of fire blight by fruit cargo crates. The idea that *E. amylovora* could survive on crates as ooze for any significant time was quite conjectural, and it was even less likely that it could be transmitted from them. This theory had persisted in the literature because of opinions expressed by the very first British scientists dealing with the first fire blight outbreak in Europe, but he was not aware of any further research on the issue. The many European experts on fire blight attached no practical importance to this idea.

Question 32: Are there reasonably available methods to inspect imports of mature apple fruit for fire blight contamination? Would routine inspection of shipments at import be feasible to detect the presence of internal or external fire blight bacteria in or on apple fruit imports?

6.170 **Dr Geider** answered that routine inspection of apples after harvest for fire blight symptoms was not reasonable. It was possible to take samples and to try to detect *E. amylovora*, but even if a few bacteria were unexpectedly detected this would not cause the establishment of fire blight at the place of consumption for the reasons already given.

6.171 **Dr Hale** stated that there were no recognized methods for inspection (e.g. visual) of imports of mature apple fruit for contamination with *E. amylovora*. It might well be possible to develop technologies for sampling and PCR-based detection – although the time necessary to process samples might make them unworkable. Consequently routine inspection of shipments at import to detect the presence of *E. amylovora* in or on apple fruit would be difficult.

6.172 **Dr Hayward** noted that there were no inspection methods which would routinely detect fire blight on mature, symptomless fruit at the point of entry. Tests to examine the calyx end of fruit for low numbers of *E. amylovora* would require a dedicated laboratory.

6.173 **Dr Smith** indicated that the levels of contamination concerned were too low for there to be a reasonably available method to inspect imports of mature apple fruit for fire blight contamination. Such inspection would necessitate impossibly large samples.

Question 33: How does Japan's 1999 PRA compare with the IPPC Guidelines for Pest Risk Analysis of 1995 (Exhibit JPN-30) and the IPPC Pest Risk Assessment standard of 2001 (Exhibit USA-15)?

6.174 **Dr Geider** stated that it was not possible to prove the total absence of a pathogen in plant material. Nonetheless, it was not reasonable to assume that bacteria on a fruit's surface could establish fire blight. He indicated that both PRAs tried to define risk of pest, the Japanese PRA with more concern than the US PRA. He questioned whether a general PRA was appropriate for fire blight, since too many assumptions were open for describing the problems with that disease. Most risk assessment assays could not consider all the steps and random events in fruit harvest, processing, trade and consumption. Remote risks could be estimated by considering historical events in disease distribution, pattern analysis of strains and through consideration of the absence of fire blight in the countries of the Southern hemisphere except New Zealand.

6.175 Dr Geider was of the opinion that a decision to remove most restrictions on importation of apples from fire blight countries should take into consideration that Japanese apple production is highly sophisticated based on a demand for high quality apples, and the import of low quality apples into Japan at cheap prices could undermine that country's disease controls, regardless of the low risk of disseminating fire blight with apples. As such, he personally favoured the importation of apples from inspected US-orchards, without pre-treatment of the fruits. While chlorine treatment would certainly decrease epiphytic bacterial populations, chlorinated by-products could be unfavourable to human health and such treatment was not justified to protect Japan from fire blight.

6.176 **Dr Hale** noted that Japan's PRA was in three parts: (1) Fire Blight – details of the disease and cause; (2) Pest Risk Analysis concerning *E. amylovora*;

and (3) Pest Risk Analysis for quarantine measures on *E. amylovora* for US fresh apple fruit. The PRA followed, to a certain extent, the 1996 IPPC Guidelines for Pest Risk Analysis. However, it did not address the commodity that was under dispute, i.e. mature, symptomless apple fruit, nor did it address a number of the issues that were required to be addressed according to the IPPC Pest Risk Assessment Standard of 2001.

6.177 Dr Hale stated that it appeared that Japan had prejudged the outcome of its risk assessment in that it had stated that phytosanitary measures were required based on the possibility, rather than the probability, of introduction of fire blight. It therefore did not fulfil the second requirement of a risk assessment (IPPC Pest Risk Assessment Standard of 2001) as it did not evaluate the likelihood (probability) of entry, establishment and spread through the importation of mature, symptomless apples. The PRA should also focus on mature, symptomless apples, and not on all other types of fruits (immature), leaves, pears etc., as this was the product that the United States wished to export. In his opinion, the following key steps had been overlooked for the probability of entry:

(i)   identification of the relevant pathways;

(ii)   probability of fire blight being associated with the pathway of origin;

(iii)   probability of survival during transport and storage;

(iv)   probability of fire blight surviving existing pest management procedures; and

(v)   probability of transfer of fire blight to suitable hosts.

Japan had not provided an evaluation of the likelihood that the steps necessary for entry of fire blight bacteria would be completed. Their analysis of establishment and spread was similarly not an evaluation as the likelihood of entry, establishment and spread needed to be evaluated according to the measures that might be applied. Some measures to reduce risk had been identified but not evaluated.

6.178 Dr Hale further observed that available scientific evidence that mature, symptomless apples do not transmit fire blight had not been taken into account. Thomson (2000) had stated that it has never been demonstrated that mature apple fruit were involved in dissemination of *E. amylovora* or served as a source of new fire blight infections in orchards. It was also considered extremely unlikely that contaminated fruit could be responsible for establishing new outbreaks of fire blight.

6.179 According to **Dr Hayward,** Japan's 1999 PRA was of necessity based on the 1996 IPCC Guidelines for Pest Risk Analysis. There were substantial differences between these guidelines and the later version (IPCC Pest Risk Assessment Standard of 2001). Notably, stage 2: Pest Risk Assessment was almost entirely different in the two documents. The first version had seven sub-headings in Stage 2, the later document 36. Pest risk analysis had evolved with experience of its application in the years between the first and second guidelines and it had been found necessary to break down the elements of the process into their component parts. The first eight sections in the later document were concerned with "Pest Categorization" (absent from the 1996 Guidelines, and also absent from the 1999 PRA from Japan). There then followed probabilistic assessments of the entry of the pest; identification of pathways by which this might occur; probability of the pest being associated with the pathway at origin; probability of survival during transport or storage; probability of pest survival during pest management procedures; probability of transfer to a suitable host; probability of establishment; probability of spread after establishment. Such a stepwise analysis would ideally be based on quantitative data but in the absence of data there could be semi-quantitative or qualitative assessments. Probabilities for each component could be given a rating of "very low", "high" or "moderate", etc. Estimates for the probability of importation and the partial properties of distribution, establishment and spread could be combined using a simulation-based approach to give an overall estimate of the unrestricted annual risk associated with a particular pest. The importing country then had to decide whether the unrestricted risk was above or below the appropriate level of protection for that particular pest. The Japanese PRA of 1999 contained much of the information which would be required for a PRA in terms of the 2001 Guidelines, but the stepwise probabilistic assessments were lacking.

6.180 **Dr Smith** considered that the Japanese PRA satisfactorily addressed most of the necessary aspects, notably the identity, probability of establishment, potential loss etc. However, nobody contested that *E. amylovora* presented a real risk for Japan, and that it could be carried in international trade. According to the 1996 IPPC standard (section 3), "a list of options for reducing risks to an acceptable level should be assembled", "the efficacy and impact of the various options in reducing risk to an acceptable level should be evaluated", "the positive and negative aspects of the options should be specified", "countries should take particular note of the Minimal Impact Principle". The Japanese PRA did not consider the measures as "options". It was principally concerned to show that each of the measures already in place was effective in some respect, and concluded that all should therefore be applied. The question of whether any single measure, or a combination of fewer measures, could reduce the risk to an acceptable level was not addressed. Comparisons were made with measures used in other parts of the world, but only to verify their effectiveness, not to establish their appropriateness for one particular pathway (imported fruits). Some of the measures referred to were in fact used for the risk management of other commodities, such as nursery material. The Japanese approach did not seem to allow for the possibility of adjusting measures for different commodities presenting different risks. The IPPC 2001 standard (section 3.4) stated that "the measures should be as precise as possible as to consignment type (hosts, parts of plants) and origin so as not to act as barriers to trade by limiting the import of products where this is not justified". It envisaged single measures in the first instance, since it then continued "Combinations of two or more measures may be needed ...". The Japanese PRA had not clearly explained why all the measures it applied were needed.

6.181 Dr Smith further noted that Japan referred to the "systemic approach" (more usually, "Systems Approach"), which was now covered by IPPC standard ISPM No.14. Since a Systems Approach was by its nature a combination of measures (or options, in the language of the PRA standards), it should not be regarded as a single measure or option. A Systems Approach might be unnecessarily restrictive by comparison with its component measures and so not respect the minimum impact principle.

Question 34: Stage 3 of the IPPC Guidelines for Pest Risk Analysis of 1995 (Exhibit JPN-30) deals with risk management options. The first step outlined at section 3.1 of the Guidelines is the assembly of a list of options for reducing risks to an acceptable level. The second step outlined at section 3.2 of the Guidelines is to evaluate the efficacy and impact of the various options in reducing risk to an acceptable level. In your view, does the Japanese Pest Risk Analysis of 1999 list options for reducing risks ? Furthermore, does the Japanese Pest Risk Analysis evaluate the efficacy and impact of various options in reducing risk to an acceptable level?

6.182 **Dr Geider** observed that section 3.1 sounded legally reasonable, but wondered whether or not the listed options had been verified. For fire blight, phytosanitary inspection of apple orchards could be a compromise between parties with restrictive and liberal fruit import regimes. Post-harvest inspection was not useful to detect fire blight symptoms. Prohibition of entry from a specific origin could be applied only to areas without fire blight inspections. It could be assumed that liberalized access for apple imports to Japan would attract also other fire blight countries, where inspections might be needed for some time. Of course, there was also some concern about the method and impact of inspections. For example, did a necrotic branch of an apple tree mean fire blight? If confirmed, should this tree endanger the harvest of a whole orchard with hundreds or thousands of trees? Also inspection by specialists might not detect low levels of fire blight, and the disease could appear afterwards or increase later in the season. The principle of measures resulting in minimum impediments to trade could lead to a reasonable compromise between opposing opinions about severe restrictions or unregulated apple importations.

6.183 **Dr Hale** stated that in Japan's 1999 PRA the following risk management options had been considered: (1) designated areas - fire blight-free sites and buffer zones; (2) preventative measures for post-harvest contamination; and (3) labelling after disinfection and inspection. However, in Japan's 1999 PRA the following risk management options had not been not considered:

- treatment at point of entry, inspection station, place of destination;
- detention in post-entry quarantine (may not be feasible for perishable commodities, although apple fruit could be stored);
- post-entry measures (restrictions on use of commodity);
- prohibition of entry of specific commodities from specific origins.

Many of the options for reducing risk to an acceptable level were embedded in Japan's 1999 PRA, but did not appear to have been effectively addressed. Japan had identified some measures but had not provided an evaluation of the efficacy and impact of the options in reducing risk to an acceptable level in terms of the factors listed in the 1996 IPPC Guidelines for Pest Risk Analysis. Information on some of the factors affecting various risk management options could be found in the PRA but the efficacy and impact of the options (rather than of the disease itself) had not been evaluated. Japan had ranked the efficacy of import inspections very highly but this was the option that would be most difficult to achieve without the development of rapid molecular *E. amylovora* detection systems for checking samples of imported fruit.

6.184 **Dr Hayward** noted that a section of Japan's 1999 PRA was devoted to "Pest risk management for *E. amylovora*". This section highlighted the difficulty of detecting the pest and its potential for rapid growth from a low population level. It was designated as a pathogen subject to import prohibition. In the next part of the PRA, Chapter 3, pages 18-22, some of the risk management options considered necessary, such as designation of pest free production areas, the need for a buffer zone, the need for post-harvest chlorine treatment of fruit, and the need for adequate labelling were included. However Japan's PRA did not include an adequate evaluation of the efficacy and impact of the various options in reducing risk to an acceptable level as specified in the IPPC Guidelines of 2001.

6.185 **Dr Smith** replied by referencing his answer to Question 33.

Japan's disease-free status

Question 35: Please comment on the divergence in opinions regarding the occurrence of fire blight in Japan, including Mizuno, et al (2002).

6.186 **Dr Geider** noted that the paper of Mizuno *et al.* (2002) had reviewed possible fire blight events in Japan. In a recent paper for the Proceedings of the International Symposium in Asian Pears 2001 (Geider *et al.*, 2002), Dr Geider had discussed the possibility that the report from 1903 could have really been based on fire blight events. It was the published opinion of his laboratory that a pear disease in Japan (not officially admitted) was not fire blight (Beer *et al.*, 1996), but related to Asian pear blight from Korea (Kim *et al.*, 2001a). The pathogen of 1903 could well have been fire blight, because the pathogen was reported to have been isolated from apple, which was barely susceptible to Asian pear blight (Rhim *et al.*, 1999; Kim *et al.*, 2001b). Mizuno *et al.* had discussed several options for the causative agent of the disease in 1903. There were always difficulties with Gram-staining in laboratories and this was the main reason why *E. amylovora* was taxonomically incorrectly called *Bacillus amylovorus* for a long time. According to Dr Geider, it was not a valid argument to say that positive Gram-stains around 1900 in Japan subsequently ruled out the presence of *E. amylovora*. However, he noted that an answer to this question did not provide information about fire blight in Japan at the present time. The recently considered pear disease was not identical with fire blight and other reports about additional bacterial pathogens such as *E. amylovora* were not known for Japan.

6.187 For **Dr Hale**, the evidence suggested that Bacterial Shoot Blight of Pear (BSBP) was very similar to fire blight but could be distinguished in physiological, biochemical and pathogenicity characteristics. Molecular techniques could be used to differentiate between isolates and eventually the taxonomic position of the Japanese isolates in relation to *E. amylovora* would be determined. The early reports on whether or not the disease was caused by *E. amylovora* or various fungi could not be verified and so should not be considered in this dispute.

6.188 **Dr Hayward** noted that Mizuno (2002) had concluded that the disease reported to be fire blight of apple in Japan was apple canker caused by *Valsa ceratosperma* and that the alleged fire blight of pear was either a twig blight caused by *Diaporthe* sp. or bacterial shoot blight of pear. In the past 15 years, the taxonomy of bacteria had become increasingly reliant on the use of DNA-based methods. There was evidence that the bacterium that caused shoot blight of pear in Hokkaido, Japan, was distinct taxonomically from *E. amylovora*, the cause of fire blight of apple and pear and *Rubus* sp. in North America and elsewhere. They may all have shared a common ancestor, and it would be interesting to know the sequence of evolutionary events given that fire blight was first recognized over 200 years ago in the United States, whereas the other two pathogens apparently originated in Korea and Japan.

6.189 **Dr Smith** noted that it was commonplace to find that a pest had been recorded in a country in the relatively early days of plant pathology and had not been later confirmed. Scientific knowledge advanced, diagnostic techniques improved and the observations of earlier scientists proved to be simply mistaken. In addition, it was quite common for there to be early records which seemed to be convincing, followed by a long period when the pest in question was not reported again. It was then inferred that it had disappeared. So the early records of fire blight in Japan could simply be disregarded with respect to any understanding of the present situation. The problem with the agent of "bacterial shoot blight of pear" was that it did appear, bacteriologically, to have been *E. amylovora* - maybe a distinct strain or pathovar with a different host range and a different aggressiveness, but still the same species. This raised interesting questions of where it had originated and if there were other distinctive *E. amylovora* strains elsewhere in the world. But the disease no longer occurred, and the pathogen could no longer be found. Furthermore, the presence of *E. amylovora* in Japan would not as such invalidate measures that Japan might take with respect to imports from other countries, provided that it was "not widely distributed" (bacterial shoot blight was only found in Hokkaido) and equivalent official control was applied within Japan (principle of non-discrimination).

Question 36: How do the findings regarding disease symptoms observed in apple shoots in the United States (at low percentage when they were injected with high-concentration bacterial suspensions) compare with the findings of fire blight in mature apples (eg, when inoculated with high concentrations of E. amylovora) as reported in various experiments and studies?

6.190 **Dr Geider** stated that plant inoculation could (and often did) result in no appearance of fire blight symptoms. Statistically, the pathogen did not always multiply at the inoculation sites. This could depend on the experimental conditions, on the strains applied, and on the apple variety or shape of the plant used. Young shoots often reacted to bacterial injections at an intermediate to high level. Bacteria in mature apple could certainly survive for a certain time in a moist and sterile environment.

6.191 **Dr Hale** noted that Beer *et al.* (1996) had produced a low percentage of infection (typical symptoms of fire blight) in apple shoots inoculated with high concentrations of BSBP bacteria. However, the evidence suggested that the Japanese isolates were much less virulent on apples than on pears in Japan, and consequently should be designated as pathogenic variants of *E. amylovora*. There were other known pathogenic variants of *E. amylovora*, isolated from *Rubus* species, that did not cause disease symptoms on apples and pears. Based on greenhouse studies, the strains of *E. amylovora* from Hokkaido exhibited a range of host specificity towards apple cultivars not previously recognised. In addition, their microbiological and molecular biological characteristics were distinct.

6.192 Dr Hale further stated that there were some reports (Anderson 1952; Dueck 1974; Nachtigall *et al.*, 1985) that apples had developed blight symptoms in storage. However, in all of these cases the fruit were wounded and high inoculum levels (c10^9 cfu/ml) had been injected into the apple cortex. These conditions did not reflect the conditions likely to be encountered naturally or the levels at which *E. amylovora* would be likely to be associated with mature, symptomless apple fruit. Van der Zwet *et al.* (1990) had reported that fruit collected from fire-blight free orchards developed internal blight symptoms in storage. However, they had also noted that symptoms were difficult to distinguish from those of other rots and they did not isolate *E. amylovora* from the blight-like symptoms to confirm the causal agent. Van der Zwet (Exhibit USA-18) also stated that heavily infected trees were nearby those from which the fruit were harvested. Roberts (2002) had repeated the storage trials in commercial cold storage using mature, symptomless fruit from orchards containing sources of fire blight inoculum. None of the fruit had developed either internal or external disease symptoms in storage and *E. amylovora* had not been isolated from any of the fruit sampled.

6.193 **Dr Hayward** observed that Beer *et al.* (1996) had reproduced "typical symptoms of fire blight in response to inoculation with the Hokkaidian strains" in shoots of European and Asian pear plants. Four of the 220 vigorously growing apple shoots inoculated with the Hokkaidian strains had developed typical symptoms of fire blight, when inoculated at high concentration (billion cfu per ml). There were examples in the literature of phytobacteriology of misleading results being obtained in pathogenicity tests when very high concentrations of inoculum were used to inoculate non-host plants. The best known phenomenon was the hypersensitive response elicited by pathogenic bacteria in non-host plants. In his opinion, there might be similar doubts about experiments where fire blight had been produced in apples when inoculated with a massive concentration of inoculum.

6.194 **Dr Smith** did not express an opinion but noted that it depended on the type of inoculation. He further noted that all sorts of strange results could be obtained by artificially inoculating plants with high concentrations of pathogens – which was one of the reasons why the demonstration of Koch's postulates could be so difficult.

VII.   INTERIM REVIEW

A.   *Introduction*

7.1   The Panel issued the draft descriptive sections of its report (factual and arguments) to the parties on 6 February 2003, in accordance with Article 15.1 of the DSU. Both parties offered written comments on the draft descriptive sections on 24 February 2003. The Panel noted all these comments and amended the draft descriptive part where appropriate. The Panel issued its interim report to the parties on 20 March 2003, in accordance with Article 15.2 of the DSU. In communications dated 3 April 2003, both Japan and the United States requested that the Panel review precise aspects of the interim report. Neither of the parties requested an interim review meeting. On 11 April 2003, Japan and the United States provided written comments on each other's comments on the interim report, as permitted by the Panel's working procedures. The Panel carefully reviewed the arguments made. They are discussed in this section and, to the extent necessary, are reflected in the findings section below, in accordance with Article 15.3 of the DSU.[180]

B.   *Comments by Japan*[181]

1.   *Burden of Proof*

7.2   Japan's first comment relates to our statement in paragraph 8.44 according to which:

> "We do not see the greater expertise of the exporting country as a factor which should automatically justify a different allocation of the burden of proof."

7.3   Japan requests that we review that conclusion because of the difficulties it faces in conducting field experiments on its territory and because of the problems occurring when cooperation from exporting country governments is required. We have explained, in paragraphs 8.45-8.46 below, why we believe that such an argument is not compelling under the circumstances of this case. We would like to add that the United States is not the only country where fire blight is present and where scientific experiments could be performed.

---

[180]   Section VII of this Report entitled "Interim Review" therefore forms part of the findings of the final panel report, in accordance with Article 15.3 of the DSU.
[181]   This section is divided according to the sections of the findings on which comments have been made.

7.4   Japan's argument would imply in practice either that a more demanding standard of proof to establish a prima facie case be imposed on the United States, or that Japan either be granted a different standard of proof when rebutting the US arguments or be relieved of rebutting the US claim. Neither of these suggestions is supported by the approach on burden of proof defined by the Appellate Body in *EC – Hormones* and recalled in paragraph 8.42 below. Moreover, nowhere does the *SPS Agreement* provide for a specific standard of proof in relation to dispute settlement.

7.5   We also consider that our statement in paragraph 8.44 does not imply that an exporting country will be "allowed to prevail by merely contradicting the evidence the importing country has".[182] We applied the principle of allocation of burden of proof as identified by the Appellate Body in *United States - Shirts and Blouses* and recalled, as mentioned in paragraph 8.42 below, in the context of the *SPS Agreement* in the Appellate Body Report on *EC – Hormones*. The requirement that the complainant make a prima facie case is the same in a dispute relating to the *SPS Agreement* as under any other WTO agreement. In *EC - Hormones*, the Appellate Body described the establishment of a prima facie case as follows:

> "In accordance with our ruling in *United States – Wool Shirts and Blouses*[183], the Panel should have begun the analysis of each legal provision by examining whether the United States and Canada had presented evidence and legal arguments sufficient to demonstrate that the EC measures were inconsistent with the obligations assumed by the European Communities under each Article of the *SPS Agreement* addressed by the Panel, i.e., Articles 3.1, 3.3, 5.1 and 5.5. Only after such a prima facie determination had been made by the Panel may the onus be shifted to the European Communities to bring forward evidence and arguments to disprove the complaining party's claim."[184]

This is exactly what we requested from the parties in this case.

2.   Article 2.2 of the SPS Agreement

7.6   Japan requests us to review our assessment of the 1990 article of van der Zwet *et al.* in paragraphs 8.127-8.128 below. We did not find Japan's arguments in support of its request sufficiently convincing. In particular, Japan's allegation that Professor van der Zwet admitted in Roberts *et al.* (1998) that the tested apple fruit in van der Zwet *et al.* (1990) were mature and symptomless is not supported by the information contained in that very article. On the basis of the nature of the information reported in the articles, the experts' views and the comments of

---

[182]   Japan's comments, 3 April 2003, para. 3.
[183]   Adopted 23 May 1997, WT/DS33/AB/R, pp. 14-16.
[184]   (*original footnote*) Our finding that the Panel erred in allocating the burden of proof generally to the Member imposing the measure, however, does not deal with the quite separate issue of whether the United States and Canada actually made a prima facie case of violation of each of the following Articles of the *SPS Agreement*: 3.1, 3.3, 5.1 and 5.5. See in this respect, footnote 180 of this Report.

Professor van der Zwet himself in his statement of 16 July 2002, Exhibit USA-18, we see no reason to change our assessment of van der Zwet *et al.* (1990) and of Roberts *et al.* (1998).

7.7   In response to comments from both parties, we revised our findings in section D.

3.   *Article 5.7 of the SPS Agreement*

7.8   In its comments of 3 April 2003, Japan contests our reasoning under Article 5.7 of the *SPS Agreement*. Japan first claims that it should be possible to invoke Article 5.7, for example, in situations where the process of scientific discovery is at work and thus available scientific evidence is not conclusive, even though the quantity of the evidence is more than little.

7.9   We have no reason of principle to reject the hypothesis suggested by Japan, although we note that the process of scientific discovery is by its nature an ongoing process. It is possible that, in a given situation, a lot of scientific research may have been carried out on a particular issue without yielding sufficiently "relevant" – within the meaning of Article 5.7 - or reliable evidence. In such a case, however, there is little or no reliable evidence on the subject matter at issue. This is not the case here. There is a great deal of "relevant" scientific material available. What Japan addresses in its comment on paragraph 8.219 is, in fact, a question of weighing the evidence before the Panel. We have carefully reviewed the material submitted in this case and found that the present situation was one where a lot of "relevant scientific evidence" had already been accumulated. Our assessment was not simply quantitative; it was also qualitative, as demonstrated by the position we have taken on van der Zwet *et al.* (1990) on the basis, *inter alia*, of the opinion of the experts consulted by the Panel.[185]

7.10   Japan also argues that we should not include, in our assessment under Article 5.7, scientific evidence which has become available after the date of entry into force of the *SPS Agreement* in 1995. We do not see in the text of Article 5.7, or of Article 2.2 for that matter, any reason to limit our assessment of the "relevant scientific evidence" to evidence available before 1995. On the contrary, since Article 5.7 provides for an exception to Article 2.2, and an assessment of the compatibility of a measure with Article 2.2 is made at the time the matter is reviewed by the Panel, there is no justification for assessing any alleged provisional measure at a different date. If we were to agree with Japan, a measure could be indefinitely maintained on a provisional basis under Article 5.7, and the requirement that Members seek to obtain the additional information for a more objective assessment of risks and review the phytosanitary measure accordingly within a reasonable period of time would become ineffective. Such a selective interpretation of Article 5.7 is not acceptable.

---

[185]   See para. 8.127, below.

4. Article 5.1 of the SPS Agreement

7.11 Japan argues that, contrary to what is mentioned in paragraph 8.247 below, the conformity of a PRA under Article 5.1 should be assessed in light of information available at the time when the PRA was conducted, and no later evidence should be considered.

7.12 We corrected paragraph 8.247 as far as the representation of Japan's arguments is concerned. However, we do not agree with Japan's position that no information subsequent to the completion of a PRA should be taken into consideration by a Panel, particularly if, as in the present case, that PRA is already almost four years old at the time it is reviewed. Some assessment of the subsequent evolution of the scientific evidence is not only acceptable, it is also necessary, if only to monitor the development of any new evidence which might require a revision of the risk assessment. One must not lose sight of the purpose of a risk assessment, which is to serve as a basis for regulatory actions. If the scientific evidence evolves, this may be an indication that the risk assessment should be reviewed or a new assessment undertaken. It would be also legally inconsistent to require, on the one hand, that phytosanitary measures not be maintained without sufficient scientific evidence pursuant to Article 2.2[186] while, on the other hand, accepting that risk assessments not be renewed in the face of new scientific evidence.[187] Even though new evidence may not always justify a new risk assessment, it would be contrary to the purpose of risk assessments under the *SPS Agreement* to follow the approach advocated by Japan.

7.13 In relation to our findings on Article 5.1, Japan further argues that the Panel was wrong in stating in paragraph 8.271 that "the 1999 PRA is not sufficiently specific to the matter at issue [apple fruit] to constitute a proper risk assessment under Article 5.1 of the *SPS Agreement*". According to Japan, the 1996 and 2001 IPPC Guidelines admit the initiation of a PRA by the identification of a pest, as well as the identification of a pathway. These Guidelines do not limit the scope of the PRA to a particular host of bacteria, but rather allow for assessing a variety of hosts.

7.14 We agree with Japan that the 1996 and 2001 IPPC Guidelines for PRAs do not limit consideration to just one particular host of a kind of bacteria. However, they do require that the risk relating to the particular commodity to be imported be evaluated. In its 1999 PRA, Japan evaluated the risks associated with all possible hosts taken together, not sufficiently considering the risks specifically associated with the commodity at issue: US apple fruit exported to Japan. We therefore see no reason to change our findings in this respect.

---

[186] We note in this respect that "in connection with Article 2.2, Japan believes that the provision requires a measure to be based on sufficient scientific evidence available at the time of the finding of the Panel." (Japan's reply to question 4 of the Additional Questions from the Panel, 28 January 2003).
[187] We note in this respect that the Appellate Body in *EC – Hormones*, recalled that "Article 2.2 and 5.1 should constantly be read together. Article 2.2 informs Article 5.1: the elements that define the basic obligation set out in Article 2.2 impart meaning to Article 5.1." (Appellate Body Report, para. 180)

7.15   Moreover, Japan contests our finding in paragraph 8.280 that "Japan's PRA does not evaluate the likelihood of entry or spread of fire blight through the importation of apple fruits" because Japan's 1999 PRA does not suggest any precise evaluation of the degree of potentiality or probability for the occurrence of the event and fails to provide more than an indication of a potential for entry or spread, or does not assess the probability of such events occurring. Japan argues that, even though the 1999 PRA's use of the terms "suggest" or "can" to describe probability might have been misleading, Japan stated in its first written submission to the Panel that the 1999 PRA addressed not a theoretical possibility but the likelihood of the introduction and spread of fire blight through apple fruit.

7.16   We consider that the fact that Japan further elaborated before the Panel on the meaning of the terms it used in its 1999 PRA cannot correct the fact that the 1999 PRA itself did not use the terms used by Japan before the Panel and actually did not sufficiently evaluate the likelihood of entry, establishment or spread of fire blight, as well as the associated potential biological and economic consequences, within the meaning of Article 5.1 and Annex A, paragraph 4 of the *SPS Agreement*. It is not merely the use of some terms that is at issue here, it is the whole approach followed by Japan in undertaking the 1999 PRA. We recall that, in *Australia – Salmon*, the Appellate Body insisted that a conclusion of mere possibility of entry, establishment or spread of a disease was not sufficient to meet the requirements of Article 5.1[188], just as *some* evaluation of the likelihood of entry, establishment or spread was not sufficient either.[189] Likewise, the Appellate Body recalled that the existence of unknown or uncertain elements did not justify a departure from the requirements of, *inter alia*, Article 5.1.[190] In the light of the relatively strict standard applied by the Appellate Body in *Australia – Salmon*, we see no reason to reconsider our findings.

7.17   Japan further contests our reasoning and conclusions in paragraph 8.285 below. Japan claims that in 1999, it considered the US proposal to narrow the width of the buffer zone and to reduce the number of field inspection routines. However, such consideration is not apparent in the 1999 PRA.

7.18   In essence, Japan considers that, once a measure is in place, the analysis and evaluation will inevitably focus on the existing measure, in the absence of alternative proposals. Japan seems to suggest that it was up to the United States to bring to the attention of Japan the existence of alternative measures or options. We cannot agree with either of these points. Regarding the first one, there is no technical reason why, once a measure is in place, it would not be possible to consider alternatives. Japan argues as much, by stating that the analysis "will inevitably focus" on the existing measure. Yet, information on alternative options does not become less available because one measure has been put in place by a Member. Likewise, nothing in the text of Article 5.1 and Annex A,

---

[188]   Appellate Body Report, para. 123.
[189]   *Ibid*, para. 124.
[190]   *Ibid.*, paras. 129-130.

paragraph 4, suggests that alternative options have to be proposed by the exporting Member. On the contrary, given the importance of the PRA to support the imposition of a measure, it is in the interest of the importing Member to consider alternatives on its own initiative.

7.19   We do not consider either that a requirement to consider alternative options would create a situation where a Member could not be confident, at any time, of the consistency of its PRAs with Article 5.1 of the *SPS Agreement*. First, this requirement does not result from the reasoning of the Panel, but from the terms of Article 5.1 and Annex A, paragraph 4 of the *SPS Agreement*, which refer to "the SPS measures which might be applied", thus making it clear that a Member has an obligation to consider other measures than those it actually applies. Whether such a requirement could actually create a problem of legal certainty for a Member performing risk assessments is not an issue before us. Indeed, since Japan did not appear to have considered measures other than those it applies[191], it clearly did not meet its obligation and it is not necessary to determine how far it should have gone in identifying "SPS measures that might be applied" to comply with Article 5.1 and Annex A, paragraph 4 of the *SPS Agreement*.

5.   Article 7 of the SPS Agreement

7.20   Finally, we took note of the factual information provided by Japan regarding Article 7 and Annex B to the *SPS Agreement*, as well as the additional comments of the United States. As a result we revised our findings on this claim.

C.   Comments by the United States[192]

1.   Requests for Additional Findings

7.21   The United States requests the Panel to make a number of additional findings, most of which are essentially factual. As a general remark, we believe that panels are bound by their terms of reference, but they need only make the findings which they deem necessary for the resolution of the case. As a result, while we agreed with some of the US requests, we did not find it necessary to make all the additional findings that the United States requested in its comments.[193] We do not, for example, consider it necessary to make a finding that the United States has raised a presumption that there is no scientific evidence that mature apples have ever been the means of introduction of fire blight into a previously fire blight-free area, and Japan has failed to rebut that presumption. While we have some reliable indication that this statement by the United States might well be correct, we see no need to make a specific finding on this question. Rather, we will use the information available in support of our finding as to whether apples exported from the United States into Japan could

---

[191] See para. 8.285, below.
[192] This section is divided according to the sections of the findings on which comments have been made.
[193] In addition to the discussion in this paragraph, see para. 7.25 below.

serve as a pathway for the entry, establishment or spread of fire blight within Japan.

2.   Comments on Specific Paragraphs of the Report

7.22   The United States also made a number of specific comments on paragraphs of the findings. In this respect, we clarified or corrected, as necessary a number of paragraphs. This was the case with paragraph 2.1. Regarding paragraph 2.22, we have recognized the definition contained in *International Standards for Phytosanitary Measures No.5: Glossary of Phytosanitary Terms*, FAO, Rome 2002. However, we have clarified that, for the purposes of this case, we have relied on an alternative definition given during the Panel meeting with the experts which differentiates between infection and infestation.[194]

7.23   The first specific comments of the United States on the findings relate to our identification of the elements composing the phytosanitary measure at issue (paragraphs 8.22 to 8.25). We originally were of the view that the two elements which the United States wants us to include in the measure[195] were not worth considering in an assessment of the measure *as a whole*, since their economic impact was very limited and these types of measures are commonly used by Members. However, we agree with the United States that, even though they are part of a broader measure, they are phytosanitary measures within the meaning of Annex A, paragraph 1 of the *SPS Agreement*. Since they also were identified by the United States in its request for establishment of a panel, they ought to be listed among the elements composing the phytosanitary measure at issue. We accordingly modified paragraphs 8.24 and 8.25.

7.24   The United States makes a second comment in relation to paragraph 8.25 and requests that we make a finding that the prohibition of imports of US apples from states other than Washington or Oregon is not rationally related to any scientific evidence of a risk of introduction of fire blight via imported apples. The United States argues that the failure of the United States to provide documentation relating to other quarantine pests cannot justify the maintenance of a fire blight restriction limiting importation from the states of Oregon and Washington exclusively.

7.25   We understand the position of Japan to be that what prevents the importation of apples from states other than Oregon and Washington is not their fire blight status, but the status of other quarantine pests. Japan argues that if proper documentation were submitted by the United States with respect to those other pests, shipments of apples from states other than Oregon and Washington could be exported to Japan under the same conditions which apply to apples from Oregon and Washington.[196] We agree that failure to provide documentation

---

[194]   Annex 3, para. 67.
[195]   The two elements are: (1) the certification by US plant protection officials that fruits are free of fire blight and have been treated post harvest with chlorine; and (2) the confirmation by Japanese officials of the US officials' certification and inspection by Japanese officials of disinfection and packaging facilities.
[196]   See para. 4.132, above.

on other quarantine pests than fire blight cannot justify the imposition of restrictions based on fire blight, but if a product cannot be exported for other phytosanitary reasons, the fact that it could be free of fire blight will not make it exportable. The United States did not demonstrate that Japan was imposing measures relating to fire blight in relation to other quarantine pests. We therefore see no reason to make the ruling requested by the United States.

7.26   We also clarified paragraphs 8.84 and 8.88 to reflect what the United States had to demonstrate under Article 2.2 of the *SPS Agreement* in this particular case. Paragraph 8.90 was also modified to reflect more accurately the position of the United States. However, we did not find it necessary to modify paragraph 8.106 on burden of proof. Likewise, we find it relevant to state in paragraph 8.212, that Japan, as the party invoking Article 5.7 of the *SPS Agreement*, bears the burden to make a prima facie case. The fact that the issue of burden of proof was not addressed by the parties or that Japan clearly did not meet the four cumulative requirements in order for the measure at issue to qualify for the exemption under Article 5.7 does not relieve the Panel from applying the standards recalled by the Appellate Body in *United States – Wool Shirts and Blouses*. Each party has to prove its allegations. This principle applies whether the provision invoked is or is not an exception. In this case, Japan invoked Article 5.7; it had the burden to establish its claim prima facie and failed to do so.

7.27   We also did not find it appropriate to amend the last sentence of paragraph 8.196. Indeed we consider that the two propositions of this sentence are logically connected. If surface *E. amylovora* is found rarely on apples coming from severely infected orchards, the risk of entry, establishment or spread of fire blight within Japan through apples coming from severely blighted orchards can only be very low (assuming, as we did, that endophytic bacteria would not be found in mature, symtomless apples).

7.28   The United States also claims that, even though its request for establishment of a panel referred to "US apples" in general, it advanced arguments only relating to mature, symptomless apples. The United States considers as a result that we need not address the issue of other apple fruit with respect to which the United States presented no evidence. The United States requests that we remove our finding in paragraph 8.161.

7.29   As mentioned in paragraph 8.33, we consider that the US claims are based on two assumptions: (a) that mature, symptomless apples are not a pathway for fire blight; and (b) shipments from the United States to Japan only contain mature, symptomless apples. These assumptions were largely confirmed in our findings.

7.30   This said, the position defended by the United States in its request for review seems in this respect to be contradictory. On the one hand, it claims that requiring the importation of mature, symptomless apples should be sufficient to meet the level of protection sought by Japan in light of the established risk, thus assuming that only mature, symptomless apples will ever be exported. On the other hand, it claims that it did not address the issue relating to non mature or damaged apples. In our opinion, these issues are two sides of the same coin, and the United States actually had to address the issue of control to support the assumption that it exports only mature, symptomless apples.[197] Indeed, the United States provided considerable information regarding its control procedures.[198] As a result, we do not believe that we go beyond our terms of reference by considering the risk that apple fruit other than mature, symptomless apples could be exported to Japan.

7.31   Moreover, even if we were to agree with the United States that the matter before us is limited to mature, symptomless apples, we do believe that we are entitled to address Japan's position that a risk of entry, establishment or spread could result from a malfunction in the sorting of apples or of an illegal action in the country of exportation. We cannot agree that we should concentrate our findings exclusively on that very product simply because the United States apparently limits its claims, arguments and evidence to it. The purpose of phytosanitary measures is to prevent the introduction of diseases into the territory of the Member imposing them. As recalled by the Appellate Body in *Australia – Salmon* with respect to Article 5.6 of the *SPS Agreement*,

> "The determination of the appropriate level of protection, a notion defined in paragraph 5 of Annex A, as 'the level of protection deemed appropriate by the Member establishing a sanitary … measure', is a *prerogative* of the Member concerned and not of the panel or of the Appellate Body."[199]

7.32   If we were to restrict our findings to "mature, symptomless apples", we would disregard the position of Japan that the protection to be achieved by the measure should be equivalent to that of an import prohibition. It seems to us legitimate to consider all the aspects referred to by Japan in relation to the importation of apples from the United States. This issue is addressed in our discussion of Article 2.2, paragraphs 8.119-8.122.

7.33   We agree with the United States that our remarks regarding developmental or technical circumstances prevailing in the importing Member in paragraph 8.239[200] were more an *obiter dictum* than a consideration necessary

---

[197]   See, e.g., paras. 4.188-4.190.
[198]   See, eg., paras. 4.182, 4.187-4.189, and the footnotes relating to these paragraphs.
[199]   Appellate Body Report on *Australia – Salmon*, para. 199.
[200]   This paragraph and the following paragraph previously read:
        "It might be observed, in this context, that the requirement that the risk assessment be 'appropriate to the circumstances' has been considered to leave some flexibility for an assessment of risk 'on a case by case basis, in terms of product, origin and destination, in particular country-specific destinations'. The Panel is of the view that 'appropriate to the circumstances' might also be with regard to the developmental or technical circumstances prevailing in the importing Member. For example, what might be expected in terms of a risk assessment put forward by a developing country with limited plant protection services and trained professional staff may not be 'appropriate' with respect to an importing country with sophisticated plant protection services and highly trained professional staff. Furthermore, the access the importing country has to relevant data and scientific information might be relevant in consideration of whether a risk assessment is 'appropriate to the circumstances'.

for the resolution of this case. In paragraphs 8.45 and 8.46 we already considered that Japan was not put at a disadvantage in terms of submission of evidence by the fact that its territory was free from fire blight. We therefore adjusted paragraphs 8.239-8.240.

7.34   We also clarified the US position as presented in paragraphs 8.265 and 8.284, even though it seemed quite obvious from the context that the statements concerned originated in Japan's 1999 PRA.

7.35   Finally, we clarified the arguments of the United States in paragraph 8.295.

VIII. FINDINGS

A.   Approach Followed by the Panel

8.1   The United States raises the following claims:

   (a)   Japan's measures on US apples are inconsistent with Article 2.2 of the *SPS Agreement* because they are "maintained without sufficient scientific evidence";

   (b)   Japan's measures on US apples are inconsistent with Article 5.1 of the *SPS Agreement* because they are not based on a risk assessment;

   (c)   by failing to take into account certain information in its assessment of risks, Japan has acted inconsistently with Article 5.2 of the *SPS Agreement*;

   (d)   Japan's measures are inconsistent with Article 5.6 of the *SPS Agreement* because they are more trade-restrictive than required to achieve Japan's appropriate level of protection;

   (e)   Japan has failed to notify changes to its fire blight measures and to provide information as required by Article 7 and Annex B of the *SPS Agreement*;

   (f)   in addition, the United States developed, at the first and second substantive meetings with the Panel, two of the claims against Japan that it had listed in its request for establishment of a panel but not developed in its first written submission: the violation of Article XI of GATT 1994 and of Article 4.2 of the Agreement on Agriculture.

8.2   Japan makes the following main arguments in response:

   (a)   Japan requests that the claims contained in the request for establishment of a panel but not raised in consultations and/or not

---

'In this dispute, the Panel notes that both parties are developed countries with highly sophisticated plant protection services and skilled professional staff. Furthermore, the Panel has already found no evidence that Japan did not have ready access to the relevant scientific evidence necessary to conduct an appropriate risk assessment."

developed in the first written submission of the United States be "removed" from the proceedings of the Panel;

(b)   Japan's measure is not "maintained without sufficient scientific evidence" and is consistent with Article 2.2 of the *SPS Agreement*. Alternatively, Japan's measure is justifiable as a provisional phytosanitary measure under Article 5.7 of the *SPS Agreement*;

(c)   Japan has conducted a risk assessment ("Pest Risk Analysis" – "PRA") compliant with Article 5.1 of the *SPS Agreement*;

(d)   Japan's PRA is consistent with the requirements of Article 5.2;

(e)   Japan's measure is consistent with Article 5.6 of the *SPS Agreement*;

(f)   Japan acted in compliance with Article 7 and Annex B of the *SPS Agreement* regarding transparency.

8.3   Having regard to the arguments of the parties, we will first define what we consider to be the phytosanitary measure at issue and the product subject to this measure. We will then address the procedural issues raised by the parties, in particular the treatment of the burden of proof and the preliminary rulings requested by Japan.

8.4   Thereafter, giving due consideration to the order in which the parties have argued the case and consistent with the opinions of the Appellate Body in *EC – Hormones* and in *Australia – Salmon*[201], we will address the issues before us in the following order:

(a)   We will first address the application of Article 2.2 of the *SPS Agreement* to the phytosanitary measure at issue. However, we note that Japan presented an alternative defence under Article 5.7 of the *SPS Agreement*, in the event that the United States should successfully establish violation of Article 2.2. We recall that, in *Japan – Agricultural Products II*, the panel faced a comparable situation where Japan had presented a defence under both Article 2.2 and Article 5.7. In that case, the panel refrained from making a final finding of violation of Article 2.2 until it had reached a conclusion on the application of Article 5.7. It recalled that Article 2.2 of the *SPS Agreement* provides that Members shall ensure that any phytosanitary measure "is not maintained without sufficient scientific evidence, *except as provided for in paragraph 7 of*

---

[201] Appellate Body Report in *EC – Hormones*, para. 250, where the Appellate Body expressed its surprise at the fact that the panel began its analysis of the whole case with Articles 3 and 5, and not by focussing on Article 2 that is captioned "Basic Rights and Obligations", an approach that, to the Appellate Body, appeared "logically attractive".

In *Australia – Salmon* case, at para. 138 of its report, the Appellate Body considered that:
"by maintaining an import prohibition on fresh, chilled or frozen ocean-caught Pacific salmon, in violation of Article 5.1, Australia has, by implication, also acted inconsistently with Article 2.2 of the *SPS Agreement*."

However, we do not read this finding as implying that we *should* address the US claim of violation of Article 5.1 before its claims on Article 2.2.

Article 5" and concluded that it had to examine whether the measure at issue was a measure meeting the requirements in Article 5.7. If the measure at issue met these requirements, it would not find a violation of Article 2.2.[202] We believe it appropriate to follow, in this case too, the approach of the panel *in Japan – Agricultural Products II*. There is only one situation where it may not be necessary to address Article 5.7. This is if we find that the measure or measures as a whole is/are "not maintained without sufficient scientific evidence" within the meaning of Article 2.2. If we were to find, however, that part or all of the measure or measures at issue is/are maintained without sufficient scientific evidence, we would suspend our final conclusion on the consistency of the measure(s) at issue with that provision until we have completed our examination under Article 5.7 of the *SPS Agreement*.

(b)   In that context, our analysis of the conformity of part or all of the phytosanitary measure(s) at issue with Article 5.7 will immediately follow our analysis of the US claim under Article 2.2.

(c)   At that juncture, should we find the measure or measures at issue to be inconsistent with both Article 2.2 and Article 5.7, we could legitimately abstain from making any findings on the other claims of the United States. However, we are of the view that findings regarding, more particularly, the claims raised with respect to Japan's obligations in terms of risk assessment may assist the Dispute Settlement Body (DSB) in making sufficiently precise recommendations and rulings so as to allow for prompt compliance, in order to ensure effective resolution of the dispute.[203] This is why we will also address the claims relating to those obligations, beginning with Article 5.1 (risk assessment).

(d)   We will then continue our assessment of the matter with the examination of the claims regarding Article 7 and Annex B to the *SPS Agreement*. For reasons explained in Section G below, we will not review the US claims under Article 5.6.

(e)   Finally, for the reasons explained in Sections I and J, we do not intend to make findings with respect to the US claims on Articles XI of the GATT 1994, Article 4.2 of the Agreement on Agriculture and the other claims not developed by the United States in its submissions before the Panel.

---

[202]   *Japan – Agricultural Products II*, para. 8.41, emphasis in the original.
[203]   See Appellate Body Report in *Australia – Salmon*, para. 223.

B.   The Measure at Issue and the Product Subject to this Measure

1.   The Measure at Issue

(a)   Summary of the Arguments of the Parties[204]

8.5   According to the United States, Japan maintains measures restricting the importation of US apples in connection with fire blight or the fire blight disease-causing organism, *Erwinia amylovora* (hereafter *E. amylovora).* The United States has identified nine specific prohibitions or requirements imposed by Japan:[205]

(a)   The prohibition of imported apples from US states other than apples produced in designated areas in the states of Oregon or Washington[206];

(b)   the prohibition of imported apples from orchards in which any fire blight is detected on plants or in which host plants of fire blight (other than apple trees) are found, whether or not infected;

(c)   the prohibition of imported apples from any orchard (whether or not it is free of fire blight) should fire blight be detected within a 500-meter buffer zone surrounding such orchard;

(d)   the requirement that export orchards be inspected three times yearly (at blossom, fruitlet, and harvest stages) for the presence of fire blight for purposes of applying the above-mentioned prohibitions;

(e)   a post-harvest surface treatment of apples for export with chlorine;

(f)   production requirements, such as chlorine treatment of containers for harvesting and chlorine treatment of the packing facility;

(g)   post-harvest separation of apples for export to Japan from fruits destined to other markets;

(h)   certification by US plant protection officials that fruits are free of fire blight and have been treated post harvest with chlorine; and

(i)   confirmation by Japanese officials of the US officials' certification and inspection by Japanese officials of disinfection and packaging facilities.

---

[204] A detailed account of Japan's measures and of the arguments of the parties can be found in paras. 2.17-2.19, and paras. 4.17-4.33, respectively.

[205] US Request for Establishment of a Panel, WT/DS245/2; US First Submission, para. 19; US Answers to Additional Questions from the Panel, 28 January 2003, para. 2.

[206] The United States contends that paragraph 25 of the Annexed List to Table 2 of the Plant Protection Law Enforcement Regulations limits the importation of fresh fruit of apple from the United States to Golden Delicious and Red Delicious apple varieties. The Panel, however, notes that there is disagreement between the parties as to the English translation of the aforementioned paragraph 25. The English translation of paragraph 25 provided by Japan makes no mention of the Golden Delicious and Red Delicious variety requirement. Ministerial Ordinance No. 73: Plant Protection Law Enforcement Regulations, Annexed List, para. 25 (Exhibit JPN-21 and Exhibit USA-9).

8.6   Japan does not dispute the description of the requirements at issue made by the United States. Japan recalls, however, that points (h) and (i) above are not included in its description of its fire blight requirements since "certification or declaration by officials of the exporting country" and "confirmation by Japanese officials" are mere procedural steps to ensure compliance with the substantive requirements and are common for all phytosanitary measures. On the other hand, Japan describes the disinfection of the harvest containers and the disinfection of the packing facilities (item(f)) as two separate elements of its requirements.

8.7   The United States considers that the means through which Japan maintains these restrictions and requirements consist of: (i) the Plant Protection Law (Law No. 151; enacted 4 May 1950), as amended; (ii) the Plant Protection Regulations (Ministry of Agriculture, Forestry, and Fisheries Ordinance No. 73, enacted 30 June 1950), as amended; (iii) Ministry of Agriculture, Forestry and Fisheries Notification No. 354 (dated 10 March 1997); and (iv) related detailed rules and regulations, including Ministry of Agriculture, Forestry, and Fisheries Circular 8103.

8.8   The United States argues that Japan prohibits the importation of apples from the United States unless all of the requirements referred to above are satisfied. While this cumulative requirement is, in its view, contrary to the *SPS Agreement*, the United States also contends that each of the nine specific requirements listed above could be considered as a separate phytosanitary measure and that each of them is inconsistent with Japan's obligations under Article 2.2 of the *SPS Agreement* because they are maintained without sufficient scientific evidence.

8.9   Japan does not dispute that the measure is covered by the *SPS Agreement*. However, Japan argues that its requirements constitute a "systemic approach".[207] The systems approach consists of approving only those apples produced in environmental conditions that will not allow the presence of fire blight bacteria, both outside and inside of apple fruit, at various stages from blossom to growth, harvest and shipment. Japan therefore disputes the allegation of the United States that each aspect of the measure could be addressed in isolation. Even though each requirement is technically independent, some of the components are interrelated. As a whole they are, in Japan's view, cumulative, inseparable and integral parts of a single measure.[208]

(b)   Analysis of the Panel

8.10   Before going any further, we need first to clarify the relevance, in our assessment, of treating the Japanese requirements and restrictions at issue as one single measure or as a combination of several individual measures. As stated by

---

[207]   Hereafter "systems approach". ("The integration of different pest risk management measures, at least two of which act independently, and which cumulatively achieve the appropriate level of phytosanitary protection". *International Standard for Phytosanitary Measures No.5: Glossary of Phytosanitary Terms* , FAO, Rome, 2002).

[208]   Japan, Response to Additional Questions from the Panel, 28 January 2003, Question 1.

the Appellate Body in *Australia – Salmon*[209], our findings must assist the DSB in making sufficiently precise recommendations and rulings so as to allow for prompt compliance, in order to ensure effective resolution of the dispute. In that context, given the number of requirements identified by the United States, it may be relevant to address each of them as a separate "measure". However, we note that Japan insisted on the fact that those requirements are part of one single systems approach. Furthermore, some of the requirements are clearly interrelated. For example, the requirement of a buffer zone is directly related to the requirement that the export orchard be disease-free.

(i) One or More Measures?

8.11   We recall that the concept of "measure" is not defined in the DSU, even though the term "measures at issue" is found in Article 6.2 regarding the establishment of a panel. The use of the term "measures at issue" in plural suggests that a matter brought before the DSB may refer to several "measures". This said, Article 19.1 refers to "a measure" that is found to be inconsistent. The definition of the concept is the result of the practice of panels and the Appellate Body under the GATT and the WTO. "Measure", for the purpose of dispute resolution under GATT and the WTO, has generally been understood to refer to an action in which there was "sufficient government involvement".[210]

8.12   We note that Annex A, paragraph 1, of the *SPS Agreement* provides a definition of "phytosanitary measure". In *Australia – Salmon*, the Appellate Body, by referring to the "sanitary measure at issue in this dispute", seems to have implied that a "measure" in a phytosanitary case should be defined with reference to the definition of "phytosanitary measure" in the *SPS Agreement*.[211]

8.13   Paragraph 1 of Annex A of the *SPS Agreement* defines as a phytosanitary measure "all measures applied to protect animal or plant life or health within the territory of the Member from risks arising from the entry, establishment or spread of pests, diseases, disease-carrying organisms or disease-causing organisms". However, this definition provides little direct guidance in determining whether we should treat the several requirements identified by the United States together as one measure or separately as individual measures.

8.14   We recall, however, that panels and the Appellate Body have in the past considered as one single "measure" legal requirements comprised of several obligations, some simply prohibiting importation, some allowing importation under certain conditions. In *Australia – Salmon*, the Appellate Body considered that the measure at issue was a text called QP86A, as confirmed by an Australian decision of 1996. As mentioned by the Appellate Body, QP86A "impose[d] an

---

[209]   Appellate Body Report, para. 223.

[210]   Panel Report in *Japan - Film*, paras. 10.55-10.56, referring to GATT panel reports *Japan – Semiconductors*, para. 102 and *EC – Restrictions on Imports of Dessert Apples* (Complaint by Chile), para.126.

[211]   We also note that in *Japan – Agricultural products II*, the Appellate Body characterised varietal testing as a regulation, within the meaning of paragraph 1 of Annex B, implicitly identifying it as a "measure" under paragraph 1 of Annex A.

import prohibition, [but also] delegate[d] authority to the Director of Quarantine to allow imports that have been subject to such treatment as is likely, in his opinion, to prevent the introduction of any disease".[212] The Appellate Body nonetheless described the measure as a whole as an "import prohibition".[213]

8.15   We note that in this instance, on the one hand, the United States does not suggest that it would be inappropriate for us to treat the nine "requirements" it identified as one single measure. Indeed, it considers that none of those requirements is justified, as long as the exported product is mature, symptomless apples. On the other hand, Japan objects to our reviewing each of these requirements separately, as it considers them to be the necessary elements of a systems approach.

8.16   We further note that these requirements cumulatively constitute the measures *actually applied* by Japan to the importation of US apple fruit to protect itself against the entry, establishment or spread of fire blight within its territory. As noted above, they are interrelated, and it is this entire set of requirements that must be met in order for US apples to be exported to Japan. We recall in this respect the Appellate Body's statement, in *Australia – Salmon*, that "the SPS measure at issue can *only* be the measure which is *actually* applied to the product at issue".[214]

8.17   In the light of the above, we consider that there is no legal, logical or factual obstacle to treating the requirements identified by the United States as one single phytosanitary measure within the meaning of the *SPS Agreement*. There are, on the contrary, good reasons to do so, in particular the fact that both parties themselves have argued the case as an "all or nothing" exercise. We note in this regard that the United States did not argue that part or all of the requirements it identified were not "necessary" within the meaning of Article 2.2 of the *SPS Agreement*. Rather, the United States argues that there was not

---

[212]   Appellate Body Report in *Australia -Salmon*, para. 98.

[213]   The Appellate Body rejected the description of the measure by the panel as two sides of the same coin because part of the measure (the heat treatment requirement) did not actually apply to fresh salmon (see paras. 103-104). On the treatment of a legislation with several requirements as one measure, see also Appellate Body Report in *EC – Asbestos*, para. 64 :

> "In our view, the proper legal character of the measure at issue cannot be determined unless the measure is examined as a whole. Article 1 of the Decree contains broad, general prohibitions on asbestos and products containing asbestos. However, the scope and generality of those prohibitions can only be understood in light of the exceptions to it which, albeit for a limited period, *permit, inter alia*, the use of certain products containing asbestos and, principally, products containing chrysotile asbestos fibres. The measure is, therefore, *not* a *total* prohibition on asbestos fibres, because it also includes provisions that *permit*, for a limited duration, the use of asbestos in certain situations. Thus, to characterize the measure simply as a general prohibition, and to examine it as such, overlooks the complexities of the measure, which include both prohibitive and permissive elements. In addition, we observe that the exceptions in the measure would have no autonomous legal significance in the absence of the prohibitions. We, therefore, conclude that the measure at issue is to be examined as an integrated whole, taking into account, as appropriate, the prohibitive and the permissive elements that are part of it."

[214]   Appellate Body Report in *Australia - Salmon*, para. 103 (emphasis in the original).

sufficient scientific evidence to support any of those requirements. Treating the requirements at issue as one measure is, therefore, appropriate, especially in the context of Article 2.2 of the *SPS Agreement*, provided that we determine that the measure as a whole is – or is not – compatible with the *SPS Agreement*.

8.18   However, we do not exclude that, as we carry out our analysis, especially under Article 2.2 of the *SPS Agreement*, we may be apprised of scientific evidence to support certain aspects of the measure and not others. In this regard, the Panel is guided by the opinions of the experts which it appointed to serve as scientific and technical advisers.[215] While this may, in principle, justify specific findings on those aspects of the measure, we recall that neither the United States nor Japan have taken the view that the phytosanitary measure at issue could be partly justified under the *SPS Agreement*. The United States' position is that none of the aspects of the measure is justified with respect to the importation of mature, symptomless apple fruit. Japan argues, on the contrary, that each of the components of the measure is inseparably part of a systems approach.

8.19   We may of course conclude that one aspect of a measure is illegal and not others, even when the complainant argues that the measure as a whole is illegal. Indeed, since the *SPS Agreement* establishes different rights and obligations, it may be also appropriate, depending on the provision at issue, to consider the specific requirements individually. However, to assume such a subdivision would disregard the way in which those requirements are presented by the parties and applied, i.e., as one single measure.

8.20   For these reasons, we find that we should consider together the requirements identified by the United States as the phytosanitary measure at issue in this dispute.

(ii)   Elements Constituting the Phytosanitary Measure at Issue

8.21   We note that the parties disagree as to the actual number of requirements imposed by Japan with respect to the importation of US apples. We recall that the United States listed nine requirements and that although Japan lists the requirements differently, Japan does not dispute the description made by the United States, except with regard to two items.

---

[215] Noting that this Panel involved scientific or technical issues, and noting that both parties acknowledged that the Panel may need to consult with scientific and technical experts, we decided, pursuant to Article 13.1 of the DSU and Article 11.2 of the *SPS Agreement*, to select and appoint specialists in the field of plant pathology and pathogenic bacteria. The procedure followed for the selection and consultation of the experts is described in paras. 6.1-6.4 above. The experts appointed by the Panel were: Dr Klaus Geider, Professor of Molecular Genetics and Phytopathology, Max-Planck-Institut für Zellbiologie, University of Heidelberg, Ladenburg, Germany; Dr Chris Hale, Science Capability Leader, Insect Group (Plant Health and Fire Blight) HortResearch, Auckland, New Zealand; Dr Chris Hayward, Consultant on Bacterial Plant Diseases, Indooroopilly, Queensland, Australia; and Dr Ian Smith, Director-General, European Plant Protection Organization, Paris, France. Consistent with the principles recalled by the Appellate Body regarding burden of proof, the opinions of the experts were used by the Panel to assess the factual allegations raised by the parties in support of their claims.

8.22   Concerning the first one (certification by US plant protection officials that fruits are free of fire blight and have been treated post harvest with chlorine), we agree with Japan that it is essentially a procedural requirement and that phytosanitary certificates are common practice in international trade. Indeed, we note that the relevant international standards setting body in this respect, the Interim Commission on Phytosanitary Measures, has adopted standards for such certificates.[216] Furthermore, we note that the US Apple Export Act provides for the issuance of phytosanitary certificates for apples exported from the United States that are of a certain grade and quality. In this respect, our opinion is without prejudice as to what exactly should be certified.

8.23   Regarding the second item (i.e., the confirmation by Japanese officials of the US officials' certification and inspection by Japanese officials of disinfection and packaging facilities), it appears that they do not entail significant additional obligations for the United States compared with the other requirements identified.

8.24   However, we note that both requirements fall within the definition of phytosanitary measures contained in Annex A, paragraph 1, of the *SPS Agreement*, which includes "inspection, certification and approval procedures". We also note that the definition in Annex A, paragraph 1, does not consider the trade effect of a given measure as a factor to determine whether such a measure is or is not a phytosanitary measure. While such requirements are common practices and, on their own, may not have justified the initiation of this case by the United States, we note that they are part of the measure as a whole and that, in combination with other elements of that measure, they may contribute to the restrictive effect of the measure at issue.

8.25   For these reasons, we conclude that the measure at issue is composed of the following elements:

(a)   **Fruit must be produced in designated fire blight-free orchards. Designation of a fire blight-free area as an export orchard is made by the United States Department of Agriculture (USDA) upon application by the orchard owner. Any detection of a blighted tree in this area by inspection will disqualify the orchard. For the time being, the designation is accepted only for orchards in the states of Washington and Oregon[217];**

---

[216]   Op. cit., ISPM 12.

[217]   Japan argues that the current phytosanitary requirements against fire blight can be applicable to apple fruit produced in other States, but that the United States has not submitted documentation on the status of other quarantine pests for states other than Washington and Oregon. As such, Japan argues that this is a procedural matter. (Japan, Response to Questions from the Panel, 13 November 2002, Question 47) The United States argues that Japan prohibits the importation of US fruit other than fruit produced in designated export orchards within either of the two states of Washington or Oregon. The United States has in the past requested that Japan expand the list of states eligible to export apple fruit to Japan, to no avail. While there is scientific evidence that fire blight bacteria are not associated internally or externally with mature, symptomless apple fruit from the state of Washington, there is not a rational or objective relationship between the scientific evidence and

(b)   the export orchard must be free of plants infected with fire blight and free of host plants of fire blight (other than apples), whether or not infected;

(c)   the fire blight-free orchard must be surrounded by a 500-meter buffer zone. Detection of a blighted tree or plant in this zone will disqualify the export orchard;

(d)   the fire blight-free orchard and surrounding buffer zone must be inspected at least three times annually. US officials will visually inspect twice, at the blossom and the fruitlet stages, the export area and the buffer zone for any symptom of fire blight. Japanese and US officials will jointly conduct visual inspection of these sites at harvest time. Additional inspections are required following any strong storm (such as a hail storm);

(e)   harvested apples must be treated with surface disinfection by soaking in sodium hypochlorite solution;

(f)   containers for harvesting must be disinfected by a chlorine treatment;

(g)   the interior of the packing facility must be disinfected by a chlorine treatment;

(h)   fruit destined for Japan must be kept separated post-harvest from other fruit;

(i)   US plant protection officials must certify that fruits are free from fire blight and have been treated post harvest with chlorine; and

(j)   Japanese officials must confirm the US officials' certification and Japanese officials must inspect packaging facilities.

2.   *The Product Subject to the Phytosanitary Measure at Issue*

(a)   Summary of the Arguments of the Parties[218]

8.26   The United States argues that the commodity subject to the measure at issue is the product it allegedly exports, i.e., "mature, symptomless apples". Japan contests the notions of "mature" and "symptomless" as subjective. The United States replies that these notions are scientifically supported.

Japan's prohibition of apples other than those harvested in the states of Washington or Oregon (US First Submission, para. 58).

[218] For a more detailed account of the arguments of the parties see, *inter alia*, paras. 0, 4.63-4.64 and 4.99.

(b)   Analysis of the Panel

8.27   On the basis of the information before us, we understand that Japan's concern is that fire blight could be introduced into its territory through apples imported from the United States and their containers (e.g., crates).

8.28   Japan argues that:

(a)   fire blight bacteria are capable of long-term survival inside or on the surface of "mature, symptomless" apples, such that the apple fruit could develop fire blight symptoms sometime after their selection and packing for export. Hence, apple fruit could be contaminated and yet be found fit for exportation. Once introduced into Japan, fire blight would have ample potential for growth and infection with major negative, irreversible consequences[219]; and that

(b)   there is a very real risk of accidental contamination or erroneous grading, which could lead to the introduction of infected or infested apples in a shipment of otherwise mature, symptomless apple fruit bound for Japan, or to the contamination of crates.[220]

Hence, in the absence of an appropriate quarantine inspection method or internal apple disinfection treatment technique, Japan considers that a systems approach is the only viable alternative (short of import prohibition) to ensure that there is no presence of fire blight bacteria either inside or outside of apple fruit shipped to Japan.[221]

8.29   We recall the argument of the United States that it exports only mature, symptomless apples, which it claims have been proven not to be a pathway for fire blight (i.e., they are not capable of transmitting fire blight to other hosts). We understand the US position to be that, in that context, none of the requirements contained in the measure at issue is compatible with the *SPS Agreement*.

8.30   In light of the claims and arguments of the parties, we consider it essential to identify precisely the "product" subject to the measure at issue.[222] Indeed, if we consider that "product" to be limited to "mature, symptomless apple fruit", as claimed by the United States, many aspects of the measure at issue might, *ipso facto*, lose their *raison d'être* and may become incompatible with the *SPS Agreement*. This could be the case for most of the requirements, which under the measure currently applied by Japan, take place before harvesting. If, on the contrary, we conclude that the product at issue is "any apple to be shipped to Japan from the United States", then we actually need to address the justification of the requirements imposed by Japan as a whole.

8.31   We note that some requirements may appear to relate to the apples that *cannot* be exported (prohibitions), whereas some others apply only to those that

---

[219]   Para. 50.

[220]   Para. 190.

[221]   Paras. 19-20.

[222]   We note in this respect that an approach aiming at identifying precisely the product subject to the measure was confirmed by the Appellate Body *in Australia – Salmon*, paras. 94-95.

can be exported. If we follow the US definition of the product at issue, we run the risk of reviewing only the requirements applying to mature, symptomless apples, which would be illogical.

8.32   We also note that the request for establishment of a panel submitted by the United States only refers to "US apples", which is less specific than "mature, symptomless apples".[223] The request for establishment of a panel is the document that defines our mandate. It is not exclusively a limitation to our jurisdiction, it defines it positively too. The fact that the United States intended to address "only" mature, symptomless apples in its submission does not affect our mandate.[224] We also recall the arguments of the parties and the experts regarding the notion of "mature" and "symptomless" apple fruit, and the fact that the susceptibility of apples to infestation or infection by *E. amylovora* is related to the maturity of apples. In this respect, the experts were able to provide definitions of, and to distinguish between, "physiological" and "commercial" maturity. Furthermore, the experts confirmed that there were widely used and accepted objective methods for determining the maturity of apples.[225]

8.33   Without prejudice to our discussion of the merits of this case, we feel bound at this early stage of our reasoning not to prejudge our conclusions by unduly restricting the scope of our findings to mature, symptomless apple fruit. Indeed, we believe that the US claim that the product at issue is "mature, symptomless apples" is based essentially on two assumptions: (a) mature, symptomless apple fruit are not a pathway for fire blight and (b) shipments from the United States to Japan only contain mature, symptomless apples. In our opinion, these assumptions can only be verified through a review of the merits of the case, in particular the central question of whether, and under which conditions, apples may or may not act as a pathway for fire blight.

8.34   We therefore conclude that we should consider the measure at issue as applicable to apple fruit produced in the United States for exportation to Japan.

C.   Procedural Issues

1.   Introduction

8.35   In its first submission, Japan requested the Panel to address three "procedural issues".[226]

---

[223]   See WT/DS245/2: "Japan currently maintains measures restricting the importation of *US apples* in connection with fire blight or the fire blight disease-causing organism, *Erwinia amylovora*" (underlining added).

[224]   We note in this respect that Japan claims that it was made aware of the concept of "mature, symptomless apples" during the consultations. This suggests that, by the time the United States requested the establishment of this Panel, it could have referred specifically to "mature, symptomless apples".

[225]   Dr Hale, para. 6.5.

[226]   Japan first submission, paras. 17-34.

8.36   Japan requested that we exercise our authority under paragraph 9 of our Working Procedures[227] to seek clarification from the United States of the time as of which it considers that the Japanese measure at issue was no longer supported by sufficient scientific evidence. The United States subsequently stated in reply to a question from the Panel that it considered that the measure had never been compatible with the *SPS Agreement.*[228] As a result, we find that it is no longer necessary to address this request by Japan.

8.37   Japan also requested in its first written submission that we "remove", in accordance with paragraph 10 of our Working Procedures, two documents submitted by the United States as evidence in its first submission.

8.38   Moreover, Japan requested that, in accordance with paragraph 10 of our Working Procedures, we "remove" from the "scope of our proceedings" all the provisions that the United States did not address in its first submission.

8.39   In addition, while it seems undisputed by the parties that the United States bears the burden of presenting a prima facie case for each of its claims, Japan has, on several occasions[229], raised questions relating in particular to the administration of evidence, including the accessibility of the information, the fact that scientific evidence should not be limited to "direct evidence" and the standard of proof to be applied by the Panel. Since these questions are primarily of a procedural nature, we consider it appropriate to address them at this stage.

8.40   As a result, in this section we will:

(a)   Under a heading regarding burden of proof, recall the general obligations of the parties in terms of burden of proof, including with respect to the question of the general access of Japan to scientific information;

(b)   Under a heading relating to Japan's requests made under paragraph 10 of our Working Procedures, recall our decision regarding the treatment of the two communications the admissibility of which is contested by Japan and address Japan's request on the scope of our mandate in relation to the US claims not developed in the first submission of the United States.

2.   *Burden of Proof*

8.41   At the outset, we find it important to clarify that, as recalled by the Appellate Body in *EC – Hormones*, there is not any necessary connection between "the undertaking of Members to ensure, for example, that SPS measures are 'applied only to the extent necessary to protect human, animal or plant life or health …' and the allocation of burden of proof in a dispute settlement proceeding. Article 5.8 of the *SPS Agreement* does not purport to address burden

---

[227]   The Working Procedures for the Panel are reproduced in Annex 1 and the Working Procedures for the consultation of experts are contained in para. 6.2 of the Report..

[228]   US Response to Questions from the Panel, 13 November 2002, para.87.

[229]   Japan first submission, paras. 17-34, 47-50, 129-141, Japan Second Submission, paras. 1, 38-47.

of proof problems; it does not deal with a dispute settlement situation".[230] A distinction must therefore be made between the obligations of Members in adopting and maintaining the measures concerned and the separate issue of burden of proof in dispute proceedings.

8.42   As a result, we shall apply the principles of allocation of the burden of proof as identified by the Appellate Body in *EC – Hormones*:

> "The initial burden lies on the complaining party, which must establish a prima facie case of inconsistency with a particular provision of the *SPS Agreement* on the part of the defending party, or more precisely, of its SPS measure or measures complained about. When that prima facie case is made, the burden of proof moves to the defending party, which must in turn counter or refute the claimed inconsistency."[231]

8.43   We nonetheless note that Japan raised some specific questions regarding the burden of proof in general and the nature of admissible evidence.

8.44   Japan argues that the United States, as the exporting country affected by the disease, would "naturally" have more information on the *E. amylovora* bacteria. We do not see the greater expertise of the exporting country as a factor that should automatically justify a different allocation of the burden of proof or the imposition of a heavier burden of proof on one party.

8.45   We do not disagree that specific pieces of scientific evidence may be more readily available in some countries than others, and in the case of a disease-free country, that evidence relating to the spread of that disease may naturally be less extensively developed within that territory than in a country with direct exposure to the disease. However, this should not mean that a Member should be exempted from an obligation to provide evidence of its allegations simply because its territory is free from a particular disease, or that a heavier burden of proof should be imposed *ipso facto* on a Member simply because its territory is not disease-free. Indeed, a number of developing countries affected by a pest or disease may not have the resources to gather information on that pest and may need to rely on information gathered in other countries.

8.46   We note, moreover, that Japan could have sought to perform or commission research on *E. amylovora* in third countries. Japan has in the past undertaken studies in relation to fire blight-like diseases of pears, and in 2002 regarding fire blight in apples. Furthermore, Japan proposed and engaged in joint field experiments with the United States regarding fire blight in US apples.[232]

8.47   In addition, Japan has been arguing that evidence should be limited to public information. In the case of scientific evidence, it should have been peer reviewed by other scientists. We note that virtually all of the evidence presented

---

[230]   Appellate Body Report in *EC – Hormones*, para. 102.
[231]   Appellate Body Report in *EC – Hormones*, para. 98. See also the Panel Report in *Australia – Salmon - Article 21.5 (Canada)*, para. 7.37 and the Panel Report in *Japan – Agricultural Products II*, para. 8.13.
[232]   See discussion in paras. 4.174-4.178.

in this case, with the exception of the most recent research undertaken by both countries[233] and the clarifications sought by the United States[234], is publicly available.

8.48   As a result, we do not consider that Japan should be exempted from its obligation to sufficiently support its allegations or that a heavier burden of proof should be imposed on the United States for the reasons alleged by Japan above. In drawing this conclusion, however, we bear in mind the duty of all parties in a dispute to cooperate in the proceedings, including, as necessary, in the gathering of information relevant to the Panel's assessment of the matter.

8.49   A related question is whether the Panel should consider evidence that became available only after the establishment of the Panel. Our approach in this respect should be pragmatic. Besides the situation contemplated in paragraph 11 of our Working Procedures, we decided not to reject evidence submitted by a party on which the other party had had an opportunity to comment, whether it took advantage of such an opportunity or not. This is without prejudice to the admissibility of such evidence on other grounds or the weight that we might eventually give to such evidence.

8.50   However, our discussion above does not dispose of the question of the actual standard or level of proof that must be satisfied for each claim to succeed. As recalled by the Appellate Body in *US – Wool Shirts and Blouses*:

> "In the context of the GATT 1994 and the *WTO Agreement*, precisely how much and precisely what kind of evidence will be required to establish [a prima facie case] will necessarily vary from measure to measure, provision to provision, and case to case."[235]

8.51   We are therefore of the view that this aspect will be more appropriately addressed in the sections regarding each claim.[236]

---

[233]   Exhibits JPN-33, JPN-39, JPN-42, USA-32 to USA-39.

[234]   Exhibits USA-18 and USA-19.

[235]   Appellate Body Report in *US – Wool Shirts and Blouses*, p. 335.

[236]   This is without prejudice to the standard of review for fact-finding to be applied in this case. As recalled by the Appellate Body in *EC – Hormones*:

> "The standard of review appropriately applicable in proceedings under the *SPS Agreement*, of course, must reflect the balance established in that Agreement between the jurisdictional competences conceded by the Members to the WTO and the jurisdictional competences retained by the Members for themselves. To adopt a standard of review not clearly rooted in the text of the *SPS Agreement* itself, may well amount to changing that finely draw balance; and neither a panel nor the Appellate Body is authorized to do that.
> ... In our view, Article 11 of the DSU bears directly on this matter and, in effect, articulates with great succinctness but with sufficient clarity the appropriate standard of review for panels in respect of both the ascertainment of facts and the legal characterization of such facts under the relevant agreements.
> So far as fact-finding by panels is concerned, their activities are always constrained by the mandate of Article 11 of the DSU: the applicable standard is neither *de novo* review as such, nor 'total deference', but rather the 'objective assessment of the facts'. Many panels have in the past refused to undertake *de novo* review, wisely, since under current practice and systems, they are in any case poorly suited to

3.   Japan's Requests for Preliminary Rulings

(a)   Introduction

8.52   As mentioned above, Japan requested that we issue a preliminary ruling on two issues, in accordance with paragraph 10 of our Working Procedures. First, Japan requested that we "remove" two documents submitted by the United States as evidence[237] essentially:

(a)   because these documents were submitted in such a way that Japan was prevented from discussing them during consultations, with the consequence that it was denied an opportunity to settle the matter in good faith through bilateral consultations; and

(b)   because the probative value of those communications is questionable, given the conditions in which they were obtained.[238]

Indeed, Japan contends that the declarations at issue were pre-worded by the United States to suit its position.[239]

8.53   Second, Japan requests that we "remove" from the "scope of our proceedings" all the provisions that the United States did not address in its first submission.

8.54   At our request, the United States submitted written comments before our first substantive meeting.[240] The issues were further addressed by the parties at our first meeting and subsequently by Japan in its second written submission and during our second substantive meeting with the parties.

(b)   Japan's Request that we "remove" Certain Pieces of Evidence from the Proceedings

8.55   With regard to Japan's first request, in a letter dated 15 January 2003, we informed the parties of the following:

"The Panel refers to Japan's request for a preliminary ruling concerning the admissibility of two exhibits submitted by the United States with its first written submission, namely the declaration from T. van der Zwet (USA – 18) and the letter from S. V. Thomson (USA – 19).

The Panel notes that, as a matter of principle, the parties are entitled to submit evidence in support of their arguments. Having considered the arguments of the parties, the Panel is not convinced that, in this particular instance, it should exclude the

---

engage in such a review. On the other hand, 'total deference to the findings of the national authorities', it has been well said, 'could not ensure an 'objective assessment' as foreseen by Article 11 of the DSU'" (paras. 115-117).

[237]   These documents are (a) a declaration by Dr Tom van der Zwet (Exhibit USA-18) and a letter by Professor Sherman Thomson (Exhibit USA-19).

[238]   A detailed account of the arguments of the parties can be found in paras. 4.6-4.16.

[239]   Comments of Japan on Experts' Responses, 23 December 2002, paras. 13 and 17.

[240]   Reply of the United States to the Request by Japan for Preliminary Rulings, 16 October 2002. See paras. 4.7, 4.8, 4.10, 4.12, 4.13.

aforementioned exhibits from the proceedings *a priori*. This decision is without prejudice to the weight, if any, that the Panel may ultimately ascribe to these documents, including in light of Japan's comments.

Japan may, if it deems necessary, make further representations or ask additional questions regarding the contents of these documents in the course of the second substantive meeting."

8.56   We confirm our decision not to reject the two pieces of evidence submitted by the United States as Exhibits USA-18 and USA-19. We are of the view that our obligation, pursuant to Article 11 of the DSU, to make an objective assessment of the matter before us, including an objective assessment of the facts of the case, imposes on us an obligation not to exclude *a priori* any evidence submitted in due time by any party. However, the fact that we accepted the evidence at issue as a matter of principle is, as stated in the letter above, without prejudice to the weight that we will ultimately give to these exhibits in our discussion of the substance of this case. We also note that, consistent with the practice of panels, we provided Japan with the opportunity to comment on the substance of these documents.

(c)   Japan's Request Regarding some Claims not Developed by the United States in its First Submission

(i)   Summary of the Arguments of the Parties[241]

8.57   Japan requests that we "remove" from the scope of our proceedings a number of claims contained in the request of the United States for the establishment of the Panel. With respect to Article 4.2 of the Agreement on Agriculture and Article 5.5 of the *SPS Agreement*, Japan argues that no bilateral consultations were held. Regarding Article XI GATT 1994, Article 4.2 of the Agreement on Agriculture and Articles 2.3, 5.3, 5.5, 6.1 and 6.2 of the *SPS Agreement*, Japan argues that the United States should not be entitled to develop those claims during these proceedings since it did not address them in its first submission.

8.58   The United States argues that there is no basis for the Panel to remove claims that are within the Panel's terms of reference as established by the DSB. There is, in its view, no obligation under the DSU to consult on a particular claim in order to include that claim in the Panel's terms of reference. The purpose of consultations is to provide a better understanding of the facts and circumstances of a dispute. Logically, then, a party may identify new claims in the course of consultations and include them in the request for establishment of a panel.

---

[241]   A detailed account of the arguments of the parties can be found in paras. 4.1-4.5 of this Report.

(ii) Analysis of the Panel

8.59   We understand that Japan wants us to declare that the claims at issue are either not properly before the Panel or should otherwise not be addressed by the Panel. In other words, Japan wants us to interpret our terms of reference, as defined by Article 7 of the DSU and the US request for establishment of a panel. Japan's request seems to be based on two reasons:

(a)   Some of those claims (those regarding Article 4.2 of the Agreement on Agriculture and Article 5.5 of the *SPS Agreement*) were not found in the initial request for consultations contained in document WT/DS245/1 (hereafter "Request (a)"); and

(b)   Some of those claims (those regarding Article XI GATT 1994, Article 4.2 of the Agreement on Agriculture and Articles 2.3, 5.3, 5.5, 6.1 and 6.2 of the *SPS Agreement*) were not developed in the US first written submission (hereafter "Request (b)").

-   Request (a)

8.60   Concerning the claims referred to under (a) above, we first recall that, even though the United States included Article 5.5 in its request for establishment of a panel, it did not submit any argument or evidence in support of that claim. As a result, it is not necessary for the Panel to issue any ruling on the admissibility of a claim that was not addressed by the complaining party.

8.61   Regarding the claim of the United States under Article 4.2 of the Agreement on Agriculture, we consider that, in the light of our findings on the merits of this case[242], it is not necessary to decide on the admissibility of that claim.

8.62   For these reasons, we refrain from making any finding on Japan's request that those claims be "removed" from these proceedings by the Panel because they were not found in the initial request for consultations.

-   Request (b)

8.63   As regards the claims referred to under (b) above, we first note that we are bound by our terms of reference.[243] We also note that the Appellate Body in *EC – Bananas* stated that:

> "There is no requirement in the DSU or in GATT practice for arguments on all claims relating to the matter referred to the DSB to be set out in a complaining party's first submission to the panel. It is the panel's terms of reference, governed by Article 7 of the DSU, which set out the claims of the complaining parties relating to the matter referred to the DSB."[244]

---

[242]   See para. 8.336 below. See also paras. 8.63-8.66.

[243]   Appellate Body Report in *India – Patents (US)*, paras. 92-93.

[244]   Appellate Body Report in *EC – Bananas*, para. 145. This position has been reaffirmed recently in the Report of the Appellate Body in *EC – Sardines*, para. 280 and in the Report of the Appellate Body in *Chile – Price Band System*, para. 158.

8.64   Therefore, it is well established that a complainant is not prevented, as a matter of principle, from developing in its second submission arguments relating to a claim that is within the terms of reference of the panel, even if it did not do so in its first written submission.

8.65   In the present case, the United States made arguments in relation to its claims under Article XI GATT 1994 and Article 4.2 of the Agreement on Agriculture only during our two substantive hearings with the parties. Such a tactic may seem questionable since nothing prevented the United States from presenting arguments on these claims in its first submission, and such an approach may significantly limit the possibility for the defending party to argue in response, depending on the circumstances of the case, or at least could unduly delay the proceedings.

8.66   Taking into account the established practice on issues such as this, and having given due consideration to Japan's request, we decided that the most appropriate way to deal with this issue was to give Japan sufficient opportunity to reply. We declined to rule on this issue at the first substantive meeting and made the following statement at our second meeting with the parties:

> "Referring to the letter we sent yesterday [reproduced in paragraph 8.55 above], we addressed only one of the issues on which a preliminary ruling had been sought by Japan. We did not address the other point as we intend to address that in the findings. Since one party referred to this other issue this morning, the Panel notes that it is still open to the parties to make further comment on it at this meeting or within the deadlines for comment on matters arising from this meeting by close of business Tuesday 28 January"[245].

The US claims under Article XI GATT 1994 and Article 4.2 of the Agreement on Agriculture are discussed in Sections I and J below.

D.   Article 2.2 of the SPS Agreement

1.   Summary of the Arguments of the Parties[246]

(a)   United States

8.67   The United States argues that Japan's fire blight measure is inconsistent with Article 2.2 of the *SPS Agreement* because it is maintained without sufficient scientific evidence, contrary to the last requirement of that Article.

8.68   The United States argues that in *Japan – Agricultural Products II*, the Appellate Body interpreted the relevant part of Article 2.2 in light of the ordinary meaning of the word "sufficient" ("of a quantity, extent, or scope adequate to a certain purpose or object") and in the context of Articles 5.1, 3.3 and 5.7. The

---

[245]   Statement by the Chairman of the Panel, Mr Michael Cartland, at the Panel meeting with the parties on 16 January 2003.
[246]   A detailed account of the arguments of the parties can be found in paras. 4.48-4.137 of this Report.

Appellate Body affirmed the conclusion of the panel that the obligation in Article 2.2 not to maintain an SPS measure "without sufficient scientific evidence" requires that "there be a rational or objective relationship between the SPS measure and the scientific evidence" which is to be determined on a case-by-case basis and will depend on the particular circumstances of the case, "including the characteristics of the measure at issue and the quality and quantity of the scientific evidence".[247]

8.69   The United States argues that there is no evidence that the apple fruit sought to be exported from the United States, i.e. mature, symptomless apples, have ever transmitted and or would transmit fire blight disease to Japan.[248] All of the scientific evidence shows that mature, symptomless apples are not a pathway for the disease.

8.70   The United States adds that scientific evidence is borne out by real world experience. Over the past 35 years, there has not been a single reported instance of fire blight spread through export of US apples. Thus, there is no rational or objective relationship between the scientific evidence and the Japanese fire blight measures.

8.71   The United States further argues that mature, symptomless apples do not serve as a "pathway" for fire blight disease. The International Plant Protection Convention defines a pathway as "[a]ny means that allows the entry, establishment or spread of a pest". Phytosanitary measures under the *SPS Agreement* must, by their nature, address a risk that arises due to an identifiable pathway.

(b)   Japan

8.72   Japan argues that each of the current requirements on the importation of US apples to prevent the entry of fire blight is reasonably supported by scientific evidence, similar measures taken by other countries and international standards. As such, Japan contends that there is a "rational or objective relationship" between the measure and the evidence.

8.73   Japan argues that a variety of published literature on the ecology, properties and survivability of *E. amylovora* establish that the bacteria is evidently capable of long-term survival inside or on the surface of what the United States termed "mature, symptomless" apple fruit. The fact that bacteria could exist and survive inside mature, symptomless apple fruit means that the fruit could cause fire blight symptoms later on. As such, apple fruit could be contaminated and yet be found fit for exportation. Once introduced into Japan, fire blight would have ample potential for growth and infection and lead to major negative, irreversible consequences. Previous instances of trans-oceanic dissemination of fire blight showed the survivability of bacterium and no ecological study had pin-pointed the exact pathway for transmission of the

---

[247] US first submission, para. 22.
[248] *Ibid.*, para. 23-24.

diseases in those cases. As such, apple fruit could not be ruled out as a vector for the transmission of fire blight.

8.74   Japan also contends that the United States places too much weight on "direct evidence" in assessing the risk of introducing fire blight with apple fruit. If one considers also the "indirect" scientific evidence, then Japan argues that there is evidence that contaminated apple fruit can go through each of the steps necessary for it to eventually cause fire blight in the importing country.

8.75   Japan further argues that the US criteria of mature, symptomless apple fruit is ambiguous. "Immature" and "mature" apples are not two clearly separate phenomena. Japan contends that maturation is a "continuous process". Such an ambiguous concept is therefore, in the view of Japan, unworkable.

8.76   Apple export data supplied by the United States are misleading, according to Japan. Japan notes that the top ten markets for US apples have very different climatic conditions from Japan (eight being found in the tropical region and the other two in desert climes). As such, none has favourable conditions for the establishment of fire blight, unlike Japan.

2.   *Approach of the Panel with Respect to the Review of the Phytosanitary Measure at Issue under Article 2.2 of the SPS Agreement*

(a)   Preliminary Remarks: Limitation of Findings to whether the Measure is Maintained "without sufficient scientific evidence"

8.77   Having reviewed the arguments of the parties, we note that the US claim regarding the violation by Japan of Article 2.2 of the *SPS Agreement* is limited to the allegation that the measure at issue is maintained "without sufficient scientific evidence". We are therefore not requested to identify a violation, or the absence thereof, of any other requirement of Article 2.2 of the *SPS Agreement*, such as whether the phytosanitary measure is based on scientific principles, even though these other requirements may be useful in understanding the extent of Japan's obligations under that Article. This said, it is essential to recall, as a first step of our analysis, what the parties must demonstrate in relation to this very specific aspect of Article 2.2.

8.78   In this respect, we should also be careful not to confuse the requirement that a measure is not maintained without sufficient scientific evidence with the requirement of Article 5.6 of the *SPS Agreement* that the measure is "not more trade-restrictive than required to achieve [Japan's] appropriate level of ... phytosanitary protection". In other words, while we might find that some specific requirements of the measure at issue are not supported by sufficient scientific evidence, our findings should be limited to Article 2.2.

(b)   Determining whether the Measure at Issue is (or not) "maintained without sufficient scientific evidence"

(i)   Introduction

8.79   The relevant part of Article 2.2 of the *SPS Agreement* reads as follows:

"Members shall ensure that any sanitary or phytosanitary measure … is not maintained without sufficient scientific evidence, except as provided for in paragraph 7 of Article 5."

8.80   First, we recall that, as mentioned above, Japan has argued that the measure would still be justified under Article 5.7 of the *SPS Agreement*, even if it were found to be maintained without sufficient scientific evidence. We have already discussed the interrelation between Article 2.2 and Article 5.7 in the section regarding our general approach to this case. The arguments of Japan regarding Article 5.7 will be addressed immediately after this section. At this stage, we will address the claim made by the United States specifically under Article 2.2 of the *SPS Agreement*, i.e., that Japan maintains the measure at issue without sufficient scientific evidence, and Japan's arguments relating specifically to that provision.

8.81   Second, it is clear that we must determine in general whether the phytosanitary measure at issue is maintained without sufficient scientific evidence. However, before we can address the evidence submitted by each party, it is necessary to identify *what*, in substance, needs to be demonstrated.

8.82   Third, we will need to determine *how* parties can demonstrate their respective views. We note that the parties have extensively discussed the question of the evidence that may be submitted in these proceedings. In this respect, we note that the term "sufficient scientific evidence" contains a number of elements that need to be taken into consideration:

(a)   First, the very notion of "scientific evidence" seems to exclude elements of information that cannot be considered as "evidence". The same notion also seems to exclude any evidence that is not "scientific".

(b)   Second, the term "sufficient" seems to address not only the quantity and quality of the evidence as such, but also the "causal link" between the phytosanitary measure at issue and the scientific evidence establishing a phytosanitary risk and justifying the measure.

8.83   We will therefore need to address the question of (a) the nature of the evidence that may be accepted and (b) the quality of the evidence to be accepted.

(ii)   What Needs to be Demonstrated in Substance?

8.84   We note that the approach followed by the United States in order to demonstrate that the phytosanitary measure at issue is maintained without sufficient scientific evidence consists, in substance, of trying to establish that there is no evidence that "mature, symptomless apples" have introduced or could serve as a pathway for the entry, establishment or spread of fire blight by alleging that:

(a)   There is no evidence that mature, symptomless apple fruit can be infected by E. amylovora;

(b)   there is no scientific evidence that mature, symptomless apples can be endophytically[249] infested by the bacteria;

(c)   scientific evidence shows that presence of epiphytic[250] bacteria is rare and limited to apples harvested on or very close to blighted trees; and

(d)   there is no evidence that apples, even on those rare occasions that epiphytic bacteria is present, can act as a pathway for the dissemination of fire blight. Indeed, such bacteria are unlikely to survive normal commercial handling, storage and transport of fruit. In addition, even if the infested apple is placed near a suitable host that is receptive to an infection, there is no dispersal mechanism or vector to allow movement of such bacteria from the fruit to that host.

8.85   Japan, on the contrary, argues that:

(a)   Fire blight can be harboured in or on mature, symptomless apple fruit;

(b)   apple fruit is a possible pathway for the transmission of the disease;

(c)   trans-oceanic dissemination of the disease has previously occurred; and

(d)   it must also protect itself against failures in the control systems of exporting countries which could lead to the introduction of contaminated apples.

In the absence of any reliable quarantine inspection methods to detect fire blight in or on mature, symptomless apples, Japan views a systems approach as necessary.

8.86   A first issue to consider is, therefore, whether there is sufficient scientific evidence, within the meaning of Article 2.2 of the *SPS Agreement*, to support the view that "mature, symptomless apple fruit" can harbour the bacteria causing fire blight. If the United States were to demonstrate that this is not the case, most of the restrictions imposed by Japan would not be justified.

8.87   However, even if it were the case that mature, symptomless apples cannot be infected and do not harbour endophytic or epiphytic populations of bacteria susceptible of transmitting fire blight to a host plant in Japan, this may not

---

[249] See definition of endophytic and epiphytic, para. 2.10.
[250] *Ibid.*

exclude the possibility that fire blight-free apples become contaminated after they are harvested, nor does it exclude a risk of failure in the control procedures which normally lead to the exportation of only "mature, symptomless apples". This consideration implies that we have previously established that apples other than "mature, symptomless apples" could pose a higher risk and, thus, that we do not limit our analysis to mature, symptomless apple fruit.

8.88   Conversely, even if the United States were to fail to demonstrate that there is not sufficient evidence supporting the view that mature, symptomless apples have introduced fireblight or could serve as a pathway for the entry, establishment or spread of fire blight, this would not, *ipso facto*, imply that the Japanese measure *as a whole* is maintained with sufficient scientific evidence. We recall that this measure is composed of a number of elements all of which Japan presents as indispensable in the framework of a systems approach. If we were to find that some of these elements are redundant, i.e., that their imposition in the context of the phytosanitary measure at issue is not justified as such in response to a scientifically established risk, or that other elements of the measure already serve the same purpose, we may find that these elements are maintained without sufficient scientific evidence. Under such circumstances, the measure as a whole, at least to the extent it includes those "redundant" requirements, would be deemed to be imposed without sufficient scientific evidence.

8.89   In order to address this question, we will assess the following five elements:

(a)   As a preliminary matter, whether the notion of mature, symptomless apple fruit is scientifically supported and whether it is appropriate to restrict our examination of the measure at issue to its application to mature, symptomless apples;

(b)   whether mature apple fruit can be infected;

(c)   whether endophytic bacteria may be found in mature apple fruit;

(d)   whether mature apple fruit may harbour epiphytic bacteria;

(e)   whether infested or infected apple fruit harbouring endophytic or epiphytic bacteria can complete the fire blight transmission pathway, i.e. whether the bacteria can survive commercial handling, storage and transportation and whether, once it has entered Japan, it can transmit the bacteria to host plants at a receptive stage (apple as a pathway).

(iii)   How to Demonstrate the Existence or Absence of Sufficient Scientific Evidence?

-    "Scientific evidence"

8.90   We note that previous cases have essentially dealt with the question of *sufficient* scientific evidence. In this case, however, both parties have addressed the question of the *nature* of the evidence that should be considered. The United States argues that evidence under Article 2.2 must be scientific, i.e. valid according to the objective principles of the scientific method. Circumstantial evidence should, in its view, be rejected. Japan argues that the US approach to "evidence", limited to "direct" evidence, is inappropriate. In Japan's view, "indirect" evidence should also be taken into account. Japan defines "direct" evidence as "conclusive scientific discovery", whereas "indirect" evidence would be, for instance, evidence that would show the ability of contaminated apple fruit to go through each step of the pathway that could eventually cause fire blight in the importing country.

8.91   Starting with the notion of "scientific" evidence, we do not see the positions of the United States and Japan as fundamentally incompatible. It seems to us that Japan refers to scientific evidence when it points to both "direct" and "indirect" evidence. The only difference between "direct" and "indirect" evidence if we follow Japan's view is, in a sense, the degree of relationship of the evidence with the facts that Japan wishes to demonstrate with this evidence. In any event, indirect evidence may be scientific, even if it does not directly prove the facts.

8.92   We consider that, in accordance with the general principles of interpretation of public international law, we must give full meaning to the term "scientific" and conclude that, in the context of Article 2.2, the evidence to be considered should be evidence gathered through scientific methods, excluding by the same token information not acquired through a scientific method. We further note that scientific evidence may include evidence that a particular risk may occur (e.g., the entry, establishment or spread of the bacteria that causes fire blight disease) as well as evidence that a particular requirement may reduce or eliminate that risk (e.g., the effectiveness of chlorine treatment in eliminating the bacteria).

8.93   Likewise, the use of the term "evidence" must also be given full significance. Negotiators could have used the term "information", as in Article 5.7, if they considered that any material could be used. By using the term "scientific evidence", Article 2.2 excludes in essence not only insufficiently substantiated information, but also such things as a non-demonstrated hypothesis.

8.94   We note that the parties and the experts have discussed the notion of "circumstantial evidence". In this respect, we recall the view expressed by Dr Smith regarding the relevance of "circumstantial evidence" as far as the study of fire blight is concerned:

> "... fire blight is a well studied disease, much observed and so that there is a very large body of direct evidence concerning fire blight. The existence of this body of direct evidence gives one a perspective in evaluating indirect evidence and in judging and insofar as you cannot necessarily draw a sharp dividing line in deciding whether circumstantial evidence is useful in trying to decide whether what is the risk of a certain scenario. In plant health it is important to keep one's feet on the ground, to consider the direct evidence first and to evaluate conjectural scenarios rather carefully in relation to what is really known about, for

example, fire blight. We live in a world now in which various risks have been recently identified - risks of the entry of alien species from other continents, risks of the movement of living modified organisms - where there is little direct evidence and most of the evidence that has to be used is of a circumstantial kind. Where there is no direct evidence, it is not possible to use it as a kind of counterweight in one's judgements. But in plant health there is direct evidence. A lot of work has been done and it does assist one in making judgements in relation to evidence which is less certain."[251]

8.95   We find that this statement supports, in this particular case, an approach that favours relying on scientifically produced evidence rather than on purely circumstantial evidence. At the very least, Dr Smith's statement suggests that, in the case of fire blight, any circumstantial evidence should be considered in the light of the substantial body of scientific evidence already available.

8.96   We do not believe that our approach is overly restrictive or that it could lead to the sort of scenario suggested by Japan, where a Member could only protect itself against known, well established dissemination pathways.

8.97   First, our approach is consistent with the structure of the *SPS Agreement*, which allows a Member to invoke Article 5.7 when it does not yet have "sufficient scientific evidence", and in those circumstances to rely on "available pertinent information". We recall in this respect that the Appellate Body stated that:

> "Article 5.7 operates as a *qualified* exemption from the obligation under 2.2 not to maintain SPS measures without sufficient scientific evidence. An overly broad and flexible interpretation of that obligation would render Article 5.7 meaningless."[252]

8.98   Second, requiring "scientific evidence" does not limit the field of scientific evidence available to Members to support their measures. "Direct" or "indirect" evidence may be equally considered. The only difference is not one of scientific quality, but one of probative value within the legal meaning of the term, since it is obvious that evidence which does not directly prove a fact might not have as much weight as evidence directly proving it, if it is available.

8.99   On the basis of the above, we conclude that:

(a)   We will consider all relevant evidence that can be considered "scientific", and do not exclude *a priori* that "indirect" evidence may be pertinent to our assessment, provided that it is scientific in nature;

(b)   This is without prejudice to the probative value to be ascribed to each piece of evidence in the course of our assessment.

---

[251]   Transcript from Panel meeting with experts of 13 January (afternoon) and 14 January (morning) 2003 (hereafter Annex 3), para. 338.
[252]   Appellate Body Report in *Japan – Agricultural Products II*, para. 80 (emphasis in the original).

- "Sufficient" scientific evidence

8.100 The requirement that a measure not be maintained without sufficient scientific evidence has been addressed by panels and by the Appellate Body in other cases. Therefore, we find it appropriate to consider from the outset the conclusions they reached to the extent that they have already clarified the meaning of the terms in which we are interested. Indeed, reports adopted by the DSB have discussed the meaning of those provisions in accordance with the general principles of international law regarding the interpretation of treaties – as set out in Articles 31 to 33 of the Vienna Convention on the Law of Treaties – pursuant to Article 3.2 of the DSU. Therefore, we see no reason to perform the same analysis again if it is not necessary. We further interpret the provisions of Article 2.2 of the *SPS Agreement* only to the extent that their meaning has not been fully clarified in previous adopted reports, as was the case for the terms "scientific evidence".

8.101 We first note that the meaning of the term "sufficient" in the expression "sufficient scientific evidence" has been addressed by the Appellate Body in *Japan – Agricultural Products II* as follows:

> "The ordinary meaning of 'sufficient' is 'of a quantity, extent, or scope adequate to a certain purpose or object'. From this, we conclude that 'sufficiency' is a relational concept. 'Sufficiency' requires the existence of a sufficient or adequate relationship between two elements, *in casu*, between the SPS measure and the scientific evidence."
>
> ...
>
> "The context of the word 'sufficient' or, more generally, the phrase 'maintained without sufficient scientific evidence in Article 2.2, includes Article 5.1, as well as Articles 3.3 and 5.7 of the *SPS Agreement.*"

8.102 When addressing the meaning of the term "sufficient", we thus enter the realm of the relationship between the phytosanitary measure at issue and the "scientific evidence" relating to the risk that the phytosanitary measure is supposed to address. An *adequate relationship* is thus required between the restriction on imports of apples applied by Japan and the relevant scientific evidence. Such an adequate relationship would not be satisfied in a situation where only *patent insufficiency* would be considered as not "sufficient".[253]

8.103 It should be recalled that the adequate relationship between the SPS measure and the scientific evidence requires "a rational or objective relationship". As recalled by the Appellate Body,

> "Whether there is a rational relationship between an SPS measure and the scientific evidence is to be determined on a case-by-case basis and will depend upon the particular circumstances of the

---

[253] Appellate Body Report in *Japan – Agricultural Products II*, para. 82.

case, including the characteristics of the measure at issue and the quality and quantity of the scientific evidence."[254]

8.104 From the above, it appears that the term "sufficient" is clearly to be considered in relation to the phytosanitary measure itself. This said, we should not leave aside the fact that scientific evidence relates to a risk and is supposed to confirm the existence of a given risk. In the present case, the United States denies that mature, symptomless apple fruit carry the risk of transmitting fire blight. The United States also argues that there would be possibilities to successfully eradicate fire blight, as suggested by the experience of Norway and Australia, if it were introduced by accident into Japan. Japan disputes this contention and identifies a series of risks that are ignored by the United States: contamination of mature, symptomless apples; contamination of crates; inclusion by mistake of a contaminated apple in an otherwise healthy consignment bound for Japan, transfer of bacteria by birds or insects and, ultimately, the risk of introduction of fire blight on a territory which is, for the moment, free from it.

8.105 However, neither party denies the ecological and economic impact that the introduction of fire blight could have in Japan. Under those circumstances, we should, when determining the weight of the evidence before us, "bear in mind that responsible, representative governments commonly act from a perspective of prudence and precaution when risks of irreversible ... damages ... are concerned".[255]

8.106 Japan argues that, in order for the United States to establish a prima facie case under Article 2.2, it has to positively prove the "insufficiency" of scientific evidence. The United States claims that there is simply no scientific evidence supporting the measure at issue. Under these circumstances, and in application of the reasoning of the Appellate Body in *Japan – Agricultural Products II*, we consider that the United States should raise a presumption that there are no *relevant* scientific studies or reports in order to demonstrate that the measure at issue is not supported by sufficient scientific evidence.[256] If Japan submits elements to rebut that presumption, we would have to weigh the evidence before us.

8.107 Japan also argues that we should take into account the requirements of Article 4 of the *SPS Agreement* when considering whether the measure at issue is supported by sufficient scientific evidence. We agree that other provisions of the *SPS Agreement* are part of the context of Article 2.2, as recalled by the Appellate Body in *Japan – Agricultural Products II*.[257] However, Article 4 deals with the specific question of the recognition of equivalence of measures. Unlike Articles 3.3, 5.1 and 5.7, the purpose of Article 4 is clearly different from that of Article 2.2. We also note that the United States did not raise any claim under Article 4 and that this Article is not a defence against violations of other provisions of the *SPS Agreement*. As a result, we see no reason to consider

---

[254] *Ibid.*, para. 84.
[255] Appellate Body Report in *EC – Hormones*, para. 124.
[256] Appellate Body Report in *Japan – Agricultural Products II*, para. 137.
[257] *Ibid.*, para. 74.

Japan's arguments regarding Article 4 in our assessment of Article 2.2, other than to the extent that Article 4 might form part of the relevant context in the interpretation of Article 2.2.

8.108 On the basis of the above, we conclude that:

    (a) The United States should raise a presumption that there are no *relevant* scientific studies or reports supporting the measure at issue in order to demonstrate that the measure at issue is not supported by sufficient scientific evidence. If Japan submits elements to rebut that presumption, we would have to weigh the evidence before us.

    (b) There is no reason to consider Japan's arguments regarding Article 4 in our assessment of Article 2.2, other than to the extent that Article 4 might form part of the relevant context in the interpretation of Article 2.2.

        3.   Preliminary Question: the Relevance and Consequences of the Notion of "mature, symptomless" Apple Fruit in the Assessment of the Phytosanitary Measure at Issue under Article 2.2

        (a)   Summary of the Arguments of the Parties[258]

8.109 The United States argues that the product it exports to Japan is "mature, symptomless apple fruit". It adds that there is a long established scientific, commercial and horticultural basis for the use of the concepts of physiological and commercial maturity. In the US view, this distinction is relevant because mature fruit, unlike immature fruit, is not susceptible to contamination by *E. amylovora* and cannot host or develop fire blight.

8.110 Japan challenges the concepts of "mature" and "symptomless" apples. Japan argues that the concept of maturity is inherently subjective and that there is an ambiguity in using it, since "physiological maturity" and "commercial maturity" should be distinguished. Japan considers that maturity is a continuing process. Japan is of the view that endophytic bacteria found in physiologically immature apples are likely[259] to survive until "commercial maturity" in light of the ecology and other known properties of the bacteria. Japan adds that close-to-mature apples have been found to harbour *E. amylovora* and even display signs of serious infection, such as bacterial ooze. Japan also claims that the United States has not submitted any scientific explanation for the fact that the bacteria *E. amylovora* can be found in close-to-mature apples, but allegedly not in mature apples.

---

[258] A detailed account of the arguments of the parties can be found in paras. 4.90-4.102 and 4.192-4.198 of this Report.
[259] Japan second submission, 13 November 2003, para. 27.

(b)   Analysis of the Panel

(i)   Introduction

8.111 When discussing the product at issue in this case in paragraphs 8.26-8.34 above, we considered that we could not prejudge our conclusions by unduly restricting, from the outset, the scope of our findings to mature, symptomless apple fruit. In the context of Article 2.2 we consider that the discussion of the parties raises two main issues: one is the relevance of the concept of "mature, symptomless" apple in terms of risk of fire blight transmission; the second is the risk related to apples other than mature, symptomless apples, such as immature or damaged apples.

8.112 If we find that there is pertinence in differentiating "mature, symptomless" apples from other apples (e.g. immature or damaged apples), we will proceed with a specific analysis of the risks attached to each category.

(ii)   Mature, Symptomless Apples v. Other Apples

8.113 We note that the experts commented, at our request, on the concept of maturity and whether a naturally infected apple could develop into a healthy looking fruit.[260] Regarding the concept of maturity, Dr Hale confirmed that there were accepted definitions for determining if an apple fruit is physiologically and commercially mature. An apple will be deemed to be physiologically mature when it reaches the point at which, if picked, it will ripen. If an apple is not mature at the time it is harvested, then it will not ripen. It will shrivel and be unacceptable.[261] Maturity assessment includes colour, starch index, soluble solid content, flesh firmness, acidity, and ethylene production rate. Dr Hayward stated that there were objective methods for the determination of the maturity of apples which formed the basis of the OECD international guidelines.[262] For Dr Hayward, as for Dr Hale, an apple fruit was physiologically mature when it was at the stage of development where, even when detached, it continued to develop and ripen.[263] Having regard to the evidence submitted by the parties and the opinions of the experts consulted by the Panel, we consider that the concept of maturity is relatively well defined as the moment when the apple fruit is at a stage where it will ripen even if detached from the tree. We conclude from this that it is scientifically possible to differentiate between mature and immature apples.

8.114 However, the experts noted that maturation was a continuous process.[264] We understand from the opinions of the experts that they considered this issue to be relevant with regard to the *susceptibility* of the apple to fire blight. Dr Smith agreed with Dr Geider that whatever made an immature apple permissive to the

---

[260]   Paras. 6.5-6.10.
[261]   Para.6.5.
[262]   Para. 6.6.
[263]   *Ibid*.
[264]   Annex 3, Dr Hale, para. 91.

introduction of the bacteria did not necessarily have much to do with what later made it physiologically mature or commercially mature.[265] According to these experts, it is clear that very young apples are susceptible to *E. amylovora,* but that by the time they have reached commercial maturity, they are no longer susceptible. At some point in between immaturity and commercial maturity, they lose that susceptibility.[266]

8.115 As a result, we consider that the differentiation between mature and immature apples is relevant in terms of the risk of contamination of the fruit.

8.116 We also note that the experts stated that fruits infected at fruitlet level would not develop into healthy looking fruit.[267] Dr Geider considered that a dormant persistence of *E. amylovora* in fruit was not documented and was difficult to demonstrate.[268] Naturally infected fruits would be small, shrivelled, might show some lesions, and would not mature. Consequently, they were highly unlikely to develop into healthy-looking fruit.[269] In addition, when natural infections occur at an advanced growth stage in apples, e.g. as a result of hailstorms, the apples begin to rot and ooze (exudate).[270]

8.117 The experts did indicate that if the bacteria remained confined to the outside of the fruit, including in the calyx at the blossom end, a healthy looking fruit could develop. However, none of the experts reported knowing of any scientific studies where the bacteria on the surface of the fruit or harboured in the calyx had ever infected the inside of the apple. Likewise, attempts to develop infection by cutting the pedicel of the apple and placing a large quantity of *E. amylovora* on the cut pedicel failed to convincingly demonstrate infection of the inside of the apple.[271]

8.118 As a result, we consider that the concept of "symptomless" is also scientifically pertinent. Indeed, insofar as dormant persistence of *E. amylovora* has not been documented, any infection is very likely to be visibly identifiable.

(iii)   Relevance of Addressing the Risks Related to Both Mature, Symptomless Apples and Other Apples

8.119 The above discussion tends to suggest not only that mature, symptomless apples may present a low risk of acting as an effective pathway, but also that apples other than mature, symptomless apples may carry a higher risk in terms of contamination. We recall that Annex A, paragraph 1 of the *SPS Agreement* defines as a phytosanitary measure "any measure applied to protect plant life or health within the territory of a Member from risks arising from the entry,

---

[265]   Annex 3, Dr Geider, Dr Hale, Dr Smith, paras. 89, 91, 95.
[266]   Annex 3, Dr Smith, para. 95.
[267]   For the purpose of this case, the terms "symptomless" and "health-looking" will be used indifferently.
[268]   Para. 6.7.
[269]   See also, Dr Hale, para. 6.8.
[270]   Dr Geider, para. 6.7.
[271]   Annex 3, Drs Geider, Hale, Hayward, Smith, paras. 178, 180, 181, 182.

establishment or spread of pests, diseases, disease-carrying organisms or disease-causing organisms." This definition does not limit the scope of application of phytosanitary measures to the product that the exporting country claims to export. In order to be effective, a phytosanitary measure should cover all forms of a product that may actually be imported.

8.120 We recall in this respect that in *EC – Hormones*, the Appellate Body considered it legitimate for the European Communities to consider not only the *scientific risks* arising from the ingestion by human beings of residues of hormones in meat, but also the closely related risks arising from the failure to observe the requirements of good veterinary practice in the administration of hormones for growth promotion purposes, in combination with multiple problems relating to the detection and control of such failure.[272] We recognize that the Appellate Body expressed this view in the context of a risk assessment under Article 5.1 and 5.2. However, we first note the central role of Article 5.1 in the *SPS Agreement*.[273] Second, the following statement of the Appellate Body is, in our view, indicative of a general application of this principle under the *SPS Agreement*:

> "We consider that the object and purpose of the *SPS Agreement* justify the examination and evaluation of all such risks for human health, whatever their precise and immediate origin may be."[274]

8.121 Under those circumstances, it seems to us legitimate to consider all the aspects referred to by Japan in relation to the importation of apples from the United States, including human/technical errors in the sorting of apples or illegal actions which would lead to the importation of infested/infected apples.[275]

8.122 On the basis of the above, we conclude that it is not only useful, but also relevant to differentiate, in our assessment of the evidence regarding transmission of the disease, between the risks related to physiologically mature and apparently healthy apple fruit on the one hand, and the risks related to other apples (immature, mature but damaged) on the other hand, even if the latter may only accidentally enter the territory of Japan.

---

[272] Appellate Body Report in *EC – Hormones*, para. 205.

[273] See Appellate Body Report in *EC – Hormones* para. 180, where the Appellate Body mentioned that:

> "180. At the outset, two preliminary considerations need to be brought out. The first is that the Panel considered that Article 5.1 may be viewed as a specific application of the basic obligations contained in Article 2.2 of the *SPS Agreement*[160], which reads as follows:
>
>> Members shall ensure that any sanitary or phytosanitary measure is applied only *to the extent necessary to protect* human, animal or plant life or health, is *based on scientific principles* and is not maintained without *sufficient scientific evidence*, except as provided for in paragraph 7 of Article 5. (underlining added)
>
> We agree with this general consideration and would also stress that Articles 2.2 and 5.1 should constantly be read together. Article 2.2 informs Article 5.1: the elements that define the basic obligation set out in Article 2.2 impart meaning to Article 5.1."

[274] Appellate Body Report in *EC – Hormones*, para. 206.

[275] However, since the importation of immature, infected apples may only occur as a result of a handling error or an illegal action, we address the question of the contamination only in relation to the completion of the pathway.

4. *Infestation and Infection*[276] *of Mature, Symptomless Apple Fruit*

    (a)   Infestation

    (i)   Endophytic Bacteria

8.123 According to the United States, numerous studies indicate that mature, symptomless apple fruit do not harbour endophytic populations of the bacteria, even when harvested from blighted apple trees. These results reflect the biology of the disease. Apples infected with the bacteria do not mature. Immature apples may contain detectable levels of endophytic fire blight, but mature, symptomless apples would not harbour internal populations of bacteria. Van der Zwet *et al.* (1990), on which Japan relies, did not distinguish between immature and mature fruits. The United States further argues that the attempt to recover endophytic bacteria by Tsukamoto *et al.* (2003) was not successful.[277] The preliminary results showed that *E. amylovora* had not been found. The study did not provide additional information with respect to steps in Japan's hypothetical pathway, which experts have concluded could not be completed.

8.124 Japan argues that the United States only demonstrated that risk may not be present in certain, limited circumstances. The bacteria is capable of surviving in varying conditions. In addition, Japan, relying on van der Zwet *et al.* (1990), argues that endophytic *E. amylovora* had been found in mature apple fruit. Such findings were confirmed by Roberts *et al.* (1998). Japan argues that the United States has not explained how endophytic *E. amylovora* could be found in close-to-mature apples and disappear in the few days or weeks before maturation. Japan also recalls that Tsukamoto *et al.* (2003) have conducted experiments to clarify the ability of *E. amylovora* to invade and multiply through the pedicel (stem).[278]

8.125 We note that the views of the experts on this question is that there is no evidence that mature apple fruit will harbour endophytic bacteria.[279] Dr Smith added that a few papers described endophytic bacteria, but the experts consulted by the Panel were not convinced by those descriptions.[280]

---

[276] In para. 6.8 above, Dr Hale stated that it was important to make a distinction between infected and infested fruit. Infected fruit were diseased whereas infested fruit were contaminated with *E. amylovora* but not diseased. See also Dr Smith, para. 6.10, who defined infection as meaning not just the presence of bacteria, but an active process of pathogenesis. Dr Hayward, Annex 3, para. 67: "if I can quote definitions given in a guide to the terms in use in plant pathology: 'Infection is the entry of an organism or virus into a host, the plant, and the establishment of a permanent or temporary parasitic relationship'. Whereas infestation means, or to infest: 'To overrun the surface of a plant. When used in reference to micro-organisms or virus particles on plant surfaces, there is no implication that infection has occurred." As indicated in para. 2.15, the Panel will use the definition used by the experts.

[277] Exhibits JPN-39 and JPN-42.

[278] *Ibid.*

[279] Annex 3, paras. 28, 29, 54, 57, 59, 63, 75, 76, 80, 82, 83, 360-363. See also paras. 6.72-6.75.

[280] Annex 3, para. 363.

8.126 The experts consulted by the Panel also stated that *E. amylovora* did not occur as an endophyte in healthy-looking mature fruit.[281]

8.127 Based on the scientific evidence available to us in these proceedings, we note that the observation of the existence of endophytic populations in mature apple fruit is based essentially on one single study whose findings in this respect are not clear and are disputed: van der Zwet *et al.* (1990).[282] That study, although it recorded the isolation of *E. amylovora* from harvested fruit, did not specify the degree of maturity of the fruit or whether it was symptomless or not.[283] The study also appeared to report in a single paper different series of experiments in different locations and conditions, and not to contain a sufficiently precise description of the conditions of the experiment to allow for a precise conclusion to be drawn from them.[284] This in itself made its conclusions relatively confused, difficult to interpret or even unconvincing, as was suggested by the experts consulted by the Panel.[285] Furthermore, clarifications sought by the United States from the main authors of this study cast further doubt on conclusions that *E. amylovora* was found inside commercially mature fruit.[286] The Roberts *et al.* (1998) study cited by Japan simply reports on the findings in van der Zwet *et al.* (1990) and does not report on any new evidence in this regard. The fact that van der Zwet collaborated in Roberts *et al.* (1998) does not, in our view, affect the conclusion drawn from the experts' views and the author's comments of 16 July 2002.

8.128 We therefore conclude, on the basis of the information made available to the Panel, that there is not sufficient scientific evidence to conclude that mature, symptomless apples would harbour endophytic populations of bacteria.

(ii) Epiphytic Bacteria

8.129 The United States claims that a review of the scientific literature suggests that the presence of epiphytic bacteria on mature, symptomless fruits at harvest is extremely rare. In those few instances where external bacteria had been detected, the fruit had been harvested from or within 10 meters of an infected tree in severely infected orchards. The United States concludes that in most cases, mature, symptomless apples, even when harvested from infected trees or orchards, would not be externally contaminated with fire blight bacteria.

8.130 The United States also argues that the biology of the fire blight bacteria and the disease cycle is such that the bacteria shows a decline in population counts as the season advances and the conditions turn less hospitable, becoming

---

[281] Paras. 6.15-6.19 and 6.72-6.75; Annex 3, paras. 59, 76 and 82.
[282] Paras. 6.72-6.75.
[283] Annex 3, Dr Smith, para. 53.
[284] Dr Smith and Dr Geider, Annex 3, paras.54, 56, 57.
[285] Dr Hale and Dr Smith, paras. 6.77-6.79, 6.81-6.84, 6.86-6.87 and 6.89, respectively.
[286] We note that while these declarations confirm our conclusion that the results of this study are unclear, our conclusions in this respect are not dependent on them.

extremely rare on fruits at the time of harvest. The scientific evidence indicates that bacteria on the surface of fruits die within a short time.[287]

8.131 Japan does not agree with the conclusion that the external presence of the bacteria is extremely rare. Japan refers to Sholberg *et al.* (1988) to claim that *E. amylovora* may be present on symptomless fruit at harvest under certain conditions.

8.132 In this regard, we note Dr Hayward's remark that Sholberg's study showed susceptibility only when apple trees were inter-planted with heavily infected pear trees[288] and that the very different management practices pertaining to apple and pear fruit apparently preclude interplanting of the two crops.[289]

8.133 The United States argued that mature apples will rarely harbour epiphytic bacteria, even when harvested in heavily blighted orchards.

8.134 We recall that the experts did not exclude that bacteria could be found on the surface of apples in heavily infected orchards.[290] They also observed that epiphytic bacteria could result when early infection of blossoms did not lead to the development of fire blight and some of the bacteria remained confined in the calyx. Some of the experts questioned whether these surface or calyx populations could be considered as real epiphytic populations capable of transmitting fire blight. Indeed, "epiphytic" implied that the bacteria could persist and even reproduce at low levels over a period of weeks or months, which did not seem to be the case with surface *E. amylovora*.[291]

8.135 We note in this regard that the experts concurred in considering that even apples harvested very close to sources of inoculum did not harbour large populations of epiphytic bacteria.[292]

8.136 We therefore conclude, on the basis of the information made available to the Panel, that there is not sufficient scientific evidence to conclude that mature, symptomless apples are likely to harbour epiphytic populations of bacteria capable of transmitting *E. amylovora*.

(b)   Infection

8.137 Japan argues that there could exist mature, apparently healthy, but infected fruits. The United States claims that scientific evidence shows that mature apples cannot be infected.

8.138 We note that the information before the Panel tend to demonstrate that it is unlikely that a mature apple will be infected. If an immature apple is infected, it will not develop into a mature, healthy-looking fruit. If it does, then it is likely that the bacteria will not have developed.[293] The experts consulted by the Panel

---

[287] Dr Hayward, para. 6.36, Dr Hale, para. 6.121, Dr Hayward, para. 6.122, Dr Smith, para. 6.123.

[288] Annex 3, Dr Hayward, para. 205.

[289] US answers to Additional Questions from the Panel, 28 January 2003, para.44.

[290] Dr Hale, paras. 6.24-6.25 and 6.113-6.114

[291] Dr Smith, paras 6.18-6.19.

[292] Para. 6.17; Annex 3, paras. 364-367; see also paras. 223-236.

[293] Dr Smith, paras. 6.10 and 6.19.

have also agreed that there was no scientific evidence that a mature harvested apple fruit will be subsequently infected.[294]

8.139 We therefore conclude, on the basis of the information made available to the Panel, that mature apples are unlikely to be *infected* by fire blight if they do not show any symptoms.

5.   *Risk of Entry, Establishment or Spread of Fire Blight within Japan by Imported US Apple Fruit (apple fruit as a pathway)*

(a)   Introduction

8.140 The United States argues that not only is there no evidence that mature, symptomless apples have ever spread fire blight, but there is also no evidence that mature fruit could be a pathway for the spread of the bacteria. The evidence concerning infestation and infection of mature apples does not support Japan's proposed pathways. Japan contends that pathways may or may not be direct; contaminated cargo crates were a possibility, as was propagation from fruit to other plants in the environment.

8.141 The parties and experts have primarily discussed the risk of transmission by mature apples, because this is the commodity normally exported and on which scientific experiments have been performed. However, for the reasons mentioned above, we also find it necessary to assess the risk of transmission through apples other than mature, symptomless apples: essentially immature, infected or infested apples.

8.142 Since we have reached the conclusion that infection of mature apples has not been established, that populations of endophytic bacteria have not been found in mature apples and that ephithytic bacteria populations are very rare, we need to address at this stage only the two last steps of the pathway for fire blight transmission: (a) the survival of the bacteria through commercial handling, storage and transportation; and (b) the existence of a vector permitting the contamination of a host plant in Japan by the imported apple.

8.143 We are mindful of the indirect pathways suggested by Japan. However, with the exception of the contamination by blighted apples of crates subsequently re-used in Japan, we consider that they are all dependent on the existence of a vector allowing the contamination of a host plant by an imported apple once in Japan. With respect to indirect contamination by infested or infected cargo crates, we consider that the evidence before us does not support the opinion that they could operate as a vector of transmission. On the contrary, the evidence shows that *E. amylovora* is not likely to survive on crates. [295]

---

[294] Annex 3, paras. 355, 356, 357, 358.
[295] Paras. 6.26, 6.32-6.35, 6.166-6.169, Annex 3, Dr Smith, para. 241.

(b)   Mature, Symptomless Apple Fruit

8.144 The United States argues that the scientific literature reveals that there is no evidence that mature, symptomless apple fruit ever transmitted fire blight disease, i.e. provided inoculum for an outbreak of fire blight.[296] The risk is, according to the authors, "negligible", "unlikely", "very remote", "insignificant", "extremely low" or "extremely unlikely". The United States considers that by describing the risk of transmission as "negligible" rather than "zero", the scientific reports merely reflected "the uncertainty that theoretically always remains [that an event may occur] since science can never provide absolute certainty" that an event may never occur.[297] Both the panel and the Appellate Body in *EC – Hormones* concluded that theoretical uncertainty is not the kind of risk which a risk assessment and, therefore, an SPS measure, is to address.[298]

8.145 The United States argues that it is not established that the four instances identified of trans-oceanic dissemination of fire blight were attributable to apple fruit.[299] Indeed, in relation to one of these, it disputes that it even constitutes a case of trans-oceanic dissemination.

8.146 Japan argues that there is no ecological study available on the possible dissemination of fire blight via apple fruit. Japan argues that, as a matter of common sense, it could be envisaged that *E. amylovora* could be transmitted to nearby host plants, either by way of rain, wind, insects, etc. Once such fruit was introduced into Japan, the bacteria would be exposed to its environment at all the stages of distribution, storage, consumption and disposal of the fruit, causing a real risk of dissemination.[300] Japan adds that there is no scientific evidence documenting trans-oceanic dissemination. The absence of evidence attributing the cause to apple fruit does not demonstrate that the bacteria was transmitted only via budwood or nursery stock. This indirect or circumstantial evidence, together with van der Zwet *et al.* (1990), suggests a risk that endophytic *E. amylovora* in fruit could survive trans-oceanic shipment and later cause fire blight in foreign destinations.

8.147 In light of the elements before us in these proceedings, we conclude that there is scientific evidence suggesting that epiphytic bacteria could be found on mature, symptomless apples. However, the number of apples contaminated with epiphytic bacteria in severely blighted orchards has been found to represent a very small percentage[301] and it is not clear whether this form of bacteria could actually transmit the disease to a host, in other words, whether the successive steps of the pathway could be completed.[302] In fact, Dr Hale and others reported that large-scale experiments to cause infection via surface and calyx-infested

---

[296] Exhibits USA-4; USA-5; USA-28; USA-42.
[297] The United States refers to the Appellate Body Report in *EC – Hormones (United States)*, para. 186.
[298] Appellate Body Report in *EC - Hormones (United States)*, para. 186; Panel Report in *EC - Hormones*, paras. 8.152-8.153.
[299] Paras. 4.68-4.72.
[300] Exhibit JPN-14.
[301] Annex 3, Dr Hale, para. 202.
[302] Paras. 6.69-6.71.

fruits had all been unsuccessful.[303] We note in this respect that in its risk assessment under Article 5.1, Japan itself failed to clearly identify transmission pathways for apples.[304]

8.148   Japan also insists on the resilience of the bacteria and its capacity for rapid reproduction. However, the experts consulted by the Panel have expressed doubt on this matter and contested the notion that the bacteria is actually that resistant.[305] *E. amylovora* does not seem to be capable of surviving the competition with other bacteria involved in the apple decomposition process.[306]

8.149   Drs Geider, Hale, Hayward and Smith categorically stated that there was no evidence to suggest that mature apple fruit had ever been the means of introduction (entry, establishment and spread) of fire blight into an area free of the disease.[307] The experts further agreed that the historic and scientific evidence suggested that the likelihood of fruit being a pathway for introduction of fire blight was negligible.[308] Dr Hayward indicated that the standard scientific definition of "negligible" was a likelihood of between zero and one in one million.[309] In Dr Smith's view, "not only was there no evidence that fruits had ever introduced fire blight to an area, but there was also no necessity to invoke such an improbable pathway since there were much more probable alternatives".[310] Dr Geider explained "new establishment of the disease by other than sequential distribution was so rare that it was not possible to conduct ecological studies".[311]

8.150   We also note the comment of Dr Geider that in his view, the highest risk of fire blight contamination is from travellers to Japan bringing in contaminated plants or fruits which are not likely to be detected by phytosanitary controls.[312]

8.151   We note, however, that Dr Geider has expressed the view that apples should not be exported if they were picked from a fire blighted orchard, so as to avoid the probably very low risk of accidental contamination.[313] He added that it was not advisable for phytosanitary reasons to export apples picked in orchards with severe fire blight, although such apples might be harmless as regards disease distribution.[314]

8.152   We also note that many factors can interfere in the transmission process described by Japan, and we are mindful that, as recalled by the experts, it may be

---

[303]   Annex 3, Dr Hale, para. 238; paras. 364-381; see also para. 6.101, Exhibits JPN-8 and JPN-29.
[304]   See section F.2 below.
[305]   Paras. 6.36, 6.108-6.111, 6.124-6.127.
[306]   Paras. 6.71, 6.109-6.111.
[307]   Paras. 6.20-6.23.
[308]   Paras. 6.37-6.40, also Annex 3, paras. 382-385.
[309]   Annex 3, para. 332.
[310]   Para. 6.31. The most probable route identified by the experts was the entry of infected planting materials.
[311]   Para. 6.61.
[312]   Annex 3, paras. 263, 398 and 431.
[313]   Para. 6.42.
[314]   Para. .6.112.

very difficult to experimentally replicate all possible pathways and combinations of circumstances and thus exclude categorically all possibilities of transmission.

8.153 We conclude from these elements that the scientific evidence presented to the Panel show that, with respect to mature, symptomless apple fruits, the risk that the transmission pathway be completed is "negligible". Nevertheless, the experts consulted by the Panel, while firmly considering that transmission by mature apple fruit is unlikely, suggested, *inter alia*, that apples from severely blighted orchards (the only documented situation of relatively heavy infestation of mature apples) not be exported.

> (c) Apples Other than "mature, symptomless apple fruit"
>
> (i) Capacity of Infected Apple Fruit to Serve as Pathway

8.154 We have already concluded above that the risk that mature, symptomless apple fruit be a vector for the entry, establishment or spread of fire blight within Japan is negligible, even if infested with epiphytic *E. amylovora*. We understand Japan's argumentation to imply that an infected apple could serve as a vector for the entry, establishment or spread of fire blight within Japan. We note that the United States did not claim that infected apples would not act as a pathway. As we have mentioned above, the US position in this case is that it exports only mature, symptomless apple fruit to Japan. Even though the United States did not submit evidence regarding transmission of fire blight through immature apple fruit, it argues that the pathway is unlikely to be completed. Having regard to the arguments of the parties, it is necessary to determine, even before we proceed to address the possibility of an error or illegal action, whether there is a more than theoretical possibility that infected apple fruit could be a vector for the introduction of fire blight into Japan.

8.155 According to the experts, the primary condition for transmission of fire blight is heavy contamination, either on the surface[315], or internally, in order for the bacteria to survive through all the various steps in a sufficiently large number to be capable of later contaminating a host plant or fruit. However, this does not mean that large numbers of bacteria are necessary to contaminate a host plant.[316]

8.156 The information before the Panel relates essentially to mature apples. Immature apples are hardly ever used in scientific experiments. We have noted that most of the obstacles to the survival of the bacteria and, later, the contamination of a host plant referred to by the experts relate to the progressive disappearance of bacteria capable of reproducing and contaminating a host plant (lengthy storage in cold but humid conditions[317], handling, limited capacity of *E. amylovora* to compete in a hostile bacterial environment, such as in decaying fruit or unsterilized soil). We recall, however, the prudence expressed by the

---

[315] Dr Geider, para. 6.68, Dr Hale, para. 6.69, Dr Smith, para. 6.71.
[316] Dr Geider, Annex 3, para. 235.
[317] Annex 3, paras. 208-216.

experts regarding the exportation of apples harvested in blighted orchards. Under these circumstances, if survival of epiphytic bacteria on mature apples throughout their commercial handling, transportation and storage cannot be totally excluded, *a fortiori*, survival in an *infected*, immature apple of most probably much larger quantities of bacteria is possible too. We note in this respect the comment of Dr Smith that "a conceivable short-cut [to contamination through epiphytic populations harboured by mature, symptomless apples] might occur if fruits became internally infected and these fruits were not detected. If this ever happened (which is debatable), then there was a stronger possibility that viable bacteria remained in the fruit during storage and shipping".

8.157 We therefore conclude that infected apples are capable of harbouring populations of bacteria which could survive through the various stages of commercial handling, storage and transportation.

(ii)   Error of Handling and Illegal Action

8.158 Japan further argues that the risk of accidental contamination or erroneous grading is very real, and cites as an example the recent report of codling moth being found in a shipment of US apples to Chinese Taipei.[318]

8.159 The United States argues that fruit for export are subject to multiple human and machine-based examinations, which along with the strict grading requirements it applies, make it extremely unlikely that immature fruit would be exported. Furthermore, the United States contends that Japan's current measures do not counter the "unestablished and hypothetical" risk of accidental or intentional shipment of immature, infected fruit.[319]

8.160 We recall that the Appellate Body in *EC – Hormones* deemed consideration of the risk of error of handling or of illegal action legitimate in the SPS context. [320] We note that in this case too, the experts have admitted the possibility of an error of handling. The Panel recalls the comments by Dr Smith that:

> "… people often suppose that inspection is efficient, 100 per cent efficient even, at a given moment. Sometimes, in special cases, it is. There are some pests which you can be certain to find when you examine an infested item, but this is exceptional. In plant quarantine, in general terms, whether you are inspecting trees in an orchard or fruits in a crate or plants being shipped you cannot be 100 per cent certain by inspection that the unit you are inspecting is healthy. So you automatically in the system have a certain tolerance and run a certain risk of some infected plants. The only way you can improve your chances is to look at more plants so basically you have to select a sampling system which gives you a certain level of security. This is what is inherent in the idea of

---

[318]   Para. 4.191.
[319]   Paras. 4.188-4.190, 4.192-4.193.
[320]   Appellate Body Report in *EC – Hormones*, para. 205.

managed risk which I mentioned earlier yesterday. Managed risk implies that whatever you do, there is a small risk of missing what you are looking for. You recognize that what you are doing is not 100 per cent efficient but you have to do a trade-off between practicality and cost on the one hand and the risk which you are running on the other."[321]

Furthermore, Dr Smith stated that:

" ... there will be a certain small risk that, if such infected fruit were present, they will not be detected but will in some way pass through the system."[322]

Moreover, Dr Geider considered that surface contamination could not be excluded and might be caused naturally by insects but also by handling during or post harvest.[323] On the other hand, the Panel recalled the view of Dr Geider that the highest risk of fire blight contamination was from travellers to Japan bringing in contaminated plants or fruits.[324]

8.161 We therefore conclude that errors of handling or illegal actions are risks that may be, in principle, legitimately considered by Japan. These risks have been acknowledged by the experts, even though they consider them to be "small" or "debatable".[325]

8.162 We now need to determine whether one or more infested or infected apple fruit entering Japanese territory could actually transmit fire blight to a host plant, i.e. complete the pathway.

(d) Risk of Completion of the Pathway

8.163 It is our understanding that epiphytic bacteria could apparently survive commercial handling, storage and transport in the calyx, but their number would be reduced by commercial storage that combines cool temperatures and high humidity to avoid dessication.[326] In some circumstances, bacteria will apparently no longer be discernible.[327] According to Dr Smith, there is a stronger possibility that viable bacteria remained in the fruit during storage or shipping if the fruit was internally infected.[328] Survival of an epiphytic population of *E. amylovora* seems to depend also on the quantity of bacteria in the calyx. The chance of retrieving bacteria after commercial storage depends on the quantity that existed originally. The experts mentioned in this respect that experiments use artificial inoculation of large quantities of bacteria.[329]

---

[321] Annex 3, para. 303.
[322] Annex 3, para. 266. See also para. 327.
[323] Para. 6.15.
[324] Annex 3, paras. 263, 398 and 431.
[325] Annex 3, Dr Smith, para. 266; and para. 6.71.
[326] Annex 3, paras. 208-216. Diminution in the number of bacteria is less in cold but dry conditions.
[327] Annex 3, Drs Hale, Hayward, Annex 3, paras. 209, 212.
[328] Para. 6.71.
[329] Annex 3, Drs Hale, Geider, Annex 3, paras. 211, 215.

8.164 This seems to imply that the likelihood that a naturally infested apple will contain a population capable of transmitting fire blight when it reaches Japan is apparently limited, even though survival is not excluded.[330] The risk seems to be more important in the case of infected apples.

8.165 The second point to address is the existence of a vector to transmit the bacteria to a host plant. The parties have addressed the situation where the fruit would be released as juice or discarded. They have also addressed contamination though rain splashes, insects or birds.

8.166 We note that experiments trying to reproduce the conditions applicable to discarded apples have not led to any visible contamination,[331] even when ooze was reported to exist. The experts themselves listed a number of cumulative conditions for a successful completion of the pathway.[332] While the experts agreed that short distance contamination was possible through rain splash or bees, this essentially related to contamination at the flowering stage, not to contamination from apple fruit. Contamination by birds was not established.[333] In light of these conditions, the experts considered the completion of the pathway to be unlikely.

8.167 We note in this respect that Japan did not submit sufficient scientific evidence in support of its allegation that the last step of the pathway had been completed or was likely to be completed. The evidence submitted by Japan was essentially circumstantial or deemed unconvincing by the experts.

8.168 We therefore conclude, on the basis of the evidence submitted to the Panel, that it has not been established with sufficient scientific evidence that the last stage of the pathway (i.e. the transmission of fire blight to a host plant) would likely be completed.

6.   Intermediate Conclusion

8.169 On the basis of the above, we note, in light of the elements placed before us by the parties, as well as in light of the comments of the experts appointed by the Panel, that the scientific evidence suggests a negligible risk of possible transmission of fire blight through apple fruit.

8.170 In making our assessment, we consider that the quality and quantity of scientific evidence at issue is relevant. We note in this respect that, although we did not exclude the relevance *a priori* of indirect evidence, there appears to be, in this instance, a significant amount of direct evidence, including through extensive trade in apples to blight free areas, suggesting that such contamination is unlikely. By contrast, scientific evidence, direct or indirect, to suggest the possibility of contamination in the various scenarios envisaged above is

---

[330] Annex 3, Dr Hale, para. 211.
[331] Dr Hale, para. 6.69.
[332] Dr Hayward, para. 6.70, Dr Smith, para. 6.71.
[333] Annex 3, Dr Smith, para. 241 and Dr Geider, para. 263.

significantly more limited. The elements submitted by Japan are in fact largely hypothetical or circumstantial.[334]

8.171 In particular, the following points can be highlighted:

(a)   If infection or infestation of immature apple fruit is not contested, infection of mature, symptomless apples has not been established;

(b)   the possible presence of endophytic bacteria in mature, symptomless apples is not generally established;

(c)   the presence of epiphytic bacteria in mature, symptomless apples is considered to be extremely rare;

(d)   assuming that either of the situations of infection or infestation listed above would arise, the entry, establishment or spread of the disease as a result of the presence of these bacteria in or on apple fruit would require the completion of an additional sequence of events which is deemed unlikely, and which has not even been experimentally established to date.

8.172   We further recall the opinion of the experts that due to the development of new scientific research tools, in particular DNA-based methods, they were more confident than ever before that there was only a negligible chance of fire blight being transmitted through apple fruit.[335]

8.173 Nonetheless, we note that even if the scientific evidence before us demonstrates that apple fruit is highly unlikely to be a pathway for the entry, establishment and spread of fire blight within Japan, it does suggest that some slight risk of contamination cannot be totally excluded. The experts all categorized this risk as "negligible".[336] Dr Smith observed that "from a scientific position, the logical conclusion of saying that there is an absolutely negligible risk of movement of fire blight with fruits is in fact a completely unrestricted trade".[337] However, none of the experts were comfortable with the notion of eliminating "in one step" all phytosanitary controls, taking into account Japan's island environment and climate.[338]

8.174 Furthermore, we note that Japan is concerned as well with the risk that something other than mature, symptomless apples may actually be imported. The latter risk would seem to arise primarily as a result of human or technical error, or illegal actions. Responding to a question from Japan regarding "uncontrollable risks based on real world experience" such as the finding of codling moth in US apples exported to Chinese Taipei, Dr Smith replied "... when the phytosanitary system is changed it should be changed under circumstances that retain some degree of control on what is happening and not in a single step that removes control altogether".[339]

---

[334]   Exhibit JPN-40.
[335]   Annex 3, para. 342; Dr Smith, para. 343.
[336]   Annex 3, paras. 382-386.
[337]   Annex 3, para. 419.
[338]   Annex 3, paras. 386, 389, 409, 411, 413, 414, 419, 423, 424, 426 and 429.
[339]   Annex 3, para. 423.

8.175 We do not agree with the United States that the scientific prudence displayed by the experts should be completely assimilated to a "theoretical risk" within the meaning given to that terms by the Appellate Body in *EC – Hormones*. On the other hand, we can only note that Japan did not submit "sufficient scientific evidence" in support of its allegation that the pathway could be completed.

8.176 On the basis of the information made available to the Panel, we conclude that there is not sufficient scientific evidence that apple fruit are likely to serve as a pathway for the entry, establishment or spread of fire blight within Japan.

7. *Conformity of the Phytosanitary Measure at Issue with Article 2.2 of the SPS Agreement*

(a) Absence of a "rational relationship" between the Scientific Evidence Available and the Measure at Issue

8.177 We recall that the claim of the United States under Article 2.2 is that the phytosanitary measure at issue is maintained "without sufficient scientific evidence" We also recall that the United States argues that *none of the requirements* contained in the measure has a basis in science.

8.178 We recall the position of Japan that each individual requirement contained in the phytosanitary measure at issue is essential to prevent the risks of entry, establishment or spread of fire blight within Japan *and* that all these requirements are applied cumulatively, and not alternatively, by Japan to apple fruit imported from the United States.

8.179 In paragraph 8.20 above, we concluded that we should consider the requirements identified by the United States together as the phytosanitary measure at issue in this dispute. Our finding of whether the phytosanitary measure at issue is not maintained without sufficient scientific evidence pursuant to Article 2.2 should, consequently, relate to the measure as a whole, not to individual requirements thereof, even though, as acknowledged by the Panel, each of these elements may be considered to individually constitute a phytosanitary measure within the meaning of paragraph 1 of Annex A to the *SPS Agreement*.

8.180 As mentioned in paragraphs 8.101-8.103, above, a *rational or objective relationship* is required between the phytosanitary measure at issue applied by Japan and the relevant scientific evidence. Such a rational or objective relationship is to be determined on a case-by-case basis and depends on the particular circumstances of the case, including the characteristics of the measure at issue and the quality and quantity of the scientific evidence.[340] We understand this requirement to mean that a measure as a whole should be considered to be

---

[340] Appellate Body Report in *Japan – Agricultural Products II*, para. 84.

maintained "without sufficient scientific evidence" if one or more of its elements are not justified by the relevant scientific evidence addressing the risk at issue.

8.181 In paragraph 8.176 above, we concluded, on the basis of the elements before us, that there was *not sufficient scientific evidence* to support the view that apples are likely to serve as a pathway for the entry, establishment or spread of fire blight within Japan. Given the negligible risk identified on the basis of the scientific evidence and the nature of the elements composing the phytosanitary measure at issue, the measure on the face of it is disproportionate to that risk.

8.182 More particularly, having regard to the arguments of the parties and the opinions of the experts, we have found that the following requirements are instances of elements of the measure at issue which are most obviously "maintained without sufficient scientific evidence", either as such or when applied in cumulation with others, taking into consideration the risks to be addressed:

(a)   The prohibition of imported apples from any orchard (whether or not it is free of fire blight) should fire blight be detected within a 500-meter buffer zone surrounding such orchard; and

(b)   the requirement that export orchards be inspected at least three times yearly (at blossom, fruitlet, and harvest stages) for the presence of fire blight for purposes of applying the above-mentioned prohibitions.[341]

(i)   The Prohibition of Imported Apples from any Orchard (whether or not it is free of fire blight) Should Fire Blight be Detected within a 500-Meter Buffer Zone Surrounding Such Orchard

8.183 The United States argues that since mature, symptomless apples are not a pathway for the introduction of fire blight, even if picked from a highly infected tree, buffer zones are not relevant. According to the United States, the EPPO requirements on which Japan relies to justify the obligation to set up a 500-meter buffer zone around orchards are part of an eradication programme, not a protection against transmission through imported fruits.

8.184 Japan argues that the practice of buffer zones is recognized by the IPPC Requirements for the Establishment of Pest-Free Places of Production and Pest Free Production Sites.[342] The 500-metre buffer zone is supported by scientific evidence that *E. amylovora* could be found at some distance from points of inoculum.[343] Furthermore, buffer zones are necessary to ensure that host plants

---

[341]   Para. 8.25.
[342]   *International Standard for Phytosanitary Measures No.10: Requirements for the Establishment of Pest Free Places of Production and Pest Free Production Sites*, FAO, Rome 1999 (Exhibit JPN-24).
[343]   Exhibit JPN-25; JPN-26, JPN-27; JPN-19.

are grown in a disease-free environment. Japan submitted a number of elements justifying in its view a 500-meter buffer zone.[344]

8.185 We have found above that there is not sufficient scientific evidence supporting the view that infested or infected apples are likely to serve as a pathway for the entry, establishment or spread of fire blight within Japan. However, even if this were not the case, we are of the opinion that the prohibition of imported apples from any orchard (whether or not it is free of fire blight) should fire blight be detected within a 500-meter buffer zone surrounding such orchard is not supported by sufficient scientific evidence.

8.186 We note that the agreed purpose of a buffer zone is to avoid the contamination of a fire blight-free orchard by bacteria carried from outside by creating a zone that will be difficult for the bacteria to cross, e.g. by removing any potential host plants from the buffer zone.[345]

8.187 We recall that the experts have noted the relevance of a buffer zone for disease eradication purposes.[346] However, measures for an eradication programme are not necessarily the same as those required to reduce the risk of fire blight transmission through imported, mature, symptomless apple fruit. In that context, we cannot assume, as Japan does, that the suggestion made in the studies of Meijneke (1979)[347] and Zeller (1987)[348] for a 500-meter *eradication countermeasure* in Europe is necessarily relevant for justifying a buffer zone to ensure that apple fruit is free of bacteria. Even if one were to rely, as proposed by Japan, on van Vaerenbergh *et al.* (1987),[349] which showed dispersion of *E. amylovora* for 250 meters in humid weather, and on the measures required by the United States against citrus canker for Unshu oranges (400-meter buffer zone), a 500-meter buffer zone for apples is still not scientifically supported.[350]

8.188 We also note that the experts have stated that buffer zones are useful to protect nursery stocks over several years. Dr Smith noted that buffer zones are more suitable for nurseries where one is looking at a situation where the nursery should be free and remain free over a period of years, since fire blight can develop rather slowly on planting material.[351] At the same time, infected nursery

[344] Japan First Submission, paras. 158-165.
[345] Annex 3, Dr Geider, para. 319. Dr Hayward quoted ISPM 5 (1999) *Glossary of Phytosanitary terms*, according to which a buffer zone was "An area in which a specified pest does not occur or occurs at a low level and is officially controlled, that either encloses or is adjacent to … a pest free area, a pest free place of production or a pest free production site, and in which phytosanitary measures are taken to prevent spread of the pest."
[346] Annex 3, paras. 314, 319 and 320.
[347] Exhibit JPN-19.
[348] Exhibit JPN-27.
[349] See para. 4.115.
[350] Dr Hale, Dr Hayward and Dr Smith concur in their assessment that the epidemiology of fire blight was different from that of many bacterial diseases such as citrus canker (Dr Hale, para. 6.139, Dr Hayward, para. 6.140, Dr Smith, para. 6.141). The experts also considered that the zone size recommended for citrus canker had no relevance for fire blight (Dr Hayward, para. 6.140; Dr Smith, para. 6.141).
[351] Annex 3, para. 320, see also para. 6.137.

stocks are known to be the most common pathway for the introduction of fire blight into regions not adjacent to infected areas.[352]

8.189 However, the experts expressed doubts as to the usefulness of a buffer-zone to protect an orchard from fire blight. Dr Hale recalled that Roberts (2002)[353] had shown conclusively that no buffer zone of any size was justified by the existing scientific data, as fruit harvested from blighted trees or adjacent to blighted trees had not harboured *E. amylovora*.[354] Dr Smith considered that, as far as fire blight is concerned:

> "the possibility that fire blight should enter an orchard during a given growing season from outside the orchard from a canker infection in which the bacteria multiplies and from that multiplication infects fruit is almost impossible. We already query the possibility that fruits can be significantly infected within the orchard so the fruits are very unlikely to be directly infected by inoculum coming from a joining orchard and if the inoculum comes into the orchard what it first has to do is establish itself, establish the disease in the orchard and from that the disease has to spread to the fruit and in the most favourable circumstances this could not happen until the following growing season. So for that reason I doubt whether a buffer zone is really necessary in the case of fire blight."[355]

8.190 Both the United States and the experts consulted by the Panel also referred to studies examining 30,900 mature, symptomless fruits harvested between 0 and 300 meters from fire blight inoculum sources which found that none of the fruits that were subsequently cool-stored had developed fire blight symptoms and none of the sliced fruit had yielded *E. amylovora*, even when harvested from trees directly adjacent to fire blight sources.[356]

8.191 We therefore conclude that, on the basis of the evidence before us, the requirement by Japan of a 500-meter buffer zone, to prevent contamination of US apple fruit with fire blight, does not bear a rational relationship to the scientific evidence available.

8.192 Even if a buffer zone were sufficiently justified scientifically to avoid the contamination of apple fruit, we also recall that it is applied cumulatively with other measures which are intended to ensure that the apple fruit is free of fire blight when exported, such as the surface treatment requirement or orchard inspections. In that context, the requirement of a buffer zone would be redundant.

---

[352] Paras. 6.28, 6.29, 6.31, 6.32, 6.41, 6.47.

[353] Exhibit USA-16.

[354] Dr Hale, paras. 6.134-6.135; Dr Hayward also refers to Roberts (2002, in press) which has obtained results that have indicated that a buffer zone of any size provides no phytosanitary security (Annex 3, para. 315).

[355] Annex 3, para. 314, see also Dr Geider, para. 319.

[356] Paras. 6.134-6.136.

(ii) The Requirement that Export Orchards be Inspected at Least Three Times Yearly (at blossom, fruitlet, and harvest stages) for the Presence of Fire Blight

8.193 The United States recalls that Japan requires that the orchards and buffer zones be inspected at least three times yearly, at the blossom, fruitlet and harvest seasons. The United States also notes that additional inspections are required following any strong storm (such as a hail storm). The United States argues that only a harvest season inspection that detected severely blighted orchards might be relevant for assessing the likelihood that there could be fire blight bacteria on the surface of mature, symptomless apples. However, the United States contends that even that inspection is unnecessary because there is no scientific evidence that mature, symptomless apple fruit can act as a pathway for the entry, establishment or spread of fire blight within Japan.

8.194 Japan argues that field inspections are necessary to ensure the efficacy of the systems approach. Inspection at the blossom stage was necessary because this was when the trees were most susceptible to infection. However, infection by *E. amylovora* was most visible at the fruitlet stage. A third inspection at the harvest stage was necessary because infection could occur after the fruitlet stage and the mechanism of invasion of *E. amylovora* inside apples was not known.

8.195 We have found above that there is not sufficient scientific evidence supporting the view that infested or infected apples are likely to serve as a pathway for the entry, establishment or spread of fire blight within Japan. However, even if this were not the case, we are of the opinion that the requirement that export orchards be inspected at least three times yearly (at blossom, fruitlet, and harvest stages) for the presence of fire blight is not supported by sufficient scientific evidence.

8.196 Whilst the experts considered that inspection was necessary for identification of the disease-free status of an orchard, all of them said that three inspections were more than what was necessary to detect whether there was significant fire blight infection.[357] Even with uninspected orchards the experts thought the risk to Japan of the entry, establishment or spread of fire blight was very low as surface *E. amylovora* was found only rarely on apples even from severely infected orchards.[358]

8.197 We therefore conclude that the requirement by Japan that US export orchards be inspected at least three times yearly (at blossom, fruitlet, and harvest stages) for the presence of fire blight does not bear a rational relationship to the scientific evidence available.

---

[357] Annex 3, paras. 268, 273-283, 303.
[358] Dr Hayward, para. 6.74; Dr Hale, paras. 6.25, 6.113, 6.139, 6.145, 6.150; see also Annex 3, Dr Smith, para. 310.

(b)   Conclusion

8.198 For the reasons mentioned above, we conclude that the phytosanitary measure at issue is clearly disproportionate to the risk identified on the basis of the scientific evidence available. In particular, some of the requirements applied by Japan as integral parts of the measure at issue are, either individually or when applied cumulatively with the other requirements of that measure, not supported by sufficient scientific evidence within the meaning of Article 2.2 of the *SPS Agreement*.

8.   *Provisional Conclusion on Article 2.2 of the SPS Agreement*

8.199 On the basis of the above, we conclude that the phytosanitary measure at issue is, as a whole, maintained "without sufficient scientific evidence" within the meaning of Article 2.2 of the *SPS Agreement*.

8.200 We note that Article 2.2 of the *SPS Agreement* provides that "Members shall ensure that any ... phytosanitary measure ... is not maintained without sufficient scientific evidence, *except as provided for in paragraph 7 of Article 5*". We recall that the panel in *Japan – Agricultural Products II*, having found that the phytosanitary at issue violated Article 2.2 but noting that the defendant was also invoking Article 5.7, concluded that it had to examine next whether that measure met the requirements in Article 5.7. The panel concluded that if the phytosanitary measure at issue met these requirements, it could not find that it violates Article 2.2.[359]

8.201 We agree with this approach and refrain from making final findings with respect to the consistency of the measure at issue with Article 2.2 until we have completed our analysis under Article 5.7.

8.202 We therefore proceed with our analysis of the applicability of Article 5.7 of the *SPS Agreement* to the phytosanitary measure at issue.

E.   *Article 5.7 of the SPS Agreement*

1.   *Summary of the Arguments of the Parties*[360]

8.203 Japan argues that should the Panel find the scientific evidence insufficient to support Japan's measure under Article 2.2, the measure could be considered to be a provisional measure in the context of Article 5.7 since the date of entry into force of the *SPS Agreement.*

8.204 The United States argues that the Panel's analysis of Japan's alternative defence under Article 5.7 can begin and end with the first requirement of that Article that the provisional measure be imposed only "[i]n cases where relevant scientific evidence is insufficient". The United States contends that Japan had not

---

[359] Panel Report in *Japan – Agricultural Products II*, para. 8.48.
[360] A detailed account of the arguments of the parties can be found in paras. 4.201-4.221 of this Report.

demonstrated that the relevant scientific evidence was insufficient. Indeed, the United States argues that there has never been scientific evidence that mature apple fruit transmitted the disease.

8.205   The United States contends that the scientific evidence predated the entry into force of Japan's fire blight measures in 1994 and continued to be the same thereafter. Thus, Japan has been acting inconsistently with its commitment under Article 2.2 not to maintain its fire blight measures without sufficient scientific evidence since the entry into force of the *SPS Agreement* in 1995.

8.206   Japan recalls that its current phytosanitary requirements were introduced on the basis of an agreement between the Governments of Japan and the United States, in order to allow importation of US apple fruit while preserving Japan's appropriate level of protection. The measures were developed on the basis of proposals from the United States. As such, Japan contends that it is unreasonable for the United States to now claim that the evidence had been insufficient from the beginning.

8.207   The United States argues that it acquiesced to the fire blight measures which Japan introduced in 1994 as preferable to an outright ban on imported apple fruit, although it had recognized that the scientific evidence did not support the restrictions imposed by Japan. The United States contends that it never accepted the consistency of these measures with Japan's WTO obligations.

8.208   Japan believes that considerable scientific evidence exists to support its measure to control the risk of fire blight in US apples. And, if the Panel were to find that this evidence was not sufficient under Article 2.2, it is nonetheless "available pertinent information" in the context of Article 5.7. Together, these pieces of evidence demonstrate that a phytosanitary measure is needed to counter the risk of dissemination of fire blight via imported US apples.

2.   Analysis of the Panel

8.209   Article 5.7 reads as follows:

> "In cases where relevant scientific evidence is insufficient, a Member may provisionally adopt sanitary or phytosanitary measures on the basis of available pertinent information, including that from the relevant international organizations as well as from sanitary or phytosanitary measures applied by other Members. In such circumstances, Members shall seek to obtain the additional information necessary for a more objective assessment of risk and review the sanitary or phytosanitary measures accordingly within a reasonable period of time."

8.210   We understand Japan to be claiming that the phytosanitary measure at issue is justified under Article 5.7 "in the alternative", should the Panel find that the measure is maintained without sufficient scientific evidence within the meaning of Article 2.2. We first note that arguing in the alternative is a well-established judicial practice and arguing a point in the alternative of another point often implies that there may be some contradictions between the two lines of argumentation if they were presented concurrently.

8.211 In this instance, we have determined above that Japan's measure is maintained without sufficient scientific evidence within the meaning of Article 2.2, which is the circumstance in which Japan invokes Article 5.7 in the alternative and claims that this provisional measure has been in place since the date of entry into force of the *SPS Agreement* in 1995.

8.212 We will therefore now consider whether the measure at issue can be justified as a provisional measure within the meaning of Article 5.7 of the *SPS Agreement*. Before doing so, however, we find it relevant to recall that the burden is on Japan, as the party invoking Article 5.7 to make a prima facie case in support of its position.

8.213 We recall that the Appellate Body in *Japan – Agricultural Products II* noted that Article 5.7 sets out four requirements which have to be met in order for a measure to be justified as a provisional measure. These requirements, cumulative in nature, are the following:

(i)   The measure is imposed in respect of a situation where "relevant scientific evidence is insufficient";

(ii)   the measure is adopted on the basis of "available pertinent information".

Pursuant to the second sentence of Article 5.7, such a provisional measure may not be maintained unless the Member which adopted the measure:

(iii)   "seek[s] to obtain the additional information necessary for a more objective assessment of risk; and

(iv)   "review[s] the ... measure accordingly within a reasonable period of time."

The Appellate Body added that "whenever *one* of these four requirements is not met, the measure at issue is inconsistent with Article 5.7".[361]

8.214 We note that we may begin our examination with either the requirements of the first sentence or of the second sentence of Article 5.7.[362] However, in the light of the arguments of the parties, we proceed to consider the first requirement under Article 5.7, first sentence, i.e. that the measure is imposed in respect of a situation where "relevant scientific evidence is insufficient".

8.215 We first note that the existence of a situation where "relevant scientific evidence is insufficient" cannot be merely presumed on the basis of the fact that

---

[361] Appellate Body Report in *Japan – Agricultural Products II*, para. 89 (emphasis in the original).

[362] In *Japan – Agricultural Products II*, the Appellate Body confirmed that the panel could begin its analysis with any one of the four requirements mentioned above. It concluded that:

"...the Panel did not err in its application of Article 5.7 by first examining whether the varietal testing requirement meets the requirements of the second sentence of Article 5.7. Having established that the requirements of the second sentence of Article 5.7 are not met, there was no need for the panel to examine the requirements of the first sentence." (Appellate Body Report in *Japan – Agricultural Products II*, para. 91).

the measure at issue has been found to be maintained "without sufficient scientific evidence" pursuant to Article 2.2. The fact that a particular measure, in this instance the set of requirements applied by Japan to the importation of US apple fruit, is found to be maintained without sufficient scientific evidence may not necessarily dispose of the separate question, under Article 5.7, of whether the situation is one where "relevant scientific evidence" is insufficient.

8.216 We recall from our discussion regarding Article 2.2 that the "situation" addressed by the measure at issue in this case is not one where the measure is imposed in respect of a situation where "relevant scientific evidence is insufficient", but where, on the contrary, a wealth of information is available. It should be noted first that Article 5.7 refers to "relevant scientific evidence" which implies that the body of material that might be considered includes not only evidence supporting Japan's position, but also evidence supporting other views. In the course of our analysis under Article 2.2 we have come across an important amount of relevant evidence, including scientific studies and reports on the risk of transmission of fire blight through apples. This information was submitted not only by the parties but also by the experts consulted by the Panel. The fact that this information may not all support Japan's opinion is in our view not pertinent in the context of this first requirement of Article 5.7. It is indisputable that a large amount of relevant scientific evidence is available. [363]

8.217 We note that Japan argues that, on certain aspects of the dissemination of the bacteria, the evidence is not sufficient. Japan argues, for instance, that there is limited evidence on what happens to *E. amylovora* inside immature apples that would ensure it was not found in mature apples. Likewise, Japan argues that not enough studies have been performed on the potential completion of contamination pathways.

8.218 We recall that the requirement concerning scientific evidence relates to the insufficiency of relevant scientific evidence regarding what the Appellate Body in *Japan – Agricultural Products II* describes as a "situation"[364] and Article 5.7 even more generally as a "case". From the use of these terms, we conclude that the term "insufficient relevant scientific evidence" is meant to refer to evidence *in general* on the phytosanitary question at issue, in this instance the risk of transmission of fire blight through apple fruit.

8.219 The current "situation", where scientific studies as well as practical experience have accumulated for the past 200 years, is clearly not the type of situation Article 5.7 was intended to address. Article 5.7 was obviously designed to be invoked in situations where little, or no, reliable evidence was available on the subject matter at issue. With regard to fire blight, not only a large quantity but a high quality of scientific evidence has been produced over the years that describes the risk of transmission of fire blight through apple fruit as

---

[363] See, for example, Annex 3, Dr Smith, para. 338:
"Well, I would certainly support Geider in his view that fire blight is a well studied disease [Annex 3, para. 336], much observed and so that there is a very large body of direct evidence concerning fire blight."
[364] Appellate Body Report in *Japan – Agricultural Products II*, para. 89.

negligible.[365] Moreover, this is evidence in which the experts have expressed strong and increasing confidence. We therefore are of the view that the first condition of the first sentence of Article 5.7 is not met.

8.220 Even if we were to accept Japan's arguments that "relevant scientific evidence" in Article 5.7 may refer to a specific aspect of a phytosanitary problem, we recall that the experts have indicated that even on the specific scientific questions raised by Japan, there is a large volume of relevant scientific evidence. This is the case regarding the absence of endophytic bacteria in mature apple fruit[366] and the risk of transmission of fire blight by apple fruit.[367] As mentioned above, the fact that it does not support Japan's views is of no relevance. Article 5.7 does not refer to evidence supporting the views of the Member wishing to impose SPS measures.

8.221 For these reasons we conclude that the present "situation" is one where there is sufficient relevant scientific evidence available, and that the first condition for invoking Article 5.7 is consequently not met.

8.222 We therefore find that, since the first requirement of the first sentence of Article 5.7 is not met, and since the requirements of Article 5.7 are cumulative, Japan has failed to establish that the phytosanitary measure at issue is a provisional measure justified under Article 5.7 of the *SPS Agreement*.

3. Final Conclusion on Article 2.2 of the SPS Agreement

8.223 In paragraph 8.199 above, we provisionally concluded that the phytosanitary measure at issue is maintained without sufficient scientific evidence, within the meaning of Article 2.2. We have found in the preceding section that the phytosanitary measure at issue was not a provisional measure maintained in accordance with the requirements of Article 5.7.

8.224 Consequently, we conclude that the United States has made a prima facie case that, by maintaining the measure at issue "without sufficient scientific evidence", Japan has violated its obligations under Article 2.2 of the *SPS Agreement*. Japan has failed to rebut that presumption.

8.225 We note in this respect that our conclusion is based on the evidence submitted by the parties and the opinions of the experts consulted by the Panel. This conclusion relates to the application of the measure at issue *as a whole*. This conclusion does not imply that no SPS measure would be compatible with Article 2.2, nor does it prejudge the question whether certain elements of the measure at issue could, individually or in combination with others, be compatible with Article 2.2.

---

[365] Annex 3, Dr Hale and Dr Smith, paras. 342 and 343.
[366] Annex 3: Dr Geider, paras. 63, 115, 355, 360; Dr Hale, paras. 356, 361; Dr Hayward, paras. 357, 362; Dr Smith, paras. 358, 363. See also paras. 6.7-6.10, 6.15-6.19.
[367] Paras. 6.20-6.25 and 6.37-6.40.

8.226 Indeed, we recall that the experts considered, *inter alia*, that it would be appropriate not to export apples from (severely) blighted orchards[368] and that they would not be comfortable with a complete and immediate removal of the phytosanitary measures imposed by Japan, given the phytosanitary situation of that Member.[369]

8.227 For the reasons mentioned in paragraph 8.4(c) above, we now proceed with an examination of the US claims regarding Japan's risk analysis.

F.   Articles 5.1 and 5.2 of the SPS Agreement

1.   Introduction

8.228 The United States submits that the measure at issue is inconsistent with Articles 5.1 and 5.2 of the *SPS Agreement*, in that it is not based on a risk assessment, as required under these provisions.

8.229 The relevant paragraphs of Article 5 read as follows:

> "1.   Members shall ensure that their sanitary or phytosanitary measures are based on an assessment, as appropriate to the circumstances, of the risks to human, animal or plant life or health, taking into account risk assessment techniques developed by the relevant international organizations.

> 2.   In the assessment of risks, Members shall take into account available scientific evidence; relevant processes and production methods; relevant inspection, sampling and testing methods; prevalence of specific diseases or pests; existence of pest- or disease-free areas; relevant ecological and environmental conditions; and quarantine and other treatment."

8.230 These provisions directly inform each other, in that paragraph 2 sheds light on the elements that are of relevance in the assessment of risks foreseen in paragraph 1. In addition, the notion of risk assessment is defined in Annex A of the *SPS Agreement*. The relevant part of paragraph 4 of Annex A reads as follows:

> "4.   *Risk assessment* – The evaluation of the likelihood of entry, establishment or spread of a pest or disease within the territory of an importing Member according to the sanitary or phytosanitary measures which might be applied, and of the associated potential biological and economic consequences; ..."

8.231 We also recall the Appellate Body's observation that Article 2.2 informs Article 5.1 and that they should "constantly be read together".[370] We will therefore examine the US claims under Article 5 paragraphs 1 and 2 in light of

---

[368] Annex 3: Dr Smith, paras 266, 411 and 429; Dr Hale, paras. 269, 410 and 414; Dr Geider, paras. 409 and 413.
[369] Annex 3: Dr Geider, paras. 409 and 424; Dr Hale, para. 410; Dr Smith, para. 419.
[370] Appellate Body Report in *EC – Hormones*, para. 180.

each other, bearing in mind also, to the extent relevant, our analysis under Article 2.2 above.

8.232 We will first turn to Article 5.1, which contains the general requirement for Members to base their measures on a risk assessment. However, because Article 5.2 imparts meaning to the general obligation contained in paragraph 1 to base measures on an "assessment ... of risks", we may also consider elements contained in Article 5.2 in the course of our analysis under Article 5.1.

8.233 As has been noted by previous panels, the general obligation reflected in Article 5.1 contains two elements:

(a)   an assessment of risks; and

(b)   that Members ensure that their SPS measures are *based on* such an assessment.

8.234 These two elements will be considered in turn.

2.   Japan's Risk Assessment

(a)   Requirements of a Risk Assessment under Article 5.1

8.235 As noted above, Article 5.1 requires an assessment "as appropriate to the circumstances, of the risks to human, animal or plant life or health, taking into account risk assessment techniques developed by the relevant international organizations". In this instance, the measure at issue is a phytosanitary measure.

8.236 Accordingly, taking into account the relevant definition of a risk assessment in Annex A paragraph 4, the risk assessment in relation to the measure at issue involves an evaluation of:

(a)   "the likelihood of entry, establishment or spread of a pest or disease within the territory of an importing Member according to the sanitary or phytosanitary measures which might be applied, and of the associated potential biological and economic consequences" (Annex A paragraph 4);

(b)   whether this risk assessment is "as appropriate to the circumstances";

(c)   whether the risk assessment takes "into account risk assessment techniques developed by the relevant international organizations".

8.237 The last two factors, in our view, pervade the entire assessment of the risk, as defined in Annex A, paragraph 4. Their consideration is therefore generally relevant to our assessment of the risk assessment itself as a whole, and we will consider them first.

(b)   A Risk Assessment "as appropriate to the circumstances"

8.238 As noted above, the measure at issue is a phytosanitary measure, where the risks are with regard to plant life and health. Neither party contends that there is any risk to human or animal health from fire blight disease, nor risk of "other damage to the territory" of Japan. An appropriate risk assessment must therefore focus on the risks related to plant life and health.

8.239 It might be observed, in this context, that the requirement that the risk assessment be "appropriate to the circumstances" has been considered to leave some flexibility for an assessment of risk "on a case by case basis, in terms of product, origin and destination, in particular country-specific situations".[371]

8.240 A relevant circumstance in this case is, in our view, the fact that Japan is considered to be fire blight-free, as well as its specific climatic conditions, which make it a potentially favourable environment for the spread of fire blight, should the disease enter the country.[372]

> (c) International Risk Assessment Techniques Developed by Relevant International Organizations

8.241 We recall that Article 5.1 requires the "risk assessment techniques developed by the relevant international organizations" to be "taken into account". We note first that this expression does not impose that a risk assessment under Article 5.1 be "based on" or "in conformity with" such risk assessment techniques. This suggests that such techniques should be considered relevant, but that a failure to respect each and every aspect of them would not necessarily, *per se*, signal that the risk assessment on which the measure is based is not in conformity with the requirements of Article 5.1. Nonetheless, reference to these risk assessment techniques can provide very useful guidance as to whether the risk assessment at issue constitutes a proper risk assessment within the meaning of Article 5.1. In particular, it can shed useful light, in this dispute, on the US argument that Japan has failed to evaluate the likelihood of entry because it failed to consider all the steps in the pathway that would lead to apple fruit being a vector for the entry and transmission of the disease.

8.242 In this instance, it is not disputed that the relevant international organization is the IPPC.[373] However, the parties have referred to two separate instruments. The United States has referred to the most recent International Standard for Phytosanitary Measures (ISPM) developed by the IPPC for Quarantine Pests, namely ISPM 11 on Pest Risk Analysis for Quarantine Pests, adopted in 2001. Japan, on the other hand, has noted that the relevant standard at the time of conduct of its own pest risk analysis was ISPM 2 on Guidelines for Pest Risk Analysis. Both of these instruments are described in more detail in section II. C. 2 above.[374]

---

[371] Report of the Panel in *Australia- Salmon*, para. 8.71.
[372] We note in this respect that these factors relate to some of the factors required to be taken into account under Article 5.2 of the *SPS Agreement*, which refers *inter alia* to "prevalence of specific diseases or pests; existence of pest- or disease-free areas; relevant ecological and environmental conditions".
[373] See para. 2.20.
[374] Paras. 2.24 ff.

8.243 With regard to the question of whether ISPM 2 or ISPM 11 should be taken into account in this case, we note that both instruments describe pest risk analysis as involving three stages: (1) the identification of a pathway that may allow the introduction and/or spread of a quarantine pest, and the identification of that pest; (2) an examination of the specific pest in light of the criteria for quarantine pest status; and, finally, (3) the determination of the appropriate phytosanitary measure. Compared to the previous guidelines, ISPM 11 sets out in more detail (and in a manner more closely resembling the definition of a risk assessment under the *SPS Agreement*), the specific steps involved in a PRA which include an assessment of the probability of introduction and spread. The assessment of the probability of introduction itself is indicated as requiring an analysis of each of the pathways for entry with which a pest might be associated.[375]

8.244 Although the 2001 ISPM provides a greater degree of detail to guide the conduct of a specific PRA, both parties agree that both build on the same framework, and that the detailed differences between them are not significant to this dispute, although for opposite reasons. In Japan's view, the Japanese PRA took into account the 1996 guidelines and did not need any review as a result of the 2001 instrument. In the US view, Japan's PRA does not meet the standard of either of the two instruments. We shall therefore not seek to analyse *a priori* the details of the differences between the two guidelines, but rather focus on the key issue of whether Japan's PRA sufficiently identifies and assesses, as suggested under both instruments, the possible pathways for the introduction and spread of fire blight through apple fruit and the likelihood/probability for their being realized.

(d)   Japan's   Risk   Assessment   in   Light   of   the Requirements under Annex A, paragraph 4 of the *SPS Agreement*

(i)   Introduction

8.245 As noted by the panel in *Australia – Salmon* and endorsed by the Appellate Body, an evaluation of the "likelihood of entry, establishment or spread of a pest or disease within the territory of an importing Member according to the sanitary or phytosanitary measures which might be applied, and of the associated potential biological and economic consequence" encompasses two distinct elements, which together constitute the relevant risk assessment in relation to phytosanitary measures: (1) an evaluation of the likelihood of entry, establishment or spread of a pest or disease within the territory of an importing Member according to the sanitary or phytosanitary measures which might be applied; and (2) an evaluation of the "potential biological and economic consequences associated with such entry or spread".[376]

---

[375] *Ibid.*
[376] Panel Report in *Australia – Salmon*, para 8.72, and Appellate Body Report in *Australia – Salmon*, para 120.

8.246 These elements will be considered in turn. First, however, we should determine the factual elements on which our assessment of Japan's risk assessment should be based. In this respect, we note that Japan has conducted two risk assessments of relevance to the entry and spread of fire blight: one in 1996, concerning various pests, including fire blight, and another in 1999 concerning specifically fire blight on apples imported from the United States (hereafter the "1999 PRA").

8.247 We note that the parties agree that the 1999 PRA is the main relevant document. Contrary to the United States, however, Japan does not agree that conformity with Article 5.1 can be also assessed in light of subsequent information. We also recall that a Member is not required to perform its own risk assessment under Article 5.1, but to base its measure on a risk assessment appropriate to the circumstances.

8.248 In this instance, Japan has conducted its own risk assessments, and the parties have particularly focused on Japan's most recent and most specific PRA, conducted in 1999. We will thus consider principally the 1999 PRA as the relevant risk assessment in this case, but we do not exclude that other elements, including subsequent information, could also be of relevance.

8.249 Having determined that these are the relevant elements to consider, we now turn to an examination of the various elements of Japan's risk assessment in order to assess whether the United States has made a prima facie case that Japan's measure is not based on a risk assessment within the meaning of Article 5.1.

8.250 The Appellate Body has clarified that, on the basis of the definition of a risk assessment contained in Annex A, paragraph 4, first sentence (which is the relevant one in this instance):

"a risk assessment within the meaning of Article 5.1 must:

(1)   *identify* the diseases whose entry, establishment or spread a Member wants to prevent within its territory, as well as the potential biological and economic consequences associated with the entry, establishment or spread of these diseases;

(2)   *evaluate the likelihood* of entry, establishment or spread of these diseases, as well as the associated potential biological and economic consequences; and

(3)   evaluate the likelihood of entry, establishment or spread of these diseases *according to the SPS measures which might be applied*."[377]

8.251 These will be considered in turn.

---

[377] Appellate Body Report in *Australia – Salmon*, para. 121. In *Japan – Agricultural Products II*, the Appellate Body endorsed the aforesaid three-pronged test. See para. 112. This test was also used by the Panel in *Australia – Salmon (Article 21.5 – Canada)*, para. 7.41.

(ii)   The Disease at Issue and the Potential Biological and Economic Consequences Associated with its Entry, Establishment or Spread

8.252 The United States does not dispute, in this instance, that Japan's risk assessment fulfils the first of the three conditions listed in paragraph 8.250, in that it has "identified fire blight as the disease whose entry, establishment, or spread Japan wants to prevent within its territory as well as potential associated biological and economic consequences".[378]

8.253 However, the United States considers that Japan has failed to meet the other requirements of a risk assessment under Article 5.1, namely the evaluation of the likelihood of entry, establishment or spread of that disease (item (iii) below); according to the SPS measures which might be applied (item (iv) below).

(iii)   The Likelihood of Entry, Establishment or Spread of the Disease

8.254 The United States argues that Japan has failed to evaluate the likelihood of entry, establishment or spread of fire blight within Japan, in particular because it has, in its view, "fail[ed] to focus on scientific evidence relating to the importation of apples, making only general statements of possibility rather than an assessment of probability of entry, establishment or spread".[379] The United States recalls in particular the Appellate Body's observation that "it is not sufficient that a risk assessment conclude that there is a possibility of entry, establishment or spread of diseases and associated biological and economic consequences" ... it "must evaluate the 'likelihood', i.e., the 'probability' of entry, establishment or spread ...".[380]

8.255 Japan responds that the US arguments are groundless, and that Japan's risk assessment "reflects available evidence and reasonably supports its current phytosanitary requirements".[381] Japan considers that the 1999 PRA had addressed not a theoretical possibility but the likelihood of the introduction and spread of fire blight through apple fruit.

8.256 We understand the United States to argue both that the risk assessment at issue lacks the required "specificity" in relation to the product at issue/the source of the risk, i.e. the importation of apples, and also that the assessment performed does not sufficiently evaluate the *likelihood* of entry, establishment or spread, as required under Article 5.1.

8.257 With regard to the specificity required of a risk assessment under Article 5.1, we note first that it has been clarified on previous occasions that the risk assessment must be specific to the disease at issue, and, where several diseases

---

[378]   US first submission, para. 66.
[379]   *Ibid.*, para. 69.
[380]   Appellate Body Report in *Australia – Salmon*, para. 123.
[381]   Japan first submission, para. 211.

are at issue, specific to each disease.[382] In this instance, the United States does not challenge the specificity of the risk assessment in relation to the disease at issue, but rather in relation to the product whose importation would lead to the introduction of the disease at issue: the United States thus argues that no evidence is presented as to the probability of entry, establishment or spread of the bacteria *through apple fruit*[383], and, in particular, the relevant paragraph entitled "Probability of Transmission via fresh apples", does not "distinguish between evidence relevant to the exported commodity from other evidence".[384] More generally, the United States notes that a proper risk analysis should have focused on the probability of US apples being infested or infected with fire blight, rather than focusing on damaged fruit, immature fruit, apple leaves, etc.[385]

8.258 Japan notes in response that the risk analysis "obviously took into account all available scientific evidence that relates not only to apple trees but mature and immature, visibly blighted and symptomless apple fruit as well – including van der Zwet *et al.* (1990)".[386]

8.259 With regard to the assessment of the "likelihood" of the entry, establishment or spread of the disease, the United States argues that there is no evidence of spread from apples in the past, and no evidence that the hypothetical pathway of spread through mature apples could be completed. The United States also argues that Japan's PRA ignores key steps in the assessment, and in this respect also has failed to evaluate the likelihood of entry, establishment and spread of the disease.

8.260 Japan contends that the 1999 PRA identified the steps in the pathway necessary for fire blight to be disseminated via mature, apparently healthy apple fruit imported from the United States.[387] Japan notes that the very objective of the assessment in the 1999 PRA was to assess US apple fruit as a potential pathway. Furthermore, while the 1999 PRA did not estimate numerical probabilities of contamination by the bacteria, the PRA had qualitatively evaluated the probability.[388]

8.261 We will first examine the relevant parts of Japan's 1999 PRA before assessing it in light of the parties' arguments.

-     Japan's 1999 PRA

8.262 Examining Japan's 1999 PRA, we first note that it refers in its subtitle to "Fresh apples produced in the United States of America". We note that the structure of this document is to focus first on a description of the disease, followed by a general pest risk analysis for *E. amylovora*, before addressing quarantine measures for "US fresh apple fruit", and finally including a chapter on

---

[382] Panel report in *Australia – Salmon*, para. 8.74.
[383] US first submission para. 73.
[384] *Ibid.*, para 74.
[385] US first submission, para. 75.
[386] Japan first submission, para, 203.
[387] *Ibid.*, paras. 202-211.
[388] Japan second submission, paras. 58-67.

"Pest risk analysis for quarantine measures on *E. amylovora* for US fresh apple fruit". The initial chapter describing fire blight contains a section entitled "Probability of transmission via fresh apples". In this section, reference is made to the possibility for immature fruit to be infected through natural openings in the skin, lenticels or diseased branches. Reference is also made to a number of studies describing the isolation of *E amylovora* from apple fruit ("mature fruits harvested in severely infected orchards" (Hale *et al.* 1997), "fresh apple fruit" (van der Zwet *et al.* 1990) or "young apples") as well as reports describing the survival of *E. amylovora* on fresh mature apple fruit (McLarty, 1922).[389]

8.263 The general PRA contained in Chapter 2 begins with an analysis of the susceptibility of Japan to fire blight, were it to be introduced into the country (i.e. the presence of host plants, favourable climatic conditions, and an estimation of the probability for expansion) and on the potential impact, should this expansion occur (Section 2-2-3). A subsequent section focuses on the "Introduction potential" (Section 2-2-4). In the first part of that section, "the parts of plants which can be infected with *E. amylovora*, namely, fresh plants (including fresh fruit, flowers ...)" are identified as some of those that can introduce *E. amylovora* into Japan.[390] In this section, it thus appears that fresh fruit is considered to be a "host plant", alongside cut flowers or nursery stock. Within the same section, under the heading "Main uses of plants after importation" the different types of "plants" are referred to. With regard to fruit, it is noted that :

> "fresh fruit are used for raw food or processing and supplied through markets .... However, not all of them are distributed or consumed completely by such usages. In the course of the distribution, processing and consumption, some can be released to the natural environment as leftovers, waste or useless materials.
>
> In this way, if imported stocks and pollen are contaminated with *E. amylovora*, they become the direct cause for the occurrence of fire blight because they are directly brought into agricultural production area. When contaminated cut flowers and fresh fruit are released as juice, leftovers, waste, useless materials in the fields surrounding ranches or in a natural environment, they can be the source of the disease."[391]

8.264 The conclusions reached in light of the general PRA for *E. amylovora*, were that imported host plants should not be infected with *E. amylovora* and that "to avoid the introduction of *E. amylovora*, it must be designated as pathogen subject to importation prohibition ...".[392]

8.265 The following and final chapter of the 1999 PRA is devoted to a "Pest risk analysis for quarantine measures on *E. amylovora* for US fresh apple fruit". The introduction to this section indicates that Japan needs "to review whether or not 'plant quarantine measures against *E. amylovora* concerning US fresh apple

---

[389] Exhibit JPN-32, para 1-1, page 5.
[390] *Ibid*, para. 2-2-4-1.
[391] *Ibid*, para. 2-2-4-3.
[392] *Ibid*, para. 2-3-2.

fruit', which have been taken by Japan based on the proposal by the US government since 1994[393], are adequate as an alternative to lift the import prohibition measures against *E. amylovora*"[394] A section is then devoted to each of the measures in place, which concludes that they provide a level of protection equivalent to the import ban.

-    Assessment of Japan's Risk Assessment

Specificity of the PRA

8.266 We first turn to the US argument that the 1999 PRA fails to focus specifically on the product at issue, namely fresh apple fruit.

8.267 We first note in this respect that it has been recognized, in prior cases, that a risk assessment conducted under Article 5.1 of the *SPS Agreement* should be sufficiently specific to the risk at issue. In particular, we recall the findings of the panel in *EC - Hormones*, as upheld by the Appellate Body, that studies relating to the carcinogenicity of certain hormones in general, without an evaluation of the specific potential for carcinogenic effects arising from the presence of hormones in food or meat products, were insufficient to support the measure at issue.

8.268 In this instance, the United States notes that Japan's PRA refers to a number of possible hosts of fire blight (such as cut flowers, shoots, plants), rather than focusing on apples. We first note in this respect that Japan's PRA, which in part describes in general terms the risk of entry, establishment or spread of the disease through various possible hosts, including but not exclusively apple fruit, often either addresses these other hosts or includes the consideration of apple fruit within a broader category, as one of the possible "plant hosts", without specifically distinguishing it from other potential sources of infection, for the purposes of evaluating the general likelihood of entry, establishment and spread of the disease. Japan states that while the objective of the 1999 PRA was to assess US fruit, all potential pathways were considered.

8.269 While we do not exclude that a consideration of other possible hosts of the disease may be relevant in a risk assessment directed at the evaluation of the likelihood of entry, establishment and spread through apple fruit, it could be expected that the possible relevance of these other hosts/factors to contamination through apple fruit would be explained, and that conclusions relating to the likelihood of entry, establishment or spread specifically through apple fruit would be clearly identified, since the announced objective of the assessment is precisely to evaluate the risk in relation to that particular product.

8.270 In this respect, we note in particular that Chapter 2 of the 1999 PRA, which contains the general pest risk analysis concerning *E. amylovora*, includes

---

[393] The United States, however, argues that it accepted the fire blight measures imposed by Japan only reluctantly, recognizing that the scientific evidence did not support the restrictions. See para. 4.29 above.
[394] Exhibit JPN-32, para. 3-1.

very general conclusions that "*E. amylovora* is risk Grade A (extremely high)". This conclusion, however, is based on an overall assessment of possible modes of contamination, where apple fruit is only one of the possible hosts/vectors considered. As cited above, only one paragraph in that chapter specifically addresses fresh fruit, simply noting that not all fruit are distributed or consumed totally and "in the course of distribution, processing and consumption, some can be released to the natural environment as leftovers, waste or useless materials".[395] Thus, although the risk assessment is intended to be conducted, as indicated by its very title, in relation to the importation of US fresh apple fruit, the main portion of the PRA is conducted on the basis of a general assessment of possibilities of introduction of fire blight into Japan, through a variety of hosts, including - but not exclusively - apple fruit.

8.271 There is no clear indication in the document as how the other possible vectors might be of relevance to an assessment of the likelihood of entry, establishment or spread through apple fruit specifically. Indeed, the conclusion of the PRA does not purport to relate exclusively to the introduction of the disease through apple fruit, but rather more generally, apparently, through any susceptible host/vector. The scientific evidence submitted by both parties leaves no doubt that the risk of introduction and spread of the disease varies considerably according to the host plant, with nursery stock and budding material identified as known sources for the spread of fire blight in some cases. We therefore conclude that, in this respect, the 1999 PRA is not sufficiently specific to the matter at issue to constitute a proper risk assessment under Article 5.1 of the *SPS Agreement*.

Evaluation of likelihood (possibilities vs. probabilities)

8.272 Turning now to the actual evaluation of "likelihood" of entry, or spread of fire blight through the importation of apple fruit, as reflected in the 1999 PRA, we recall the US argument that Japan's risk assessment falls short of the requirements of Article 5.1 in that it identifies mere "possibilities" rather than "probabilities" of entry, establishment or spread, as required under Article 5.1.

8.273 We recall in this respect that Annex A, paragraph 4, requires a risk assessment, with respect to phytosanitary measures, to contain an evaluation of the "likelihood" of entry, establishment or spread of the disease. As has been clarified by the Appellate Body, this evaluation of likelihood involves more than a mere identification of "possibilities". It requires an assessment of *probability* of entry, and, in the words of the Appellate Body, "probability implies a higher degree or a "threshold of potentiality or possibility".[396] It is also understood, however, that such probability need not be expressed in quantitative terms, but may be expressed in qualitative terms.

8.274 Japan has used in the context of its PRA, a general "scale" of grades in order to rank the risks at issue, ranging from A (extremely high) to D (extremely

---

[395] *Ibid*, para 2-2-4-3.
[396] Appellate Body Report in *EC Hormones*, para 184.

low). In this instance, the general PRA on *E. amylovora* leads, as already mentioned, to an overall ranking for the "total assessment of *E. amylovora*" of a "Grade A (extremely high)" risk. However, as noted above, that conclusion does not appear to specifically evaluate the likelihood of entry, establishment or spread through apple fruit, which is at issue here. In those parts of the PRA that do relate directly to the probability of entry specifically through apple fruit, the report does not suggest any precise evaluation of the "degree of potentiality" or probability for the occurrence of the event. Thus, in a section entitled "Probability of transmission via fresh apples", it is noted that "immature apples *can* be infected ..." (emphasis added), and that a number of studies report the presence of *E. amylovora* in association with apple fruit. In conclusion, it is noted that:

> "Those reports, therefore, *suggest the probability* of transmission via fresh apple fruit. Although several reports have described that the *possibility* of transmission of *E. amylovora* by fresh apple fruit can be denied or ignored, these reports have only mentioned that 'symptomless mature fruit' (McLarty 1922, Dueck 1974) 'apparently healthy mature fruit' (Roberts et al. 1989), and 'the fruit harvested in fire blight symptomless orchards' (van der Zwet *et al.* 1990) are safe."[397] (emphasis added)

8.275 Although the term "probability" is used here to describe the conclusion to be drawn from the cited studies[398], it does not seem to reflect any particular assessment of the degree of likelihood of the event. Indeed, the reference to "probability" is even made in a somewhat hypothetical mode (probability is "suggested"). Similarly, the following paragraph appears to confirm that the cited studies lead to the identification of a possibility of apple fruit acting as a possible pathway for the entry of fire blight, but it does not indicate any quantitative or qualitative assessment of the probability of this occurring:

> "As mentioned above, the mature apple fruit harvested in fire blight occurring orchards *can* carry *E. amylovora* and, in addition, the mature fruit not carrying *E. amylovora can* be contaminated by harvesting operation, etc., in the orchard where there are sources. In particular, when scarred fruit is infected with *E. amylovora* and becomes rotten, it *can* be considered to exude bacterial ooze. Such fruit *can* be the source of transmission after being imported."[399] (emphasis added)

8.276 These terms clearly point to the identification of a possibility of entry, establishment and spread, but do not, in our view, amount to an evaluation of the likelihood of entry within the meaning of Article 5.1 of the *SPS Agreement*, in that they do not assess the probability of such entry beyond the identification of the potential for entry, establishment or spread. In particular, they do not address

---

[397] Exhibit JPN-32, para. 1-1, p.7.
[398] Note this is translated from the Japanese language. The text used here is the version provided by Japan.
[399] Exhibit JPN-32, para 1-1.

the likelihood of an apple becoming contaminated by the harvesting operation, nor the likelihood that a damaged fruit will be included in the export shipment, nor the likelihood that such a fruit, were it to be shipped, would become rotten.

8.277 Another section of Japan's PRA purports to consider the probability of introduction through "normal transport method". Fruit is mentioned as one of the potential sources of entry along with other "host plants" through "normal transport method", so that if the importation of these plants is not prohibited, "it can easily increase the probability of introduction of *E. amylovora* into Japan together with host plants".[400] Finally, the PRA identifies the possibility for fruit to be disposed of, or discarded in, possible host areas and concludes that it thus "can" be the source of contamination after importation. These elements, which are dispersed throughout the PRA along with consideration of other possible vectors for the entry, establishment or spread of fire blight within Japan, provide some evaluation of various possible steps for the entry, establishment and spread of fire blight though the importation of apple fruit.

8.278 However, these appear to be intertwined with other possible vectors, which have otherwise been identified much more clearly as potential sources of contamination (such as nursery stock or plants), and it is difficult to discern, from the structure and contents of the PRA, an effort to evaluate specifically the likelihood of entry, establishment or spread from the importation of apple fruit. Furthermore, to the extent that it might be considered to identify the potential for each of the relevant steps to be completed, the PRA fails, as noted above, to provide more than an indication of a potential for entry, establishment or spread, and does not assess the probability for such events to occur, as required under Article 5.1.

8.279 We further recall the inadequacies in the 1999 PRA identified by Dr Hale and Dr Smith. According to Dr Hale, the following key steps had been overlooked for the probability of entry:

- **identification of the relevant pathways;**
- **probability of fire blight being associated with the pathway of origin;**
- **probability of survival during transport and storage;**
- **probability of fire blight surviving existing pest management procedures; and**
- **probability of transfer of fire blight to suitable host.**[401]

8.280 In light of the above, we conclude that Japan's PRA does not evaluate the likelihood of entry, establishment or spread of fire blight through the importation of apple fruit, as foreseen in Article 5.1 and Annex A, paragraph 4, of the *SPS Agreement*.

---

[400] Section 2-2-4-1 of the 1999 PRA.
[401] Dr Hale, para. 6.177. See also Dr Smith, para. 6.181-6.181.

(iv)   According to the SPS Measures which Might Be Applied

8.281 As noted above, Article 5.1 and Annex A, paragraph 4 of the *SPS Agreement* require measures to be based on an assessment of risks "according to the SPS measure which might be applied". In this instance, the United States contends that Japan's risk assessment does not comply with this condition because, although it clearly identifies some SPS measures that might apply to US apples, it does not "in any substantial way, evaluate their relative effectiveness in reducing the overall disease risk" as required under Article 5.1.[402] The United States also notes that Japan failed to consider any alternative measures to those that it was already applying, and in particular did not consider some alternative measures proposed by the United States in 1997.

8.282 Japan notes that the current measures (in particular the limitation of imports of apples from the states of Oregon and Washington) were established on the basis of a proposal by the United States itself. It also notes that the "mature, symptomless" criteria now mentioned by the United States was not proposed at any stage prior to the consultations held in April 2002.

8.283 With regard to the requirement that the evaluation be conducted "according to the sanitary or phytosanitary measures which might be applied", we note that this expression refers to the measures *which might* be applied, not merely to the measures which *are being* applied. This suggests to us that it cannot be assumed that it would be sufficient, under this provision, to simply consider the particular measures that are already in place, to the exclusion of other possible alternatives.

8.284 In this instance, it is apparent from the introductory paragraph of the last chapter of Japan's PRA that it has aimed specifically to assess "whether or not 'plant quarantine measures against *E. amylovora* concerning US fresh apple fruit', which have been taken by Japan based on the proposal by the US government since 1994, are adequate".[403]

8.285 We note, in this respect, that Japan does not appear to have considered any alternative measures other than these existing measures. We recall that the requirement that the risk assessment be "appropriate to the circumstances", has been considered to leave some flexibility for an assessment of risk, "on a case to case basis, in terms of product, origin and destination, in particular country specific situations".[404] Arguably, in this instance, part of the circumstances of this particular risk assessment was the fact that the overall Japanese scheme involves an *a priori* prohibition of imports of host plants of fire blight and that this risk assessment was being conducted specifically to verify the viability of a specific set of measures, in order to lift the ban in circumstances suggested and identified by the exporting country itself. The terms of this provision, which

---

[402]   US first submission para 83, citing Appellate Body Report in *Australia – Salmon*, para. 133.

[403]   1999 PRA, Section 3-1. The United States, however, argues that it accepted the fire blight measures imposed by Japan only reluctantly, recognizing that the scientific evidence did not support the restrictions. See para. 4.29 above.

[404]   Report of the Panel in *Australia – Salmon*, para 8.71.

refers generally to the measures which "might be applied", suggest to us, however, that consideration should be given not just to those specific measures which are currently in application, but at least to a potential range of relevant measures. Japan has not, in this instance, attempted to identify any other risk-mitigating measures than those actually applied as a result of its discussions with the United States. In this respect, Japan has not, in our view, properly evaluated the likelihood of entry "according to the SPS measures that might be applied".

8.286 With regard to the actual evaluation performed by Japan in relation to those measures which it *has* identified, we recall the Appellate Body's observation in the *Australia – Salmon* case that "some" evaluation of the likelihood of entry [according to the SPS measures which might be applied] is not enough.[405] We also note that in reaching its conclusion that the Australian risk assessment did not, in that case, meet the third requirement for risk assessments of this type (i.e. an evaluation *according to the SPS measures that might be applied*), the Appellate Body highlighted the following observations of the panel with regard to the quarantine policy options considered to reduce the total risk associated with the disease of concern:

> "the ... Report does not substantively evaluate the relative risks associated with these different options. Even though the definition of risk assessment requires an "evaluation ... according to the sanitary ... measures which might be applied", the ... Report identifies such measures but does not, in any substantial way, evaluate or assess their relative effectiveness in reducing the overall disease risk."[406]

8.287 In this instance, each of the measures applied is considered and described in turn in Japan's 1999 PRA, and a brief conclusion is drawn in respect of each of them. While this analysis might be considered to provide "some" evaluation of the risk of entry, establishment or spread and its mitigation through the relevant measure, it seems to suffer from flaws in part linked to the insufficiency of the evaluation of the likelihood itself, and provides only a cursory assessment of some of the proposed measures. The evaluation "according to the measure which might be applied" is considerably less substantial in terms of consideration of the relevant scientific evidence than that found to be insufficient in the *Australia – Salmon* case.

8.288 We also note that a general conclusion is drawn that "so long as [the group of measures under consideration] are adequately obeyed, there is no possibility that fresh apples exported to Japan would be infected with or contaminated by *E. amylovora* through any of cultivation, harvest, selection of fruit, packing or transportation, and *E. amylovora* could never, of course, be introduced via those fruit".[407] However, no attempt is made to assess the "relative effectiveness" of the various individual requirements applied, and the assessment appears to be based on the assumption from the outset that all these measures

---

[405] Appellate Body Report in *Australia – Salmon*, para. 134.

[406] *Ibid*, para. 133, citing from panel report para 8.90.

[407] 1999 PRA, section 3-2-3.

would apply cumulatively. In our view, however, an assessment "according to the SPS measures that might be applied" suggests that it would not be sufficient, where a number of distinct measures are considered, to simply draw a general conclusion on their overall combined efficiency, without any analysis of their relative effectiveness and whether and why all of them in combination are required in order to reduce or eliminate the possibility of entry, establishment or spread of the disease.

8.289 We further recall the opinions of Dr Hale and Dr Smith that the 1999 PRA "appeared to prejudge the outcome of its risk assessment"[408] and that "it was principally concerned to show that each of the measures already in place was effective in some respect, and concluded that all should therefore be applied".[409] Dr Smith in particular noted that "the question of whether any single measure or combination of fewer measures, could reduce the risk to an acceptable level was not addressed".[410] He further concluded that: "the Japanese PRA had not clearly explained why all the measures it applied were needed".[411]

8.290 In light of the above, we find that Japan's 1999 PRA concerning fire blight in relation to fresh apples produced in the United States does not meet the requirements of a risk assessment within the meaning of Article 5.1, as defined in Annex A, paragraph 4, of the *SPS Agreement*.

3.   Is the Measure "based on" a Risk Assessment?

8.291 In light of our finding above that Japan's PRA does not amount to a risk assessment within the meaning of Article 5.1, we must also, as a consequence, conclude that Japan's measures are not "based on" a risk assessment. We therefore do not examine this issue further.

4.   Conclusion

8.292 In conclusion, we find that the United States has made a prima facie case that Japan has violated Article 5.1 of the *SPS Agreement*, which Japan has not rebutted. In light of this finding, we do not find it necessary to consider whether the measure at issue is also in violation of Article 5.2 of the Agreement, which identifies further specific factors that Members are required to take into account in their assessment of risks.

---

[408]   Dr Hale, para. 6.177.
[409]   Dr Smith, para. 6.180.
[410]   *Ibid.*
[411]   *Ibid.*

G. Article 5.6 of the SPS Agreement

1. Summary of the Arguments of the Parties[412]

8.293 The United States claims that Japan has acted inconsistently with Article 5.6 of the *SPS Agreement* because Japan's fire blight measures are more trade-restrictive than required to achieve Japan's appropriate level of phytosanitary protection. The United States contends that restricting importation to mature, symptomless apple fruit is an alternative measure that is reasonably available, achieves Japan's appropriate level of protection (ALOP), and is significantly less restrictive to trade than Japan's fire blight measures.

8.294 The United States contends that the fact that Japan's fire blight measures are more trade-restrictive than necessary is also evident from the range of other possible measures that could be envisaged that are less trade-restrictive and that would more than achieve Japan's appropriate level of protection. The United States identified four possible measures:

(a) Japan could require a phytosanitary certificate that the exported commodity (mature apple fruit) is free from fire blight;

(b) Japan could require that imported mature, symptomless fruits be harvested in the states of Washington or Oregon;

(c) Japan could require that imported mature, symptomless fruits be harvested at least 10 meters from a source of inoculum;

(d) Japan could require that imported mature, symptomless fruits be treated with chlorine.

8.295 The United States adds that as the scientific evidence established that apple fruit had never transmitted fire blight and that mature, symptomless fruit are not a pathway for the disease, any of these less trade-restrictive measures would more than achieve Japan's appropriate level of protection. However, for the same reason, the United States argues that, with the exception of the alternative measure in 8.294(a) above, they would also be more trade-restrictive than necessary. Hence, the United States believes that a requirement that exported US apples be mature and symptomless, including through the submission of a phytosanitary certificate, would constitute the only requirement that could be considered as necessary given the scientific evidence.

8.296 The United States argues that its grading standards and law, enforced by federal and/or state inspectors, require exported apples to be mature and symptomless. Apples exported from the United States are inspected for compliance and each fruit passes multiple human and machine-based examinations which categorically exclude immature fruit.

8.297 Japan argues that the exportation of "mature, symptomless" apple fruit to Japan would not achieve Japan's appropriate level of protection. The alternative proposed by the United States is (1) not based on scientific evidence, (2) not supported by real life experience, (3) not practical to implement, and (4) not

---

[412] A detailed account of the arguments of the parties can be found in paras. 4.181-4.200 of this Report.

scientifically sound. Japan claims that the United States has not defined exactly what "mature, symptomless" fruit would mean. Nor has the United States defined specific means to produce, select and export only such apple fruit. Consequently, Japan requests the Panel to consider the "mature, symptomless" criteria as ambiguous and easily manipulated. Japan argues that the "mature, apparently healthy" apple fruit criteria could offer security only when the mechanism by which the bacteria did not exist in such fruit was identified.

8.298 Japan believes that the risk of accidental contamination or erroneous grading is very real. As such, the United States is proposing to replace Japan's current phytosanitary requirements with something: (1) the efficacy of which is questionable; and (2) the quality of which the United States does not guarantee. On this basis, Japan argues that it would be a grave mistake to assume the US proposal would achieve Japan's appropriate level of protection or would provide security at a level comparable to that of the current requirements.

2. Analysis of the Panel

8.299 We have already found above that the phytosanitary measure at issue (i.e. Japan's measure as a whole), breaches Articles 2.2, 5.7 and 5.1 of the *SPS Agreement*. We note that, as stated by the Appellate Body in *Australia – Salmon*,

> "a panel has to address those claims on which a finding is necessary in order to enable the DSB to make sufficiently precise recommendations and rulings so as to allow for prompt compliance by a Member with those recommendations and rulings 'in order to ensure effective resolution of disputes to the benefit of all Members'."[413]

8.300 Therefore, we find it relevant to consider the merits of making a finding in relation to Article 5.6 of the *SPS Agreement*. As recalled by the Appellate Body *in United States – Wool Shirts and Blouses*, "a panel need only address those claims which *must be* addressed in order to resolve the matter at issue".[414] Therefore, we must determine whether this additional finding would be necessary for the formulation of sufficiently precise recommendations and rulings so as to allow for prompt compliance by Japan.

8.301 We note that Article 5.6 of the *SPS Agreement* provides as follows:

> "Without prejudice to paragraph 2 of Article 3, when establishing or maintaining sanitary or phytosanitary measures to achieve the appropriate level of sanitary or phytosanitary protection, Members shall ensure that such measures are not more trade-restrictive than required to achieve their appropriate level of sanitary or phytosanitary protection, taking into account technical and economic feasibility."[footnote 3]

Footnote 3 to Article 5.6 of the *SPS Agreement* reads as follows:

---

[413] Appellate Body Report in *Australia – Salmon*, para. 223, quoting Article 21.1 of the DSU.
[414] Appellate Body Report in *United States – Wool Shirts and Blouses*, p. 340.

> "For purposes of paragraph 6 of Article 5, a measure is not more trade restrictive than required unless there is another measure, reasonably available taking into account technical and economic feasibility, that achieves the appropriate level of sanitary or phytosanitary protection and is significantly less restrictive to trade."

8.302 We recall that what we are reviewing in this case – including with respect to the US claim under Article 5.6 - is the phytosanitary measure at issue *as a whole*, not certain elements of it. In particular, we are not expected to reach a conclusion as to whether some elements of that measure would individually meet the requirements of Article 5.6. Likewise, we are not mandated to find whether some alternative measure would be compatible with the *SPS Agreement* while meeting Japan's phytosanitary objectives.[415]

8.303 We have already found that the phytosanitary measure at issue is maintained without sufficient scientific evidence, in contravention of Article 2.2. In other words, this measure cannot be maintained as such by Japan. A finding under Article 5.6 would not add anything in terms of legal implications.[416] In particular, it would not automatically mean that any alternative measure that could be identified would be the only acceptable alternative to Japan's phytosanitary measure in terms of the requirements of Article 5.6. Such a finding would simply establish that Japan's phytosanitary measure *as a whole* is more trade-restrictive than required to achieve Japan's appropriate level of phytosanitary protection. In a context where it has already been established that the phytosanitary measure at issue cannot be maintained, another finding to the same effect that the measure cannot be maintained would be of no practical advantage and thus would be of no assistance to the DSB.

8.304 We therefore decide to exercise judicial economy with regard to the US claim under Article 5.6 and refrain from making any finding.

H.   Article 7 and annex b of the sps agreement

1.   Summary of the Arguments of the Parties[417]

8.305 The United States claims that Japan has acted in violation of Article 7 and Annex B, paragraphs 5 and 7 of the *SPS Agreement*, in that it has not notified changes introduced to its fire blight measures since the entry into force of the *SPS Agreement* in 1995. More specifically, the United States considers that Japan should have notified to WTO Members the changes effected through Japan's MAFF Notification No. 354, dated 10 March 1997, because it changes

---

[415] See para. 8.225.

[416] We recall in this respect that our recommendations are limited, pursuant to Article 19.1 of the DSU, to recommend that the Member concerned bring its measure into conformity with the *SPS Agreement*.

[417] A detailed account of the arguments of the parties can be found in paras. 4.222-4.223 of this Report.

Japan's fire blight restrictions and imposes a regulation not based on international standards.

8.306 The United States notes that Japan has substantively changed its fire blight measures since 1995, and has failed to notify these changes. The United States points to four distinct measures by which Japan imposes its requirements regarding fire blight measures: the Plant Protection Law No. 151, Article 7; the Plant Protection Law Enforcement Regulations, Article 9 and Annexed Table 2; the MAFF Notification No. 354; and the MAFF Detailed Rules for US Apples. The United States argues that the latter two of these measures "appear to have been amended or introduced since 1995 without being notified to WTO Members".[418]

8.307 Japan considers that, contrary to the US assertions, it did not substantively change its fire blight measures since the entry into force of the *SPS Agreement* in 1995. It further notes that it had notified that it would designate *E. amylovora* as one of the diseases that trigger import prohibition as of 1 April 1997, in accordance with the requirements of Article 7 and Annex B.[419] In Japan's view, the amendments to the notification and the Detailed Rules in 1997 were technical rephrasing of the regulations reflecting the designation of the bacterium, which did not modify in any way the phytosanitary requirements against fire blight.

8.308 In response, the United States observes that this notification "provided notice that Japan's Plant Protection Law Enforcement Regulations would be amended to designate *E. amylovora* as a pest subject to import prohibition"[420], but that in its view, a notification of changes to the Plant Protection Act could not be considered as a notification of changes to *other* fire blight measures.

2.   Assessment by the Panel

8.309 Article 7 of the *SPS Agreement* provides as follows:

> "Members shall notify changes in their sanitary or phytosanitary measures and shall provide information on their sanitary or phytosanitary measures in accordance with the provisions of Annex B."

8.310 Annex B to the *SPS Agreement* contains a number of provisions relating to transparency of SPS measures, including notifications. More specifically, paragraph 5 of Annex B foresees the notification of SPS regulations if a number of conditions are cumulatively met, i.e.:

> (a)   where a relevant international standard does not exist or the content of the proposed measure is not substantially the same as the content of an international standard, guideline or recommendation, *and*

---

[418] US first submission, para. 114.
[419] Notification contained in G/SPS/N/JPN/19.
[420] US answers to additional questions from the Panel, 28 January 2003, para. 42.

(b)   if the regulation may have a significant effect on trade of other Members.

Paragraph 7 of Annex B, which the United States also argues has been violated by Japan, provides that notifications shall be in French, Spanish or English. The Committee on SPS Measures has adopted recommended guidelines with regard to paragraphs 5 and 6 of Annex B.[421]

8.311   We understand the US claim in respect of Article 7 and Annex B to be limited to two measures only: MAFF Notification No. 354 of March 1997 and the Detailed Rules for US Apples of April 1997, replacing prior similar instruments. In the US view, the notification made by Japan in respect of its Plant Protection Law Enforcement Regulation does not "cover" these separate instruments. Japan, for its part, has indicated in response to a question from the Panel that this notification has no relationship or relevance to the measures at issue, because the change in the regulatory status of *E. amylovora* (i.e. its designation as one of the pests that automatically triggers importation prohibition of host plants) did not in any way affect the measure at issue, which was already in place.

8.312   Both parties thus seem to agree that although Japan made, in 1997, a notification through which it identified fire blight as a pest triggering import prohibition under the Plant Protection Act, this notification is not directly relevant to the measures whose notification is a issue here, i.e. MAFF Notification No. 354 and the 1997 Detailed Rules for US Apples. The question before us is therefore whether these two instruments, which are subsequent to the entry into force of the *SPS Agreement*, should have been notified under Article 7 and Annex B.

8.313   It is not disputed that the present situation is one where "an international standard, guideline or recommendation does not exist [regarding *E. amylovora*] or the content of a proposed sanitary or phytosanitary regulation is not substantially the same as the content of an international standard, guideline or recommendation". Therefore, we must determine whether the changes identified above constitute changes which are required to be notified under Article 7 because, *inter alia*, they "may have a significant effect on trade of other Members" in the context of the chapeau to Paragraph 5 of Annex B.

8.314   We consider that the most important factor in this regard is whether the change affects the conditions of market access for the product concerned, that is, would the exported product (apple fruit from the United States in this case) still be permitted to enter Japan if they complied with the prescription contained in the previous regulations.[422] If this is not the case, then we must consider whether the change could be considered to potentially have a *significant* effect on trade of other Members. In this regard, it would be relevant to consider whether the change has resulted in any increase in production, packaging and sales costs,

---

[421]   G/SPS/7/Rev.2, April 2002, and earlier recommendations.

[422]   This approach is in line with the discussion of the concept of "significant effect on trade of other Members" in the notification procedures adopted and revised by the SPS Committee G/SPS/7/Rev.2, para. 7).

such as more onerous treatment requirements or more time-consuming administrative formalities.

8.315 We note that the United States essentially states that Japan "substantially changed its fire blight measures since the entry into force of the *SPS Agreement*". The United States adds that Japan appeared to have amended or introduced MAFF Notification No. 354 on 10 March 1997, which set the requirements for imports of US apples into Japan, and MAFF "Detailed Rules for US Apples" on 1 April 1997, which implemented Notification No. 354. However, the United States did not specify in what respect Japan had "substantially changed" its fire blight measures. On the other hand, Japan does not admit that it changed its phytosanitary measures for fire blight since 1994.

8.316 We recall that, in *EC – Hormones*, the Appellate Body noted that

"… Panels are inhibited from addressing legal claims falling outside their terms of reference. However, nothing in the DSU limits the faculty of a panel freely to use arguments submitted by any of the parties – or to develop its own legal reasoning – to support its own findings and conclusions on the matter under its consideration."

8.317 However, the Appellate Body clarified in *Korea – Dairy* that "[B]oth 'claims' and 'arguments' are distinct from the 'evidence' which the complainant or respondent presents to support its assertions of facts and arguments".[423] We note in this regard that the party making an allegation must provide sufficient evidence in support of this allegation, and that a panel should not entertain a claim for which a prima facie case has not been made.[424] In the present case, the United States has effectively argued that Japan had substantially changed its fire blight measures since the entry into force of the *SPS Agreement*. However, the United States limited its argumentation to mention that new regulations had been implemented and to attach translations of the regulations to its first written submission. It did not specify in what respect these new regulations departed from the previous ones.

8.318 Indeed, either the United States knows in which respect the 1997 texts differ from the ones they replace – in which case it could and should have mentioned it in its submissions - or it does not, in which case it cannot be deemed to have established a prima facie case. In either situation, for the Panel to examine the regulations at issue to identify differences would be equivalent to "making a case" for the United States, something we are not allowed to do. For these reasons we conclude that the United States did not establish a prima facie case in relation to the violation of Article 7 and Annex B of the *SPS Agreement*.

8.319 Even if we were to address that claim, we do not consider that a violation of Article 7 and Annex B has been established. Article 7 of the *SPS Agreement*

---

[423] Appellate Body in *Korea – Dairy*, para. 139.
[424] Appellate Body Report in *Japan – Agricultural Products II*, para.126.

requires Members to notify "changes" in their SPS measures.[425] We note that the MAFF Notification No. 354, dated 10 March 1997, replaced MAFF notification No. 1184, of 22 August 1994.[426] Similarly, the Detailed Rules for US Apples, dated 1 April 1997, replaced the MAFF Detailed Rules for US Apples of 22 August 1994.[427] We note that both of the preceding instruments predated the entry into force of the *SPS Agreement*. We should therefore consider whether the new instruments adopted in 1997 (subsequent to the entry into force of the Agreement) introduced changes in Japan's SPS measures such that they should have been notified to WTO Members under Article 7 of the *SPS Agreement*.

8.320 In comparing the MAFF Notification of 1997 with that of 1994, it seems that they both overall follow a very similar structure and contents. Nonetheless, it can be noted that: (1) in the definition of the plants and areas, the 1994 Notification requires that the designation of the area of production as "under intensive pests and diseases control", whereas the 1997 Notification refers to areas "where intensive control for coddling moth is conducted and also where the US plant protection authority inspect at proper times" (para. 1); (2) the phytosanitary certificate required under the 1994 Notification refers to codling moth only, whereas the 1997 certificate refers both to codling moth and fire blight; and (3) a requirement for the fruit surface to be sterilized was added in the 1997 Notification, compared with the 1994 Notification.

8.321 We recall that the MAFF Notification of 1997 has included a requirement for the fruit surface to be sterilized which did not appear in the 1994 MAFF Notification as such. Yet, this requirement was already applicable to apples exported from the United States pursuant to another legal instruments: the 1994 MAFF "Detailed Rules for US Apples", at paragraph 6(2).

8.322 We note that a phytosanitary certificate which included only the information required according to the 1994 MAFF Notification would presumably no longer be acceptable since it did not contain the specific information regarding also fire blight required according to the 1997 notification. We note however, on the basis of information submitted by Japan at the interim review stage, that the additional requirements resulting from the 1997 Notification are limited and unlikely to "have a significant effect on trade" in apples from the United States.

8.323 Finally, we note the differences in the definitions of plants and areas in the 1994 and the 1997 Notifications. Since measures were already applied in relation to fire blight before 1997, we do not consider that the change in definitions that we identified would be such as to "have significant effect on trade" in apples from the United States.

8.324 We conclude, therefore, that the MAFF Notification of 1997 may reflect a change in a phytosanitary measure whose content is "not substantially the same as the content of an international standard". However, we do not consider that

---

[425] In this respect, we do not believe that changes of legal instruments require, in all instances, notification.
[426] Exhibit US-11.
[427] Exhibit US-12.

those changes "may have a significant effect on trade of other Members" and that Japan was required to notify them in accordance with Article 7 and Annex B of the *SPS Agreement*.

8.325 As for the MAFF Detailed Rules for US apples, the 1994 rules already refer to designated areas as areas "with no infection and non-export area or buffer zone in accordance with the following conditions for fire blight" and defines buffer zones and disease-free status for these areas. These appear to be unchanged in the 1997 Detailed Rules. The 1994 Detailed Rules already clearly contain detailed requirements specifically concerning fire blight, and some of these are adjusted in the 1997 Detailed Rules, although it is difficult to judge how substantial such changes actually are.

8.326 We note that most of the changes in the MAFF Detailed Rules for US Apples do not appear to have resulted in any further change which might have affected the access of US apples to Japan. However, when considering the Detailed Rules that have been translated into English from the Japanese language it is difficult to determine whether a change is strictly editorial or whether a more substantial change has been introduced. We are therefore unable to reach any conclusion as to whether Japan was required to notify the changes in the MAFF Detailed Rules for US Apples introduced in 1997.

8.327 For these reasons, we find that the United States failed to make a prima facie case in relation to the violation of Article 7 and Annex B of the *SPS Agreement*.

I.   Article XI of GATT 1994

8.328 We have found above that the phytosanitary measure at issue violates Articles 2.2, 5.7 and 5.1 of the *SPS Agreement*. Under those circumstances, we find it appropriate to exercise judicial economy as previous panels did in similar situations in relation to alleged violations of provisions of GATT 1994.[428]

8.329 Since we have found that the phytosanitary measure at issue is inconsistent with the requirements of the *SPS Agreement*, we see no need to further examine whether this measure is also inconsistent with Article XI of GATT 1994.

J.   Other Claims Included in the Request for Establishment of the Panel

8.330 We recall that the United States' request for establishment of a panel contains, in addition to the claims already addressed above, the following claims:

> "These measures appear to be inconsistent with the commitments and obligations of Japan under … Article 4.2 of the *Agreement on Agriculture*, and Articles … , 2.3, … , … , 5.3, 5.5, … , 6.1, 6.2 … of the *Agreement on the Application of Sanitary and Phytosanitary*

---

[428] Panel Report in *EC – Hormones (Canada)*, para. 8.275; Panel Report in *Australia – Salmon*, para. 8.185.

Measures (SPS Agreement). Japan's measures also appear to nullify or impair the benefits accruing to the United States directly or indirectly under the cited agreements."[429]

8.331 Out of these claims, only one – the violation of Article 4.2 of the Agreement on Agriculture - was briefly addressed by the United States in its oral submissions before the Panel.

8.332 As mentioned above[430], we are mindful that our findings must assist the DSB in making sufficiently precise recommendations and rulings so as to allow for prompt compliance, in order to ensure effective resolution of the dispute. Since we have found that the phytosanitary measure at issue is inconsistent with several provisions of the *SPS Agreement*, we see no particular reason to address the claim of the United States regarding Article 4.2.

8.333 Therefore, we exercise judicial economy and refrain from making any findings with regard to Article 4.2 of the Agreement on Agriculture.

8.334 Regarding the other provisions referred to in the US request for establishment of a panel, namely Articles 2.3, 5.3, 5.5, 6.1 and 6.2 of the *SPS Agreement*, we recall that they were not addressed by the United States in any of its submissions. While they could be considered to be within our terms of reference, we note that, in order for us to make a finding on these claim, the United States should have made a prima facie case for each of them. The United States did not make such a prima facie case for each of these claims.

8.335 Under these circumstances, we refrain from making any finding regarding the consistency of the phytosanitary measure at issue with Articles 2.3, 5.3, 5.5, 6.1 and 6.2 of the *SPS Agreement*.

8.336 Finally, since we found a violation of the *SPS Agreement*, we see no need to determine whether Japan's measures also nullifies or impairs the benefits accruing to the United States directly or indirectly under the cited agreements in the absence of violation.

IX.   CONCLUSIONS

9.1   In light of the findings above, we reach the following conclusions:

(a)   **Japan, by maintaining the phytosanitary measure at issue, violated Article 2.2 of the *SPS Agreement* not to maintain phytosanitary measures "without sufficient scientific evidence, except as provided for in paragraph 7 of Article 5";**

(b)   **the phytosanitary measure at issue does not comply with the requirement under Article 5.7 of the *SPS Agreement* that relevant scientific evidence be insufficient in order to justify the application of the phytosanitary measure at issue as a provisionally adopted measure; and**

---

[429]   WT/DS245/2 (emphasis in the original).
[430]   See, e.g., para. 8.4, referring to the Appellate Body Report in *Australia - Salmon*, para. 223.

    (c)   **the phytosanitary measure at issue is not based on a risk assessment within the meaning of Article 5.1 of the *SPS Agreement.***

9.2   Article 3.8 of the DSU provides that "[i]n cases where there is an infringement of the obligations assumed under a covered agreement [including the *SPS Agreement*], the action is considered prima facie to constitute a case of nullification or impairment". We note that Japan failed to rebut this presumption. We conclude that, to the extent Japan has acted inconsistently with the *SPS Agreement*, it has nullified or impaired the benefits accruing to the United States under the *SPS Agreement*.

9.3   We recommend that the Dispute Settlement Body request Japan to bring the phytosanitary measure in dispute into conformity with its obligations under the *SPS Agreement*.

ANNEX 1

JAPAN – MEASURES AFFECTING THE IMPORTATION
OF APPLES (DS245)

Working Procedures for the Panel

1.   In its proceedings the Panel shall follow the relevant provisions of the Dispute Settlement Understanding (DSU). In addition, the following working procedures shall apply.

2.   The panel shall meet in closed session. The parties to the dispute, and interested third parties, shall be present at the meetings only when invited by the Panel to appear before it.

3.   The deliberations of the Panel and the documents submitted to it shall be kept confidential. Nothing in the DSU shall preclude a party to a dispute from disclosing statements of its own positions to the public. Members shall treat as confidential information submitted by another Member to the Panel which that Member has designated as confidential. Where a party to a dispute submits a confidential version of its written submissions to the Panel, it shall also, upon request of a Member, provide a non-confidential summary of the information contained in its submissions that could be disclosed to the public.

4.   Before the first substantive meeting of the Panel with the parties, the parties to the dispute shall transmit to the Panel written submissions in which they present the facts of the case and their arguments. Third parties may transmit to the Panel written submissions after the first written submissions of the parties have been submitted.

5.   At its first substantive meeting with the parties, the Panel shall ask the United States to present its case. Subsequently, and still at the same meeting, Japan will be asked to present its point of view. Third parties will be asked to present their views thereafter at the separate session of the same meeting set aside for that purpose. The parties will then be allowed an opportunity for final statements, with the United States presenting its statement first.

6.   All third parties which have notified their interest in the dispute to the Dispute Settlement Body shall be invited in writing to present their views during a session of the first substantive meeting of the Panel set aside for that purpose. All such third parties may be present during the entirety of this session.

7.   Formal rebuttals shall be made at a second substantive meeting of the Panel. Japan shall have the right to take the floor first, to be followed by the United States. The parties shall submit, prior to that meeting, written rebuttals to the Panel.

8.   Within seven days following the submission or presentation concerned, each of the parties and third parties shall provide the Panel with an executive summary of the claims and arguments contained in their written submissions and

oral presentations. The executive summaries will be used only for the purpose of assisting the Panel in drafting a concise arguments section of the Panel report to the Members. They shall not in any way serve as a substitute for the submissions of the parties in the Panel's examination of the case. The executive summaries of the written submissions to be provided by each party should not exceed 10 pages in length each and the executive summaries of the oral presentations should not exceed 5 pages in length each. The summary to be provided by each third party shall summarize their written submission and oral presentation, and should not exceed 5 pages in length.

9.   The Panel may at any time put questions to the parties and to the third parties and ask them for explanations either in the course of a meeting or in writing. Answers to questions shall be submitted in writing by the date(s) specified by the Panel. Answers to questions after the first meeting shall be submitted in writing at the same time as the written rebuttals, unless the Panel specifies a different deadline.

10.   A party shall submit any request for a preliminary ruling not later than its first submission to the Panel. If the complaining party requests such a ruling, the respondent shall submit its response to the request in its first submission. If the respondent requests such a ruling, the complaining party shall submit its response to the request prior to the first substantive meeting of the Panel, at a time to be determined by the Panel in light of the request. Exceptions to this procedure will be granted upon a showing of good cause.

11.   Parties shall submit all factual evidence to the Panel no later than during the first substantive meeting, except with respect to evidence necessary for purposes of rebuttals or answers to questions. Exceptions to this procedure will be granted upon a showing of good cause. In such cases, the other party shall be accorded a period of time for comment, as appropriate.

12.   The parties to the dispute have the right to determine the composition of their own delegations. The parties shall have the responsibility for all members of their delegations and shall ensure that all members of the delegation act in accordance with the rules of the DSU and the Working Procedures of this Panel, particularly in regard to confidentiality of the proceedings.

13.   The parties to the dispute and any third party invited to present its views shall make available to the Panel and the other party or parties a written version of their oral statements, preferably at the end of the meeting, and in any event not later than the day following the meeting. Parties and third parties are encouraged to provide the Panel and other participants in the meeting with a provisional written version of their oral statements at the time the oral statement is presented.

14.   In the interest of full transparency, the presentations, rebuttals and statements shall be made in the presence of the parties. Moreover, each party's written submissions, including responses to questions put by the Panel, shall be made available to the other party.

15.   To facilitate the maintenance of the record of the dispute, and to maximize the clarity of submissions, in particular the references to exhibits submitted by parties, parties shall sequentially number their exhibits throughout

the course of the dispute. For example, exhibits submitted by the United States could be numbered USA-1, USA-2, etc. If the last exhibit in connection with the first submission was numbered USA-5, the first exhibit of the next submission thus would be numbered USA-6.

16.   Following issuance of the interim report, the parties shall have two weeks to submit written requests to review precise aspects of the interim report and to request a further meeting with the Panel. The right to request such a meeting must be exercised no later than at that time. Following receipt of any written requests for review, if no further meeting with the Panel is requested, the parties shall have the opportunity, within a time-period specified by the Panel, to submit written comments on the other party's written requests for review. Such comments shall be strictly limited to responding to the other party's written request for review.

17.   The following procedures regarding service of documents shall apply:

(a)   Each party shall serve its submissions directly on the other party. Each party shall, in addition, serve its first written submission on third parties. Each third party shall serve its submissions on the parties and other third parties. Parties and third parties shall confirm, at the time a submission is provided to the Panel, that copies have been served as required.

(b)   The parties and the third parties should provide their written submissions to the Dispute Settlement Registrar by 5:30 p.m. on the deadlines established by the Panel. The parties and the third parties shall provide the Panel with 10 paper copies of their written submissions. All these copies must be filed with the Dispute Settlement Registrar, Mr Ferdinand Ferranco (Office 3154).

(c)   At the time they provide paper copies of their submissions, the parties and third parties shall also provide the Panel with an electronic copy of the submissions on a diskette or as an e-mail attachment, if possible in a format compatible with the Secretariat's software (e-mail to the Dispute Settlement Registrar at Dsregistry@wto.org, with a copy to the Secretary of the Panel, Mr Michael Roberts at michael.roberts@wto.org, Ms. Gretchen Stanton at gretchen.stanton@wto.org, Ms. Kerry Allbeury at kerry.allbeury@wto.org and Mr Yves Renouf at yves.renouf@wto.org)

(d)   Parties and third parties shall provide the Panel with written copies of their oral submissions no later than the day following the date of the presentation. Written replies to questions shall be submitted by a date to be decided by the Panel.

ANNEX 2

ABBREVIATIONS USED FOR DISPUTE SETTLEMENT CASES REFERRED TO IN THE REPORT

SHORT TITLE	FULL TITLE
Australia – Salmon	Panel Report, *Australia – Measures Affecting Importation of Salmon*, WT/DS18/R and Corr.1, adopted 6 November 1998, as modified by the Appellate Body Report, DSR 1998:VIII, 3407.
Australia – Salmon	Appellate Body Report, *Australia – Measures Affecting Importation of Salmon*, WT/DS18/AB/R, adopted 6 November 1998, DSR 1998:VIII, 3327.
Australia – Salmon (Article 21.5 – Canada)	Panel Report, *Australia – Measures Affecting Importation of Salmon – Recourse to Article 21.5 of the DSU by Canada*, WT/DS18/RW, adopted 20 March 2000, DSR 2000:IV, 2035
Brazil – Aircraft	Appellate Body Report, *Brazil – Export Financing Programme for Aircraft*, WT/DS46/AB/R, adopted 20 August 1999, DSR 1999:III, 1161.
Chile – Price Band System	Panel Report, *Chile – Price Band System and Safeguard Measures Relating to Certain Agricultural Products*, WT/DS207/R, 3 May 2002, adopted 23 October 2002, as modified by the Appellate Body Report, WT/DS207AB/R.
Chile – Price Band System	Appellate Body Report, *Chile – Price Band System and Safeguard Measures Relating to Certain Agricultural Products*, WT/DS207/AB/R, adopted 23 October 2002.
EC – Asbestos	Appellate Body Report, *European Communities – Measures Affecting Asbestos and Asbestos-Containing Products*, WT/DS135/AB/R, adopted 5 April 2001.
EC – Bananas III	Appellate Body Report, *European Communities – Regime for the Importation, Sale and Distribution of Bananas*, WT/DS27/AB/R, adopted 25 September 1997, DSR 1997:II, 591.
EC – Hormones (Canada)	Panel Report, *EC Measures Concerning Meat and Meat Products (Hormones) – Complaint by Canada*, WT/DS48/R/CAN, adopted 13 February 1998, as modified by the Appellate Body Report, WT/DS26/AB/R, WT/DS48/AB/R, DSR 1998:II, 235.
EC – Hormones (US)	Panel Report, *EC Measures Concerning Meat and Meat Products (Hormones) – Complaint by the United States*, WT/DS26/R/USA, adopted 13 February 1998, as modified by the Appellate Body Report, WT/DS26/AB/R, WT/DS48/AB/R, DSR 1998:III, 699.
EEC – Dessert Apples	Panel Report, *European Economic Community – Restrictions on Imports of Dessert Apples – Complaint by Chile ("EEC – Dessert Apples)*, adopted 12 July 1983, BISD 30S/129.
EC – Sardines	Appellate Body Report, *European Communities – Trade Description of Sardines*, WT/DS231/AB/R, adopted 2002.

SHORT TITLE	FULL TITLE
India – Patents (EC)	Panel Report, *India – Patent Protection for Pharmaceutical and Agricultural Chemical Products – Complaint by the European Communities*, WT/DS79/R, adopted 22 September 1998, DSR 1998:VI, 2661.
India – Patents (US)	Panel Report, *India – Patent Protection for Pharmaceutical and Agricultural Chemical Products*, WT/DS50/R, adopted 16 January 1998, as modified by the Appellate Body Report, WT/DS50/AB/R, DSR 1998:I, 41.
Japan – Agricultural Products II	Panel Report, *Japan – Measures Affecting Agricultural Products*, WT/DS76/R, adopted 19 March 1999, as modified by the Appellate Body Report, WT/DS76/AB/R, DSR 1999:I, 315.
Japan – Film	Panel Report, *Japan – Measures Affecting Consumer Photographic Film and Paper*, WT/DS44/R, adopted 22 April 1998, DSR 1998:IV, 1179.
Japan – Semi-Conductors	Panel Report, *Japan – Trade in Semi-Conductors ("Japan – Semi-Conductors")*, adopted 4 May 1988, BISD 35S/116.
Korea - Dairy	Panel Report, *Korea – Definitive Safeguard Measure on Imports of Certain Dairy Products ("Korea – Dairy")*, WT/DS98/R and Corr.1, adopted 12 January 2000, as modified by the Appellate Body Report, WT/DS98/AB/R/, DSR 2000:I, 49
US – Wool Shirts and Blouses	Appellate Body Report, *United States – Measure Affecting Imports of Woven Wool Shirts and Blouses from India*, WT/DS33/AB/R and Corr.1, adopted 23 May 1997, DSR 1997:I, 323.

ANNEX 3

TRANSCRIPT FROM PANEL MEETING WITH EXPERTS
OF 13 JANUARY (AFTERNOON) AND 14 JANUARY (MORNING) 2003

MONDAY, 13 JANUARY

Chairman

1.   Good afternoon. I would like to welcome the parties and our four experts to this meeting of the Panel on Japan – Measures Affecting the Importation of Apples. First of all I would like to say a word about interpretation and microphones. The Panel has acceded to the Japanese delegation's request for them to provide continuous and consecutive modes of translation between Japanese and English. The English channel, for the benefit of the experts, is channel 1. May I request Japan to confirm that all necessary arrangements are in place? Thank you. Partly because of the interpretation and because the proceedings are recorded, and the tapes form part of the record of this Panel, I would request everyone taking the floor to make use of the microphone, to switch the microphone on when they begin to speak and off when they are finished. Let me now go to introductions. I would like to begin by introducing the members of this panel. On my right is Dr. Kathy-Ann Brown of the Mission of St. Lucia; and on my left, Mr. Christian Häeberli of the Swiss Federal Office of Agriculture; and myself, Michael Cartland, from Hong Kong, and I am Chairman of the Panel.

2.   Assisting the Panel in its work are the Panel Secretary, Mr. Michael Roberts, aided by Mrs. Gretchen Stanton from the Agriculture and Commodities Division, and the Legal Adviser, Ms. Kerry Allbeury, supported by Mr. Yves Renouf, who will be joining us later, from the Legal Affairs Division.

3.   I would like to identify and introduce the four experts. We have first Dr. Klaus Geider, Professor of Molecular Genetics and Phytopathology from the Max-Planck Institute for Cell Biology at the University of Heidlelberg in Germany. Secondly, we have Dr. Chris Hale, a Science Capability Leader, Insect Group, Plant Health and Fire blight, Hort Research, Auckland, New Zealand. Third we have Dr. Chris Hayward, Consultant on Bacterial Plant Diseases, Indooroopilly, Queensland, Australia. I hope I got the name of the place correct. Dr. Ian Smith, finally, is Director-General of the European and Mediterranean Plant Protection Organization, in Paris.

4.   Perhaps for the benefit of the experts, I could also invite the heads of delegations to introduce themselves and the other members of their rather large delegations. If your delegation has not already done so, it would be appreciated if you could submit a list of your delegation's members to the Panel Secretary. I will begin with the United States please.

United States

5.   Thank you Mr. Chairman, on behalf of the United States. My name is Juan Millán. I am an Assistant General Counsel with the office of the US Trade Representative in Washington D.C. The gentleman to my right, my peripatetic colleague is Stephen Kho from the US Mission here in Geneva, and I will ask the remainder of the members of my delegation to please introduce themselves seeing as we are quite strung out along the length of this room.

My name is Dr. Rodney Roberts, I am a plant pathologist with the Agricultural Research Service in Wenatchee, Washington.

Alan Green, Assistant Deputy Administrator, Plant Protection and Quarantine.

Mike Guidicipietro, Trade Specialist on Phytosanitary Issues, USDA, APHIS.

Dr. Kenneth Vick, US Department of Agriculture, Washington, D.C.

Paul McGowan, Trade Director for Asia, Plant Protection and Quarantine.

Garrett Weiner, Legal Intern, at the US Mission to the WTO.

Lynn Alfalla, with USDA, APHIS. I am Director for Asia Trade Policy.

Anne Dawson, I'm the Japan Desk Officer for the Foreign Agricultural Service, USDA.

Gregg Young. I am with the US Mission here – Agriculture.

Chairman

6.   Thank you very much. Perhaps I could now invite the delegation of Japan to perform the same function.

Japan

7.   Thank you, Mr. Chairman and members of the Panel. My name is Masatoshi Sakano. I am Deputy Director-General of Agricultural Production Bureau, Ministry of Agriculture, Forestry and Fisheries of Japan. Now I will let each of the Japanese delegation introduce themselves.

My name is Noboru Saito, Director, Plant Protection Division, Ministry of Agriculture, Forestry and Fisheries.

Masaru Kitamura, Legal Adviser, Ministry of Agriculture, Forestry and Fisheries.

My name is Masao Goto, Plant Bacteriologist and Professor Emeritus of Shizuoka University.

Akira Sugiyama, Director of WTO Dispute Settlement Division, Ministry of Foreign Affairs.

Yayoi Matsuda, Dispute Settlement Officer here in the Mission in Geneva.

My name is Hiromichi Matsushima, Agriculture Counsellor, Japanese Mission, here.

My name is Katsuhiro Saka, Agriculture Attaché, Japanese Mission in Geneva.

My name is Junichi Taniuchi, Deputy Director, Plant Protection Division, Agricultural Production Bureau, Ministry of Agriculture, Forestry and Fisheries.

My name is Hiroyuki Yamaguchi. I am from Plant Protection Division, Ministry of Agriculture.

My name is Akifumi Mizuno, Ministry of Agriculture in Tokyo.

My name is Kenji Shinoda, Official and Attorney, International Agreements Division, Treaty Bureau, Ministry of Foreign Affairs.

My name is Akira Uchida from the WTO Dispute Settlement Division, Ministry of Foreign Affairs.

My name is Ryosuke Hirooka, International Affairs Bureau in Agriculture Ministry.

Aya Iino, covering dispute settlement issues in Japanese Mission here.

Chairman

8.   Thank you very much. Turning now to the establishment of the Panel and Terms of Reference, as a preliminary matter I should recall that at its meeting on 3 June 2002, the Dispute Settlement Body decided in accordance with Article VI of the Dispute Settlement Understanding, to establish a panel pursuant to a request by the United States. I further recall that the Panel held a first substantive meeting with the parties on 21 October 2002. Both the panel and the parties recognized the need for the panel to consult with experts possessing specialized scientific expertise on the issues arising in the dispute. In conjunction with the parties, the panel agreed on working procedures for its consultations with scientific and technical experts. These working procedures were communicated to the parties on 18 October 2002. After consultation with the International Plant Protection Convention and having received the views of the parties, the panel appointed Drs. Geider, Hale, Hayward and Smith to serve as scientific experts in this dispute. In accordance with the working procedures and after comment by the parties, the panel communicated questions to the experts. The experts were requested to reply by 12 December 2002, and these replies were communicated to the parties. Comments received from the parties on the experts' replies were circulated to the experts. I hope that reflects everyone's understanding of what has actually happened so far.

9.   Conduct of the meeting. The purpose of today's meeting is for the experts to meet the panel and the parties, and to discuss their written responses to the questions and to provide further information. Today's meeting will proceed as follows: Firstly I should like to request the experts to make introductory or general remarks and then I will open the floor to the parties. We hope that after the parties have completed their questions, we will be able to take a short break of fifteen minutes or so, after which the panel will ask certain questions to the experts. I should say at this stage that we do envisage the need to reflect on the

outcome of today's session, and we would appreciate the opportunity to come back for a further session with the experts tomorrow. I think that if we could convene in this room at 11 o'clock for that purpose tomorrow that would be a convenient arrangement.

10.   The experts are welcome in their introductory remarks to address any point where they believe further clarification is needed, particularly in the light of the parties' comments to any of the expert responses to the panel's written questions. Finally, at the end of our session tomorrow, I shall of course allow the experts time to make any closing remarks that they should wish. I would like to recall that the meetings of the panels in the WTO are tape recorded. I have mentioned this already at the beginning. The only point is to remember to use your microphones. I would also further remind the parties and I would wish to draw the attention of the experts to the fact that the proceedings of this panel are confidential, as provided for in Article XVIII of the DSU. Unless there are any comments or questions at this stage, we can now proceed. Japan.

Japan

11.   Thank you Mr. Chairman. I am sorry to pose questions first before we go into the substance but we would appreciate it very much if you would clarify a bit further how exactly the floor will be open to the parties. Is it going to be alternate one question by one question or substance by substance? These kinds of matters need to be clarified. Thank you.

Chairman

12.   I have proposed to give the floor to each delegation in turn to ask all the questions that they wish to ask, and then I will give the floor to the other delegation to ask all the questions that they wish to ask, so in fact we will take it one delegation at a time. [Discussion within the Panel and with the Secretariat.]

13.   I am inclined to start with the United States, asking them to present an issue, or a series of issues. If Japan has questions on the same subjects, then we will stay on those subjects until we have exhausted them, and then Japan can ask a question on another subject. Are the parties content to do that, on an alternating basis?

United States

14.   Subject-matter by subject-matter would seem to us to make more sense than a strict alternating question by question. However, we would also be open to asking all of our questions in sequence, so I'll give you another 15 seconds to decide.

Chairman

15.   No, no, I think we have decided. I think we have spent long enough on that.

Japan

16.   We are in your capable hands, Mr. Chairman, of course, but your suggestion of subject by subject seems to make more sense to us. Thank you.

Chairman

17.   Thank you. I suggest we hear from the experts in alphabetical order, starting with Dr. Geider, for the introductory comments. I think I have already observed that the panel does not envisage that we are going to finish this afternoon. The process today is for the introductory comments and for the questions from the parties to the experts, and after a break the Panel will put some questions. That said, I think I will now invite the experts to take the floor with their opening remarks, and perhaps I can begin with Dr. Geider. Dr. Geider, thank you, you have the floor.

Dr. Geider

18.   Thank you, Mr. Chairman. Of course it is difficult for a scientist to take this issue in parts, but one hopes that there could be a final solution. When we talk about fire blight we have to distinguish two situations. One is short-distance distribution which is mainly thought to occur with insects, especially with bees visiting flowers, with wind and with birds. I think here we should not discuss much about short-distance distribution, unless fire blight is established from a long-distance distribution, which is very rare. We think that the trade of imported latently infected host plants are mainly the cause of fire blight establishment in remote areas. And when we come to some sort of message we can contribute in this case, we have carefully, as far as we could, investigated the spread of fire blight in Europe and the Mediterranean region. What we can say is that fire blight occurred at certain points which were the source of the disease and then it spread sequentially. I think that this sequential spread was noted by the US delegation and it was also noted in one of the reports of New Zealand. So that means fire blight occurred in England and it occurred in Egypt and then no novel occurrence was visible until recently in central Spain and northern Italy, and I think in these two cases we could certainly assume that fire blight was established by import of plants from nurseries. And we know by the patterns we use to dissect the strains that these nurseries were probably located far from northern Italy and far from Spain, probably from Belgium. And these are exceptions, but in all other cases fire blight spreads from the source in England and the source in Egypt to other countries. Of course we cannot go back to the original situation. What happened that fire blight came to England and what happened that fire blight came to Egypt? Actually, in the recent issue of the International Workshop on Fire blight which was held in New Zealand, Eve Billing made some speculations about the origin of fire blight in England, and it is somehow of course getting a little bit into the argumentation of the Japanese delegation, that fire blight might have occurred by import of contaminated pears and that the pears leaked out and wood caskets were contaminated and afterwards they were used in farms for collecting apples.

19.   The other point is does fire blight stick to mature apples and what are the data and what are the reasons? Of course I think when fire blight, which means *E. amylovora*, is getting to the apples, it could happen that the pathogen will stick there for quite a bit of time. We have actually done a few experiments in that direction, but I have noticed that the Japanese scientists in Yokohama have

done similar things in that they have inoculated apples and found that the pathogen can stick with these apples for quite a bit of time, that means for weeks and maybe even for a couple of months.

20.   In our hands we did not really see a systemic spread of fire blight or *E. amylovora* in the apple. It was located in the inoculation sites and the symptoms which appeared were very minor. There was a little bit of browning and maybe a little of fungus growth but not a systemic spread on the whole apple. Therefore we think that when an apple is getting somehow contaminated accidentally in the harvest it can carry the disease further on, but I think it is not really a source of the disease because we have no examples that any apple that was spreading fire blight in Europe or in countries we have notice on.

21.   What I proposed in my comments on the questions of the panel were a couple of measurements that can be used in order to control the contamination and persistence of *E. amylovora* on apples, and the delegations might consider if those experiments are meaningful and they might be done in one or the other lab and we are also open to help on this occasion. Because in a few of my comments my colleagues were somehow accused of doing things not extensively and not too carefully, it is of course the sort of science in which it is very difficult to get to a judgement and things can happen or they cannot happen the next time and therefore it is a very difficult decision what is really getting on an apple which is infected or inoculated with fire blight.

22.   At the end I want to make a few comments about fire blight in Germany. The fire blight started in the north and it was slowly carried on to the south and now it is heavily in the south and almost disappeared in the north. The old question if fire blight was in Japan or has been in Japan or is still in Japan is a little bit difficult to answer because there are not really widespread observations about the disease and there are not too many samples which were taken. Also I cannot really judge how the scientists in Japan deal with possible necrotic diseases on apples and pears. Of course when Tom van der Zwet is stating in the first chapter of the fire blight book that Japan has had fire blight since 1903, I would somehow object this notation although I feel that fire blight in 1903 might have occurred but it disappeared. I think what we have in Japan as an Asian fire blight is probably something else, and we have accumulated a lot of data and published them in a couple of journals and the last one came out this month, that the disease which exists in Japan is probably different from fire blight. So I think fire blight, in my opinion, disappeared when it was in Japan in 1903. So that is what I want to comment.

Chairman

23.   Thank you very much Dr. Geider. Can I just clarify that when you use the word "we" that you are referring to your team at the Max-Planck Institute?

Dr. Geider

24.   Yes, right.

Chairman

25.   Let me now invite in alphabetical order, Dr. Chris Hale, to take the floor for introductory remarks.

Dr. Hale

26.   Thank you Mr. Chairman. I would like to preface my remarks by just giving you some idea of my area of expertise. I am a plant pathologist by training and in particular have worked on bacterial diseases of plants and the epidemiology of these bacterial diseases. I have been involved in science management for a period of about twenty years in the area of plant protection and during this time I have managed a number of programmes on the ecology of *E. amylovora* and on the epidemiology of fire blight.

27.   I would like to thank the panel for the opportunity to provide responses to a number of questions. My responses were in the form of opinions in most cases, rather than direct answers, as the panel specifically requested, in most cases, opinions. The expert advisers were expected to provide these opinions and I realize that the parties will also have opinions and that these may differ. There are a number of points arising from the comments on the expert advisers' responses to the panel's questions, which will no doubt be addressed at various stages during the meeting. For example, fruit maturity, endophytic bacteria, export practices, possible pathways for introduction of fire blight, orchard inspections and buffer zones. I am not a plant physiologist and consequently cannot provide detailed information on fruit maturity and marketing and my responses in this area are consequently limited. However, in the area of maturity of fruit, comprehensive objective maturity parameters were discussed within the New Zealand answer to question 2 from the panel, and these have been certainly adopted by the industry in New Zealand. I am under the impression that similar systems apply also to the United States. The details of the various practices are given in the New Zealand response to questions, which was New Zealand Exhibit No.13.

28.   On endophytic bacteria, my group has found no evidence of multiplication of bacteria within fruit, and there doesn't seem to be any evidence of mature symptomless fruit disseminating endophytic *E. amylovora*. Of course we have this question about endophytic bacteria. In the work that we have done over many years, we certainly can find bacteria on tissue in the calyx of the fruit, but there does not seem to be any evidence of multiplication and I don't consider this to be convincing evidence of endophytic bacteria.

29.   In the work of Tom van der Zwet, I really feel that, having read that paper, it fails to convince me that *E. amylovora* is in fact endophytic. Just to move on, to a continuation of that part of the work, I was quite surprised to find in the comments of Japan on the expert responses, that the letters or the declaration by Dr. van der Zwet and the letter by Professor Thomson were supposedly pre-worded letters. This was completely new knowledge as far as I was concerned, and I think this goes for the rest of the experts as well.

30.   As far as export practices are concerned, the comments by Japan relating to codling moth larvae in the US apples exported to Chinese Taipei are also new to the procedure. I don't think the situation was brought up in the second written submission of Japan, dated 13 November, and I presume this was because the information was not generally available at that time.

31.   On the pathway of possible introduction of fire blight into countries where the disease has not been recorded, a lot of the work that we have done recently has been experimental research on discarded fruit and it is very difficult to do this work unless artificial contamination of fruit is used. In fact, in our work we have used heavily infested fruit, and large numbers of them, and placed them in orchards. If you are trying to use naturally infested or naturally contaminated fruit, it is very difficult because you cannot actually detect whether there are any bacteria present until the fruit have been destructively sampled. There is also, in our view, no evidence that survival in artificially infested fruit is any different from that in naturally infested fruit in the environment.

32.   And then on to the effect of discard of blighted cores. In my opinion there appears to be very little evidence of any core infection of mature, symptomless fruit. In the area of orchard inspections, I agree that orchard inspection and fire blight-free orchards are important. However, I realize that there is a divergence of opinion on timing of inspections. On the area of buffer zones, in New Zealand buffer zones were put in place as a requirement for apple exports to Japan at the request of Japan Ministry of Agriculture, Fisheries and Forestry. It is very difficult to inspect such large buffer areas in New Zealand due to the relatively small size of orchards and the frequent difficulty in traversing adjacent mountains and rivers. I think that leads on to the work by Roberts which was reported in 2002, where infected pears were kept in orchards to continuously provide a source of inoculum and there seems to be no evidence that buffer zones provided any additional phytosanitary security. Mr. Chairman those are some of the remarks that I wanted to make at this early stage.

Chairman

33.   Thank you very much, Dr. Hale. Perhaps I could now invite Dr. Hayward for any introductory remarks.

Dr. Hayward

34.   Thank you, Mr. Chairman. For the past 40 years my principal research interest has been in the plant pathogenic bacteria and the diseases they cause. As the first bacteriologist to be appointed to what was then the Commonwealth Mycological Institute at Kew in January 1959, I was charged with the isolation and identification of bacteria from a great variety of moribund plant material. My background is in microbiology and plant pathology. In my last year at Kew, which was 1964, the warm and wet spring provided conditions ideal for epidemic fire blight in the south west London suburbs extending from Kew (including the Royal Botanic Gardens) through Richmond and on to Hampton Court Gardens. Fire blight was widely manifest in home gardens and roads, along roadsides on cotoneaster, pyracantha, *Sorbus* species and many other

ornamental members of the Rosaceae. I moved to Australia in 1965. Fire blight does not occur in Australia and there were no further opportunities to witness the effects of the disease except on visits to the United States and British Colombia. Since 1965 I've worked on phenotypic diversity and more recently genetic diversity and phylogeny, using DNA based methods, in bacterial pathogens of importance in the tropics and sub-tropics, particularly *Ralstonia solanacearum* the cause of wilts in many economically important crop plants. I now work as a consultant on bacterial plant diseases.

35.   Almost two years ago, I was asked by the Department of Agriculture, Fisheries and Forestry, Australia, to provide technical advice to the risk analysis panel considering the application made by the Government of the Philippines to export fresh green bananas to Australia. One of the diseases of concern is a bacterial disease known as Moko caused by *Ralstonia solanacearum*. I've looked in detail at the likelihood of the entry and establishment and spread of Moko disease as well as the associated potential biological and economic consequences. There are some similarities and several major differences between green bananas as a possible pathway for entry of Moko disease and the matter of mature apples and fire blight. Now to the matter we're dealing with here.

36.   Since preparing responses to questions 1 to 36 posed by the Panel, I've obtained copies of all the documents not available to me at the end of November last year. Most importantly, I have the paper by Mizuno *et al.* (2002) published in the journal of General Plant Pathology, Japan, which relates to question 35. I can add comments now, but I think probably it would be better later when I expect this question will be considered. Thank you.

Chairman

37.   Thank you, Dr. Hayward. I would now like to invite Dr. Smith to make his introductory remarks.

Dr. Smith

38.   Thank you Mr. Chairman. Working as I do for an international organization, the European and Mediterranean Plant Protection Organization, I have a responsibility to advise member governments of our organization on the measures which they may take in relation to quarantine pests, and in particular to advise them on how to conduct pest risk analysis, which is an internationally agreed procedure for deciding which pests require measures and for justifying those measures. And it is in this area, pest risk analysis, that I would like to make a few comments.

39.   First of all, the question has been raised concerning the proof of a scientific phenomenon. It has been said several times in the documents that it is impossible to prove that a rare event can never happen and this is clearly accepted. But I would like to add that it is also very difficult to prove that a rare event is happening, because it is rare. If scientists have to design experiments to observe such events and be satisfied that they are really occurring in the way that they predict, those experiments have to be very strictly controlled indeed to make sure that the very occasional events that they observe really confirm the

hypothesis, or that they might not be due to some other cause (experimental error, interaction with some other factor or whatever). So, from my point of view, it is very difficult to set out to conduct scientific research on unlikely rare events and it is by no means certain that some questions can ever be satisfactorily settled.

40.   Coming now to the process of pest risk analysis, there are international guidelines for this, two international standards under the International Plant Protection Convention. At the moment, we could say that the second one, which is International Standard No. 11, is the one which is in force and is the most recent and the most important. Throughout this document, it is stressed that pest risk analysis is first of all concerned with data obtained from areas where pests occur. Basically, observations are made on how pests behave where they occur, and then inferences are made about how they might behave in another place.

41.   The text of these standards has been structured in this way precisely to discourage wilder flights of conjecture about events which might occur and to try to keep the scientific arguments firmly on the ground. In this particular case, we are talking about a pathway which is the import of apple fruit. And, in the international standards, it is advised that in a pest risk analysis, the analyst should allow for known pathways and should also consider other possible pathways. One of the reasons for investigating other pathways is that their role in carrying pests from one country to another may in fact be quite different from what was initially supposed. Therefore the analyst should examine all possible pathways to make sure the pest is not entering easily by some other path which is different from the one which is mainly under consideration. In the present case we have the opposite situation, however. The pathway which is of main interest is one which is considered by most people to be an unlikely one, and one which has not been found in practice to occur in reality. It still needs to be evaluated, but its evaluation could lead to various conclusions. It could lead to the conclusion that this pathway is real and that it should be taken into account in taking phytosanitary measures. But it could also lead to the conclusion that this possible pathway is of no importance in practical terms, that there are no practical measures to be taken and so this pathway can be ignored. So when the PRA standard says that known pathways should be considered and also possible pathways should be considered, it does not mean to say that measures have to be taken for all pathways. It means that each has to be evaluated for its importance and, in relation to its importance, strict measures may be appropriate or mild measures may be appropriate or no measures may be appropriate. That is the purpose of the analysis.

42.   Now, finally, I would like to refer again to the standard on pest risk analysis which mentions a principle called the Principle of Managed Risk. I think this principle has not particularly been invoked in the documents which have been presented so far. It is one of the principles appearing in International Standards on Phytosanitary Measures No. 1. This principle says "because some risk of introduction of a quarantine pest always exists, countries shall agree to a policy of risk management when formulating phytosanitary measures". In the text of Standard No. 11 it is also written "since zero risk is not a reasonable

option, the guiding principle for risk management should be to manage risk to achieve the required degree of safety that can be justified and is feasible within the limits of available options and resources". I think it is important to bear in mind that pest risk management, according to international standards, should take into account this Principle of Managed Risk. Not only the Principle of Minimal Impact which has already been mentioned, but also the Principle of Managed Risk. And on the basis of this principle it should be possible to manage risks which are open to some uncertainty. Part of the problem in the case we are considering is that there is uncertainty about the possible importance of apples as a pathway. Pest risk management still has to try to find the most appropriate way to manage that risk despite the uncertainty. This is a kind of uncertainty management, we might say. So I do underline that the text of these international standards have foreseen many such situations and that it may be useful to quote them in further consideration of the problem which we face at the moment. Thank you, Mr. Chairman.

Chairman

43.   Dr. Smith, thank you very much. I'd now like to open up the meeting by inviting the parties to pose questions to the experts. As I said earlier, I propose that the parties be given the opportunity to pose their questions taking issues in alternate order and starting with the applicant, the United States. United States, you have the floor for the first issue.

United States

44.   Thank you, Mr. Chairman. Before I start with the first topic it occurred to me that it might be useful for my delegation to confer briefly in light of what the experts have said, to consider the questions that we had prepared and whether or not we might adjust or even not ask certain of the questions. It might be more efficient to the proceedings. Could we take a short break of no more than five minutes?

Chairman agrees.

Chairman

45.   Let's resume and let me thank the US delegation for keeping to the five minutes, and invite them to continue with questions on their first issue.

United States

46.   Thank you, Mr. Chairman. I thought you were going to charge me for taking six minutes so I appreciate the comment. Let me start by briefly thanking the experts for the evident care with which they have prepared answers to the Panel's questions and, in particular, for their citations to the scientific evidence which certainly made it easier for mc and the United States, and I believe probably the Panel as well, to understand and evaluate those answers. The Panel suggested that we take this session as an opportunity to dialogue with the experts, so I will try not to repeat comments of the United States that we previously submitted on the experts' answers or some of the major points on

which we found the experts to be in agreement, some of the major points in this dispute.

47.   Instead, and it may be a little chopped up because of the format of this session, what I would like to do is to turn to particular steps in the hypothetical pathway that's been proposed for transmission or introduction of fire blight via imported apple fruit and ask some questions for clarification of the scientific evidence or lack thereof. So, the first subject matter of my questions relates to endophytic presence in mature apple fruit.

48.   In response to question 11 from the Panel, Dr. Smith noted that van der Zwet *et al.* (1990) is, and I'll quote from your answer Dr. Smith, "the only published paper to my knowledge which records isolation of *E. amylovora* from core sections of fruits". And the paper itself, in combination with Dr. van der Zwet's declaration, tells us that this isolation was only from developing or immature fruit.

49.   If I may pause here briefly. Dr. Hale, you mentioned the description of this declaration as pre-worded. In submissions to the Panel we have made clear the process by which this declaration was developed. Japan has chosen to characterize that declaration as pre-worded. In fact, as we have described the process, questions were posed to Dr. van der Zwet and Professor Thomson. They provided answers and those answers were reduced to writing and then sent to the two gentlemen who reviewed the answers, which were their own oral answers, and made changes. We then asked whether we would be able to use these documents, make them public and use them in this procedure, and they both agreed, and having made changes to their answers they then signed these documents and permitted the United States to submit them as exhibits. So I'm not certain how the characterization of pre-worded can really be made, but that's the situation for your information.

50.   To return to my question, as I said, the paper in combination with this declaration tells us that these isolations from core sections of fruit was only from developing or immature fruit. Dr. Smith, I'd like to ask you whether, after reading the other experts' answers as well as the Parties' comments on those answers, this is still your view of the experiments reported in van der Zwet *et al.* (1990).

Dr. Smith

51.   Mr. Chairman, I had originally understood that the experts would answer in order, but I take it that you wish me to reply directly to this point.

Chairman

52.   This point has been specifically directed to you so perhaps on this occasion and on all occasions where it's specifically directed the expert to whom it's directed can reply first, and then we'll revert to the alphabetical order for the others to address the same question.

Dr. Smith

53.   In this article, Mr. Chairman, in several instances *E. amylovora* has been re-isolated from the core sections of fruits under conditions which should make sure, in principle, that there is not a contamination from the surface of the fruit or from some other part of the fruit. What is not made clear in the paper is, first of all, whether the presence of those bacteria is associated with any symptoms or not. My inference is that there are no symptoms. I think that if there had been symptoms they would have been described. That would seem to imply that the fruits are not in fact diseased and that small numbers of bacteria have somehow entered the fruit and have remained there. And in the paper itself, the maturity of the fruit concerned was not specified, but then the later declarations make it clear that the fruits concerned were not mature. For me, the most significant point about these observations is that the fruits are not diseased, so we are talking about very low levels of contamination by bacteria. Bacteria have been re-isolated from the fruits but that does not mean to say that there are large populations of bacteria there. Are they more or less important than bacteria which you can re-isolate from the surface of the fruit? It is not really possible to tell. If those bacteria had been causing symptoms, if it could be shown that they were damaging the fruits and multiplying in large numbers inside the fruits themselves, the risk could be much greater, but this is not recorded in the paper.

54.   I have said that these are the only results to my knowledge where has been recorded from core sections of fruits but also that other published papers refer to such internal infections only casually. There are other remarks in other papers about bacteria being recorded from the insides of fruits, but I think that this van der Zwet paper is the only one which tried to investigate the phenomenon generally. My main emphasis is that the data as presented does not show more than a low level of contamination in those cases and correspondingly a low risk. In general, I have made it clear in my reply that I feel that the results of van der Zwet *et al.* (1990) are confused, that the materials and methods of that paper describe various procedures which they said they would follow but for which no results are subsequently reported, and one is left with a feeling of dissatisfaction that the experiments were set up with a certain purpose and yet the experiments were not completed and for one reason or another the results are not presented. This is really the basis for my feeling that this research did not go exactly according to plan and when research does not go to plan it is sometimes better not to publish it. If you do publish it maybe you should continue the research and do better experiments in order to obtain clearer conclusions on issues which are certainly important.

Chairman

55.   Thank you, Dr. Smith. Can I ask Dr. Geider if you wish to say anything in response to this question?

Dr. Geider

56.   Nothing at all. I agree with Dr. Smith that this paper was probably written as a collection of data without getting a good feeling that everything which was

claimed in that paper was scientifically verified. I think the main problem in science is that methods of course change, and at the end you're not sure if the old papers still have the same impact as papers with new methods. In this case I think there is too much emphasis put on the question if this paper is really a message. I would say it's a possibility that these things could have happened and it might not exactly be what is claimed in the paper.

57.   We, that means my lab, are quite cautious about endophytic bacteria because you really have to show that they are endophytic and this is not so easy to do. I think these bacteria have to be labelled and not just plated. There is something and this is probably fire blight, although in this case, you have to carefully examine individual colonies to find out if this is fire blight or something else. In the older days, in 1990 and the paper is going back into the 1980s, the methods were not so advanced and, therefore, it could really have happened that it was put up by contamination and other things. And we have to look to the authors who are Tom Van der Zwet and Sherman Thomson and Gordon Bonn, all three of them are advanced scientists. I personally don't think that they have done the experiments themselves, so they trust other people and I don't know with three different complicated labs if everything that was published was really exactly what was extracted here by the Panel. For those reasons I would agree to be very cautious to use that paper as *the* document that *E. amylovora* can be endophytic.

Chairman

58.   Thank you, Dr. Geider. Dr. Hale, on this subject?

Dr. Hale

59.   I'd like to reiterate what Dr. Geider has said. I feel very much the same. Certainly, in my laboratory we have looked at core tissue and we have found no *E. amylovora* in core tissue, apart from in the calyx end of a core taken through an apple from an orchard with a high level of fire blight in the trees. One of the points that Dr. van der Zwet admitted in his declaration is that the fruit, in fact, was taken from, or fairly close to, areas in the orchard where there were fire blight-affected trees. It is quite possible, from work that we have done as well, that the calyx, in fact is infested, not infected but infested, and very low numbers of *E. amylovora* are present. Also when the core tissue was being taken right the way through the fruit, the calyx end tissue is the area where most of the bacteria are likely to be found. Again, from reading the paper, I'm not totally convinced that this is showing us that there were endophytic bacteria in the fruit.

Chairman

60.   Thank you very much. Dr. Hayward?

Dr. Hayward

61.   Thank you Mr. Chairman. I didn't have the courage to respond to this question in my document, in my responses last November. However, having heard Dr. Smith and having read what he's written, I think I support that quite strongly. He says that "it may be noted that the experiments reported in the paper

were performed by different scientists at four widely separate locations in several years". I think that gives us some hint as to the problems that may have occurred. And later he says "It is my conclusion that overall the study reported in this paper fails to convince. Experiments are said to be performed and procedures followed and no results are reported". I think I support this. Thank you.

Chairman

62.   Thank you very much. I think I would like at this stage to interject a question from the Panel to get clarification about some of the terms that have been used. So, the question is this: Would it be right to conclude that if an apple fruit is infected with *E. amylovora*, this means it has fire blight disease? If an apple is infested with *E. amylovora*, this means that *E. amylovora* bacteria is present but the fruit is NOT diseased? If the fruit is infested, the bacteria may be present either inside the tissues of the fruit, endophytic contamination, or on the surface of the fruit, epiphytic contamination? Would those be correct understandings? Perhaps I can do it in the alphabetical order, Dr. Geider?

Dr. Geider

63.   I think, in general, the scientific claim of endophytic bacteria is still not very well established. Many of my colleagues have had similar intentions to show that the bacteria is inside of plant tissue but very few have really shown that they're inside. I think it's scientifically, or via lab work, very difficult to dissect what is infected. And of course when there are symptoms, you may say the symptoms are coming from the pathogen or they may be coming from something else and we all have to deal with bacteria, viruses and of course with fungi. The question is "Is not everything you see really is a disease?" When you say infested, it could be on the surface, it could be somewhere but to my knowledge, nobody has ever really shown that bacteria, especially *E. amylovora* inside and is in the tissue. And for those reasons I think we are getting a little bit into a very sophisticated argumentation – what is there? And it doesn't answer the question "Does that spread fire blight?" I think that in the end it doesn't really matter to go into scientific details here, what is symbiotic and endo-symbiotic or what is outside. I think it's finally: "Is it spreading fire blight?" And I would say there is no evidence that endo-symbiotic bacteria, like *E. amylovora*, can really be found and that they can be connected to spread of fire blight. I'm maybe not answering your question completely; perhaps somebody else can pick it up again. Thank you.

Chairman

64.   We come to Dr. Hale now and perhaps he could address the question because I think it was from him that I heard the terms "infected" and "infested".

Dr. Hale

65.   Yes, again I really have very little more to say than Dr. Geider has said. My feeling has always been that if we have an infection, we have a fruit which is infected, then it is diseased in some way. Whereas, if we have an infested fruit, it is contaminated and may be carrying low levels of bacteria but the fruit or plant

part is not actually diseased. So, I think, infested is really more a contamination rather than a disease-causing part of the overall strategy of the bacterium. I have no more to say than that.

Chairman

66.   Thank you very much. Dr. Hayward?

Dr. Hayward

67.   Mr. Chairman, if I can quote definitions given in a guide to the terms in use in plant pathology: "Infection is the entry of an organism or virus into a host, the plant, and the establishment of a permanent or temporary parasitic relationship". Whereas infestation means, or to infest: "To overrun the surface of a plant. When used in reference to micro-organisms or virus particles on plant surfaces, there is no implication that infection has occurred."

Chairman

68.   Thank you. Do you have anything to add, Dr. Smith?

Dr. Smith

69.   I would just add a word about epiphytic and endophytic. I think it is generally understood that an infesting or contaminating population on the surface of a plant is epiphytic, if in some sense it persists. This implies that it is alive, that it is multiplying, that it has some existence in time, whereas infestation or contamination could actually be temporary. And, in the same way, I would say that an endophytic population in a plant is present somehow within the plant, between the cells or in spaces that exist inside the plant. If it is endophytic this implies that it is surviving, persisting and perhaps even multiplying. Otherwise, it is again simply a contaminant and may die out after a certain time. But these are difficult questions to investigate, to know exactly how a population of bacteria behaves inside a plant tissue. If you observe that it remains at the same level over a period of time, are the same cells staying alive for a very long time or are they turning over slowly? This is the kind of question that is very difficult to answer. But certainly both epiphytic and endophytic imply survival whereas contamination does not necessarily imply survival. A contaminant population may die out rather quickly.

Chairman

70.   Thank you very much. I was interrupting the United States' questions on that first issue. Do you wish to continue with that? Japan, you have a reaction on this point?

Japan

71.   Certainly we can respond but ...

Chairman

72.   Sorry, I understood you'd asked for the floor, but if this is not the case ... Sorry, yes. This is still continuing on the first issue I presume.

United States

73.   Sorry, Mr. Chairman, I'd lost my place briefly. I was actually going to ask the other experts to address the question that I'd placed to Dr. Smith. I really only have at this time one more question in this subject area of endophytic presence and maybe I'll start with Dr. Hayward. I believe in your written response to Question 2, you had said that the evidence on presence of *E. amylovora* as an endophyte in apple fruit is not monolithic and then later in your answer to Question 10 you said that, assuming the positive fruit in van der Zwet *et al.* (1990) to be immature, "I know of no studies that report the detection of endophytic bacteria in mature symptomless fruit". And so I wanted to ask you first, and then the other experts as well, whether there is any scientific evidence that endophytic *E. amylovora* has been isolated from mature apple fruit.

Dr. Hayward

74.   Mr. Chairman, I didn't use the word monolithic in the answer to Question 2 – it was somewhere else, but that's not really important. I stand by what I wrote then. I don't have any evidence. Sorry, what was the question which you posed? Relating to my response to Question 10 or Question 11?

United States

75.   I believe it was in your answer to Question 10 that you wrote "I know of no studies that report the detection of endophytic bacteria in mature symptomless fruit" assuming that the results from van der Zwet were wrong.

Dr. Hayward

76.   Yes, well I don't have any other evidence.

Chairman

77.   I assume that doesn't call for any response from the other experts?

United States

78.   Can we assume then that the experts agree with that statement?

Chairman

79.   I thought we were simply confirming the wording that had been put into the experts' answers. Do the others have anything to say? Dr. Geider.

Dr. Geider

80.   Just to repeat my statements. I think here in the audience it is very easy to talk about endophytic bacteria but in scientific terms it's very difficult. I spent quite some time in cooperation with some lab in Aberdeen, Scotland and they were claiming that you can see endophytic bacteria, but we were not sure at the end there what we really saw. It was not really connected to the presence of *E. amylovora* in fruit, but at least it was in the special forms of the bacteria in plant tissue. Finally, we could not make a final decision what endophytic is and for those reasons I think we are getting beyond science here. We just feel that there must be something inside an apple and it will get out and then we have the

disease, but I don't think that is the case here. I think this is artificial and it's not what can be really followed in the lab.

Chairman

81. Thank you. Dr. Hale?

Dr. Hale

82. Certainly based on the experience that we've had working with bacteria associated with fruit, I agree entirely with what Dr. Hayward said. I have no evidence whatsoever from any work that we've done, whether it be reported or published or not, or whether it's just laboratory work, that we could say there were any endophytic bacteria in mature, symptomless apple fruit.

Chairman

83. Dr. Smith? Nothing to add? Thank you. Are we finished on that topic?

United States

84. Yes, we have. Thank you.

Chairman

85. Thank you very much. Now, I would like to invite the delegation of Japan to present its first issue and questions on it. It's also open to you on the issue we've just heard. Thank you.

Japan

86. Thank you, Mr. Chairman. We also very much appreciate the efforts the experts expended in preparing the written responses, and I understand it must have taken you a great deal of time to analyze our discussions as well as the written responses to the answers to the questions by the experts.

87. I may sound a little bit less professional on the questions of plant pathology, but let me start my question in this way. It seems to me that there have been a number of definitions on maturity. In this proceeding, we heard there's a concept by the name of physiological maturity, there is another concept of commercial maturity and also the third concept of horticultural maturity, or maybe picking dates or harvest dates proposed by the United States. Let me start with a very general question, a very amateurish question first. Is maturity or immaturity, or mature apples and immature apples, do these two things reflect a dichotomy or are they in some stage of a continuum? Is this, so to speak, the transition from immaturity to maturity a continuous process, something which is in continuum?

Chairman

88. It's a reference to the first question from the Panel and the question was whether the process is a continuum, whether it is continuous.

Dr. Geider

89. I'm certainly not the best person to ask anyhow because we are not really working with apples in all stages of development. I think in terms of fire blight,

it might be a question of how permissive an apple is in which stage to distribute or at least to accept the bacteria and to multiply them. I think this is a matter of maturity but it can also be a matter of the cultivar and other circumstances. For those reasons, I think to answer that question completely will not be too helpful in order to say something about the presence and multiplication of *E. amylovora*. That is my opinion, but I'm not really the person who can define maturity of an apple.

Chairman

90.   Thank you. Dr. Hale?

Dr. Hale

91.   I think we all have problems defining the real maturity of an apple. As far as I'm concerned, I go by the response from New Zealand as to what a mature apple is, as really it relates more or less to whether the apple is at a stage where it is in fact going to ripen. The physiological maturity is a stage where once the apple is picked it will, in fact, carry on to ripen. Commercial maturity really is at the next stage, if you like, with continuation of that physiological maturity to a stage where the fruit is going to be acceptable in the marketplace. So, I guess, if you want to look at it like that, it is a continuum. But, as Dr. Geider has mentioned, whether or not the stage, whether it's physiologically mature or commercially or horticulturally mature, has any bearing on the ability of bacteria associated with that fruit to cause disease is a question which is very difficult to answer. And probably it may not be of any use for us to answer that one as far as the disease is concerned, and whether it's going to be transmitted.

Chairman

92.   Thank you very much. Dr. Hayward?

Dr. Hayward

93.   Mr. Chairman, I have nothing to add to that.

Chairman

94.   Thank you. Dr. Smith?

Dr. Smith

95.   Mr. Chairman, I think I would agree with Dr. Geider that whatever it is that makes an immature apple susceptible to fire blight has not necessarily much to do with what later makes it physiologically mature or commercially mature. I think these just represent points in time in the development of an apple. It is clear that very young apples are susceptible. It would seem that by the time apples have reached the time when they are commercially mature they are no longer susceptible and that at some point in between, they lose that susceptibility. But I would hesitate to say exactly when or exactly why they do so.

Chairman

96.   Thank you. Have you any further questions on that?

Japan

97.   Yes, I have quite a few sets of questions. I think we were talking about the beginning of the pathway. I think we finally understand from the answers that it is a very continuous process of maturing of the apple and at an earlier stage, apples are very susceptible and that that susceptibility will decrease as time goes on. So what ever does the United States mean by the term "maturity"? I recall that Dr. Smith observed that "apples tested by van der Zwet *et al.* (1990) were not mature". I think all the other experts agreed with his description of the study. May I ask each one of the experts under which definition do you believe the apples of the van der Zwet *et al.* (1990) were not mature?

Chairman

98.   Under which definition do you believe the apples of the van der Zwet *et al.* (1990) were not mature?

Dr. Geider

99.   I feel rather like a prophet to look back and to know what they considered to be mature. I think it was probably done by eye. There were some sort of opinion on that and that ok, this looks immature and this is mature. But I have to tell you that scientists of course want to pick up something peculiar and probably they said: oh, we found something that is an apple which looks mature and therefore we have now shown fire blight can exist in mature apples. I think this is a tendency we are all forced actually by publishing papers to find something new and unexpected and this might be the final solution of that paper, as I say, exaggerated a little bit, and saying: oh, we saw symptoms on apples which are mature - and another thing is that of course where there are problems with apples, they have a tendency to ripen earlier. They get into a mature stage just because they are struggling with something inside, so this could be another point, but it is all sort of guesses and I have no idea to say backwards why they said it was a mature apple.

Dr. Hale

100.   I can only go along what Dr. van der Zwet and Professor Thomson have said on this particular issue. I don't think that it is really a major point as to whether they were mature or not. I think that to try to go back and re-analyse work which was done in 1990, using some of the techniques that were available at that time, is perhaps not the way to go and I would be much happier if we had data from work which had been done more recently, using the techniques which are now available, as Dr. Geider suggested very early on. I think that my own feeling is that we are attaching probably far too much importance to this particular paper.

Dr. Hayward

101.   Again, I would refer to the declarations by Dr. van der Zwet and Professor Thomson. To answer the question from Japan directly, the fruit taken in July and August must have been by definition, immature. So I think the answer lies in the declaration by those two authorities and in their paper. The

fruit came at a time of the season when they could not have been other than immature.

Dr. Smith

102. I would support the position of Dr. Hayward.

Chairman

103. Thank you very much. Anything further on this topic? [Pause] Well, to an issue which is related to the same topic, otherwise we will go on to the next issue from the US.

Japan

104. Thank you. Let me start. When I first read about this continuation between immature apple and mature apple, my first impression was that when you are talking about the immature apples, you are talking about fruitlets or very small ones. But as the process goes on I believe if it is really a continuous process, something very near to maturity, or maybe even physiologically mature apples, could be indeed not just infested body but also infected. We have searched various websites and we found a picture of apples which show symptoms only a few weeks before the harvest stage. Has this been distributed?

Chairman

105. I only have the black and white version.

Japan

106. Exhibit JPN-41. This is a picture we saw, we found on the website of the Michigan State University, which is captioned that the fruit was infected only a few weeks before harvest. So whatever it is, it must be very close to whatever maturity it is, or even maybe physiologically mature. And it seems to me that these two fairly large apples show serious symptoms.

Chairman

107. Is the question clear?

Japan

108. No, it is not a question.

Chairman

109. I think we should stick to questions. We seem to be on much the same issue that the US was on at the beginning. I thought we had agreed that we would alternate the issues. Do you want to start an issue which is different, because we still seem to be mining the same topic; have we finished with that topic now and can we go on to another one?

Dr. Geider

110. Just to make a comment on that apple, or apples. I think I did not have to look at the internet. I actually presented not a Korean brown apple but a brown apple in my report; I think that those things can really happen that apples get

sorts of fire blight and they get ooze when fire blight is striking a tree. But on the other hand, there are several questions coming up and one is of course, that I have to admit that even in my apples I presented in my report, we have never shown that the ooze which is coming out was caused by *E. amylovora*. It could have been something else. This picture was taken in 1988, in the fire blight outbreak in July in the Heidelberg area of Germany and of course it was quite obvious that this all and the same as here looks like what we would expect from fire blight and I have no personal reason to disprove that assumption. On the other hand the question is this apple really mature? To me it is looking quite green and for those reasons it could be immature. I don't know, they don't even say the variety or what they used, it could be Granny Smith, or what, anyhow, I think it's you see the difficulty. They make the statement a few weeks before harvest and they say it's mature but I doubt that. I think it is still an apple in a developmental state where it is getting mature and I would not really agree on that and the same thing of course is the problem is that what is coming out here is it really ooze from *E. amylovora* or is it some sort of soft rot mixed with something else? I can't say.

Dr. Hale

111.   Just to follow up on that one, I consider many of the apples which are also in this cluster are fairly green, and I would say that they are immature. If those fruit had been infected at some stage, then that might, in fact, bring on the maturity and cause reddening as if the fruit is starting to mature. Again we have no proof that what is exuding from those apples is *E. amylovora*.

Dr. Hayward

112.   I don't have anything to add to that, Mr. Chairman.

Dr. Smith

113.   Well, Mr. Chairman, these are certainly not symptomless apples!

Japan

114.   My question wasn't really meant to ask you whether these are mature. Matter of fact it seems to me immature, but my question was this is very large, and they are at this stage it still get infected by something. It seems to me it's a fire blight bacteria. So, generally speaking even at this stage, can these apples be infected? We are not talking about only very young fruits but fairly close to maturity apples can be infected. Am I correct to say that, or do the experts agree?

Dr. Geider

115.   Actually when I commented to the first question or the first part of the Panel's question, I said that apple is not very susceptible and actually we are not using it all in the lab to look to screen strains of *E. amylovora*, or mutants or whatever we do. I think apple is not so susceptible that it is a lab tool. It is something which you can notice in nature and I don't know what other labs, we cannot ask Dr. Hayward, but Dr. Hale is using apples in the lab. So I think the experience in the lab about apple as a tool to look for fire blight is very limited

and for those reasons I cannot answer the question is an apple in this stage is susceptible to show fire blight symptoms.

Dr. Hale

116.   Mr. Chairman, I really can't add too much more to that. I think that we again find it very difficult and I mentioned this in my response, to infect apples as they become mature, but I agree with the comment that Dr. Smith made, this is not a symptomless fruit, and in most of the comments I made I am talking about mature, symptomless apple fruit from orchards which are not showing fire blight symptoms. My feelings in looking at that picture is that the orchard must have had fairly high levels of fire blight in it.

Dr. Hayward

117.   Mr. Chairman, this illustration refers to the fire blight epidemic in South West Michigan. We are told nothing about it. There must have been some severe meteorological disturbance I should think, perhaps severe hail damage. Indeed, the illustration you provide Dr. Geider, in your, I think 'After Hail Damage'. Well, we know nothing about the history of this particular crop. There must presumably have been some severe damage. That is all I'm going to say about that.

Chairman

118.   Since you have brought that up, perhaps I could go back to Dr. Geider because in the answer to Question 12 from the Panel, you made reference to van der Zwet's successor at the US Department of Agriculture, in Kearneysville as having informed colleagues about late growth stage infection of apples with fire blight after a hail storm. I wonder if you could expand on the source of this information and its relevance to the claim that mature apples are symptomless?

Dr. Geider

119.   Ok, what happened was actually that there was a severe hail-storm and Dr. Norelli informed a couple of colleagues that they are facing fire blight problem. I don't know if somebody else here in the audience was informed. It was actually there were many pictures taken with hail and impressive glass damage of greenhouses and very little bit of fire blight. Of course you can expect that. When hail is coming into an orchard there is damage, fire blight may occur two weeks or later and for those reasons I think this was not too impressive for an outbreak of fire blight. The only message which is coming out is that a hail storm can really cause outbreaks which are unpredictable. I think is spring when there are flowers and when there are insects visiting flowers, so the distribution of fire blight is quite clear, but later on when there is a hail storm those things can happen and its really not in our hands what will be coming up with fire blight or if there is nothing coming up and for those reasons I think we should be always aware that late events which could even occur just before harvest could affect all the fire blight in orchards.

Chairman

120.   To go back to Dr. Smith, please take the floor on that.

Dr. Smith

121.   I think Mr. Chairman, that one of the important points is that when fire blight bacteria multiply and infect apple fruit they cause symptoms, and you can see they are there, you can see that something is happening. Under the normal situation in which fruit is being inspected and certified for movement, such fruit would not be accepted.. There may be certain extreme situations (orchards with a very high level of fire blight or extreme weather situations) in which fruit which is not very small and very immature but rather older, may become infected. But then you see something like this and I think this is why the insistence is that what is really safe is mature symptomless fruit. Fruits like these, whether they are mature or not, clearly present a danger, but they should not be traded.

Japan

122.   Thank you. So since Dr. Hayward raised the question of damage, external damage which may be a conduit to the bacteria inside the fruit and as we read the experts' opinions we understand that there are possibly two possible ways of bacteria reaching the apple fruit. One is contamination of the stigma during the flower stage and the possible external damage. We wondered whether those two are the only possible roads of infestation and we did a little bit of experiments very recently which has been provided and distributed to you as Exhibit No.39 and 42.

Chairman

123.   Have these been made available to the experts and to the other parties?

Japan

124.   Yes. There are some pictures here in colour!

United States

125.   May I ask a quick question Mr. Chairman? I notice that Japan's questions started with definitions of maturity. Now we are moving on to different ways in which fruit may become infected. I am happy to let Japan ask another question, although I have lost track in my notes whether this is four or five. And can I just confirm that we will have the opportunity to pose a question of our own at some point? Thank you.

Chairman

126.   Absolutely yes. I think we want to try to break the continuum at some stage otherwise we won't be able to alternate the issues.

Japan

127.   Well, in fact, the next set of questions will complete the cycle.

Chairman

128.   Ok

Japan

129.   Thank you and so we wonder whether there will be any possible other roads of infestation or entry of bacteria inside apple fruits and we found, so we did a little bit of research projects and the results already are out, and I wish to introduce Professor Goto to explain the results and purpose and some discussions of the study, if I may.

Chairman

130.   So your question is what's the experts' reaction to these?....

Japan

131.   Yes, yes ....

Professor Goto (Japan)

132.   Thank you Mr. Chairman, members of the Panel and all of the experts. I read carefully all the literature cited in the documents of both parties to this dispute as an adviser of the Japanese delegation to this meeting. As a result I noticed a question which was not satisfactorily explained in the literature. The question is on the infection and all infestation of apple fruit via pedicel or stem. Most attention of the past studies was focused exclusively on calyx, fruit surface and fruit itself and the infection and/or infestation of apple fruit via pedicel or stem was rarely discussed. Perhaps the only exception was the data listed in Table 4 of van der Zwet *et al*. 1990.

133.   Therefore I requested the scientists of Yokohama Plant Protection Station of Japan to conduct preliminary experiments on the infection, multiplication and movement of *E. amylovora* in pedicel of mature apple fruits. The experiment was conducted through to evaluate the ability of *E. amylovora* to invade fruit pedicel, to multiply in this tissue and to further to move inside of apple fruit. The materials and the method are explained in the paper distributed to you submitted as Exhibits JPN-39 and JPN-42. The results were that *E. amylovora* clearly showed rapid ingress into the pedicel and active multiplication there. Moreover, it was suggested that the bacteria further moved into fruit within several days because *E. amylovora* was detected in the vascular tissue. These pictures show that if an apple tree has an internal *E. amylovora* population, the fruit are continuously exposed to introduction of the bacteria through pedicel, regardless of the maturing stage of fruit, until they are harvested. Although further investigation is necessary, the route of the introduction of *E. amylovora* into apple fruit may not be limited to stigmas of flowers in early season and accidental injuries of fruit surfaces thereafter. I cannot fail to emphasize that the results of this experiment are clearly consistent with some of the experimental results of van der Zwet *et al*. (1990), especially in the pathological survey that detection of *E. amylovora* in upper core was clearly correlated with that in stem with regards to Rome Beauty apples harvested from blighted Utah orchard.

134.   Also, the results of the storage experiment can be explained by the same discovery, namely it is considered that *E. amylovora* remaining in pedicel or upper core later caused the fruit blight inside of apple fruit during the cold

storage. Unfortunately *E. amylovora* couldn't be detected inside of apple fruit in the first experiment. However, the bubble formation on top of the apple fruit suggests that physiological activity of fruit was depressed by invasion of *E. amylovora* and that caused induction and the propagation of anaerobic bacteria. This phenomenon occurred because the apple fruit were harvested in Japan which had rich micro-flora and the high humidity and different results will be obtained in the United States with a relatively poor micro-flora.

135.   To sum up, these results of these very recent experiments indicate that the available information on the fruit infection is far from enough to draw any decisive conclusion, in spite of enormous number of articles on fire blight in the long history of research. Thank you.

Chairman

136.   Can I clarify what the question is therefore, for the experts?

Japan

137.   Yes, Do you have any comments?

Dr. Geider

138.   I agree with Dr. Goto that this type of experiment has not been routinely performed in labs and therefore it is somehow novel or maybe a parallel approach of old data of Tom van der Zwet. Of course what I would expect is when you cut the pedicel and you put *E. amylovora.* solution on top it will be sucked in and it will somehow be in the apple after some time and afterwards of course you can ask for symptoms. I think I would agree with the first part that *E. amylovora* is in and the bacteria which are presented here in the sort of MS medium look like *E. amylovora* and therefore things are ok and there is not doubt on that but I have to say that the pedicel tissue is of course something different from the apple although it belongs usually to the apple. Yes I think we all eat apples which are not harvested without pedicels so this could some sort of attraction for fire blight which is in the stem which is getting to this part of the apple and it will stick there. The other part which are the figures 6 and 7 look a little bit unusual to me, a thing is foaming at the left side is from my opinion not typical for fire blight at all. I think it could be some other micro organism and you say you find these apples rich in micro-flora it might be something else but I have never seen *E. amylovora* foaming on a plant surface like that although I can be wrong by doing not the same experiment.

139.   The next pictures which are of brown apples look to me quite rotten and of course I have to believe you that this is fire blight and we see those symptoms coming up from *E. amylovora*. If you don't mind we can repeat that experiment at home with labelled *E. amylovora* and find out if everything which is seen here is really *E. amylovora* or something else and for those reasons I think we should keep this as an interesting experiment in the lab but a little bit cautious in interpretation if this clearly shows that apple can be infected just from fire blight coming from the stem section through the pedicel into the apple. I would be a little bit cautious in saying that.

Dr. Hale

140.   Yes, I would like to just follow that up because I think that Dr. Geider is quite right. If you cut the surface and you put a pure suspension of *E. amylovora* on that cut surface then it is likely to be sucked into that vascular system. It may well be because of this sudden impact of large amounts of *E. amylovora* in that area that there is some tissue breakdown and what is happening then is that the anaerobic or fermentative bacteria are breaking down carbohydrates around that area at the top, or breaking down the plant tissue, releasing carbohydrates which may, in fact, enhance the growth of *E. amylovora* at that stage. But I think it really is quite an artificial situation to cut the surface like that and then just let the bacteria get sucked in.

Dr. Hayward

141.   Mr. Chairman, I agree with what both the previous speakers have said, but I would like to refer to the last paragraph in the discussion to this paper, which seems to me to make an assumption which is not warranted. The paragraph begins: "We consider that this phenomenon, (and the authors are referring to the figure 6, left) we consider the gas formation due to possibly anaerobic bacteria, possibly other Enterobacteriaceae . We consider that this phenomenon might develop because these apples were harvested in Japan, which has complicated and rich micro-flora under high temperature and humidity and different results will be obtained from apples harvested in the United States which has rather micro-flora." I can't see that that is a scientific statement. We don't have the experience the experiments haven't been done in the United States. The comparable experiments have not been done. How can it be said that the micro-flora is poor in one part of the world as compared with another, without having I don't understand that statement. Thank you.

Dr. Smith

142.   I think Mr. Chairman, that experiments done under artificial conditions of this kind can give one some insights into what might happen, but the first point in my mind, is what is supposed to happen in nature? Apples in fact are mainly attached to the trees by their pedicels. They are not cut and so the question is, supposing that there were a canker on the branch, can the bacterium spread through the pedicel into the fruit under those conditions? And such an experiment would also have to be done to see whether the results obtained in the laboratory have any relation to a natural situation. In the comments that I made earlier, I said that all kinds of strange results can be obtained by artificially inoculating plants with high concentrations of pathogen. Such experiments can guide you as to what might happen, but they do not really provide conclusive evidence of what is happening on an apple tree.

Chairman

143.   Thank you very much. Are we now at the point where we can go onto another issue, or are we still on .. You have another question relating to the same topic? So you have a question back to the experts on what they have just said? Please go ahead.

Professor Goto (Japan)

144. Dr. Smith, I would like to ask a question about your comment. I think that every expert would agree to the fact that there is latent infection with *E. amylovora* on branch in nature. Also, various studies have reported the existence of very small cankers on branch in nature. Then, do you think that *E. amylovora* can move from a canker on branch into fruit through xylem?

Dr. Geider

145. Ok, I probably got at least the end of the question.

Chairman:

146. Would you like to have it repeated?

Dr. Geider

147. No, no it is ok. It is always a question how does *E. amylovora* move in plants and we did quite a bit of work showing that the bacteria are moving towards the root system and it is unexpected but it is in agreement with data which were before obtained by Bob Goodman in Missouri. So I think the question that it's moving from a canker in the stem up and getting into branches and finally into fruits is very unlikely. I think all our data are objective against this assumption, I think the only thing which could be assumed is that a tip of a shoot is getting newly infected with fire blight and the bacteria are moving down and they are hitting apples and then they get this way into the pedicel and finally into the fruit. But in general, shoots are not this much any more in the late part of the season, that means in August, September shoots are mature and they do not sprout any more and for those reasons I think fire blight is restricted to older parts of the plant and this movement can do at least to the data we have in the lab cannot occur.

Dr. Hale

148. I have nothing to add to that.

Dr. Hayward

149. I have nothing to add to that.

Chairman

150. Any more questions from Japan?

Professor Goto (Japan)

151. I would like to ask a question about Dr. Hayward's comment. As I mentioned at the beginning, this experiment is a preliminary one. In the last paragraph of the paper on the preliminary experiment, we stated that *Clostridium* sp. could be involved in the bubble formation. We have considered that if the infection occurs like this and a lot of ethylene would come out, anaerobic condition could be produced. Then, *Clostridium* sp. could multiply under anaerobic condition. Of course, Enterobacteriaceae could multiply and form the

bubble. I think that both can occur. Dr. Hayward, do you think that neither situation can occur under this condition?

Dr. Hayward

152.   Thank you Mr. Chairman. I don't have any quarrel with the statement made by Professor Goto. I merely drew attention to the last paragraph in relation to the comment made about the micro-flora in the United States. That is why I raised the matter. I think the interesting phenomenon is its clearly a gassy response implying fermentation of soluble sugars, maybe polysaccharides from the fruit by bacteria which could be, as suggested I think, facultative anaerobes or even possibly anaerobic bacteria, and the comparison was made in the last paragraph with the known Clostridium sp. response on potato. So I have no disagreement I think either possibility that Professor Goto has raised is likely. But that is not really why I raised the matter.

Dr. Geider

153.   A short question about this browning. To me it looks that there is some sort of saprophyte coming up and its just colonised the tissue and I would say this could be explanation that this sort of foam is coming out. Would you agree on that?

Dr. Hayward

154.   Yes.

Chairman

155.   You are talking about these pictures here? Yes. Thank you. Japan, any more? This is the last one?

Japan

156.   Let's forget the mature, immature distinction of continuum or continuous process for a while. Nonetheless in some of the experiments bacteria were isolated inside the apple. I wonder what would happen to maybe a small population of bacteria in the following few weeks. Would they die or would they somehow multiply and how quickly they will complete whatever process?

Dr. Geider

157.   Just to repeat the question – how were the bacteria introduced into the fruit just by damaging the fruit outside or by the pedicels? Is that it?

Japan

158.   I am sorry, I am referring to van der Zwet *et al.* (1990). In van der Zwet *et al.* (1990) some very small population of bacteria were recovered from fruits and the question is what the fate of those bacteria would have been? Would they have died, or would they have survived and multiplied in whatever it is and how long would it have taken for the bacteria to perform that process?

Dr. Geider

159.   I think it is getting back to the old problem with that paper. In 1990 of course they did probably some plating assays there to find out that there is *E. amylovora*. Really I am unable to comment how this bacteria behaved before – were they in the fruit, were they epiphytic or were they just a contamination by hands getting to the fruit? I think we really dwell now on a paper a little bit difficult in terms of how it was created and how all the data were interpreted. Usually to our opinion and I agree on that with many of my colleagues, including Jean-Pierre Paulin, saying that persistence of fire blight in plant tissue is a very difficult issue, you cannot really judge here what is going on there. Is the population staying? Is it going up or down? And actually we discussed that issue when there was transient occurrence of fire blight in the Botanic Garden of Melbourne if plants which were imported and put into the garden could have carried fire blight for decades, maybe thirty years or so, and finally we gave up. I think there is no real research on the point about persistence of this pathogen, specifically *E. amylovora*, in plant tissue. The only point is that there is something in the population increases and you get symptoms and you see the symptoms and you say that's fire blight.

Chairman

160.   Thank you. Dr. Hale, in asking you to address this question, can I add a related question from the Panel? In your reply to Question 10 from us, with reference to Thomson (2000), you stated that endophytic bacteria can "multiply in internal tissues without causing disease". So the question is, can these bacteria nonetheless spread the disease to other hosts?

Dr Hale

161.   Right. I'm not necessarily talking about fire blight in this situation. This is a situation of endophytic bacteria in plant tissue generally and not necessarily fire blight.

Chairman

162.   Do you have anything else you wish to say on the question as originally formulated?

Dr. Hale

163.   Can you just go back to that question again? The original question? I don't really have any information on that other than to corroborate what Dr. Geider has said.

Chairman

164.   Dr. Hayward?

Dr. Hayward

165.   Mr. Chairman, I have nothing to add to what Dr. Geider said.

Chairman

166.   Dr. Smith?

Dr. Smith

167.   I think that, in van der Zwet *et al.* (1990), as far as we can infer, the fruits were symptomless. Of course it's impossible to say with any certainty what eventually might have happened to those fruits. But, because, in general, internal infections with fire blight are not found in mature fruits, we would suppose that nothing would have happened to those bacteria; they would simply have stayed there at the same level or perhaps declined. But I am really making a conjecture there because I do not think that this is a situation which has been investigated. But I would suppose that the population could not increase, so that the situation of those bacteria as a phytosanitary risk would not be very different from those that might be in the calyx or which might be on the outside.

Chairman

168.   Thank you very much. Can we now bring that particular discussion to a close and revert to the United States to the questions on their next issue.

United States

169.   Thank you Mr. Chairman. We do wish to move matters along. It did seem to us there were a couple of issues raised by the Japanese questions and the experts' responses that could bear some clarification. In particular, while I'm sorry that the Japanese scientists had to spend the holiday season conducting new research, I'm doubly sorry that the experts have not had much time to review these exhibits that were only presented on Friday and this morning. And I thought that I may have heard perhaps a slight mis-statement from one or more of the experts with regards to the result of this experiment. In particular I'm looking at the one from Friday. I thought that someone had mentioned that while this really does look like fruit rot, how can you know that this is fire blight or why do you report this as fire blight and I'm looking at the discussion of this first experiment (this is Exhibit JPN-39) and actually if you refer to the colour exhibits with the plates that were passed out, you go down to number 6, you can see scoops in the cortex of the fruit. If you then read the discussion it says the discs of mesocarps were gouged out at the same intervals using a sterilised cork borer. Detection of *E. amylovora* from these discs was carried out as described above and no *E. amylovora was detected in any disc*. The cause of browning has not been clarified yet. I read this report to be that in fact they're not recording this as fire blight infection caused by *E. amylovora* because they didn't detect any *E. amylovora* within the cortex of the fruit from these discs that you can see in the colour plates that have been gouged out. But as I'm not a scientist and Dr. Roberts has not had time to properly train me on what to say, I thought that it might be expedient for me to turn to Dr. Roberts and perhaps he could give some reactions to this paper and then we could ask the Panel's experts for their reactions to that reading.

Chairman

170.   As long as this is framed in the form of a fixed question to the experts.

United States

171.   Just as Japan has phrased its questions. Thank you.

Dr. Roberts

172.   I've only had a brief time to read this paper as well but I have a couple of comments that I think bear consideration and perhaps comment by the Panel in light of their statements previously. First I would like to reiterate what Mr. Millán has indicated and that is that contrary to the claim, the fruit mesocarp was not infected by fire blight and I think perhaps the experts were under the impression that this was a fire blight infection when in fact it was not. Additionally I do not feel that infection of the pedicel occurred either. There was no ooze present. We see a little discoloration of the tissue but pedicel browning was reported primarily at the point at which the pedicel was cut for the inoculum and this is likely due to oxidated browning. Many times you cut plant tissue it turns brown, due to the production of polyphenols and so it's not at all clear or confirmed that this fruit became infected with fire blight at all. As the experts have commented, removing the abscission layer before placing the inoculum onto the pedicel removes a major barrier to infestation and invasion by many micro-organisms. That this is a totally artificial construct is reflected in the fact that stems have never been shown to harbour an internal bacteria, internal populations of the *E. amylovora*, in studies of fruit exposed to naturally-occurring inoculum, referring to Sholberg *et al.* (1988) and my own work in 1989 which, by the way, both of these studies did evaluate the presence of *E. amylovora* in stems of fruit that were harvested from trees that had fire blight, and none was found. Of course we didn't cut the ends of the stems off and put the bacterium on there, we just looked at what happens in nature. Now, the abscission layer serves as a barrier to entry of micro-organisms and also restricts the loss of water from the fruit. Removing this abscission layer allowed, apparently in this experiment, the transpiring apple to draw in the aqueous suspension of *E. amylovora*. Even so, neither infection nor infestation of the fruit cortex occurred even after 10 days of incubation under the artificial method of inoculation and incubation under near ideal conditions apparently. So I would be interested in the Panel's further reflection of the significance of this work in light of this additional, perhaps clarifying information.

Chairman

173.   Thank you. Before I ask the experts to respond to that perhaps I should first of all say that we had envisaged in fact that we would probably have come to an end of this afternoon's session by now, but we haven't done so and it is a useful process we would like to continue with but unfortunately one of our number Mr. Häberli has to leave us and he will be back tomorrow but we propose to continue with just the other two panellists. I hope that's acceptable to the parties. Dr. Geider, perhaps I could ask you to respond to the US.

Dr. Geider

174. Just maybe repeating in different statements what I said before – the browning of the fruit is caused by something else and of course I didn't have the time too much to read all the statements and there was no *E. amylovora* involved anyhow, I think this is a clear point. The other point is about this figure 7 – the left apple here which shows some sort of browning from inside, I would assume that this is very similar, that there is some sort of rotting bacterium or something else but of course you have to take samples out and the question is: was that done? An apple which has this browning and was assayed for fire blight or for *E. amylovora* or was that just kept as it is? The question is to the Japanese party.

Chairman

175. Does Japan wish to respond to that at this time? Are you able to respond to it?

Professor Goto (Japan)

176. We just started this experiment last December, so we have had only one month since then. In addition, apple fruit season has already passed. Therefore, we will study this topic intensively from autumn this year, and further examine how the browning of the fruit was caused, whether or not *E. amylovora* can be isolated by other isolation methods from the rotten part of the apple fruit and from the base of pedicel where the bubble was formed, how the bacteria can move inside of apple fruit after invasion through pedicel, etc. On the last point, Crosse *et al.* (1972) already reported that the bacteria could move quickly both upwards and downwards through main vein from the inoculated point. Dr. Roberts has pointed out that the infection of the pedicel did not occur in this experiment. We would agree with him if "infection" were defined as "oozing". We would like to emphasize, however, that pedicel could play an important role for multiplication and movement of the bacteria. Therefore, we would like to examine these issues from completely different viewpoint and wish to demonstrate what kind of role the pedicel infection with *E. amylovora* could play in infection and fruit blight inside of apple fruit.

Chairman

177. Thank you. Dr. Geider, you asked that question.

Dr. Geider

178. I have an agreement and a disagreement. I think what, I have followed the work of Goodman and personal discussions with him. *E. amylovora* is moving mainly downward, it's moving a little bit upwards but mainly downwards as a plant so I think that this is also in agreement with our results we published a couple of years ago. With ooze formation and the pedicel, I'm of course not so convinced that must happen all the time because ooze formation requires a special environment which is not always realised especially in plant tissue they can just get necrotic and showing no ooze. Ooze needs humidity and certain conditions, so I think ooze formation might not be applicable for all plant tissue tested.

Chairman

179. Dr. Hale? Anything on what has just transpired?

Dr. Hale

180. Yes, just looking at the pictures. I just feel again that we haven't really got any proof that the symptoms are caused by fire blight. Okay, admittedly *E. amylovora* placed on the pedicel, the cut pedicel, is probably being sucked into the vascular system and consequently it may multiply a little there, particularly as the fruit is breaking down. So, one would expect to find *E. amylovora* there. However, just looking at the rot-type symptoms now, the fact that nothing has entered the mesocarp, and also that picture No. 7 certainly, to me, looks far more like a fruit rotting than it does to symptoms caused by fire blight.

Dr. Hayward

181. I don't really have anything to add. I think it was useful for Dr. Roberts to point it out that those cork borer extracts, none of that resulted in isolation of *E. amylovora*. And looking at the paper I see that the results are actually in the fourth paragraph of the discussion.

Dr. Smith

182. One interesting thing about what's done here is that these symptoms do result from inoculation of the pedicels with *E. amylovora*. I assume that in the control apples nothing happened. So this is evidence of some kind that if you introduce *E. amylovora* into an apple in various ways you can actually trigger infection of the apple by saprophytic bacteria which are not *E. amylovora* and various strange phenomena can be obtained. I recall van der Zwet *et al.* (1990) who found that, when they surface-sterilized apples and put them into store, those which had been exposed to *E. amylovora* beforehand rotted much more than those that had not and yet the surface sterilization is supposed to destroy the bacteria. So, there is no doubt that strange things can be done and the interactions between *E. amylovora* and other bacteria may cause strange effects. But whether these correspond to anything in nature, I am inclined to doubt.

United States

183. At this time our preference would actually be to whether we could stop proceedings for today and begin tomorrow only because we have additional questions along this subject-matter but we just feel it would probably be more appropriate and given procedurally useful since this is an oral discussion and discourse here for all 3 panellists to be present, so if that is alright with you and with Japan, that is our preference.

Chairman

184. The problem is that time will be limited tomorrow and it's not tonight, so if we give up this time now we may come to the end of the available time without having asked all the questions and having given everybody the opportunity ...

United States

185.   We understand that but again, just looking at our questions and maybe I don't know how many questions – this is why we're raising this now, to see what other, what the Panel's view is and what Japan's view is but, I mean, we feel that tomorrow would be sufficient time to cover, at least our questions and then some, but I don't know, maybe both either the Panel or Japan may have just an overwhelming amount of questions – I just think in this situation it is useful to have all 3 Panellists present when there's nothing on record here.

Chairman

186.   The time-limit again for Mr. Häberli tomorrow is 2 p.m. so after 2 p.m. he will not be available so we would then have to, if we are going to start at 11, we would really only have a couple of hours. I would ask you to take that into consideration.

187.   We are prepared to make a proposal that would hopefully address the concerns. We suggest that we resume with all 3 Panel members at 9 a.m. tomorrow morning and hopefully aim to complete the process by the end of the morning and we would adjourn now. Any problems with that?

United States

188.   Mr. Chairman, just to confirm then that we would be able to have an opportunity to go through the procedure as you laid it out in the beginning, I mean through that time-period. For example, should there be a problem and we are not able to get through closing statements by the experts, will we still make time for that as well? Because after what you've said we consider that we were not aware that we only had limited time tomorrow as well.

Chairman

189.   Well the situation is that we are still in the questions from parties to experts and we are going to follow the procedure as laid out, so the next stage after that will be, once the parties' questions are all exhausted, will be a brief suspension while the Panel reflects for 15 minutes or so and then we will come back with our questions. Just on that, it would be helpful to know whether there are still a lot more questions to come from the Parties or whether we've made good progress, or whether we've only just begun.

United States

190.   Depending on how you define questions, we have 3 questions only to ask. This might be 3 subject matters but I don't think these questions will take very long. It's more multiple questions, because as drafted we might pose a question to an individual expert and then ask the other experts to comment as well, so we would only have 3 questions for you, for the experts.

Japan

191.   Well if we try to reduce specific questions, we have quite a few more questions, however I'd say several questions.

Chairman

192.   How many is several? Less than ten? Less than five?

Japan

193.   It's a continuum!

Chairman

194.   I think that the best we can say is that we can try to advance the process, hoping that we can finish between 9 and 2. Of course it's still open to go on with the other 2 Panellists. We have no control over our colleague's commitments but I don't think we can offer more than that really. We're quite prepared to go on tonight but if you would prefer to start in the morning then I think that proposal we made would maximise the available time. So we will adjourn now and resume at 9 tomorrow morning unless there's any....

United States

195.   Your proposal's fine with us.

Chairman

196.   So we'll adjourn now and resume in this room at 9 tomorrow morning. Thank you very much.

TUESDAY, 14 JANUARY

United States

197.   Yesterday we started to follow the hypothetical pathway for fire blight and we asked whether there was any scientific evidence of endophytic populations of bacteria in harvested mature fruit. The experts replied there was none. Today's questions will address epiphytic populations of bacteria along each step of the hypothetical pathway – that is, mature, harvested fruit. With reference to panel question 19, I want to focus on what evidence there is of the hypothetical risk of epiphytic *E. amylovora* on apple fruit. A question to Dr. Hale with regard to Thomson (2000): In your answer you stated that you agreed with Thomson's conclusions that "contamination of mature fruit is rare and only occurs when there are active sources of fire blight either in the orchard or close by. Wherever *E amylovora* has been detected on mature fruit it has been associated with fruit from orchards with high levels of fire blight infection". Dr. Hale, based on our reading of Thomson (2000), we assume that the literature you were considering in making this statement was Hale *et al.* (1987), Sholberg *et al.* (1988), and van der Zwet *et al.* (1990) because these three active sources of fire blight and severely blighted orchards?

Dr. Hale

198.   Yes.

United States

199.   And "rare" because most of the literature which attempted to isolate or recover live *E. amylovora* from mature fruit harvested from blighted trees and orchards did *not* isolate *E. amylovora*?

Dr. Hale

200.   In subsequent observations, we have only found epiphytic *E. amylovora* in calyxes when harvested from New Zealand orchards with high populations of *E. amylovora* and severe fire blight symptoms.

United States

201.   With reference to the studies of Thomson (2000), Hale et al (1987) and Sholberg *et al.* (1988), there were different levels of infection in the orchards. In your 1987 study Dr. Hale, your results were from a highly infected orchards and *E. amylovora* was only found in the calyxes of less than 1 per cent of apples. In Hale and Taylor's 1999 study of a severely infected orchard, 2 per cent of fruit had *E. amylovora* isolated from them using two different techniques. These confirm that any findings of *E. amylovora* are rare?

Dr. Hale

202.   The results of the 1987 paper were from a heavily infected orchard with 75 strikes per tree and we found *E. amylovora* in the calyxes of less than 1 per cent of fruit from blighted trees. For fruit from a highly infected orchard harvested in 1999, less than 2 per cent of fruit had epiphytic *E. amylovora* in the calyx. PCR (Polymerase Chain Reaction) had been used to positively identify the bacteria, but PCR will give positive results even if the bacteria are dead. A further enrichment technique was also used for detection.

United States

203.   Thank you. I would like to ask the other experts whether they would agree with these conclusions of Thomson (2000) and Dr. Hale. Dr. Smith, you wrote that "The conclusions of Thomson (2000) seem well reasoned". Could you confirm that you were considering these conclusions?

Dr. Smith

204.   I support my written answer. Thomson (2000) seems well-reasoned.

Dr. Hayward

205.   Nothing to add to my written reply. Thomson found that the pistil surface was the most susceptible for *E. amylovora*. I am not aware of any work which disputes Thomson's study. Sholberg's study showed susceptibility only when apple trees were inter-planted with heavily infected pear trees.

Dr. Geider

206.   Many smear effects if the orchard is heavily blighted. Bees and insects can carry bacteria and leave bacteria sitting on apples. Rain also. So heavily

blighted orchards should not be used for export of apples. I agree with Thomson's conclusions.

United States

207. My understanding from your responses is that epiphytic bacterial populations may rarely be recovered from calyxes of mature fruit harvested from severely infected orchards with nearby sources of active inoculum. The next step in the hypothetical pathway would be that this epiphytically contaminated fruit is cleaned, sorted, sized and graded, etc. and put into cold storage. In fact, to be exported to Japan, US apples are required to undergo cold storage at less than 2.2° C for 55 days before shipping. On the effect of cool storage, I'd like to clarify whether there may be some divergence of opinion among the experts re the effect of cold storage. In Dr Geider's reply to Question 30, he commented that "cool storage will increase survival, whereas moisture and other microorganisms will add to the decay of the pathogen". In considering Dr. Geider's response, and contrary to our previous comment on this answer, it's come to our attention that, in fact, commercial cold storage of apples is at relatively high relative humidity levels: 85-95 per cent. For example the "Operations Guide for Export Apples" for Fresh New Zealand states that commercial cold stores in New Zealand use 90 per cent relative humidity plus or minus 5 per cent. Information from the University of Maine show 90-95 per cent humidity used. The reason being that apple fruit stored at low temperature and low humidity would shrivel and shrink, reducing fruit quality. Are any of the experts familiar with relative humidity in commercial cold storage?

Dr. Geider

208. Not doing survival studies on apples but other surfaces – plastics, agar etc- in a defined environment can show that *E. amylovora* survives at low humidity and in a sterile environment. General rule, cold and sterile better for survival than moist and the presence of other micro-organisms.

Dr. Hale

209. In Hale & Taylor (1999) apples were studied in commercial storage conditions to look at survival in the calyx end associated with dried up flowers. Fruit from a naturally infected orchard included about 2 per cent with *E. amylovora* on calyx before storage. Cold storage at 2°C for 25 days is the requirement for codling moth disinfestations of apples required by Japan. After cold storage, we found no evidence of fire blight bacteria in the calyx. We postulated that phenolic compounds from the re-hydrated dried-up flower remnants may affect the survival of the bacteria. I know that apples are stored at relatively high humidity to avoid desiccation.

United States

210. Given cool storage conditions of 55 days for codling moth in the US case what is the likelihood of *E. amylovora* surviving in calyxes?

Dr. Hale

211.   The likelihood of survival is reduced but we can't, as scientists, say there is no risk. You certainly reduce the number of bacteria surviving. When apples were artificially inoculated before cold storage at the highest dose of 10 (to the power of 7) and then left in retail conditions for a further 14 days we found a further drop off in numbers of bacteria surviving.

Dr. Hayward

212.   Sholberg *et al.* (1988) found that cool storage reduced *E. amylovora on* Newtown apples to below detection levels. I'm not sure if it was under commercial storage conditions though…..

Dr. Smith

213.   Concerning the effects of cold storage reducing *E. amylovora,* I think we need to know the initial levels we are starting from. Normally, *E. amylovora* levels would drop even under regular conditions over time. If it is cold and dry, numbers would drop less quickly; if there is high humidity, levels would drop more.

Dr. Hayward

214.   I can't find the reference for Sholberg *et al.* (1988). I don't recall any reference to the relative humidity in the study as being controlled.

Dr. Geider

215.   Reducing levels depends on where we start from . If you start with high doses of inoculum, for example 10 (to the power 8), you will find something . Is low number of bacteria meaningful to spread disease? The answer is no. If you inoculate at high levels you will find something at the end.

Dr. Smith

216.   All experiments done on fruit use high inoculum levels before passing the fruit directly into cold storage. Under real conditions fruit would be handled and then put into cold storage. This would be at ambient temperatures. So the levels of *E. amylovora* on the fruit would already be falling by the time the apples reached cold storage.

United States

217.   I'd like to turn now to the step in the hypothetical pathway relating to the fruit once it has arrived in Japan. Again, my understanding from your previous responses is: There is no scientific evidence of endophytic *E. amylovora* bacteria and only rarely is epiphytic bacteria found in calyxes. Epiphytic bacteria is reduced by handling and storage. What happens when it arrives? The experts were unanimous in that there was no risk of transfer from discarded fruit to an orchard. Looking at Japan's description of potential pathways in Exhibit JPN-14, Japan indicates that imported fruit with endophytic or epiphytic bacteria result in infected fruit that produce ooze. Is there any scientific evidence of ooze from apples with *E. amylovora* in the calyx ?

Dr. Geider

218. No. To get ooze from mature apples has not been described. Unrealistic even if artificially inoculated with high number. I was never able to get infection and have never seen ooze.

Dr. Hayward

219. I agree. It is highly unlikely that you could get ooze from residual populations in the calyx.

Dr. Smith

220. I would agree.

Chairman

221. On this question on the presence of *E. amylovora* and ooze, the Panel would be most grateful if you would assist us in our understanding of the terms bacteria, ooze and inoculum in relation to the transmission of fire blight? In particular, is the simple presence of bacteria on an apple sufficient to constitute a risk of transmission by any vector ? Or must the bacteria be in the form of ooze to be infectious to a host plant?

Dr. Hayward

222. Ooze consists of large populations of bacteria and exopolysaccharide. Ooze is the outcome of a severe infection on a susceptible host.

Dr. Hale

223. Bacteria associated with ooze are in a very active stage of multiplication. This is not the case with the bacteria found in the calyx of the apple.

Dr. Geider

224. Ooze is beneficial for *E. amylovora* bacteria to stop them from drying out. Polysaccharides in the ooze provide nutrients and help protect against the plant's natural defence mechanisms. However even naked bacteria not covered by ooze can multiply and infect if they find a suitable environment – but *E. amylovora* suffer without ooze protection.

Dr. Smith

225. No-one has observed the production of ooze from the calyx of an apple. The bacteria would have to multiply massively, and they could do this only if they infected the apple leading to visible symptoms. In the calyx you have perhaps tens or hundreds of bacteria surviving, whereas in a little ooze you have got thousands of millions of bacteria. The quantities are of a completely different order of magnitude. The bacteria have multiplied intensively; they are there in enormous numbers and the reason why ooze is much more infective is primarily because of these enormous numbers.

Dr. Hayward

226. Mr. Chairman can I add to that. I agree with that entirely. I was a little bit cautious about attempting to put numbers in ooze from say a pear or an apple or

indeed a fire blight strand, but in the context of the kind of diseases I work with we talk about bacterial ooze from infected potatoes with brown rot and you are talking about of the order of 10^{10} per millilitre. Does anybody have a figure for ooze?

Dr. Geider

227.   We are getting a little bit diverse in this respect and of course when you see something like ooze it is a mass of bacteria, of polysaccharides and of water so this is what you can see by eye when you look with a microscope you can see a little bit more when they are very small droplets but when you use a higher solution even with a microscope you can stain capsules and you still see that there is something around bacteria which is finally visible as ooze on a branch or whatever where the infection occurs. So I think ooze in one sense is a visible accumulation of many bacteria in this complex mixture but it can be turned down to a single cell which is covered over with a capsule which is composed of exopolysaccharides which is finally the form which is the ooze which we see. So I think these are all stages. One is the macroscopic status, the other one is the microscopic stage but in both cases we have exopolysaccharides and without those exopolysaccharides the bacteria are a little bit helpless and they suffer from their environment.

Chairman

228.   So does the ooze or perhaps the polysaccharides in the ooze attract other vectors such as birds, insects or bees?

Dr. Geider

229.   The answer is no in this sense because it does not contain sugars which are attractive. I have never tasted it but people think what attracts insects is the moisture. There is something which is humid and they go to that and then they get contaminated but I think by itself the exopolysaccharides are too large to be sensed as something useful for insects.

Dr. Hayward

230.   Can I just add a little bit. It is a water-loving substratum. It's hydrophilic isn't it. Recalling van der Zwet (1972) where they describe the appearance or enhancement of fire blight strand formation which is allied ooze. Fire blight strand formation by application of an oil spray and these strands were coming out from length cells and stigma and other natural openings. Now I think in that paper there is quite precise data about the amount of plant polysaccharide, the numbers of bacteria. Strand is a manifestation of ooze is it not? So there should be data somewhere.

Dr. Smith

231.   I would like to add some more remarks concerning the production of ooze from the bacteria in the calyx. Now first of all nobody has observed it but we can still argue about what would be happening if it were possible. You start with, as I said, some hundreds of bacteria that you can recover from a calyx and if ooze is to form those bacteria have got to multiply themselves from a few hundreds to

hundreds of millions and how can they do that? They can only do it by infecting the apple because bacteria can only grow if they are actively using a substrate and the only substrate available to them in an apple fruit is the apple tissue. So that is only possible if they infect and in fact if the apple is diseased. So between the bacteria in the calyx and the production of ooze there must be a phase of infection which would be visible also as a blighting of the fruit which then finally leads to the formation of ooze or bacterial strands. So it is not conceivable that ooze could be formed without some other symptoms that could be detected.

Chairman

232.   Moving on from that, you've talked about the high concentrations of bacteria in ooze. Are you aware of any studies on the concentrations of bacteria needed to infect the host plant whether or not it's in use. In fact how likely is it that fire blight bacteria would be found at such concentrations if they are definable on mature epiphytically infested apples.

Dr. Smith

233.   The question of the inoculum needed to infect is a very technical one and I defer to my colleagues to reply to you on that one.

Dr. Hayward

234.   I don't have data relating to apples but Crosse and Goodman (1972) described an experiment where they took young apple leaves and cut them at the apex just at the apex and cut the apex of the leaf off and sprayed inoculum at different concentrations and they found a minimal dosage of 38 cells. I think that is correct.

Dr. Geider

235.   Of course I think this is an endless question in phytopathology. How many pathogens do you need to cause a disease? I still think when the environment and everything is appropriate and ideal for multiplication you can go down to very low numbers and we have published data with slices from immature, freshly harvested pears and you can easily go down to about 50 bacteria in order to produce symptoms which means they will multiply and they will produce ooze and you can see that after a couple of days. So I think a low number of bacteria is still capable to produce symptoms in the environment which is suitable. In natural environments many bacteria have to visit flowers or leaves and damage them this is less known. I think the experience is the more bacteria you use the more often you get symptoms when you cut down the number you will have to work hard to see anything because the bacteria will disappear and nothing will happen so I think the experience is not to go to very low numbers otherwise you can work forever without seeing anything, but still back to the question is it possible to cause symptoms with very few bacteria I think in certain environments like immature pear slices it is.

Dr. Hale

236.   I agree entirely with what Dr. Geider has said and it really depends a lot on the environment as to whether or not you are going to get infection.

United States

237.   I think it was Dr. Geider and it was sort of suggested by Dr. Hale, you talk about different environments under ideal conditions or a cell applied directly to certain flower parts and I am wondering about suitable environments. In the hypothetical pathway we were talking about epiphytic populations in the calyx and Dr. Smith has said, how is it even conceivable that you would have epiphytic populations multiplying in a calyx that would result in fruit infection?. There must be something sort of intervening so I guess the question is how suitable is the calyx for bacterial multiplication such that you might get numbers sufficient that it would conceivable that it would transferred and this really goes to the work that you did Dr. Hale where you tried to find movement of bacterial populations in a calyx to a susceptible host.

Dr. Hale

238.   From the work that we have done we have never found any multiplication of bacteria in the calyx of fruit. Even when we have put high levels of bacteria in the calyx we have not found multiplication and the numbers usually decrease. They don't increase. Then of course somehow the bacteria have to get out of the calyx end of the fruit and on to a susceptible part of a plant under conducive conditions for infection. As Dr. Geider pointed out it could be very low numbers that are required to get there, but the number of steps which are required suggests to me that the chances are very slim and the work that we have done and the discard paper show that we have not been able to find a means of getting from reasonably high numbers of bacteria in a calyx end of a fruit through to infecting a flower or any shoot tissue or even getting onto the surfaces of plant tissue.

United States

239.   And your point about the high bacterial numbers is to distinguish it from what you would expect to find in the calyx of an apple that has been imported and gone through all of the steps we discussed?

Dr. Hale

240.   Exactly, yes. I consider the numbers would be very low and, as Dr. Smith has pointed out earlier, we are not talking about large numbers of bacteria associated with the calyx end of a fruit even if it has come from an orchard which is heavily infected with fire blight.

Dr. Smith

241.   I would like to illustrate the way that this has been thought about in the past. Two of the pathways that have been invoked for the introduction of fire blight into new areas are firstly being carried by birds and secondly contaminated fruit crates. Now both of these have been suggested without any firm proof but they have been suggested by plant bacteriologists as plausible pathways and in both cases the supposition has been quite clearly that it must have been ooze which was involved. The only way in which you could imagine that bacteria could survive on a crate is if they were contaminated with ooze. In other words sufficiently large numbers of bacteria protected by the ooze could

perhaps survive. Similarly the idea that birds might have carried fire blight between different European countries is based on the idea that in perching on infected trees their feet were contaminated by ooze and it was this ooze which was carried from one country to another and the bacteria survived because they were protected in the ooze. Neither of these pathways invoke the idea that small numbers of bacteria could have been carried by either of these pathways. The only way to make these pathways plausible is to invoke the idea of ooze - in other words very large numbers of bacteria.

Dr. Hayward

242.   The only thing I would like to add is that the calyx is dead tissue is it not? And it is dry tissue and it at best is only a possible protected site for survival, not for proliferation as you have pointed out.

Chairman

243.   So by that you mean that it is protected from other things like rain or access by insects or birds.

Dr. Hale

244.   And also protected from UV light which is UV radiation which is quite important as far as bacterial survival is concerned and even on the surface of the fruit as well.

Chairman

245.   This explains why you see the calyx as the most highly infectious part.

Dr. Hale

246.   No, the part which may be infested.

Dr. Hayward

247.   Could I add to that the matter of protection is a matter of access. When the question of sterilization of apples with chlorine and other compounds was considered several people raised, Dr. Smith, Dr. Hale, Dr. Geider, that in fact there isn't a ready access of the surface sterilizing substance fluid because of air bubbles and so on in the calyx - is that correct?

Dr. Hale

248.   Certainly there is no access to those parts of the calyx tissue which are not exposed to the surface. The calyx of an apple fruit - if you look at an apple fruit - the parts of the calyx are on the outside of the fruit and parts of the calyx are within the cavity at the calyx end of the fruit. If there are bacteria on the calyx which are on the exposed part then I think there was a paper in the US which shows sterilization treatment such as chlorine will, in fact, remove those bacteria. However, we have found that the bacteria inside the calyx or on the calyx tissue is unexposed to the outside of the fruit, are those parts which are difficult to get at with the surface sterilant.

Chairman

249. So that does not count as epiphytic if it is on the inside part of the fruit?

Dr. Hale

250. No, because the calyx is essentially not part of the internal tissue of the fruit.

Chairman

251. Still epiphytic?

Dr. Hale

252. Yes.

Dr. Smith

253. To clarify that you can imagine the remains of the calyx as a little pocket folded into the fruit. Its surface is continuous with the outside but it nevertheless is protected because air or liquid can only enter this little cavity through the terminal opening. I must say that my written remarks about bubbles or the rough surface of the calyx are just common sense. They are not based on any investigation as to what happens when liquid is placed on apples. I do not know of any study as to how well a surface sterilant penetrates into the calyx. But one can see that the surface may repel water to a certain extent, and for one reason or another the surface sterilant may not penetrate fully into the calyx.

Chairman

254. Have we completed the questions?

United States

255. That completes our questions and I want to thank the experts for helping me walk through some of that scientific evidence and we look forward to an opportunity to pose follow-up questions later in this session. Thank you.

Chairman

256. Thank you very much. Can I now turn to the Japanese delegation and invite Japan to put whatever remaining questions they have to the experts. You have the floor.

Japan

257. Thank you. So it doesn't have to be epiphytic bacteria. Thank you.

258. It seems to me just listening to the discussions that there may be some divergence of opinions about the number of bacteria required to cause new infections somewhere else. Some experts believe that ooze is essential whereas Dr. Geider seems to believe that that question depends on the variety of factors inherent in the environment. Let me take one step backwards and revisit the discussions we had yesterday. I recall there was a consistency amongst the experts that the concept of maturity is something of a continuous process. Apples start maturing and then later on ripen and perhaps as I recall it was Dr. Smith

who pointed out that the issue will be whether there will be any symptoms. Probably if symptoms are there that should be detectable and it will never be exported into Japan. Having said that let me start with the question of survivability of the bacteria. You might recall you saw this picture of fairly heavy infection of young maturing apple fruits and it seems to me some of the fruits are exuding ooze here. Suppose that this apple was mistakenly harvested and put into commercial storage for 55 days at a high level of humidity at 2°C and after completing all the commercial processing just assume that this apple was mistakenly put into commercial storage. Can bacteria on these apple fruits survive?

Dr. Geider

259.   I am afraid I have to repeat from yesterday. We have to assume that all the symptoms we see on this apple are coming up from fire blight and nothing else which is open to discussion. Usually, you don't get this extensive rot because *E. amylovora* is not a soft rot but what we call a dry rot or necrotic-type so all the soft *E. amylovora* can produce those symptoms. But anyhow let's assume that most of the bacteria or the ooze is composed of *E. amylovora* the question is do they contribute to spread of fire blight when packed into a harvest which is exported. I would say when those heavily infected fruits are exported there is of course a chance that things will survive and get into another country and I think otherwise the disease would never get distributed and I refer to Eve Billing's article about fire blight in England where she was saying that this most probably caused by oozing pears which were brought from the US into England and they leaked out into the caskets and finally these were used in farms for apple production. So I think when you have those circumstantial events it cannot be excluded that something must happen. On the other hand of course, and that is my intention in my comments, we have to cautious to avoid those things. To avoid heavily blighted orchards and to avoid suspicious fruits and what I understand from harvesting that all the fruits are inspected as they are visibly OK and I agree with Dr. Smith that fruits which are without any symptoms are probably not heavily infected with fire blight. I think this would be a very artificial assumption which has never been realized and I think that will never probably happen that the food which is looking completely healthy is heavily infected. I think this is out of scientific scope and therefore we can say this apple which is on the internet is probably a danger, but it would not be exported.

Dr. Hale

260.   I agree entirely. I think that it is unlikely that those fruits would pass through picking, packing, harvesting process and so on and the inspection processes which go on before the fruit become ready to ship. Those fruit would not, in fact, be likely to be shipped or exported.

Dr. Hayward

261.   I agree entirely with what the two previous speakers have said and I have nothing to add.

Japan

262.   So my next question was how likely it is that shippers will be able to successfully detect symptoms. I am sure symptoms - will they be large or small and lighter? Dr. Smith said in the context of discussions on epiphytic bacteria that if there are going to be any ooze there could be symptoms that could be detected. How certain is it that farmers or shippers will assure or ensure that apples with symptoms will never be exported into Japan, or for the next 25 years?

Dr. Geider

263.   Of course you can make the worst scenario and what will happen when somebody overlooks something and these things can occur but many things can occur. My feeling is the highest danger coming from fire blight is from tourists. They take something which is contaminated and they bring it into the country and touch other things and then the disease might get infested in a way which we cannot overlook. I think with all these things an apple which is somehow contaminated or infected with fire blight, going through all the controls and finally ending up in a market is thinkable, but all the experience we have, and I pointed out in my introduction that even in Europe with all these fruits activities back and forth, we cannot see that in any country fire blight was reintroduced by looking at the pattern which is coming up in European countries that they are all well organized and no mixing, so that means fire blight is certainly distributed widely with all sorts of activities and in Europe we can include also activities with whole plants so I think fire blight is really something which is ordered and rarely distributed outside orchards by insects or birds and wind.

Dr. Hale

264.   I think another aspect of this is probably something that Dr. Geider pointed out earlier on. In order to have fruit showing symptoms it is more than likely that the orchard had relatively heavy symptoms during the year. Inspection processes hopefully would eliminate the export of fruit from heavily infected orchards.

Dr. Hayward

265.   Nothing to add on this point.

Dr. Smith

266.   I think that the process in which fruit is harvested, sorted and selected for export is a process which can be audited and indeed is. So that a certain degree of quality can be guaranteed. Nevertheless there will be a certain small risk that, if such infected fruit were present, they will not be detected but will in some way pass through the system. That is the reason why those who regulate in relation to fire blight are also interested in the general condition of the orchards in which the fruits are taken. We have heard that the conditions of heavily infested orchards are almost necessary for you to get this kind of symptom on fruits. The requirement is often made that fruit should come from orchards which are fire blight free. Now from my point of view what is necessary is to ensure that the

orchard is free from fire blight. It is only heavily infested orchards where you have such risks. There is no doubt that to avoid this chance of a mistake in the sorting process you take one step up the line and inspect the orchard as well and make sure no active fire blight is in the orchard. How severely you apply this and what extent, how many inspections, how many years you maintain those inspections, whether you have a buffer zone or other questions can be argued over. In relation to fruits I would say that such an inspection regime of the orchard can be fairly light. It can be much lighter than the regime that would be used for inspecting nurseries where you are looking for the possibility of infected plants as oppose to infected fruits. This is a different issue and as a point of principle your best protection against the mistakes in the sorting process is to work with fruits from clean orchards in the first place.

Chairman

267.   Can I just take you on a little bit further from there. You've talked about precautionary measures and said it is arguable how necessary they are but there must be a relationship between those and the degree of risk involved. Could you comment for example on the question of designated areas being inspected - orchards being inspected say three times yearly - is that a sufficient requirement for the circumstances or is it more than necessary for the sort of risk that you have in mind and is there any other scientific evidence that would relate to the degree of such controls that are necessary in relation to the risk?

Dr. Smith

268.   There are many options that can be taken in applying such precautionary measures. The first is the number of inspections, of which the minimum would be one, but according to circumstances such inspections sometime apply up to three in a season and sometimes they go back to the preceding season. I am not talking about fire blight but the most general case. In extreme cases the requirement is sometimes made that the disease in question has never been seen on the land concerned. There is also a geographical criterion. It may be sufficient to inspect only the trees which have been harvested which would be a minimum requirement or you could make the requirement for the whole field which is concerned but is not always the case that fruit from a single field goes to the same destination - it may be divided later and go to different places with different requirements. The requirement may be made not only for the field, it may be made for the whole place of production so that although other parts of the place of production may not be exporting apples you could ask that all of the place of production was inspected the appropriate number of times. A further step is to ask for immediate vicinity freedom which implies that there is a buffer zone of a certain size around the place of production which must also be free from disease and you could take it even further and ask for radius freedom which means over quite a considerable defined distance the disease should not be found. So there are many variables that you can play with in deciding on the level of intensity of your inspection. This is a case-by-case question and the authorities have to work out in each individual case what they think is necessary. It is finally a matter of judgement by comparison with equivalent cases that have

been used in the past and I think it difficult on a purely scientific basis to be able to declare that for the certain disease there are good scientific reasons for insisting on three inspections when two or one would be sufficient. It comes finally to a question of expert judgement and experience. If I take the example of nurseries under European conditions, requirements of this kind are made for propagating material which is exported from nurseries. The European regime for this material is a severe one - it concerns the whole place of production and a zone around it. There is one inspection regime for the place of production, with two inspections in the growing season, and a different regime for the surrounding zone. That I would call a fairly heavy regime, which is appropriate for plants intended to be planted because if they have fire blight, it is very likely the disease will express itself where they are used. If it were a question of applying such requirements for orchards, I would say fairly categorically that the regime which is appropriate for nursery plants is more severe than is needed for orchards. That is for the simple reason that the intended use of the fruits is to be consumed, processed or destroyed - not to survive, and so manifestly it is not necessary to apply measures of such stringency in the case of fruits. But I would hesitate to advise exactly what should be the inspection regime for an orchard. Turning it round, I would say that a single inspection of the orchard in the growing season, without the buffer zone would give you a good guarantee that the orchard was not heavily infested by fire blight and we have been hearing that infection of mature fruits only happens in orchards that are heavily infected. So from those conclusions an expert might reasonably decide that to avoid the possibility that there would be heavily infected fruit coming out of an orchard it is enough to make sure that the orchard itself is not heavily infected by a single season growing inspection.

Dr. Hale

269.   No I don't really have anything to add - I think Dr. Smith has summed that up very, very well - very clearly and I think that that is exactly the way I would feel about things as well.

Dr. Geider

270.   I think it's of course a matter of trust and harvest efforts with fire blight outbreaks in the orchards it would be really a pity when they are doing that so I hope that there are some standards and of course to keep the standards some inspections might be useful and beneficial. To my experience, just to find fire blight in the area is often not so easy. I asked colleagues in Eastern Canada to show me fire blight orchards and we had to drive hundreds of kilometres to find the next orchard which was really in a bad shape where fire blight persisted but in all other orchards around there was no fire blight at all and I think all inspections would have been good and without any concern so I think it is a little bit a matter of personal feeling and balance and finally of course we have to trust farmers that they are not doing completely wrong and I don't know this impact is really applicable in trade or is it that farmers try to sell everything - that is sometimes the feeling that people develop on the market here.

Dr. Hale

271. Just following up on what Dr. Geider said and with my own experience as far as New Zealand is concerned. We do not try to sell everything - it would be a ridiculous situation for us to sell everything. We only sell the highest possible quality to the markets which pay the highest prices. So, as far as New Zealand is concerned, that is what happens and I would assume that the United States has a similar situation.

Dr. Smith

272. An orchard or any other plot of land should be inspected. This has the administrative consequence that the Plant Protection Authorities in the exporting country must know that that producer intends to export to a given destination because they have to be warned in advance of the need to inspect. Otherwise they will not carry out the inspection and they will not be able to certify. This system has to be controlled and in such a system farmers have no freedom of action in this respect. If they have not been inspected and the certificate is not delivered, then they cannot export. The authorities need at the beginning of each growing season to determine which farmers are intending to export to which destinations in order to be able to put in place the necessary inspection regime. So I do not think there should be any serious concern in this case. The administrative aspects of the system normally function very well.

Dr. Hayward

273. We are considering question 23, aren't we on the orchard inspections? And Dr. Smith said earlier that one inspection should be sufficient, but my question would be what is the optimum time for making that inspection at flowering, at a later stage - can I ask that?

Chairman

274. Yes!

Dr. Smith

275. Well Mr. Chairman I didn't know that this was a session where the experts ask each other questions! I must say that I am an expert on phytosanitary regulations, but not an expert on fire blight and so I cannot answer that question. But perhaps my colleagues here who have looked at a lot of fire blight in orchards are in a better place to be able to confirm my suggestion that you should be able by a single inspection to tell whether an orchard is heavily infested with fire blight and what would be the best time.

Dr. Hale

276. If it was going to be one inspection I would say that inspection should be done at harvest time because if it is a heavily infected orchard there is no way that the grower can have pruned out all infections within that orchard. I think my answer originally to the question was that I have always felt that an early season inspection, whether it be at flowering or at the fruitlet stage, is quite important for two reasons: one it alerts the grower or the exporter to the fact that the

orchard is not going to be suitable and consequently the grower is not going to export to a specific market; and secondly, because of the information, the grower or exporter can then divert that fruit to markets where there is no problem as far as fire blight is concerned. It is very important when dealing with large quantities of fruit for logistical purposes to be able to make those decisions relatively early in the season and it is certainly the case that we in New Zealand were looking at. However, I realize that the costs and so on of more than one inspection are high and consequently if we were going to go to a single inspection I would say that the pre-harvest inspection would be adequate.

Chairman

277.   So other inspections at blossom time and harvest time would be overkill perhaps?

Dr. Hale

278.   I think the minimum would be the pre-harvest and the maximum requirement would be an earlier season inspection as well.

Chairman

279.   So that is two?

Dr. Hale

280.   Yes, that would be a maximum of two, but I think , from experience, that the pre-harvest inspection would be adequate. An earlier season inspection from a commercial point of view, would be useful because, as I mentioned, the fruit from those orchards would not be harvested and sent to a country which had specific regulations as far as fire blight is concerned. There are very few of those in the world.

Dr. Geider

281.   In my statement I favoured the time after flowering for the scientific reasons. One is when you do inspection during flowering you can be misled by other symptoms - there are other necrotic bacteria which can cause blackening of flowers and therefore this can be misleading what you see. At harvest time it is a very important time because this is telling about the quality of the apples for against fire blight but I feel it is not an easy to see. I think no farmer would leave all necrotic branches until harvest - he has to do something - prune them or otherwise it would be endangering his whole orchard so I don't know Dr. Hale means - if they are pruned branches would that be an indication that there was fire blight so therefore the orchard is suspicious or is it just that you expect that at the harvest there would still symptoms available which can be seen by inspectors.   For those reasons, I think after flowering maybe three, four, five, six weeks would be a good time because then it is clear when there are necrotic symptoms coming up and there is even ooze connected with these symptoms it is a good time for fire blight and this is clear - all other stages are difficult and for those reasons I personally favour this period.

Dr. Hale

282.   Yes, I agree with Dr. Geider. I think that if there is going to be a single inspection, then perhaps the earlier one would be more useful and cover both fire blight and logistics.

Dr. Smith

283.   Well, Dr. Hale has put his finger on another aspect of such an inspection regime which is that it has to be organized in the exporting country. The fact of doing it at all is the main constraint because it requires that orchards should be individually identified, that they should be registered, that the authority has to keep a register of them, has to have a whole system for following what is going on and to put such a thing in place where otherwise it would not exist is a heavy task. On the other hand I rather have the impression that, whether you are in New Zealand or the United States, if you are exporting apples those orchards are in any case bound to be under surveillance. So that, for the authorities of the exporting country, once the orchards are part of the system, whether they inspect early or late, once or twice, does not make such a very great difference to the task they have to undertake. They may choose to do it as Dr. Hale suggests in a way which is most convenient for the growers by doing it early. All sorts of other considerations come into play in deciding how to organize the inspection of an orchard or nursery in the most efficient way possible.

Chairman

284.   There was mention made of pruning of infected branches that were discovered in these inspections. Could you tell us what is the effect on the possible level of infection of fire blight in apples from pruning such branches?

Dr. Smith

285.   Well, I have to refer to my colleagues who know the question directly. All I can say is that the basic purpose of pruning away infected branches is to reduce the risk of fire blight. The question is: does it do it primarily in the current season or does it carry over to the next season? I would have thought that the main purpose was for future seasons because by the time you have pruned them away they may already have caused whatever undesirable effects you might expect in the current season.

Dr. Geider

286.   Of course I think this is a delicate question in practical approaches. That depends how the growers do that. Do they sterilize their scissors and whatever they use carefully and otherwise they might carry the disease onto other trees and in other parts of the tree. This is not so easily done because you are somehow climbing a tree and you prune something and then you have to disinfect your scissors and how do you do that? You use alcohol or chlorine solutions and so this is already a difficult point. The next point which was pointed out by Bob Goodman is that of course pruned branches have a tendency to shoot again and therefore open for secondary infections though it is a little bit a balance what is the best way to do. I cannot give recommendations and think there must be

experience which is coming up by growers - how they see the development of fire blight in orchards and I don't know if…

Dr. Hale

287.   What Dr. Geider says is correct. Unless you are going to prune out properly and sterilize between cuts then, of course, the disease may manifest itself even more obviously within the orchard.

Chairman

288.   I will now hand the floor back to Japan. Thank you.

Japan

289.   The concepts of heavy infection on orchards may raise some questions. It is arguable to what sort of percentage infection would be heavy or substantial and there ought to be some fairly artificial limits of how many percentages or in our case our preference is zero - no tolerance. I wonder, this question is certainly based on science, but may also apply to the level of protection which Japan wants. That is my impression. Is that the kind of statement that experts would agree: that the level of protection should be something which definitely needs to be considered in determining the level of infection from zero to something ?

Dr. Smith

290.   Well, naturally the criterion used in practice is whether any infection is found. An inspector follows a procedure and if he finds any infection the orchard is disqualified. What determines the level of tolerance is the intensity of the inspection. So a protocol has to be set out which lays out how an orchard is inspected and how many trees are examined, in what way, what samples are taken. Such protocols exist for fire blight. You can devise a light protocol or a heavy protocol. A light protocol would only detect a heavy infection, while a heavy protocol would detect a light infection. However, I do not mean to imply that there is a qualitative difference between the heavily infected and lightly infected orchards . There is not. In the end, the only discriminating factor you can use is the intensity of your inspection.

Dr. Geider

291.   I somehow agree on that. I wonder about no tolerance. It is very difficult to judge from a necrotic branch is that is fire blight. You have to be very careful of excluding other possibilities which means the inspection has to be followed by some sort of reliable assays and even these assays must be a little bit higher level otherwise people can easily claim that they have seen something so therefore this orchard is disqualified. I think just to get the whole process in a meaningful way - it is still complicated and I don't know how the inspection should occur. If the Japanese people will come to the United States and then I see something and they will take samples and they will give it to a lab in the States or they bring it back to Japan - probably not do that - so the question is a little bit difficult and therefore would still agree in this respect that the symptoms must be a little bit more than once or twice there must be really a good indication that this is fire blight and can be identified and controlled pretty much after the inspection.

Dr. Hale

292.   To reiterate what Dr. Geider has said - I agree with the notion there. It has got to be not only the inspection but certainly a follow-up on identification of what is causing possible symptoms. As Dr. Geider pointed out there are a number of organisms which can cause symptoms similar to fire blight and if you look at question number 35 where some of the early reports of fire blight in Japan have since been attributed to fungal diseases. Thank you.

Dr. Hayward

293.   I think the question from Japan was really asking how do we define the intensity of infection so isn't this defined in terms of the number of strikes per tree? How do you define the level of intensity of infection - people like plant breeders must be able to define the level of resistance in a new cultivar. How do you it? When you say you have a heavily infested orchard what do you mean by that?

Dr. Hale

294.   In the work we have done we have talked about a heavily infected orchard in which we have said there are 75 to 100 strikes per tree. So this is a heavily infected orchard. If we only find the odd strike in the orchard, that is a lightly infected orchard, and if we find nothing we are assuming that it is, in fact, an orchard free of symptoms of fire blight.

Dr. Smith

295.   I stress that, in practice, all the inspection protocols used for phytosanitary purposes of this kind are effectively working with zero tolerance. That is to say that when you follow the protocol, if you find a single strike, the orchard is considered to be infected. In view of Dr. Hale's description of a heavily infected orchard, you hardly need an inspection protocol at all. So, quite a light inspection procedure would be enough to ensure that you were dealing with orchards that are not heavily infected.

Japan

296.   I would like to invite Professor Goto to discuss.

Professor Goto (Japan)

297.   I would like to thank the experts for your broad debate. I really appreciate that as an academic in phytopathology. I would just like to confirm the consensus reached by the experts that for the fruit exporting country the important point is that the orchard is blight free. Is that true? Is that the consensus reached by the experts? Another question that I have to the experts. For any bacterial disease or any disease for plants from the beginning of occurrence up to harvest of that plant the situation of the disease would fluctuate continuously depending on what environment they are exposed to during that period. So sometimes the disease would inadvertently increase in occurrence and at other stages that might decline. Is that also the agreement by the experts?

Dr. Geider

298.   In this case, the answer is yes because what we discussed about the fire blight in orchards there can be a period where fire blight is heavy - you can of course try to get rid of the symptoms by pruning for instance and finally it might be very low or not visible any more. So this, with all diseases, is always a problem - when is the peak and that is the best time to detect it and we all know from medicine here that even doctors have the same problem. The disease cannot be picked up and they are not in the right level so this is the same for plant disease. For those reasons, there is no proof to say there is no fire blight in an orchard. That means you have to inspect everything in terms of analysis, in very broad scale and you might be lucky to find something which is fire blight, confirm that, and say I did all my best and I found fire blight symptoms and could confirm it so I think to prove the absence of a disease is almost impossible. The only thing you can say is I see something and they are symptoms so this could be disease and then I identify it to be what I expect.

Professor Goto (Japan)

299.   Thank you. Well if that is the case - just one-time inspection at the time of harvest is something that I would like to raise the question to the experts because some of the experts might say that one time at the harvest would be the follow-up of all the previous stages before harvest but that has been discussed before for a grower. If he or she sees an occurrence of a disease then of course a grower's natural desire would be to control that so that there would be pruning of that branch. Therefore, a one-time inspection would not be able to really check the occurrence of the disease from the budding to the harvesting stage of that plant because that means there will be some kind of a latent infection or small lesion remaining on the field from the start of the early stage of this plant to the actual harvest because if the grower proves at the beginning stage when he or she sees the disease then there might be some of that latent infection or the small lesions are remaining in the field. So from the importing country's standpoint the more times, the more frequent the inspection the better. That is the view of the importing country, but what do the experts say on this point?

Dr. Geider

300.   I think in theory I agree, but for practical reasons we disagree. I think it is almost impossible to follow the development of a disease in orchards from blooming to harvest. That means the inspector would have to live on the farm and he has to be very clever to find out and quickly drive to get to a point where fire blight might occur. Practically that is impossible. So I think we have to compromise in some way otherwise you have to say it is impossible to export any apples because there is always a low risk that something might have happened in the orchard so the whole thing is fictitious.

Dr. Hale

301.   One of the reasons I have always been a proponent of a reasonably early season inspection is that what we are really worried about - or could be worried about - is calyx infestation. With infection of fruit during the season - those fruits

are unlikely to be harvested in any case. An early season inspection would pick up any likelihood of calyxes actually carrying bacteria and I think that any other fruit during the season becomes infected it is not going to be harvested. So, that is one of the reasons I have always been a proponent of an earlier inspection. I still think a pre-harvest one is a final check on the status of that orchard.

Chairman

302.   But you put the limit at two? Thank you. Now Dr. Smith.

Dr. Smith

303.   In discussing these questions, Mr Chairman, people often suppose that inspection is efficient, 100 per cent efficient even, at a given moment. Sometimes, in special cases, it is. There are some pests which you can be certain to find when you examine an infested item, but this is exceptional. In plant quarantine, in general terms, whether you are inspecting trees in an orchard or fruits in a crate or plants being shipped you cannot be 100 per cent certain by inspection that the unit you are inspecting is healthy. So you automatically in the system have a certain tolerance and run a certain risk of some infected plants. The only way you can improve your chances is to look at more plants so basically you have to select a sampling system which gives you a certain level of security. This is what is inherent in the idea of managed risk which I mentioned earlier yesterday. Managed risk implies that whatever you do, there is a small risk of missing what you are looking for. You recognize that what you are doing is not 100 per cent efficient but you have to do a trade-off between practicality and cost on the one hand and the risk which you are running on the other.

Dr. Hayward

304.   The thing I would add is that Professor Goto in his question referred to latent infections which were not recognized and these latent infections were present at the time of harvest - I would doubt very much whether they have any relevance at all to the health of the fruit.

Professor Goto (Japan)

305.   Thank you very much for those comments of all the experts and what I meant in my previous questions is not exactly what Dr. Geider said in his comments. In other words, I do not mean that the inspectors should live in the orchards throughout the growing season up to the actual harvest time. That would be in a quite extreme case. I am not meaning that. What I mean, in effect, is that compared to a single inspection - either it is at the beginning of the season or towards the late stage near about to harvest time - compared to that single inspection, three times inspections certainly seem to be better. As Dr. Smith said, if three times inspections are conducted during the season that can quite certainly and effectively reduce the risk of remaining infection of the disease that is from the importing country's viewpoint. I would like to know if it is also the opinion of these four experts? Is it?

Dr. Smith

306.   I think we have been over this ground.

Dr. Geider

307.   We have been over this ground. I don't really know what else I should say. I think three inspections are more effective than one inspection. I personally would say it is much more effort without much more value. This is my opinion.

Dr. Smith

308.   I have nothing to add to this.

Professor Goto (Japan)

309.   Thank you very much. I would just like to go back to Dr. Hale's comments regarding the cost of those inspections. Obviously if the exporting countries of the fruit conduct three times inspection the cost would increase compared to just one single inspection. However, for the importing countries of these fruits if the inspection time is just kept to once and consequently, if the diseased fruit imported into importing countries and if consequently the disease in question makes an occurrence in that case the cost for the importing countries would increase exponentially and it is almost impossible to compare to the cost of let us say three times inspection. I would like to know what the four experts think of this particular case.

Dr. Smith

310.   Well, I am not sure I will answer that question directly, but rather by trying to say that in some way you have to match the intensity and costs of measures to the risks. I mentioned already that the inspection regime with which I am familiar is the one which is used in Europe for nursery plants. In the case of a nursery the European Union recommends two inspections. I point out again that if a plant in a nursery is infected and exported, planted and used, if that plant carries fire blight then it will nearly certainly introduce fire blight into the country to which it is exported. So the risk from such plants is very high indeed; whereas if a single infection of a tree in an orchard is accidentally missed then the probability that the fruits from that tree will be infected and will after transport, storage and use will transmit fire blight is many thousands, even millions times lower than the risk from that nursery plant which is being exported. So if two are enough in the EU for nursery plants, it seems to me three are too many for fruit.

Dr. Geider

311.   Something about the nursery plants even in this case fire blight might not always spread out of one plant. We have such examples, in my report, that a plant which is imported from Belgium got fire blight and we noticed that and identified the disease unambiguously and there was no occurrence in the environment. There were many orchards of BBA nearby which is dealing with insect diseases and we still couldn't see anything in the other plant. So the risk even in an infected plant to distribute fire blight is not 100 per cent. It is something between 0.1 and something higher.

Dr. Smith

312.   Yes, I accept that. I have overstated my point.

Japan

313.   Two more questions. One is about the buffer zone or how effective a buffer zone could possibly be. Hearing all the discussions I think the issue is how effective an inspection can be and what level of protection these inspections will provide. Isn't a buffer zone a mechanism to ensure the high quality of inspections inside an orchard? Would the experts agree with that description? If there is a buffer zone surrounding an orchard and there is an orchard which we want to be fire blight free wouldn't a buffer zone ensure the quality of inspections to be done inside the orchard? Would the experts agree with that description?

Dr. Smith

314.   It is clear that if a buffer zone is put in place around the place of production this increases the security to a certain degree. But creating such a buffer zone and administering it and inspecting it is in itself a costly procedure and therefore one must be certain that it is necessary to do this and that the added value of a buffer zone is justified. Now if you think about the scientific justification of a buffer zone, it lies in the possibility that the pest concerned could rather easily move into the field or orchard concerned from outside. Between the time at which the last inspection was carried out and the time at which fruits were exported, there would be a significant possibility that the pest would enter. For some insects that is a real possibility. They can indeed fly in and multiply rapidly so that in those extreme cases there are good reasons for buffer zones. I would say in the case of fire blight the possibility that fire blight should enter an orchard during a given growing season from outside the orchard, form a canker infection in which the bacteria multiply and, from that multiplication, infect fruit is almost impossible. We already query the possibility that fruits can be significantly infected within the orchard so the fruits are very unlikely to be directly infected by inoculum coming from an adjoining orchard. If the inoculum comes into the orchard, what it first has to do is establish the disease in the orchard and from that the disease has to spread to the fruit and in the most favourable circumstances this could not happen until the following growing season. So for that reason I doubt whether a buffer zone is really necessary in the case of fire blight.

Dr. Hayward

315.   Chairman, we do have evidence that Roberts (2002) in press has obtained results that have indicated that a buffer zone of any size provides no phytosanitary security.

Chairman

316.   Does the panel have a copy of that? We do. There was one other document you cited yesterday that I am not sure the Panel has got. It was a directory of phytosanitary terms.

Dr. Hayward

317.   Yes, the British Society of Plant Pathology 1973 publication. I can provide that. And Mr. Chairman there were also one or two other papers that were not presented by any of the parties. For example, Crosse and Goodman (1972) which I think might have been ...

Chairman

318.   If you could let the Panel secretary have those. Any other comments from the experts on those questions.

Dr. Geider

319.   Of course I agree with Dr. Smith that a buffer zone increases security and it's a little bit difficult to follow that up too. On the other hand of course the definition of buffer zone is also very difficult. We have many measurements and the terms are very strict in laws and quarantine so they tried to avoid fire blight by removing all sorts of host plants and potential hosts of fire blight, but it did not really help. So I think for those reasons buffer zones have to be really strictly defined and all host plants which could be eventually harbouring have to be removed and finally I think it would be a very big effort to realize that.

Dr. Smith

320.   That is true, but I do stress also the buffer zones that Dr. Geider is referring to have the purpose of protecting nurseries, not orchards. Even their original purpose was to attempt to eradicate fire blight altogether. For example in Switzerland measures of this kind were used 10 or 15 years ago when fire blight first appeared. Even in the case of the same disease, the value of a buffer zone depends on the product you are talking about - whether about fruits or plants for planting. It is much more important in the case of propagating material that the nursery should be free and remain free over a period of years. But, as fire blight can develop rather slowly on planting material and your security depends not only on the state of the nursery in the given season but also in the past, you are looking at a situation in which a nursery remains free from fire blight for a long period to give you the level of security that you need.

Japan

321.   The final question has to do with post harvest treatment by chlorine. Is there any reason that any of the experts is opposed to post harvest treatment for phytosanitary purposes?

Dr. Geider

322.   Actually in my report I had one reason which was a little bit a personal one saying that chlorine treatment is not good for health. This is a personal point, not so important. The other point is that this treatment will also change the micro-flora, epiphytic on the apples and our experience is this is usually not very beneficial for the firmness and the durability of the apples. They just get easier exposed to soft rots and all sorts of things and for those reasons I would not

really favour this treatment just to be sure that fire blight has been removed if present.

Dr. Smith

323.   I think, in terms of efficacy, then there is evidence that these treatments will destroy fire blight bacteria on the surface of fruits. The question is how should such measures be used. I believe that some countries which import apple fruits require treatment as the only measure they apply. Indeed it could be argued that such a disinfection treatment is quite adequate to remove the phytosanitary risk by itself. Conversely, if the system is already in place that ensures that the fruits are taken from a fire blight free orchard, treatment of the fruit with a disinfectant is superfluous. I think in many circumstances one would look on these as alternatives rather than as complementary to each other. Putting both measures into place is asking for a very high level of phytosanitary security. One can argue whether it is necessary to combine measures in this way or whether a single method would be sufficient in the circumstances of fruits.

Dr. Hale

324.   I agree with what Dr. Smith has said. We have evidence that the surface of the fruit can be disinfested by a chlorine treatment but as Dr. Smith says, if we take fruit from an orchard which has been inspected and is not showing any symptoms of the disease then the probability of any of those fruits either being contaminated on the surface or in the calyx is extremely low and the use of a further treatment is, in my opinion, unnecessary and from Dr. Geider's point of view environmentally and health wise it is not a good thing at all.

Dr. Hayward

325.   The only thing I would add is that if cold storage for 55 days at 2°C is as effective as it seems to be in reducing any residual population, that would be far preferable to any chemical treatment.

Chairman

326.   Just arising from one of your earlier questions there is one follow-up point I would like to bring up with Dr. Smith. This actually comes from your answer to question No. 27 in which you stated that what is important is clearly to maintain the identity and integrity of batches and thus to ensure that fruits from a significantly infected orchard are not mistakenly certified as coming from a fire blight free orchard. I think this was touched on in the discussion about infected fruit being accidentally included and I think it was probably a reference to the same thing, but how feasible is it to ensure this identity preservation? Is it common practice to ensure it or what is the incidence of mistakes?

Dr. Smith

327.   The authority which is responsible for phytosanitary certification has an obligation to maintain the identity and integrity of batches. The whole system of phytosanitary certification depends on this. Under the International Plant Protection Convention, countries are required to have in place systems which enable them to do this effectively, by employment of qualified staff and so on.

This is set out in some detail in international standards. Having said that, of course, one cannot totally exclude the possibility that these systems sometimes go wrong. There is a small risk that batches of lots of fruits or materials could be confused. For this reason, both the national authorities and sometimes the authorities of the importing countries like to put in place occasional audits to make sure that everything is functioning correctly. This aspect of phytosanitary security is vital. One absolutely depends upon it and it has to function correctly in relation to any material which is certified.

Chairman

328. So would you characterize the risk which you have mentioned as being remote unlikely to occur in practice or how would you characterize it?

Dr. Smith

329. I would characterize it as remote, because in the present case we are dealing with a high profile commodity exported from the US to Japan, where the authorities of both countries are very much concerned that everything should proceed safely.

Dr. Geider

330. Just to add something. Even with the leftover of a very remote occurrence that something is going wrong the question is does that affect the distribution of the disease and I still would say that there is a sort of feeling which was expressed here yesterday that this chance is also extremely low so I think altogether it is not an essential question that we have to rely on.

Dr. Hale

331. Yes, I would agree with the two previous speakers. I think the chances are remote. That's all I can say really.

Dr. Hayward

332. Maybe we should use the term negligible. That is the standard term of a likelihood of between zero and one in a million.

Chairman

333. Now we have reached the point where we have actually completed the questions from the parties to the experts. As it happens we have also exhausted most of the questions that the panel had. We actually asked most of our questions in writing ahead of the session and we have had very good comprehensive written answers from the experts for which we are very grateful. We had a number of points for clarification but most of those have now gone. I think we have just two remaining and I think if we put those orally now we can dispense with having a 15-minute break. These are questions to all the experts and the first one is: as you are no doubt aware of reading of the arguments of the parties a distinction in the notion of scientific evidence between direct and indirect scientific evidence has been made. Without commenting on any legal issues which may be associated with this distinction could you please elaborate on what type of information you believe to constitute scientific evidence whether this

direct/indirect distinction has any significance and if so what in scientific terms? Can we get the precise reference to where that distinction was made? OK. Thank you. Can we go on? Dr. Geider just to clarify this. This distinction between direct and indirect scientific evidence was made in several places, but this is paragraph 18 of the Executive Summary of the statement of Japan at the first substantive meeting in October and they are quoting the US or at least referring to the US in saying the United States apparently believes that any scientific evidence must be direct evidence without such evidence the US argues that Japan must immediately abolish its phytosanitary measures. And this is from US answers to questions from the Panel and it's at a footnote 67 to paragraph 89 which is replying to question 38. The evidence Japan cites is circumstantial not direct or scientific evidence and Japan makes no assessment of the relative effectiveness of this measure on reducing the likelihood of entry or overall disease risk. Would the US want to say something about this before we...

United States

334.   Yes, in fact if you would like to read the full footnote that would be fine, but I have the first submission in front of me and will give you the sentence the proceeds the sentence that you started: This is in the first written submission of the US, paragraph 85, subparagraph numbered 6 where we are listing the various restrictions that Japan applies and we say here with respect to chlorine treatment of containers for harvesting Japan claims that the requirement is necessary to avoid contamination of fruit by contaminated harvest containers. The evidence Japan cites is circumstantial not direct or scientific evidence and Japan makes no assessment of the relative effectiveness of this measure on reducing the likelihood of entry or overall disease risk. I will read the footnote references if you like or ...

Chairman

335.   I hope that that has said enough to clarify the question.

Dr. Geider

336.   Things would be so easy that we not be here! Maybe I can cite one of my colleagues, Eve Billing, who is one of the experts of fire blight and she was citing the philosopher Feyneman. The value of science and the same scientific knowledge is a body of statements of varying degrees of certainty some most unsure, some nearly sure, none absolutely certain. So this is the right answer on the problem. I would say with fire blight we are in a difficult situation because long-distance transmission rarely happened and for those reasons we do not have scientific data and we cannot of course do experiments on that issue. I think no country in the world would be willing to allow this experiment without having a very good reason - maybe some island in Japan or somewhere else is suited to doing this experiment to import apples, discard them and find out if something will happen to the trees. So I think we are really in a very difficult situation on a scientific terms what is direct and indirect evidence and both parties are somehow right but I have the feeling the Japanese party is a little bit squeezing things in a way that all thinkable events can happen and this can be realistic and

for my feeling is this is a little bit too much. All the experience we have accumulated to 200 years about fire blight is that the risk of spread is not so extreme, it is not an Ebola virus - even with Ebola virus it is ending suddenly in an environment so for those reasons we feel that the Japanese argumentation is a little bit too far going for scientific evidence and the American one is maybe somehow reasonable saying there is no proof but I have to say there can be no final proof that these things which is proposed by the Japanese delegation can never happen and I think we somehow agree on that in the discussions too.

Chairman

337.   Any other comments on that? Dr. Smith?

Dr. Smith

338.   Well, I would certainly support Geider in his view that fire blight is a well studied disease, much observed and so that there is a very large body of direct evidence concerning fire blight. The existence of this body of direct evidence gives one a perspective in evaluating indirect evidence and, insofar as you cannot necessarily draw a sharp dividing line, in deciding whether circumstantial evidence is useful and in trying to decide what is the risk of a certain scenario. In plant health, it is important to keep one's feet on the ground, to consider the direct evidence first and to evaluate conjectural scenarios rather carefully in relation to what is really known about, for example, fire blight. We live in a world now in which various risks have been recently identified - risks of the entry of alien species from other continents, risks of the movement of living modified organisms - where there is little direct evidence and most of the evidence that has to be used is of a circumstantial kind. Where there is no direct evidence, it is not possible to use it as a kind of counterweight in one's judgements. But in plant health there is direct evidence. A lot of work has been done and it does assist one in making judgements in relation to evidence which is less certain.

Chairman

339.   Thank you. I think that is leading into or even addressing my final question which is: has there been any significant change in the relative scientific evidence regarding apple fruit as a pathway for the transmission of fire blight since the inception of the Phytosanitary Agreement in 1995?

Dr. Geider

340.   I think the tools to identify bacteria have probably got improved there are more ways of course PCR was published in 1992 but maybe not so widely used in 1995 or did not get it into this contribution at that time so I think there are more tools about existence of the pathogen in this case *E. amylovora* in fruits and in other environments. Maybe the idea if this is really saying something about distribution of fire blight I think it might not really have changed in that time.

Dr. Hayward

341.   I would just like to add to that that I think that the field of investigation that Dr. Geider refers to, the sensitivity and specificity of the methods used

which are DNA based have improved dramatically and one can anticipate that they have already shown a potential to be automated for processing of plant material. This will advance. It's a little bit like your new computer; it's out of date as soon as you have bought it and I think the field of molecular identification or DNA based identification has advanced dramatically in the last five years in particular and we can anticipate that it will advance greatly in the next five years.

Dr. Hale

342.   As a practitioner in the work on ecology and epidemiology of the organism and the disease the modern detection techniques have revolutionized what we can actually find out. Certainly in the area of looking at parts of the potential pathway for transmitting the disease, I think we have shown in a number of the exhibits that have been put forward that we have advanced since 1995 and, in fact we are much more confident now than perhaps we would have been seven years ago in the fact that there is a negligible chance of the disease being transmitted in fruit.

Dr. Smith

343.   I would certainly agree with Dr. Hale that if the same discussion had taken place ten years ago, the information then available would probably have led to a disagreement along rather similar lines. The information that has been published since then establishes as a result of scientific experimentation how bacteria in fact behave on fruits, how they survive, whether there can be epiphytic infection, what happens to bacteria in calyx and so on. Although maybe scientists ten years might have asserted fairly categorically that they did not think that these things would happen, since 1995 or the early 90s papers have been published which confirm that they do not. So scientists would be satisfied now that their conclusion that fire blight is very unlikely to be carried by fruits in international trade was supported by scientific results whereas ten years ago it was supported more by their own convictions of what was likely or unlikely.

Chairman

344.   Now in the time that you have been dealing with these questions, actually the Panel has thought of one more question not necessarily related to the one we have just been dealing with but will put this quickly to you and ask for your patience in addressing it. How do the experts view the IPPC standards 1995 and 2001 for risk assessment techniques in practical terms? Do you have experience or information on cases at hand? Are such risk assessments common practice today or is the Australian risk assessment of New Zealand apples rather an exception?

Dr. Hayward

345.   Although procedures used in Australia are highly confidential, like they are here, they adopt the same rigour of pest risk analysis to mangos, pineapples, fresh green bananas as they do to apples from New Zealand so I think Australia is a strong player in this field. They have used ISPM 11 of 2001 and I think that

is a very considerable advance on the first document of 1995. I think the reason is that there has been experience gained by various countries and to me there is no comparison between the two documents. The later document of 2001 I have used myself and has been modified and fine tuned by various people but it is a useable document and extremely helpful in my experience.

Dr. Hale

346. This is nothing to do with any argument between Australia and New Zealand. The pest risk assessment methods that have been put in place are adopted by New Zealand for a number of diseases and with just as much rigour as the Australians as well. Yes, I think that the changes that have come about between 1995 and 2001 as far as assessments are concerned are is an important advance.

Dr. Smith

347. In the framework of the phytosanitary regulations of the EU such pest risk analysis methods are now regularly used in relation to the development of any new measure. It has taken a few years for this to come into operation, but as things are now, any new measure which is proposed (and even an emergency measure or provisional measure) is subject to a form of pest risk analysis. A question arises concerning measures which have been in place for many years, before the modern techniques of pest risk analysis were available. They were put in place by the use of a scientific judgement which was in many respects equivalent to pest risk analysis. In any cases where there is some doubt about measures which are in place at the moment, the scientific experts in the EU would call on PRA Standard No. 11 as their reference point for deciding on the validity of their measures.

Chairman

348. Thank you very much. There are no other comments on that. I would like to thank you for your patience and the specific way you have addressed the panel's questions. Before I proceed any further I would like to know whether either of the parties wish to put any further additional questions to the experts? The US?

United States

349. May I just clarify with you what the procedure would be for the remainder of this session?

Chairman

350. I believe that the next stage would be to invite the experts to make final comments and if they wish to do so and then propose to close the meeting.

United States

351. If this would be our only opportunity to ask follow-up questions as yesterday could I request we have a short recess so that I can gather with my delegation?

Chairman

352. I suggest we take 10 minutes if you can keep to that for your purpose. Ten minutes and then after that any final questions to the parties.

Chairman

353. Thank you. Can we now resume at the point where we were inviting the parties to put any final questions they might have to the experts. The US?

United States

354. Thank you Mr. Chairman and thanks for your indulgence of our break period. This may feel a bit repetitive to the experts but hopefully it is something that we could do fairly quickly because I expect you will have yes or no answers. I am not threatening you just trying to lay out the parameters of my questions. The first is and is to all of the experts so if you each could respond that would be appreciated. The first relates to the fruit itself and it is: is there any scientific evidence that a mature harvested fruit will be infected?

Dr. Geider

355. I would say no, but I pointed out apples are anyhow difficult to do ... and get symptoms so I think at this stage apples that are immature are not very open like pears are so I think the evidence to my experience, I can say no.

Dr. Hale

356. If we are talking about a mature fruit that is harvested? Then my answer is no.

Dr. Hayward

357. No such evidence.

Dr. Smith

358. And nor have I.

United States

359. I thank the experts very much. The second question is: is there any scientific evidence that mature fruit harvested from an orchard will harbour internal populations of fire blight bacteria - these are the endophytic populations we were discussing earlier.

Dr. Geider

360. I think even in this case we discussed in a little more detail and the answer was as far as I got the point was no.

Dr. Hale

361. I agree with that.

Dr. Hayward

362. No such evidence.

Dr. Smith

363. To be more precise, papers describing such evidence have been considered but we are not convinced by this evidence.

United States

364. The third question is we discussed earlier that there was some scientific evidence that from severely infected orchards with active sources of inoculum that rarely epiphytic populations could be isolated from the calyx of such fruit. My question is: is there any scientific evidence that epiphytic calyx populations can infect a mature harvested apple fruit?

Dr. Geider

365. I would say no. Of course I think the point is that the same fruit that the calyx is infested and the fruit is sent out and I think that has not been reported and nobody has seen that and therefore I would say no here.

Dr. Hale

366. I have no evidence of this and I have extensively used experimentation which has put … in the calyx end fruit and have never found any infection.

Dr. Hayward

367. I also think it's highly unlikely that you could get transition from the calyx. It is a small population in a dead substratum and is not an active population.

United States

368. So you say highly unlikely and so is there any scientific evidence?

Dr. Hale

369. I have nothing that would support such an idea. No.

Dr. Smith

370. I know of no evidence.

United States

371. The next question: is there any scientific evidence that any epiphytic calyx populations in a harvested mature apple fruit that hypothetically would survive through importation into an importing country can be vectored through from a discarded apple fruit to a susceptible host?

Dr. Geider

372. I think this is also very remote. It is close to zero but of course in theory it cannot be excluded by all means, but I still would say it's almost zero.

United States

373.   So when you say it's almost zero is that there is no scientific evidence that this vectoring has …

Dr. Geider

374.   No, this is actually a very difficult experiment to do here. I think to look for apples which are infested in the calyx and get them to a garbage deposit and find out if there is carrying the disease I think this is a scientifically impossible experiment so we have to be honest in saying we don't see that there is a good chance but it is close to zero but not zero.

United States

375.   Perhaps we could turn to Dr. Hale to describe such a difficult experiment.

Dr. Hale

376.   We have done difficult experiments like that and we have reported them. We have no scientific evidence from the work that we have done that there is any transmission, but as Dr. Geider has pointed out, as scientists, it is very difficult to say that it is totally impossible.

United States

377.   No, I appreciate that and in fact would not expect a scientist to ever say that something can be totally excluded.

Dr. Hayward

378.   I think the likelihood is negligible as we defined previously between zero and one in a million.

United States

379.   OK and could you answer the question of whether there is any scientific evidence of vectoring?

Dr. Hayward

380.   I have no evidence of that at all, no.

Dr. Smith

381.   Equally, I think there is no evidence of this and in any case it appears exceedingly unlikely.

United States

382.   I thank the experts and Dr. Hayward actually you kind of predicted what my final question would be in your answer to this last question. Given the foregoing answers to my questions I was wondering whether the experts could please tell us what is the risk of introducing fire blight that is entry establishment or spread of *E. amylovora* to an importing country via imported harvested mature apple fruit? What is the risk of introducing fire blight? Any imported mature apple fruit?

Dr. Geider

383.   I think it is referring to your last question then. Still it is very low yes or negligible.

Dr. Hale

384.   Yes, I would say negligible too.

Dr. Hayward

385.   I would say negligible.

Dr. Smith

386.   I would also say negligible, but would add provided that the systems were in place in the exporting country to ensure that what is exported does exactly correspond to what is specified.

United States

387.   Just a clarification there. You are saying that in fact mature fruit is a mature fruit that is it is not infected.

Dr. Smith

388.   Well no I think I am saying a bit more. Certainly that it is mature fruit, but also that [pause]. Mr. Chairman this puts me in a slightly difficult position. The implication behind this question is that, provided one knew that the fruits were mature, they could be exported without any phytosanitary measure. Now I don't believe that fruits should be exported without any phytosanitary measure in these circumstances. At the very least one would suppose that they were accompanied by a phytosanitary certificate. The phytosanitary certificate attests first of all that the fruits are free from quarantine pests including fire blight and it attests also that any requirements that are made are satisfied. I would not make an absolute statement that no requirements are needed for mature apples. I believe there are certain requirements to be made by the exporting country to certify the export of mature apples according to the standard procedures used under the International Plant Protection Convention and if those certification procedures are followed then yes the risk is negligible.

Chairman

389.   Can I just clarify that the other three experts were also speaking in subject of the same qualification. Yes.

United States

390.   I want to thank the experts very much and Dr. Smith for that clarification which I think was very helpful to us and this concludes our follow-up questions. Thank you Mr. Chairman.

Chairman

391.   Can I now invite the Japanese delegation to put any final questions they may have to the experts.

Japan

392. Thank you Mr. Chairman and thank you for your patience. The first question: would the infested apple fruits bear the risk of disseminating the disease into the importing country?

Dr. Geider

393. In fact that means there are symptoms too? I think when it really happens that an apple which shows fire blight symptoms which are advanced is important - it is a risk, but I think this is coming back to the old question. Is this a normal event or a negligible event and I think we all agreed to some point this should not occur but as outlined with millions of efforts there might be something which can come up in this way so it cannot be completely excluded. On the other hand, even in this case, I am not convinced that this automatically implies that fire blight will come up in that country where the apples are finally on the market so I think even that risk of heavily infected apples it must be a lot of additional circumstances that fire blight get established in the environment of this apple so I would say it is still negligible that this event can occur.

Dr. Hale

394. I think that what Dr. Geider has said is absolutely correct and the situation is that we are pretty well convinced that a mature apple fruit which is of export quality and likely to be exported would not, in fact, be carrying the disease and cause an outbreak in another country.

Dr. Hayward

395. I think the question refers directly to Exhibit JPN-14. As I understand it with ISPM 11 you could do a probabilistic assessment of each step in the pathway assuming that pathway can be completed and that is extremely uncertain. I think if you did that - I can't really anticipate that - but based on the evidence we have I would agree that the possibility is negligible.

Dr. Smith

396. I would support the other statements Mr. Chairman.

Japan

397. Is there any serious possibility or risk that apples with symptoms may go undetected through export procedures for the next 25 years?

Dr. Geider

398. You are asking us a little bit too much in the future. Of course I am always wondering when I read the paper of Tom van der Zwet and others. Rodney Roberts already made the statement that the likelihood is 35,000 years and a little bit more and that is a precise answer to an event. Of course mathematically I think it is probably correct to do this judgement. On the other hand of course fire blight is not really predictable and just to get something which I have in my summary towards the end. It is of course a big question - what will happen when apples trade between the US and Japan is liberalized

completely and fire blight will be in Japan afterwards. Can somebody say this was due to the import of apples or was it another event which finally came up to introduce fire blight and I would still say the other event is much more likely but both events will come together and you have apple imports and you have fire blight. This is a very difficult situation which cannot be foreseen and it cannot be really answered right now, but I still think that both events can happen that apples will be in Japan, but fire blight is coming by other means to the country and I cannot really say what we should do afterwards. Would you blame us that we were not strict enough to seize that situation and this is the situation which cannot be foreseen?

Dr. Hale

399.   I would just like to concur with Dr. Geider because I think it is a very difficult question for us to answer and I don't think we are really in a position to do so.

Dr. Hayward

400.   Since zero tolerance is not an option we are talking about something a little bit above that.

Dr. Smith

401.   Apples and pears have been traded as fruits between many countries in the world for the last 50 to 100 years, sometimes with strict requirements and sometimes with no requirements, and it was our initial view as experts that in no case have fruits been known to introduce fire blight. However, international trade is intensifying. It is difficult for us, as phytosanitary experts, to calculate in terms of volume of trade and intensity of measures how we can compare the past period with the one that's coming. Nevertheless I think the past period does reassure us to a certain extent that fruits have not carried fire blight, and lead us to suppose that by maintaining measures it should be possible to continue to protect countries which do not have fire blight provided that they are in an isolated situation. Fire blight has spread in Europe because the countries are contiguous and no human activity could stop it because it was being spread by wind, rain and birds. But Japan is an island, Australia is an island. It is a perfectly reasonable endeavour to suppose that it is possible by phytosanitary measures to continue to exclude fire blight from them.

Dr. Geider

402.   An additional remark to that is that of course it is remarkable that most countries in the southern hemisphere are without fire blight except New Zealand. I am asking the question, I would assume that the import restrictions for fruits and plants in South America are not very high so Chile has a lot of apples which actually we get into Germany and Argentina and Brazil there is also some growth of apples which might not be as big as the other two countries. The question still is they didn't get fire blight. Is that because they are not carefully enough if they have some or is it for sure that even with strict detection methods there is no fire blight in South America.

Dr. Hayward

403.   New Zealand has had fire blight since 1919. Now the Australian quarantine and inspection service attempts to prevent movement of fresh fruit and vegetables from any external source but I think their estimates are that they only intercept perhaps 10 per cent of all vegetable material. I don't have an exact figure but it is obvious it should be self-evident that no quarantine, no inspection service at port of entry, airports, docks, etc. could possibly given human nature intercept all introductions of fresh fruit and vegetables. There must during that 80 years have been at least some fresh fruit brought in from New Zealand. We cannot quantify this can we? It is all very theoretical. Anyway we can say that fire blight from whatever source has never got into Australia by that means through port of entry whereas citrus canker for example been found on plants in the Northern Australia on at least five or six occasions and has been eradicated. It has not been brought in - it has been detected on fruit at port of entry - citrus canker on citrus fruits but the only incursions were in Northern Australia resulting in eradication of those plants.

Dr. Hale

404.   Just as a follow-up we have had exactly the same situation in New Zealand where citrus canker did appear and has been eradicated but that was on plants and not fruit.

Dr. Smith

405.   I think the comment from Japan was posing the question whether you can rely on the correct implementation of phytosanitary measures in long term. Is there an adequate guarantee that systems will continue to function? Obviously one cannot say this categorically. But past experience does show that by the use of phytosanitary measures, countries have excluded fire blight. They have excluded it for the last 50 to 100 years. I who work in plant quarantine specifically believe that it is a worthwhile activity and it can be conducted successfully. The measures which exporting and importing countries take can be successfully used in the long term.

Dr. Geider

406.   Just to ask the US delegation what are the restrictions or regulations between the US and South America? Is there free export of apples and pears or are they many regulations or no?

Chairman

407.   Sorry, but this is a discussion which started with the Japanese question perhaps we can just keep it in that direction. Let us come to that later.

Japan

408.   I am confused. A couple of hours ago you were discussing and you said you were in agreement that fire blight free orchards will be effective and will be important to protect against the risk of spread of the disease. Are you still in that position or are you now suggesting that we should abolish that?

Dr. Geider

409. I think it is probably you feel that sort of compromise. We are saying even with uninspected orchards the chance to transmit fire blight to Japan is very low. On the other hand we do not feel that we could squeeze Japan into that situation and saying we are now helpless to all apple imports from other countries. I don't know, maybe in five or ten years these restrictions can be abolished and no measurements are necessary and for those reasons for a transition time it would be a good decision to keep into that measurement and do inspections to make sure that you have done something and I think we all agree that you cannot do everything and this is just what is the most reasonable approach at the present time.

Dr. Hale

410. I am sure Dr. Smith is going to want to talk about what I was going to mention and that is the fact that export phytosanitary regulations will prevail in any case and I just feel like Dr. Geider that we probably do need some phytosanitary regulation in place.

Dr. Smith

411. Well it has to be said that apple fruits in Europe are traded completely freely between different European countries. There is no inspection of orchards, no registration of orchards, no phytosanitary certificate, no interference of plant health authorities in any way at all in the trade in apples. Apples in theory in Europe could be taken from a heavily infected fire blight orchard and traded. Perhaps that has happened (though ordinary commercial quality standards for fruits should reduce the risk). Despite this, nobody can cite an instance when fruits have transmitted fire blight. So certainly the European position is that you do not need measures for fruits in trade. However, it is accepted that different countries have an appropriate level of protection which they decide for themselves. We can reasonably expect that Japan would in fact have a higher level of protection for this disease than the European countries. If a measure is needed, the requirement that the fruits should come from an orchard free from fire blight appears from my point of view the most effective single measure that could be put in place.

Japan

412. Thank you for the clarification. So having heard what you have told us this morning my final impression is that Japan is entitled to have a different level of protection and in order to achieve that level of protection the requirement of shipments from a fire blight free orchard with inspections is a reasonable one to achieve the level of protection and that it is something experts would recommend.

Dr. Geider

413. Of course I think it is reasonable when you feel Japan is threatened by fruits imports that you have to be careful to prevent any risk which is not zero so I think really you should do this measurements for at least some time and get

more acquainted. I think the problem is, and the same for Australia, the people are not acquainted with fire blight and don't know enough of what are the symptoms, how do I see and detect a level which is fast and efficient so there are a couple of problems and would still say to be safe some sort of measurements are reasonable at this time.

Dr. Hale

414.   My only qualification would be not inspections but inspection.

Dr. Hayward

415.   I wish we could play back the answer that Dr. Smith gave just a minute or two ago. On the basis of what you said and the experience of European trade in apples it might be unreasonable to expect any special treatment. Am I putting words into your mouth? Didn't you just say that in spite of massive unregulated, uninspected, untreated trade in apples there has been no introduction of fire blight.

Dr. Smith

416.   Well, the declaration that no case has been known in which fruits have carried the disease is a negative statement based on the fact that, where the disease has been introduced from one country to another, we can find other explanations. The overall pattern of spread does not appear, in the way that it manifests itself geographically, related to the fruit trade. However, in a continent where there is a lot of fire blight, it is impossible to say that it has never happened, or that an infected fruit was never carried in trade and in some way or another infected an orchard. The general background is one where you would not see this event. All we can say is as far as we know that in new areas in which fire blight did not previously occur, when it was introduced it does not seem to have been by this pathway, but we have not done a systematic study to say were apples traded between those particular countries at the time. If it was important for us in Europe to answer this question, we would have to analyse it further. In my written replies, I used the wording "appropriate level of protection" because the Members of the WTO have the possibility of deciding on different measures on the basis of the same scientific evidence if they choose to do so. Although from a scientific point of view it might appear to us as experts that there was inconsistency in the approaches of the authorities in different countries, countries have the sovereign right to decide that they will take more stringent measures in the face of the same risk.

Chairman

417.   ... Subject to the provisions of the SPS Agreement.

Japan

418.   So in essence you feel Dr. Smith, there is some risk which may have to be accidental contamination in infected fruits carried over or in some cases where farmers, shippers and growers cheat and that would be accidentally included in shipments and brought onto Japanese soil. It is unquantifiable, but I believe it is a risk because I might remind you that Taiwan recently discovered codling moth

for the first time in the past 25 years. It was supposedly those apples were codling moth-free but it happened. I would imagine it was an accident, but it indicates or shows some evidence that whatever procedure, export guarantees or inspections may never be an adequately established level of safety. Is it to counter that risk that you feel a fire blight free orchard would be an appropriate response to that?

Dr. Smith

419.   I think that a country which opens a new trade which did not previously exist, subject to certain phytosanitary requirements, can reasonably wish to monitor the operation of what goes on during the course of such trade for a certain time to be satisfied that all the components of their phytosanitary protection is working correctly. Whether it is safe to import mature apples depends on a satisfactory phytosanitary system in the exporting country which can provide guarantees. So it maybe, as Dr. Geider has suggested, that in 10 or 20 years time the Japanese phytosanitary authorities might come to the conclusion that they are perfectly happy with the movement of apples from the United States if experience shows them that in actual fact there are never any incidents and nothing is found. Then they may then ultimately change their regime. There are now quite heavy and multiple requirements in place. If there were to be a substantial lightening of those requirements, the country concerned would wish to maintain some protection initially. From a scientific position, the logical conclusion of saying that there is an absolutely negligible risk of movement of fire blight with fruits is in fact a completely unrestricted trade. Now, even as a scientist looking at this, I find it hard to see that one would make this change in one step! There should be phytosanitary control, i.e. at least phytosanitary certification of fruits. To remove measures altogether takes away any control, and leaves everything to the discretion of growers and traders. It is difficult for experts to make judgements on what should be the phytosanitary policies of countries. These policies are conditioned by concerns which go beyond those which we have been discussing and the SPS Agreement must take into account the necessity for such policies. I think it is not for us as scientific experts to try to make judgements on what governments should or should not do in those cases.

Chairman

420.   Thank you very much.

Japan

421.   Perhaps you can tell me why you feel that some measure will be necessary? Is it because there ought to be some compromise? Or is it because there is some need for a compromise or because there is some uncontrollable risk, nevertheless, based on the real world experience, such as finding codling moth apple?

Chairman

422.   Do you feel you have answered this question already or is it

Dr. Smith

423. Well Mr. Chairman I think I have answered this question. Until a particular system applied to phytosanitary security is put into place one is only trying to forecast how it operates. For that reason, when the phytosanitary system is changed it should be changed under circumstances that retain some degree of control on what is happening and not in a single step that removes control altogether. This is not a precautionary principle but just ordinary prudence. I am not sure that this is something that has to be argued on scientific terms. It is a matter of public policy.

Dr. Geider

424. I think I made remarks on that too and it legally asks the Americans about South America. I think we still can learn of course from other habits and grades of apples if the risk is really so high and it is a little pity that nobody from South America is here that the Panel can ask these people what is your policy on American apple imports so I still would say in the case of Japan if you really feel that there is a risk and the other is saying the risk is very low that you are entitled to impose regulations in some way but I still, for my personal feeling, these regulations should be not so high that they are very difficult and costly to perform and that will finally end up in a barrier of trade and I think we discussed that a couple of times and Dr. Hale pointed out three inspections are a lot and finally it is getting into impossible measurements and would really abolish trade of apples from the US to Japan and I understand that the reason we are here is that restrictions right now are so high in the level that Americans feel that this should be changed in some way.

Chairman

425. Thank you. The reference to South America - I believe the point is covered in a reply to the Panel's question to Brazil, third party question. There was only one question put by the Panel to Brazil and the answer you will find addresses the point you are referring to you. Are there any other comments on the Japanese question? Dr. Smith.

Dr. Smith

426. I would like to say that the IPPC provides for phytosanitary certificate. It does not regard them as a special phytosanitary measure or requirement but as being a normal and regular way of ensuring that plants and plant products can be traded safely. It makes sure that the exporting country does identify consignments and inspect them, and verify their state before they are exported. I think the greatest risk that might arise for apples that were exported to Japan would be that they would be taken from infected orchards. In an unregulated trade of apples you would not know where the apples were coming from. Phytosanitary certificates partly give you a phytosanitary guarantee and partly a guarantee of identity and integrity. Any importing country can reasonably require this identity guarantee which it is a very minimal level of security and perfectly justifiable in this case.

Japan

427.   Perhaps I was misunderstanding you. So export certificates certainly ensures that all the requirements are met and what I am interested in is what sort of requirements would be, should be, and based on the discussion I am hearing, the suggestion is that some sort of fire blight free orchard with inspection or inspections - once again I am repeating my other question but am I right to understand the response that way?

Chairman

428.   If this is a repeat of the question you might consider whether you need to offer any further answer to what you have already said.

Dr. Smith

429.   That's right. I think that if a system of phytosanitary certification is in place then the requirement that the fruit should come from a healthy orchard is a reasonable requirement. That is partly because the simple inspection of the fruit may not be an adequate measure for you to determine if they were mixed or contaminated by fruit from infected orchards.

Chairman

430.   This now brings us to the final stage of the meeting. Before closing the meeting I would like to offer the experts an opportunity to make any final comments that they wish to make and let me clarify first of all that the Secretary of the Panel will prepare a summary of your written responses and a record of today's meeting and each of you will be asked to review this summary to confirm that it is correct and correctly reflects what you have said both in the written and the oral answers that you have given. So perhaps with that said I could proceed to invite Dr. Geider first if there are any final comments you wish to make.

Dr. Geider

431.   Of course I think it is difficult now to say something new. So I think we all agreed that in the novel introduction of fire blight in countries are very rare and the reasons for introductions can be guessed and we somehow agreed it was probably mainly or only due to trade of plants which were latently or even obviously infected by the disease and although the disease is somehow bound for a while to the species where it first appears and it's obvious in Italy it is sticking to pears, in other countries it is sticking to apples and I am a little bit wondering that the Japanese delegation did not pick up that there is a substantive growth of Nashi pears in the country which are obviously although hosts for the disease and since there are no pathovars of *E. amylovora* all the host plants can be affected and of course we should not only talk about apples and pears, it could be also a target for the disease and therefore the Japanese should of course also look that there is some sort of remote danger for the pear production of this fire blight. OK, so this is one point and of course the other point is appearance and disappearance of fire blight and there is this one example of Australia. The other point is about Japan 1903 and I think we do not have to discuss that further on except that it was fire blight or something else - obviously whatever it was this

disappeared and to my opinion, but I am not certainly entitled to make a comment on pear disease in Japan, there could be something else and I don't know if this is endangering other pear productions in the world or not? OK, so this one point. Another point is disappearance of fire blight in Norway, but I have learnt from my colleagues in these days that fire blight reappeared in Norway so it is unpredictable in many instances and what could happen in New Zealand is that fire blight is not obvious for a couple of seasons and then will reappear so it's a disease which is really unpredictable and of course there are many events that some sorts of strains which are located in areas like we found in Northern Italy that disappeared and others took over, and Al Jones, who is another fire blight expert in America, told me that certain strains will move very slowly to other parts where they originated so it is back and forth with many events which are considering fire blight. At the end I would really summarize it once more that import of fruits cannot be blamed, at least to our best knowledge we expressed in these days, for new outbreaks of fire blight in a country. A very final point I wanted to make is, since we are talking about, is big risks of fire blight in some countries. We should be a little bit cautious in a way. In modern times we are all publicly exposed and we all know about these big discussions about terrorism in the world and I think even Japan is not free - not in political terms, that people try to do something bad for a country. When we really expose the fire blight to be a big threat of half of the world I think that would also be not very wise. Fire blight is not I think to be or not to be. It can be managed in many ways and I think it would be really a bad thing when we give other people the impression that fire blight is something so special that they get attracted to do hostile actions in a country and I think this is certainly not a point here in this Panel to come to a statement, but it should be somewhere considered in the background that this is also of course a way to deal with fire blight and it would be a pity when those things would occur, in countries which do not have fire blight, in the future.

Chairman

432.   Thank you Dr. Geider. Now Dr. Hale.

Dr. Hale

433.   Thank you. I haven't a huge amount to say, but just to pick up on what Dr. Geider was saying. We have about 220 years of history of fire blight and we have no evidence of transmission with fruit and as Dr. Smith pointed out there are many effective ways in moving fire blight around and fruit is not one of them. I was interested in the comment which was brought up about direct evidence. It is interesting to note that there is a huge amount of research which has gone on with this particular disease and it is important, I think, to note that the detection techniques which we have developed over the last few years are providing far more confidence than we previously had in ecological and epidemiological studies. I think that we now are able to almost categorically say that there will be no movement of fire blight through fruit which is taken from healthy orchards. There are risk management systems and pest risk analysis and we have been through those in a fair amount of detail so good mechanisms are

available and these are universally agreed now through the International Plant Protection Convention and I think this is important that these are in place. I think that it is very important also that the work that was carried out in the United States, which showed that buffer zones do not provide any real phytosanitary security, is taken into account and it is interesting that this has not been a topic which has been discussed in great detail at this meeting. As Dr. Smith pointed out, in Europe there appear to be no need for measures to be put in place for fire blight and the possible transmission as far as fruit is concerned. I agree with what most other people have said about the level of protection which is sought by various countries and through their sovereign rights they have this available to them. I realize that Japan is certainly not used to being able to cope with fire blight and consequently seeks high levels of protection rather than unrestricted trade in fruit until Japan has confidence in the fact that healthy fruit will not be transmitting the disease. That's really all I have to say. I would just like to thank the Panel for the questions that they have put and also for the discussions that we have had with the US and Japan over the last two days. Thank you.

Chairman

434. Thank you very much Dr. Hale.

Dr. Hayward

435. I have listened very carefully over the last two days to the comments that everybody has made on all sides and the first point I would like to make is I see no reason to modify what I have put in my responses to questions 1-36. The second point is that we didn't cover all the questions and there is no problem in that - obviously the discussion was going to focus on the central issues concerning trade in apples and the risks and consequences. I was particularly interested in questions 35 and 36 and Dr. Geider mentioned that there was a record in 1903 which might have been the fire blight in Japan. Having read the review by Mizuno *et al.* (2002) on the status of fire blight and the status of that record I accept their suggestion that there was a misidentification or confusion with a fungal canker. Also in relation to this I read the United States responses to the Panel's 36 questions and in relation to question 35 I think the United States suggested that it was a controversial matter - I am referring to bacterial shoot blight of pear in Hokkaido and the status of the berry strains in the United States. I think we need to rethink the relationship of all these organisms in the light of modern evidence on genetic relationships. Modern taxonomy of bacteria is polyphasic ideally - polyphasic meaning that it is a combination of phenotypic - looking at the all the external properties of an organism - its phenotype and then looking at its basic genetic constitution and so that is the genotype and all this information is integrated together. Now speaking as a microbiologist when I look at all this evidence it is not controversial at all. When I look at the paper by Mizuno *et al.* (2002) in the journal of General Plant Pathology - to me it is not controversial at all. The evidence is solid and very sound, but the problem is we don't have a nomenclature which copes with the differences - these are quite different agents and the nomenclature doesn't cope with it. I think it might foreshadow a system where you have not perhaps pathovars or biovars but sub-

species being covered by the code of the nomenclature and subspecies would sit better in phytosanitary regulations. I mean you would have say a subspecies amylovora for the apple and pear strains from North America you would have a subspecies rubi for the raspberry strains and then you'd have a subspecies pyri perhaps but I think I shouldn't say, but question 35 wasn't covered. To me it is not controversial. The status of these different organisms as described in various publications recently is to me quite clear as a microbiologist. These are different agents that the nomenclature we have for these different agents isn't adequate at this stage, in my opinion.

Chairman

436.   Thank you very much Dr. Hayward. Last, but not least, Dr. Smith.

Dr. Smith

437.   Well I have been associated with the development of the International Standards of Phytosanitary Measures which have been put in place by FAO at the direct instigation of the World Trade Organization and so I would like to underline that there are several such standards which are very relevant to this case. These include Standard No. 1 (principles of plant quarantine in relation to international trade) and also Standards 2 and 11, but I think mainly 11, which is the standard for pest risk analysis. Now until the present time I have not heard of any formalized dispute in relation to measures where these standards were applied. It is important, I think, now that these standards have been accepted internationally, that they should indeed be respected. One purpose of drawing up these standards was to create conditions in which disagreements could be settled . So if I am allowed to urge the Panel to do anything in particular, I would urge them to take good account of these international standards in their decision because we in the phytosanitary sector depend on their application in future and it is very important to us that they should be well interpreted and well implemented.

Chairman

438.   Dr. Smith thank you very much. After this meeting the Panel will of course want to reflect very carefully on everything that has transpired here yesterday and today as well as on all the written material which has preceded the meeting. This is obviously not something we can do immediately but as a result of this I cannot rule out the possibility that we might want to revert to the experts with additional questions if that review seems to warrant it. If we do so we will try to do so as soon as possible and we would hope that the written replies would also be available as soon as they can be produced and we would see that they were copied to the parties with an opportunity to comment on the replies and the questions. So we are reserving the right to possibly revert back to you. That said, I would like on behalf of the Panel to thank our four distinguished experts very sincerely for your enormous effort so far. We found the very thorough exhaustive written replies you have given extremely helpful and as far as we were concerned they enabled us to reduce our own questions to a minimum in this Panel meeting. So thank you very much and before I close the meeting I

would just like to remind the parties that we will be meeting with them again on Thursday in this same room - starting at 11am and not 10am as originally communicated to you. If there are no other matters with my thanks again to the experts. Thank you all of you for your cooperation today. This meeting of the Panel is now closed.

Cumulative Index of Published Disputes